Silence as Language

Verbal silence touches on every possible aspect of daily life. This book provides a full linguistic analysis of the role of silence in language, exploring perspectives from semantics, semiotics, pragmatics, phonetics, syntax, grammar and poetics, and taking into account a range of spoken and written contexts. The author argues that silence is just as communicative in language as speech, as it results from the deliberate choice of the speaker, and serves functions such as informing, conveying emotions, signalling turn switching and activating the addresser. Verbal silence is used, alongside speech, to iconically serve linguistic functions in all areas of life, as well as being employed in a wide variety of written texts. The forms and functions of silence are explained, detailed and illustrated with examples taken from both written texts and real-life interactions. Engaging and comprehensive, this book is essential reading for anyone interested in this fascinating linguistic phenomenon.

MICHAL EPHRATT is Professor of Linguistics at the University of Haifa, Israel. Her research interests include language and life: neologisms, iconicity, pragmatics, proper names and linguistic models in psychoanalytic theory and practice. Her major research focus is on the study of silence as a means of expression.

Silence as Language
Verbal Silence as a Means of Expression

Michal Ephratt
University of Haifa

CAMBRIDGE
UNIVERSITY PRESS

Shaftesbury Road, Cambridge CB2 8EA, United Kingdom

One Liberty Plaza, 20th Floor, New York, NY 10006, USA

477 Williamstown Road, Port Melbourne, VIC 3207, Australia

314–321, 3rd Floor, Plot 3, Splendor Forum, Jasola District Centre, New Delhi – 110025, India

103 Penang Road, #05–06/07, Visioncrest Commercial, Singapore 238467

Cambridge University Press is part of Cambridge University Press & Assessment, a department of the University of Cambridge.

We share the University's mission to contribute to society through the pursuit of education, learning and research at the highest international levels of excellence.

www.cambridge.org
Information on this title: www.cambridge.org/9781108458214

DOI: 10.1017/9781108650779

© Michal Ephratt 2022

This publication is in copyright. Subject to statutory exception and to the provisions of relevant collective licensing agreements, no reproduction of any part may take place without the written permission of Cambridge University Press & Assessment.

First published 2022
First paperback edition 2025

A catalogue record for this publication is available from the British Library

Library of Congress Cataloging-in-Publication data
Names: Ephratt, Michal, author.
Title: Silence as language : verbal silence as a means of expression / Michal Ephratt.
Description: Cambridge, United Kingdom ; New York, NY : Cambridge University
  Press, 2022. | Includes bibliographical references and index.
Identifiers: LCCN 2021039267 (print) | LCCN 2021039268 (ebook) |
  ISBN 9781108471671 (hardback) | ISBN 9781108458214 (paperback) |
  ISBN 9781108650779 (epub)
Subjects: LCSH: Silence. | Nonverbal communication. | BISAC: LANGUAGE ARTS
  & DISCIPLINES / Linguistics / Semantics
Classification: LCC P99.7 .E476 2022 (print) | LCC P99.7 (ebook) | DDC 401/
  .4–dc23/eng/20211118
LC record available at https://lccn.loc.gov/2021039267
LC ebook record available at https://lccn.loc.gov/2021039268

ISBN   978-1-108-47167-1   Hardback
ISBN   978-1-108-45821-4   Paperback

Cambridge University Press & Assessment has no responsibility for the persistence or accuracy of URLs for external or third-party internet websites referred to in this publication and does not guarantee that any content on such websites is, or will remain, accurate or appropriate.

Uzzi
Love that never told can be
(William Blake)

Contents

List of Figures and Tables   *page* x
Preface and Acknowledgements   xi

1   Introduction   1

2   The Different Sorts of Silence   5
    2.1   Silences External to Interaction: Stillness   5
    2.2   Silences within Interaction   7
       2.2.1   Muteness as a Symptom   8
       2.2.2   The Intermediate Plane: Pauses as Paralinguistic Silences   9
       2.2.3   The Content Plane   15
          2.2.3.1   The Unsaid   16
          2.2.3.2   Empty Speech   19
       2.2.4   The Verbal Plane   22
          2.2.4.1   Silencing   23
    2.3   Scheme: Silences in Interaction   27

3   Verbal Silence: Forms   30
    3.1   Verbal Silence: An Intuitive Glance   30
    3.2   The Forms of Verbal Silence   36
       3.2.1   Phonetic Verbal Silence   50
       3.2.2   Morphological Verbal Silence   57
          3.2.2.1   Isolated Bound Morphemes as Stumps   58
          3.2.2.2   Morphological Stumps in Light of the Zero   60
       3.2.3   Morphosyntactic Verbal Silence   69
          3.2.3.1   Definiteness: The Definite and Indefinite Articles   70
          3.2.3.2   The Passive Voice as Verbal Silence   78
       3.2.4   Syntactic Verbal Silence   96
          3.2.4.1   Leaving the Subject and Predicate Constituents Uninstantiated   101
          3.2.4.2   Leaving the Subject's Constituent Uninstantiated   102
          3.2.4.3   Leaving the Sentence's Entire VP or Only Its Head Uninstantiated   111
          3.2.4.4   Leaving the Verb Complements or Adjuncts Uninstantiated   132
          3.2.4.5   Leaving Syntactic Function Words – Prepositions and Connectives – Uninstantiated   163

	3.2.4.6	Leaving a Conjunct of a Coordinating or a Subordination Construction Uninstantiated	171
	3.2.5	Lexical Verbal Silence	190
		3.2.5.1 Speech and Silence Lexical Entries Signalling Verbal Silences	192
		3.2.5.2 Intertextuality as Verbal Silence	207
		3.2.5.3 Verbal Silence Pointing to Taboo	218
		3.2.5.4 Proper Names and Verbal Silence	226
		3.2.5.5 Part–Whole Relations and Verbal Silence	240

4 Verbal Silence: Functions — 248

- 4.1 The Referential Function — 249
- 4.2 The Emotive Function — 254
  - 4.2.1 The Diminutive — 262
- 4.3 The Conative Function — 264
  - 4.3.1 Conative Roles Served by Verbal Silence as the Unmarked Means — 267
    - 4.3.1.1 Turn-Switching: A Verbal Silence Discourse Marker — 267
    - 4.3.1.2 The Silent Treatment — 268
    - 4.3.1.3 Silence as Consent — 269
  - 4.3.2 When Speech and Verbal Silence Jointly Complement to Produce an Illocution — 271
  - 4.3.3 Conative Roles Served by Verbal Silence while Speech Is the Unmarked Means — 272
    - 4.3.3.1 Propadverts: Propaganda + Adverts — 272
    - 4.3.3.2 Question–Answer Adjacency Pair — 275
- 4.4 The Phatic Function — 283
- 4.5 The Poetic Function — 293
  - 4.5.1 Poe's 'The Raven': Verbal Silence Projected to Build the Ballad's Poetic Sequence — 295
  - 4.5.2 Haiku — 301
  - 4.5.3 The Mono-Dialogue — 306
- 4.6 The Metalinguistic Function — 308
  - 4.6.1 Pointing to a Mismatch between Code and Meaning — 309
    - 4.6.1.1 The Passive Pointing to a Mismatch between Subjecthood and Agenthood — 309
    - 4.6.1.2 Uninstantiated Syntactic Function Words Pointing to the Structure of the Code — 310
    - 4.6.1.3 Partial Binary Code Accenting Its Counterpart — 310
    - 4.6.1.4 Taboo: The Words Pointing to the Prohibited Code — 310
    - 4.6.1.5 Distorted Code as Metalinguistic Verbal Silence — 311
  - 4.6.2 Activating the Addressee as an Encoder — 311
    - 4.6.2.1 The Unmarked Turn-Switching Discourse Marker — 312
    - 4.6.2.2 Intertextual Stumps Metalinguistically Activating the Addressee as an Encoder — 314
    - 4.6.2.3 Formal Stumps Activating the Addressee as an Encoder — 315
  - 4.6.3 The Metalinguistic Verbal Silence: Dot Dot Dot — 316
    - 4.6.3.1 The Paradigmatic Role of the Three-Dot Mark — 316
    - 4.6.3.2 The Syntagmatic Role of the Three-Dot Mark — 316

	4.6.3.3 The Three-Dot Mark Signifying Authentic Metalinguistic Void	318
	4.6.4 The Shortage of Words	321
	4.6.5 The Right to Silence	326
4.7	The Circumstantial Function	328
5	Ṣ Ṣ Ṣ	334

References   335
Literary Works   351
Index   354

Figures and Tables

Figures

2.1	Silence in interaction	*page* 28
3.1	'M rmite'	32
3.2	'm ss ng'	50
3.3	SEE in ASL	64
3.4	DET/NUM C-commanding a (sister) empty noun node as a syntactic forerunner	100
3.5	'O'er all the hilltops / $\mathcal{S}$ is quiet now': subject vs	105
3.6	'After' connecting two sentences: speech $\mathcal{S}_{vx}$ after long silence $\mathcal{S}_{vy}$	115
3.7	'Get beaten': 2018 World Cup	127
3.8	Theresa Hak Kyung Cha, *Aveugle Voix*, 1975, performance	143
4.1	UK visa application form for 'visit and short term stay'	250
4.2	That silence which I carry	257
4.3	Baker's (1955) model of the silences in the field of language	285
4.4	The less semantic content the more intimate knowledge sets	287

Tables

2.1	Key differences between the six categories in Figure 2.1	*page* 29
3.1	Four-way distinction – the message from (Saville-Troke)	40
3.2	Matrix showing dyadic interaction (Kurzon)	45
3.3	Milestones of language	51
3.4	Main verb and its continuation in English translations of Genesis 4:8	153
3.5	Silences from Huxley's *Eyeless in Gaza* (pp. 176–177)	193
4.1	Poe, 'The Raven': prosodic patterning illustrated with the opening stanza	296
4.2	Poe, 'The Raven': lexical verbal silences	300

Every effort has been made to contact the relevant copyright-holders for the images reproduced in this book. In the event of any error, the publisher will be pleased to make corrections in any reprints or future editions.

Preface and Acknowledgements

I became involved in the study of silence through my interest in language and life, that is language as symptom and symptom as language, language as a prism to the speaker's inner life and hes intersubjective and social contacts and not language as a means.

Tuning my academic attention to verbal silence such that shares, on the one hand, key traits with other silences (such as the stillness of nature) and on the other hand is an integral part of language, I felt like the child from Andersen's tale 'The Emperor's New Clothes'. Embracing and acknowledging the absences within language, gave way to investigating those silences as something rather than nothing. As I deepened my explorations, verbal silence emerged as a varied phenomenon, with many types, forming diverse relationships with speech and with the real world (iconicity).

I now hand the book over to you, the reader. I do hope that you will find it interesting, relevant, and that while reading you will identify an idea, an analysis, or an example significant to you, enriching you as a person and/or contributing to your endeavors as a scholar. As I say in Chapter five, I do hope that this book will be a beginning: inviting ideas, discussions and collaborations.

Studying silence requires attention to pauses, slow time, incubation, introspection as well as voids in the hope that such will be met with astonishment. I wish to thank The University of Haifa (Israel) for granting me sabbatical leaves which afforded me the space required to enable the writing of this book; I thank my many colleagues around the world, some of whom I met in person at conferences and some of whom, unfortunately, only through continuous e-mail exchanges. Contacts and ongoing discussions with these dear colleagues – devoted to the study of silence within their disciplines and interests – were most stimulating, rescuing me from the experience of the lone child in Andersen's tale and challenging and enriching my perspective on silence. I thank the students who enrolled in the Master's seminars on 'silence as language' which I taught over the years. Teaching this course is always an inspiring experience: where students studying linguistics evolve from an often suspicious or ignorant group with regard to silence, through the stages of puzzlement and discovery, to enthusiasm, curiosity and sometimes MA theses.

Last but not least, I warmly thank Helen Barton and Isabel (Izzie) Collins of Cambridge University Press for their endless patience and wise and helpful guidance throughout the process of compiling and producing this book. Special thanks to Dr Lynne Porat, Head of the Interlibrary Loans department of Younes & Soraya Nazarian Library at the University of Haifa, who went out of her way to help me obtain access to books and materials, enabling me to submit the final draft on time, overcoming the local and worldwide closings of international borders and academic libraries during the Covid-19 lockdowns.

Michal Ornan-Ephratt

1   Introduction

This book is devoted to the linguistic study of verbal silence (hereinafter – vs). The uniqueness of this study lies in its focus on expected and unexpected cases within the normal course of interaction when the addresser chooses to use vs, that is, silence as a verbal means of expression. The speaker[1] skilled in choosing for each communicative exchange between realising or not realising a linguistic component is also habituated, when making use of the latter, to signal to the addressee hes choice of silence as a means of expression.[2] It is also part of the listener's proficiency to identify this silence as a verbal means of expression and to determine its function and meaning. When silence is a means of expression, it stands as figure.

The contribution of this study is, first of all, the completion of the extensive study of the realised forms in language in general, and in specific languages in particular, by focusing on and hence elucidating this unique verbal means. The study describes and discusses vs in accordance with the conventional division of linguistics into phonology, semantics, morphology, syntax and pragmatics. Our examination reveals that vs does not constitute a homogeneous means of expression: it is not shapeless and void of content but rather constitutes a diverse verbal means serving all linguistic functions. Another contribution gained from incorporating the study of vs in linguistic exploration is that the study of absence as something (rather than nothing) sheds new light on linguistic phenomena, thereby contributing to the discovery, refinement and conceptualisation of broadly as well as negligibly studied linguistic issues.

Verschueren (1985: 73) opens his chapter on 'The Semantics of Silence' by asserting: 'There is more to silence than the absence of speech. Silence can be

---

[1] The term 'speaker' is used in this study both to denote the generic speaker of a language and to refer to the addresser of an utterance (whether s/he communicates that utterance realising speech or using vs, aurally or in writing; using the spoken channel or visual sign language channel).
[2] To adopt non-discriminatory language while avoiding convoluted formulas, the following notations replace the gender-signed pronouns: the form 'hes' covers 'her' and 'his'; the form 'hem' covers 'her' and 'him'; and, accordingly, the form 'hemself' includes 'herself' and 'himself' (this seems to coincide with Middle English pronouns used, for example, by Chaucer, see Horobin 2012: 579–580 note 4).

golden, deathlike, tomblike, solemn, and even pregnant; but it is rarely neutral. That is, when silence is talked about or even noticed'. This results from the fact that the silences noticed are those that are not trivial.

Deborah Tannen (1985) entitles her article on silence, 'Silence: Anything But'. The word 'silence' is used in English to denote many different notions, some of which have nothing to do with language (e.g. stillness), while others form part of interaction but are not a means of communication, and hence are not vss (paralinguistic pauses, silence as symptoms, the unsaid, empty speech and silencing, see §2.2). Whatever the term may be, each one of us – as a person, an addresser and an addressee – encounters vss, identifies them in discourse and uses them in many different ways. They are living and kicking, informative or poetic, present in our hearts and experiences, ranging from memories of pleasant and intimate experiences involving silences to harsh and distant ones. Most importantly, we all distinguish between the different silences and recognise that 'silence can be either optional or constrained. But only the former type is communicatively meaningful' (Rescher 1998: 91).

As a basis for navigating the field of vs we begin by familiarising ourselves with the area. To this end, we draw on studies undertaken and published by linguists and other scholars who devoted their expertise to the study of silence. These reveal the broadest common denominators, as well as the distinctive, unique perception of silence and framework of investigation imparted by each such contribution in advancing the understanding of silence, in general, and of silence as a means of expression, in particular.

Silence and its varied phases have preoccupied thinkers, artists, writers, poets and playwrights, as well as researchers, jurists and therapists in diverse fields. This study focuses on one of its many states: silence as a means of expression, reflecting the choice of the addresser (and not the listener) to use an unarticulated signifier as a means of verbal expression.

This silence serves communication within interaction. It is used together with or alongside speech (words) to convey messages, for emotional sharing, for activating the other and as an aesthetic means. Vss also serve metalinguistically to structure and process discourse. In addition, such silences may serve as situational-register devices pragmatically pending on the particular circumstances and contexts of the specific exchange. Vs is available and used in all areas of life: in the many contacts of spontaneous interpersonal discourse as well as in public and collective discourses, such as speeches and judgements. Vs is also employed in a wide variety of written texts.

In all these settings, vs occurs not because the addresser has nothing to say or wishes to conceal something from the audience but rather because of the addresser's deliberate choice to express what s/he wishes to share using vs. Sometimes such a choice is motivated by iconicity; sometimes it is the outcome of the shortage of words; while at other times the addresser's preference for vs over speech reflects stylistic or conative considerations.

This study of vs is a direct outcome of viewing vs as a linguistic-verbal signifier that shares with speech the task of expression and verbal communication and is of equal value and effect to speech. Vs as a verbal signifier is therefore silence that occurs where speech is expected; sometimes it is the silence of a single phone, sometimes the silence of a word or a sentence and sometimes the silence of an entire discourse.

Thus, this study seeks to present a systematic and comprehensive investigation of vs, paralleling the ongoing, massive and copious studies of speech. In this sense, the study of silence as a means of expression should be equivalent to the exploration in descriptive linguistics of speakers' linguistic competence – a skill we use from the moment we begin to mumble. In view of the immense linguistic literature devoted to speech and its mechanisms, the lack of an adequate parallel linguistic study of vs is all the more glaring. This underscores the gains that can be achieved for the study of language and speech through an extensive study and understanding of vs alongside speech.

The book is organised according to the conventional linguistic areas. It examines silence as form (the verbal signifier plane) and the functions played by that signifier (the content plane). Vs as a signifier is studied and presented from the level of a single phoneme to the level of a complete discourse or text, and examined in light of the specific language functions and meanings it serves and the cooperative maxims it fulfils.[3] All these are explained and illustrated using examples from spoken languages and signed ones, and from a wide variety of written texts, ranging from ancient scriptures (such as the Old and New Testaments) to literary works; from poetry to novels and prose; from private personal letters to manifests of historical value; and from adverts and political propaganda to web blogs and chats. The singularity of vs is significantly valuable when exploring its iconic power.

Throughout the book we point to the contribution of the linguistic study of vs to theoretical linguistics. The study of language, through the dimension of silence – the lack of the articulation of an expected verbal signifier – sheds new light on linguistic phenomena in general, and on two groups of phenomena in particular. The first group includes phenomena that have been overlooked, or rather not seen, by linguists. By contrast, the second group consists of phenomena familiar to linguists but where the confining of their investigation to

---

[3] To minimise inflation of bibliography references only a few major publications are mentioned, which also leads to their use as references to theories and statements which they mention or cite but do not necessarily support. Primary sources (literary works) are referenced by author's name and the title's first word. Secondary sources (references) are references by author's name and year of publication.

the prism of articulated signifiers (speech) yields only a partial picture, and in some instances conceals the real matters involved. In such cases, bringing vs to the fore sheds new light on the linguistic form, requiring us to re-examine our understanding of linguistic notions – a process that reveals new linguistic issues and challenges familiar issues. This process entails the reconsideration of the phenomenon in light of the examination of vs in a complementary distribution to speech, and in light of the extraction of speech from its status as the sole verbal means of expression. In some instances the contribution is confined to the identification of the challenge, while in others the study of vs also offers a solution to that challenge. A key contribution is the insight that there are certain silences that do not ground speech but rather – like speech – are figure, and as such constitute verbal signifiers. This insight illuminates the relationship between figure and background and between speech and these silences.

Before we delve into vs, we must acknowledge explicitly and unequivocally the dominance of speech (vocalised or signed) as the primary means of human communication in general, and verbal communication in particular. While it might seem that this primacy goes without saying (trivial silence ...), it is only accentuated in light of the verbosity needed to present vs. This study does not seek to deprive speech of its precedence but to enhance our understanding of its loyal and junior helpmate – vs – and show that together they do more than complement each other: together they create a unique thirdness.

2 The Different Sorts of Silence

Focusing here on VS, that is, silence as means of expression, we must first distinguish between this silence and other phenomena termed 'silence'. Such a distinction must be explicit, since unlike English words such as 'speech', 'phones' or 'words', which refer exclusively to language, this is not the case in the speech of ordinary people nor in the linguistic nomenclature regarding the English word 'silence'.

The primary measure serving here to distinguish between the different notions denoted using the word 'silence' is whether the referent so denoted is situated within interaction (§2.2) or external to it (§2.1).

2.1 Silences External to Interaction: Stillness

Stillness is not the absence of speech (verbal signifiers) but rather the absence of sounds, and therefore its antonym is not 'speech' but 'noise' (Kurzon 1998: 15; Jaworski 1993: 26). Stillness includes numerous states external to the human body, such as the stillness of nature

[~1^{German}]   Über allen Gipfeln / Ist Ruh (Goethe, *Goethe Werke*, I, p. 142);

[~81$^{German-T}$]   O'er all hill-tops Is quiet now (Longfellow, *The Complete*, v, p. 617; and see [~81$^{German-T}$] §3.2.4.2)[1]

or the silence of a CD player following an electrical short circuit. Being external to communication, the question of choice and selection (as a signifier) is extraneous regarding stillness.

The musician John Cage argues that 'there is no absolute silence, there is always something that produces sounds' (1961: 9). To illustrate this position, Cage wrote '4'33"' – a four-minute and thirty-three-second piano composition

---

[1] Examples are numbered sequentially. The language of non-English examples is indicated after the number. 'T' following a language indicates that the English example is not original but a translation. Examples belonging to a single source share a single number. Letters following that number indicate chunks from the same text, while tags indicate my paraphrases (but see note 9). In the case of idioms, the letters indicate the specific contexts making use of the idiom.

(comprising three movements) during which the pianist places hes fingertips on the piano keys but deliberately refrains from vibrating the strings and so produces no sounds. In Cage's opinion, sounds such as the squeaks of the seats or coughs that fill the concert hall during this time span support his claim that there is never absolute silence. Clearly, this claim is not directed at the music itself, which in this case has nothing to do with the concept of silence (but see Kurzon 2007: 1683) but rather to do with what happens in the concert hall.

For Poyatos (2002: II, 302), silence and stillness are major categories (alongside what he describes as a triple communication structure consisting of language, paralanguage and kinesics). But examined from a physical perspective, stillness is the absolute lack of acoustic vibration, and accordingly the absence of motion is a key feature of that silence. Such an observation places kinetic stillness and acoustic stillness (silence) not as two distinct and mutually exclusive phenomena but as type (stillness – the absence of motion) and token (stillness – the absence of acoustic motion). Returning now to Cage's argument, stillness, so described, strongly associates the absence of sounds with the inanimate. This is why concert halls are not the typical locations where stillness – that is, absolute silence – emerges. Naturally, stillness may occur in remote locations far from urban areas.[2] In fact, stillness takes place irrespective of whether there are people attesting it or not.

Such experiences are recurrently reported by persons taking part in expeditions to uninhabited lands. Says Captain Scott of his 1904 mission to Antarctica,

[~2] I have never witnessed a more impressive sight; the sun was low behind us, the surface of the ice-sheet in front was intensely white, and in contrast the distant sea and its forking leads looked almost black. The wind had fallen to a calm, and not a sound disturbed the stillness about us. (Scott and Wilson 2014: II, 347)

Likewise, experiences of stillness stand out in reports following natural disasters such as volcanic eruptions or earthquakes:

[~3] We heard this most horrifying sound, it was like a train but came from so deep, just so powerful. [...] and then I felt this tack, tack sound of falling

---

[2] Due to the ongoing noise noticeable in urban settings, when such background noise is unexpectedly missing it draws attention placing the stillness as figure. Pribram (1971: 51) reports of such 'deafening silence':

> For many years there was an elevated railway line (the 'El') on Third Avenue in New York that made a fearful racket; when it was torn down, people who had been living in apartments along the line awakened periodically out of a sound sleep to call the police about some strange occurrence they could not properly define. The calls were made at the times the trains had formally rumbled past. The strange occurrences were, of course, the deafening silence that had replaced the expected noise.

rocks and you know I just felt, 'This is it. I'm going to be buried alive'. They kept on piling on top of me and then finally there was this stillness, this complete stillness, and I knew I was alive (the photographer Roberto Schmidt describes his experience in the 2015 Himalayas earthquake).[3]

The *Oxford English Dictionary* (OED) describes this silence as 'the state or condition when nothing is audible; absence of all sound or noise; complete quietness or stillness' (OED: Silence, N.2a).[4] Because stillness is the absolute silence of nature, unlike other silences stillness is not gradual but total: either no sound is heard (see stillness in [~160^a] §3.2.5.1 and Table 4.2 in §4.5.1) or sounds are heard (some sounds, soft ones, distinct ones, etc.).

Stillness is external to interaction. Moving now to interaction and interactants, other silences emerge.

2.2 Silences within Interaction

The OED lists the following under the major entry for 'silence': 'The fact of abstaining or forbearing from speech or utterance (sometimes with reference to a particular matter); the state or condition resulting from this; muteness; reticence; taciturnity' (OED: Silence, N.1a). Clearly, the silences itemised in this list differ from stillness in that they all refer to absence of speech (or utterances) and so all fall in the realm of interaction. But here their similarity ends. A careful examination of these notions in terms of their place and role within interaction, the matter of choice and the nature of the silence exposes diverse sorts of silences.

We use as a starting point for outlining the various categories of silence the parallelism between stillness and muteness Charles Lamb applied when urging his readers to join him in a Quakers' meeting:

[~4]   READER, wouldst thou know what true peace and quiet mean; wouldst thou find a refuge from the noises and clamours of the multitude;
[...]
What is the stillness of the desert compared with this place? What the uncommunicating muteness of fishes? – Here the goddess reigns and revels. (Lamb, 'Quakers', pp. 58–59)

Three sorts of silence stand out in Lamb's correspondence: stillness, muteness and peace and quiet. Having excluded stillness from interaction, we now move on to muteness.

---

[3] https://correspondent.afp.com/im-going-be-buried-alive (accessed 10 July 2017). Throughout this study, ellipsis marks added to the source are indicated using square brackets.

[4] This is the second, not the first, of the OED's definitions for 'silence' (see §2.2.3). Entries from the OED are indicated by 'OED' followed by the OED's lexical entry, its category and the meaning's number and letter. The entries were accessed between 2010 and 2020.

2.2.1 Muteness as a Symptom

Bodily conditions, emotional dispositions (e.g. trauma or detachment) and cognitive deficits or communication disorders, such as falling in the extreme pole of the autistic spectrum disorder, can result pathologically in the speaker[5] refraining from interaction altogether or temporarily ceasing speech or communication. This is alluded to in the OED's definition cited above as 'muteness' (see also Bruneau 1973 'psycholinguistic silences'; Zeligs 1961). 'Muteness' is further defined in the OED as 'the quality or condition of being mute or silent; inability to speak or make a sound; wordlessness, silence' (OED: Muteness, N.1).

This definition shows prima facie the generality in which the word 'silence' is used. It then points to a clear distinction between muteness and other silences. Muteness surfaces within interaction; but not only does muteness not serve interaction, it actually lies outside the free choice of the speaker. Muteness is a pathological symptom that within interaction, when speech and verbal expression are expected, results in silence. Muteness is a symptom and silence its signifier.

Following Peirce (1965: §§2.277–2.286), a major class of indices are defined as symptoms. An index is a sign 'which signifies its object solely by virtue of being really connected with it', such as cause and effect (Sebeok 1994: 48–50).

Symptomatic silences associated with a person who stutters or is undergoing strong emotional experiences of disassociation, let alone symptoms caused by such physiological conditions as brain damage, all fall outside communication and interaction.

To take just one example, when at the Battle of the Wilderness (1864 Virginia Civil War), unlike other men who dived for cover, General John Sedgwick stood up and caught a bullet in his face, his last words are said to have been

[~5]   They couldn't hit an elephant at this dist –

Not concluding articulation ('distance') is by no means here the outcome of an intentional choice serving communication but a factual reflection of General Sedgwick's instant death preventing him (among other things) from concluding the word (see Robinson 2003: 31).

From a pragmatic-communicative point of view, symptoms are not signs. Authors, such as playwrights and poets, may indeed make iconic use of symptomatic behaviour, including symptomatic silences, as verbal means

---

[5] We deliberately refrain here from dealing with volition. As Freud has taught the world, no person and no deed are free of the unconscious.

2.2.2 The Intermediate Plane 9

(see [~31]–[~33] §3.2.1; [~160ʲ] §3.2.5.1; [~103^{b-δ}] §3.2.4.4.1; [~105] §3.2.4.4.2 note 69).

One such example is:

[~6] I will have such revenges on you both,
That all the world shall – I will do such things –
What they are, yet I know not, but they shall be
The terrors of the earth! (Shakespeare, *King Lear*, II.iv.275–277, Norton³, p. 1418)

Only an author such as Shakespeare, ingeniously familiar with the illocutionary felicity of threats (see §4.3.2), could put these lines in King Lear's mouth to portray the king's tragic disposition straggling old age, grief, loss of control and fear of insanity. Lear's lengthy verbosity, with its camouflaging of the threatening deeds using general words (see §3.2.5.1.6), and his explicit admission of ignorance ('what they are yet, I know not') all result in symptomatic silence enacting a declining sovereign, father and man on the verge of a mental and emotional storm ('let not women's weapons, water drops, / Staine my mans cheekes').

Goffman's (1959: 2) distinction between what he views as 'radically different kinds of sign activity' seems most helpful for our investigation of the distinction between silences internal and external to the verbal code. According to Goffman, 'given information' consists of the verbal symbols (or their substitutes) which the addresser uses admiringly and solely to convey the information the interlocutors are known to attach to those symbols. 'Given-off information', says Goffman, 'involves a wide range of action that others can treat as symptomatic of the actor, the expectation being that the action was performed for reasons other than the information conveyed in this way'. The addressee, noticing the performance of such symptomatic or paralinguistic silences (pauses) by the expected addresser, may infer meanings concerning the addresser or concerning subjective or objective circumstances regarding the interaction. But, as Goffman stresses, unlike 'given information', these non-intentionally communicated impressions either convey no given information or fall outside the (given) information conveyed in that way. Goffman's distinction seems most helpful when examining the differences between paralanguage and language in general and pauses and speech in particular.

2.2.2 *The Intermediate Plane: Pauses as Paralinguistic Silences*

The third class alluded in ([~4]) are pauses (Lamb's 'peace and quiet'). The OED distinguishes between technical and general uses of the term 'pause'. The primary general use denotes 'an act of stopping or ceasing for a short time in a course of action; a short interval of silence or inaction, *esp.* one arising from uncertainty, doubt, or reflection; an intermission; a delay, a hesitation' (OED: Pause, N.II.5a). The primary technical use refers to 'a break or rest made for effect, according to the sense, in speaking, reading, or signing; a similar break made in playing instrumental music' (OED: Pause, N.I.1a). Examining the general and technical uses, it appears that the term 'pause' is by no means unique to communication and speech; rather, it denotes the suspension of an activity with the intention of resuming it (e.g. 'coffee break' or 'spring recess'). As stated in both definitions, one such pause is the suspension of speech. Speech constitutes interaction, and so pause as the suspension of speech is at all times within interaction. 'Pause' referring to the suspension of speech bears all the essential characteristics shared by all the other sorts of pause; only the fact that the action suspended is speech positions these pauses as part of interaction, when during a verbal exchange between interlocutors the addresser holding the floor suspends the speech expected of hem.

If we take paralanguage as an intermediate plane between pure symbol and pure icon, or rather as an intermediate sign incorporating both a symbolic and an iconic relation between signifier and signified, the paralinguistic classification of silence (pauses) may be confirmed as not accidental.[6] Hence, paralanguage falls between communicating and not-communicating. Indeed, this plane covers the various pauses which seemed to be in the focus of the dealings of scholars of nonverbal communication with silence (see later in this section).

Some of the components identified by scholars as belonging in the paralinguistic plane are voluntary; others are activities that the speaker is caught into. Moreover, a cry or laugh may accompany speech, supporting or contrasting it, but may also be detached from it. At times they may be a burst of emotion that the experiencer does not wish to share with anyone (such as embarrassing laughter or crying in public).[7]

Mehrabian (1972: 1–2) differentiates between what he considers a more accurate sense of nonverbal behaviour and the broader traditional sense of the concept. He suggests that the former refers to actions as distinct from speech, while the latter also includes a variety of subtle aspects of speech, such as paralinguistic or vocal phenomena. These vocal qualities (including fundamental frequency range and intensity range, speech errors or pauses, speech rate and speech duration) are, according to Mehrabian, implicit aspects of speech.

Some of the paralinguistic vocal devices accompany the act of speech itself, colouring or differentiating it, such as a high voice, a whisper or sibilating. Others, such as coughing or belching, belong in the facet of voices because

---

[6] Cf. Peirce's (1965: §2.283) classification of genuine indices as secondness.
[7] With the advent of live media, cases of publically circulated shots of officials bursting into tears at press conferences or during formal meetings are no longer rare.

2.2.2 The Intermediate Plane

they, too, are produced using the speech organs. However, not only are they not phones or words, but it is merely accidental that they are produced using the speech organs. In essence, they are just like other body-reflected sounds not produced using the speech organs (such as abdominal cramping, farting or even finger-clicking, see Scott 1958).

In a short monograph dedicated to prosodic and paralinguistic systems in English, Crystal and Quirk (1964: 41) describe them as occupying a continuum: from the most prosodic (features such as intonation which easily integrate with other linguistic structures) to the extreme paralinguistic end (where such integration is not possible). They claim that in order to produce the latter (such a laughter and cry), habitually, the addresser stops the course of hes speech. But they claim that it is also possible to speak through these properties, or in other words to integrate these qualities in the language.

Some paralinguistic silences fracture speech because of internal failures, such as difficulties encountered in decision-making and planning concerning speech; difficulties in its production; emotional overflow or difficulties coping with exterior; or failures that depend on the listener or the surroundings.[8]

O'Connell and Kowal (2004) seek to refute the association made between silences and phenomena involving speech blockage, disfluency or perplexes. They oppose the practice of many scholars who examine and evaluate spoken language in general, and silences in particular, relative to written texts (see note 16). They argue that in spoken languages pauses are an oral phenomenon; examining them there and in signed languages (irrespective of writing) will illuminate paralinguistic silences not as a failure but rather as positive devices for the handling of speech and facilitation of communication. O'Connell and Kowal include in what they consider positive means the silences that Bruneau classified as temporary halts initiated by the speaker to serve hes semantic or syntactic decision-making: silences as temporary spacing initiated by the addresser to facilitate decoding processing and needs.

Using here the measure of interaction, it must be stated that what O'Connell and Kowal rightly point out as silences supporting contact are not part of the utterance. As Leathers (1997: 169) plausibly clarifies, such silences are related to speech and interaction. It is therefore appropriate to conclude regarding these behaviours and silences (including pauses) that they appear during speech and interaction alongside language, and hence belong on the paralinguistic rather than the linguistic plane. As interlocutors, we experience paralinguistic silences on a daily basis. This can be illustrated by citing a passage from Rebelle's novel *Light of the Waxing Crescent*, relating a computer pad

---

[8] It may be assumed that Bruneau's (1973) association of these shortcomings with silences explains his inclusion under the term 'silence' of phenomena such as word change, repair or repetition that are clearly not incidents to do with the absence of speech or the absence of sounds.

conversation in the year 2086 between the singer Apollo Powers, who has just returned to earth with his band from a galactic concert tour, and his agent:

[~7^S]   Apollo Compad chimed. He went over to it and answered it, 'Hello.'
  'Apollo,' said his agent. 'It's Chuck. Are you familiar with Clara Jarosova?'
  Apollo froze where he stood. His mind raced. 'Very.' He paused. S_1 'What about her?'
  There was a pause at the other end of the line as his agent chose his words. 'S_2 Her agent just contacted me. It seems that she's a huge fan of yours and would like to arrange a date.'
  Apollo was silent for a moment. 'S_3 Seriously?' He looked at Sonya. 'Any specific place or time?'
  'Mars,' said Chunk. (p. 89)[9]

Three pauses appear along the course of this computer-mediated exchange: S_1 signals the pause breaking Apollo's speech. This pause resulted from the overwhelming emotions of astonishment evoked by the mention of Clara Jarosova. This paralinguistic silence parallels the physical symptomatic stillness of the speaker holding the floor (Apollo): freeze. As the text tells us, S_2 is a planned pause paralinguistically serving the addresser's selection of his coming words (which in fact also covers the ruling out of other words that might have been on the tip of Chuck's tongue). Using silence as the unmarked discourse marker indicating the switching of speech turns (see §4.3.1.1), Apollo is now the speaker expected to respond to Chuck's announcement. Had we as addressees heard this conversation, we would have heard the pause (S_3); noticed the suspension of Apollo's reply; and so the narrator's clause 'Apollo was silent for a moment' would have been superfluous, especially retroactively upon hearing his suspicion ('Seriously?').

In addition to a textual illustration of three different paralinguistic pauses (S_1 astonishment: caught unprepared; S_2 decision-making; and S_3 uncertainty) citation [~7^S] neatly demonstrates the distinction between the kinetic and the paralinguistic components of communication. Vargas (1986: 86) offers an operational test:

A man stands inside of a closed glass phone booth. You cannot hear a word he says, but you can see his postures, gestures, and facial expressions. You see his *kinetics*. Now imagine that you are on the other end of the telephone line. You cannot see any nonverbal communication, but you can hear more than his words. You can hear his *paralanguage*.[10]

---

[9] The initial S (also followed by an index number) is used throughout as the 'vs sign'. It is inserted within citations and texts to designate textual silences and to facilitate references to them in our discussion. S following examples' numbers (within brackets) indicate that only the 'vs sign' was added to the text.

[10] Unless stated otherwise, emphasis is in the original.

2.2.2 The Intermediate Plane

Returning now to pauses within paralanguage, citation ($[\sim 7^S]$) also illustrates that, unlike stillness, paralinguistic silences take place within the particular speaker's speech turn; yet, being paralinguistic, they are not in themselves means of expression and interaction. While stillness is external to interaction, suspension of speech is a (temporary) departure from interaction and communication.

Because the practical function of pauses in speech is to take time off within an interaction to admit the necessary space to attend to non-communicative demands, these pauses have an iconic basis and are thus indexical (see Bruneau 1973 on psycholinguistic and interactive pauses). At the same time, when the addresser purposely maintains them to elicit their corresponding meaning – 'I realise that my line of argumentation might be tricky and so I pause to allow you – the listener – time for processing' – such pauses may acquire a symbolic character. Such characteristics may be attributed to these pauses only if the addresser is assumed to be undertaking an intentional (but see note 5) communicative act (given information as opposed to given-off information) in initiating such pauses.

Excerpt ($[\sim 8^S]$) from a marriage counselling session (Fanshel and Moss 1971: 47, 64) exemplifies our case:

$[\sim 8^S]^{11}$	235 THERAPIST:	What happened before that episode?	
	236 MR. P:	(becomes guarded) Before, you mean, before I went ... ?	$\leftarrow S_1$
	237 THERAPIST:	Yes ... the subway incident ... had life been piling up?	$\leftarrow S_2 \leftarrow S_3$
	238 MR. P:	Ya ... an ...	$\leftarrow S_4$
	239 THERAPIST:	What was exactly going on for you?	
	240 MR. P:	Well, guess I was pretty lonely. I guess the culminating thing was some gal I was going around with who ... threw me overboard.	$\leftarrow S_5$

This short exchange illustrates the correspondence between content and form regarding both speech and pauses. These lines make up a fragment of the session when, in an attempt to convey to Mr Porter the legitimacy of expressing his anger, the therapist encourages him to talk about his past suicidal attempt (when he threw himself in front of a subway train). Vocally, two sorts of pauses are attested: unfilled (unvoiced) pauses (indicated here by '...' (S_2, S_3 and S_5 237, 240 in $[\sim 8^S]$)) and a filled (voiced) pause 'ya ... an ...' (S_4 238). At first sight, the notion of 'voiced pauses' may seem to be an oxymoron (as, conversely, would vs). Yet taking pauses in the paralinguistic plane as iconising the object's state of affairs in the real world (factual or

---

[11] In order not to shadow the ellipsis mark, the silence sign plus an arrow is placed facing the relevant mark at the end of the relevant line.

fictional), filled pauses, although not typical, are still not an oxymoron (see Figure 2.1). As seen here, Mr Porter is ambivalent: he wishes to share with his therapist and with his wife the painful experience of his attempted suicide, and so cooperates with the therapist in answering her question, but on the other hand he becomes guarded, probably fearing emotions such as shame which might accompany his disclosure. His actual wording as well as his filled and unfilled pauses express his state of mind. His words seem to paraphrase the meanings iconically conveyed by these paralinguistic pauses. They do so regarding the dilemma of telling the story or hushing it up: life piling up, feeling lonely, being with someone yet being thrown over by her. The therapist's pauses (S_2 and S_3) convey her own ambivalence in dealing with this trauma, and also indicate to Mr Porter that she is not rushing him.

We use this example to further comment on the paralinguistic peculiarity concerning filled pauses. Typically the pause extends from the termination of one speech event to the beginning of the subsequent one. In that time stretch, the speaker does not usually produce any sounds. This is why the phenomena of filled pauses puzzles scholars (see, e.g. Crystal and Quirk 1964: 49; Druckman et al. 1982: 49–50; Poyatos 2002: chapter 7; on filled pauses in signed languages see Winston 2000). The term 'filled pauses' refers (see S_4 [~8^s]) to pauses containing nonverbal sounds (e.g. 'e ... e ... ', 'em ... m', 'ya ... an ... ' and 'a ... ', see O'Connell and Kowal 2004). Mr Porter's filled pause ('ya ... an ... ') iconically reflects his ambivalence in that particular interaction. Adell et al. (2007) investigated the phenomenon of filled pauses as part of disfluent speech to be integrated in a speech synthesis model they generated to closely mimic natural speech. To this end, they analysed data drawn from authentic speech comparing the differences in prosodic settings and in durations of filled and unfilled pauses. Adell et al. have shown that filled pauses differ from their unfilled counterparts in distribution and internal structure. They observed that filled pauses result from the speaker's need to gain time. Since the maximal duration of a syllable and that of an unfilled pause are limited (the upper limit being approximately 500 ms) to gain more time (such as for planning), the speaker must stretch the syllable preceding the pause to its upper limit, lengthen the unfilled pause to its upper limit and fill in the additional time needed by inserting the nonverbal sounds. As they point out, this suggests that speakers must have an estimation of the overall time they need.

A difficulty arises regarding the relationships between Adell et al.'s chronometric explanation of the filled pauses phenomenon and the iconicity-based explanation suggested here in regard to Mr Porter's filled pause (S_4). Unfortunately, addressing this question requires the measuring of durations in such iconic dispositions and comparing them with the measures and analyses presented by Adell et al. It is anticipated that, unlike their cases, unfilled pauses involving overwhelming emotional turmoil that mitigates against planning will be found to exceed significantly the upper limit stretch expected for the entire duration of all pauses. This prediction is partly supported by daily experience, in which we as interlocutors identify such states because they exceed the default chronometric length.

To sum up the phenomena of stillness, symptomatic silences and paralinguistic pauses, it is important to note that just as not all pauses belong in the paralinguistic plane, so not all pauses are signs. Examples of the latter include pauses that involve the suspension of speech as one of many actions suspended, such as a person not communicating because s/he is sleeping, is alone (see Jaworski 1993: 77, 105; Bilmes 1994: 79) or is meditating (but see Jaworski 1993: 18–20). These pauses, not limited to speech, are not part of communication, and thus do not form part of the paralinguistic or any other plane of communication.[12]

Druckman et al. (1982: 43) define paralanguage as 'the content-free vocalizations and pauses associated with speech'. Saville-Troike points to the crucial difference between these context-free silences and context-sensitive ones:

Silent communicative acts are to be distinguished from the pauses which may or may not occur in conversational turn-taking, or between questions and responses [...] Silent acts are part of the verbal code, and pauses part of the nonverbal. (1982: 144)

Goffman's (1959: 2) distinction between 'given information' and 'given-off information' is most helpful when applied to the addressee's handling of paralinguistic silences (pauses). These are external to the (given) information conveyed by the addresser. This distinction, crucial for weeding out silences that not being (verbal) signifiers have no signified attached to them, serves us now to deepen our investigation focusing on silences within interaction.

2.2.3 The Content Plane

Silence may relate to phenomena in which there is speech within interaction, yet there is silence in regard to the expected-relevant content.

The typical situation occurs when an addresser who has something to say and wishes to share it with hes addressees uses verbal signifiers denoting the particular content. This is the use of speech within the verbal plane. To this end, the addresser holding the floor communicates content (facts, emotions,

---

[12] Following this line of argument, it is maintained that the cases Bruneau (1973: 41) lists as 'places of silence' and Kurzon's 'textual silences' (2007: 1679–1681), like readers reading text in a library or prayers in religious services, even when they all silently go through the same text, are not cases of silences within interaction because there is no interaction.

speech-acts, etc.) using conventional signifiers agreed upon and jointly understood within the specific language community (see the earlier quote from Goffman 1959:2, in §2.2.1). The typical obverse case is one in which having nothing to say or not wishing to communicate results in the conventional expected absence of speech. An illusory dichotomy emerges whereby having content is met by a matching form (verbal signifiers), whereas lacking content is matched by the absence of such form. The presence of atypical cases, however, shows such a dichotomy to be inaccurate.

Studies in diverse fields present, alongside paralinguistic silences and vss (see §2.2.4), concepts relating to silence on the part of contents. The first definition of 'silence' provided by the OED refers to silence as 'the fact of abstaining or forbearing from speech or utterance (sometimes with reference to a particular matter)' (OED: Silence, N.1a).[13] Examining here the notions of silence belonging in the content plane, we focus on 'silence with reference to a particular matter'. Such silences, taking place within interaction, emerge not as suspended speech but as refraining from speaking about a particular matter. The most prominent of these are the 'unsaid' and 'empty speech'. In both categories speech goes on, but this is not the speech expected regarding particular content. Such silences resist or even counter expression and cooperation (Grice 1989; Ephratt 2012).

2.2.3.1 The Unsaid

Having something to communicate in a dialogical context and wishing to share it typically results in its articulation by means of speech. Conversely, having nothing to say or not wishing to communicate results in the absence of speech.

'The unsaid' is a category of silence in which there is content – the addresser has something to say about a particular issue – and that specific speech exchange is initiated in the expectation that the addresser will give this information. The event is held and the addresser speaks and gives information on other relevant matters; but contrary to the underlying anticipation, that addresser deliberately chooses to abstain from relating to the particular matter. This expected but deliberately left-out content constitutes 'the unsaid'. Zerubavel (2006) identified this unsaid with 'the elephant in the room': all participants are definitely aware of this unsaid, it is impossible not to notice it, yet the addresser deliberately avoids it as if it were not there.

Private and public life offer many examples of the unsaid. No doubt every reader has hes own examples of the unsaid. We regularly encounter the unsaid when a public figure giving a public speech, interview or statement at the

---

[13] See also the OED definition of the noun silence: '3a.: Omission of mention, remark or notice in narration'; and the definition of the verb silence '4.: To leave unmentioned or unnoticed; to pass over in silence, to omit' (if these actions are performed intentionally).

2.2.3 The Content Plane

height of an inflaming incident mentions and talks about all relevant topics except for the most relevant and expected one (see Jaworski 1993: 98–114; Rescher 1998: 92–93). Dressen (2002) examines the eloquence of the unsaid surfacing in academic publications by scientists who ignore a relevant and expected reference or scholar, refraining from mentioning them as academically expected in their work.

A special context of the unsaid is the 'argument from silence' (Latin: *argumentum ex silentio*), referring to conclusions based on the absence of (an expected) mention in historical, biographic, commercial and other documents. The classic example is the claim that Marco Polo was never in China, a claim based on the fact that in his detailed report on China, Marco Polo never mentioned ubiquitous features such as the Great Wall of China or tea (see McGrew 2011: 64–65).

The unsaid is also apparent in discourses taking place in intrasubjective and intersubjective settings. Common incidents are when, following an emotional turmoil such as a bitter quarrel between couples, between parent and child or among co-workers, the conversation then continues as if nothing happened, despite everyone involved knowing that something has indeed happened. This nature of the unsaid being silence is exemplified in Theodor Reik's report (1927: 177) on a Viennese actress Josefine Gallmeyer, who requested of her table companion, who had sat beside her in complete silence for over half an hour:

[~9]   Let's be silent about something else!

Clearly Gallmeyer's companion had something to say: there was content and verbally available form articulating that content, but something in him resisted his inclination to disclose that content. In her phrasing – expressing her wish to make the unsaid absent by replacing it with something else – Gallmeyer voices her awareness of her companion's internal (psychological) dilemma presenting the unsaid as given information (see also [~161] §3.2.5.1). In line with Zerubavel's (2006) 'elephant in the room' image, and [~9], the unsaid is a deliberate silence originating in the addresser.

Special attention should be paid here to the difference between the unsaid as an iconic sign and what is left out assuming one way or another that it is known, irrelevant, not worth mentioning or could be otherwise implied. Rescher (1998: 93) claims:

In verbal communication we never have enough time and space at our disposal to make it all explicit [...] and this means that for reasons of communicative efficiency and economy we have to let silence do some of the communicative work [...] and so the natural presumption is that what we do actually say is the most important part of the matter [...] and this means that in many declarative settings silence implies *normalcy*.

Rescher's thesis is confined to the sphere of speech as the typical means of verbal communication and does not allude to the unsaid, which intensifies, rather than normalises, the presence of that absence.[14]

As in speech, the hearer can interpret the unsaid in many different ways not included in Goffman's given information, yet constituting given-off information. Since both the given information and the given-off information are delivered in the case of the 'unsaid' using absent verbal code, the question arises as to how the hearer detects and determines the information given as the 'unsaid'. Bilmes (1994: 82) explains the mechanism of silence using a relevance model:

> Constituting silence has become a major occupation of social scientists. We find topics or points that the speaker or the author might have mentioned, things that he might have said, but didn't, and we note his silence. We create silence by creating relevance.

Sperber and Wilson see relevance as a relational feature balancing efficiency contextual effect and required effort (1986: 153). Relevance is assessed with regard to context: the relevance A of B in context γ (see Ephratt 2014a). When, as in [~9], a particular content B is expected but missing in context γ, it comes to the fore as the most and only relevant topic.

'The unsaid' seems to coincide with Kurzon's 'thematic silence', a type of silence in which 's/he chooses silence instead of talking about the topic. [...] In this type of silence, the theme or topic of the text is known, and perhaps the contents are also known' (2007:1677). Kurzon asserts that since a unique feature of what he terms 'thematic silence' is that it cannot be timed (the addresser does not stop talking), it is metaphorical. We have to disagree with this claim. When we place 'the unsaid' in the content plane, namely looking at the content not said rather than its form (time-consuming), the question of time proves irrelevant. The absence of mention, when that mention is most relevant and so definitely expected, makes this absence become present.

Genocidal traumas elicit silence. The Holocaust engenders many sorts and forms of silence: silence iconically enacting the void of the black hole; silence reflecting what cannot be verbalised; silence due to fear of mistrust; and silence as the wish to enable a new start by letting go of horrific personal and collective losses and memories. The silence of Holocaust survivors may be the most powerful illustration of the presence of the unsaid as concrete (non-metaphorical). As Zerubavel (2006: 86, after Jasper 1997: 139) suggests: 'In fact, we may one day come to remember the Holocaust not so much for the

---

[14] See Saville-Troike's (1985: 10) reference to Abrahams 1979 on silence as an intensifier. The argument just directed at Rescher seems to apply to Tyler's view on 'The Said and the Unsaid' (1978) as representing the topic and comment uttered and the presuppositions and implications drawn from that (1978: 459–465).

2.2.3 The Content Plane

number of its victims as for the silence surrounding it' (see §4.6.4). The unsaid surrounded the Holocaust in real time when head of states, religious authorities such as Pope Pius XII and the Vatican, and other European institutions refrained from speaking out against what they witnessed during the Third Reich era, and in some cases refrained from taking actions against the horrors.

In the personal realm, the unsaid elephant in the room was the silence surrounding both the Holocaust survivors and the second generation. Bar-On (1995: 20) describes this as 'A sort of "double wall" [that] forms between the two generations: parents do not tell; children do not ask'. Helen Epstein, who dared ask, tells of her mother, a Holocaust survivor who emigrated to the States:

[~10] Whenever I asked her what it had felt like to arrive in New York, Franci invariably replied that the trip had taken twenty-six hours, that the temperature was over 100 degrees, that she was sweating under all those clothes. [...] She never mentioned any emotions. (Epstein, *Where*, p. 305)

These accurate details are not irrelevant to the experience, thus constituting a cooperative answer to the daughter's question. In light of the accurate memorised details, what struck Epstein, standing out as the unsaid, was that her mother 'never mentioned any emotions' (see also Wiseman and Barber 2008: 79–94).

In summary, silences in the content plane are inter alia atypical. The unsaid is the typical option of this atypical plane. It stands out not because of chronometric pauses suspending speech altogether, nor because of irrelevant speech, but because of the silence in place of the anticipated most relevant content. We now move to a converse phase of silence within the content plane: empty speech.

2.2.3.2 Empty Speech

If, in the content plane, the 'unsaid' is the more typical strategy accessible to the addresser who does not wish to communicate what is most expected of hem – 'empty speech' is the atypical of the atypical. To give a first impression of empty speech, we compare [~10] above with [~11] as told by Ruth Wajnryb (2001: 30–31), where she relates her personal memories as a second-generation survivor:

[~11] When 'the topic' came up, it was especially important to look solemn and not say anything. [...] I certainly did not realise in any conscious way that all the family talk about the historical circumstances of war allowed everyone to camouflage the way we avoided probing the personal. Under that talk, the wound was allowed to grow scar tissue and everyone knew better than to pick at it.

Speech is the typical verbal means of communication and saying nothing is the typical strategy for not-communicating (a particular topic or all topics), thus matching the lack of content with absence of speech. The unsaid is an atypical strategy because it uses speech to communicate but keeps silent on a specific required matter. Empty speech is the unsaid's atypical semiotic convergence. A comparison of [~10] and [~11] reveals that whereas the information communicated in [~10], though not the anticipated, is not irrelevant, in [~11] there is again an unfulfilled expectation of relevant content but unlike [~10] (and the unsaid) the speech in [~11] is void of *any* relevant information. As Wajnryb states, this speech does not inform or share but rather camouflages.

From the content plane, we have here a signifier with no signified. In the empty speech, as in the unsaid, there is content (signified) expected to be communicated in that conversation exchange – which, despite being most relevant, the addresser chooses not to communicate. However, unlike the cases of the unsaid, in the empty speech cases there is no correspondence between the addresser's choice to silence this content and the absence of the signifier. What is special about this speech is that these are not the signifiers corresponding to the silenced signifier. In §4.4, we introduce 'small talk' which, despite being a signifier void of matching content, is nevertheless functional; it is there not to communicate but to preserve the communication channel.

However, unlike small talk, empty speech does not come as a kind of speech. Says Jaworski, 'speech represents here the lack of expected silence (about something)' (1993: 76).

Saville-Troike (1985: 6, after Searle) explains it thus: 'one can utter words without saying anything'. Content-wise, the meaning conveyed by empty speech is not the words uttered but its emptiness. Clear examples of intersubjective empty speech are the exchanges between the characters in Beckett's *Waiting for Godot* (Hassan 1967; Amir 2014: 107–110; and see [~272] §4.3.3.2.1) and, regarding public discourse, the ongoing televised reporting of 9/11 (Jaworski et al. 2005). Susan Sontag (1969: 12) comments: '[The art of] our time is noisy with appeals for silence [...] one recognizes the imperative of silence, but goes on speaking anyway. Discovering that one has nothing to say, one seeks a way to say *that*'.

This brings out an additional peculiarity concerning empty speech. As humans, we are accustomed to viewing speech and silence as two opposites (see earlier in this section), such that speech is meaningful and silence insignificant. Empty speech as a chain of signifiers lacking content is a case of meaninglessness, and thus empty speech. Incorporating empty speech as silence (within the content plane), we find that empty speech can last from

2.2.3 The Content Plane

seconds to a flood of words not allowing the spaces expected to puncture and ground that speech, and on to the duration of an entire lengthy discourse performed to flood the listener or to occupy time. The filibuster is no doubt the extreme case of empty speech, and its record length is the longest empty speech silence and noise.[15]

Jacques Lacan coined the term '*parole vide*' (as opposed to '*parole pleine*') to capture speech that reflects the immanent split of the subject from hes desire. Lacan explains: 'where the subject seems to be talking in vain about someone who, even if he were his spitting image, can never become one with the assumption of his desire' (1956: 50). Empty speech is, according to Lacan, the exemplary illustration of a chain of signifiers as the absence of '*das Ding*' (the thing), namely the desire (see §4.5.1).

Empty speech damages communication as it masks the absence of contact with noise, concealing the shortcoming and futility of language. Harold Pinter described it as 'a constant stratagem to cover nakedness' (Ceramella 2014: 36 note 4). A good example comes from two scenarios Bilmes (1994) illustrates differentiating between what he terms two kinds of conversational silences: 'explicit silence' and 'implicit silence'. In the first scenario, when I show you a picture I have drawn for you, you do not express any praise but simply hand back the picture without saying a word; this constitutes explicit silence. But if, in the same situation (Bilmes continues), you give the picture back to me with some irrelevant remark about the weather or suchlike, a first priority response will still be missing, and I will draw the same conclusion as I would in the case of explicit silence (namely that you did not care much for the picture). This response constitutes implicit silence (Bilmes 1994: 82). Bilmes concludes his illustration by noting that 'some silences are obscured by words'. This is also captured in Khalil Gibran's opening verse to his poem 'On Talking': 'You talk when you cease to be at peace with your thoughts, and when you can no longer dwell in the solitude of your heart' (see [~268] §4.4). To this, Jensen (1973: 253) adds that some silences reveal the person's attempt to escape from hemself, from reality around hem.

Summing up the content plane, we see that it focuses on the content (signified): that is, the plane prior to language. Focusing on the content plane in general, and on the silences specific to that plane in particular, we find that alongside the possibility to communicate verbally that s/he does not want to talk about it (see [~9]), the addresser may decide to employ the typical strategy offered in the content plane, namely the unsaid: iconically articulating the

---

[15] See https://en.wikipedia.org/w/index.php?title=Filibuster&oldid=1011123871 (accessed 9 March 2021).

absence of content using the absence of form (signifiers). An atypical, and therefore non-transparent, strategy is empty speech, which entails a discrepancy between the particular expected content that is not denoted and another extraneous signifier that denotes nothing. Last but not least, empty speech and the unsaid are by definition cases in which speech accompanies silence: the addresser does not stop speaking (see Kurzon 2007: 1679). Indeed, as with other extralinguistic signs, speech may accompany the extralinguistic sign (such as kinesics or gaze; see on linearity, §4.6.3.3.3).

The following questions posed by the psychoanalyst Theodor Reik bridge the silences in the content plane and the focus of our investigation – silences in the verbal plane. After noticing that he has 'here handled silence as if it were a means of expression like speech, even though it is the opposite of speech', Reik asks:

But speech is then so unequivocal? When a person speaks, does he always say something? Doesn't speech just as often serve the one purpose of obscuring our thoughts as the other of expressing them? (1927: 183)

These questions spotlight empty rather than full speech. Reik's tentative answers to the above questions touch on the unsaid, and finally seem to lead to vs. Reik continues (1927: 183):

In analysis we come familiar enough with patients whose continuous speech has the sense of not saying precisely the most important things. Their speech is like those nets through whose large mesh just the most valuable things escape. If this is so, it will not surprise us that, on the other hand, silence can take over the function of expression.

We are thus led to recognize a singular antinomic relationship between speech and silence. Speech expresses this antinomy variously: there is meaningless speech and meaningful silence.

Only when the addresser uses silence admiringly as a verbal symbol (or its substitute) to communicate does such silence constitute vs belonging in the verbal code (see the quote from Saville-Troike 1982: 144 in §2.2.2).

2.2.4 The Verbal Plane

The verbal plane is strongly identified with language. As the most intuitive verbal signifiers, words are the typical means of that plane. Words being verbal signifiers are threefold: (1) form – phonetic sequences[16] and morphological

---

[16] Alphabetic writing systems, being visual representations of the oral media, do not constitute a special language (such as 'written English'). This is probably not the case regarding pictograms, emoji and SMS-specific notations.

2.2.4 The Verbal Plane

structure; (2) semantic content – meaning or grammatical functions attributed in a specific language and linguistic context to the specific form, and (3) the interpretation of form – meaning relations.

But, in addition to this typical manner, the addresser of the language also has at hes disposal an atypical option: to use silence as a verbal means of expression. The quality of vs as the outcome of the addresser's calculated choice to use it as a means of expression within hes speech places vs in given – rather than given-off – information.

Vs is the silence which Cicero, the master of rhetoric, regarded as 'one of the great arts of conversation'. Tannen (1985: 95) cites: 'if you don't understand my silence you will not understand my words'. This silence is part of the discourse: not the complete absence of sounds (stillness), not paralinguistic pauses suspending speech and not the silencing of content (the unsaid and empty speech), but a verbal means chosen by the addresser alongside words and phrases to communicate.

When, within an interaction, the content, phrasing, articulation or intonation of what our interlocutor says takes us by surprise, our response can take on different forms. Surprise can cause us to withdraw into ourselves, temporarily cutting ourselves off from the interaction (pause), or it can render us speechless (symptom). Alternative responses might include the use of words to communicate to our interlocutor that we are surprised or even feel that we are speechless. In addition, we can choose to respond by using silence: this is vs, which in this instance iconically acts out our reaction to the surprising content in the real world. Such a silence can last an entire speech turn, or be the starting point or final part of a speech turn complemented by matching metalinguistic verbalisation of that silence such as, e.g.,

[~12^s] S_1 I feel lost for words / ('I feel lost for words S_1').

Such verbalisation does not eliminate the vs that precedes or follows it but illuminates it. This is probably what Robert Blackmur (1957: 152) meant when he commented that 'meaning is what silence does when it gets into words'.

Before focusing on vs, it is worth differentiating between vs and silencing. In various interactions the two may surface identically, but they originate from two contradictory sources and motives.

2.2.4.1 Silencing

Searching the keyword 'silence' in databases and publications from the last hundred years shows that the majority of references retrieved a link to silencing.

Verschueren (1985: 75–76) argues that while English has no genuine lexical items denoting verbs describing a person being silent (what Verschueren terms '*verba tacendi*'), the verb 'to silence' does describe (usually linguistic) acts performed in order to cause somebody else to be silent (see also Zerubavel 2006; Ben-Ze'ev et al. 2010).

The syntactic-semantic feature shared by all actions involving silencing is that not only is the silence not the product of the person's free will and inner need for expression, but it is actually externally imposed on hem by a genuine or fake power as a means of controlling individuals' speech (in general or in specific contexts, see §4.7). This is the crucial difference between silencing and vs.

From the outset, societies and administrations have recognised the value of expression in general, and speech in particular, as resources of power. The resource of speech and its denial were and still are a central tool in the hands of all, especially those who hold power, alongside exclusion in general, as well as other means such as granting or denying freedom of movement and the right to assembly. According to Bruneau (1973: 39), a great deal of political power is derived and even maintained by the use of silence. He supports this claim by weighing the use of silencing as a power by the authorities against the use of the subordinates of silent protests as a countermeasure neutralising the power of the authority's silencing. Silencing and the breaking of silence are central and recurring themes in the platforms of various social movements.

Because power is not confined solely to silencing but also extends to control over resources of speech and silence, it is sometimes silence (rather than speech) that constitutes power. Typical examples of this are the silent treatment and sectional or personal boycotts (see §4.3.1.2).

As noted regarding pauses, here too the issue at stake is not silence and silencing but a more general matter: social conduct and solidarity, in which speech and its denial are just one incident (other incidents include dress code and gaze appropriateness).

The feature shared by silencing and vs that distinguishes them from stillness and paralinguistic silences, such as pauses, is that they both occur within interactions in which the addresser has something to say and wishes to communicate that message. While the defining features of silencing may seem almost trivial, we outline them here in order to mark the differences between silencing and vs. Silencing and vs are opposites concerning free will. Whereas vs is a choice the addresser makes towards expression, silencing counters the speaker's will to communicate.

Externally imposed silencing can be explicit, such as rules or censorship, or indirect, such as restricting access to public media or sabotaging communication channels. Implicit silencing should also cover silence events that on the surface seem to be the product of an individual or of a group of people internalising externally imposed silencing. Closer investigation, however, reveals that these result from submissiveness. A severe example of this is the silence of victims of sexual abuse (see battered woman, §3.2.3.2.2).

2.2.4 The Verbal Plane

The 'spiral of silence' stands for a social dynamics forming public opinion that, according to Noelle-Neumann (1974), takes place by virtue of the unique junction between the individual's need for belonging and hes fear of isolation, on the one hand, and on the other the immense power possessed by the media on which that individual is almost entirely dependent as a source of information gathering and which fully controls the disclosure or non-admission of that information. By commanding this power, the media constructs reality. According to Noelle-Neumann, this spiral dynamics of the media amplifies the opinions favoured by their owners, so that other opinions, even those held by the majority, do not receive equal exposure. Noelle-Neumann claims that 80 per cent of the individuals whose beliefs differ from those propagated by the media submit to the dynamics of adaptation. This results in silencing their genuine voice.

The result of the two manners of silencing original and genuine beliefs is a spiral dynamics strengthening the viewpoint voiced by the media. Needless to say, this spiral works in the same way when it comes to personal issues such as fashion, norms, popularity and in-group acceptance discussed in personal circles.

The 'spiral of silence' falls half way between external silencing and self-silencing. Other cases in which individuals might silence themselves include the silencing of internal codes in order to match and assimilate external codes, or the acceptance of restrictions by way of vows. As we detail (in §3.2.5.3), another category of silencing that falls midway between the external and the internal, between the collective and the personal, and even between speaking and keeping silent, is the category of taboo and derogatory words (see e.g. Jaworski 1997: 392–394).

Disparate roles are played by free will in silencing and vs. Regarding silencing, the speaker makes the choice (be it genuinely or only ostensibly free) to accept and follow the external imposition. The case of vs differs from the former in that here the speaker is not only determined to speak but will also take action to carry out hes intention. The choice faced in the case of vs is not between communicating and not communicating but relates to the form that this message will take: speech (words and phrases) or vs.

Jensen's (1973: 249) wake-up call, that 'numerous factors of context and also cultural influences will of course also play a role in the various functioning of silence, so we must ascribe functions with caution', must be taken seriously.[17]

---

[17] Understanding speech and silence in the socialisation context, it will come as no surprise to find that opposite incidents entailing silence when speech is expected also count as anti-social deeds. One recent example (2015) is former Labour leader Jeremy Corbyn standing silent for the British national anthem during the Battle of Britain memorial service at St Paul's Cathedral. See, for example, *The Guardian*, www.theguardian.com/politics/2015/sep/15/jeremy-corbyn-silent-during-national-anthem-battle-of-britain-service (accessed 3 July 2017).

As silencing is a tool used by the superior to control or limit the inferior's acts, 'breaking the silence' is a strategy that seeks to repel that silencing. Due to the worldwide trend for the granting of rights the weight has shifted in modern times from the very struggle for the right of expression – that is, breaking the silencing – to the struggle for the right to talk about specific content (that is, a shift from the linguistic and paralinguistic planes to the content plane, see Figure 2.1, and see Jaworski 1993: 115–139).

This marks a move from passive submissiveness (being silenced) to actively voicing one's presence. As Saville-Troike points out, 'where institutionally determined power is accorded voice, silence is often indicative of passivity and powerlessness' (1994: 3945). Such breaking of silencing entails a refusal to comply with the ban to speak, be it external (explicit or implicit) or internal.

The following text illustrates a move from collective silencing (involving the unsaid) to breaking that silence:

[~13]   After months of telling me that race doesn't belong in a court of law, Kennedy McQuarrie took the elephant in the room and paraded it in front of the judge. She squeezed it into the jury box, so that those men and women couldn't help but feel the pinch.
   I stare at the jury, all lost in thought and utterly silent. Kennedy comes to sit down beside me, and for a moment, I just look at her. My throat works while I try to put into words everything I am feeling. What Kennedy said to all those strangers, it's been the narrative of my life, the outline inside of which I have lived. But I could have screamed it from the rooftops, and it wouldn't have done any good. For the jurors to hear it, really hear it, it had to be said by one of their own. (Picoult, *Small*, p. 467)

This passage seems self-explanatory, though it is worth highlighting the revelation undergone by Ruth (the African-American nurse on trial) as she expresses it in her closing words. Not only can the unsaid be the outcome of self-silencing or external silence internalised by the speaker, but the resonance of its breaking turns out to be a function of the identity of whoever breaks it and the magnitude of that elephant. The more racism is ignored the stronger the significance of its breaking (as reflected in the jury's astonishment and ensuing silence).

As apparent from the above outline, and as evident from observing real life, silencing is frequently misconstrued as silence itself. Heading towards our focused study of vs, we have perused silencing to elucidate the difference between the two. An important point concerning this difference surfaces from Raufman and Ben-Cnaan's (2011) analysis of Grimm's fairy tale 'The Twelve Brothers'. The authors chose not to be dragged into the feminist and postmodern inclination to rewrite the narratives placing women in what have customarily been stereotyped as masculine roles (e.g. speaking as an action). Instead, they offer an alternative reading that focuses on the liberating power of silence. The most important contribution of their analysis is the understanding that what seems on the surface to be a case of silencing (the decree to refrain from all forms of speech for seven years, externally imposed on the princess by the witch's spell) is in fact an active and forceful tool serving the heroine's end as a means of connection and communication. This silence acts as a dynamic and expressive means alongside or in place of speech (see [~235$^{\text{German-T}}$] §3.2.5.5.1). This common sense insight from 'The Twelve Brothers' and other folk stories will accompany us throughout our exploration of the forms and functions of vs.

2.3 Scheme: Silences in Interaction

To conclude the overview of the different categories covered by the term 'silence', we cite Verschueren (1985: 73), who turns to geology in order to support his linguistic interest in the semantics of silence:

> Though for a geologist the complete set of holes in the surface of the earth does not form a natural category, it consists of a number of subsets (e.g. volcanic carters, holes caused by the impact of meteorites, those caused by earthquakes, etc.) [...] Similarly, thought all instances of linguistic silence,[18] taken together, do not constitute a natural linguistic category, it is linguistically significant to get an overview of the complete set.

The scheme in Figure 2.1 and the entire study focusing on vs pick up this gauntlet. Figure 2.1 is a graphic summation of the various issues discussed in this chapter, mapping the addresser's different silences in interaction onto typicality within the three planes and the involvement of sounds. Having exhausted the typical options of interacting (speech) and not interacting (pauses), silences in the content plane are inter alia atypical.

Excluding stillness exterior to interaction, this scheme delineates the multifaceted relations that the various modes of speech and of silences may assume within interaction and at its peripheries. This explains why categories in which sounds or even a voice is audible but where the articulated signifier is null because it does not connote the content on the agenda, or where the voices do not constitute words in the language, must be regarded as forms of silence and not forms of speech. Evidently, speech is the only category in this scheme that is not a form of silence (Table 2.1).

---

[18] Verschuren's use of 'linguistic silence' covers not only the different silences taking place within interaction (see Figure 2.1) but also silencing; this includes vs as a subset, but is by no means identical with it.

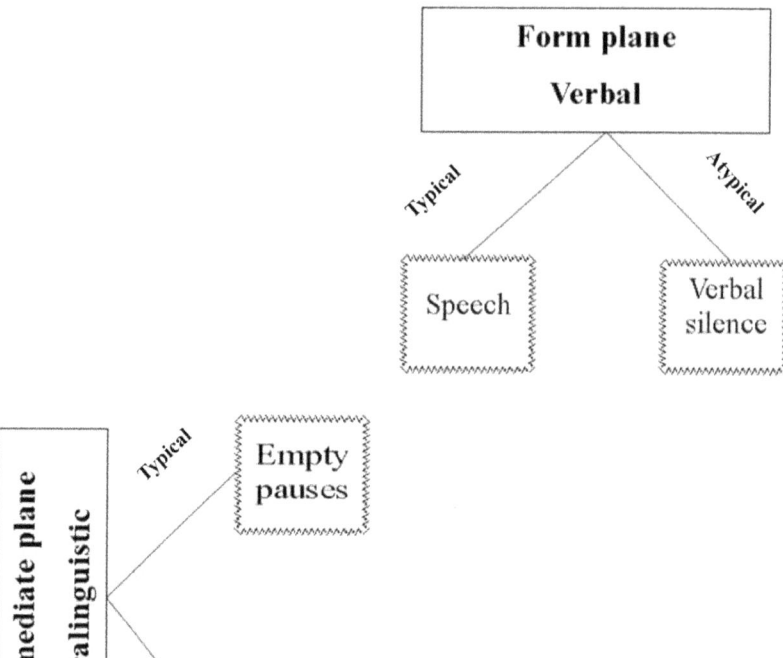
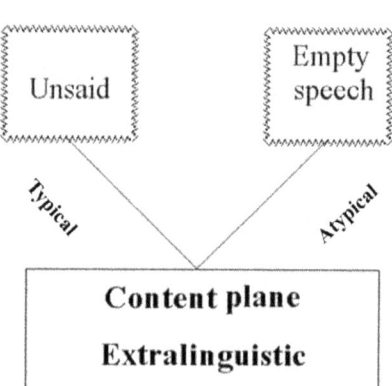

Figure 2.1 Silences in interaction.

2.3 Scheme: Silences in Interaction

Table 2.1. *Key differences between the six categories in Figure 2.1*

Object	Form plane		Intermediate plane		Content plane	
Term	Speech	Vs	Empty pauses	Filled pauses	Unsaid	Empty speech
Typicality: markedness	Typical	Atypical	Typical	Atypical	Typical	Atypical
Interaction	Genuine part	Genuine part	Suspend	Suspend	Genuine part	Genuine part
Phonetic: what sounds are produced	Verbal	No sounds	No sounds	Nonverbal sounds	Verbal	Verbal
Semantic: there is a specifically expected content	Yes	Yes	No	No	Yes	Yes
Semiotic: the form and content match	Yes	(Yes, When Iconic)	Yes	(No)	(Yes, in terms of relevance)	No
Chronometric: the form takes up time	Yes	(Only when enacted by a pause)	Yes (only when enacted by a pause)	Yes	No	Yes

3 Verbal Silence

Forms

After presenting the different sorts of silence and the relationships between them, we now delve into the realm of vs. This chapter presents the different forms of vs according to the chief linguistic concepts used for describing speech.

The chapter comprises two parts. Following a more intuitive presentation of some examples of vs, §3.2 provides a systematic linguistic classification and analysis of vs. An equally detailed account of the varied functions fulfilled using vs making extensive use of pragmatics is the focus of Chapter 4.

3.1 Verbal Silence: An Intuitive Glance

The simple and intuitive qualities of vs are shared naturally by the speakers of a language. Using words, clauses, discourse markers, intonation and other articulated verbal signifiers – as forerunners – the addresser signals to hes addressee hes choice of silence as a means of expression. These addressees' proficiency in the language enables them to identify these signifiers as the forerunners of vs and to determine the form of that silence, the local function it serves and the broader meaning it carries in the interaction.

Although vs constitutes the absence of articulation, the unique combination of the speech surrounding the particular instance of vs (its forerunner) and its meaning imbues vs with many verbal forms and functions. Each of the phenomena outlined intuitively here will be examined systematically in the latter parts of our study.

[~14^s] SPEAKER A: 'Good evening S_1'
          SPEAKER B: 'Good evening S_2'

The vs at the centre of example [~14^s] has no bibliographic reference as it – or variants thereof – participate in every verbal exchange. Focusing on vs, the issue here is not the identical formulaic greeting performed by both interlocutors but rather a far more commonplace, yet important, practice, namely the use of vs as a discourse marker. S_1 stands here for the unmarked turn-switching marker: in ordinary discourse, the speaker holding the floor does

3.1 Verbal Silence: An Intuitive Glance

not use words (such as 'Roger' in military discourse for received, or Latin '*dixi*' 'I have spoken') to acknowledge the successful termination of the current turn. In discourses involving fragments longer than [~14^s] S_2 too designates a turn-switching discourse marker. But if [~14^s] presents the entire exchange then S_2 is interpreted as a marker indicating the final closure of that discourse (not performing a speech-act allocating the next speaker; see §4.3.1.1 and §4.6.2.1).

These discourse markers occur in most turn-switching and discourse closure contexts, although as default forms they are not explicitly marked in the transcriptions of discourses. Compare the rewrite of lines 235 and 236 of excerpt [~8^s] discussed in Chapter 2:

[~8']   235 THERAPIST: What happened before that episode?

235' S_0

236   MR. P: (becomes guarded) Before, you mean, before I went ... S_1?

236' S_2

S_0 and (new) S_2 follow a question. In English, as in many other languages, a question is marked using interrogative intonation. Note, however, that the orally elevated intonation in spoken languages and the facial and brows configuration in signed languages do not designate the switch of turn to the person to whom that question is directed (here the therapist or Mr Porter): after posing the question, the current speaker may go on talking (answering that question, making a further statement or adding questions). It is the vs discourse marker (such as S_0 and S_2) that initiates the turn-switching shift.

The next example, strongly associated with silence in language, is the zero sign (ø). Jakobson (1937: 152), following Bally, defined the zero sign as 'a sign invested with a particular value but without any material support in sound'. In many synthetic languages the zero sign conventionally designates the unmarked grammatical inflection of minimal verbal pairs, though it is also found in other contexts. This use is illustrated in the opposition between the masculine 'actor' and the feminine 'actress':

[~15^a]   Casey Affleck won the 2017 Oscar for best actorø.

[~15^b]   Emma Stone won the 2017 Oscar for best actress.

In accordance with the diagrammatic maxim: additional content (or grammatical information) materialises in additional form (signifiers), it is the unmarked form that takes on the zero sign. This seems to become more challenging in cases such as the opposition:

[~16]   Widowø / widower.

32   Verbal Silence: Forms

Contrary to the grammatical tendency in English to identify the masculine form with the unmarked lexical entry, here the zero sign attaches to the feminine form – 'widowø' – while the agent morpheme is added to the masculine: 'widower'.[1] This is by no means accidental: the opposition between the zero sign and the agent morpheme ('er') diagrammatically reflects the reality that, due to the difference in life expectancy, significantly more wives outlive their husbands than vice versa. Pragmatically speaking, feminine rather than masculine is the unmarked case when it comes to widowhood. Because the zero sign is prescribed by grammar and so not a product of the addresser's verbal choice (see §3.2.2.2), while it functions verbally it does not constitute as vs.

The following examples illustrate three incidents of vs announced using linguistic incompleteness: phonetic lipogram ([~17], see Figure 3.1), syntactic incompleteness ([~18]) and lexical incompleteness ([~19^s]).

[~17]

Figure 3.1 'M rmite'.
Reproduced with kind permission of Unilever PLC and group companies[2]

---

[1] This should not be mistaken for Bloomfield's (1933: 217–218) explanation of French masculine formation as a secondary derivation by what he termed as a 'minus-feature'.
[2] https://twitter.com/marmite/status/608934650912849921 (accessed 11 July 2017).

3.1 Verbal Silence: An Intuitive Glance

Verbal signifiers constitute a coherent and fixed sequence of phones conventionally linked to a specific lexical meaning. Paralinguistic infinitesimal pauses or juncture groundings envelop the lexical signifier, leaving it intact and in no way penetrating it. However, the vs in [~17] serves as iconic means: the rupture of the signifier (in Figure 3.1 the logo 'Marmite' and 'extract') is analogous to the rupture of life caused by the loss of blood.

To signify iconically the need for blood donations and the potential for the public to fill in the vital gap, logos of famous products and signposts appeared silencing the letters 'A' and 'O', representing the required blood types. The choice to use famous logos and signposts made the missing phones (letters) in the lipogram stumps salient.

Example [~17] illustrates the iconic faculty of vs to convey a message and conatively activate the addressee (see §4.3). This end is reached using phonetic vs: leaving out phones as means of expression (see §3.2.1).

The next case portrays vs announced using syntactic incompleteness:

[~18]   Avis. We try harder.

This is the fifth most famous advertising slogan of all time. The deliberate use of a comparative adverb ('harder') dictates a syntactic construction of comparison (S_1: 'than Δ'):

[~18^S]   Avis. We try harder S_1.

This syntactically and semantically obligatory constituent is left out (see §3.2.4.4). The goal of the Avis campaign was to move Avis from being the second-ranked car-rental service in the USA to the first by overtaking Hertz.[3] In this context, 'Hertz' is necessarily the only entry successfully instantiating the complement. But this by no means makes this a case of redundancy: had the content of the comp-element [S_1, 'than Hertz'] been redundant, the slogan would have been trivial all together. The vs not only avoids mentioning 'Avis' and 'Hertz' side by side, which would position them as equal competitors, but it also implies that the contest is over: Hertz has vanished as a contestant and Avis has taken over. As a case of iconicity, S_1 belongs in the code: in what is said as given information (Goffman 1959) also fulfilling Grice's (1989) cooperative principle (see Ephratt 2012).

While [~18^S] illustrates a forerunner constituting an incomplete truncated syntactic (grammatical) structure, the next case portrays lexical vs (S_1: 'on first thought'):

[~19^S] S_1 On second thought, I'll stick with my Diet Pepsi.

---

[3] *Time*, 24 July 1964: www.time.com/time/magazine/article/0,9171,939058,00.html (accessed June 2011).

The grammatical-syntactic structure is fully articulated in [~19^s]. The expression 'on second thought' placed at the opening indicates a series of which the second constituent is articulated, thus serving as a lexical forerunner pointing to the unarticulated first constituent (S_1) – an idea – which, as a preliminary, is irrational and triggered by emotions.[4] Clearly, this vs signifies – but does not articulate – 'Coca Cola'. Here, similar to [~18^s], an iconic quality of vs is exploited: an unarticulated signifier denoting the nullification of the signified (S_1).

Although both vss ([~18^s] and [~19^s]) – as all vss – have no sound, they are not identical signifiers. While the first stands for a comparison complement, the second stands for the initial element of a series (see §3.2.5.5.2). Let us now add a third instance:

[~20^s] S_1 Easy come S_2 S_3 easy go.

Here it is the sum of the vss (and not a single clear-cut form) that produces the idiomatic flavour of the utterance, attaining an illuminating accord between form and content. At least three incidents of vs partake in the construction of this idiom.[5] The idiom comprises two parallel clauses, each lacking a subject (syntactic SUBJECT as well as thematic topic, S_1 and S_3), and jointly missing an obligatory connective (S_2) responsible for binding the two propositions to produce a single coherent statement. Unlike impersonal constructions denoting actions not performed by agents (having no doer), or those performed by a non-specific agent or by an unknown agent (a textbook example being English 'It rains'; French '*Il pleut*'), [~20^s] is not an impersonal form (one cannot replace it with the PRONOUN 'it'). This instance ([~20^s]) lacks any referent, whether personal or impersonal. The absence of a syntactic-logical connective hampers our ability to determine the nature of the association between the two propositions (e.g. which of the first-order predicate calculus connectives holds true for [~20]: a conjunction, a disjunction, an opposition, a conditional such as cause and effect or equivalence). The failure to clarify the relationship between the two constituents prevents the possibility of extracting a new cohesive proposition. Unlike symptomatic silences or paralinguistic silences, however, these syntactic and logical absences are not accidental and do not end in deficiency. On the contrary, the combination of the local (S_1 and S_3) and general (S_2) vss produces a sense of arbitrariness (see §3.2.4.5). The idiom in [~20] communicates nothingness and a sense of being left up in the air (much like the two parallel constituents and the interlocutors). The form and the

---

[4] Compare Wallace Stevens' 'first idea' as the suspension of intellect, a state of zero degree of mental activity surrendering of sheer sensation (Eeckhout 1996: 266–267).

[5] For example, 'come' and 'go', at least when functioning as genuine motion verbs, may require origin, destination and root as complements.

3.1 Verbal Silence: An Intuitive Glance

iconic character of the idiom enable the speaker to communicate hes subjective modal stances, such as toning down or ruling out the matter discussed as easy come easy go: irrelevant, unsustainable and short-lived.

The last example in this section dedicated to an intuitive presentation of vs is an instance of vs as a direct speech-act:

[~21$^{\text{Japanese-T}}$]   A: Please marry me.
           B: [Silence; head and eyes lowered] (acceptance).

Saville-Troike (1985: 8), who cites this case (after Williams 1979), explains that in this very emotional situation, which occurred between Japanese speakers, for the girl (B) to have said anything would have been considered very inappropriate (see also Saville-Troike 2003: 133–134, and see [~21$^{\text{a-Japanese-T}}$]).

The exchange in [~21$^{\text{Japanese-T}}$] illustrates the case of vs as consent (see §4.3.3.2.1). As Saville-Troike (2003: 133) explains, 'He was not really asking her a question and expecting an answer, but declaring his decision to marry her'.

Silence may also function as a verbal speech-act admitting guilt:

[~22]   A: Who ate all the cookies?
        B: [silence]
        A: I knew it was you. (Jaworski 2006: 378)

The juristic practice '*Qui tacet consentire videtur*' – 'he who keeps silent is assumed to consent' (and see also in the Talmud, *Yevamot* 87b), is also a direct speech-act of admission of guilt performed using vs. Vs as a means for performing a direct speech-act of consent is rooted in judicial practices in which the burden of proof rests on the defendant or accused.[6] From a communication efficiency point of view, vs acting as an anaphoric PRO for the entire speech-act (its expositional part and its referential part) consumes near to no energy, and far less than performing the act phonetically ('I admit P', see §4.3.1.3).

Another important characteristic worth noting is that when vs signifies a direct speech-act, such as consent (both in intersubjective contexts, as for example in [~21$^{\text{Japanese-T}}$]) and in formal judicial settings [~22]), it occupies an entire speech turn, whether as an answer or a response. In this case, as illustrated in [~14^{S}] and [~8'], this turn is also preceded and followed by silence as a (turn-switching) discourse marker (see also §4.3.3.2.1).

Sampling diverse forms of vs and examining the communicative roles they play, it now becomes apparent that although all incidents of vs are soundless,

---

[6] For an interpretation of its relationship to the 'right to silence', see §4.6.5.

they are not uniform (signifiers): their forms differ according to the verbal code they stand for and the verbal context grounding them as figure.

The intuitive presentation of vs shows that vs is used regularly as part of the given information of the verbal code. Speakers, copywriters, authors and orators use vs signifiers, relying on the addressees' linguistic competence to handle vss, that is to identify and decode them, integrating them as part of the message.

This observation calls for the thorough systematic examination of the forms and functions of vs.

3.2 The Forms of Verbal Silence

> [...] Words, after speech, reach
> Into the silence. Only by the form, the pattern,
> Can words or music reach
> The stillness [...] (T. S. Eliot, 'Burnt Norton')

Two forms of silence may participate in speech, playing a linguistic role in verbal communication: phonetic punctuation and vs.

Phonetic intervals are minimal breaks segregating small verbal units within larger units, such as words within compounds or clauses within utterances.[7] Compare:

[~23^a]   [ə#ˈneɪm] (A name)
[~23^b]   [ən#ˈeɪm] (An aim).

We cannot manage without these extremely short sparks of silence: they are essential for destroying continuity and thus enabling the cognitive-mental decoding of speech (Bruneau 1973: 18). Yet being integrated in the code and being extremely short, they often remain unnoticed. Compare:

[~24^a]   Light housekeeper
[~24^b]   Lighthouse keeper (Haiman 1983: 781)

Only when something goes wrong – for example, when the expected punctuation is missing, dislocated or stretched disproportionately – do these silences attract attention. Phonetic punctuation may also be noticed when junctures are deliberately contrasted, for example in order to form an equation or be equated

---

[7] While phonetic punctuation is primary, as Poyatos (2017: 60–61) shows, orthographic punctuation marks represent conscious efforts to symbolise spoken discourse. Accordingly, they are only partial and leave a large proportion of audible or silent constructs unrepresented (see also [~75]–[~77] in §3.2.4 and §4.6.3).

3.2 The Forms of Verbal Silence

to build sequences producing poetic affects (see §4.6 and §4.5) as in Wyatt's 'Each man me telleth':

[~25]   My word nor I shall not be variable
        But always one, your own both firm and stable.[8]

Gregerson (2013: 157) ties the poetic effect of the play between [ˈvá-ri-able] and [ˈvə-ri##ˈable] with iconic open voicing, saying that 'The pull between plain váriable and the rhyming back formation of very-áble, [...] enacts in miniature the selfsame instability that is the subject, and the larger method, of this poem' (see also §4.6.1.5).

A humorous play on juncture is illustrated in:

[~26]   I scream, you scream, we all scream for ice-cream![9]
[~26'] [ˈaɪ#ˈskɹiːm##u##ˈskɹiːm##wiː#ɔːl#ˈskriːm##fɔːr#ˈaɪs#kriːm##].

To illustrate acting out with words (and determining relevance, see §4.1), Wilfred Bion (1970: 13) cites a psychoanalytic verbatim revolving on this same juncture:

[~27]   Thus A says he could buy no ice-cream. Six months later he says he cannot even buy ice-cream. Three days later he mentions his being too late to buy ice-cream: there was no ice-cream left. Two years later he says he supposes there was no ice-cream. Had I known, when the topic was mentioned first, what I know now I might have noted the time and place of the reference, but I did not know and therefore could not attend to this statement or note it. When I did, it was because of the obtrusive 'I scream' theme. It was later still that I grasped the significance of 'no – I scream'.

Comparatively longer intervals, yet still extremely short, break up larger chunks, such as sentences. Indeed, Zellig Harris (1951: 14) defines an utterance as 'any stretch of talk, by one person before and after which there is silence on the part of the person'.

Notice, however, that unlike silence as a discourse marker introduced by the addresser to generate turn-switching (see [~8'] and §4.3.1.1), phonetic punctuations are not in themselves a product of the addresser's verbal choice. Accordingly, while they function verbally, they do not constitute as vs.

Vs covers:

Unarticulated verbal signifiers chosen by the addresser, that is, the speaker (holding the floor) as a verbal means of expression (in place of particular articulated speech) signifying meaningful content.

---

[8] The reference for this poem is Gregerson (2013), see note 96 on reference.
[9] A 1927 rhyme, see http://rwj-b.stanford.edu/song/i-scream-you-scream-we-all-scream-ice-cream (accessed 6 July 2017).

Being verbal means of expression, vss belong in the linguistic inventory; they are part of its given information (see §2.2.1) and play an active role in verbal communication.

A review of the tables of contents of linguistic textbooks leaves the impression that linguistics is confined to the study of articulated verbal signifiers: morphemes, words, clauses, sentences and utterances, as well as entire discourses and texts. This impression is further enhanced when examining the analyses of the examples provided in such textbooks, which are attuned to the sounds of speech yet leave the forms of silence in the background.

This unbalanced picture, which obscures the active role played by vss as part of the linguistic code, may be explained (though not justified) once we understand that for vs to serve as a signifier, it must be bounded within speech (articulated verbal signifiers). As examples [~8'] and [~14^s] through [~22] show, the speech stretches which ground vss may range from single phones or words to entire discourses – but vs cannot stand on its own, let alone function in isolation.

The addresser who chooses to employ vs as a signifier undertakes to inform hes addressee of the coming silence, that is the deliberate absence of the expected linguistic grammatical or lexical element(s). To this end, s/he plans hes utterance so that the speech surrounding that silence, and particularly the speech preceding it, will serve as its background, marking the coming silence as figure. Accordingly, the addresser makes the coming vs apparent by the use of speech forerunners pointing to the coming silence (see Saville-Troike's (1985: 4, observation (1)).

Forerunners are grammatical or lexical stumps signalling the location, category and content of the vs in the specific utterance.[10]

These can be a ruptured word, ripping apart the coherence of its phonological sequence ('M rmite' in [~17]), or a forerunner taking the form of a grammatical or lexical particle that is articulated without its required complementation (see examples [~18^s] and [~19^s]). Non-terminal intonation should also be included, in English and other languages, within grammatical particles. This forerunner is typically used by teachers as an interrogative intonation marking, alongside an incomplete sentence, what Saville-Troike (1985: 7; 2003: 117) terms 'fill-in-the-blank structure', as in:

[~28]   And your name is _____?[11]

---

[10] Kurzon (1998: 6) uses the term 'forerunner': 'Zero is taken as a "forerunner" of silence' to refer to the silence signifier or signified. Likewise Poyatos (2017: 27, 57) uses the term 'anticipator' to denote silence and non-verbal constituents serving as receptacles of coming words or activities. Here 'forerunner' is used in an inverse sense to denote articulated speech marking the coming vs.

[11] This vs, being a variable to be filled by the addressee, belongs in the conative function (see §4.3).

3.2 The Forms of Verbal Silence

Lexical entries such as 'silence' (see for example [~163] §3.2.5.1.1 – 'The rest is silence') may also be used to designate the coming vs and so act as lexical forerunners.

Linguists and other scholars who relate to vs (that is, those who identify the uniqueness of vs as a verbal signifier) must account for the relations between vs and speech.

Jaworski (1993), who confines his study only to silences taking place within interaction, claims that silence and speech do not stand in total opposition. He therefore presents them on a continuum ranging from the most typical cases of the addresser's speech (what he terms 'straightforward talk') through the least typical (or most atypical) speech and silences, to what Jaworski considers as the most typical cases of the addresser's (not the listener's/addressee's) silences; those in which silences, when communication is assumed to be taking place, are not interpreted as violations of any communicative norms.

A close examination of the silences Jaworski considers as most typical reveals that these include diverse sorts of silences. These include instances Jaworski classes as 'formulaic silence', which do not stand by themselves and require other nonverbal behaviours; silence as a state, which, despite taking place within interaction and when speech is expected, plays a negative – rather than a positive – role in that what replaces speech is not that silence but other nonverbal channels (visual: kinesics, proxemic); and silences as activities, including the unsaid (see §2.2.3.1) as well as incidents in which, according to Jaworski (1993: 82), 'someone's silence may effect changes in other people's behavior or attitudes'. However, the latter form includes symptoms and other forms of unintentional silences, and therefore belongs in given-off information rather than silence as given information (see §2.2.1). The continuum laid out by Jaworski is not a two-dimensional model of verbal communication but a three-dimensional one of personal communicative interaction.

Saville-Troike's detailed attention to silence as a key topic yielded many clear statements not previously heard in linguistics. She begins (1985: 4) with two constitutive statements about silence: (1) 'we can view silence as itself a valid object of investigation, bounded by stretches of verbal material which provide boundary marking for its identification'; and (2) 'just as with speech, silence is not a simple unit of communication, but is composed of complex dimensions and structures'. As reproduced in Table 3.1, Saville-Troike (1989: 145, figure 4.1; cf. Saville-Troike, 1982: 143, figure 4.1; Saville-Troike 2003: 116, figure 2) differentiates between code and channel (i.e. the mode of production),[12] yielding the oppositions verbal/nonverbal and vocal/nonvocal.

---

[12] Unfortunately, Saville-Troike uses the term 'channel' both for the mode of production (vocal versus nonvocal) and for the mode of transmission (face-to-face, telephone, tape recording, etc.).

Table 3.1. *Four-way distinction – the message from (Saville-Troke)*

		CHANNEL	
		Vocal	Nonvocal
CODE	Verbal	Spoken language	Written language (Deaf) Sign language Whistle/drum languages Morse code
	Nonverbal	Paralinguistic and prosodic features Laughter	Silence Kinesics Proxemic Eye behavior Pictures and cartoons

Saville-Troike (1989: 145, figure 4.1), reproduced with permission from John Wiley & Sons Limited.

Bearing in mind observations (1) and (2), as well as Saville-Troike's statement that 'within communicative events, not all nonvocal communication is nonverbal, so that a further distinction should be made between verbal silence and nonverbal silence' (1985: 5),[13] the following questions arise regarding her fourfold categorisation presented in Table 3.1. First, under this categorisation, where should vs be placed? Second, what does nonverbal nonvocal silence stand for?

In a detailed analysis of [~21$^{\text{Japanese-T}}$], Saville-Troike (2003: 133–134) describes its message's form and content as follows:

[~21$^{\text{a-Japanese-T}}$]   MESSAGE FORM:
    Verbal – spoken Japanese; silence
    Nonverbal – kinesics; eye gaze
   MESSAGE CONTENT AND SEQUENCE:
    P1: Holds P2's hand (optional)
      Looks at P2
      Says 'Please marry me'
    P2: Stands with head down
      Silence

Since sociolinguistically this is, as she argues, the only appropriate option within such an exchange, this silence is indeed the unmarked verbal response. If so, then this excerpt and Saville-Troike's analysis seem to offer a precise illustration of her sound judgement that 'each component that can call for a different form of speech can also permit or prescribe silence' (1985: 14). This

---

[13] For her definition of 'verbal', see Saville-Troike (2003: 19).

3.2 The Forms of Verbal Silence

silence is then part of the code (here Japanese) and not the silent counterpart of spoken languages (see §4.3.1.3).

Having shown vs conformity to spoken languages we now proceed to examine silence in sign languages. Saville-Troike states concerning sign languages[14] (such as American Sign Language (ASL)) – which, with good reason, she categorises as verbal nonvocal – that a nonverbal dimension of its form includes the silence deliberately introduced by eye closure or the aversion of gaze. Based on studies on non-manual markers in sign languages (e.g. Sandler 2010) eye blinking and gaze do not function uniformly in all sign languages. In some they are strongly associated with the prosodic paralinguistic dimension (see §2.2.2). In addition, such markers may function as nonverbal, such as breaking down contact due to hard feelings. They are often attested as verbal conative markers metalinguistically marking turn-switching (see §4.3.1.1 and §4.6.2.1) and in specific languages (such as Israeli Sign Language (ISL)) as syntactic markers (marking topicalisation, relative clauses, parentheticals, etc., e.g. Nespor and Sandler 1999: 23). That is, eye blinking and gaze shift (as well as hand relaxation) may cover different sorts of silence in signed languages.

It then follows that eye behaviour in signed languages functioning as verbal means (e.g. a grammatical WH-marker) or paralinguistic prosodic means are distinct, and thus not contained in the nonverbal and nonvocal 'eye behaviour' of Table 3.1. This multicity (which as shown later in this section occurs also concerning paralanguage and silence) is the outcome of a non-exclusive classification confusing function and mode of transmission. Moreover, silences in sign languages are not confined to non-manual markers. As Koulidobrova (2017) shows concerning ellipsis, for example, not only does ellipsis as a syntactic non-realisation occur in ASL, but its use is not limited to cases of redundancy (such as agreement constituents, see §3.2.4); it also serves as a verbal means for introducing newfangled constituents and notions. As in spoken languages, iconic void is extensively portrayed in signed poetry.

Our example of silence as poetic means of expression in British signed poetry comes from Sutton-Spence's (2005: 145–147) discussion of Dorothy Miles's use of personation as a poetic rule-breaking device (poetic licence). To achieve role shift (what Miles terms 'personation' – the sign language technique in which the signer becomes the person or thing s/he is talking about when s/he is doing straight description or narrative; 2005: 145), Miles impersonates the second character in her poem 'Total Communication'[15] by placing

---

[14] This term should be in the plural, and not as Saville-Troike (Table 3.1) denotes in the singular.
[15] 'Total Communication' alludes to the philosophy and practice encouraging the use of oral-manual in the education systems for the deaf children and among deaf people in their communities.

that person (lover) in a separate – empty – space in which she signs lexical items that normally require a body contact for their location. Sutton-Spence (2005: 147) explains this semiotic absence:

> There is no body-contact there, so the sign is technically ill-formed. The audience is obliged to imagine the second body that should provide the location for the sign, while at the same time accepting that the lack of the body implies the absence of the character.

This serves Miles to enact the failure of the central character 'I' to connect emotionally and mentally and reconcile with her lover (addressed throughout the poem as 'you'). We may return here to Saville-Troike's (1985: 14) claim cited above, and her statement (2006: 379) that:

> [silence] is an essential component of communication [...] Silence is a 'signifier' in Saussure's sense of a meaningful element that is linked to a referent by cultural convention. As with spoken language, the linkage between silence and meaning may be symbolic, indexical, or iconic.

Sutton-Spence's analysis of the poetic silencing of the grammatical contact in Miles' 'Total Communication' shows that sign languages, like spoken languages, tolerate and use vss marked by absence of expected grammatical or lexical forms (see also Klima and Bellugi 1976).[16]

Re-examining Saville-Troike's analysis of $[\sim 21^{\text{Japanese-T}}]$ and $[\sim 21^{\text{a-Japanese-T}}]$ and her mention of eye blinking in signed languages, the answer to our first question points to the identity between the functions of silence in spoken and signed languages. Unlike the relations outlined in Table 3.1, despite the difference in channel (vocal versus manual), both sets of verbal languages are accompanied with a paralinguistic plane, and both incorporate vss as part of their verbal plane.

To answer the second question (what does nonverbal nonvocal silence stand for in Table 3.1) we refer to two more events that Saville-Troike (2003: 135–137) analyses as communicative events. The first is a ritual in response to lightning practised among the Bukidons of the southern Philippines. According to Saville-Troike the response includes as its message form silence as well as cutting and burning of locks of hair. She notes that the rules of interaction for this event demand absolute silence. As a ritual practised to avoid punishment for doing something unnatural, and directed towards the evil spirits (whose arrival is signalled by lightning and thunder), no verbal

---

[16] Saville-Troike's example of sign languages is a classic example of verbal nonvocal communication systems. On the other hand, the classification of written languages as verbal nonvocal is justified only for written systems that are independent of spoken languages. A writing system corresponding to a spoken language – and more so Morse code, which is always language sensitive – is not a system in its own right but a visual means for mediating speech (see also note 16 in §2.2.4).

3.2 The Forms of Verbal Silence

interaction is expected. In fact, all activities – other than the self-selection of the individual performing the ritual and the cutting and burning of the hair – are suspended. The suspension of speech in this event does not differ from the suspension of eating or dancing. It seems that despite Saville-Troike's terminology ('communicative event') this event cannot be regarded as a communicative exchange between interlocutors; it is not a discourse situation. And thus, not only should silence not be mentioned here but also, silence does not and should not constitute a category of its own (see Table 3.1). This becomes apparent when compared with vs as a response in the Japanese communicative event ([~21$^{\text{Japanese-T}}$] and [~21$^{\text{a-Japanese-T}}$]), and silence as the counterpart of speech in the next example.

Saville-Troike (2003: 135–136) analyses a condolence event among Igbo speakers in Nigeria on the occasion of a 'premature' death to illustrate a communicative event that takes place with no speech at all. The event is performed to express sympathy and to manifest innocence of responsibility for the death. Saville-Troike classifies this event's message form as consisting of silence and proxemics (see Table 3.1). The act sequence described for this event proceeds as follows: the deceased's family members stand inside the house while hes spirit hovers nearby. A mourner enters and stands before the bereaved family members and the deceased's spirit. He then sits silently among the other (adult male) mourners. He presents himself again to the family and spirit, after which he leaves.

Among the rules of interaction which Saville-Troike lists for this communicative event is the rule that mourners should not speak. Concerning norms of interpretation, she mentions that verbal reference to death increases grief. Unlike the classification of the message form of the silence for [~21$^{\text{a-Japanese-T}}$] as 'verbal' (alongside spoken Japanese), Saville-Troike does not classify the silence in this Igbo condolence event as verbal. Sharing the message form with proxemics, could this constitute the nonvocal nonverbal silence listed in Table 3.1? The silence in the Igbo condolence event differs from the silence in the lightning of the Bukidons in that it is situated in a human context of interaction and so speech is potentially an option. Such silence resulting from the prohibition to speak is the counterpart of speech: it is not an independent category (nonvocal nonverbal) but the negation of the verbal category (in fact, it is here the negation of spoken Igbo speech, though it could easily incorporate a form of conventional or sporadic signed Igbo). Moreover, the Igbo condolence event illustrates the difference between proxemics as an independent nonvocal nonverbal device and silence as a dependent counterpart of speech. Finally, a subtle distinction should be noted between the silence in the Japanese marriage offer and the silence in the Igbo condolence event: while the silence in the marriage offer is a response – in that culture constituting the conventional equivalent of the verbal phrasing 'I do' – the silence in the Igbo condolence event is not a verbal means of phrasing but a deliberate strategy employed to refrain from phrasing. While proximity communicates sympathy, silence as negation of speech repels the danger of charge with involvement and responsibility for that death.

Dennis Kurzon has published important contributions to the linguistic and pragmatic studies on silence. In a sense, Kurzon's programmatic monograph, *Discourse of Silence* (1998), departs from Saville-Troike's (2006: 379) peak: dealing with silence as a sign. Using the semiotic square, based on Aristotle's square (Kurzon 1998: 8–18), to test the semiotic relations between speech and silence, Kurzon challenges intention on the one hand and the relation between signifier and signified on the other. Accordingly, he postulated that:

> [...] normal human conversation is made up of the sequence:
>   speech silence speech ...
> When one person speaks, the other in order to listen should be silent [...]
>   (1998: 10)

Kurzon goes on to assert:

> one cannot speak and be silent at the same time; this is necessarily an either/or relationship [...] non-speech may have one of two meanings. If it means the lack of communication, then it cannot imply silence in the sense in which I am analysing it – as a communicative activity. Secondly, if non-speech means non-verbal communication, which includes kinesics and body language, proxemics [...], paralinguistic cues (such as intonation, tone of voice, pitch and volume), as well as chronemics (timing and rhythm) of which silence is usually considered a part, then such behaviour may also accompany speech, and in the case of paralinguistic cues) must do so. (1998: 11)

Kurzon then differentiates between nonverbal and coverbal behaviour. In fact, classifying as coverbal all communicative behaviours that accompany speech (or silence), he classifies intentional silence as nonverbal, being complementary to speech: silence alternates with speech (1998: 18; according to Kurzon, unintentional silence contrasts with noise).

At the end of a lively discussion, Kurzon (1998: 18, figure 7) formulates a matrix clarifying his reading of the relations between silence and speech. He bases that matrix on oppositions he adopts from Malandro et al. (1989: 6) (Table 3.2). These oppositions coincide with the oppositions chosen by Saville-Troike (see Table 3.1).[17]

Recruiting identical oppositions (code – verbal/nonverbal and channel – vocal/nonvocal) highlights a striking difference concerning the position of

---

[17] Saville-Troike first published a matrix of the message form including silence as an independent constituent in 1989 (see Table 3.1, and compare with Saville-Troike 1982: 143). This is the same year as Malandro et al. However, Malandro et al. did not mention 'silence' in their matrix (see 1989: 6, figure 1.1) nor did they refer to that matrix in their description of silence (1989: 250–256). Kurzon (1998) does not mention Saville-Troike's classifications.

3.2 The Forms of Verbal Silence

Table 3.2. *Matrix showing dyadic interaction (Kurzon)*

	Verbal	Non-verbal
Vocal	Speech	Paralinguistics
Non-vocal	Silence	Body movements, etc.

Kurzon (1998: 18, figure 7), reprinted by permission of John Benjamins.

silence between the classification proposed by Saville-Troike (Table 3.1) and that proposed by Kurzon (Table 3.2). Saville-Troike classifies silence as nonverbal and nonvocal, whereas according to Kurzon silence is verbal and nonvocal.

Kurzon agrees with Saville-Troike on the voice matter, but they differ concerning the verbal standing of silence. Kurzon's matrix epitomises his sharp view that both speech and silence being verbal signifiers alternating as verbal communicative codes belong in the verbal plane. Kurzon's chief grounds for placing silence alongside speech in the verbal plane is his observation that silence – unlike paralanguage and body movements – cannot be coincident with speech: 'one cannot speak and be silent at the same time; this is necessarily an either/or relationship'. Accordingly, he contends that speech and silence do not accompany each other; rather, they alternate with each other (the relations between them is paradigmatic substitution).

An apparent difficulty with this scheme (Table 3.2) is that while paralinguistic voice qualities and features are confined to vocal verbal communication (assuming that Kurzon limits his matrix to spoken communication – see earlier in this section on paralinguistic signed communication), kinetic properties such as body gestures and blushing may accompany both speech and silence (see, e.g. Saville-Troike's analysis of [~21[a-Japanese-T]]).

A key issue requiring attention, however, is the nature of the difference between speech and silence in terms of the channel. What is meant by placing speech in the vocal channel and silence in the nonvocal channel (a minimal difference in Kurzon's matrix)?

On the face of it, this distinction is justified and inherent: the content signified using silence as a (verbal) signifier is communicated without voice (the verbally expected phones, words or phrases are not articulated). But this is only the shell: defining silence as a signifier belonging in the nonvocal channel is contingent on the understanding that this value ('nonvocal') differs from the absence of voice in nonvocal languages such as those based on the visual channel (e.g. sign languages or kinetography). As discussed and illustrated earlier concerning sign languages, typically voice is not part of the components of those languages (see Pfau and Quer 2010 on mouthing). The opposite holds for spoken languages (see note 16) founded on the human/animate voice. The value 'nonvocal', pertaining to silence as a verbal signifier in oral languages (sharing the code with speech), refers to the instantiation of a negative value to the variable VOCAL. Being a binary acoustic/articulatory variable, VOCAL can take on the positive value (describing speech) or the negative value (describing VS). This captures the essence of VS as the part of the verbal code which signifies by not articulating particular expected speech. This is much like the opposition between 'voiced' and 'unvoiced' phones instantiating a positive or a negative value to the binary phonetic feature VOICED depending on whether the laryngeal cords vibrate (/d/ versus /t/);[18] or the values 'plus nasal' or 'minus nasal' for the NASAL variable (/n/ versus /d/). As is apparent, VOCAL, VOICED and NASAL are extraneous to visual languages (which utilise features involving SPACE, e.g. SHAPE, LOCATION).

In summary, the scholars' account of silence as the product of the addresser's choice to so communicate specific content when speech (articulation) is expected (see, e.g. Courtenay 1916; Dauenhauer 1980; Saville-Troike 1985, 2006; Jaworski 1993; Bilmes 1994; Kurzon 1998) shows that VS belongs in the verbal plane, that is, in the linguistic apparatus. As both the fourth-century BC grammarian Pāṇini and de Saussure show, the entire linguistic system relies on oppositions between that which is present and that which is absent (see §3.2.2.2 'something versus nothing'). Oppositions function at all language levels. In fact, VS carries semiotic discursive meaning because of the active role it plays within the verbal sequence. In this sense, VS does not coincide with speech, indicating that it does not belong in the paralinguistic plane, nor in other communicative clues (such as kinetic) that may accompany speech (and silence). Just as one cannot articulate two phones, words or clauses simultaneously, because each such pair instantiates one and the same variable and requires one and the same resource, so one cannot simultaneously materialise speech and silence. This is why, examined from the paradigmatic articulation axis, speech and VS exclude each other, but seen from the syntagmatic axis the unique non-linear quality of VS emerges (see §3.2.5.1.3 and §4.6.3.3.3).

Clearly, the preceeding discussion supports and complements the key criteria for VS, namely that of all silences only VS is chosen by the addresser as a means of expression when (specific) speech is expected. Clearly, this dictates that there is specific content the addresser wishes to communicate and the VS fills in for the speech expected to convey that content. As shown in §2.2.1, the case is not one of muteness or situations in which speech is expected but the anticipated speaker is silenced (see §2.2.4.1, see also Jaworski 1993: 3;

---

[18] The feature VOICED refers to the involvement of the laryngeal cords in the production of the phone and not to 'vocality'; see also Kurzon 1998: 18 note 6.

3.2 The Forms of Verbal Silence

Kurzon 1998). This is also not the case in which the addresser chooses not to share that content with others (see §2.2.3). Yet scenarios such as the shortage of words (phrasing) which that silence substitutes do form part of 'expected speech' (see §4.6.4).

Because vs is a signifier characterised by the absent expected articulation (and in written equivalences), its essence is the lack of form. That is to say, vs is a sign that is regular in terms of its content and functions but irregular in terms of its form. It is not accidental that this description matches Melčuk's (1976: 52) definition of suppletion as '[t]he relationship between any two linguistic units A and B which meet the following condition: the semantic distinction between A and B is regular, while the formal distinction between them is not regular'. The integration of vs as a signifier at all levels of language and the examples throughout our study illustrate the complementary relations between speech as the regular, expected verbal means of expression and vs as its strong suppletive counterpart. This also exemplifies the contribution gained from incorporating the study of vs in linguistic exploration into the refinement of the notion of suppletion.

As seen, due to this regularity of the content (that which the addresser wishes to express using vs), the description of the meanings and functions of vs is identical with that of speech (see Chapter 4). Yet the attempt to implement the linguistic tools conventionally used for describing verbal forms faces difficulty: in terms of phonetic, morphological, syntactic, lexical and discursive descriptions all vs signifiers seem to have one and the same form: no-form. The challenge to be taken up here is to extrapolate the strategies employed by the addresser for communicating the message to hes interlocutor in such a way that that message will be accessible and so successfully deciphered. To do this the addresser must signal to hes addressees the involvement of a vs signifier in that message. The clues provided in the form generated by the addresser rely on hes anticipated-interlocutor's linguistic competence to identify these forerunners and process them adequately.

The verbal plane, that is, where speech is expected, being the language speaker's and listener's starting point is accordingly the starting point of our formal investigation. As the intuitive examples presented in §3.1 illustrate, at times vs may be affective or cooperative (Grice 1989; Ephratt 2012) as its articulated counterpart, or it can exceed the expected (articulated) speech. In other cases the supremacy of vs as a signifier is that it expresses that content which is beyond words. As speakers, we know that a verbal exchange may even start with silence, proceed in silence and end in silence, but this entire exchange must be situated within speech. The vs detected as figure and its specific form are derived by its relation with the speech serving as its ground.

The speech particles grounding vs and thus acting as its forerunners are grammatical or lexical stumps signalling the location, category and content of the vs in the specific utterance (see note 10). Stumps ranging from single phonemes up to truncated discourses serve the addresser to signal coming vs. In most cases vs does not consume time (i.e. surface as acoustic gaps or their orthographic equivalents, such as blanks marking void). The forerunners are the stumps – residual speech – retained to announce the silence: its form and function. Forerunners are language, grammar and context sensitive, but by no means do they licence a free-for-all framework. Unlike the speech expected, an addresser using vs articulates only the sufficient stump needed to signal the coming silence. This vs as a verbal signifier as well as its forerunner are included in the given information, and are thus not to be considered as given-off information (see §2.2.1) or derived by implicature (see Ephratt 2012). We may compare [~18^s] where the superlative adverb ('harder') is a stump of a syntactic construction of comparison and serves as a forerunner informing the forthcoming vs (S_1: 'than Δ') with the full articulation ('Avis. We try harder than Hertz') in which there is no vs to show that the two do not communicate the same message. It is only that which includes vs as part of its given information that communicates Avis's iconic resolve to take over Hertz and eliminate Hertz as a contestant.

The forerunners of vss attain their faculty to point to the vs signifiers and to indicate their form and content by triggering the grammatical rules, lexicon and usage of that language. Beneath these we may also find phonetic forerunners recognised as partial articulations of words or the rupturing of phonetic sequences. All in all, forerunners cover all language levels from the phonetic level up to entire discourses (see [~241'] §3.2.5.5.2).

As we show, a form not articulated because it is found redundant or trivial is not considered vs: this silence is not chosen as means of expression and thus is not part of the underlying code. The exploration of the forms of vss and their forerunners will furnish a valuable refinement of known distinctions pursued in linguistics, examples being suppletion and onomatopoeia; the distinction between the use of pronouns, elliptic sentences and passive constructions involving vss and such usage unrelated to vss. The criteria for distinction include the requirement that, in the specific text, context and co-text, the verbal constituent is either phonetically, structurally, semantically or pragmatically obligatory, that the (verbal) silence is a motivated means of expression (meaningful rather than technical) and that it is the choice of the addresser.

Because the starting point for this study is the form criterion, that is, the verbal (linguistic) component expressed by the vs signifier, this chapter proceeds along conventional linguistic lines from the minimal linguistic unit to the largest unit. The discussion of the forms of vs is language sensitive.

3.2 The Forms of Verbal Silence

Typological differences set the make-up of the VS signifiers in each language (or language family) and shape accordingly the forms of their forerunners.

What seems, at this introductory stage, the most straightforward case illustrating the dependency of the identification of an absent verbal constituent as a VS signifier on the typology of the language is a case unique to French, namely French grammar ordering the deletion of inanimate complements of simple and compound prepositions, which results in a null pronoun. The following example, cited and analysed by Adler (2007: 183–184), comes from *La fée Carabine* by Daniel Pennac. It illustrates the employment of VS – deliberately violating grammar rules – as a means for reaching an iconic verbal expression:

[~29^{French}] *Un type* se baladait avec un rasoir dans Belleville. Il coupait les vieilles dames en deux, sous le nez de l'inspecteur Van Thian, et l'inspecteur Van Thian n'arrivait pas à mettre la main *dessus*.[19]

As Adler points out, the deletion here of the animate complement '*sur lui*' from the end of this sentence, contravening grammar, is a forerunner signalling that 'criminal' is treated as an inanimate noun excluded from the class of humans (animate, rational).

The identification of the uninstantiated PP object ('*sur lui*') which places the PREP '*dessus*' as stumps of a complement VS signifier (see §3.2.4.4.2) and the interpretation of the given information it carries is a unique outcome of French and its grammar rules.

We are now in a position to detail the inventory of verbal means serving as VS's forerunners. This inductively extrapolates the deciphering process performed by the addressee (based on the interplay between hes linguistic competence and the forerunner which the addresser inserts in hes utterance): identifying the articulated part as a forerunner, determining the category and nature of the VS signifier in the specific context and making out its meaning. The contention that VS is always attained in retrospect calls for an inventory of forms constituting the set of potential forerunners. Yet the question whether an incidence of such a form is indeed a VS signifier must be examined and answered in the specific context of each verbal exchange and in accordance with the functions of language participating in the particular context (see Chapter 4). This too simulates the strategies summoned by the addressee participating in that exchange. Since we include under 'verbal exchange'

---

[19] Due to the difference between the handling of pronouns in French and in English, this VS is not preserved in Monk's English translation, pp. 75–76.

50 Verbal Silence: Forms

spoken interactions, as well as readers of written texts, we illustrate the forms (forerunners) and vss putting forth varied excerpts and texts.

3.2.1 Phonetic Verbal Silence

Phonetic vs is a verbal signifier deliberately leaving out phonemes to signify meaningful content.

While phonetic silence can exceed a morpheme or word boundary, and thus extend over clauses and discourses, it is limited to the elision of phonetic rather than morphologic or semantic entities. The crucial semiotic distinction is that as articulatory or acoustic entities, phonemes or phones lack meaning. Thus the semiotic essence of phonetic silence derives from its presence and from the rupturing of the word unity and not from a linguistic unit of form and content left out in the stump.

Examples [~17] (see §3.1) and [~30] may illustrate the essence of phonetic silence as opposed to higher-level vs signifiers.

[~30]

Figure 3.2 'm ss ng'[20]

---

[20] www.wolverhamptonsafeguarding.org.uk/safeguarding-children-and-young-people/i-work-with-children-young-people-families/children-who-go-missing (accessed 11 July 2017). Unfortunately all attempts to contact Wolverhampton to verify the identity of the advert's licensor, and get their permission, failed.

3.2.1 Phonetic Verbal Silence

The poster in Figure 3.2 features as part of the Association of Chief Police Officers (ACPO) guidance on children who go missing. It places the Scrabble tiles not on the game's rack but on what appears to be a deserted roadside. In addition, while the rules of the game permit only complete words on the board, here iconically the word 'missing' is itself missing the two 'I's ('m$\mathcal{S}_1$ss $\mathcal{S}_2$ng'), so that this is not a word. The campaign is run to raise public awareness of this troubling and tragic problem. The lipogram silencing the letter (vowel) 'I' and the Scrabble image are recruited here to activate the addresser. This phonetic vs rupturing the word, and more specifically omitting its vowels and so negating its existence as an utterable word, mimics the campaign's conative message (see §4.3). Akin to the steps the player is expected to follow in the game (language assignment), the public is urged to follow steps starting from awareness and advancing to searching for and hopefully finding the missing child. By so doing, that individual – that I – will be transformed from being missing to being present.

Clarifying the operation of phonetic vs as a verbal signifier, it is important to note that despite the iconic force earned by the deliberate choice to forerun this vs by eliding the letters 'I' in the word 'missing', 'i' in that word does not function as a pronoun (morpheme). As a vocalic phoneme carrying the syllabic making of the word, its elision blocks articulation of the word (see [~33^{German}]). But by no means do these 'i's being phonemes carry meaning.

The minimal units of content and the minimal units of form make up the linguistic sign, but they are not in themselves linguistic signs. The smallest linguistic sign – the minimal composite of content and form – is the morpheme (see Table 3.3).

As outlined in Table 3.3, the phone as the smallest phonetic unit and the phoneme as the smallest phonological unit are both void of content. Sememes (or prototypical features) being the smallest semantic units lack form. As the bottom right square in Table 3.3 shows, the empty merger of content and form

Table 3.3. *Milestones of language*

Content Form	+	—
+	Morphology Morpheme lexeme	Phonology phonetics Phone phoneme
—	Semantics Sememe denotation	

Following Ephratt 2014b: 131.

has nothing to do with the language domain, and so lies outside the brief of linguistics.

Example [~30] illustrates the iconic faculty of vs to convey a message and conatively activate the addressee (see §4.3). This end is reached using phonetic silence: leaving out phones alluding here to the subject matter in question.

The following groups of phonetic silences signify solely by elision. As discussed in §2.2.1 (and see [~5]), silence that originates as a symptom is not a verbal means of expression. But electively converting silences from their symptomatic grounds to a literary setting transforms them into vs. And when the material silenced equals phones, this constitutes phonetic vs.

Our first illustration comes from the novel *House Mother Normal*, subtitled as 'A Geriatric Comedy' (by B. S. Johnson). The novel is uniquely structured to present the goings-on in an old-age home on one single evening. The eight residents and the house-mother are each allocated their own chapter. All the chapters are structured to uniformly reflect the residents' involvement in a particular activity at the home (dinner, singing the house hymn, occupational therapy, etc.). Each chapter opens with a clinical account: the residents are challenged by varied geriatric illnesses and pathologies, and the chapters are presented in ascending severity from the healthiest resident to the most impaired. This literary parallelism provides a detailed vertical familiarity with each inmate as well as a horizontal account of the events at the home. This double-angled configuration fosters simultaneity and parallelism and emerges as the key technique for depicting the symptoms of aphasia and dementia. Comparing the texts and content produced by the least impaired resident helps decipher the symptomatic silences. As the pathology increases, larger portions of the text are fragmented, resulting in blank patches and entire blank pages.

Being a novel – and not an authentic excerpt – the author employs these pathologies, states and settings as literary poetic devices (see §4.5). For example, a comparison of what each resident retains of the hymn shows that Johnson employed the pathologies and their severity to iconically mirror the diverse intensities of symptomatic silences as well as for discriminate omissions for the higher-functioning inmates (see [~31^b] and big chunks of random lapses for the more severely impaired (see [~31^c] and [~31^d]).

Example [~31] shows four inmates' productions when the first verse of the hymn is sung.

Phonetic silence as a verbal literary device emerges in the two intermediate cases. Comparing [~31^c] with [~31^b], it appears that unlike Ron, who omits words and phrases (as explained chosen by Johnson to convey meaning), what Sioned omits are not linguistic units: she elides phonetic sequences. Rosetta – the most severely impaired inmate – appears to be in a completely

3.2.1 Phonetic Verbal Silence

detached state: no language or phones are retained and she seems to mumble randomly and sparsely.

[~31ª] Charlie Edwards (p. 33)
    The joys of life continue strong
    Throughout old age, however long:
    If only we can cheerful stay
    And brightly welcome every day.
    Not what we've been, not what we'll be,
    What matters most is that we're free:
    The joys of life continue strong
    Throughout old age, however long

[~31ᵇ] Ron Lamson (p. 77)
    of life continue strong
    Throughout   old age, however long
    If only we can   cheerful
  Stay, And   every day.
              not what we'll
    What matters most   that we're free
    joys of life continue strong
    Throughout old age, however long.

[~31ᶜ] Sioned Bowen (p. 121)
    What matters most

        old age   long ha ah ah !

ha ha ha ha ha !

[~31ᵈ] Rosetta Stanton (p. 165)

        grymus

      hwyliog

The gradual fading of sounds ('are' → 'ars$_1$' → 'as$_1$s$_2$'), iconically imaging the transmission from voice, speech and vividness to stillness, void and disappearance, is illustrated in the closing verse of E. E. Cummings' 'Birds' (Webster 1999: 209):

[~32]   who
       s)e
       voi

       c
       es
       (
       are
       ar
       a

As Webster (1999: 208–210) observes:

The birds' voices fade into 'twilight's vastness', into 'Be' and 'now' and 'soul' until they 'are' 'a' part of silence [...] The vastness of twilight is rendered in a kind of stutter, or if you like, musical progression or crescendo, which is mirrored by the reverse stutter or diminuendo at the end of the poem: 'are / ar / a'. [...] The unpronounceable dying of the printed ending refers to the fading cries of the birds, to the dissolution of the self (addressed in the third stanza: ('Be)look / now (come / soul) into twilight, and to the paradoxical oneness of song and silence, of bird-voices and man-soul. Thus this dying fall ('are / ar / a') signifies both being ('are') and nothing ('a' – a thing unnamed and unnameable).

Focusing here on phonetic vs, it seems worth noting that only phonetic vs literally ruptures language. In the case of higher vss (complex constructs), the stump does not lose its linguistic (form+content: signifier+signified) standing. Phonetic silence, on the other hand, ruptures the word. This loss of 'wordiness' results in breaking down the linguistic linkage between form and content (see Table 3.3; see also [~17] §3.1). This explains why, for the addressee to identify the articulated stump as a phonetic forerunner pointing to an unarticulated whole, that stump must be placed in opposition to the whole. This is attained when that whole is commonly known (see 'M rmite' in [~17]), as well as in poetry, where as Jakobson (1960: 358) explained equations are used to build sequences (such as 'a' (in [~32]) and ([~283]) in the poetic function §4.5; see also §3.2.5.3.4).

Onomatopoeia is the prototypical (primary) phonetic image. Although onomatopoeias are symbols, and as such comply with the syllabic patterning of the specific language (see, e.g. de Zutter 1993), their perception is intuitive. As Tsur (2001) has shown, adaptation from one semiotic system to another necessarily requires selection, including loss. The ideal, Tsur explains, is the choice of the option closest to the source phenomena that the target semiotic system can offer (see also Jespersen 1922: 396–411).

Classic onomatopoeia are verbal symbols for cultivated animal cries (see de Zutter 1993), or for natural objects producing distinct sounds (e.g. 'tick-tack' representing in many languages a clock's sound).

Onomatopoeic silence as a verbal signifier emerges as one of the most intuitive and iconic modes of representation. Gerzi (2007: 144, 148) describes such silences as communicating the absence of registration or the registration of absence. Indeed, it is unique in the sense that, when examined on the basis of the notion of silence as void, its transition from the source occurrence to the verbal system does not involve translation (see also [~163] §3.2.5.1.1 and §4.2).

The next example illustrates the role played by onomatopoeic vs as a key actor in Ernst Jandl's poem 'schtzngrmm' and its ideological message, namely that any war is death. The poem is structured as a lipogram, solely confined to consonantal phoneme sequences that are contained in the German word 'Schützengraben' meaning trench (see Pavel 2014). The poem's closing lines are:

[~33^{German}] tzngrmm
    t-t-t-t-t-t-t-t-t
    scht
    scht
    scht
    scht
    scht
    scht
    schtzngrmm
    grrrrrrrrrrrrrrrrrrrrrrrrrrrrr
    t-tt. (Jandl, *Laut und Luise*, p. 47)

3.2.1 Phonetic Verbal Silence

As Pavel (2014: 47) points out, the consonantal onomatopoeia simulates the attack from the soldier's position sitting in the trench: 'E. Jandl constructs his work form, trying to portray by the sounds what he is writing about [...] Thus E. Yandl managed to create a complete picture of the war not with individual words, but using different combinations of sounds of only one word'. Pavel details the onomatopoeic qualities of the sibilants, clattering consonants, portraying not only the weapons employed but also the escalation of combat from the use of handguns to weapons of mass destruction. The inevitably disastrous outcome is portrayed in the poem's closing word, 't-tt', a lipogram for 'tot' (death). Pavel is right in claiming that Jandl's refusal to include vowels allows him to make the material word forms heavier. Founded on the Latin etymology of the word 'vowel' ('*vōcālis*' uttering voice, speaking), the vowels carry the word's syllabic flow (see, e.g. OED: Vowel, N.; Vocal, Adj. and N).[21] Examining the onomatopoeic role played by phonetic vs, the exclusion of vowels turns out to be most significant. Not only does it rupture the structure and intactness of the word as a linguistic entity, but it actually denies the word and the poem (void of any vowels) its voice. There is no flow and no life: phonetically silencing all vowels onomatopoeically portrays a skeleton; instead of the flesh of individual expression we encounter coarse, dry and stagnant remains.

The cases discussed here employ phonetic vss to communicate absence and void, some of which can be recovered and so repaired (cases such as [~30] in which the addressee is urged to fill in the missing objects in the real world, or Jandl's message [~33^{German}] pleading via phonetic vs to take action to cease fire and end wars). But phonetic vs can also signify and fix linguistic and semantic relations.

An important point concerning onomatopoeia has to do with diagrammaticality. In light of the relations between form and content (see Table 3.3), iconicity anticipates the addition of content to be followed by increasing form (diagrammaticality). Vs as a symbol may seem counter-iconic. But this is not the case with onomatopoeic vs when the content – the object or quality – is silence or absence itself, such as the stillness of nature, the silence of a stone and the silence of the dead (as in [~33^{German}]).

Sound symbolisms, such as synesthetic or phonaesthemes, are conveyed not by the sameness of sounds but by association based on the effect of the role played by the auditory qualities of the specific sounds and their relations (such as opposition or flow) with other sounds in the sound-vehicle (see Waugh and

---

[21] For some unexplained reason Pavel's (2014: 46) citation of the poem replaced Jadl's (*Laut und Luise*, p. 47) 'scht' with 'sect'. While the poet's name 'Ernst Jandl' may strike English speakers as lacking vowels, not only does the poem 'schtzngrmm' have no vowels at all, but it also lacks the liquid phonemes which ensure normal syllabic structure.

Newfield 1995). The exemplary case of cross-linguistic sound symbolism is the contrastive association of the high front vowel /i/ with diminutive on the one hand, and the back low (dark) /u/ vowel with augmentative on the other – for example, in the opposing size conveyed in German '*Gross*' versus '*Klein*'; English 'all' versus 'each', 'pee' versus 'poo'. As is true for all cases of sound opposition, 'it would be absurd to maintain that all words at all times in all languages had a signification corresponding exactly to their sounds, each sound having a definite meaning once and for all' (Jespersen 1922: 397). This is specifically true of the diffuse/grave opposition: /i/ does not mean 'small' and /u/ does not mean 'big', as the very case of these English words demonstrates (see Tsur 2006). Unlike onomatopoeia, in sound symbolism there are auditory qualities but no source sounds.

Through the perceived symbolic sound relationship between /i/ and smallness, /i/ has acquired this sense and so has become a derivational morpheme designating the diminutive, for example: English 'bird' – 'birdie'; German '*Vögel*' – '*Vögelien*' (see, e.g. Volek 1987; Sundén 1904; Schneider 2003). The addition of form (diminutive morpheme) accords with the iconic diagrammatic expectation that addition of content will be followed and thus matched with addition of form.

But when, as here, the content is decreased, a semiotic discrepancy is created between content and form. A concomitant reduction of form overcomes this discrepancy and secures qualitative agreement at the expense of the quantitative mismatch. The reduction of form, namely expressing a sequence of the source phones using phonetic silence, is iconic to the object's reduced size (see the quote from Strang 1962 in §4.2.1). Having confined phonetic vs to missing phonemes – and not larger units being linguistic entities – entails considering such diminutives as incidents of phonetic vs.

When such a morphophonetic strategy serves lexical enrichment and lexical dissimilation it is not the choice of the specific addresser, and accordingly no longer counts as phonetic vs. But when this strategy is initiated by the person deriving that form, such cases are indeed incidents of phonetic vs. In fact, all currently lexicalised entries started off as a speaker's means to iconically express reduction; for example:

[~34]   Wee ← wǣge (old English, weigh);

[~35]   Ok ← all correct.

The diminutive 'OK' portrays the reduction of the scope from a universal statement ($\forall(x)$) to an existential one ($\exists(x)$). It is important to note that since the significance is the iconic reduction, it is obtained also using other forms of vs, such as morphological vs (pianoforte→piano; homosexual→homo; neighbourhood→hood especially among African-American speakers denoting urban neighbourhoods).

Whether the affective meaning attached to diminutives is secondary to the size notion or the two come hand in hand, many scholars noticed and accounted for this association. Because of the universal dominance of phonetic vs to communicate affection, a detailed account on this category will follow when discussing the emotive function (§4.2.1).

Another semiotic category that is strongly associated with silence and so makes extensive use of phonetic vs is 'taboo words'.

In compliance with the Third Commandment (Exodus 20:7), the prototypical example of a taboo word is Hebrew '*yhwh*' yielding English

[~36]   G-d ← God

phonetically breaking the word sequence (and see [~211^{Hebrew}] in §3.2.5.3.4, see also Mirus et al. 2012 concerning ASL). Because the vs of taboo words rests not on its form but on its unique metalinguistic function, it is dealt in detail in §3.2.5.3 and §4.6.1.4.

Phonetic vs is the first class of vs presented. §§3.2.2–3.2.5 not only proceed to units larger than the phonemes and phones but accordingly deal with vs strategies involving linguistic units (see Table 3.3). This, on the one hand, leaves unarticulated chunks larger than phones or phonemes, or sequences thereof; on the other hand, and unlike the case of phonetic vs, it produces stumps that are themselves linguistic entities, that is, stumps in which the merge of form and continent is retained.

3.2.2 Morphological Verbal Silence

While the statement that all languages have words is universally valid, this would appear to be the only morphological generalisation that holds concerning all languages. Moreover, the nature of words varies tremendously between different language types, within individual languages and across diachronic changes.

Focusing here on morphological vs, the criteria adopted and followed are those that can distinguish morphological vs from other forms of vs. Table 3.3 is the outcome of such a deliberation. Each form is attached within the specific language to a fixed lexical or grammatical meaning, and so constitutes a verbal constituent in that language. While determining the verbal status of each form is language specific, the criteria are not.

Applying the ground and figure relations between the specific incident of vs and its forerunner, morphological vs relies on the leaving out of verbal particles (form and meaning) that are smaller than a word. Accordingly, while synthetic (fusional and agglutinative) languages offer a wide range of morphological vss, in isolating languages these functions will be achieved using lexical and syntactic vss (see §3.2.4 and §3.2.5). Since languages springing from the same family or placed in the same typological class may differ significantly regarding their morphological modules, further refinement is needed (e.g. compare English, German and French).

A key criterion for determining morphological vs is that it takes place within word boundaries. Morphological vs is defined as:

A word deliberately leaving out an expected verbal particle (morpheme or other) to signify meaningful content associated with that verbal particle.

Incorporated in the general framework of vs, morphological vs must be the product of the addresser's free choice to use it as a means of communication: for successfully delivering a message. Accordingly, morphological forerunners are word stumps (roots, basis, lexical entries or inflected forms) that remain following the leaving out of the particular particle. While forms identified in isolation as vs's word stumps are those whose well-formedness is harmed (detailed in §3.2.2.1) this is not the case with morphological vss in which the well-formedness of the isolated word is not harmed (§3.2.2.2). Because their surface forms collide with their unmarked counter-forms, the disambiguation of unharmed words – determining their status as morphological stumps – requires reference to contextual information.

3.2.2.1 Isolated Bound Morphemes as Stumps

The first group seems best illustrated by Lyn Hejinian's poem 'Writing Is an Aid to Memory'. As its title declares, and as the poem's content and form tell and echo, writing is indeed an aid to memory. Writing is not the authentic experience of the event. Among the many poetic licence resources manifested in this poem, Hejinian makes extensive and illuminating use of morphological vs placing bound morphemes in isolation, deliberately leaving out the base-word form they modify. Being clear instances of harming the words' well-formedness they are easily identified as morphological vs forerunners.

Since the poem exceeds 1,500 lines, only a few short fragments are cited here to exemplify Hejinian's unique and iconic use of morphological vs. The first citation seems at first sight transparent, both regarding the identification of its incidents of morphological vss and regarding their interpretation:[22]

[~37-5]   [...]
      rim memory and more
      all these ways painting, modeling
      guage means general
      will push **straction** one day to the left [...]

---

[22] The numbers following the hyphen refer to the poem's sections. Emphases added here (not in the original): forms for which there is no English grammatical or semantic reading that allows them to appear in isolation are presented in bold; forms that may stand for independent lexical lemmas, as well as for bound forms, appear in italics.

3.2.2 Morphological Verbal Silence 57

Whether the affective meaning attached to diminutives is secondary to the size notion or the two come hand in hand, many scholars noticed and accounted for this association. Because of the universal dominance of phonetic vs to communicate affection, a detailed account on this category will follow when discussing the emotive function (§4.2.1).

Another semiotic category that is strongly associated with silence and so makes extensive use of phonetic vs is 'taboo words'.

In compliance with the Third Commandment (Exodus 20:7), the prototypical example of a taboo word is Hebrew '*yhwh*' yielding English

[~36]   G-d ← God

phonetically breaking the word sequence (and see [~211^{Hebrew}] in §3.2.5.3.4, see also Mirus et al. 2012 concerning ASL). Because the vs of taboo words rests not on its form but on its unique metalinguistic function, it is dealt in detail in §3.2.5.3 and §4.6.1.4.

Phonetic vs is the first class of vs presented. §§3.2.2–3.2.5 not only proceed to units larger than the phonemes and phones but accordingly deal with vs strategies involving linguistic units (see Table 3.3). This, on the one hand, leaves unarticulated chunks larger than phones or phonemes, or sequences thereof; on the other hand, and unlike the case of phonetic vs, it produces stumps that are themselves linguistic entities, that is, stumps in which the merge of form and continent is retained.

3.2.2 Morphological Verbal Silence

While the statement that all languages have words is universally valid, this would appear to be the only morphological generalisation that holds concerning all languages. Moreover, the nature of words varies tremendously between different language types, within individual languages and across diachronic changes.

Focusing here on morphological vs, the criteria adopted and followed are those that can distinguish morphological vs from other forms of vs. Table 3.3 is the outcome of such a deliberation. Each form is attached within the specific language to a fixed lexical or grammatical meaning, and so constitutes a verbal constituent in that language. While determining the verbal status of each form is language specific, the criteria are not.

Applying the ground and figure relations between the specific incident of vs and its forerunner, morphological vs relies on the leaving out of verbal particles (form and meaning) that are smaller than a word. Accordingly, while synthetic (fusional and agglutinative) languages offer a wide range of morphological vss, in isolating languages these functions will be achieved using lexical and syntactic vss (see §3.2.4 and §3.2.5). Since languages springing from the same family or placed in the same typological class may differ significantly regarding their morphological modules, further refinement is needed (e.g. compare English, German and French).

A key criterion for determining morphological vs is that it takes place within word boundaries. Morphological vs is defined as:

A word deliberately leaving out an expected verbal particle (morpheme or other) to signify meaningful content associated with that verbal particle.

Incorporated in the general framework of vs, morphological vs must be the product of the addresser's free choice to use it as a means of communication: for successfully delivering a message. Accordingly, morphological forerunners are word stumps (roots, basis, lexical entries or inflected forms) that remain following the leaving out of the particular particle. While forms identified in isolation as vs's word stumps are those whose well-formedness is harmed (detailed in §3.2.2.1) this is not the case with morphological vss in which the well-formedness of the isolated word is not harmed (§3.2.2.2). Because their surface forms collide with their unmarked counter-forms, the disambiguation of unharmed words – determining their status as morphological stumps – requires reference to contextual information.

3.2.2.1 Isolated Bound Morphemes as Stumps

The first group seems best illustrated by Lyn Hejinian's poem 'Writing Is an Aid to Memory'. As its title declares, and as the poem's content and form tell and echo, writing is indeed an aid to memory. Writing is not the authentic experience of the event. Among the many poetic licence resources manifested in this poem, Hejinian makes extensive and illuminating use of morphological vs placing bound morphemes in isolation, deliberately leaving out the base-word form they modify. Being clear instances of harming the words' well-formedness they are easily identified as morphological vs forerunners.

Since the poem exceeds 1,500 lines, only a few short fragments are cited here to exemplify Hejinian's unique and iconic use of morphological vs. The first citation seems at first sight transparent, both regarding the identification of its incidents of morphological vss and regarding their interpretation:[22]

[~37-5]   [...]
       rim memory and more
       all these ways painting, modeling
       guage means general
       will push **straction** one day to the left [...]

---

[22] The numbers following the hyphen refer to the poem's sections. Emphases added here (not in the original): forms for which there is no English grammatical or semantic reading that allows them to appear in isolation are presented in bold; forms that may stand for independent lexical lemmas, as well as for bound forms, appear in italics.

3.2.2 Morphological Verbal Silence

'Memory' – one of the two words operating as the pivot of this metalinguistic poem – is fully articulated, albeit lessened by 'rim' modifying it, calling off the expectancy for an infinitely expanding memory. The form 'guage' is documented as a misspelling of 'gauge' (measuring scale). The poetic context in [~37-5] seems to tolerate and even gain from a reading incorporating the scaling gadget as a means for making generalisations. But as is not uncommon in the poetic licence use of morphological vss, here 'Sguage' also stands as a stump forerunning the poem's second pivot word: 'language' (see §4.6).

The explanation for her use of truncated words offered by Hejinian herself (2005) tallies with the definition of vs underlying our study:

[B]ecause I wanted to give – you know, 'writing as an aid to memory' – some sense of a level of language in which memory or the meaning is retroactive always. You know, things come along, and then you discover what they mean. So I wanted to show things coming into memory, or coming into meaning. So words not yet formed into their wholes.

This is captured by a morphological vs in which 'language' – as a signifier and as an object – is not articulated but instead emerges, using 'Sguage' as its stump.

Perceiving memory as the girth and words (language) as a blur displacement, or as Hejinian puts it 'a type of parallax, exists in the relation between things (events, ideas, objects) and the words for them – a displacement producing a gap' (2000: 48), is tantamount to vs, and here to morphological vs.

Hejinian's statements regarding her perception of memory and language, the relations between them and the nature of their rapport with reality, as well as the multiple lemmatisations shown for '$\{S_1\}$guage', would all seem to call for a retroactive inspection of the form '$\{S_2\}$rim' assigning it as a stump forerunning morphological readings such as '(un)trim' and 'grim'. The verse in the poem stating that 'a syllable is a suggestion / is the beginning of inclusion' coincides with the above definition of a vs forerunner. This is further illustrated by the form 'S_3straction' ([~37-5]), in which the only possible reading is as a stump suggesting the notions 'abstraction' and 'distraction'.

As Hejinian states in her writings, and as encapsulated in citations [~37] (2000: 43), this device not only bypasses the fiction of representation (and rememberability) but also rejects closure. This, in turn, foregrounds processes, thereby opening the text for the reader and for infinite possibilities:

[~37–27] [...]
    delve
    sume but *dom* or another
    duce [...]

– delve S_1sume: consuming, assuming, presuming, subsuming, resuming but S_2dom: freedom, kingdom ..., or another S_3duce [to:] conduce, seduce, conduce, produce, educe, overproduce, introduce induce, deduce.

60   Verbal Silence: Forms

The following citation illuminates a poetic practice Hejinian frequently employs supporting the stumps' forerunning morphological vss with immediate context articulating the full form, thus:

[~37–19] [...] number *rust numb* trot [...]

Using the 'neutralisation of oppositions' (which may be considered an additional morphological vs technique, see Ruipérez 1953: 244–245), 'numb' in [~37–19] being both a fully articulated verb and a nominal stump (S_1numb) forerunning 'number' communicates the specks of memory left of the total that was diminished by corrosion. The rust numb multiplicity is iconically captured by repetitions: the phonetic repetitions 'number'–'numb'; part of speech ambiguity, and the semantic repetitions 'rust'–'numb' as staleness, ruin (see Hejinian 2000: 48 after Gertrude Stein; on repetition, and see §4.5.1).

Hejinian's 'Writing Is an Aid to Memory' is fascinating in its extensive use of vss to communicate poetically the intricate relations holding between form and content, language, memory (retroactive) and reality (see also [~74^S]). Not surprisingly, vs in the form of truncated words plays a crucial role in accomplishing that which is unattainable.

In summary, morphological vs articulating bound morphemes as stumps forerunning the base-word forms they modify constitutes an explicit means for expressing issues such as lessening, impossibility, termination and gaps associated with the specific text's local or broad-spectrum content. This differs from backformation in that it is not a product of analogy, nor a means for deriving a new lexeme, and most importantly in that the partial form does not turn into a form that is independent of its base. On the contrary, its raison d'être is its being a stump forerunning the full form.

3.2.2.2 Morphological Stumps in Light of the Zero

In his important contribution on the linguistic notion of the 'zero', Melčuk (1979: 232) states that the zero morphs or lexes (Melčuk's syntactic zeros) are deficient only with respect to their signifiants (strings of phonemes or graphemes). Normally, he explains, they have a full-fledged signifié (formal semantic expression) and (for lexes) a full-fledged syntactics. They each have a specific, identifiable meaning and specific, identifiable combinatory possibilities and effects on other words.

Two issues addressed by Melčuk concerning morphological and syntactic zeros seem to require our attention before we continue our exploration of morphological vss (§3.2.2), morphosyntactic vss (§3.2.3) and syntactic vss (§3.2.4). The first – more general – issue is the relation between Melčuk's zeros and vss; the second – more specific – matter concerns his use of the trait deficiency. Melčuk observes that the correspondence between forms in which the signifiers are empty strings (zero) and their usually non-empty meanings (signified) represents a normal linguistic correspondence which overlaps with the relations between non-empty

3.2.2 Morphological Verbal Silence

signifiers and non-empty meanings (signified). This postulation is the canon dictating the notion of vs as a means of expression. Nevertheless, the relations between Melčuk's zeros and vss must be clarified. As shown in detail concerning the morphological zero (§3.2.2.2.1), morphosyntactic vss such as the definite article and the passive (§3.2.3) and syntactic vss (§3.2.4), some of the zeros covered by Melčuk are not the product of the addresser's free choice as means of expression but are themselves signifiers dictated by grammar rules or pragmatic realia. The latter are not cases of vs. In addition, vs ranges over a much broader scope than fixed zero morphs and lexes and includes numerous phenomena not covered by zeros. The second issue, not unrelated to the matter of choice, is Melčuk's treatment of the empty (zero) signifier as a deficiency. Melčuk emphasises that zeros (morphs or lexes) are deficient only with respect to their signifiants. The iconic capabilities of vs to communicate absence and deficiency, as the most suitable or sometimes even the only available means of expression within the particular linguistic apparatus, render vs anything but a deficiency.

Accordingly, in order to describe cases of morphological vs involving stumps not articulating expected bound morphemes, we must first determine the nature of the zero sign as an unarticulated symbol and its relations with vs.

3.2.2.2.1 Is the Zero an Instance of Verbal Silence?

Jakobson (1937: 152), following Bally, defines the zero sign as 'a sign invested with a particular value but without any material support in sound'. This citation hinges on these authors' structural method and theory regarding paradigmatic relations. Jakobson (1937: 151), referring to de Saussure, states:

> According to the fundamental formula of F. de Saussure, language can tolerate the opposition between something and nothing and it is precisely this 'nothing' that is in opposition to 'something' or, in other words, the zero sign, which lead to certain of the personal and fertile concepts of Charles Bally.

The following are some examples of the zero sign as a verbal signifier in English designating the unmarked member of a category:[23]

[~38]   catø / cats (see [~42]);

[~39]   bakeø / bakes / baked / baking;

[~40]   bigø / bigger / biggest;

and

[~41]   actorø /actress (see [~15^a] and [~15^b], and see discussion later in this section).

---

[23] Our focus here is on morphology, and accordingly we ignore morphophonetic operations as well as irregular forms (including suppletion, but see §3.1).

The zero sign (ø) in [~38] to [~41] designates the obligatory absence, as opposed to morphological vs, which we designate using the 'ṣ̌' notation.

Greenberg's (1963: 94) 35th universal states that the zero sign is a widespread integral part of grammatical descriptions:

> There is no language in which the plural does not have some nonzero allomorphs, whereas there are languages in which the singular is expressed only by zero. The dual and the trial are almost never expressed only by zero.

Pāṇini, the famous fourth-century BCE Indian linguist, was the inventor of many basic linguistic terms. His ordered formal grammar is clearly the source of the linguistic notion of the 'zero' (ø).

On the surface, the structural notation of the zero sign and Pāṇini's notion of the zero seem one and the same. However, a careful inspection of these notions in the specific contexts in which they were set reveals that the two are actually completely different.

Al-George (1967) emphasises that despite the similarity between the zero sign as described and used within the structuralist paradigm and Pāṇini's notion of the zero, the two are not identical either in theory or practically. Al-George maintains that recognition of the Sanskrit language as an integral part of the Indian ontology and worship contextualises Pāṇini's clear-cut distinction between an ideal plane and a sensible (material) one in a much broader context than his linguistic notions and grammar rules. As Al-George explains (1967: 120–121):

> According to Pāṇini, the full structure of the word exists *a priori* in every available form as an inherent reality. When the available form shows differences from the ideal one, Pāṇini introduces the idea of a substitute, and if the difference consists in a diminution, the respective absence is considered as being only apparent, the bare place of an invisible entity. The blank indicates or represents the original unit, being its substitute. *Lopa* is equated by Pāṇini to what is invisible, [...] *Lopa* indicates the category which exists though not embodied in a concrete form, suspended as a pure virtuality at the border between existence and non-existence.

Unlike the structuralist's zero sign, in the context of Pāṇini's Indian-Vedic doctrine, the zero is not a device – an *a posteriori* descriptive notation – but rather an *a priori* philosophical entity. According to Al-George (1967: 123), 'the substitute zero appears more as a natural or logical sign than as a linguistic signifier'. *Lopa* as a substitute is a natural sign referring – like the algebraic zero – to the abstract form and not limited to the absent signifier. The *lopa* is not identical with the concrete form: equated with the invisible – the virtual wholeness – it constitutes more than the sum of its parts.

This construct incorporating the individual, the shape and the class-essence differs from the structuralist linguistic zero sign in that Pāṇini's zero is not the form articulated (and thus inflected) in a specific grammatical context (see also

3.2.2 Morphological Verbal Silence

Scharf 1996: 174). Located in the plane of the ideal wholeness, Pāṇini's zero is void of any sort of grammatical information. In fact, it extends the linguistic definition of the lexeme as a theoretical entity onto the ideal and metaphysical plane.[24]

Understood within this broad Vedic philosophical context, and unlike the zero sign of structuralism, Pāṇini's zero does not stand solely for an individual referent, as 'catø' in

[~42]   The catø sat on the matø (and see [~38]);

or the shape: the form 'cat' (such as when contrasted with other forms, such as 'mat' or 'rat'). Pāṇini's zero stands for the generic sense of cathood, covering existing cats and non-existing ones; masculine and feminine, single and multiple (see also §3.2.3.1.1 on the definite article).

Now that we have introduced the structuralists' and Pāṇini's notions of the zero and clarified the differences between them, it is time to examine the above in light of our definition of morphological vs. It immediately becomes clear that neither of these notions meets the two essential properties of vs:

1. Vs being the product of the addresser's choice. The addresser's use of the structuralist zero sign to refer to the unmarked constituent of oppositions is the product of activating a grammatical rule and not a reflection of hes free will. The case of Pāṇini's zero is even more significant, first because it is not dependent on textual context, but also because its linguistic grammatical settings and materialisations are only one instance of a much broader extralinguistic context.
2. Vs standing in place of expected verbal articulation. As a conventional notation designating the unmarked constituent of the paradigm, the structuralist zero sign is clearly a case in which no speech, let alone specific linguistic articulation, is expected.[25] Given the extralinguistic nature of Pāṇini's notions of the zero when applied to grammar, the possibility of speech (articulation) as an alternative is theoretically ruled out.

So while the structuralist zero sign is indeed a verbal signifier, it is not an instance of vs.[26] Pāṇini's zero is not a verbal signifier, and naturally also not an instance of vs.

---

[24] Examined within the Vedic context, it becomes apparent that Pāṇini's other discoveries, such as the root and phoneme (all being theoretical – not materialised – entities) follow the same line and serve the same rationale as the zero. See also Prasad (2009).

[25] It is worth noting that Kurzon (1998: 7) and Poyatos (2017: 57) use of the term 'zero sign' for cases such as someone responding with silence to a question or a greeting by no means coincides with the grammatical notion of the 'zero sign' in which – as detailed here – no speech is expected (and see §4.3.3.2).

[26] Sobkowiak (1997: 45) excludes the zero sign from his discussion of silence and markedness on the grounds that including morphological and syntactic issues in relation to silence entails an extremely wide and hence unwarranted definition of silence. Although the outcome produced by Sobkowiak's argument seems to be identical to the outcome yielded by our discussion,

64 Verbal Silence: Forms

3.2.2.2.2 Stumps Not Articulating the Expected Bound Morphemes

It emerges that in addition to showing that both the structuralist zero and Pāṇini's zero are not cases of VS silence, a further exploration of the relationships between the three forms the foundation for an original contribution to the study of morphological VS as well as definiteness morphosyntactic VS silence (see §3.2.3.1.1).[27]

Example [~43^S] will serve to illustrate morphological VS and its relation to – though not identity with – the structuralist zero sign. We will then illustrate morphological VS in relation to – but not identical with – Pāṇini's zero.

[~43^S]   Two boyS_1 but one bodyø

The above caption heads a short but emotional video clip shared on YouTube.[28] The short clip shows the daily life of Shivanath and Shivram, Siamese twins from Tonk region in Rajasthan who each have a head and four limbs but who share a single torso (Dicephalic Parapagus).

Examining this short text in light of the structural zero sign, the difference between the null articulation in 'body' ('bodyø') and that in 'boy' ('boyS_1') is striking and thus indicative. 'Body' being a single referent of its kind is

---

Sobkowiak's argument actually differs in all respects from the considerations pursued here (see §4.1).

[27] As in spoken languages, in sign languages too there is a zero sign. Its functions are the same as those of spoken languages: it denotes the unmarked members of categories but its use and implementation differ according to the grammatical peculiarities of the language. As in spoken languages, sign languages may also use morphological VS as means of expression. Interestingly, in addition, some sign languages (for example, ASL and ISL) make an additional distinction, that between the zero sign and a morpheme zero. This is illustrated, with Aronoff et al. (2004: 22) (Figure 3.3).

 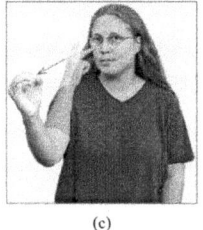

(a)   (c)

Figure 3.3 SEE in ASL.
(a) SEE is the unmarked zero sign form; (c) is the affixed form: SEE-ZERO, 'not see at all'.
Reprinted by permission from Springer Nature.

[28] www.youtube.com/watch?v=NUwa4pVKK_Q (accessed 2 April 2018).

3.2.2 Morphological Verbal Silence

grammatically marked by the zero sign as the unmarked constituent of its category: one – single – body. As such the zero sign and not any other speech form is expected. However, 'two boy' being a case of multiple references is morphologically marked, and so requires the articulation of the expected nominal plural morpheme ('s'). The absence of this expected plural morpheme is clearly not a case of the zero sign. Ruling out the attribution of this text ([~43^s]) to grammatical error or graphical elision, there is good reason to assume that it is the product of the addresser's choice to use morphological vs to iconically express the unique circumstances of the lives of these twins as it unfolds in the video clip. Their being two separate individuals is captured by the quantifier 'two'; their indivisible unity is expressed using the morphological silencing of the plural form.

We now move to the relations between morphological vs and Pāṇini's zero, which as described originate in Vedic philosophy and are extralinguistic, belonging on the ideal and not the material plane.

We first refer back to example [~15] (§3.1), which served earlier as an intuitive introduction to more familiar extracts employing vs. We may now examine the same example systematically. The grammatical opposition between the masculine in [~15^a] and feminine in [~15^b] is a clear case of a verbal sign ('ø') determined by grammar, and hence not the product of the addresser's choice to use vs as means of expression. Examining [~15^c] in light of [~15^a], [~15^b] and Pāṇini's zero,

[~15^c]   Emma Stone is a famous actor$_1$, she won the MTV 2017 best actor$_2$ award,

the following picture unfolds: from a lexical and grammatical point of view, the feminine morpheme 'ess' is indeed expected, and so 'actor' is here identified as a stump ('actress'). While the zero sign (as in [~15^a] 'actorø') is a verbal signifier prescribed in the grammar (and thus expected, see §3.2.2.2), 'actor$_1$' and 'actor$_2$', ([~15^c]) are morphological vss. The textual context, as well as MTV's decision to eliminate what became a tradition of segregation between men and women performers, results in the distribution of a single award (rather than two gender-segregated awards). Example [~15^c] serves here to introduce the speaker's widespread practice of using morphological vss to nullify oppositions and to communicate such neutralisations. In [~15^c] this neutralisation served the idea(l) of equality and non-discriminatory behaviour (especially in respect to groups and individuals assessed as minorities). This is why the nullification should not only be done but also shown: the addresser uses vs placing it as the figure to be accentuated.

This use does not overlap with Pāṇini's zero, but its use of morphological vs captures Pāṇini's notion of zero as referring to an idea: 'the category which exists though not embodied in a concrete form, suspended as a pure virtuality' (see the citation from Al-George 1967 in §3.2.2.2.1).

In light, on the one hand, of the morphological dull marking in English grammar in general, and in modern Englishes across genres in particular, and on the other the more persistent morphological (and morphosyntactic, in the third-person pronouns) gender markings that coincidently appear to become the flagship of politically incorrectness, gender morphological vs appears to be the epitome of morphological vs in English.

It is no coincidence that [~43^g] and [~15^c] involve instances relating to gender or number marking, which are commonplace expected nominal morphemes, and do not involve Modern English verbal inflectional morphology. Compared with other Indo-European languages and languages of other families, English's verbal inflection appears to lack a system of clitic morphemes each marking a specific grammatical role such as person and tense (and in cases aspect).[29]

Using here the present simple inflection as an example, it appears that French and German index all the forms of their present simple paradigm (no form is left unindexed, i.e. with no affix). Turkish differs from this pattern in two respects. First, as an agglutinative language, it attaches one morpheme indicating the present simple and a separate (portmanteau) morpheme indexing person and number. Second, within the present simple paradigm the third-person singular has a zero marking in the second portmanteau morpheme slot. Returning now to English, it stands out that while the non-indexed Turkish exemplar unequivocally designates a single constituent of the category, the English exemplar has the essence of a mirror image. In English the morphological indexing of the present simple inflection is actually the exception (only the third-person singular attaches grammatical morphemes). A comparison to Modern French, a language which like English requires personal pronouns before the verb, emphasises that this absence cannot be attributed to the explicit mention of the personal pronoun. Interestingly, this mirror image extends further as, in both languages, it is the third-person singular which differs from the remaining constituents. Mayerthaler's (1987: 28) wake-up call urging that 'we must be wary of the current English terminology, which fails to distinguish between "unmarked form" and "form without marker"' seems most relevant to the issue at stake. By no means should it be considered accidental that languages tend to correlate indexation with the more complex and less regular constituents. To use Mayerthaler's (1987: 28) distinction, English, being the mirror image of the Turkish case, is therefore not an instance of a zero sign for the unmarked option but a constellation exhibiting grammatical information left without marking.

As argued concerning the zero sign, because the nature of indexing – using a zero sign (for the unmarked option), using articulated morphemes (for all options or the unmarked ones) or not marking (as is the case for English) –

---

[29] The languages differ as to the morphological or phonological properties which dictate the final inflected form. Such are, for example, the different French conjugations and issues involving modality (subjunctive); Turkish is even more complicated, exhibiting vowel harmony as well as modal and other constructs.

3.2.2 Morphological Verbal Silence

is grammar rule-governed and not the product of the addresser's free choice, these are not cases of morphological vs.

As recalled, despite the clear-cut distinction between morphological vs and the zero sign and Pāṇini's zero, the latter may semiotically inspire morphological vs (see [~43^s] and [~15^c]). The widespread absence of marking in the Modern English verbal inflectional paradigm considerably reduces the likelihood of it inspiring morphological vs. In such grammatical and contextual settings, where the prevailing cases are not marked, a potential incidence of morphological vs, instead of being salient and so designated as a forerunner, will most probably be overlooked and so merge with the default grammatical notation. From a qualitative perspective, the no-marking grammatical convention assigned to the marked – rather than the unmarked – form seems to mitigate against the expression of ideal or generalisation meanings expressed using morphological vs.

Because only the present simple, the past simple and the continuous aspect are indexed in English using clitic morphemes (as opposed to auxiliaries and modals), it appears that practically[30] the only morphological forerunners informing the coming morphological vs involving tense and aspects are deliberate switching between these forms, such as the use of the present form for the past, continuous form (' – ing') for punctual aspects, and concerning strong verbs (verbs not inflected using ' – ed') use of different aspects of the past tense (such as simple versus perfect).

We first reflect on Harrison's (1856: 330–333) words concerning 'broke' and 'unsmote' of the final stanza of Lord Byron's 'The Destruction of Sennacherib' (p. 181):

[~44]   And the widows of Ashur are loud in their wail,
          And the idols are broke in the temple of Baal;
          And the might of the Gentile, unsmote by the sword,
          Hath melted like snow in the glance of the Lord!

Denouncing what he considers a literary substitution of the verb for the participle that causes a great deal of mischief, Harrison cites this as a case of 'corruption in its full aspect of deformity'. Harrison concludes his prescriptive words by saying that '[m]any examples of this kind [...] form an anomaly not to be found, one would hope, in the language of any other civilized people on earth'. Harrison's words concerning the grammatical facts, as well as poets such as Byron and Milton, present a normative stance ruling out poetic licence

---

[30] 'Practically', because, probably ever since tense differentiation was formed, there has been no form equivalent to the Vedic or Ancient Greek '*aorsit*' (a verbal form unmarked regarding tense, see, for example, Hewson 1997: 59–61). On the interesting aetiology and correspondence between the '*aorist*' and Pāṇini's zero, see Prasad (2009).

and leaving no room for an examination of the reasons and function of such deliberate and erudite usage.[31]

In line with the attitude voiced by Harrison, while critics have noticed Lord Byron's use of 'broke' and 'unsmote' in place of the expected 'broken' and 'unsmitten', they have offered no explanation for this choice. The appearance of this deliberate switch of tenses in the final stanza describing the outcome of the destruction of Sennacherib seems unlikely to be accidental, and indeed the application of the principles of morphological vs confirms that the choice of these two particular verbs is a clever poetic choice performed by a master wordsmith. From a grammatical point of view, we would naturally expect a participle in both these slots. The unexpected morphological vs creates an iconic parallelism between form and content. By breaking and smiting grammar, the form both symbolises the reality it describes – the breaking and dissolving of Ashur – and conveys the message that this reality is a *fait accompli*.

Our understanding of this use of the participle in this example will help us as we consider the next:

[~45$^{a\text{-}\delta}$] Sergei Skripal's cat and guinea pigs dieδ_1 after police sealδ_2 house.

This is the wording of the headline of a front-page news item in the *Guardian*.[32] We should compare the tense of the heading with that of the lead:

[~45^b]   Two guinea pigs found dead at Salisbury home of ex-spy while a cat needed to be put down,

and that of the opening paragraph of the *Guardian*'s news item:

[~45^c]   Two guinea pigs belonging to Sergei Skripal died and his cat was put down after the Salisbury nerve agent attack, the government has revealed.

These examples shed light on the deliberate use of morphological vs in newspaper headlines. Headline [~45$^{a\text{-}\delta}$] uses 'die' and 'seal' (present, but see later in this section); the lead [~45^b] uses an elliptical form of the passive perfect 'found dead' ('had been found dead') and the phrasing in the opening of the article ([~45^c]) uses the past simple: 'died'.

Chovanec, who specialises in the grammar of newspaper headlines, contends that in headlines the present tense is the unmarked tense for referring to

---

[31] A clear distinction should be observed between cases of zero sign, dialectical or social-based markerless behaviour and deliberately leaving out a morpheme as a forerunner serving morphological vs. A case of an 's' third-person present singular markerless behaviour is explained by Trudgill (1974: 55–63) as a sociolinguistic characteristic of lower working-class dialects of East Anglia.

[32] www.theguardian.com/uk-news/2018/apr/06/sergei-skripal-cat-guinea-pigs-die-police-sealed-house-salisbury-spy (accessed 8 April 2018).

past events (2003). He explains that the present tense has an 'atemporal' character (see also Wolfson 1989: 145 'timeless'). Chovanec, along with other scholars, suggests that the use of the present tense to refer to past events in newspaper headlines secures such functions as enhancing the most dramatic aspect of the event and acting as a shifter to synchronise the time of the event and the reader's pragmatic time.

The question of choice, which is an essential prerequisite for vs, should also be considered regarding the apparent absence of past tense forms in headlines in general, and in [~45^{a-s}] in particular. For [~45^{a-s}] to be a case of vs it must be the product of choice. But can choice play a role if the present tense is the default unmarked tense for headlines (see Chovanec 2003)?

Chovanec (2003: 86) explicitly confines this 'grammar of headlines' to ones in which a time adverbial is absent, thus allowing the conventional shift of tenses and the eventual use of the simple present. Returning now to [~45^{a-s}], despite the explicit mention of the temporal adverb 'after', the two verbs ('die' and 'seal') appear in the present form ('die after police seal'). This effectively results in an ungrammatical formation in which [~45^{a-s}] is marked for tense.

Despite this marking, [~45^{a-s}] maintains the functions attributed earlier to tense shifts. However, an examination of the different content reflected in the acts listed in the headline ([~45^{a-s}]), the lead ([~45^{b}]) and the story ([~45^{c}]) reveals that in addition to those functions something else is going on. Being marked – deliberately diverging from the expected rigid 'grammar of headlines' – [~45^{a-s}] is indeed a case of morphological vs, rendering:

[~45$^{a'}$] Sergei Skripal's cat and guinea pigs die[d] after police [had] sealed {the} house.

As a punctual verb in terms of aspect, the verb 'die' is rarely used in the present simple (except for habitual repetitive contexts). This ungrammatical form foreruns in [~45^{a-s}] the morphological vs, conveying the latest decisive evidence for the use of Novichok on Skripal's premises, as well as the instant fatality of this nerve agent. Only such an understanding of the text and the choice of morphological vs justify the shaping and blurring of the facts as revealed when comparing the information given in [~45^{a-s}] with the facts detailed in the lead [~45^{b}] and the story [~45^{c}].

In morphologies (such as Modern English) that lie further away from synthetic language types, some of the vs forerunners involving morphology are syntax sensitive. Exceeding word boundaries, they comprise morphosyntactic forerunners.

3.2.3 Morphosyntactic Verbal Silence

Vs varies among languages mainly in the form of its forerunners. Within form it varies particularly concerning the relations between morphology and syntax, which shape the magnitude and nature of the morphosyntactic phase – when such a phase applies. As explained, in purely analytic languages this burden falls mostly on syntax and lexicon. In addition to typological properties, the language's particular conventions must also be taken into account. The literate speakers of those languages psycholinguistically perceive bound grammar morphemes written as isolated graphemes as separate words. Because such cases exceed the boundaries of a single word, they – and accordingly their vss – belong to morphosyntax and not to morphology.

Linguists differentiate between 'content words' and 'function words', as Hurford (2014: 140) explains:

All languages make some distinction between 'content words' and 'function words'. Content words carry descriptive meaning; nouns, verbs, adjectives, and adverbs are types of content word. Function words are typically little words, and they signal relations between parts of sentences, or something about the pragmatic import of a sentence.

In addition to forming part of the speakers' linguistic intuitions, this distinction is supported by theoretical contributions and empirical findings (see also §3.2.4.6).

In English, morphosyntactic forerunners take the form of a non-articulated expected function particle or a non-articulated expected form consisting of a function particle and a clitic affix (such as the definite or indefinite articles or an auxiliary verb and '-ed' verb affix expected for the passive voice). For such stumps to count as forerunners of morphosyntactic vs they must be the product of the addresser's deliberate choice to employ vs as a cooperative means to communicate meaningful content. Following this key requirement, the articulation of such function particles in pragmatic or grammatical contexts in which they are not expected, thus silencing their expected counterpart, may also serve as forerunners of morphosyntactic vs.

In addition to morphosyntactic vs involving both morphology and syntax, the fact that it is both language and script sensitive may further complicate matters. In order to offer a presentation of morphosyntactic vs that is as clear and simple as possible, the current discussion is confined to two issues: definiteness (§3.2.3.1) and the passive (§3.2.3.2). This is not an exhaustive enumeration of morphosyntactic forerunners; yet, this list includes phenomena that are not subject to disputes regarding their classification as involving function words rather than content words (Corver and van Riemsdijk 2001). Fortunately, in languages such as English, these two central issues offer interesting linguistic and pragmatic prototypical instances of morphosyntactic vss.

3.2.3.1 Definiteness: The Definite and Indefinite Articles

Extensive literature has been devoted to the definite and indefinite articles, including their functions and grammatical behaviour. We confine our

3.2.3 Morphosyntactic Verbal Silence

discussion here to aspects directly relevant to the morphosyntactic VSS that include articles.

The definite and indefinite articles are conventionally classed as function words, though they convey qualities involving meaning and denotation – dimensions more typical of the content end of the spectrum. Falling in the realm of what Corver and van Riemsdijk (2001) phrased as 'the function of content words and the content of function words', studies offer two perspectives for grouping the articles: a functional perspective and, regarding languages marked for definiteness, a formal perspective.

The functional perspective differentiating between definite and indefinite was pioneered by Russell (1905). Focusing on descriptions rather than noun types, he suggested that what we are acquainted with is obtained by denotation, while what we only have knowledge of can be obtained only using denoting phrases (1905: 479). The notion of uniqueness, stating that 'the N VP', formalised (after Löbner 1985: 189) as: $\exists x(N(x) \wedge VP(x) \wedge \forall y(N(y) \rightarrow y=x))$[33] has served as the prototypical parameter differentiating definite from indefinite referents ever since Russell (see also Hawkins 1991: 406–407; but see Jespersen 1949: vii, 482–485).

The parameter of familiarity (what we are acquainted with), is interpreted in different ways such as previous experience, salience in the specific context, shared information and so forth (see Berezowski 2009: 7, 103–104; Jespersen 1949: vii, 417–429 outlines four stages of familiarity). Uniqueness and familiarity are complementary: one must not necessarily be acquainted with unique objects, and on a regular basis, publically or privately familiar objects are not unique.

Other parameters include non-ambiguity (Löbner 1985: 291 and see Jespersen 1949: vii, 403–405 after Christophersen 1939) and inclusiveness, that is, indicating the reference to the totality of the set (Hawkins 1991: 409; see also Berezowski 2009: 32–33 on Chesterman). Parameters such as existence (Russell 1905; Hawkins 1991: 412–413) do not discriminate between the definite and the indefinite but are implied by the use of definiteness. A remnant of the demonstrative role that is inherent in the etymology of the word 'the' (Hewson 1972: 11–25; Hawkins 1978: 104–115, 267–271) can still be discerned in the English definite article (Berezowski 2009: 10, 39–47).

The formal perspective – concerning languages marked for definiteness – differentiates between articulated and non-articulated articles. Here, too, different models can be found. All scholars agree that in English there is a gradual

---

[33] Löbner (1985) argues against Russell's existence plus uniqueness account. Löbner shows concerning one of a kind, such as '*the sun*' in which the existential (initial component: $\exists x(N(x) \& VP(x))$ ranges over the same extension as the larger formula, that it also equates the indefinite ('*a*').

scale including, on the one hand, articulated articles (most prominently 'the' for the definite and 'a' for the indefinite) and, on the other hand, either a single class including all the non-articulated cases or separate classes thereof. What further complicates matters is the use of what seems to be the same morphosyntactic term (that is the same signifier) for different concepts. This is most apparent in the case of the non-articulated articles. Clearly, if all the cases in which no definite or indefinite article is attached to a noun[34] are grouped as the zero sign (ø), the use of the term is much broader than its structural use and Pāṇini's notion of the 'zero' together (see §3.2.2.2.1). This distinction is particularly valuable in the context of the note made by Jespersen's editor Niels Haislund concerning the opening lines of Jespersen's chapter on 'The Articles':

We are here in the first line concerned with the articles, the definite (or better: defining) article and the indefinite article, as well as with the use of words without either of them (zero or the zero article).
[*Note by Niels Haislund*, Otto Jespersen did not intend to use the term *zero*, but would have spoken about 'the bare word'. But in accordance with the usage and theory set forth in many linguistic works I prefer to retain the zero-term]. (Jespersen 1949: vii, 403, see also Berezowski 2009: 5ff., and see note 34)

Unfortunately, due to his illness and death Jespersen did not write or even dictate this chapter: it was written by Haislund and accordingly is coloured with his strong structuralist imprint. The question whether Jespersen – like Pāṇini – differentiated between the noun, irrespective of the context in which it serves (the bare form), and the various forms each noun type can take depending on its specific context, will remain open and unanswered. Hewson (1972: 76) does seem to share this distinction, claiming that 'the bare unqualified noun (article zero) calls into play all the potential values together'. 'Without the limiting force of the article, the noun expresses its total potential significate, limited only by the context of situation' (1972: 116).

English marks definiteness – articulating the article 'the' – before (singular and plural countable as well as non-countable) common nouns, which as Berezowski (2009: 9) characterises are used whenever they are as definite as a proper name. English marks indefiniteness before common nouns which refer to single/partial members of a countable class. The two extreme cases regarding definiteness are (definite) proper names and (indefinite) plurals and non-countable (mass) common nouns, which do not attach articles. As apparent to all English speakers, this is a crude simplification (notice, e.g. 'The

---

[34] That which Berezowski (2009) terms 'article free' and Hewson (1972: 76, following Guillaume) terms 'the bare unqualified noun'. Berezowski (2009) argues that the zero article is a myth.

3.2.3 Morphosyntactic Verbal Silence

Themes'[35] and 'a years ago'; for schematic outline of the articles and noun types, see also Yule 1998: 25). 'Stone' as in

[~46]   *A Marriage Manual: A Practical Guide-book to Sex and Marriage* was composed in 1937 by the couple Hannah Mayer Stone and Abraham Stone,

'a/the stone' as in

[~47]   A/The stone fell off the truck

and 'stone' as in

[~48]   The house is made of stone

illustrate the various possibilities: a proper name not marked for definiteness ([~46]), a count common noun marked as definite or indefinite ([~47]) and the non-countable common noun referring to the substance stone ([~48], likewise 'The Castle' 'castle' in [~231$^{German-T}$] §3.2.5.4.4).

Focusing here on morphosyntactic vs involving definiteness, a clear distinction must be made between non-articulated articles resulting from morphosyntactic or pragmatic rules and the addresser's free choice to express definiteness using vs. We therefore focus here on the latter.

Vs is effective here because the marking of definiteness (using 'the', 'a' or an unarticulated form thereof) is obligatory: a description is expected to be definite or indefinite within any given context. Hawkins's (1991: 419) operative phrasing – '*the* and *a* contrast over uniqueness. Sentences with the former entail it, sentences with the latter appear to implicate conversationally its negation' – alludes to vs forerunners.

These strategies are not limited to logical argumentations and to linguists: they primarily depict the speakers' practice. A citation from Didier (2012: 9) is brought in to illustrate how authors – while ignorant of the terms 'vs' and 'forerunner' – make explicit practical use of vs. Referring to Heidegger's account of Nietzsche's perception of 'master of the earth', Didier cites Heidegger's argument that

[~49$^{French-T}$]   Nietzsche was the first man to raise the question: Is man, as he has been and still is, prepared to assume that domination? If not, then what must happen to man as he is, so that he can make the earth 'subject' to himself and thus fulfil the words of an old testament?

This citation is immediately followed by Didier's observation and treatment of the article 'an'. He asserts:

In thus citing what he calls 'an old testament' – the substitution of the indefinite article for the definite one is pregnant with meaning, since it implies, against the witness he himself is bearing, that the God of Israel would only be one god among others.

---

[35] Unless 'the' is to be regarded as part of the name and not as an free grammatical article.

Didier's observation is particularly valuable as it concerns a case in which an article is articulated (though it is not the conventionally expected article in context). Thus this example also illuminates Hawkins's practice of regarding 'a' as implying the negation of 'the' (see just above).

We now discuss the two forms of morphosyntactic vs forerunners: the expositional occurrence of a subsequent token (§3.2.3.1.1), and the expected (definite or indefinite) article (§3.2.3.1.2). These forerunners may also blend in specific settings (§3.2.3.1.3).

3.2.3.1.1 Non-articulation of an Expositional Occurrence as Verbal Silence

English grammar rules and pragmatic conventions require the marking of unique objects, such as:

[~50]   The sun (see for example, [~2] in §2.1 and Woolf, *Waves*, pp. 1, 16, 46, 70);

[~51]   The sky (see for example, [~54]; Huxley, *Eyeless*, p. 176),

unambiguously using the definite article.[36] Likewise, circumstantially determined objects, especially in synchronic communication in which interlocutors share a set of common knowledge, are also marked from the start with the definite article:

[~52]   The king is dead! Long live the king.

[~53]   The day has come.

The explicit semantic exposition of other objects – countable and non-countable – within a specific context paves the path for contextual familiarity expressed in subsequent mentions by means of the definite article. The opening of Doris Lessing's short story 'Wine' seems to provide a straightforward illustration:

[~54]   A man and woman walked towards the boulevard from a little hotel in a side street.
The trees were still leafless, black, cold; but the fine twigs were swelling towards spring, so that looking upward it was with an expectation of the first glimmering greenness. Yet everything was calm, and the sky was a calm, classic blue.
The couple drifted slowly along.
[...]
The man yawned; the woman caught the infection [...] (*Works*, p. 87)

---

[36] But see Hewson's observation (1972: 125) that 'we enjoy *sun* or *shade* in the summer, but we sit *in the sun* or *the shade* (the place where there is sun or shade)'.

3.2.3 Morphosyntactic Verbal Silence

On the first encounter with the story, the man and woman are not known to the reader, and are thus marked using the indefinite article. Once they have been introduced, any subsequent reference to them (jointly or separately) must be marked using the definite article. Any subsequent use of the indefinite ('a man', 'a woman', 'a couple') will be interpreted as introducing new characters, rather than as referring to the former referents. 'The couple' is then a case illustrating contextual second token involving semantics. 'Spring' is a season pragmatically definite in the specific narrative, which according to English grammar renders the articulation of the definite article redundant (see, e.g. Jespersen 1949: vii, 540–542). As explained, 'sky' ([~51]) is definite as a unique occurrence of its kind. All the cases in [~54] follow English grammar rules and pragmatic conventions.

Deliberate non-articulations, as means of expression, of the first (exposition) occurrence of a token which is not one of its kind, constitute instances of vs. An interesting example comes from the title of Jerome K. Jerome's renowned novel (1889):

[~55^S]   Three Men in a Boat (S_1 To Say Nothing of S_2 the Dog).

Interestingly, the bracketed text is pregnant with vss. We focus here on 'the dog' not articulating an – expected – expositional token. Clearly, dogs are objects comprising a sort class and are not one of their kind. Placed in the book's title it may be attributed to a literary convention regarding headings, whereby not articulating the expositional occurrence of a token referring to the book's key object (such as the protagonist) has the effect of drawing the reader into the plot while passing over the intermediate exposition stage (see e.g. Jespersen 1949: vii, 560–561). Despite the fact that this is indeed a literary convention, it is the product of the author's choice and hence constitutes a case of vs. We may compare such an example as:

[~56^S] S Jack and the Beanstalk.[37]

But as is apparent, title [~55^S] does not follow the typical syntax of titles; in fact, bracketing text counters the semiotic raison d'être of titles and headings. Had Jerome K. Jerome wished to follow the headings' convention, pretending the reader is already familiar with a key protagonist (as illustrated in [~56^S]), and leaving out the expositional token of 'dog' (S_2), this vs would not have been enclosed in brackets, and hence presented as secondary.

What calls for explanation here is the combination of the parenthesis acting to dilute the importance of this information compared with the non-bracketed part, and on the other hand the two vss (on 'S_1 to say nothing of', see

---

[37] See https://en.wikipedia.org/wiki/Jack_and_the_Beanstalk (accessed 21 November 2018).

§3.2.5.1.4) positioning this message as a figure. The answer seems to come from the symbolic – non-literate – layer of the novel and its characters. Magill (2015: IV, 2428) described J. – the narrator of the novel – as the alter ego of Jerome K. Jerome. Along the same lines, Montmorency – the dog – must be placed in the devil's camp. Montmorency and the men represent two complementary opposites. Magill explains that 'Montmorency, as revealed by J., is the voice of realism on the boat. His sardonic attitude is in humorous contrast to the blustering naïveté of the human animals, J., George, and Harris' (2015: IV, 2429).

These complementary oppositions are portrayed using the diminishing brackets with the salient effect of vss. Being enclosed in brackets, the dog – the voice of realism – is set apart from the men: the blustering naïveté of the human animals. This is met with vs: leaving out the exposition of the dog makes reality salient, an option which is iconically voiced using vs. This option does not require exposition because it is, without doubt, familiar to the readers – but, as J. observes, withheld from the three men: 'To look at Montmorency you would imagine that he was an angel sent upon the earth, for some reason withheld from mankind' (Jerome, *Three Men*, p. 27). Montmorency parenthesised and declared as not talked about (see $\mathcal{S}_1$ §3.2.5.1.4) adds a significant and somewhat humorous flavour, particularly when we recall that of the four participants in the journey, it is Montmorency (standing for reality) who is a fictitious figure: Jerome's pure invention.

3.2.3.1.2   Non-articulation of an Expected (Definite or Indefinite) Article as Verbal Silence

The cases illustrated in [~46] through [~54] articulating the definite and indefinite articles, as well as those not articulating the articles (such as 'ø spring'), were rule-governed and accordingly are not cases of vs.

Recruiting a title of another seminal novel will serve here to illustrate the reverse of [~56$^\mathcal{S}$], that is, the author's decision to refrain from following the literary and advertising convention to phrase book titles using the definite article:

[~57$^\mathcal{S}$] $\mathcal{S}$ Adventures of Huckleberry Finn.

This may surprise readers who have seen copies titled *The Adventures of Huckleberry Finn*, but in fact Mark Twain published the book leaving out the definite article. This seems to raise a discrepancy between the expected form and the actual form composed by Twain, and this has not gone unnoticed. While not naming this phenomenon 'vs', readers and critics treated it as a forerunner announcing the missing (expected) article, hence leading them to decipher the meaning and significance Twain wished to convey refraining from the use of the conventional definite article.

3.2.3 Morphosyntactic Verbal Silence

Philip Young was struck by the difference, not between the general convention and Twain's practice in [~57^s] but between the latter and Twain's *The Adventures of Tom Sawyer*. He solves this puzzle by explaining that

> [...] *Adventures of Huckleberry Finn* has no definite article in its title, though one is usually put there. Tom Sawyer's adventures were *The adventures* ... but they were completed, while Huck ends his book with anticipations (never fulfilled) of further goings-on in the West. For this reason, very likely, Twain hesitated to call the job he had done definitive. (Young 1966: 212 note)

Young's explanation relies on the distinct scopes delineated by the different articles. As discussed in §3.2.3.1, while the indefinite article refers to a partial group, the definite article refers to the total, be it a whole consisting of a unique and single member or a pragmatically unambiguously determined object. Since the novel about Tom Sawyer is presented as having been composed after Sawyer's adventures were completed, these were equivalent to the entire scope, yielding the inclusive role of the definite article (see Hawkins 1991: 409). In the case of [~57^s] it is not the indefinite zero (preceding 'adventures' as a countable plural noun) that is at stake but, as Young points out, rather leaving out the expected inclusive mark. By doing so Twain's title expresses an incompleteness 'to be continued'. Interpreting the absence of 'the' as a vs forerunner, we are encouraged to twin this novel with *The Adventures of Tom Sawyer* and to take Young's observation a step forward. The opening lines of *Adventures of Huckleberry Finn* are: 'You don't know about me without you have read a book by the name of The Adventures of Tom Sawyer; but that ain't no matter. That book was made by Mr. Mark Twain, and he told the truth, mainly'. In so stating, the adventures of Tom Sawyer are incorporated by way of intertextuality (see §3.2.5.2) in the current novel, which makes *Adventures of Huckleberry Finn* incomplete from its start (and compare [~58^s]).

3.2.3.1.3 Settings in which the Two Definiteness Forerunners Combine

An illustration of the blend of the two vs forerunners (§3.2.3.1.1 and §3.2.3.1.2) comes from an account of the title Peter Carey chose for his novel – not irrelevant to questions concerning uniqueness and factuality – structured as a bunch of manuscripts:

[~58^s]   *S̶* True History of the Kelly Gang

Says McGregor (2015: 358):

> *True History of the Kelly Gang* is thus not a straightforward sympathetic account, a history told from Kelly's point of view. Carey's work is instead Kelly's story: it is history in a literal sense; *his story*, told by him. The first clue to the complexity of the novel is in the title, the missing definite article before 'true'. This could reflect a

grammatical error on the part of the uneducated narrator, but has a deeper significance in drawing attention to the first two words of the title. On a popular understanding, 'true history' is redundant because if a history is not factual, then it is fictional and fails to qualify as history. On the other hand, Eggert [...] quotes Carey's claim to have deliberately selected the title for the purpose of signalling that the work is *not* a history – the idea being that contemporary professional historians are sceptical about the transparency of history. Whichever understanding one has of 'true history', that it protests too much or that it is oxymoronic, the title serves to direct attention to the history-in-the-novel and the function the history-in-the-novel serves.

The reader is encouraged to spot the different definite and indefinite vs forerunners incorporated in [~58^s] and their different meanings, as offered in the quote from McGregor, as well as many more layers that have emerged over the many forms of publications devoted over the years to the story of the Kelly Gang.[38] The write-up in *Age* on 'The many histories of the Kelly Gang' opens more possibilities of vs forerunners. It is interesting to note that among many other things it alludes to Huckleberry Finn. Focusing on definiteness vs promotes another correlation, that of two novels capturing a narrative whose beginning is told elsewhere, and in this respect is only partial (see §3.2.5.2).

3.2.3.2 The Passive Voice as Verbal Silence

The linguistic definition, characterisation and description of the passive voice vary considerably depending on the prevailing theory and the languages involved. To help us embark on our topic, namely the passive voice as a forerunner of morphosyntactic vs, we turn first to Keenan and Dryer (2007: 352). The key cross-language characteristic they offer defining the passive voice is that 'in a passive, the subject in the corresponding active is expressed by an element that is neither a subject nor an object in the corresponding passive or is not expressed at all; if it is not expressed, its existence is still entailed by the passive'.

Two points in the above quote are worth noting. Not surprisingly, the first is that the passive is a syntactic phenomenon involving syntactic roles played by the different constituents and their arrangement. The second point to notice concerns what might seem to be the extreme case: that is, when prominent nominal roles are left out. It appears from the above that this serves as a passive forerunner grounding the absent roles.

Keenan and Dryer's characteristics explain the syntactic phase of the passive voice (and thus of vs), but as they admit, 'passives are not in general distinct from actives with regard to the position and case marking of NPs' (2007: 327). It turns out that the distinctive characteristic (e.g. the one setting

---

[38] 'The many histories of the Kelly Gang', *Age*, 28 March 2003, www.theage.com.au/national/the-many-histories-of-the-kelly-gang-20030328-gdvgap.html (accessed 3 December 2018).

3.2.3 Morphosyntactic Verbal Silence

passives apart from topicalisations and dislocations)[39] lies in the VP. What they found to be present (across languages) in these VPs is a specific passive suffix. These morphological characteristics complements the syntactic phase.

While the above characteristics focus on formal cues detecting the passive voice, the passive voice is to be weighed as a voice chosen from possible voices: a semiotic and pragmatic 'mechanism that selects a grammatically prominent syntactic constituent – subject – from the underlying semantic functions (case or thematic roles) of a clause' (Shibatani 1988: 3).

Utterances in which the syntactic roles and their organisation echo their thematic relationships as they take place in reality are more transparent than utterances that do not follow this parallelism. The most transparent, natural and cooperative construction for the interlocutor is one in which, for transitive acts, an animate agent occupies the sentence's subject slot, while the object slot is occupied by the patient of the act performed by that agent.[40] George Orwell (1946: 91) proclaimed, '[n]ever use the passive where you can use the active'. He regards discarding such habits not merely as a matter of 'good language' but as a precondition for achieving political regeneration. Not surprisingly, many authors of 'good grammar' guides base their diktats on Orwell's authoritative contention. A careful reading of Orwell elucidates that he not only excludes the literary use of language from his rules but more importantly weighs language and its forms in light of their adequacy to serve 'as an instrument for expressing and not for concealing or preventing thought'. The incentive motivating numerous scholars to engage in the study of the use of the passive voice is their understanding that in particular contexts the passive voice not only differs (semantically or pragmatically) from the active voice but is the only available option or the most suited means for expression (see, e.g. Rodman 1981; Skinner and Pludwin 2013). These studies pave the way for us to examine the relations between the passive and morphosyntactic VS.

For such passive constellations to count as forerunners pointing to VS, they must be a product of the addresser's choice to use them as means of expression. Introducing VS as a figure necessitates differentiating between cases in which the passive voice is dictated by grammar rules or by pragmatic matters and VS. Classifying this VS as morphosyntactic is justified having accounted for the fact that the use of the passive as a forerunner requires both the

---

[39] See, for example, Shibatani's (1985) argument for setting agent defocusing apart from topicalisation, and see later in this section.

[40] Such correspondence between form and content is perceived as more natural but does not constitute a universal rule. Other configurations, include VOS languages, such as Kiribatese (Micronesia), in which the subject is placed as the last constituent, are also attested (Keenan and Dryer 2007: 327).

morphological phase (affixes) and the syntactic phase (VP). Shibatani contends that the primary function of the passive voice is agent defocusing, explaining that:

> An element which requires the least amount of attention is subjected to a defocusing strategy, and the most obvious means of defocusing an element is not to decode it syntactically. The passive which omits an agent nominal represents such a defocusing strategy. (1985: 832)

Supporting his thesis with illustrations from various languages and genres, Shibatani shows that most passives are agentless, that the passive is rarely applicable to non-agentive intransitive forms and that even concerning transitive forms, in most cases for the passive to apply the (active) subject must be the agent.

The seeming disposition of the passive to silence the agent makes passive forms a common means for morphosyntactic vs. Depriving the agent of hes natural and expected position as the syntactic subject, or leaving out agentive phrases as a means of expression, not only recruits passive forms as forerunners but also exploits the differences within passives. To identify cases of the passive as vs, the major kinds of passives and the conventional meanings associated with them are portrayed alongside the twist that each such role undergoes which shifts it into vs. The 'faults' Freedman (1958: 14) attributes to what he terms 'the *deadly Passive*, or, better, deadening passive; it takes the life out of writing, making everything impersonal, eternal, remote and dead' will serve here to give a preliminary sense of these twists. It is as if, in a specific context, the addresser selects the passive voice as hes vivifying means to communicate the experience of the impersonal when the personal-human is expected, to convey the experience of death and detachment rather than death itself and to foster an appearance of eternal and absolute where, in reality, matters may be open to dispute.

3.2.3.2.1 The Passive for the Unknown Expressing Ostentatious Epistemic Ignorance

Vs functions here as a means for shaping an epistemic canard that the identity of an existing agent is not known. To see how the passive in its role as the unmarked form of cases in which the agent is unknown is employed as vs demonstrating ostentatious epistemic ignorance, we first look at the non-vs case, that is, the unmarked form for cases in which the agent is unknown:

[~59] [Headline] What to do if your bike is stolen
[Lead] Should you leave it to the police, head round with some heavies or jump on the black-market merry-go-round and buy it back?[41]

---

[41] Juliet Kemp, 2011, *The Guardian*, Environment/cycling bike blog, 22 June 2011, www.theguardian.com/environment/bike-blog/2011/jun/22/bike-stolen-what-to-do-bicycle (accessed 18 June 2018).

3.2.3 Morphosyntactic Verbal Silence

This illustrates the basic passive in cases in which the explicit mention of the agent is ruled out because at the time when the utterance is produced the identity of that agent is unknown to the addresser.[42] Such forms defy – and so lose – the natural, thus expected, thematic–syntactic order, but in turn they gain a genuine manifestation of the epistemic state of mind, that is, the lack of information regarding the agent's identity. In fact, in some languages, such as Classic Arabic, the use of the basic passive (*Majhul*, مجهول) is obligatory, thus ruling out an active counterpart in which that agent occupies the subject's slot and ruling out the possibility to append an agentive phrase, such as '*by*' complementation designating the agent (for an overview see Abd-Alkareem 2005, but see also Nofal 2011: 158ff.).

Basic passive forms, being in many languages the default grammar coupled with the unmarked epistemic case in which the agent is absent, are not the product of the addresser's choice. The same is true of the use of the passive to represent the epistemic process of unfolding perception: the object is brought to attention but not yet known. To illustrate this unmarked use of the passive we may cite Pane's (2017: 56) example from Thomas Hardy's *The Mayor of Casterbridge* (p. 292):

[~60]   Henchard, alone, gazes into a weir and sees what is later revealed to be his own effigy: 'While his eyes were bent on the water beneath, there slowly *became visible* a something floating in the circular pool'.

But in cases when there is an agent, and when the addresser knows the identity of that agent but chooses to exploit the default basic passive form as an ostentatious epistemic ignorance forerunner that is communicating that the identity of that agent should be treated as if it is not known, we have an instance of vs.

The addresser's choice to use forms such as the basic passive as vs differs from the use of the basic passive to conceal (see §2.2.4.1) the identity of the agent, in that the very message conveyed by vs is not the identity as such but the epistemic state, urging the interlocutors to allow the addresser to demonstrate ostentatious epistemic ignorance, and leaving the identity of the agent to hemself (not sharing it with hes interlocutors). Unlike the unmarked case or silencing and concealing, the message executed by vs in this particular epistemic case encourages the mutual understanding that despite the fact that the addresser knows the identity of the agent, epistemically this knowledge should be treated as absent.

Wishing to enforce the stance that '[i]t is important for the future of responsible investigative journalism that journalists are able to offer adequate

---

[42] This differs from phrasing which uses the dummy (non-specific) pronouns, such as 'someone stole his bikes'.

protection to their sources', the House of Lords' Communication Committee pronounced that:

[~61^S]   It therefore only serves to underscore the need for journalists to be professional in their use of information S_1 provided to them.[43]

'Information provided to them' is structured as a passive form in which the active agent, namely the source who provides that information (S_1), is left out as the agent/subject. Here the 'unknown' role of the passive is exploited as vs to highlight the confidentiality of the sources, granting the known doer an incognito status. When as in [~61^S] the identity of the agent (S_1) – the source – is known to the addresser (the particular journalist), ruling out the explicit mention of the agent (as the subject of the sentence or as agentive phrases) results from its iconic stance as vs expressing the safeguarding of the journalist's commitment to freedom of information, which in specific cases requires securing the confidentiality of hes sources.

The use of the passive of the unknown as vs communicating ostentatious epistemic ignorance occurs frequently in the speech of professionals such as medical staff, psychotherapists and social workers, who are committed to the collective and particularly the individual right to privacy. But this vs is also chosen and exploited as a rhetorical and poetic strategy.

The next example occupies a middle ground between professional scientific writing and poetic licence. This may seem strange, as scientific and poetic writing would seem to represent two polarised genres. This is precisely the topic of sociologist Laurel Richardson's (1993) paper. Writing an in-depth interview as a poem and constructing a play out of field notes (such as panel members' and audience comments on her presentation), as well as her own interior monologue in response to these commentaries, not only accentuate the relations between written texts and oral texts; source and conceptualisation; (lay) interviewee and professional scholar. These actions also raise matters concerning authenticity, validity and validation, scientific positivism (factuality) and poetic licence.

The passive voice in [~62] might, out of context, be interpreted as communicating an unidentified trivial agent. But examined here in its social and academic context, it reveals the use of the basic passive as vs forerunning ostentatious epistemic ignorance. That is, a most significant agent whose identity is known to the addresser but which she chooses not to articulate in order to raise questions concerning the borders between origin, authenticity and interpretation and production; objectivity versus subjectivity, arts and sciences, and selves: the interviewees and the investigator. Example [~62]

---

[43] 'The future of investigative journalism – Communications Committee', www.parliament.uk, https://publications.parliament.uk/pa/ld201012/ldselect/ldcomuni/256/25606.htm   (accessed 20 June 2018).

3.2.3 Morphosyntactic Verbal Silence

forms part of a dramatic adaptation of a discussion following Richardson's reading of a conference paper: a poetic presentation of an in-depth interview, a reading that was accompanied with a handout of the written version of the poem (see Richardson 1993: 700–701):

[~62]   MALE-5:   What Laurel Richardson has presented us is the grounds of Laurel Richardson's loyalty. The poem reflects her loyalty to Louisa May's story? Why didn't you tell us John's story?
       LAUREL: I am telling Louisa May's story. The material was collected in the context of a larger research project on unwed mothers.
       LAUREL *(Interior monologue):*
       You look satisfied with my answer. You nod your head. It is because I couched my answer traditionally. Because I spoke of a research project data set, interviews?. Because I spoke in the passive voice? Or, are you nodding because I confirmed your suspicions that I'm always on the woman's side. What if I had said, I am not interested in John's story? He is irrelevant ... Maybe that's what I am saying.

Laurel Richardson is the referent of the second-person in Male-5's direct question standing for an indirect accusation: 'Why didn't you tell us [...] ?'; She is also the explicit first-person agent in 'I am telling Louisa May's story' – immediately preceding the passive voice:

[~62$^{a\text{-}\mathcal{S}}$]   The material $\mathcal{S}_1$ was collected.

In her subsequent internal monologue, Laurel addresses her use of both the active and the passive voices. In so doing, she indicates that the interplay between the explicit mention of the agent (Male-5, and her own first clause) and the passive voice is significant and must not be overlooked as technical or trivial. The agent-referent in all cases is one and the same: Laurel Richardson. Since she is the person involved, and as reflected in her internal monologue, Laurel obviously knows the identity of her encompassed referent. She also knows that her readers know it too. Yet she chooses to write

[~62$^{b\text{-}\mathcal{S}}$]   I am telling Louisa May's story. The material $\mathcal{S}_1$ was collected [...]

rather than

[~62$^{b'}$]   I am {now} telling Louisa May's story. The material I had collected [...]

or even

[~62$^{a'}$]   I am telling Louisa May's story. The material was collected by me [...].

She does so in order to follow and support the thesis underlying her unique presentation as part of her composite identity: a professional and a profession (collective, objective) cannot be detached from the personal. Laurel Richardson ($\mathcal{S}_1$) wears multiple collective and individual hats: ethnographer, researcher, sociologist, ethics and methodology expert (referring to a paper she presented in the previous convention), presenter, discussant, poet and playwright, an individual (surfacing in her interior monologues) and a woman. As qualitative research contends, Laurel Richardson is no exception: no researcher and no subject (interviewee or other) can be detached from hes wholeness. Dismantling researchers and subjects into discrete variables is not only artificial but impossible and contrary to human nature.

Laurel Richardson uses the passive referentially (see §4.1) as an ostentatious epistemic ignorance forerunner, foregrounding and so revealing the full 'I' (S_1) – as opposed to the artificially and falsely split agent:

But to conjure a different kind of social science means changing one's relationship to one's work; *how* one knows and tells about the sociological. The distant, separate 'I' of normative sociology which objectifies both the product and the process as 'other', outside the self, won't do. That kind of constructed self can neither do the work that faces contemporary sociology, nor understand why it is important. [...] The relationship to one's work modelled by 'Louisa May' alters both social science and the self that produces it. (1993: 705)

Moreover, Richardson's deliberate use of the passive, forerunning her refusal to reduce her agency (S_1) to her role as a scientist, transforms what Male-5 intended and articulated as an accusation regarding the addresser's scientific malpractice into a portrayal of the truth of the matter: that which is not only true but should be embraced as a blessing in service of science, humanity, individualism and art.

3.2.3.2.2 From the Conventional Passive Rhetoric Role to Disclaiming the Agent as Morally Responsible for Hes Deeds

By eliminating the agent, vs deletes that agent's moral stand as the responsible doer. Linguists have offered interesting insights into the disputed issue of the subject's role: is the principle role of the passive to advance a constituent to the clause's subject slot, or is it to demote a constituent (usually the animate agent) from its unmarked position as subject (see, e.g. Keenan and Comrie 1977: 95–96; Shibatani 1988)?

As outlined in §3.2.3.2, 'good language' practice, as well as semiotic transparency considerations, position the use of the passive in place of the active as a stylistic evil to avoid. As Orwell noted, there must be good reasons justifying the use of the passive. Studies emphasise thematic figuring – agent demotion or patient promotion – as a key justification for the use of the passive. For example, one of the five motivations Jespersen (1924: 168) itemised for preferring the passive over the active is when one takes 'a greater interest in the passive than in the active subject'. In such cases the use of the passive facilitates a cooperative communication (see §4.1 on Grice's relation maxim), which results in an optimal message focused for the addressee's

3.2.3 Morphosyntactic Verbal Silence

benefit on the important new information. Leaving out the agent is accordingly considered patient promotion, which out of lesser interest results in agent demotion. This preference is made bona fide ('naturally', in Jespersen's words).

Donald Hall, the author of *Writing Well*, a guidebook that seeks to advance the student from writing to writing well, begins the section on the passive by stating that:

> When most writers use the passive, they usually subtract meaning from their prose. [...] We suppress identity, which is a particular, and we put hazy distance between implied subject and definite action. The passive voice avoids responsibility, as we sometimes claim that 'a dish was dropped in the kitchen,' rather than name the dropper. It diminishes a sentence by omitting a doer. So it can be very useful politically [...].
> (1957: 43–44)

The issue of agency and responsibility has been the subject of much discussion. Some, like Hall, believe that 'the passive voice avoids responsibility', while others claim that the implicit agent bears responsibility irrespective of hes syntactic position (for an overview see Hundt 2007: 66–67 note 18). In her monograph, *The Nature of Subjects, Topics and Agents*, Jeanne Van Oosten (1986) offers a thorough discussion of the matter. She (1986: 156) explains that '[t]he passive form, being a marked construction, marks a deviation from the prototype and so one of the marks of the prototypical agent or topic – maybe that of responsibility on the part of the agent – is asserted not to hold'.

Van Oosten also makes the connection between responsibility and control, on the one hand, and relevance, on the other. She shows how the rhetorical effect of the passive to figure the patient as the prominent focus of attention (see above Shibatani's 1988: 3 definition of voice), indicating that the agent is less relevant or irrelevant, is matched with reduction of responsibility. She concludes (1986: 173) by noting:

> The Irresponsibility Passive is a conventional use of the Transitory-Agent or the Focus-of-Attention passive, which works by downplaying the importance of the referent of the object of the *by*-phrase in the discourse, thus downplaying also the issue of whether the referent of the object of the *by*-phrase is to blame for the occurrence of the action of the predicate.

Van Oosten's examples and analysis of the agentless passive go hand in hand with our notion of the passive as a vs forerunner. In order for silence to be a means of expression a deliberate twist must occur from the conventionally motivated grammatical, lexical or stylistic form to vs. Addressees acquainted with the various genres have no difficulty recognising when the passive voice is used to focus on the non-agentive players, such as the patients and actions, and when the passive is a vs forerunner in service of eradicating the agent as morally responsible for hes deeds. Because moral responsibility still rests with the agent (see also Van Oosten 1986: 93), leaving out that underlying subject, which mentions the expected responsible agent, does not make hem unnoticed; on the contrary, its deliberate and non-naïve absence is indeed highlighted as a case of vs.

We conclude our presentation of vs forerunners eradicating the agent as morally responsible for hes deeds with examples ([~63]–[~66]) revolving around 'beaten' and 'battered'.

Martha Mahoney, in her examination of '[l]egal images of battered women: Redefining the issue of separation' (1991: 24), expresses the reservations of many professionals as well as lay persons that 'because the term "battered woman" focuses on the woman in a violent relationship rather than the man or the battering process, it creates a tendency to see the woman as the problem' (see also Winkelmann 2004: 8). This is portrayed in the words Quindlen (*Black and Blue*, p. 218) puts into the mouth of Frannie, the novel's protagonist:

[~63]   I am a recovering battered woman. God, I hate that term, all those classifications that seem to reduce our wounds to the same status as eye or hair color, that make us a type, a cover line in a magazine (see also [~64]).

Mahoney (1991: 25) provides and explains, in that study, varied motives justifying abandoning the term 'battered woman' (in fact the same reasons apply to the terms 'beaten women', 'battered children' and 'beaten children'). Renée Römkens (2000: 362), focusing on forensic psychiatric and testimonies by clinical psychologists in court, points to the consequence of treating the 'battered women' as a problem: 'In a legal context we could argue that the expert explains her in court. It is the expert who has access to valid knowledge and who is a knower; the defendant is in this respect a passive object to be known'.

The shift in the 1970s from a pathological and male-dominated perspective to the female-dominated 'battered woman syndrome' (BWS) – a traumatological perspective – replaced one passivity with another (Mahoney 1991: 36–49; Websdale 1998: 74–75). Moreover, the notion of the BWS was initiated and examined due to a male focus dominating the criminal forensic system dealing with men who were killed by their battered partner (see Römkens 2000). The pursuit of BWS was partly associated with the attempt to answer the troubling question – based on the definition of 'battered woman' as referring to a repetitive event – as to why such women do not separate from their abusers.

Reading first-hand testimonies of the women themselves (the 'battered women'), the use of the active voice to describe the actions of the abusing partner (as well as her own deeds) is apparent and clear (see, e.g. Mahoney 1991; Smith et al. 1995; Hydén 2005). Even if such women take responsibility resulting in self-blaming (what Hydén 2005: 180 termed 'the position of co-

3.2.3 Morphosyntactic Verbal Silence

offender'), they nevertheless state the partner's actions, thereby placing responsibility on them as the battering agent.

The term 'battered woman' and its subsequent occurrences as a basic syntactic passive form originate and are typically manifested in two types of sources: 'closeted' women, such as casted in movies and television episodes, and professional discourse (court, researchers, interviewers and helpers).

When such an authentic woman uses the passive, talking for example with a close friend or a close relative, her use of the basic passive is a symptom of her state (see on BWS above, and see on symptomatic silence, §2.2.1). But when it is a literary manner adopted in fiction (novels and plays, see [~64]), or when it is evoked in professional reports on 'battered women' (see [~65]), it is indeed a rhetorical strategy expressing the passivity of the victim and her tendency to disclaim her abuser as the agent morally responsible for her status as a 'battered women'. We return to Frannie from Quindlen's novel *Black and Blue* (pp. 3, 5) for one such illustration. The novel's first and third page read as follows:

[~64] The first time my husband hit me I was nineteen years old. One sentence and I'm lost. One sentence and I can hear his voice in my head, that butterscotch-syrup voice [...]
I remember going to court once when Bobby was a witness in a case. It was eleven, maybe twelve years ago, before Robert was born, before my collarbone was broken, and my nose, which hasn't healed quite right [...]
[...]
The first time he hit me I was nineteen.
I can hear his voice now, so persuasive, so low and yet somehow so strong, making me understand once again that I'm all wrong.
[...]
I can hear him in my head. And I know he's right. He didn't hit me, that first time. He just held onto my upper arm so tight that the mark of his fingertips was like a tattoo [...]

The next example illustrates the use of the passive in professional phrasing:

[~65] The list of violent acts does not always convey the grievous reality, or frightening extent, of male brutality or women's suffering, but women often are violated in appalling ways and means. A blow to the head is followed by another, and another, and another. A pregnant woman is kicked in her stomach. A girlfriend is hit by a car or pushed from a moving one. Eyes are blackened, limbs broken. (Winkelmann 2004: 16)

Excerpt [~65] is a good example of what might be considered an ambiguous usage between the passive as a rhetorical convention for patient promotion (here 'battered women') or a case demoting the responsible agent. The source of [~65] is a book devoted to *The Language of Battered Women: A Rhetorical*

Analysis of Personal Theologies. Accordingly, it is the text of an author attuned to the suffering of these woman as an immediate outcome of the male brutal acts. Having criticised the term 'battered woman' for creating 'an "identity" group whose very existence is based on the experience of physical and psychological violence' (2004: 8), the author is expected to fix the distortion articulating the brutal responsible agent as grounding the suffering of his victims. Being attuned to language matters, and to inflicted violence sufferers the author's choice of the basic passive could not be related to parapraxis nor to her desire to promote the victim. The answer seems to lie in the book's theological orientation: involving God as the agent managing suffering and faith and healing. Within such a mindset, disclaiming the human Adam's total responsibility promotes in turn the almighty agent.

Continuing our examination of the passive as a vs forerunner disclaiming responsibility, we turn to an examination of the passive forms and their meanings in the context of a beating scene raised by Freud when discussing incestuous relations or relations with significant-authority figures. At the heart of Freud's paper, 'A child is being beaten: contribution towards an understanding of the inception of sexual perversions' (1919a and 1919b, 'Ein Kind wird geschlagen') lie oedipal psychosexual relationships: the associations formed in the child between hes genitals and libidinal drives and gratification. Our interest here is the use Freud makes of the various syntactic voices (active/ passive; the different persons occupying the agent/patient roles) as a vs forerunner to describe the nature of the fantasy of beating as part of various stages in the awakening of the congenital libidinal drives and the origins of sexual perversions.

Freud lists the various transformations[44] in the beating fantasies (*Das Geschlagenwerden*) and in the relations between those he refers to as 'the author of the fantasies', their object, their content and their significance. He first outlines the stages regarding girls, while towards the end of the paper (1919a: 195–204) he notes the particularities and similarities regarding boys.

Freud expresses the entire fantasy using the basic passive voice (the following are both Freud's German phrasing and their authorised English translation):

[~66ª]   A child is being beaten (*ein Kind wird geschlagen*).

He then dissembles the girl's fantasy into three distinct phases. Freud contends that the first phase (presumably between 2–4) captures the early child's fantasy that an indeterminate adult beats a child. Freud points out that the person who

---

[44] It seems interesting to point out that Freud's (1919) mapping of these psychic convergences onto the various agency transformations preceded Chomsky's notion and formation of transformational grammar.

3.2.3 Morphosyntactic Verbal Silence

is linguistically presented as an indeterminate adult beater appears unequivocally as the girl's father:

[~66ᵇ]   My father is beating a child (*Der Vater schlägt das Kind*).

In this primal phase, the child in the fantasy is never the girl producing the fantasy. In fact, it is most often a younger sibling of that girl, thus:

[~66ᶜ]   My father is beating a child whom I hate (*Der Vater schlägt das mir verhaßte Kind*).

Freud phrases the little girl's fantasy as follows:

[~66ᵈ]   My father does not love this other child, he loves only me (*Der Vater liebt dieses andere Kind nicht, er liebt nur mich*);

[~66ᵉ]   (My father) loves only me, and not the other child, for he is beating it (*Er (der Vater) liebt nur mich, nicht das andere Kind, denn dieses schlägt er ja*).

This primary stage prematurely choosing the object of incestuous love, and mounting feelings of rivalry, love and hate, fosters the stage of genital organisation (second phase):

[~66ᶠ]   I am being beaten by my father (*Ich werde vom Vater geschlagen*).

On which Freud says:

Profound transformations have taken place between this first phase and the next. It is true that the person beating remains the same (that is, the father); but the child who is beaten has been changed into another one and is now invariably the child producing the phantasy. The phantasy is accompanied by a high degree of pleasure, and has now acquired a significant content, with the origin of which we shall be concerned later. Now, therefore, the wording runs '*I am being beaten by my father*'. It is of an unmistakably masochistic character. (1919: 185)

Freud verbalises the changes that the girl and her psychic awareness undergo, epitomised in the transition from 'my father is beating a child' ([~66ᵇ]) to 'I am being beaten by my father' ([~66ᶠ]):

[~66ᵍ]   My father loves me (*Der Vater liebt mich*)

meant in a genital sense transforms, owing to regression, in the second phase to:

[~66ʰ]   No, he does not love you, for he is beating you (*Nein, er liebt dich nicht, denn er schlägt dich*).

To simplify matters, and to confine the discussion to our linguistic concern, the girl's fantasy in this period of incestuous love is that 'He (my father) loves only me, and not the other child, for he is beating it' ([~66ᵍ]), which paves the way for repression and an emerging sense of guilt. Freud asserts that '[t]he sense of guilt can discover no punishment more severe than the reversal of this triumph: "No, he does not love you, for he is beating you"', which transforms the sadistic being beaten by her father fantasy of the initial phase to a masochistic fantasy – coming with by pleasure – in this phase:

[~66^i]   My father is beating me (I am being beaten by my father) (*Der Vater schlägt mich (ich werde vom Vater geschlagen)*).

Says Freud:

'My father loves me' was meant in a genital sense; owing to the repression it is turned into 'My father is beating me (I am being beaten by my father)'. This being beaten is now a convergence of the sense of guilt and sexual love. *It is not only the punishment for the forbidden genital relation, but also the regressive substitute for that relation*, and from this latter source it derives the libidinal excitation which is from this time forward attached to it, and which finds its outlet in masturbatory acts. (1919a: 189)

The final (third) stage, in which the girl producing the fantasy appears almost as a spectator, is one which Freud does not verbalise (186, 191) but explains, thus:

[~66^j]   Instead of one child that is being beaten by grown-ups {father substitutes, such as teacher}, there are now a number of {unspecified} children present {the imagining child substitutes}.

Examining in short the differences between the two sexes, Freud notes among other psychologically crucial differences that the girls' [~66^f] ([~66^h]) starts off as boys'

[~66$^{k\text{-boy}}$]   I am loved by my father (*Ich werde vom Vater geliebt*).

Owing to the masculine oedipal complex, the regression transforms this into a boy's conscious passive form deriving from the boy's attitude towards his father:

[~66$^{l\text{-boy}}$] I am being beaten by my mother (*Ich werde von der Mutter geschlagen*).

Freud concludes that both the girls' and the boys' beating fantasies originate in incestuous attachments to the father. Freud is not a linguist. He went to pains to outline this systematic mapping of the morphosyntactic structures of the various active and passive transformations onto the child's progression of oedipal psychosexual relationships in order to support his clinical hypothesis regarding the latter.

Two particularities of the children's phrasing trigger discussion of the beating fantasy and of the passive as a vs forerunner pointing to the ambivalence of responsibility and thus blame and punishment. First,

3.2.3 Morphosyntactic Verbal Silence

the passive voice is excluded from the initial stage, and predominates the girls' and boys' (second) intermediate phase as well as the boys' final stage. Second, unlike the passive for the unknown, as vs expressing ostentatious epistemic ignorance (§3.2.3.2.1), the passive forms here specify the agent by use of the agentive 'by'-phrase ([~66^f], [~66^i] – '(being beaten) by my father'; [~66$^{k\text{-boy}}$] – '(loved) by my father'; [~66$^{l\text{-boy}}$] – '(being beaten) by my mother'.

The key to both peculiarities is that in the intermediate phase 'this being beaten is a convergence of the sense of guilt and sexual love' (1919a: 189). Freud contends that pleasure and suffering in general (see Freud 1920), and psychosexual pleasure in childhood in particular, are associated with a sense of blame, which in turn is perceived as deserving punishment. It is not fortuitous that the passive voice is used when the child producing the fantasy (the girl, and even more so the boy) is identified with the beaten child (the girls' second phase and the boys' corresponding phase). In line with Freud's explanation of the shift from a sadistic fantasy to a masochistic one, sadism and masochism evolve around the subject's agency alternating objects of hes pleasure and suffering. As Loewenstein (1957: 199) suggests and illustrates, passivity is not the result of masochism but, on the contrary, a prerequisite for it. The passive (including here the agentive phrase), with its syntactic reversal of roles, here depicts the reversal of roles in the fantasy. The agent of the fantasy – the child producing the fantasy – is the child in the intermediate stage. The passive 'being beaten' (and with the masculine reversal 'being loved') depicts the child's prematurely detached sexual function. The beating and the beater are thus depicted using the passive voice as an instrument (rather than action and agent) creating the pleasure and blame of which the child is the agent. The passive form (including the agentive by phrase) is then a means of vs formed by the child's masochistic state, denying the parent's agency and responsibility. In place of the parent as the agent, passive vs depicts and expresses the child's agency of pleasure, blame and fear, which requires the admission of responsibility. As Loewenstein (1957: 199) explains (following Horney), '[t]he tendency to passivity and helplessness may have the implicit aim of appealing to the mercy of the threatening and protective parental figure'. Defining passivity as 'the readiness to comply with the will of other people', Loewenstein adds that 'by the same token, it permits sexual gratification by apparently eliminating all responsibility for it' (1957: 199).

The case of the 'battered woman' and that of the 'beaten child' seem very far removed from each other: the former is an assault occurring in reality between two adult partners, while the latter is an early childhood fantasy. Still, in both narratives the passive as a vs forerunner expresses the reassignment of agency and responsibility. Interestingly, in both cases the passive as vs serves on the one hand to disclaim the adult beater's responsibility, and on the other as a vs forerunner. Given the anticipation of the impending explicit mention of an agent, its deliberate and non-naïve absence indeed foregrounds the agent's responsibility. In the 'battered woman' scenario, this serves a masculine dominance social norm, while regarding the 'beaten child', it serves a 'masochistic' disposition akin to the evolving psychosexual stages of the young child.

3.2.3.2.3 Middle Voice Portraying the Absence of a Willing Agent

We focus here on vs when it assumes the role of the middle voice as an iconic portrayal of passivity. To this end, we confine our short introduction to the fundamental issues crucial for the subsequent discussion.

The ostensible dichotomy between passive and active has formed the basis of canonical transformation grammar as well as earlier grammars. Many scholars and studies not only challenged the categorical dichotomy between active and passive but proposed various parameters showing that the delimitation is not necessarily binary. Givón's (1993: II, 75) four-point criteria for inclusion of a form as middle voice is adopted as a starting point:

1. The verb involved is inherently a *transitive* verb.
2. The grammatical subject is a *patient*.
3. There is no clearly discernible *responsible agent*, and thus no *action*.
4. While the discernible agent is absent, the construction is *not* used primarily as an *agent-demoting* device.

The system said to best epitomise the middle voice is Classical Greek (Kemmer 1993, and see note 45). While English never exemplified the full range of the different grammatical and semantic roles attributed to the passive and the middle, textbook examples of middle voice include [~67^d], [~68^c] and [~68^d]):

[~67^a] David opened the door (active)
[~67^b] The door had been opened S_1 {, by David} (passive)
[~67^c] {After much effort} the door was opened S_1 (passive)
[~67^d] The door opened (middle voice)
[~68^a] The Chilean security forces forcibly disappeared 1,198 people (active)
[~68^b] 1,198 people were forcibly disappeared S_1 {, by the Chilean security forces} (passive)
[~68^c] 1,198 people disappeared (middle voice)
[~68^d] The smell disappeared (middle voice).

As is clear from examples [~67] and [~68], there are no morphosyntactic signs indicating the difference between active forms and the middle voice.

3.2.3 Morphosyntactic Verbal Silence

A comparison between the passive cases ($[\sim67^b]$, $[\sim67^c]$ and $[\sim68^b]$) and the middle voice ($[\sim67^d]$, $[\sim68^c]$ and $[\sim68^d]$) shows that while they both differ from the active cases in that whatever occupies their subject slot is the affected (rather than the agent), they differ in that the middle has no agent, as if the act were performed spontaneously by itself. This explains why scholars group the middle together with the reflexive, the reciprocal and the impersonal (see Shibatani 1985; Givón 1993; Kemmer 1993).[45]

An important characteristic of the middle voice which emerges, in line with Givón's third point, is that unlike the prototypical active and passive voices, in which there is an agent (though hes identity might not be known or not made available in the utterance's wording ($\mathfrak{S}_1$)), the middle voice is characterised by the absence of a clearly discernible agent. Accordingly, the middle (unlike the other forms) does not allow complementation with agentive phrases.

The question now arises as to how ruling out the existence (let alone mention) of an animate agent is reconciled with the use of the middle voice as a means of expression. Here lies the crucial difference between authentic middle voice constructions and vs as the choice of the addresser. For the middle to serve as a vs forerunner (expressing passivity), not only must the verb governing the utterance be transitive (as for the middle, see Givón's first point), but also (and unlike the middle – Givón's third point) the context of that transitive verb must raise an expectation that it will be twinned with an animate competent agent ($\mathfrak{S}_1$). The absence of such an expected agent in the subject position, or even as the object of the agentive phrase (NP: '*by* object'), is a forerunner for the impending vs. Thus, choice comes into play when, contrary to Givón's fourth point, the addresser chooses to use the middle construction primarily as an agent-demoting device. If in reality the deed is spontaneous (occurring without an agent), this is the middle and no silence is involved. Vs takes places if the choice to leave out an existing agent (as a subject or as the agentive complementation) presents that agent ($\mathfrak{S}_1$) as one that is not an agent but passive: absent from hes own deeds. This explains the extensive use of the basic passive or passive complemented by an agent phrase in verbs and idioms describing the idleness in being drawn into something or expelled from something:

[~69]   Dragged by one's own tail / feet/ heels /coat-tail.[46]

[~70]   Backed / driven into a corner.

But for vs to take place the agent must be wittingly left out.

The passive as vs iconically portraying the absence of a willing agent can be manifested in the following two situations: first, in psychological dissociation,

---

[45] For a somewhat surprising thread elicited by the classical Greek middle in the interpretation of a psychoanalytic session, see Greenberg (2005).
[46] Notice that the '*by*' clause stands for an instrument and not for an agent.

94   Verbal Silence: Forms

when while a person is physically alive, s/he is detached from hes own will and needs and thus does not perform as an agent; and second, when by actual death a living human or animal ceases to be an animate, competent, willing agent.

Our first example of the first situation comprises fragments from Jona Oberski's novel *Kinderjaren* describing how the child and his ill hospitalised mother, who had lost contact during World War II, meet again after the war:

> [~71]   'That water's not fit to drink. You want me dead, don't you?' it was shouted from the bed. [...]
> They are my potatoes. I must have them back', it was shouted. (Cornelis 1997: 1)

Cornelis (1997: 1–4) offers a detailed analysis of the role played by the passive to portray dissociation and alienation the mother – a Holocaust survivor. While Cornelis does not use the term 'vs' or allude to the semantics of the middle voice, he, no doubt, turns to the use of the passive in *Kinderjaren* in the first place and explains its significance. This is a good example of treating absence (here the absent of the agent) as a deliberate verbal means chosen by the narrator.

Alejandra Pizarnik's poem 'Silence' adds to the experience of detachment also the impression of abyss. The poem was written in Spanish, and [~72$^{Spanish-T}$] is a close translation by Cecilia Rossi:[47]

> [~72$^{Spanish-T}$]   silence
> I become one with silence
> I have become one with silence
> and let myself be made
> be drunk
> be said

The extensive use of what seems to be a middle voice is immediately apparent. The five-line poem opens with two lines which differ only in tense: while the opening line reports an act in process, the second line tells of its completion. Unlike the remaining three lines, these first two lines instantiate the complement 'silence'. Once the speaking subject has become one with silence, the vs signalled by what seems to be a middle voice governs the remaining lines, communicating the absence of a willing agent. Turned into an object, the speaking subject not only belittles hes selfhood, life and life drive (depicted using middle voice), but more so the three prototypical acts through which humans master the world and their selfhood in that world: doing ('make'); physiological intake and nourishment ('drunk' but not 'to get drunk'); and communicating ('say') are all left uninstantiated (see more on complement vs

---

[47] I am most grateful to Dr Fiona J. Mackintosh of the University of Edinburgh for her help locating this translation.

3.2.3 Morphosyntactic Verbal Silence

in §3.2.4.4.6). While the second line is longer than the first, once the speaking subject has become one with silence, the lines shorten. The uninstantiated complements of the passive-middle voice verbs, the declining length of the lines and the absence of a full stop or other final punctuation mark and even the absence of the (grapheme's) initial capital letter all create the impression of abyss. This interpretation stands in its own right, sprouting from the text and its analysis in light of passive (middle voice) silence. Alejandra Pizarnik's personal biography, and particularly her psychological difficulties and her suicide at the age of forty-six, add a further tragic layer to that analysis.

An example of the second situation, that of the death of the agent, comes from a story that Ernest Hemingway submitted to a contest for the shortest and best short story:

[~73]   For sale: baby shoes, never worn.

As Gilead (2008) shows, the tension between this text as a literary artwork and as an advert (leaving out practical details is proof that the writer has no practical intentions) embodies many losses. Gilead sums up saying (2008: 124–125) that '[t]he closer that words approach silence, the greater the effect that they can convey [...] Much remains in silence, and yet this kind of silence is full of reality, thoughts, emotions, and feelings It is pregnant with innumerable unspoken words [...] And this silence speaks; this silence echoes each word to the utmost'. One of these silences, he claims is stillness, as if following this untimely death, nothing can change (in the parents' life). No relief is possible. The only consolation, says Gilead, lies in its artistic beauty. To Gilead's detailed and illuminating analysis we add here the vs use of the role (not form) of the middle. Death and loss are expressed, among other types of vs, by situating the baby as the object left out of the passive forerunner. This passive form ('never warn'), alluding to the role of a middle voice, depicts the sense of the life-opportunity missed: the baby did not live to become an agent.

Nowhere in this remarkably powerful utterance is the baby present as a potential, human agent. The baby as a signifier is placed not as the core object of the NP but only as a syntactic modifier of 'shoes'. It is the shoes (which are in this advert the object of transaction) which make present the otherwise absent baby. Moreover, associating the middle voice with shoes is by no means accidental; a baby habitually is dressed right after birth, but only when it stands on its feet – becomes physically stable and independent – does it receive its first pair of shoes. The deliberate allusion to the middle voice – when it is semantically and pragmatically obvious that there is an agent – functions as a forerunner dramatically depicting this loss.[48]

---

[48] For a discussion of the vss complying in [~73] with the Grice's (1989) cooperative principle and particularly with its maxims of manner (see Ephratt 2012: 77).

3.2.3.2.4 Pointing to the Taboo Signifier of the Agentive Agent

As we detail (§3.2.5.3), taboo words are verbal signifiers, and due to their performative force their articulation is banned. While the primary taboo euphemisms are lexical vs forerunners, in cases in which the forbidden signifier stands as an agent occupying the syntactic subject position the passive may serve as a forerunner announcing the silence of taboo signifiers. A straightforward illustration comes from Matthew 7:7:

[~74^S] Ask, and it shall be given S_1 you; seek, and ye shall find; knock, and it shall be opened unto you $S_{2=1}$.[49]

The agent of these deeds is no doubt God (referred to in 11 as 'your Father which is in heaven' and 'him'). Clearly, this is not a case demoting the agent. In fact, on the contrary, being unarticulated signifiers renders taboo words an exceptional trait which Freud (1913: 18) captured using the collocation 'holy dread'.

3.2.4 Syntactic Verbal Silence

Syntax focuses on the sentence. One can approach syntactic parsing top down or bottom up. Both approaches yield a definition of the syntactic-thematic roles played by the individual elements as well as their roles when grouped with other elements to form syntactic constituents such as Ss (sentences), NPS (noun-phrases), VPS (verb-phrases), AJDPS (adjectival phrases) and PPS (prepositional phrases).

The function of pauses to break continuity signals segmentation, which results in groupings (and so mapping) of the syntactic constituents to the morpho-lexical elements (and vice versa). These paralinguistic (ground) pauses materialise orally as variations in the tempo and prosody of speech, segmenting the various constituents and their hierarchy. Harris (1951: 14) defines an utterance as 'any stretch of talk, by one person before and after which there is silence on the part of the person' (see §3.1).

Halliday (1985: 9) argues that 'silence is a systematic feature of the rhythm of spoken English [...] the silent beat also plays a part in grammar, in making a contrast between different meanings'. Examples are:

[~75] I meet the man on the corner. (Lees 1963: 51 note 32)

And the following, somewhat humorous, sentences:

[~76] I must eat Mummy./!
[~77] I miss my parents Jesus Christ and Bloody Mary.

---

[49] Throughout this study, the King James Version will be the source for all citations from the Old and New Testaments, unless indicated otherwise. These citations will be issued a number without indicating the source language.

3.2.4 Syntactic Verbal Silence

In an earlier publication, Halliday and Hasan (1976: 233) discuss the transition from speech to writing, delineating the written sentence as 'extending from capital letter to full stop'. In the former publication, Halliday details (1985: 3):

> The spaces that separate them – narrow spaces between letters (at least in print), wider spaces between words, and still wider spaces, with accompanying full stop, between sentences – serve to mark units off one another. The spaces and stops are not part of the substance of writing; they are signals showing how it is organized.

Such pauses are paralinguistic (see §2.2.2), and we must therefore distinguish them from vss. To determine whether a missing syntactic constituent points to syntactic vs, speakers and linguists alike must first detect the syntactic forerunners impending an empty category, and then ensure that it results from the addresser's choice and that s/he made this choice to serve (verbal) expression.

Of all the linguistic fields, morphology and syntax would seem to attract most controversy, yielding incongruent theories and techniques (even concerning one and the same language). The term 'ellipsis' (from the Greek ἔλλειψις, 'omission'), too, is trapped in this controversy.

According to Merchant (2001: 1), '[e]lliptical processes capitalize on the redundancy of certain kinds of information in certain contexts, and permit an economy of expression by omitting the linguistic structures that would otherwise be required to express this information' (see also Melčuk 1979: 246).

Other scholars emphasise a formal-syntactic prerequisite that limits ellipses to forms in which the elided constituents are structurally required. Both Bréal and de Saussure (2006: 67) refer to form when discussing the ellipsis of thought. Bréal, who in 1877 used 'ellipsis' to denote the condensations of whole ideas, explains that 'in terms of grammar, we name as *ellipsis* the omission of a word necessary in the sense of the sentence' (Bréal and Jules 1877: 301). De Saussure says that 'we know at the outset how many terms a sentence *should* be made up of, and that by comparing the actual terms it contains we work out the shortfall' (2006: 67). Thomas (1979: 43) defines ellipsis 'as a communicative option to omit from sentences contextually available elements that are structurally required by the elements that do appear in those sentences'.[50] Melčuk (1979: 246) adds that ellipsis involves '(obligatory and optional) nonappearance in surface syntax of specific deep syntactic actants'.

Since ellipsis is, on the one hand, formally expected/required, and on the other referentially redundant, recoverability constitutes a crucial constraint on

---

[50] Thomas (1979: 43) further differentiates between 'ellipsis' and 'elision': 'optional omission of specific elements that may be supplied from our knowledge of the language system without the aid of context'. He also distinguishes between the two and 'non-realization', which he defines as 'the optional total absence of potential elements from a sentence'.

ellipsis: the deletions must be recoverable (see, e.g. Chomsky 1965: 177, 188). Wilson (2000: 18) widens the scope of ellipsis recoverability to cover in addition to '(a) omitted elements recoverable from the linguistic context' also '(b) other potential syntactic forms, (c) the situational context', that is, meanings made explicit by related context.

A theory in which ellipsis – though not termed as such – plays a central role is Chomsky's (1981) *Lectures on Government and Binding*. Chomsky opens his last chapter by declaring that 'a major preoccupation throughout this discussion has been the status of categories that have no intrinsic phonetic content. Two types of such empty categories have been considered: trace and PRO' (1981: 321). Empty categories are s-structures, representations that are assigned no intrinsic phonetic content. In fact, Chomsky (1981) assumes a single basic empty category, in which the distinction between trace and PRO is that while PRO is base-generated, trace is a left-behind of a movement rule. Subsequently, unlike PRO, trace must have an antecedent that limits move-α to a non-free projection (1981: 184–185).

Whether 'ellipsis' is used loosely to designate any sort of deletion, or employed in a restricted sense within a particular theoretical framework, this term appears to denote an economically motivated practice resulting in the omission of recoverable syntactic or semantic (discursive) material. As Chomsky states (1981: 227 note 43), such an omission is obligatory:

there appears to be a general discourse principle of the rough form (iii) with the corollary (iv):
(iii) Avoid repetition of R-expressions[51], except when conditions warrant
(iv) When conditions warrant, repeat.

Thomas (1979), alluding to what Jespersen termed 'ellipsomania', warns that for ellipsis to be of interest or use, a distinction must be made between all the cases referred to as 'obligatory ellipsis' (to be excluded from the discussion) and obligatory elements. Obligatory ellipsis necessarily results in elements that could not appear in any sentence, and so we cannot compare it to any utterance or context in which the (assumed) elliptic elements would appear. This captures the fundamental difference between ellipsis and syntactic vss:

Syntactic vss *are syntactic constituents whose instantiations are left out by the addresser as a means of expression.*

An essential prerequisite for vs is that it is a communicative option. Only such a concept of ellipsis comes close to our argument concerning vs.

In addition, the reader may notice that, unlike ellipsis, syntactic vs is not restricted to omissions of predetermined obligatory syntactic constituents

---

[51] 'R-expressions' are NPs with referential heads (for example, *John, wood sincerity, book*).

3.2.4 Syntactic Verbal Silence

(such as subject or verb (INFL)) but also includes leaving uninstantiated other expected constituents in the specific context. The requirement that syntactic gaps must represent obligatory elements could mean that in addition to necessarily stipulating a precise verbal equivalent, syntactic vs also requires that the relevant syntactic gaps carry local and communicative value (see Thomas 1979; and see note 50). The two also differ regarding recoverability. While recoverability is a key economical requirement motivating ellipsis it plays an entirely different role in the processing of syntactic vss. Proper government demands the elision of any constituent that is bound to an antecedent, while an antecedent – that is, redundancy – is ruled out concerning syntactic vs. Two non-redundant items must be recovered for syntactic vss: form (determining government relations) and content (thematic roles (θ), without necessarily stipulating the precise lexical equivalents).

Dealing here with constituents larger than words, a distinction must be made between what Radford (1988: 103–104) terms 'elliptical sentences (=sentences containing empty categories)' and 'sentence fragments' (consisting of full phrases). Vss are such that the articulated forms – forerunners – grounding them (be they a word or a phrase) are overtly fragmented, and so perceived as complete only once the vs component is assumed. Halliday and Hasan (1976), examining cohesion, devoted a chapter to 'ellipsis',[52] observing that 'the essential characteristics of ellipsis is that something which is present in the selection of underlying ("systematic") options is omitted in the structure – whether or not the resulting structure is in itself "incomplete"' (1976: 144). This insight is valuable for our discussion of syntactic vss (see §3.2.4.4.4).

Last, but not least, Melčuk's (1979: 246) argument that while zero is a sign conveying meaning (see discussion in §3.2.2.2), 'ellipsis normally does not change meaning but is required by grammatical or stylistic considerations', encapsulates the crucial difference between ellipsis and syntactic vss. The non-instantiated constituent does count as vs: it is not only the content of this constituent that carries meaning and forms part of the given information but also the fact that it is not instantiated.

In order to examine syntactic vss, we follow the widest common syntactic denominators. The silences' forerunners are presented here according to the highest node, that is, the maximal syntactic constituent left out of the instantiation of the full sentence to serve communication and expression.

Before we delve into the silencing of specific syntactic roles (such as subjects NP; predicates VP and VERB (inflected verbs as heads); and

---

[52] Halliday and Hasan define 'ellipsis' as 'that form of a substitution in which the item is replaced by nothing' (1976: 88, and equally stated as 'substitution by zero', see 89, 143). When detached from the context of cohesion, this definition seems far too broad (covering morphological or even phonetic entities).

100   Verbal Silence: Forms

complements or connectives), we may examine example [~78], which offers a good starting point for syntactic vs in general and nominal head vss (NP as subjects, objects and other complements) in particular.

Example [~78] comes from Joyce's description of the encounters between the narrator and his schoolmate, who together with a third mate (Leo Dillon) decided to 'mich' school to spend a sunny June day roaming around Dublin:

[~78]   When we came to the Smoothing Iron we arranged a siege; but it was a failure because you must have at least three. We revenged ourselves on Leo Dillon by saying what a fuck he was and guessing how many he would get at three o'clock from Mr. Ryan. (Joyce, *Dubliners*: 'An Encounter', p. 22)

No doubt the absence of two NPs stands out:

[~78$^{a-\text{S}}$]   [...] you must have at least three S_1.

And

[~78$^{b-\text{S}}$]   [...] guessing how many S_2 he would get.

In both instances there is no syntactic antecedent. The first instance ('at least three S_1') could be recovered recruiting contextual effort: the two of us (the narrator and his friend Mahoney) plus (at least) Leo Dillon (who stayed back). But this absence should by no means be attributed to redundancy; on the contrary, it fits well with Joyce's view of language as gnomon (see Vanderbeke et al. 2017 note 4 after Booker). Moreover, leaving out S_1(NP/N) iconically enacts the absence of the needed individuals. The failed attempt to recover a trace for the numeric determiner ('three') signals a syntactic forerunner (Figure 3.4).

Likewise, [~78$^{b-\text{S}}$] involves a vs complement, which again falls in the realm of a failed syntactic trace attempt and Joyce's attraction to (verbal) silences. But unlike [~78$^{a-\text{S}}$], it turns out that in 'how many S_2 he would get' ([~78$^{b-\text{S}}$]) no source for recoverability can be found, even in the more distant context. This usage is an instance of Joyce's literary excellence as he tells the stories of

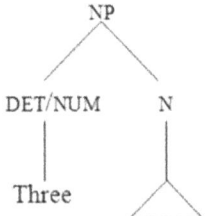

Figure 3.4 DET/NUM C-commanding a (sister) empty noun node as a syntactic forerunner.

3.2.4 Syntactic Verbal Silence

Dublin and Dubliners, not only through narratives and encounters but also by engaging the lexicon and the verbal form to reproduce an authentic Irish-Dublin language and style. The boy (homodiegetic narrator) miching a day in the high-reputation authoritarian Dublin school, like all other Dubliners, knows exactly what's left out saying 'how many S_2 he would get': this is not only a matter of euphemism, let alone redundancy, but alludes more specifically to the fact that corporal punishment was not administrated in class; instead, the teacher would write down in secrecy the number of blows (strokes on the boy's hand with a strap, see Gifford 1982: 38, for reference).

Examples [~78^{a-S}] and [~78^{b-S}], in which the NP directly dominating the categories DET/NUM directly dominates a non-overt or syntactically non-recoverable noun node, illustrate a very common form that serves as a forerunner for the impending syntactic VS. The same applies to cases in which categories such as ADJ or MOD precede an empty (non-recoverable) noun node.

Modern English displays two crucial features affecting the form of syntactic VSs and their forerunners. The first is that English is not a PRO-DROP language; the second concerns the grammatical insertion of an AUX whenever the VP head is not a finite verb.

In non-trivial cases (such as imperatives and interjections), when English speakers – lay speakers, and all the more so professionals such as poets and orators – deliberately defy the PRO-DROP limitation, this is an apparent forerunner pointing to syntactic VS. In cases in which PRO-DROPs are activated to gain the communicative effects of VS and the VP head happens to be non-finite, the auxiliary will also be dropped. A distinction must be made between cases in which the subject (NP directly governed by s) is left uninstantiated, or both the subject and the auxiliary are not instantiated as a means of VS, and cases in which it is only the subject which is in the focus of VS, while the omission of the auxiliary is a non-significant technical derivative of the subject drop. Such a distinction establishes that the latter cases are to be confined to VSs, leaving the subject's constituent not instantiated (§3.2.4.2) while excluding those which involve the main clause (subject and predicate or subject and VP head, see §3.2.4.1). In §3.2.4.3 we focus on VS involving the predicate and its head; in §3.2.4.4 we focus on VS involving complementation and §3.2.4.5 and §3.2.4.6 deal with VSs of function words and dyadic coordinating constructions.

3.2.4.1 Leaving the Subject and Predicate Constituents Uninstantiated

We begin with an enlightening yet straightforward example taken from the title Vargas (1986) chose for her textbook on nonverbal communication:

[~79]   Louder than words

Vargas opens her introduction (1986: 10) by citing Birdwhistell's claim that only 35 per cent of interpersonal communication (carried out between two speakers) is conveyed using words; the remaining 65 per cent is communicated nonverbally. She then lists what she terms 'nine nonverbal languages' which 'contribute significantly to all human communication, regardless of the spoken language they accompany': the human body, kinesics, the eyes, paralanguage, silence, tacesics and stroking, proxemics, chronemics and colour (1986: 10–11). She devotes her introductory book to presenting these 'languages'. The linguistic-communicative view explored in our study classifies silence differently than Vargas, particularly insofar as we identify vss as verbal means alongside speech.[53] Her title

[~79^S] ς louder than words

uses vs, skilfully sharing the burden of communication between words and non-words. The absence of the subject and the predicate's head – two essential sentential constituents – exemplify the book's thesis on nonverbal communication but is not in itself nonverbal. It speaks and states verbally using vs that

[~79^S] ς [Nonverbal communication speaks] louder than words.

It does so using syntax and grammar as a (verbal) forerunner. Despite various disagreements among scholars, they unanimously agree that without a subject and a finite verb as predicate head a sentence is ungrammatical. The absence of these syntactically required constituents, hinting at phrases such as 'a picture speaks louder than words' or 'actions speak louder than words', are clear indications that, here, it is vs – and not nonverbal communication – which does the work. This does not lessen the cleverness of overcoming the limitations of a title (using words) to iconically represent the 65 per cent nonverbal communication using words.

3.2.4.2 Leaving the Subject's Constituent Uninstantiated

In terms of successful cooperative communication, an addresser is expected to initiate an utterance on the basis of common knowledge. Customarily, this common knowledge occupies the subject or thematic topic slot. Having provided this common basis, the addresser can then introduce the new information: the rheme that conventionally occupies the comment predicate role.

Two features characterise the syntactic vs of the subject's constituent (hereinafter – 'subject vs'). The first is the distinction between sentences which leave the subject (the NP immediately dominated by s) uninstantiated as a means of expression (vss) and sentences having no syntactic subjects (such as

---

[53] As seen, Vargas's silence stands apart from paralanguage. Reading carefully, though, we soon realise that Vargas isolates as a special separate system silences that are different from the above: she states, '[i]nterpersonal silences that are independent of verbal communication defy classification' (1986: 77).

3.2.4 Syntactic Verbal Silence

impersonal phrases, holophrases and interjections) and PRO-DROP manifestations, such as imperatives and coordinatives. The second issue concerns forerunners pointing to subject VSs. This issue arises given the unique form (in English and many other languages) of the syntactic subject.

Also worth mentioning is that passives as VSs (see §3.2.3.2) display an overt syntactic subject in the s-structures, while the cases we are examining here leave the subject's constituent uninstantiated (the sentence's s-structure is missing a subject).

In many languages, including English, the subject's constituent differs from all other NPs in that it is morphologically unmarked. Moreover, overlooking special syntactic or contextual constraints, the fixed SVO sentential word order identifies the initial (bare) NP as that sentence's subject. As explained, forerunners are articulated grammatical or lexical stumps signalling the location, category and content of the VS in the specific utterance (see §3.2, note 10). Given the unique form of the English nominative (syntactic subject), the absence of case marking fails to produce a contrast and thus cannot serve as the forerunner for the subject VS. However, syntactic and morphological dependencies between the (left out) subject's head and overt categories may stand out as forerunners grounding the sentence's subject VS. Intermediate manifestations skirt the shortcoming of the morphologically bare NP, thus presenting a contrast which meets the role of the forerunner of the subject VS.

After noting a straightforward and ordinary instance, we shall discuss subject VS as it emerges in four classic literary texts.

In examples [~80^S] and [~81$^{S\text{-German-T}}$], a finite verb instantiating the VP verb head not matched by an overt subject (NP) anticipates the coming subject VS. The first example of an uninstantiated subject of a finite verb concerns taboo (see at length in §3.2.5.3). Due to its performative force (enacted in the third commandment: 'thou shalt not take the name of the LORD thy God in vain'), the subject 'god' is left out in every day phraseology, such as:

[~80^S]   So help me Ŝ.

The effect is heightened when intonation suggests a second-person (vocative) reading:

[~80']   [[God$_i$] [ϵ_i help me so]].

The subject constituent is left uninstantiated twice: once due to a grammatical/pragmatic ellipsis (ϵ) rule concerning the matter of appellatives, and once as the NP's noun head.

The example, in which (like [~80^S]) a finite verb not matched by an overt subject is the VS forerunner, comes from Longfellow's (*The Complete*, Vol. V, p. 617) translation of the opening verse of Goethe's 'Wandrers Nachtlied II':

[~81^(German-T)] O'er all the hilltops / Is quiet now,
In all the tree-tops / Hearest thou / Hardly a breath;
The birds are asleep in the trees:
Wait; soon like these / Thou too shalt rest.

The poem is acknowledged to be one of the lyrical gems of world literature. Its theme gradually proceeds from the universal to the particular, and accordingly leads from the distant to the close, from the external to the internal, and from the inanimate to the human. The first scene is one of stillness (see [~1^(German)] §2.1), typified by the mineral kingdom – hilltops:

[~81^(S-German-T)] O'er all the hilltops / S̷ Is quiet now,

Lacking an active verb, the German *'Über allen Gipfeln'* is an asyndetic embedded prepositional phrase setting the physical location and emotive atmosphere and texture. Goethe's main clause, *'Ist Ruh'*, articulates only an AUX serving as copula (*'ist'*) and the noun *'Ruh'*. Longfellow goes by Goethe's syntax regarding the asyndetic nominal embedded clause – 'O'er all the hilltops' – but he diverges from Goethe's main clause in structure, amount and content.

Unlike German *'Ruh'*, which is unequivocally a noun (and hence serves as the subject of the main clause of Goethe's original), English 'quiet' can stand as a noun, a finite verb or an adjective. Longfellow's decision to add 'now' as the VP clause's 'quiet' adverb[54] not only defies Goethe's minimalism but also rules out the nominal reading of the English ambiguous 'quiet'. Left with the adjectival and verbal readings, 'is' preceding 'quiet' takes over the VP's head (verb) and establishes 'quiet' as the ADJP's head. This surely obscures the impression reflected by Goethe's nominal reading, as it thins the stillness and weakens its significant salience.

From the perspective of VS, however, what at first sight may seem paradoxical – the English translation's rejection of the opening verse's NP reading, thus stressing its VP reading – syntactically highlights the absence of an expected subject. But while Longfellow dared to add to Goethe's original 'now' as an ADV, he did not dare to add the PRO (or quasi-PRO) semantically void 'it'. From a VS perspective, this suggests that Longfellow could not enact the stillness (the theme of the poem's opening verse) using the English semantic equivalents translating *'Ruh'* (e.g. 'silence', 'quiet' and 'calm'), because these all share a categorical ambiguity. Accordingly, he compensated for this loss by emphasising the VP constituent (and see note 54) in order to make apparent the uninstantiated nominal component forerunning the subject VS (Figure 3.5).

---

[54] Silz (1956) hypothesises that Longfellow added 'now' for the sake of rhyming ('now'/'thou' substituting for the original-German *'Wipfeln'/'Gipfeln'*).

3.2.4 Syntactic Verbal Silence

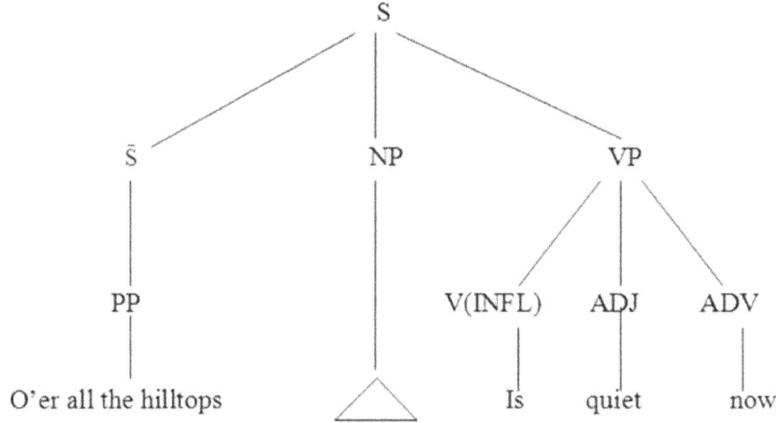

Figure 3.5 'O'er all the hilltops / S̄ is quiet now': subject vs.

Leaving the subject uninstantiated in such a syntactic constellation highlights the uniqueness of the mineral kingdom, differing it from the remaining kingdoms in its absolute stillness, without any vivid or animate figure as agent. We conclude this case with Elizabeth Wilkinson's (1949: 318) words (referring to Goethe's original): 'The verse does not describe the stillness of evening, it has become the stillness of evening; the language is evening stillness itself' (see also Ephratt 2017: §3).

The next example, probably the most quoted piece of English prose, illustrates vs leaving the subject of an independent sentence uninstantiated:

[~82ª]   To be or not to be

Hamlet's (III.i.55–59) words open his contemplation on life and death, suffering and choice:

[~82]   To be or not to be: that is the question.
Whether 'tis nobler in the mind to suffer
The slings and arrows of outrageous fortune,
Or to take armes against a sea of troubles
And by opposing end them. To die, to sleep, [...]. (Shakespeare, *Norton³*, p. 1232)

These immortal words have inspired vast studies. We humbly delineate here an angle offered by syntactic vs.

Hamlet's spoken words could be read as a rational deliberation within existential philosophy, but Shakespeare crafts them at the height of a tragic intersubjective drama in which the speaking Hamlet is an individual person: hurt son, young lover, nephew and so forth. Moreover, although Hamlet spoke in the presence of Ophelia, his words in [~82] are classified as 'soliloquy' (see *Norton*³, p. 1232 note 5). Seen thus, we cannot possibly interpret [~82ᵃ] as an impersonal statement. It is a cry uttered by a tortured individual trapped in what he experiences as a severe personal dilemma (see the emotive function, §4.2).

Examined syntactically, the opening of this soliloquy appears to be structurally ambiguous, paraphrased as:

[~82^{b'}]   To be, or not to be;
That is the question:
Whether 'tis nobler in the mind to suffer [...]. (see *Norton*¹, p. 1705)

or as

[~82^{b''}]   The question is [whether]: to be, or not to be;
Whether 'tis nobler in the mind to suffer [...].

The s-structure of [~82] is ambiguous because it tolerates simultaneously two readings (two LFs): [~82^{b'}] reveals a form in which [~82ᵃ] constitutes an independent phrase using vs to (emotionally) voice the most fundamental dilemma. 'That is the question': thus serves as the head of a new independent sentence whose subject is 'the question' and which dominates a chain of asyndetic WH-phrases, logically specifying the details of 'The' question, with its pros and cons.

In [~82^{b''}], 'To be, or not to be' is a constituent in the above chain. Since emotionally and semantically this is the question in focus – the meta-question – it is raised outside its syntactic location within the chain.

Constituting an independent sentence in [~82^{b'}] and a (raised) WH-phrase in [~82^{b''}], the infinitives 'to be, or not to be' point to an empty subject.

In the impersonal collective-philosophical reading (ruled out here), it equals:

s [PRO₁ VP [S̄ COMP [NP₁ ϵ] VP INFL be]].

In the personal reading it equals:

s [NP ϵ] [VP INFL be].

Shakespeare's syntax allows the use of independent non-finite clauses, according to which the infinitive forms ('to be', 'not to be') tolerate (subject) PRO-DROP. This choice of the infinitive form is a vs forerunner pointing to the content of the dilemma: the eros life drive ('be I/me') or the thanatos death drive resulting in the obliteration of the self ('not be I/me').

As should be apparent, this observation agrees with, rather than opposes, the prevailing interpretations of Hamlet's soliloquy and the entire drama. The strength of the evidence coming here from the vs angle lies not in it being another piece of evidence merging with previous ones but in its novelty, introducing what Hempel (1966: 34) termed 'varied evidence'. To appreciate this point, we cite from Greenblatt's (2016: 1183) explanation of Hamlet's soliloquy:

3.2.4 Syntactic Verbal Silence 107

[T]he celebrated lines that begin 'To be, or not to be: that is the question' (3.1.55ff) have the structure of a formal academic debate on the subject of suicide: prudently considering both sides of the question and rehearsing venerable commonplaces, Hamlet does not once use the words 'I' or 'me.' Yet here and elsewhere his words manage with astonishing vividness to convey the spontaneous rhythms of a mind in motion. [...] But in its moral complexity, psychological depth, and philosophical power, *Hamlet* seems to mark an epochal shift not only in Shakespeare's own career but in Western drama; it is as if the play were giving birth to a whole new kind of literary subjectivity.

This subjectivity – the sense of being inside a character's psyche and following its twists and turns – is to a large degree an effect of language, the product of dramatic poetry and prose of unprecedented intensity. In order to convey a traumatized mind straining to articulate perceptions of a shattered world, Shakespeare developed a complex syntax and a remarkably expanded diction.

Greenblatt's description is akin to the explanation presented above based on vs. The novelty introduced by vs rests here on two matters. The formal matter supplies formal indications (here flouting the English pro-drop constraints) which ground the coming vs and its linguistic nature (here the subject as a syntactic constituent). The second matter is the semiotic significance (and particularly the iconic relationships) introduced to the interpretation using in the particular context vs (rather than speech) as means of expression.

As the comparison between Greenblatt's description and our syntactic vs offered here reveals, the formal and semiotic analysis of vs seeks to explore what is left uninstantiated, how this absence is signalled, what is its nature (is it a matter of an obligatory grammar rule, is it the outcome of redundancy?) and finally what is its significance. All these aspects illuminate an aspect taken for granted and left implicit, despite the fact that it plays an iconic role in these interpretations. Defying English PRO-DROP constraints makes the absence of the subject instantiation stand out syntactically and semiotically. This is the anchor on which the entire dilemma, soliloquy and drama – as well as personal being – revolve.

The last illustration of the subject vs comes from Emily Dickinson's prevalent calculated use of 'self'-reflexive pronouns as syntactic forerunners pointing to an uninstantiated subject. [~83] exemplifies a poetic ambiguity in which the referent of the subject of the reflexive pronoun could be either syntactically recoverable or interpreted as a case of vs:

[~83]   No Prisoner be –
        Where Liberty –
        Himself – abide with Thee – (Dickinson, *Complete*, p. 353)

The absence of verbs in the first two lines stands out even on a cursory initial reading of this poem. This comes as no surprise for Dickinson's readers, familiar with her extensive poetic handling of dashes and syntactic ellipsis (see, e.g. Miller 1987; Crumbley 1992; Schmit 1993). Dickinson's practice in [~83] is consistent with English grammar. In its literal physical senses, such as presence (living) and location (abide), and in its mental non-literal meanings (such as moral or spiritual), the existential 'be' is morphologically adjusted:

[~83$^{a'}$] No Prisoner is –

Alternatively, read as the head of a modal verb/auxiliary, such as 'can' or 'shall', it is automatically recovered, yielding:

[~83$^{b'}$] No Prisoner can/shall/may be –

As minimal binding grammars and cognitively motivated explanations advocate, the next line is recovered assuming parallelism:

[~83$^{a''}$] No Prisoner is –
         Where Liberty is –

or

[~83$^{b''}$] No Prisoner can/shall/may be –
         Where Liberty can/shall/may be –

or

[~83^{c}] No Prisoner can/shall/may be –
         Where Liberty is –

Options [~83$^{a''}$]–[~83^{c}] all fall within the category of syntactic ellipsis, which is frequently evidenced in Dickinson's poems and grammar (Miller 1987: 28–29; Schmit 1993). Such syntactic existential parallelism expresses the truism that the notions of imprisonment and liberty exclude each other (be they physical or mental).

Line three opens with a reflexive pronoun ('himself'), which not instantiating a subject as an antecedent thus seems detached (unbound):

[~83^{d}] Himself – abide with Thee –

Following binding theories, the most straightforward practice is to assume that its recoverable subject is one of the two preceding nominatives: '{no} prisoner' and 'liberty'.

'Abide with Thee' resonates with readers familiar with Christian culture, as Dickinson herself was (see, e.g. Miller 1987: 132–138), given its recurrence in the Scriptures and assimilation in many hymns, intertextually (see §3.2.5.2) alluding to the sinner. This automatically renders 'prisoner' a potential antecedent of 'himself' ([~83^{d}]). The seemingly missing agreement between the singular form 'himself' (prisoner) and the plural verb form 'abide' is effortlessly settled if we follow – as in [~83$^{b''}$] and [~83^{c}] – Dickinson's practice of excluding auxiliaries and models. However, two crucial matters remain unsettled. The first is that reflexive (self) pronouns in general, and 'himself abide' in

3.2.4 Syntactic Verbal Silence

particular, cannot bind once the object is disaffirmed (no object: 'No prisoner'). The second matter is that a reading such as

[~83$^{d'}$] [No / ϵ_i The prisoner$_i$] himself$_i$ [will/shall/may] abide with Thee

counters both the above analysis and the spirit of the parable (see, e.g. Ecclesiasticus (Apocrypha) 12:13–15). We proposed above that imprisonment and liberty are incompatible. Assigning 'existence within location' as the θ-role of 'abide' renders the poem's reading a self-contradictory deduction. Adding now the context in which 'abide with thee' is incorporated leaves no doubt as to Ecclesiasticus' stand: one must not associate ('tarry') with a sinner. Thus, a prisoner who is indeed a sinner is not the sort of person who is a morally liberated person. Moreover, as Sirach warns, whoever defiles with a sinner risks being perceived as one ('who will pity?').

Following the grammatical convention to bind the PRONoun with the nominal antecedent adjacent to it results in matching 'himself' with 'liberty':

[~83$^{d''}$] [ϵ_j liberty$_j$] himself$_j$ [will/shall/may] abide with Thee

This reading, too, faces grammatical mismatches: as in ([~83$^{d'}$]), number convention is disrupted. In addition, a mismatch in gender agreement arises, given that ever since the Roman goddess Libertas, 'liberty' has been perceived as feminine. However, such agreement mismatches are common in Dickinson's poetic grammar, which also relies on unconventional syntactic shuffling (see Miller 1987: 61–63; Schmit 1993: 108–110; Freeman 1996: 196–197 on reformulation).[55]

In light of these failed attempts, and perusing further Sirach's parable, we are both forced and encouraged to move away from ellipsis and seek resolution in vs. Contrary to standard syntactic theories, such as binding theories' practice, the automatic syntactic recovery practices fail: the reflexive antecedent cannot be found in the immediate syntactic structure or in the broader context. This failure is a clear vs forerunner. The antecedent – the subject of 'himself' – is expressed using vs:

[~83']   No Prisoner [can/shall/may] be // [is]
         Where Liberty [can/shall/may] be // [is]
         [ϵ_k God$_k$/Christ$_k$] Himself$_k$ – abide with Thee –

Such a reading not only captures the very message of the Sirach parable, but it also strongly supports the Christian spiritual sources that inspire Dickinson.[56]

---

[55] Freeman (1997) confines her valuable analysis of Dickinson's use of 'self' reflexives in light of mental spaces theory to self anaphors, and hence does not account for non-anaphoric self reflexives such as those detailed here. See also [~278] and Figure 4.4).

Once we employ this mode of vs, other instances of Dickinson's reflexive pronouns are also resolved.

The clause 'abide with thee/me/us' recurs in the New Testament with God or Christ as its subject (see, e.g. Luke 24:29), fitting perfectly with the poem's message: a (non-sinner) worshipper/person will not be alone – God/Christ will abide with hem. This reading is easily maintained taking account of Dickinson's persistent practice to adjoin the reflexive singular pronoun ('himself') referring to God with a plural verbal form.

Having arrived at the vs reading of the poem, filling in the uninstantiated subject, we must now revisit the dashes (see Crumbley 1992). The dashes in the first two lines signalled and elicited the recovery of the ellipsis; but what do the dashes of the third line communicate within vs?

[~83$^{d\mathcal{S}}$] $\mathcal{S}$ Himself – abide with Thee –

The first dash, juxtaposing the subject vs with the reflexive pronoun, acts here as a vs forerunner. But this is not its sole function; together with the second dash, it serves to distance, and so to open up possibilities. Emily Dickinson was raised on the Bible and religious faith, but she also questioned this faith and its commitment as imprisonment, endangering free choice (personal, as well as female, liberty, see Zapedowska 2006: 25–26). The dashes serve here to break clichés: God/Christ will abide with the pure – non-sinner – worshipper (see [~83']) and yield a further transformation, stated not as a cliché but as a possibility (the final dash):

[~83"]   Thee are [be] No Prisoner
          Where Liberty Himself – [to worship/or not to worship God/Christ] –
          abide with Thee –

Here the vs of the subject iconically presents god (and (religious) doctrine) as a prisoner (compare 'He put the belt around my life / I heard the buckle snap' – the opening poem 273, *Collected*, p. 124).

This journey through Dickinson's poem [~83] suggests a significant contribution to linguistic theory illustrating the clear difference between ellipsis recoverability and vs. The latter comes into play when syntactic recoverability collapses. Only when linguists, linguistics and readers switch from grammatically based discussion of ellipsis to vs can they recognise that not all cases in which a syntactically required constituent is left uninstantiated are indeed cases of ellipsis.

---

[56] This reading ([~83']) seems to be reinforced by Dickinson's successive poem (poem 721).

3.2.4 Syntactic Verbal Silence

Schmit (1993: 106) differentiates between 'recoverability' and 'insertion'. The former denotes 'the recognition of unique and unambiguous elided words or phrases', while the latter refers to 'a form of systematic recoverability violation and an interpretive device that is informed by the grammar but operates outside of it' (1993: 107). The notion of 'insertion' shares with syntactic vs the role of clues of grammatical ill-formedness as forerunners announcing the uninstantiated constituent. But the two notions diverge in two essential respects: (1) like recoverability, but unlike syntactic vs, insertion demands that all the elided words or phrases must be traced in the text itself (or in an adjacent text, see also Wilson 2000: 18); and (2) that insertion, unlike syntactic vs and recoverability, does not tolerate a unique and unambiguous recognition. Syntactic (or other) vss are not a matter of the number of (admissible) readings; indeed, in the overwhelming majority of cases, vs expresses a specific single idea which is often distilled in a unique lexical form.

3.2.4.3 Leaving the Sentence's Entire VP or Only Its Head Uninstantiated

Textbook examples of VP and verb elision invoke various syntactic phenomena related to VP-ellipsis, such as gapping, and with main verb ellipsis, a form of pseudogapping, all involving explicit or implicit verb or VP antecedents. Syntactic vss leaving the VP or its head (the verb) uninstantiated as a verbal means of expression may be described as comprising of constellations for which there is no antecedent (§3.2.4.3.1 and §3.2.4.3.2); non-technical omission of AUX (§3.2.4.3.3); and finally, a failed copy attempt (§3.2.4.3.4). The latter is the most interesting instance for our purposes.

3.2.4.3.1 Not Instantiating an Entire VP or Its Head in an Initial Position, or One for which There Is No Licensed Antecedent

English tolerates VP-ellipsis as well as the omission of only the verb head. Chomsky's general discourse principle dictating the avoidance of repetition of R-expressions (see §3.2.4) results in obligatory ellipsis. In addition, in some stylistic traditions, forms originating in such omissions have frozen and so being the *façon de parler* are no longer perceived as ellipsis.

Obligatory omission of the verb occurs when the verb is a repetition of an identical instantiated form. Following Chomsky's above principle, binding licences designate that form as that verb's antecedent eliding that verb. Examples of stylistic freezes come from classic high language as well as colloquial use. The following are two short examples.

Old English's practice of omitting the infinitive forms of motion verbs (see Kjellmer 2002) accounts for Shakespeare's frequent use of 'will away', such as:

[~84] Warwick [aside] Alas, I am not cooped here for defence.
[To king Edward] I will away towards Barnet presently,
And bid thee battle, Edward, if thou dar'st (Richard Duke of York, V.i.112–114, *Norton*[1], pp. 357–358)

[~85] Dinner was not till half-past seven. (Woolf, *Room*, p. 21)

Leaving the verb 'served' uninstantiated is another freeze. Since cases such as [~84] and [~85] are not the product of the addresser's choice, they are not a matter of vs.

We now examine [~86^s], in which the addresser leaves a verb in initial position, uninstantiated, as means of expression. A verb left uninstantiated in its initial position naturally has no previous mention which can count as its potential antecedent:

[~86^s] S_v 30 pounds in only 2 weeks!

Be it thirty pounds or twenty, in two weeks or in ten days, such commercial slogans advertising diet plans make use of vs to iconically communicate slimness. The verb is left out not because it is a repetition of a former mention, and not because this verb is pragmatically recoverable (though it is; or at least a set of potential candidates can be easily assembled), but because reducing the sentence's length iconically captures the potential reduction of weight. Unlike the deliberate apparent absence of the expected verb, the omission of the subject is not a matter of vs but a syntactic and pragmatic practice concerning speech-acts directed to activate the addressee as the second-person ('you', see §4.3). To show that the reduction, loss or dropping of the (syntactically and semantically) expected verb is not motivated by the prospect of pragmatic recoverability but by the iconic force gained by the uninstantiation, we compare [~86^s] with

[~86'] Earn/gain 30 pounds in only 2 weeks!

Sure enough, when the goal is to increase income, or a premature baby or an adult need to gain weight, the verb 'earn', 'gain' (as well as 'increase', 'add' and the like) will be articulated in full.

We now examine the iconic and poetic part played, in Yeats's poem 'After Long Silence', by leaving verbs in initial position uninstantiated:

[~87] Speech after long silence; it is right
All other lovers being estranged or dead,
Unfriendly lamplight hid under its shade,

3.2.4 Syntactic Verbal Silence 113

> The curtains drawn upon unfriendly night,
> That we descant and yet again descant
> Upon the supreme theme of Art and Song:
> Bodily decrepitude is wisdom; young
> We loved each other and were ignorant.

As is common practice regarding the syntax of poem headings (and other headings, see [~45] §3.2.2.2.2), the title 'After Long Silence' omits the sentence's central constituents: NP and V(P). We focus here, however, not on the heading but on the poem's opening verse. Parsing this line, and analysing it alongside the poem in its entirety, the consideration of VS adds a unique thematic and poetic gain that is otherwise lost. We use VS and the text (wording and trope) not to negate the 'conventional' interpretations but to expose inherent but hitherto dormant possibilities in the poem.

This moving poem is no doubt closely related to Yeats's personal biography. It is sparked by sixty-four-year-old Yeats's renewed encounter with his former lover (Olivia Shakespeare),[57] many years after their affair ended. During the intervening period they corresponded but did not talk or meet in person. Their renewed meeting not only evoked personal feelings in both protagonists but also encompassed the universal essence of life, love, age and knowledge (and their negations). The poem contrasts the qualities of old age and youth: youth has its external physical merits (such as appearance), alongside its mental weaknesses (such as ignorance, though Yeats suggests that in the context of youth this may actually count as a positive feature). Old age, on other hand, has the demerit of physical infirmity (not to mention death) but offers compensation in the form of wit and refinement: 'Bodily decrepitude is wisdom' (again Yeats presents a more subtle message by recognising that wit may not be appreciated). The wit and maturation acquired in old age elevate the love experienced through its transformation as 'Art and Song' to a blessing of this stage of life. The longing for youth, passionate bodily love and ignorance portrays their current old-age love as somewhat philosophical or remote. The night – 'The curtains drawn upon unfriendly night' – is no longer a cosy place and time for love-making. The only possible and partial compensation for the lost ignorant love could be love that is displaced and reduced to discussion and aesthetics: 'That we descant and yet again descant / Upon the supreme theme of Art and Song'.

We now parse the poem's opening line in light of VS. Scholars who have analysed this short poem looked into every word, stress and punctuation mark; frequently, they went back to drafts and previous editions to trace the emergence of each form and figure through to the final outcome. Yet surprisingly,

---

[57] The prevailing position among scholars appears to be that the object of Yeats's love was Olivia Shakespeare. For an interesting alternative, see Clark (1977: 156–157, 171).

no one appears to have noticed the fact that syntax dictates a verb constituent in this construction, yet the expected verbs are missing in the opening line. This marvellous phrase, placed in the particular poetic-linguistic setting in which it is set, points to vs both as a theme and a means:

[~87$^{a\text{-}\text{б}}$]   Speech Ѕ_{v1} after long silence Ѕ_{v2};

The poem's title, being even more elliptic (leaving out the sentence's subject 'speech' as well as its verbs), does not offer any antecedent. Neither do the poem's subsequent verses.

The question would seem to be not whether the verbs are left uninstantiated, but what is their meaning and why are they not instantiated? The interpretations tagged above as 'conventional' may settle for '{finally/surprisingly/ø} comes/regains/is heard' as possible instantiations for Ѕ_{v1}, and accordingly either 'persisted/prevailed/clouded' or 'had been silenced/ceased/ended' as instantiations fitting Ѕ_{v2}. Such lexemes can fit either interpretation, both the emphasis on the virtue of old-age love and the focus on young ignorant love. As for the question why the verbs are not instantiated, we may propose various aspects and considerations. One straightforward answer concerns metrics and prosody: additional phonetic material at the very start of the poem would hamper the metric's aesthetics, which are achieved partly by means of such omissions. The preventative character of this consideration clearly cannot constitute the raison d'être of vs (see §4.5). Not instantiating the verbs as a means of expression is justified since it iconically captures the message of the line itself: that speech took over and silence was silenced. The left out Ѕ_{v1} is enacted by the actual speech (compare here the title and the first line). Likewise, the uninstantiated Ѕ_{v2} is enacted by that speech as it overrides the long preceding silence (see Clark 1977: 151–152).

Vendler (2007: 13–14), who emphasises the longing for ignorant love as the poem's theme, argues that the narrative of the couple's renewed meeting ('speech after long silence') is concluded in the poem's six lines. The last two lines, she claims, introduce a new narrative uttered outside the present tryst. She says: '[o]ld-age decrepitude is poised between two narratives – the present-tense one of mutual speech, the past-tense one of mutual youthful love'. Focusing on the two final lines and particularly the lexical and metric difference between 'we [...] were ignorant' and the preceding lines, Vendler concludes that:

Yeats's bold use of 'ignorant' to end this poem puts us on a new plane entirely [...] a plane of acerbic forgiveness for their lack of wisdom in youth [...] 'Art' and 'Song' are forgotten, here at the end, in the resigned pairing of early sexuality and life-ignorance, the one not possible without the other. (2007: 15)

As Vendler shows, the poem's closing verse does not remain in the present tryst and the context of the accomplishment of matured old age in general, and

3.2.4 Syntactic Verbal Silence

the couple's reunion in particular. Examined now from the perspective of vs, in which the fact that the syntactically expected verbs are left uninstantiated is a significant means of expression, what Vendler described as 'a new plane entirely' can herald not a change of plane but refer to an inevitable progression. The old-age speech 'That we descant and yet again descant', part of which discussed in high language their old-age reminiscences of their youthful sexual and ignorant love, cannot go on ('and yet again') forever. Reminiscing their lost youth gives voice – in vs – to the fear and vision of the coming loss of life: the eternal silence, when they shall join the lovers that are now dead ('All other lovers being estranged or dead'). This reading is easily accommodated once the first line is parsed as a parallel syntactic construction in which 'after' is the connective of two independent (sister) sentences (Figure 3.6).

Such a scheme is iconic to the chronological progression placing the constituent which 'comes after' as second:

[~87$^{a-\delta}$] Speech $\mathcal{S}_{v1}$ after long silence $\mathcal{S}_{v2}$.

The instantiated verbs offered above shift tenses: 'came/regained/was heard' for $\mathcal{S}_{v1}$, and accordingly either 'will persist/prevail/cloud'. 'Had been silenced/ceased/ended' now switches to instantiate $\mathcal{S}_{v1}$.

This reinterprets the former readings as:

[~87$^{a-\delta\delta}$] Speech $\mathcal{S}_{v2}$ after long silence $\mathcal{S}_{v1}$.

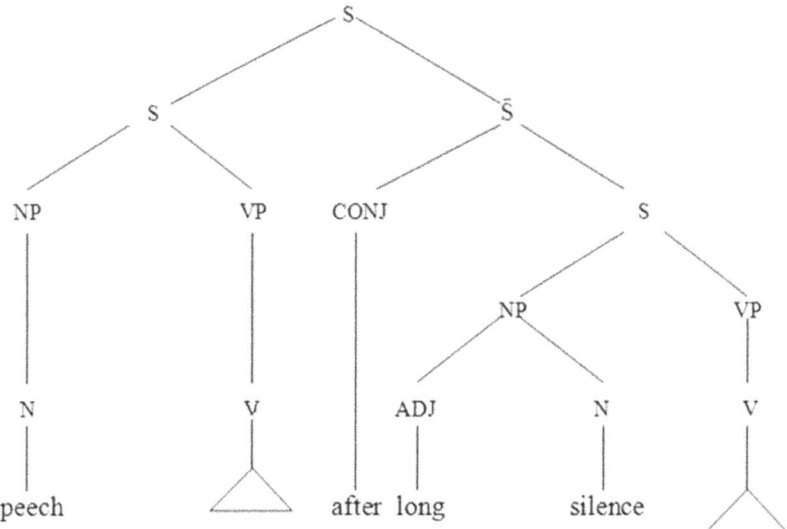

Figure 3.6 'After' connecting two sentences: speech $\mathcal{S}_{vx}$ after long silence $\mathcal{S}_{vy}$.

This alternative interpretation emerges from the grammatically licensed parsing: first came speech (and afterward) long silence (follows/ed), suggesting that first comes/came X and then follows/followed Y.

Examining this reading not only reveals that it fits perfectly with the biographical background of this poem and with its universal import. More importantly, it offers a new non-trivial interpretation. This reading also seems to be supported by the poem's title, which as recalled leaves uninstantiated not only the verbs but also 'speech', signalling that while speech and silence extend over a lifespan, with death this chain terminates and only a (deadly) silence remains. As long as syntax and text license a poetic reading, poetry tolerates (or rather encourages) ambiguity, so fortunately both readings can coexist.

A poem illustrating a unique iconic value of VS in a non-initial position is Lord Tennyson's 'Tears, Idle Tears' – a poem within a poem:

[~88]
> Tears, idle tears, I know not what they mean,
> Tears from the depth of some divine despair
> Rise in the heart, and gather to the eyes,
> In looking on the happy Autumn-fields,
> And thinking of the days that are no more.
> Fresh as the first beam glittering on a sail,
> That brings our friends up from the underworld,
> Sad as the last which reddens over one
> That sinks with all we love below the verge;
> So sad, so fresh, the days that are no more.
> Ah, sad and strange as in dark summer dawns
> The earliest pipe of half-awaken'd birds
> To dying ears, when unto dying eyes
> The casement slowly grows a glimmering square;
> So sad, so strange, the days that are no more.
> Dear as remember'd kisses after death,
> And sweet as those by hopeless fancy feign'd
> On lips that are for others; deep as love,
> Deep as first love, and wild with all regret;
> O Death in Life, the days that are no more. (Richter 1985: 139)

To show the iconic role played by VS, we chose Richter (1985) as our starting point. In his examination of iconic syntax, Richter seeks to show how the thematic sense of absence and loss in general, and particularly the unsolved anxiety, are conveyed by playing with syntactic iconicity. He shows (1985: 138) how the following sentence pattern:

NP + COP + ADJP$_1$ + and + ADJP$_2$

is transformed to form

ADJ$_1$ + as + NP$_1$ + , (comma) + ADJ$_2$ + as + NP$_2$ + ; (semicolon) + so + ADJ$_2$ + , (comma) + NP$_3$

3.2.4 Syntactic Verbal Silence

Richter noted additional structural peculiarities, such as the fact that the refrain-like NP₃ 'the days that are no more' forms the syntactic subject of each stanza. Thus this delayed subject is common to all four stanzas. Richter adds that a homograph of the absent yet expected verb ('are') is in fact present in the line. In the subject's line, he explains, 'the "are" we get [...] is the wrong "are"' – not the copula but an active verb meaning 'to exist' (1985: 140). Being the subject and reoccurring NP₃

[~88ª]   The days that are no more

deserves our attention.

'No more' serves in this structure as an ADV (not a PRO or an ADJ). As the OED (C1c.) explains it is 'a predicate: no longer in existence; dead'. The OED comments that this use is now chiefly poetic or ironic. One such example is:

[~89]   TITINIUS No, this was he, Messala,
             But Cassius is no more (Shakespeare, *Julius Caesar*, V.iii.59–60,
             Norton³, p. 1176)

The Shakespeare quote ([~89]) like Tennyson's NP₃ ([~88ª]) and like all other such adverbials leave out the verb ('exists') iconically depicting the non-existence of the dead ('{is} existing no more'). Because of its poetic conventionality, this elided form has frozen to yield an idiomatic phrase, and as such this is no longer an instance of VS chosen by the addresser (though the iconicity of silence is still apparent). This may explain why Richter (like other scholars) does not comment on this absence, and this in turn may have diverted the scholars from the true VS: the nature of the main clauses' VP (V).

Pointing to the syntactic role of NP₃ ([~88ª]) as the reoccurring subject, Richter makes the important observation that in this intricate construction it is indeed the delayed subject, but on other hand, following the natural expectancy of subjects (as theme grounding rheme), it may also point forward. On the basis of this observation and the iconic pact between the poem's form (syntax) and contents, we can conclude that the main verb of each stanza's subject is the adjectival verb commencing the subsequent stanza, thus:

[~88ᵇ']   The days that are no more are fresh [...] {and are} sad
[~88ᶜ]   The days that are no more are dear.

Our focus on the role of the main VP (V) left uninstantiated as an iconic means of expression raises the question as to what is the verb in the final stanza. Its main verb is silenced, conveying the aching frustration of irresolvable regret. The discomfort inherent in the entangled syntax, the creation of an expectation and the final descent iconically replicates the feeling of remorse. As the reader progresses, s/he generates the sentence accordingly, but facing the tangled and unresolved structure s/he is compelled to abandon the thread and begin a new search. As this is the last stanza, we may find ourselves regretting the tactics we have hitherto employed, instantiating the forms from each subsequent stanza as the main VP (v) collapses. The only solution is the acceptance of a void epitomising death in life (the registration of absence, Gerzi 2007: 144, 148). Our examination on the basis of vs reveals a crucial syntactic difference not between the first stanza and the last three, but instead between the first three and the final stanza. This appears to offer strong and innovative support for Richter's (1985: 141) observation that 'the grammar floats – not unlike the poet himself who cannot anchor himself either to life or to death, to the present or to the past'.

The next illustration of vs signalled by a verbless form VP (V)s, for which there are no antecedents to be instantiated, also comes from poetry: Ezra Pound's poem 'In a Station of the Metro'.

[~90]   The apparition of these faces in the crowd;
        Petals on a wet, black bough (Chilton and Gilbertson 1990: 229)

In 1914 Pound recollects the birth of this poem:

Three years ago in Paris I got out of a 'Metro' train at La Concorde, and saw suddenly a beautiful face, and then another and another, and then a beautiful child's face, and then another beautiful woman, and I tried all that day to find words for what this had meant to me, and I could not find any words that seemed to me worthy, or as lovely as the sudden emotion. And that evening, as I went home along the Rue Raynouard, I was still trying, and I found, suddenly, the expression. I do not meant that I found the words, but there came an equation ... not in speech, but in little splotches of colour (1914: 203)

After telling of his encounter with *hokku* as a 'one image poem', Pound (1914: 205) adds that:

I found it useful in getting out of the impasse in which I had been left by my Metro emotion. I wrote a thirty-line poem, and destroyed it because it was what we call work 'of second intensity.' Six months later I made a poem half that length; a year later I make the following *hokku*-like sentence: –

   'The apparition of these faces in the crowd:
   Petals, on a wet, black bough.'

The poem's resemblance to *hokku* is not accidental. Pound wrote it with *hokku* (Haiku) in mind. This inspiration raises expectations, only some of which are met by this poem, such as the absence of connectives (see §4.5.2). We here focus on the poem being verbless. Chilton and Gilbertson (1990), examining the making of this poem in light of its drafts, remark that the poem

foregrounds the relationship between its two lines by omitting any verbs and supplanting them with a semicolon. The result is a tentative relationship – a relationship the

3.2.4 Syntactic Verbal Silence

poem itself puts in question even as it suggests it. The poem makes that relationship its real subject, even as it disallows any final articulation of it. (1990: 235 note 21)

Thus they claim that the verbs omitted in the two lines are supplanted with a semicolon. But as seen in [~90] there is only a single semicolon (at the end of the first line, but see the colon in Pound's 1914: 205 citation). Two methods may help us examine their claim: a local method based on comparison and a general method incorporating the notion of vs and its forerunners.

Fortunately, Chilton and Gilbertson (1990: 231) provide the following quote from Pound's 'Laudantes Decem Pulchritudinis Johannae Temple':

[~91]   the perfect faces which I see at times
        When my eyes are closed –
        Faces fragile, pale, yet flushed a little, like petals of roses.

Following this citation, they comment that Pound uses an image similar to that in 'In a Station of the Metro', albeit in a less condensed manner. A careful comparison points to crucial differences between the two – extending beyond the magnitude of condensation. We use this similarity to examine Chilton and Gilbertson's claim regarding the missing verbs supplanted by the semicolon. To this end, the VP (V) constituents explicit in [~91] are replicated in 'In a Station of the Metro':

[~90$^{a"}$]   The apparition [, I see {at times} ,] of these faces in the crowd [{are} like]
              Petals on a wet, black bough.

This attempted reconstruction is based on a local comparison. Clearly, the two ([~90] and [~91]) originate from separate poems. Moving to the general, the comparison serves not to signal the particular verbs but to abstract the syntactic construction incorporating their VP (V) constituents. This results in:

[~90$^{a-\mathcal{S}}$]   The apparition $\mathcal{S}_1$ of these faces in the crowd $\mathcal{S}_2$
                         Petals on a wet, black bough.

$\mathcal{S}_2$ may consist of the semicolon replacing the verb or it may follow an uninstantiated verb (and not replace it). In either case, it is apparent that $\mathcal{S}_1$ is a VP(V) not supplanted by a semicolon (in fact, compared with [~91] it stands for NP +VP (V): 'I see').[58] As for the second line, if we confine ourselves to 'like petals of roses' of [~91], no missing verb is suggested. But sensitivity to the VS forerunners easily reveals that unlike [~91] the elaboration in [~90] 'Petals on a wet, black bough' includes a PREP ('on') which is a preposition signalling

---

[58] In terms of idea and experience, leaving the syntactic subject and main verb constituents uninstantiated raises the precise instant ('the apparition') from its embedded role as the VP's object (NP) to a position as the subject.

locality. A VP(V) constituent is expected between the NP ('petals') and the PP (PREP+NP). The verb expressing this locality or an AUX is not instantiated.

[~90$^{a\text{-}SS}$] The apparition S_1 of these faces in the crowd S_2
Petals S_3 on a wet, black bough.

Additional possible instantiations for these VP(V) constituents may be:

[~90$^{a\text{-}SS'}$] The apparition S_1 [seen / surfacing / unfolding,] of these faces in the crowd S_2
[picture / resemble / remind me]
Petals S_3 [are / rest / placed / scattered / reflecting] on a wet, black bough.

It now goes without saying that just as those verbs may instantiate the absent VP(V) nodes, moving away from [~90] other instantiations are not ruled out.

For Pound, though, it is not the particular instantiations of these VP(V) constituents (such as [~90$^{a'}$] and [~90$^{a\text{-}SS}$]) that serve imagism; what matters is the phenomenon of non-instantiation per se (see [~90$^{a\text{-}SS}$]).

We now focus on S_2, to show that the crucial element is not the semicolon but the three VSs (S_1, S_2 and S_3); this is consistent with the manner in which traditional Haiku refrain from the use of connectives, punctuation, titles, AUXs and finite verbs (see §4.5.2). In the final draft, the semicolon of [~90] replaces an earlier colon (see the quote from Pound 1914: 205). Pound explains the role of that colon as an implicit indication of a metaphorical equation: 'x is like Y'. This is part of the syntactic-structural function of the colon as a punctuation mark. Once it is neglected, VS takes over, accounting for the absent metaphorical equation. We return to Chilton and Gilbertson, examining their claim in light of VS. They say:

in the couplet, the poet [...] places before us, in two brief non-predicating sentence fragments, a collocation of images held in suspension and apprehended nearly simultaneously [...] Juxtaposed, the poem's lines borrow associations and emotional overtones from one another, but the semicolon prevents us from defining the connection. The semicolon both invites and resists uniting of the first line with the second, however we are inclined to do that – logically, rhetorically, or metaphorically. (1990: 230–231)

A semicolon may designate in English original or translated Haiku a cutting word (Japanese *Kireji*, see §4.5.2). But the semicolon in [~90] may suggest the absence of S_2 of [~90$^{a\text{-}S}$]; in fact, however, it is the uninstantiated VP or verb constituent that performs this function. S_2 is worth noting not because of the semicolon but because, unlike S_1 and S_3, the uninstantiated constituent (S_2) is part of the structure rather than the content. This explains why, in addition to its VS role (as S_1 and S_3) in negating symbolist readings, leaving the VP uninstantiated also suspends definitions.

In light of VS, Chilton and Gilbertson's (1990) words may be paraphrased by stating that not instantiating any verb constituent (and supplanting such an omission with a semicolon) is a means of expression that serves an emotive, a

3.2.4 Syntactic Verbal Silence

poetic and a metalinguistic function by which the poem makes that tentative relationship its real subject. This iconic vs, leaving the VP or verb (*\$*) uninstantiated, serves Pound to enact and so implement his notion of imagism (as opposed to symbolism) in which the poet 'is trying to record the precise instant when a thing outward and objective transforms itself, or drafts into a thing inward and subjective' (1914: 205).

This statement calls for an explanation as to how the shift from the particular VP or verb instantiations to the analytic serves a subjective transformation achieving the 'one image poem'. The Haiku genre deliberately refrains from finite (inflected) verbs, confining itself to easy NPS nouns, ADJS and ADVS (see note 58). But Pound's motive in [~90] exceeds their content-semantic outcome. Such instantiations of the syntactically expected verb necessarily set a specific time and hence bind themselves to the objective outer world. This distances itself to one 'of second intensity'. This may invite symbolism, but as Pound himself (see quote above) shows, it blocks imagism. For Pound, this is the difference between the particular and the universal. The latter, which he (1914: 207) argues exists in perfection and in freedom from space and time, constitutes analytics – a new way of dealing with form. Pound (1914: 204) defines the concept of 'Vortex': '[e]very concept, every emotion, presents itself to the vivid consciousness in some primary form'. This is achieved, among other means, by ensuring 'first intensity', whereby the theme is the instant, rather than the observer-experiencer and hes intermediate ('second intensity') point of view (on the difference between this and the 'Haiku moment' see §4.5.2).

This is a good illustration of the difference between ellipsis (which as explained is content oriented) and vs, which is here oriented to form and analysis. Vs does not serve here to express a particular content; by making present the syntactically expected but uninstantiated VP or verb constituents, it facilitates an analytic form.

3.2.4.3.2 Articulating an AUX or a MOD Form but Not Instantiating Its Head (for Which There Is No Antecedent)

As in §3.2.4.3.1, this section also focuses on syntactic vs forerunners involving VP or verb constituents for which there is no antecedent (hereinafter – 'VP or verb vss'). Unlike the previous group, we now exemplify vs signalled by the articulation of the AUX (auxiliary) or MOD (modal) form not instantiating its expected verb head.

We may illustrate this with Miss Clairol's well-known hair colour advert:

[~92]   Does she or doesn't she? Only her hairdresser knows for sure.

This 1955 advert challenged linguists. Schachter took [~92] as the starting point for his squib (1977) challenging the claim arguing that because 'propredicates', that is, predicates consisting of a bare auxiliary verb, are the product of deletion under identity with a (nonanaphoric) antecedent, propredicates lacking an antecedent are impossible. While asserting that [~92] is typical of adverts, Schachter provides other examples, such as [~93], in which the interpretation of a propredicate is pragmatically controlled:

[~93]   (John tries to kiss Mary. She says:)
        John, you mustn't.

Schachter (1977: 764) contends that 'propredicates, like personal pronouns, are generated directly – i.e. without benefit of transformations – and are interpreted on the basis of contextual cues that may be either linguistic or nonlinguistic (i.e. pragmatic)'.

Schachter explains that the use of propredicates is limited, by comparison to PRO-forms such as pronouns, or pro-verbs ('do it'), because their referential range is open-ended, elevating the addresser's concern that hes message will not be successfully interpreted. Accordingly, Schachter predicts that because the referential range of nondeclaratives (such as interrogatives, or imperatives) is narrower than that of declaratives, antecedentless propredicates of nondeclaratives will be relatively well received.

Schachter does not detail the source of his quotes. But be they real or invented, the crucial difference between [~92] and [~93] is that the pragmatically controlled antecedentless propredicates, such as in [~93], are allowed because they are set in a particular situation common to addresser and addressee which serves as the pragmatic antecedent controlling the text. Since adverts (such as [~92]) are removed from real-life intersubjective contexts, adverts thus lack situational antecedents such as those that underlie [~93].

We now tie the loose ends to discuss vs. Given that adverts are commercially motivated – that is, initiated and funded to guarantee the potential clients' unequivocal semantic, and particularly pragmatic, interpretation in order to increase demand (see §4.3.3.1) – why do they use antecedentless propredicates? Why did an advert such as [~92], featuring antecedentless propredicates with no pragmatic control, prove a dazzling success, both in terms of sales and in terms of copywriting?

The answer we propose is that the very syntactic shortcoming of the antecedentless propredicates with no pragmatic control – violations of the expected – acts as a vs forerunner:

[~92'] Does she S_1 or doesn't she S_2? Only her hairdresser knows [$S_1=S_2$/ ∈ PRO] for sure.

These salient forerunners not only signal the uninstantiated referential content (the expected verb head, whether $S_1=S_2$), but more importantly point to the absence of indispensable syntactic material, causing metalinguistic tension: a

3.2.4 Syntactic Verbal Silence

riddle demanding a resolution (see §4.3.3.1 and §4.6.2). This metalinguistic unease, evoked by vs, places the uninstantiated main verb constituents as the figure. This is the essential wit of copywriting: to catch the addressees' attention and curiosity, to make hem pause and not let go until s/he resolves the riddle, and so not only to discover what it is about (make it one's own text) but also to discharge the tension triggered by the metalinguistic challenge of vs.

Having detailed the metalinguistic challenge, we can now focus on the contents expressed by vss (S_1 and S_2). In her autobiography (Polykoff 2016), which she prefers to see as a book on advertising, Shirley Polykoff describes the birth of [~92]. In addition to increasing the consumption of Clairol hair colour, the advert also created a revolution in the use of hair colour, making (S_1, S_2 = dye (one's) hair) legitimate and socially acceptable.

Polykoff (2016) experienced this in person. On her first visit to her future in-laws' home, her yet-to-be mother-in-law repeatedly pondered (in Yiddish) 'does she or doesn't she?' Does her son's girlfriend dye her hair or doesn't she? Twenty years later, as she created her campaign, Polykoff explains 'the psychology is obvious. I know from myself. If anyone admires my hair, I'd rather die than admit I dye. And since I feel so strongly that the average woman is me, this great stress on naturalness is important'.

Not instantiating the syntactic main verb constituent iconically captures the indeterminacy of the actions, emphasising the naturalness of hair colour in general or Clairol hair colours specifically. They are so natural that the action – artificially dyeing one's hair – is, so to speak, ruled out. So to speak and not categorically, since of course the result is indeed noticed. To capture this dialectic – desired – outcome, vs does not confine itself to the positive (does S_1) or to the negative (doesn't S_2). Note, however, that the action is one and the same S_1=S_2: dyeing (one's hair).

The last issue we shall consider regarding the vs in [~92] concerns taboo words. To show this, we return to Schachter's (1977) claim that because antecedentless propredicates lack contextual restrictions, they must be pragmatically controlled. Polykoff's story, as well as the advert's caption (see, e.g. Polykoff 2016), suggest that the original phrasing was confined to the one-lined advert:

[~92^S]   Does she S_1 or doesn't she S_2?

which consists solely of function words and pronouns, without a single semantically bound content word. As already discussed, the statement's character as an advert (as opposed to a real-life excerpt), together with the absence of bound content words, allows unlimited instantiations.

This makes them fit to tolerate any instantiation, including taboo (see §3.2.5.3). Because of the practical association made between silence and taboo words, the non-instantiation of the main verbs constituents in [~92^S] activates the allusion of taboo.

124   Verbal Silence: Forms

Polykoff explains that 'Only her hairdresser knows for sure' was added[59] to [~92^S] due to concern that the original advert ([~92^S]) might be interpreted as suggestive and immoral. She says:

And smack in the middle of all this understanding and middle-class morality, we placed the arresting question, the bombshell – 'Does she ... or doesn't she?'
  Then quickly to answer the question and bring the mind back from wherever it went, we followed with our second line, 'Hair color so natural only her hairdresser knows for sure.'

3.2.4.3.3 Non-technical Omission of AUX

The third group of VSs associated with VP (V) consists of AUXs not instantiated in specific syntactic constructions that rule out technical justifications and clearly function as a deliberate means of expression. The AUXs' role is morpho-syntactic, that is, either to serve as copulas or to carry morphological information which is not marked in non-finite or gerund forms. Because leaving out AUXs does not harm semantics – that is, no content is lost – efficiency, length and other practical considerations easily permit the elision of AUXs in such syntactic constructions.

The current group considers cases in which, due to iconicity or particular syntactic contexts, the non-superfluous AUXs are left uninstantiated as a deliberate means of expression, that is as VS.

We exemplify this with Mahatma Gandhi's phrase:

[~94^a]   Our languages the reflection of ourselves.[60]

Gandhi read his speech in Varanasi (India) on the occasion of the opening of the Banaras Hindu University (4 February 1916):

[~94]   I wanted to say it is a matter of deep humiliation and shame for us that I am compelled this evening under the shadow of this great college, in this sacred city, to address my countrymen in a language that is foreign to me.
[...]
I am hoping that this University will see to it that the youths who come to it will receive their instruction through the medium of their vernaculars. Our languages the reflection of ourselves, and if you tell me that our languages are too poor to express the best thought, then say that the sooner we are wiped out

---

[59] Once it was added, the constituent 'Only her hairdresser knows [P] for sure' can either be parsed and recovered as VS in which S_1 and S_2 are its (uninstantiated) antecedents ([$S_{1=}S_2$]), or as an ellipsis (ε) of a nominal or phrasal PROFORM, such as the PRONOUN 'this'.

[60] Mahatma Gandhi information website www.gandhi-manibhavan.org/gandhicomesalive/speech2.htm (accessed 20 June 2019). It is interesting to note that unlike the exact transcript in Gandhi's website, in Montefiore's (2007: 60) book the expected AUX for this text is filled in brackets, so: 'Our languages [are] the reflection of our selves'.

3.2.4 Syntactic Verbal Silence

of existence the better for us. Is there a man who dreams that English can ever become the national language of India? Why this handicap on the nation?[61] Just consider for one moment what an equal race our lads have to run with every English lad.

We compare

[~94^b]   [...] a language that is foreign to me
[~94^c]   [...] if you tell me that our languages are too poor to express the best thought,
[~94^d]   Is there a man who dreams that English can ever become the national language of India?

in which the AUX is retained as grammatically expected ([~94^b] 'is'; [~94^c] 'are' and [~94^d] 'can') with [~94^a] in which the grammatically expected AUX ('are') is left uninstantiated. Such comparison clarifies that [~94^a] does not reveal a poor mastery of English, nor does it result from cross-language interference (such as the imposition of Hindi grammar on English). In nominal phrases (such as [~94^a] and [~94^b], [~94^c] and [~94^d] MOD), AUXs act as a copula linking two nominal forms. But as a signifier, they separate the two constituents. This distancing is appropriate when communicating the foreignness of a language ([~94^b]), serving to distance Hindi from the accusation that it is unfit for academic expression ([~94^c]) and equally to distance English – as a foreign language – from India and its national identity ([~94^d]), but it is counter-iconic regarding one's own language [~94^a]. By leaving the distancing signifier uninstantiated:

[~94^{a-S}]   Our languages *S* the reflection of our selves.

Vs communicates here the essential difference between our languages – the reflection of our selves – and what is foreign, and so can be detached. A language that is part of one's personal or collective self cannot be detached or usurped. This is the theme of Gandhi's speech, and it is enacted using AUX VS.

This text, which may be regarded as illustrating a very frequent syntactic practice, points to the crucial difference between ellipsis as a technical syntactic option (particularly in the context of a category such as AUX that lacks semantic content) and VS. In certain contexts, such as [~94^a], an elision often overlooked as trivial may emerge as a deliberate choice carrying meaning.

---

[61] This belongs in §3.2.4.3.1:

[~95^S]   Why *S* this handicap on the nation?

The expected VP or verb head is left uninstantiated despite the absence of a (grammatically licensed antecedent), such as 'inflict', 'impose' or 'stain'.

3.2.4.3.4 A Failed Attempt to Copy What Seems an Antecedent for the Uninstantiated Missing VP or Head

The last group includes instances when the syntactic structure offers a potential antecedent to an uninstantiated VP or verb constituent but an attempt to copy this as the licensed antecedent fails, signalling that this is not a case of ellipsis but of VS. This group is the most challenging since it has been overlooked by scholars examining ellipsis. The cases discussed are either cases where the syntactic structure (or even the pragmatic context) did not consist of any (potential) antecedents (see §3.2.4.3.1), or where a potential antecedent fitted and completed the missing component.

We illustrate VS signalled by a failed VP or verb head 'antecedent' by reference to the slogan of a welfare campaign ([~96^a] and [~96^b]) and a piece of literature ([~97]).

On the occasion of the 2018 World Cup, J. Walter Thompson London (now Wunderman Thompson UK) created a series of posters featuring blood on a female face or body, in the distinct shape of the flag or shape of a country participating in the football match. In each poster this image is matched with a slogan, such as:

[~96^a]   If England get beaten, so will she

(in this poster with the red outline of the St George cross on the union jack, see Figure 3.7).

[~96^b]   If Japan get beaten, so will she

(in this poster with the outline of the sun on Japan's flag).

The campaign highlights the horrifying correlation between football matches and domestic violence. As J. Walter Thompson London explain, reports indicate that domestic violence increases 26 per cent when England plays, and by 38 per cent when England loses.

On the face of it, this seems a straightforward case of ellipsis, in which the VP 'get beaten' instantiated in the conditional

[~96']   If [nation] get beaten

is the (exact) antecedent for the latter

[~96"]   so will she get beaten.

But syntax in general and thematic (θ) roles in particular rule out this copying attempt. Referring to a nation 'beat' of [~96'] either in the absolute form (OED: Beat, V^1.10d) or as a transitive form requires a competitor (collective team, or a representative thereof) as its complement (OED: Beat, V^1.10a), since it can mean both to win a contest, and, in the passive, to lose.

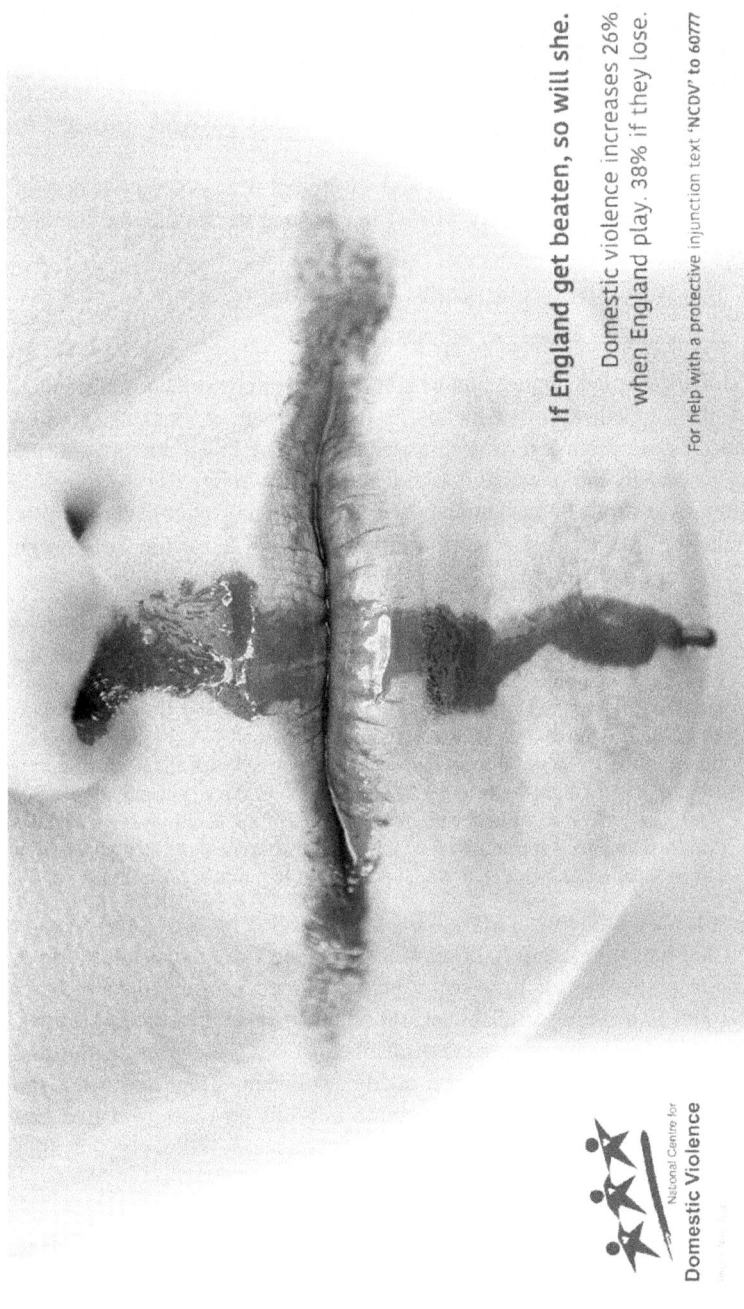

Figure 3.7 'Get beaten': 2018 World Cup.
Reprinted by permission from Wunderman Thompson UK.[62]

[62] www.wundermanthompson.com/work/the-not-so-beautiful-game (accessed 29 June 2019).

Because [~96"] switches referents – from nations and teams (as contestants) to an individual person (a woman) – the lemmas and thematic (θ) roles diverge. Lemma beaten$_1$ of [~96'] is not the same as the uninstantiated beaten$_2$ of [~96"]. The required object of the latter is confined to a living creature (a person or a beast, see OED: Beat, V^1.1a) and denotes physical striking (see 'battered women' in §3.2.3.2.2).

This intuitive copying attempt fails, and we are left with a clever use both of the benefits of speech (articulating words) and those of vs (leaving the signifier uninstantiated):

[~96$^{a"}$]   If England get beaten$_1$, so will she [get beaten$_2$]
[~96$^{a\text{-}S}$]   If England get beaten$_1$, so will she S̸.

The pros of articulation suggest 'get beaten' as a potential syntactic antecedent: act. But the immediate linguistically based rejection of this instantiation communicates the exclusion of such a possibility. The failed attempt and the resulting vs convey the message that the equation is wrong.

Our literary example of vs signalled by a failed copying attempt comes from the concluding words of the story Marlow tells of Lord Jim (in Joseph Conrad's novel *Lord Jim*):

[~97]   The two half-naked fishermen had arisen as soon as I had gone; they were no doubt pouring the plaint of their trifling, miserable, oppressed lives into the ears of the white lord, and no doubt he was listening to it, making it his own, for was it not a part of his luck – the luck 'from the word Go' – the luck to which he had assured me he was so completely equal? [...] For me that white figure in the stillness of coast and sea seemed to stand at the heart of a vast enigma. The twilight was ebbing fast from the sky above his head, the strip of sand had sunk already under his feet, he himself appeared no bigger than a child – then only a speck, a tiny white speck, that seemed to catch all the light left in a darkened world .... And, suddenly, I lost him .... (p. 253)

These words, describing what Marlow sees on boarding his boat, after he parts from Jim and bids him farewell, bring Marlow's long story to its end. Marlow, the narrator of the novel, is a sea captain who undertakes to help Jim's recovery. Jim is a white Englishman, the chief mate of the *Panta* steamer. Jim rescued himself (with other crew members) from the *Panta*, fearing the vessel would soon sink following a sudden collision. They evacuated the *Panta*, leaving on board all the passengers: pilgrims en route to a Red Sea port. The novel tells of Jim's personal consequences following this life-changing and painful event.

In [~97] Conrad presents Marlow's precise plastic description of the external scenery as well as an internal drama. We now focus on the second half of [~97]. Clearly, we expect that a VP or head (verb) will be instantiated in order for

3.2.4 Syntactic Verbal Silence

[~97^a]   then only a speck, a tiny white speck, that seemed to catch all the light left in a darkened world . . . .

to be grammatical. An immediate candidate for the current VP's antecedent is copied from its occurrence in the preceding constituent, yielding:

[~97$^{aa'}$]   he$_i$ himself$_i$ [ε$_i$ Jim] appeared$_1$ no bigger than a child – then [{he$_i$} appeared no bigger than] only a speck [appeared$_1$], a tiny white speck, that seemed to catch all the light left in a darkened world . . . .

This recovery is not grammatically supported, since it violates the basic syntactic demand that the potential antecedent and its copy have one and the same lexical meaning and share identical thematic (θ) roles. This is violated here, while 'appear' behaves in [~97$^{aa''}$] as a copula, and is in fact raised:

[~97$^{aa''}$]   he$_i$ himself$_i$ [ε$_i$ Jim] appeared$_1$ no bigger than a child
== He$_i$ appeared$_1$ {to someone/Marlow} s[{ε$_i$ is} no bigger than a child]

The latter 'appear' stems from an entirely different lemma verb denoting 'to come into sight':

[~97$^{a'}$]   then only a speck [appeared$_2$], a tiny white speck, that seemed to catch all the light left in a darkened world . . .

Compare

[~98]   Decoud lost all belief in the reality of his action past and to come. On the fifth day an immense melancholy descended upon him palpably. [. . .]
Not a living being, not a speck of distant sail, appeared within the range of his vision; and, as if to escape from this solitude, he absorbed himself in his melancholy (Conrad, *Nostromo*, p. 409)

An alternative recovery, such as

[~97$^{a''}$]   then [ε {he} appeared no bigger than] only a speck, a tiny white speck, that seemed to catch all the light left in a darkened world . . . .

retains the possible antecedent's subject ('he' – Jim) and lemma verb. Comparing [~97$^{aa''}$] with [~97$^{a''}$] makes this fault salient, 'no bigger than' acts as a diminishing ADJ having the semantically diminutive 'child' or 'a speck' (or 'a tiny white speck') as its object. But despite the loose restrictions on the s-structure of 'only', when complemented here with the above ADJ diminutives, and preceded by another ADV ('then'), the result is an ungrammatical phrase. Likewise,

[~97$^{a'''}$]   then [ε {he} appeared] only a speck, a tiny white speck, that seemed to catch all the light left in a darkened world . . . .

does not work here.

The collapse of what formally appeared to be a licensed recovery is a forerunner mandating vs:

[~97$^{a\text{-}\mathcal{S}}$] he$_i$ himself$_i$ [Jim$_i$] appeared no bigger than a child – then only a speck $\mathcal{S}$, a tiny white speck, that seemed to catch all the light left in a darkened world .... And, suddenly, I lost him ....

Once no antecedent is found (see §3.2.4.3.1), vs takes over. Many instantiations could be proposed, such as [~97$^{a'}$] ($\mathcal{S}$ = 'appeared$_2$' in its verb sense). Alternatively, another verb could be suggested, such as:

[~97$^{a''''}$] then, only a speck $\mathcal{S}$ [remained / was left], a tiny white speck, that seemed to catch all the light left in a darkened world ....

However, vs can extend even further, replacing the hyphen:

[~97$^{b\text{-}\mathcal{S}}$] he$_i$ himself$_i$ [Jim$_i$] appeared no bigger than a child $\mathcal{S}$ then only a speck, a tiny white speck, that seemed to catch all the light left in a darkened world ....

Such readings may yield:

[~97$^{b'}$] he$_i$ himself$_i$ [Jim$_i$] appeared$_1$ no bigger than a child $\mathcal{S}_1$ [he$_i$ then disappeared,] then only a speck $\mathcal{S}_2$ [appeared$_2$], a tiny white speck, that seemed to catch all the light left in a darkened world ....

So far we have focused on the syntactic mechanism in order to show that the matter at hand is vs as a deliberate means of expression, and not ellipsis. But why and how does this unique syntactic vs, in which the possible antecedent fails, accord with and contribute to the novel, and to the concluding clause of this chapter ('And, suddenly, I lost him ....')? To answer this question, we will look at the following text before returning to [~97]. [~99], immediately following [~97], consists of a condensed cluster of non-syntactic vss:

[~99] [Chapter 36] With these words Marlow had ended his narrative, and his audience had broken up forthwith, under his abstract, pensive gaze. Men drifted off the verandah in pairs or alone without loss of time, without offering a remark, as if the last image of that incomplete story, its incompleteness itself, and the very tone of the speaker, had made discussion in vain and comment impossible. Each of them seemed to carry away his own impression, to carry it away with him like a secret; but there was only one man of all these listeners who was ever to hear the last word of the story. It came to him at home, more than two years later, and it came contained in a thick packet addressed in Marlow's upright and angular handwriting. (pp. 253–254)

The enigmatic close of Marlow's story, supported by vss, did not go unnoticed. His audience sensed its incompleteness, but like Jim and Marlow himself, they were evidently lost for words. Still, the tale of Jim (up to his death), and accordingly, of Marlow, does not end there, though it is transferred to a selectively disclosed written mode.

3.2.4 Syntactic Verbal Silence

This cluster of non-syntactic VSs not only engages in dialogue with [~97]; together with [~97], the seam between the two parts of the novel, it moulds the novel's enigmatical, composition and complementation of the said and the unsaid. This is not confined to the narrated story that has just ended (initiated by a dinner at Charley's and his guests, 'after a good spread' and a box of decent cigars) and to the second part, a written mode Marlow discloses only to one privileged man.

Analysing these passages in light of the Gothic notion of the sublime, Thurber (1984: 42–43) says that 'Jim does not simply cease to be visible; Marlow loses him'. The reader, like Marlow, says Thurber, is left wondering: 'the peculiar, ambiguous resonance of this passage is by no means unique. It is characteristic [...] especially in Conrad's early work'. Focusing on language, Thurber relies on Morse Peckham's observation that 'language itself dissolves in Conrad, in ways that make the interpretive act impossible'. To this Thurber (1984: 44) adds that

we cannot respond at all if we encounter a syntactic structure that frustrates our determination of recurrent semiotic patterns – that, in other words, divorces language from the contexts we have been accustomed to using in it. [...] Conrad must for ever remain ambiguous; his language is translucent, always on the point of dissolving, he is suggestive rather than concrete, [...] all remain just beyond our knowing, part of the human world that speaks and the Conradian universe that does not.

Recalling the second half of [~97]:

[~97^c]   For me that white figure in the stillness of coast and sea seemed to stand at the heart of a vast enigma. The twilight was ebbing fast from the sky above his head, the strip of sand had sunk already under his feet [...]

Three notions trigger the unique VS at work in [~97^a]: figure, stillness and, most importantly, enigma. The failed attempts to recover what ostensibly seems to be a straightforward ellipsis ([~97^a]) reveal a VS 'syntactic structure that frustrates our determination of recurrent semiotic patterns', pointing to and enacting the enigma. This unique linguistic and semiotic VS (§3.2.4.3.4), centred on the VP verb having 'speck' as its object, iconically enacts not only the enigmatic Jim (and Marlow) but also the vast enigma concerning morals, culture and race. It enacts here what [~97^c] says concerning figure and ground, language (grammar and speech) and silence, presence and absence (appear/disappear), and white(s) and non-white(s) (we/they).

The VP verb VS outlined in [~97] (and particularly in [~97^a], ([~99]) and [~97$^{b'}$]) serves the referential function (§4.1) playing on the two lemmas of 'appear' ('appear$_1$' and 'appear$_2$') and 'disappear'. Speech and VS enact here the theme of appearance$_2$ and disappearance and appearance$_1$ (pretence, subjectively, relational) and truth (objective and absolute). These attributes are encapsulated in the notions of the 'speck', enigmatically bouncing from figure to ground, from being what is left of the diminishing figure (such as Jim, [~97$^{aa'}$])^{63} to being a (separate) figure in its own right. Jim has disappeared, and the place where Jim had been is now occupied by something else that has emerged: a speck (see OED's definition below).

This brings us back to the beginning of the novel, at the short point, prior to Marlow's story and gaze (at Charley's), in which Jim's words and gaze speak. When interrogated in court, Jim contemplates, referring to Marlow:

[~100] This fellow – ran the thought – looks at me as though he could see somebody or something past my shoulder. (p. 30)

This somebody or something seen past the shoulder is no other than the enigmatic trait of the speck and its iconic representation expressed using VP verb vs. The definition of the speck as 'a small spot of a different colour or substance to that of the material or surface upon which it appears; a minute mark or discoloration' (OED: Speck, N^1.1a) could almost have been written for [~97^a] – Jim (appearing no bigger than a child) and the speck (a tiny white speck that seemed to catch all the light left in a darkened world). The speck, a recurring feature in the novel, does not denote the original substance (here Jim) but a small spot of a different colour or substance. The OED's definition, together with verb vs, and with Thurber's (1984) observation of the role of the speck, serve to capture and convey Conradian enigmatic dissolvability of syntax-language; the speck raises issues of substance and colour. These themes are not explicit in the novel but appear$_2$ as specks through vss such as [~97]. Just as speech is taken to be the apparent and typical substance, and silence its absence, so white (Caucasian) people, culture and morals absorb and undermine all others. Conveyed through specks, Conrad neither wishes nor manages to obliterate the enigma. The great achievement is to give it voice.

With this text we conclude the sections of syntactic vs centred on the twin legs of the sentence: the subject NP and the predicate VP. We now move on to discuss the non-trivial (non-elliptic) manifestation of syntactic vss signalled by leaving other constituents uninstantiated.

3.2.4.4 Leaving the Verb Complements or Adjuncts Uninstantiated
As long as a syntactic constituent that is expected-required in the particular sentence, is left uninstantiated, there is no fundamental difference between the silence of one role or another. We discuss here five groups in which a predicative complement or adjunct required in the specific sentence and context is left uninstantiated as a deliberate means of expression.

---

[63] 'Applied to things rendered extremely small by distance or by comparison with their surroundings' (OED: Speck, N^1.1c).

3.2.4 Syntactic Verbal Silence

Syntactic complementation is primarily verb dependent. Since verb valency (the mode of combination) governs θ-roles, the major share of these cases of vs involve uninstantiated verb complements (such as NPs, Ss and PPs occupying the VPS object slot). Adjectival (ADJ) and particularly adverbial (ADV) θ-role attributors, carried over from their corresponding pre-transformed verb forms, may likewise require complementation, which if left uninstantiated may also constitute cases of complement vss (see [~18ˢ] §3.1). Moreover, in specific NP constructions and contexts that require or expect a noun, ADJ or NP complementation, deliberately not instantiating that complement will also count as syntactic vs involving complementation. One such example was [~78] (§3.2.4). An additional example is:

[~101]   Stop saying I'm someone's sister, mother, daughter: I am someone. That should be enough.[64]

The paternalistic expectation or socially required practice to identify (and so define) women in relation to men materialises syntactically as a possession construction. 'Stop saying' is an explicit form of silencing (see §2.2.4.1), yet, the emphasis here is on the syntactic vs iconically voicing an alternative standpoint:

[~101ˢ]   I am someone $. That should be enough.

According to this standpoint, a woman is an individual defined and identified independently of a male figure. The $ complementation of [~101ˢ] does not stand here for a zero (ø) morpheme but is closer to Pāṇini's notion of genericness (see §3.2.2.2). $ [~101ˢ] iconically revokes the linguistic and, more so, social dependence. It communicates that in real life a woman is a complete person in her own right. From a semiotic standpoint, a woman as the (head) of a syntactic constituent is likewise complete if a woman signifier occupies its nucleus and no male attribute is needed for its syntactic completeness 'that should be enough', as the slogan states.

As Fillmore (1968) and others show, grammar is a mapping of the verb's valency to its thematic relations (θ-roles' type and nature). It is therefore necessary to take into account that the syntactic government requirements (valency) of this verb or the other goes hand in hand with its semantics and pragmatics, dictating the manner in which they are instantiated.

For example, the thematic relations of the verb 'to eat' require an animate agent and an edible object, such as 'the cat ate the rat'. Sometimes, however, the addresser's intention is not to provide information concerning the recipient or the object of the action but to announce the very occurrence of that action:

---

[64] Designed by Daniella Culkin, see www.redbubble.com/people/daniellaculkin?ref=artist_title_name (accessed 16 July 2019).

'David ate' (contrasting, for example, with David fasted, drank or spoke). It is therefore possible to talk of valency not as a binary attribute (governed/not governed) but as a gradated one.

When one takes into account syntactic government together with semantic representation, two forms (mostly verbs) may share the same denotation, but one form instantiates syntactically each of its arguments while the complementary entry lexicalises one of its arguments, that is, incorporates that argument or referent in the denotation of that verb's lexeme. Compare, for example, 'wash textile' and 'launder'.

Another possibility is that two verbs that are identical in the action they express differ in their valency: one verb syntactically governs more arguments than the other, which includes only a section of the arguments governed by the former. The syntactic and thematic relationships between the verbs 'speak' and 'say' exemplify such as case; while they both label a speaking (verbal) agent and a specific or indefinite addressee, 'say' also requires as its complement the argument spoken.

Syntactic vss of complementing arguments or adjuncts (hereinafter – 'complement vs') will therefore include six classes: (1) cases in which a verb complement required by a specific syntactic setting and/or a specific semantic context is left uninstantiated; (2) a PP constituent (PP/NP or ADVP/NP constituent of an articulated preposition is a stump of an uninstantiated complement or adjunct; (3) vs is signalled by an adjective or adverb inflected to form a comparative while leaving the complement uninstantiated; (4) in cases involving strongly related verbs, when the more restricted verb – that is, the one requiring an additional thematic role (richer valency), not requested in its more general counterpart – is chosen but that distinctive role is left uninstantiated; (5) preferring a non-lexicalised form to its lexicalised alternative but leaving the required (syntactic) argument constituent uninstantiated; (6) a syntactic structure consisting of a sequence of multiple constituents in which each of its parts is left uninstantiated, and trace fails because the argument licensed as the instantiation of the former part is not coreferential with that of its predecessor.

We now present these classes in turn.

3.2.4.4.1 An Uninstantiated Complement Required in the Specific Syntactic Construction and or the Specific Semantic Context

The first example comes from Virginia Woolf, *A Room of One's Own*, a published and expanded essay based on 'Women and Fiction', a series of lectures Woolf delivered on October 1928 at two women's colleges (Newnham College and Girton College, both in Cambridge). As she comments on the first page of the book, the papers were too long to be read in full, and have since been altered and expanded:

3.2.4 Syntactic Verbal Silence

[~102]   The Czar and the Kaiser would never have worn crowns or lost them. Whatever may be their use in civilised societies, mirrors are essential to all violent and heroic action. That is why Napoleon and Mussolini both insist so emphatically upon the inferiority of women, for if they were not inferior, they would cease to enlarge. That serves to explain in part the necessity that women so often are to men. (p. 54)

Three syntactic-semantic forms of the verb 'enlarge' seem relevant to our discussion. These include its transitive form denoting 'to increase a person's renown' (OED: Enlarge, V.2a); its reflexive transitive and intransitive forms (OED: Enlarge, V.4a and V.4b); and, to a lesser extent, its transitive form figuratively denoting 'to widen, render more comprehensive (a person's thoughts, sympathies, affections); to expand, increase the capacity of (the mind)' (OED: Enlarge, V.3b). Examining the syntactic and semantic – literary and conceptual – context of [~102] will serve here to determine whether 'enlarge' in [~102] is an intransitive or absolute form, a case of ellipsis recoverability of the required object of transitive 'enlarge'; or alternatively, a case of vs deliberately selected by Woolf.

The PRO subject ('they') of both constituents of the conditional conjuncts

[~102^a]   if they were not inferior, they would cease to enlarge

are easily traced to the closest nominal antecedent: 'women', thus

[~102$^{a'}$]   if they$_i$ [ε women$_i$] were not inferior, they$_i$ [ε women$_i$] would cease to enlarge.

Having recovered 'women' as the PRO's antecedent, we now copy 'women' to the missing object-complement of 'enlarge' or its reflexive transformation:

[~102$^{a''}$ *]   if they$_i$ [ε women$_i$] were not inferior, they$_i$ [ε women$_i$] would cease to enlarge [ε women$_i$ / themselves$_i$].

As antonyms, 'inferior' and 'enlarge' cannot tolerate co-reference in the context of 'cease', and so attempt [~102$^{a''}$ *] must be ruled out: the subject of 'inferior' and the object of 'cease to enlarge' must be distinct. [~102$^{a''}$ *] is not an independent clause (see §3.2.4.6.2):

[~102$^{b'}$]   [...] Napoleon and Mussolini both insist so emphatically upon the inferiority of women$_i$, for if they$_i$ [ε women$_i$] were not inferior, they$_i$ [ε women$_i$] would cease to enlarge.

Moreover, [~102$^{a''}$ *] and [~102$^{b'}$] must be parsed in their broader context, that of Woolf's claim that for women to be creative authors they must have basic educational and financial independence ('a room of one's own'), and particularly that of [~102], Napoleon and Mussolini's equation of women and inferiority and men and superiority. Woolf's mirror image reflects such stands as an inverse relation whereby increasing one decreases the other. 'Men' could technically be traced as the cataphoric object of 'enlarge':

[~102ᶜ] That serves to explain in part the necessity that women so often are to men.

However, this subsequent noun is far removed, and moreover, as this ([~102ᶜ]) concluding statement states, women are needed not in their own right but it is only by downgrading women that men are enlarged:

[~102ᵃ'⁻ˢ] if they$_i$ [ε women$_i$] were not inferior, they$_i$ [ε women$_i$] would cease to enlarge ₷

in which ₷='men' reports Napoleon, Mussolini and other men's stand, but employing vs (and not initiating 'men') informs and iconically depicts Woolf's critic stand, that a woman's room of her own is not to be claimed or reached pending the will of men, it is for the women motivated by their passion to reach those preconditions and the independence that comes with it (see also [~139] §3.2.4.6.1). And, more so, this is not only in the interest of the individual woman (author or poetess) but in the interest of humanity. Because men and women are different, a male-dominated literature is deprived of women's perspectives, which are thus left unvoiced.

A skilful play between complement ellipsis and complement vs underlies Sir Thomas Wyatt's sonnet 'Hate whom ye':

[~103] Hate whom ye list for I kare not
Love whom ye list & spare not
Do what ye list & drede not
Think what ye liste I fere not
For as for me I am not
But even as one that reckes not
Whyther ye hate or hate not
For yn your love I dote not
Wherefor I pray you forget not[65]

The poem is not dated, and some scholars even question its attribution to Wyatt. Agnes Foxwell, who edited a manuscript-based collection of Wyatt's poems, argues that this poem is 'a poem without value – obviously a Court trifle' (1913: II, 164). She particularly criticises what she terms its 'like loose' rhyming and the repeated use of the same word ('not') throughout the entire poem. This may explain why this poem did not receive much attention. Looking here at vs, this poem does not come out as a jot but instead shows a skilful poetic play between complement ellipsis and complement vs (see §4.5).

---

[65] See British Library, digitised manuscripts.
www.bl.uk/manuscripts/FullDisplay.aspx?ref=Add_MS_17492 (accessed 30 July 2019).

3.2.4 Syntactic Verbal Silence

Wyatt is renowned for introducing the sonnet into English, and as such his sonnets precede English sonnets' final formulation. Whether [~103] is a sonnet addressed to Anne Boleyn, King Henry VIII's second wife and a former lover of Wyatt himself, is also uncertain. In addition to the crucial questions regarding the attribution, date and identity of this poem's addressee, the punctuation is likewise problematic. As seen from the absence of any punctuation marks in the Devonshire manuscript (see note 65), the punctuation in the poem's printed versions, as well as the spelling, are not authentic but the editors' additions and interpretations (see note 96). Regarding lines 5–10, determining punctuation is crucial for the syntactic parsing of the poem and its literary interpretation. Not being able to rely on the sonnet's (final-defining) propositional structure (in which the octave sets the premises and the tercet the resolution) is an additional shortcoming.

The sonnet's first four lines (seeming an introductory octave) consist of imperative verb forms in the second-person directed to the object of love, instructing her on her deeds. The superordinate clauses of lines 1 and 4 are complemented with their subordinate clauses 'for' explaining the addresser's (first-person, Wyatt himself) incentive for what he orders and expresses. The two intermediate lines (2–3) are structured uniformly consisting each of two coordinands (see §3.2.4.6.1), which expand the first line's main clause, that is, each includes multipart main clauses ordering the addressee. The octave lines (1–4) amount, in fact, to four truncated terminating clauses: in each the object of a transitive verb is left out. In light of the antecedent standing in each of the proceeding clauses, however, their recovery offers a textbook case of ellipsis:

[~103^a] Hate whom$_1$ ye list for I kare not [Ɛ whom$_1$ ye hate]
  Love whom$_2$ ye list & spare not [Ɛ whom$_2$ ye love]
  Do what$_3$ ye list & drede not [Ɛ what$_3$ ye do]
  Think what$_4$ ye liste [for] I fere not [Ɛ what$_4$ ye think]

Seen this way, the choice of 'not' as a refrain (criticised, see above, as a 'like loose' rhyme) contributes poetic, syntactic and iconically thematic qualities. Poetically, the single-syllable, one-sound pattern recurring throughout the entire poem communicates monotonousness. Joining now this monotonous effect and the syntactic ellipsis results in an equation which, within the poetic function, is used by projection to build a sequence (see §4.5). The monotonous effect is carried by the ellipsis (leaving out the complements, all lines end with 'not'). Yet the recovery of the various antecedents of this elliptic sequence – as a matter of selection – gives way to a combination of equivalences and differences. Examining now the themes introduced by the antecedents and their recovery, we find an additional twofold monotony: (1) the semantic-syntactic invariance of the VP predicate of the antecedent and its elliptically recovered counterpart; and (2) a lexical monotony attained limiting all the lexical verb forms to lexemes of a single semantic field.[66] This semantic field consists of the antonyms of 'care' and 'reck', and the neutral coordinate terms of the hypernyms of 'hate and love', 'list', 'dread', 'dote' and '(remember and) forget'. The three means of monotony (phonetic, syntactic and semantic) converge to indifference. This is not only the hypernym of the verbs' semantic field but also the poem's theme.

Before moving to the next line and the role played by complement vs in elaborating the experience of indifference, a note should be made regarding the poem's heading. As Foxwell (1913: Vol. II, 82) and other scholars point out, Wyatt never named his poems. Assuming that Wyatt is the author of [~103], 'He professeth indifference' inserted in some printed versions of the poem as its title, is certainly not authentic. However, it does perfectly capture this sonnet's rhythm, syntax and theme.

Returning now to the poem, its fifth line stands out as the sonnet's breaking point. The multipart syntactic pattern of lines 1–4 is missing here and the focus is apparently on the first-person speaker:

[~103^b] For as for me I am not

Bearing in mind both the final 'not' and the syntactic structure, it is clear that [~103^b] is also a truncated sentence. Deprived of authentic punctuation and reliance on the sonnet structure, it is difficult to determine whether line 5 stands on its own, in which case its syntactic recovery within line 5 yields 'me' or 'I' as antecedents complementing

[~103^b'] For as for me$_i$ I am not [∈ me$_i$/I]

Alternatively, [~103^b] is a PP resolving the vicissitude presented in the octave (lines 1–4), in which case its recoverable antecedent is

[~103$^{b''}$] For as for me$_i$ I am not [∈ whom$_j$/what$_j$ ye list].

Either way, applying Jakobson's principle of poetic equivalence, the breaking point compressed in line 5 in general, and in [~103^b] in particular, cannot be dismissed by adopting a technical elliptic (recovery) solution. Leaving out the complement 'I'/'me' not only helps the rhyme but serves here as an iconic means mirroring the obscuring of the self (the 'I', see §4.2). While, as seen in ([~103^b'] and [~103$^{b''}$]), the complement of the determiner 'not' of line 5 is easily recovered, applying Jakobson's poetic principle and the principle of iconicity encourages leaving that complement uninstantiated, thus positioning vs as part of this syntagmatic equivalence:

---

[66] Both parameters are examined bearing in mind the verb valency governing θ-roles in English in Wyatt's time (the mid-sixteenth century).

3.2.4 Syntactic Verbal Silence

[~103$^{b\text{-}\$}$] For as for me I am not $\$$

This poetic option, irresistible for line 5, retroactively unties the ellipsis determined for lines 1–4, yielding:

[~103$^{a''}$] Hate whom ye list for I kare not $\$_1$
 Love whom ye list & spare not $\$_2$
 Do what ye list & drede not $\$_3$
 Think what ye liste I fere not $\$_4$

As in line 5, the complement vs enacts a sincere – or sarcastic – indifference (see later in this section). Vs epitomises here the emptiness experienced due to the absence of a self to be hurt and to endure this agony ([~103$^{b'}$]); it expresses the absence of this self not being listed (lust/last) as the object of her positive or negative emotions ([~103$^{b''}$]). Being void in reality, any syntactic-semantic instantiation to be picked is rendered irrelevant.

Readings [~103$^{a''}$] and [~103$^{b\text{-}\$}$] herald lines 6–9. The lack of authentic punctuation, and their doubtful position as the sonnet's tercet, show up here, hampering efforts to determine whether these lines constitute a continuation of line 5, detailing its theme, or should be parsed independently. However, it seems unequivocal that lines 6–9 replicate the poetic gain attained by preferring complement vs to ellipsis. This vs depicts ignorance such that relevance does not hold and particularly so in the context of negation ('not'). The content or rather feelings denoted using such complement vs may or may not match those recovered as the elliptic antecedents:

[~103^c] But even as one that reckes not $\$$ (anaphoric – all the above: lines 1–4)
 or (complement continued in line 7: (=whyther ye hate or hate not))
 Whyther ye hate or hate not (either absolute;
 or: Whyther ye hate $\$$ or hate $\$$ not ($\$$ = whom ye list or me)).

Line 8 plays on the two meanings of 'dote' and its two predicate valences. The prime meanings denoted using 'dote' in Wyatt's time could be grouped as follows: 'to act or talk foolishly' (intransitive); 'to fool or confuse' (a person) (transitive); 'to bestow love, fondness, care' (transitive and intransitive); and 'to love and care' (transitive). In addition, the OED points to the combination of the two domains (bewilderment and love): 'to be infatuated, besotted, or foolishly in love with someone or something' (OED: Dote, V^1.2a). Integrated with the various lexical and syntactic possibilities (just outlined), line 8:

[~103^d] For yn your love I dote not

may be regarded as confined solely to the complement of love $\$_1$, using complement vs (such as 'love for me' or 'love for whom ye list'), or as expressing the negated transitive complement of 'dote' $\$_2$ using vs:

[~103$^{d\text{-}\$}$] For yn your love $\$_1$ I dote not $\{\$_2\}$

140 Verbal Silence: Forms

The reading leaving out S_2, that is, an intransitive reading of [~103^{d-8}], allows for the interpretation of line 8 as the addresser's denial of being foolishly in love. This, and the lines which follow, then become a discussion of sincerity versus sarcasm and of the poetic-iconic role played by the function words commencing the individual lines. Structure-function words (§3.2.4.5) signal the relations between syntactic constituents; they logically, syntactically and thematically tie clauses and sentences and so also serve the textual or message coherence. The missing punctuation is indeed an obstacle, but an examination of the function words

> 'For' (line 5); 'but' (line 6); 'whyther' (line 7); 'for' (line 8); 'wherefor' (line 7); 'but' (line 10)

reveals that no matter how the lines are punctuated, the function words seem conflicting (see for example lines 5 and 6). The most straightforward explanation is that the conflicting function words represent a deliberate iconic poetic means to enact – together with the syntactic and lexical choices just outlined – the sonnet's theme: emptiness and indifference. Alternatively, interpreted as a case of sarcasm (rather than a sincere case of indifference), these means reveal an extreme emotional state undergone by a speaker who is madly in love: one who is by no means indifferent but rather hurt, frustrated and jealous, left confused by his feelings of abandonment.[67] This dialectical interplay between words and forms (ellipsis and vs) tolerates and poetically enhances both narratives – indifference and unbearable suffering (see §4.2).

This explanation brings us neatly to line 9, which, like its predecessors, begins with a function word ('wherefore') and ends with a missing expected complement 'forget NP'. As above, deprived of reliable punctuation and given the sonnet's structure, the scope of 'wherefore' is undetermined: it could either range over all the above (lines 1–8, as if two octaves) or be confined solely to lines 6–8. This clearly projects on the parsing of the missing complement: forget or don't forget what.

The LF of 'forget' is a semantic surface form involving the primary sememe KNOW and a sequence of negations and causations (see [~123]) (§3.2.4.4.5):

> x forgot y == BECOME (NOT [x KNOW y]).

Examined rationally, the act of ordering his former lover (irrespective of the contents of that order) does not reconcile with indifference. Only a person who cares would urge remembrance. The left-out complement of 'forget y': BECOME (NOT [x KNOW y]) can be recovered as an ellipsis in which all its former lines (1–8) are its antecedent ('all that I have said'), or in which only

---
[67] See 'dote' above. On perplexed language – and syntax in particular – as a symptom of mental disorders, see §2.2.1.

3.2.4 Syntactic Verbal Silence   141

lines 6–8 are such. But here, too, alternating between the two dialectic states, complement vs comes into play:

[~103^{e-8}] Wherefor I pray you forget not s

[~103$^{e'}$] Wherefor I pray NOT (BECOME (NOT (you KNOW y=s)))·

The negation scoping over 'forget' equals the LF of the verb 'remember':

x remembered y == BECOME (NOT (BECOME (NOT [x KNOW y])))·

But rather than expressing the affirmation of 'remember', the poet chooses to focus on the negation of 'forget', leaving its complement uninstantiated. This not only epitomises confusion but also enacts the tension between forgetting and not forgetting. Had the complement of 'forget' been instantiated, or logically-syntactically determined (using recoverability), it would be inscribed and so the option of forgetting would be ruled out. Interestingly, for the addresser to be sincerely indifferent he must forget (and forgive): let go (see [~124']). This is enacted, from the addresser's standpoint, using vs; here the addresser orders his addressee not to forget, while the vs enacts his fear that she will forget. The next stratum ties the two: her readiness to follow his plea (see final line) is a precondition for his reaching sincere indifference, for his letting go.

Read thus, the next line

[~103^{f-8}] But love whom ye liste ffor I care not s

which is the final line summing up the sonnet, is to be read as a continuation ('but' as a connective 'and', see §3.2.4.6.1): if you – the addressee – will follow my order (not forget what I have just said) then 'love whom ye list for I care not'. As a conclusive repetition of the main clause of line 2, the left-out complement is not trivially a recovered antecedent (as in line 2: 'I care not whom you love') but is vs performing a speech-act: silence as consent (see §4.3.1.3).

Before we leave behind Wyatt's poem with its vss, the option of symptomatic confusion due to tense emotions must also be considered regarding the concluding line ([~103^{f-8}]). As explained, the nature of vs tolerates two otherwise incompatible narratives. Trivially, such lexical and structural (function words) inconstancy gives a sense of confusion. But as a deliberate iconic and poetic means, the final vs enacts symptomatic silence (see §2.2.1) in general and here the muteness of a lost, hurt and rejected self (see line 5: [~103^{b-8}]).

This poem illustrates the interplay between the recovery of syntactically required but omitted complements and vs as a poetic informative and an emotionally motivated iconic strategy. Only when the reader is led to the tip of elliptic recovery does the emphasis finally shift hem to the vs alternative.

142 Verbal Silence: Forms

The last case of VS signalled by an uninstantiated direct object-complement required in the specific syntactic-semantic context is a very common case exemplified here by the clause

[~104]   The blind sees

The valency governing θ-roles of the literary sense of the verb 'see' requires an animate agent (the perceiver) and the object of hes observation. An absolute form of this transitive verb takes place when the focus of the utterance is on the agent or on the action, while the nature and specifics of the perception are superfluous. [~104] can stand for such an absolute construction, and this is repeatedly evoked in the Scriptures in the context of miracles whereby a blind person gained hes sight:

[~104[a]] Then Jesus answering said unto them, Go your way, and tell John what things ye have seen and heard; how that the *blind see, the lame walk, the lepers are cleansed, the deaf hear*, the dead are raised, to the poor the gospel is preached. (Luke 7:22, emphasis added, see also John 9:1–7)

As seen in [~104[a]], 'the blind see' is just one exemplar of objects of a transitive (perception) action, stated in the absolute, focusing on the miracle enabling the performance of that action by the disabled agent. And accordingly,

[~104[b-French-T]] 'Onde vas, hombre?' cried the cripple on the crutches, throwing then down and running after him on two legs as goodly as ever stepped on the pavement of Paris [...] and the blind man stared him [Gringoire's] in the face with a pair of flaming eyes.
'Where am I?' cried the terrified poet.
'In the Cour des Miracles', replied a fourth specter, who had joined them. 'Miracles, upon my soul!' rejoined Gringoire. 'Here the blind see, and the lame run'. (Victor Hugo, *Hunchback*, p. 78)

But, unlike [~104[a]] and [~104[b-French-T]], the addresser may leave the required object uninstantiated as a deliberate means of expression. Such complement VS is frequently employed to iconically express impossibility. Recognising a condition (such as 'the blind see') as unattainable, no object could be produced. This doomed object is depicted using VS.

A short example can be found in Theresa Hak Kyung Cha's artwork (Figure 3.8).

Sherwood and Dungan (2005) portray Cha as a performance artist who highlights exchanges between sight, sound and gesture. Commenting on her 1975 performance *Aveugle Voix*, they explain:

The artist covers her mouth and eyes with bands of white fabric on which the words AVEUGLE (meaning 'blind', in French) and VOIX ('voice') are stencilled. The word 'voice' blinds her eyes, and the word 'blind' gags her mouth. If you say 'voix' (voice) aloud, it sounds almost identical to 'voir' (to see): to distinguish the two words, you

3.2.4 Syntactic Verbal Silence   143

would need to 'see' them written. Similarly, the title of the piece, *Aveugle Voix* ('Blind Voice'), sounds a lot like 'aveugle voit' ('the blind sees'). This rhyming of the senses is one way to highlight the interdependency between sight, sound and touch.

[~104$^{c\text{-French}}$]   *aveugle voit*

of Cha's *Aveugle Voix* artwork does not seem to be chance. Considering the cross-cultural impact of the miracles' narrative enlightened in the Christian Scriptures (see [~104^a]), as well as in Asian texts, including the Hindu scriptures, requires that the two be tied together. In light of Cha's performance, and Sherwood and Dungan's explanation of that performance, the diametrical crossing between the words seen and uttered and between their setting (AVEUGLE gagging the mouth and VOIX [*voir/voit*] blinding her eyes) indicate that vs may come into play:

[~104$^{c\text{-}\mathcal{S}\text{-French}}$]   *aveugle voit $\mathcal{S}$*.

Figure 3.8 Theresa Hak Kyung Cha, *Aveugle Voix*, 1975, performance.
Photo: Trip Callaghan, courtesy University of California, Berkeley Art Museum and Pacific Film Archive.

This complement VS moves to the fore a provocative message of the work, whereby the object of the miracles, being impossible, is non-existent. As the playing with written scripts and the sound of words results in diametrical crossing, the uninitiated object may iconically convey the message that the words of the Scriptures, or words in general, can be deceptive. Although Sherwood and Dungan overlook the possible intertextual association with the Scriptures, their report of Cha's *Aveugle Voix* also includes the following observation: 'In another photograph, Cha, blindfolded, presses her hands against a scroll, as if trying to read it by touching. The text on the scroll reads: "Words fail me."' Cha's words seem to reinforce incorporating here complement VS as an artistic means chosen by Cha to enrich her work's intertextual message (see §3.2.5.2).

3.2.4.4.2 An Articulated Preposition Being a Stump of the Uninstantiated Head of that PP Constituent

Before even considering differences across languages, it is important to note that the denotations of the term 'preposition' vary depending on the specific theory through which they are defined (see §3.2.4) (Quirk et al. 1985: 662–663; 1150–1151).

We confine ourselves here to a brief outline informing our discussion of the use of prepositions as stumps pointing to complement VS. Chomsky (1981: 48–50) employs the two categories of traditional grammar – substantives [+N] and predicates [+V] – in order to yield the following system: nouns are [+N, −V]; verbs [−N, +V]; adjectives [+N, +V] and prepositions are [−N, −V]. Chomsky argues that in English only [−N] categories, that is, verbs and PREPS, are case assigners. It goes without saying that government is a necessary condition for case assignment.

The definition of prepositions as semantically non-lexical and syntactically case assigners seems to explain their typical role determining the syntactic-semantic relations between the nominal constituent which they govern and another word.[68]

Sumner (1957) redefines parts of speech as form-classes based on characteristics typifying the structural patterns of English, and declares: 'since prepositions combine rather freely with verbs to make other verbs, they are clearly a distinct category from conjunctions' (1957: 341). More specifically:

Prepositions are parts of PH [preposition+head] structures. These must have, as minimal forms, an initial preposition and a final nominal. The PH structure may, nevertheless, act

---

[68] It is unfortunate that grammar books refrain from defining 'preposition', or do so in an unsatisfactory way (see, for example, Quirk et al.'s 1985: 958–959 negative definition; and see note 69).

3.2.4 Syntactic Verbal Silence

as an adjectival or as an adverbial, whereas MH [modifier+head] and HH [head+head] structures must, as structures, act in the same functions as their heads. (1957: 347)

From a VS point of view, since both prepositions and conjunctions serve to direct the syntactic (and as a result semantic) relations between syntactic constituents, instantiating those particles while leaving one of the constituent of such relations uninstantiated constitutes a case of complement VS. We confine our discussion here to prepositions, since while prepositions may serve as stumps impending complement syntactic VS, conjunctors as forerunners point to symmetric and asymmetric VSs (see §3.2.4.6).

Determining what is expressed using VS makes use of government and θ role assignment: whether the PREP is part of the (idiomatic or non-idiomatic) verb lexeme ('sing on pitch'; 'go on vacation'); or the head of the VP's complement, such as one of the verb's arguments ('he cycles on the wrong side of the road / on concrete'; 'she paints on glass'); or part of a sentence adjunct not governed by that VP, as for example in 'they sung on the beach' or 'she paints on weekends' (see Quirk et al. 1985: 503–514). Because PREPs mark relations, in addition to their role as stumps pointing to VS, the nature of the specific PREP indicates what the VS stands for and what is expressed by its use in this manner. Whenever a PREP is instantiated without its syntactically required (NP, or S̄) complementation (whether explicitly instantiated, recovered by ellipsis (see §3.2.4) or missing due to symptomatic behaviour),[69] this PREP constitutes a stump pointing to complement VS (see note 71).

The first example of PREP complement VS is signalled by the left out complement of the preposition 'about'. It comes from a rape case heard during Judge Lindsey Kushner's last case in court. After announcing the verdict (guilty) and sentence (six years in prison), Judge Kushner commented that as a woman judge she felt compelled to plead with women to protect themselves from predatory rapists who 'gravitate' towards drunken females. In an interview on the Victoria Derbyshire programme, Megan Clark, the rape victim in the case, explained that she understood Judge Kushner's words not as blaming her but as a warning to women (like herself) of the risk. In that interview, Megan Clark shared her experience of victim-blaming elsewhere, saying that

---

[69] An example of a (possession) PREP without its NP complementation explained as symptomatic behaviour, comes from Shakespeare's King Lear:
[~105]   EDGAR   What means this bloody knife?
          GENTLEMAN 'Tis hot, it smokes! It came even from the heart of –
                   Oh, she's dead (V.iii.199, *Norton³*, pp. 1457–1458)

The gentleman wishing to provide Edgar with an answer produces the PREP 'of' but breaks off. Overwhelmed by bewilderment he is unable to conclude the syntactically required NP: semantically identifying the dead (Cordelia). Then, possibly after regaining his breath, the gentleman does not repair this symptomatic aposiopesis; instead he produces a new sentence, referring to Cordelia: 'O, she's dead!' (and see §2.2.1).

'There is definitely still a stigma. Victim-blaming is such a big thing. I did tell people what happened and I felt judged after it'. She concluded by saying that

[~106]   People blamed my behaviour. That's why people don't talk about.⁷⁰

Though the final 'about' as an ADV is grammatical with verbs of motion such as 'walk about', 'about' is here a PP head requiring its syntactic complementation (NP or s̄). Having gone through the legal system, Megan Clark said that she was disappointed with the end result and the sentence handed down by the judge. 'I am angry and it feels so unfair. So many people go through it, people get raped, we need to deal better with it'. Megan Clark expresses using this complement VS the fear that having been raped of her body and dignity, speaking out about this rape will not win her (and other victims) the empathy and support they deserve but will only exacerbate her feelings of blame and leave her even more hurt and lonely.

The next example, illustrating complement VS impended by the PREP 'for', comes from Doris Lessing's short story 'Wine' (see §3.2.3.1.1):

[~107]   But she was again remembering that night, envying the girl ecstatic with moonlight, who ran crazily through the trees in an unsharable desire for – but that was the point.
'What are you thinking of?' he asked, still a little cruel.
'Ohhh,' she protested humorously (*Works*, p. 88)

'Desire for' is a nominal transformation of the verb form 'the girl desired NP'. Thematically, 'desire' requires a person experiencing this feeling (subject, NP) and the object of desire (object, NP, PP or s̄ – 'that' clauses):

[~107ᵃ⁻ˢ̄]   [...] the girl ecstatic with moonlight, who ran crazily through the trees in an unsharable desire for s̄

'For' is here a PREP indicating purpose.⁷¹ It stands here as a PREP stump pointing to the uninstantiated S̄:NP, denoting the purpose required by the verb 'desire' (see Quirk et al. 1985: 696). Lessing emphasises this absence graphically: 'desire for – '. 'Desire' belongs in a rich semantic field concerning 'volition'. In essence volition is directed towards a missing object, one the agent wishes to attain or possess, to have more of or not to lose. This makes the VS in [~107], leaving out the object and purpose of desire s̄ ('desire for –'),

---

⁷⁰ www.bbc.com/news/uk-39367339, John Harrison and Sarah Hatchard, *Victoria Derbyshire Programme*, 'Rape victim says judge "right about women's drunkenness"', BBC News, 28 March 2017 (accessed 1 July 2018).
⁷¹ To identify prepositions serving as VS forerunners, we – like the speakers of the language – must certify that the particle under consideration for the specific context is a PREP serving as the PP stump, and not an ADV in a prepositional adverb construction (see Quirk et al. 1985: 662–663, 1150–1151).

3.2.4 Syntactic Verbal Silence

highly significant. This complement vs iconically expresses the gap between the optimistic expectations of the young girl she had been (this emerges in the choice of the verb 'desire', which unlike 'long' assumes an object that is within reach) and what is now experienced as a lost chance to attain that purpose.

The next example ([~108]) also involves the PREP 'for' indicating purpose. Unlike [~107]), however, it is not a verb complement but an adjunct (see Quirk et al. 1985: 696). This illustrates the unequivocal sensitivity and so dependency of vs not on rigid predetermined syntactic rules but on the specific idiosyncratic context. In a specific contextual setting, leaving out a syntactically required complement may not emerge as a case of vs while elsewhere it will do so.

Excerpt [~108] comes from the HBO television series *In Treatment*.[72] The drama follows psychotherapist Dr Paul Weston's (Gabriel Byrne) weekly sessions with his patients, as well as his meetings with his own therapist. [~108] is an excerpt from his session with Sophie (Mia Nasikowska).

Sophie is referred to Paul by her lawyer for a professional opinion for an insurance report following her recent road accident. At this stage of their meetings, Sophie sticks to her (official) narrative concerning the accident (see [~108]). As she gains confidence, a therapeutic alliance builds up between her and Paul. Gradually her attitude transforms, enabling her to confront and work through her relationships with her parents, her coach Sym, her schoolmates and herself. She then admits that the incident was no accident: she broke into the road with her bike deliberately.

[~108] I am here for your professional opinion not for (Session 1, Episode 3)

Sophie could have stated, as she did in her intake:

[~108^a] I am here for your professional opinion.

Instead, she initiates:

[~108^s] I am here for your professional opinion [and] not for $\cancel{S}$

She thereby acts out her inner psychic ambivalence between official and personal, external and internal, false and true, dividing her message between the words uttered and vs. While the additional words uttered in [~108] 'not for' serve the 'official' narrative, 'for' being a purpose PREP vs stump, reverses attention, placing the uninitiated signifier 'therapy' ([~108^s]: 'not for $\cancel{S}$' =therapy) as ground, and thus introducing (the signifier and signified) 'therapy' as an option.

---

[72] www.hbo.com/in-treatment (accessed 19 August 2019).

The force of VS to enact the internal-authentic ambivalence, giving way to therapy 'where there was an external-official motive, therapy should be' (playing on Freud's '*Wo Es war, soll Ich werden*'), stands out when we compare [~108] ([~108$^\text{S}$]) to [~108$^\text{a}$], and more so when comparing [~108$^\text{a}$] to

[~108$^\text{b}$] I am here for your professional opinion [and] not for therapy

which by instantiating the negated object states its elimination as an option. In addition, we see Paul's role as a therapist, voicing and so resonating this emerging move. A mutual silence takes place between Sophie's utterance ([~108$^\text{S}$]) and Paul's words:

[~108$^\text{c}$] Not for therapy? So, let's see if I'm, uh if I'm getting this right. Are you suing the insurance company of the person who hit you?[73]

The span of silence (§4.3.1.1 and §4.6.2.1) between the two turns [~108$^\text{S}$] and [~108$^\text{c}$] encompasses: the end of Sophie's turn (in which she could have decided to initiate the NP: 'therapy'); an interactive silence, presumably for processing of [~108$^\text{S}$]; and finally phatic silence (see §4.4) harbouring the transformation just emerging.

We now focus on the adjuncts and complements in the context of complement VS. 'Am' as the verb governing [~108] does not assign thematic roles; indeed, it would seem to tolerate almost any conceivable syntactic constellation. The PPs following 'am' in general and 'for' in particular stand as adjuncts (see Quirk et al. 1985: 503–514, 696). But in a specific context such as [~108], this adjunct (like the [~107] complement) is required, thus, its uninstantiation points to VS as a deliberate means of expression.

The next example comes from Adler's (2007: 181–182; 2015: 124) paper on VS in French:

[~109$^\text{French}$] Canderel: Avec vaut mieux que sans

While in [~29$^\text{French}$] (§3.1) the complement VS involved violating French grammar rules, leaving out the animate PRO ('*[sur] lui*'), the 'Canderel' sugar substitute advert ('Canderel: with is better than without') is constructed leaving both tokens of the inanimate object uninstantiated, which places the PREPS '*avec*' and '*sans*' as stumps of complement VS. The parsimony of words iconically conveys the loss of weight achieved (a slim utterance for a slim figure) by consuming Canderel rather than sugar:

[~109'$^\text{French}$] Avec [Canderel] vaut mieux que sans [sucre]

---

[73] On questions and answers as an adjacent pair, see §4.3.3.2.

3.2.4 Syntactic Verbal Silence

As Adler points out, given that the concern here is reducing superfluous calories, standing without their required complement, these PREPs, as it were, shift from procedural grammatical entities to content words conveying the advert's message. Just as the metalinguistic (see §4.6) cutting of words does not come at the expense of information, and may even increase information, so Canderel's consumers will gain by using it (see §4.3.3.1 on its illocutionary force).

A seemingly iconic match would expect the complement of the inclusive preposition ('*avec*'-with) to be instantiated (compare [~86'] §3.2.4.3.1), while the complement of the exclusion ('*sans*'-without) to be left out:

[~109'French]   Avec Canderel vaut mieux que sans [sucre].

However, such a realisation would substantially enlarge the volume of '*avec*' (=with), overshadowing '*sans*' (=without, see Adler 2015: 124). Moreover, the concurrent structural equation would misleadingly lead to copying the former complement as the antecedent of the latter.

3.2.4.4.3 An Adjective or Adverb Inflected to Form a Comparative but Leaving the Complement Uninstantiated

Typically, English forms the comparative either lexically (using such verbs as 'exceed', 'differ' and 'go beyond', or intensifiers such as 'more' and 'less') or grammatically, using the enclitic morphemes 'er' and 'est'. Unlike derivational morphemes, comparative morphemes do not change meanings; rather they form a syntactic paradigm of degree/intensity for producing comparative structures, such as:

NP is ADJer than NP
or
NP is ADVest than NP.

While adpositions are treated in conventional linguistics as the non-case languages' equivalent of the case system (see Fillmore 1968), inflectional suffixes such as the above intensifiers are not seen as such. But it is actually the latter which behave somewhat like case markers. Using adjectives or adverbs as bases, these morphemes prompt the comparative complementation 'than NP'. The above assertion that prepositions assign thematic roles (see §3.2.4.4.2 above) holds likewise for comparatives.

The choice to inflict a base (adjectives or adverbs) to (morphologically) form the comparison has consequences for government and θ-role assignment. As Quirk et al. (1985: 711) observe, 'a comparative adjective must be related, explicitly or implicitly, to a basis of comparison. Thus we cannot say [The boy is bigger] without some such implicit relation'. Here, exactly, complement vs may take place. As demonstrated (§3.1), intuitively introducing vs, Avis's advert [~18] employs this vs ([~18^{ss}] below (S_2 = PP: 'than Hertz') to iconically depict the final stage in which Avis will become the leading car-rental company.

Examining here the forms of VS and its forerunners, an additional VS should be pointed out. The verb 'try' governs an uninstantiated INF/ing (S_1):

[~18^{SS}]   Avis. We try S_1 harder S_2

This complement VS belongs to the next group (§3.2.4.4.4) and is signalled by the choice of 'try' over a more general verb, such as 'do' ('we do better'), which does not require the additional thematic role complement demanded by the richer valency of 'try' (INF: infinitive or GER: gerund); in [~18^{SS}] it is left uninstantiated.

This, again, indicates that whatever Hertz has achieved (VP: to S_1), Avis is trying harder and so will eliminate Hertz as a competitor.[74] Eliminating Hertz as a competitor metalinguistically (see §4.6) eliminates comparison completely.

Returning now to comparative complement VS, we see that this is frequently used as a mode of VS. The following are two more American advertising slogans:

[~110]   WALMART Save money. Live better.

'Live better' was not generated by Walmart's copywriters; it is a known and widely attested collocation. The interesting feature of this collocation is that its uninstantiated complement is reflexive being coreferential to whatever will be instantiated as the thematic focus of the message (such as the addressee's life being improved by the chain store stocking everyday commodities).

Bounty paper towels,

[~111]   BOUNTY The Quicker Picker Upper

is interesting because it plays on poetic licence (see §4.5) creating an impression of increasing degree, although grammatically only the first token ('quicker') is a comparative. 'Pick up' is a phrasal verb (idiomatic collocation) meaning here 'to clean', and as a verb it could be inflected for tense, number and person. The 'er' attached to 'pick' as a verb grammatically denotes an agent: 'something or someone that picks'. The agenthood of 'er' is then carried over, yielding 'pick upper'. But this does not override 'upper' as one of the rare cases in which a preposition is 'inflected' to express comparison. In so doing, the collocation ('pick up') is broken. Its enclosure between two

---

[74] An additional (third) VS partaking in this advert is the uninstantiated conditionals:

[~18^{SSS}]   Avis. S_3 We try S_1 harder S_2 S_4:
         S_3if we try S_1 harder S_2than Hertz S_4 and succeed then we shall eliminate Hertz

(see end of §3.2.4.5). Not instantiating the conditional subordinator 'S_3 if' presents the entire situation as a *fait accompli*.

3.2.4 Syntactic Verbal Silence   151

comparatives ('quicker' and 'upper') results poetically in 'picker' contaminating this property. This repetition (of comparative 'er') results in incrementing comparative complement vs:

[~111'] Quicker than S_1; picker than S_2; upper than S_3 quicker picker upper than S_4.

Two more slogans (adverts) should be mentioned in this context of comparative complement vs:

[~112] [Apple] Think different

[~113] [Schweppes] Drink different

The reader is invited to search the web[75] for the stories behind these slogans. Sufficient to mention that by the time [~113] came out, [~112] was widely known. [~112] and [~113] seem to fit into comparative vs: 'different than S', and so metalinguistically (see §4.6) enforce a notion of unconfined and non-predetermined difference. The authors of [~113] say that they used 'different' not as a comparative but as an absolute. On the face of it, this removes the comparative vs. However, nothing in the phrasing rules out the thematic roles assigned by 'different' as a comparative, and any competent speaker of the language intuitively processes [~112] and [~113] syntactically as a comparative vs forerunner. Examining its conative force activating the addressee (§4.3.3.1), the absolute interpretation is an additional rather than an alternative one.

Comparative complement vs is a very common verbal strategy. The following example, taken from a novel, is cited here not because of its particularity but because of its routine use in such regrettably numerous circumstances. We refer here to 'keep alive longer', as in:

[~114] The Fitzgeralds have had fourteen years of being in that position – of being asked to give anything to keep their daughter alive a little bit longer.

This text is taken from Judge DeSalvo's words on the bench, in Jodi Picoult's novel *My Sister's Keeper* (p. 409). This novel presents the dilemma that faces the Fitzgerald family after the younger sister Anna was conceived in order to provide a bone marrow match for her leukaemia-stricken sister Kate. At the age of thirteen, after countless medical procedures serving her sister, Anna takes her parents to court to gain her rights over her own body and life.

[~114^S] Keep [...] alive a little bit longer S

iconically depicts the uninstantiated complement

[~114$^{a'}$] keep alive longer S [than the prognosis/as long as possible/before death comes].

---

[75] See, for example, https://en.wikipedia.org/wiki/Think_different (accessed 31 October 2019).

The steps taken or the wish to prolong the life of the sick person seek to extend one part of an equation (life) while postponing its complementary (death).

3.2.4.4.4 The Choice of the More Restricted Verb but Leaving Its Distinctive Role Uninstantiated

A concept is more specific the more semantic (or thematic) properties it attaches. The verbs 'speak' and 'say' (excluding secondary meanings such as the metaphorical) are identical in terms of the action made ('communicate verbally'), the agent (initiator) of that action (its addresser) and its recipient (its addressee), but they differ regarding the status of the content of that verbal action, that is, its outcome. Only 'say' requires, and so allocates, a $vp/\{NP, \bar{s}\}$ constituent to be filled with the content of the statement as a governed argument.

To see complement vs signalling the choice of 'say' but leaving out its distinctive-obligatory thematic role, we examine key English translations[76] of Hebrew Genesis 4:8, the story of the first death, murder and fratricide in human history. By way of background, the following are verses 8–10 from the King James Version (KJV):

[~115]   And Cain talked with Abel his brother: and it came to pass, when they were in the field, that Cain rose up against Abel his brother, and slew him. And the lord said unto Cain, Where is Abel thy brother? And he said, I know not: Am I my brother's keeper? And he said, What hast thou done? the voice of thy brother's blood crieth unto me from the ground.

Focusing now on verse 8, Table 3.4 lists the verse's main verb and its continuation in additional English translations.

Of the five translations, only two share the same verb entry. The translators chose one of four English alternatives as the main verb: 'talk' (KJV) 'speak' (ESV); 'tell' (ASV) and 'say' (RSVA and YLT). As explained, 'speak' is the hypernym stating the verbal interaction between the addresser (the agent) and the addressee. This is illustrated in [~115^{ESV}], in which the agent (Cain) and his addressee (Abel) are specified, and the thematic roles of 'speak' are thereby fully satisfied. In this case, what follows is not governed or required by the main verb and actually constitutes a new sentence. In terms of thematic roles, 'talk' ([~115]) is synonymous with 'speak'. The difference between them seems to be that while the former might suggest a reciprocal action ('talk with'), the latter is one-sided ('speak with'). [~115^{RSVA}] and [~115^{YLT}] choose

---

[76] Emphasis added. The translations were downloaded from www.biblestudytools.com/genesis/4-8-compare.html (accessed 2 September 2019). The source for the translation is indicated besides the number (and see note 49).

3.2.4 Syntactic Verbal Silence

Table 3.4. *Main verb and its continuation in English translations of Genesis 4:8*

Citation	Main VERB	Following clause
[~115 KJV]	And Cain *talked* with Abel his brother	and it came to pass, when they were in the field,
[~115ESV]	Cain *spoke* to Abel his brother	And when they were in the field,
[~115ASV]	And Cain *told* Abel his brother	And it came to pass, when they were in the field,
[~115RSVA]	Cain *said* to Abel his brother,	'Let us go out to the field'
[~115YLT]	And Cain *saith* unto Abel his brother,	['Let us go into the field;']
[~115Hebrew]	ויקן אמר להבל אחיו	ויהי בהיותם בשדה
(literal translation)	And Cain *said* to Abel his brother	And when they were in the field

'say' as the main verb. According to the above outline of the syntactic-semantic roles of 'say', in both translations a direct speech follows: 'let us go out to/into the field'. [~115ASV] uses 'tell', which like 'say' (and unlike 'speak' and 'talk') requires the content, but instead of instantiating this argument what follows is the new clause as in 'speak' and 'talk'.

We now examine these verbs and their complements in light of the original Hebrew text, which might be translated literally, that is word for word, as follows:

[~115Hebrew-T] Cain said to Able his brother (And) when they were in the field, Cain rose up against his brother Abel and killed him

As pointed, ESV ([~115ESV]) fulfils the syntactic-semantic roles for the hypernym 'speak', and so the subsequent fragment is external to the verb's valency. The same is true of KJV ('talk'). But in so doing, [~115] and [~115ESV] diverge from the Hebrew source's vs choice of 'say' (and not its hypernym). An examination of translations [~115RSVA] and [~115YLT], which follow Hebrew and use 'say', reveals that in an attempt to meet this verb's grammatical requirements, the clause 'Let us go out to/into the field' occupies the Hebrew source's uninstantiated argument theta-role. Such interpretive attempts to fill in the missing complement follow early biblical translations (such as the Samaritan, Aramaic and Septuagint versions). But looking carefully, we not only notice the brackets in [~115YLT] indicating that this is not an integral part of the text, but also that while this is here the complement of the saying, that is, its contents, in the 'speak' and 'talk' translations this content ('and it came to pass, when they were in the field') was external to the verbs' valency structured as an adjunct of an adverbial conjunction. Examined further, we see that counter to grammar requirements [~115^{ASV}], governed by the verb 'tell' (which like 'say' requires the content as complement), repeats the continuation of the 'speak' and 'talk' valency, and not that of 'say'. We also see that despite this discrepancy, of all the translations this seems the closest to the Hebrew source.

The variations pointed out should be attributed to the difficulty arising in the Hebrew source from the choice of the more restricted verb 'say' while leaving its distinctive complemented role uninstantiated:

[~115$^{\text{ś-Hebrew-T}}$] Cain said to Able his brother ś (And) when they were in the field, Cain rose up against his brother Abel and killed him

Clearly, if the biblical narrators had not wished to present the silence as a means of expression, they could easily have used the alternative hypernym 'speak' ('talk'), which does not require a complement. Moreover, integrating ś=s̄ as a vs complement ([~115$^{\text{ś-Hebrew-T}}$]) resolves the problem that faced the translators in the subsequent words, whereby they were forced to twist the text, for example by making it the content of 'say' or a detached phrase.

The biblical exegesis (*'Midrash'*) and medieval commentators noticed this vs. They attempted, as we do here, to verbalise the vs and to find out what was said leading to this constitutive murder. This incident occurred immediately after God favoured Able's sacrifice to that of Cain. Were the two incidents connected, and is this what was expressed using the vs? *Midrash Rabba* interprets 'spoke' ('say') as referring to a legal argument. The Sages listed three possible sources of conflict between the brothers: land, faith or romance (see, e.g. Cherry 2007: 87–97). The renowned biblical commentator Rashi emphasises that he is familiar with the many interpretations of this silence as offered by various commentators, but asserts that this is not a technical or accidental absence, saying 'but this is the plain meaning of the verse', that is, the biblical editor's choice – and wish – to incorporate this vs within the text must be respected. The text must be respected as such. Alter (1981: 180) adopts a similar stance in the context of biblical narrative in general, and silence in particular, noting that 'the fact of inclusion or exclusion of any particular lexical item may itself be quite important'.

The next illustration comes from Jonathan Coe's novel *The House of Sleep*. Ashdown is an old manor on a steep cliff. After it ceases to be used as a university dormitory, Gregory (Dr Dudden), one of the former students in the residence, turns the house into a clinic treating sleep disorders. More than a decade after the students leave Ashdown, convoluted circumstances reunite them for a therapeutic session at the clinic. The novel uses sleep and sleep disorders as a metaphorical prism, proceeding from wakefulness through the four sleep stages to REM as it plots each of the four protagonists' internal and intersubjective lives, past, present and future.

3.2.4 Syntactic Verbal Silence

Passage [~116] illustrating complement vs straggles the end of the first chapter ('Wake') and the opening of the second chapter ('Stage 1'):

[~116] They [Sarah and Robert] begun talking [...] it was probably, at that point, the longest conversation Robert had ever had in his life. The melancholy silence which had always enveloped him at home – his mother timid and deferential, his father morosely taciturn – had never prepared him for this kind of fluid, impulsive exchanging of confidences. By the time they had finished, he felt drunk with talk; high on confession. They had discussed everything, it seemed, and had held nothing back from each other. It had begun with the collapse of Sarah's relationship with Gregory, [...] the shared intimacies and the self-revelations coming ever thicker and faster as the subjects themselves grew larger and more complex, until Robert realized that he had trusted Sarah with secrets about himself, about his parents, about his home life, that he had never thought

   Stage One

   thought there was something strange about the rooms at the Dudden Clinic, and now realized what it was: that although they contained wardrobes, and washbasins, and dressers, and desks and easy-chairs, and all the other appurtenances of residential accommodation, they contained no beds. (pp. 55–59)

These passages come from prose, not poetry, but following Jakobson (1960: 358, see §4.5) the variation within equivalence projected – here from the axis of selection to the axis of combination – is highly significant. Two such sequences stand out (emphases added):

[~116^a] Robert *realized* that he had trusted Sarah with secretes about himself, about his parents, about his home life, that he had never *thought*

And

[~116^b] Stage One
   thought there was something strange about the rooms at the Dudden Clinic, and now *realized* what it was [...] they contained no beds.

Both 'think' and 'realise' require complements. While both tokens of 'realise' do instantiate the object of realisation, out of the two tokens of 'thought' only the object of the second token is instantiated. The absence of final punctuation and of the (expected) capitalisation of the token immediately opening the subsequent chapter may support the interpretation of that second token (being coreferential with the first) as a continuation completing the preceding sentence. However, pasting [~116^a] and [~116^b] together does not work:

Each of the tokens of 'realise' and each of the tokens of 'think' refers to a different object (four objects in total). [~116^b] is not a continuation or recovery of [~116^a] (for more on a failed recovery attempt, see §3.2.4.4.5). Both the objects of 'realise' and the object of 'think' in [~116^b] are instantiated, and so fixed and known.

In terms of the novel's plot and the reality it narrates, a transition takes place between two tokens of 'thought' (end of [~116^a] and beginning of [~116^b]), drifting from wakefulness to the first stage of sleep. We now focus on the uninstantiated token of 'thought' and complement vs. The text in [~116] suggests complements involving sharing, such as 'that he could be so open'; 'he could be drunk with talk'; or 'he could feel comfortable sharing'.

Serving the same experience, the author could have chosen verbs such as:

[~116$^{a'}$]   Realized [...] that he had never opened up
[~116$^{a''}$] Realized [...] that he had never been verbose
[~116$^{a'''}$] Realized [...] that he had never disclosed
[~116$^{a''''}$] Realized [...] that he had never shared.

Clearly, Jonathan Coe's choice to select a verb (signifier) which requires a complement, yet to leave this complement uninstantiated, reinforces the experience, informed by the division into chapters, of drifting from one state to another. Leaving the first token of the verb 'thought' uninstantiated iconically portrays the sense of drifting between wakefulness and sleep.

However, the emphasis is less on the absence of the complement per se and more on the message expressed by this vs. What does vs add in [~116^a] that would be lost in [~116$^{a'}$] to [~116$^{a''''}$]? The answer is that what Robert leaves out is what he had never done nor even took the liberty to imagine (realise and think). The uninstantiated object of the first token of 'thought' is what lies beyond Robert's psychic reach so that he cannot verbalise it: a conscious act performed while awake. This vs portrays Longfellow's (*The Complete*, Vol. IV, p. 336) reflection of 'Three silences of Molinos':

[~117]   Three Silences there are: the first of speech,
         The second of desire, The third of thought; [...]. (see [~277] in §4.4)

Applying Longfellow's three-part lesson, Robert's silencing of his own desire leads to the silence of thought, signalled in [~116] by the uninstantiated object, and finally to the silence of speech, which is bypassed in [~116] using vs as a means of expression.

3.2.4.4.5 The Preference of a Non-lexicalised Form but Leaving Its Syntactically Required Argument Constituent Uninstantiated

Lexicalisation is a semantic-lexicographic mechanism which takes a thematic role that in one specific entry constitutes a syntactic constituent and encapsulates it as a sememe of a new lexical entry (see §3.2.4.4).

Unlike the instances discussed in §3.2.4.4.4, here it is the existence of two possibilities (a syntactic realisation or a morpho-semantic lexicalisation) which forms the background to a complement vs. 'Wash textile' and 'launder' are

3.2.4 Syntactic Verbal Silence

synonymous in the sense that they denote the same action, but 'wash' and 'launder' are metonymic, not synonymous, verbs: dropping the syntactic object ('textile') that sememe is maintained in 'launder' but not in 'wash'.

Deliberately preferring a non-lexicalised form to its lexicalised alternative, while leaving uninstantiated the argument required following this choice, constitutes a complement vs forerunner.

The first case is frequently used in marketing rhetoric, as in this example from 'Stackers Burger':[77]

[~118]   Valentines Treat: Buy 1 Take 1 @ 50% OFF

The verbs 'buy' and 'take' dominate the elliptic coordination clause:

[~118']   [Є you$_i$-potential customer] buy one$_j$ [Є burger$_j$]^{78} [and] [Є you$_i$] take one$_j$ [Є burger$_j$] at 50% off.

To further analyse [~118] we look at the phrasing of other common deals, which offer bargains such as

[~119]   Buy 1 get 1 free

or

[~120]   Buy 1 take 1.

The verbs 'buy' and 'get' share roles involving 'transfer of possession':

> at time t, x possessed item y and z did not possess item y
> and at time t+, z possesses item y and x does not possess item y (any longer).

This description is also true for 'take' in the possessive sense. The verb 'get' can be synonymous with 'buy' or synonymous with 'take', but the verbs 'buy' and 'take' are not synonymous.

The difference between 'buy' and 'take' is that in 'buy' price is lexicalised as an argument. For the verb 'get' to be synonymous with 'buy', it must place a complement detailing the cost (including 'free', see [~119]) as a required syntactic constituent. The verb 'take' denotes the action transferring possession. Cost is not part of its θ-roles. This is illustrated in [~120]. 'Get' is synonymous with 'take' in the special case when the expected payment is waived (in which case [~119]=[~120]).

---

[77] www.vozzog.com/promos/264/valentines_treat_buy_1_take_1_50_off/stackers_burger_cafe (accessed 12 September 2019).
[78] 'Burger' is pragmatically recovered from information in the advert, such as the provider and the picture.

But [~118] is not such a case. The deal offers the purchase of one item at full price, and the purchase of a second item at half price. But half price is still a price. Here complement VS comes into play. The deliberate choice to pose two different verbs side by side rather than repeat the lexicalised 'buy' emphasises contrast: not 'buy and buy' but 'buy and take'. As explained, this is true when no charge is involved: when the second item is given/taken for free (see [~120]). But this is not the case in [~118], in which there is a cost, as is indeed explicitly stated in the advert parallel to the verbs, taking part in the parallel construction as the instantiated syntactic object of 'take'. Yet this again serves only to highlight the difference: while price appears in 'buy', once as a lexicalised sememe (get for money) and once as the VP's required object (NP or PP(for) detailing the amount), the verb 'take' does not take price as its object, nor is 'money' lexicalised. Moreover, semantically it cannot be an adjunct. While a second reading reveals that the purchaser is only getting 50 per cent for free (see also end of §3.2.4.5), the initial complement VS leads the potential purchaser to believe that the second item is for free and thereby attracts hes attention (and raises hes appetite).

The next example, also widespread, involves the verbs 'cooperate', 'admit guilt' and 'confess'. The example chosen here comes from Jodi Picoult's novel *A Spark of Light* (p. 8):

[~121]   Hugh McElroy, the hostage negotiator George had been talking to for hours, said George's daughter would know he had been trying to protect her. He'd promised that if George cooperated, this could still end well, even though George knew that outside this building were men with rifles trained on the door just waiting for him to emerge.

Because such uses of VS are so common, the case seems straightforward. The incident takes place in a women's reproductive health services clinic, when a gunman (George) runs in and opens fire, taking people hostage. The novel, told backwards, narrates the stories of the people caught up in the centre (staff, patients and others) and details what brought each of them to the clinic that day.

As in [~118], the syntactic-semantic relations between the verbs is not synonymity but metonymy. 'Confessing' and 'admitting guilt' constitute socially, as well as legally, a cooperative act.

The OED does not list transitive valencies for 'cooperate'. Its main intransitive meaning is 'to work together, act in conjunction' (OED: Cooperate, V1).

'Confess' has two central syntactic-semantic meanings. The first is a transitive form: 'to declare or disclose (something which one has kept or allowed to remain secret as being prejudicial or inconvenient to oneself); to acknowledge, own, or admit (a crime, charge, fault, weakness, or the like)' (OED: Confess, V.I1a; see also I1c and I1d, cited below). The second is intransitive in form, for

3.2.4 Syntactic Verbal Silence

example, '*confess to* (a thing): To plead guilty to (a charge), own to (a fault or weakness); to admit, acknowledge' (OED: Confess, V.I6a). Immediately following this the OED lists a meaning specifically relevant for our context: 'intransitive. To admit the truth of what is charged; to make a confession' (OED: Confess, V.IIspec.7. law).

Looking here at verb valency lexicalisation, the syntactic-semantic differences between the verbs stand out. While 'confess' is a speech-act verb, 'cooperate' is not. This difference shows in that 'confess' lexicalises admitting charges but also requires a syntactic constituent detailing its contents (see OED: Confess, V.I1: 'c. with subordinate clause stating the thing confessed. d. with object and infinitive complement').

Picoult's choice to make the hostage negotiator (McElroy) perform a promise to the gunman (George) in return for his cooperation, without speaking of confession, is here a complement vs forerunner, as it leaves out confession as an illocutionary act: admitting guilt, and detailing (as a required syntactic object: NP, or s̄) the fault deed (see also §4.3.3.2.1. On 'promise' as commitment, see §3.2.4.6.2).

3.2.4.4.6 Trace Fails Because the Argument's Multiple Constituents Are Not Coreferential with That of Their Predecessor

This section covers cases involving a sequence of multiple constituents in which each of the parts is left uninstantiated, but where the recovery attempt fails because the argument licensed as the instantiation of the former part is not coreferential with that of its predecessor. Examples [~122] and [~123] seem to be a good place to start, concretising and so simplifying the above theoretical description.

In *A Room of One's Own*, Virginia Woolf argues that the reason women are not renowned for phenomenological achievements is not that they are incapable of such acts, but that they had other work on their hands. She then continues, addressing young women:

[~122]   Without our doing, those seas would be unsailed and those fertile lands a desert. We have borne and bred and washed and taught, perhaps to the age of six or seven years, the one thousand six hundred and twenty-three million human beings who are, according to statistics, at present in existence, and that, allowing that some had help, takes time. (p. 169)

Each act women performed affected a different object (patient, experiences): she bore her children but bred the family; she washed her babies but also washed the floor. She did not teach the floor and probably not her husband.

Clearly this text can be read as a list of generic women's tasks in the late 1920s. But the context is not a to-do list, it is an essay by a talented and sensitive woman author. This sequence of uninstantiated transitive verbs:

'borne and bred and washed and taught' were, at the time, deeds performed solely by women, and those sorts of deeds were the only ones women did. The sense of endless, mundane, unrewarding and uncreative deeds is iconically communicated here using complement vs. The painstaking sequence of uninstantiated complements, which like reward lurk completion is left incomplete. Moreover, the syntactic straightforward practice applied to ellipsis (see §3.2.3.4) falls apart here: the recovery of the uninstantiated complement of one verb cannot be copied to the entire sequence. This syntactic (θ-role) failure depicts the fact that the objects (complementing these verbs/deeds) differ from one woman to the other. On the other hand, the fact that these objects are left uninstantiated – that is, the deeds of each woman are not detailed (unlike the contributions made by men) – depicts the ignorance of women as worthy individuals and contributors. Moreover, since the contributions attributed to men and appreciated by society are unique (performed only once in the lifetime of the contributor and once in the history of humanity), they are not only worthy of naming but also could be practically enumerated. The products of women's deeds, on the other hand, being trivial repetitive and endless could not be enumerated.

This sort of sequential complement vs is a most frequent rhetorical strategy to communicate the total absence of distinction and uniqueness. Our second example comes from Yana Stevelork's romance story, *Not Giving up on Forever*:

[~123] Nevertheless, their relationship failed. Mark graduated from University a year before his girlfriend and was on the verge of new beginnings. Ambitions and a craving to discover the world did not allow it to remain in Garth as he planned to move to the capital. Mining Great City was the main spot for young talents and dreamers of big money and freedom that goes with it. He could not admit to Anna that life in their town shaped for all as 'born – studied – worked – died' caused him nausea. He madly wanted to share all his plans with her but foreknew that in the vision of the future they cardinally disperse.

The next examples come from everyday speech:

[~124] We will not forget and not forgive

together with

[~125] We shall remember and not forgive

[~126] Lest us forget

[~127] Never again

Such expressions are strongly associated with the vow made following the Holocaust. However, they have also been used – and so become associated –

3.2.4 Syntactic Verbal Silence

with other disasters, such as the 9/11 terror attacks (2001) or India's Prime Minister Modi's statement ([~124]) after the Pulwama terror attack that killed over forty paramilitary troopers (2019).

In any case, these vows are also everyday expressions of extreme agony, involvement and commitment uttered by individuals worldwide. Their strength lies in what appears to be plain language (in terms of vocabulary and syntax) and the role played by complement vs. The non-instantiation of the complements permits their open application to any new disaster. More importantly, though, the non-instantiation plays a unique iconic role of naming and not naming. On the one hand, the addresser vows not to forgive; not to forget: to go on remembering; not to allow a second occurrence ('never again'). But on the other hand, the required objects of these private and collective deeds are left uninstantiated in order to depict the mightiness of the event: that which is beyond words, that which everyday words are doomed to lessen (see §4.6.4).

On top of this come [~124] and [~125], sequential complement vss. To see that, we now look at the verbs 'forget', 'remember' and 'forgive'. As detailed concerning [~103^{e-s}] (§3.2.4.4.1), the LF of the verb 'forget' is included in the LF of the verb 'remember'. To forget or remember something, we must first know that thing: we cannot forget or remember something we have not known. Forgetting is the process whereby that knowledge disappears. Regaining that knowledge – after it has disappeared – constitutes remembering, and this can result from the person himself or be triggered by another agent: 'z caused x to remember':

z reminded x of y == z CAUSE (BECOME (NOT (BECOME (NOT [x KNOW y])))).

The complements of the two verbs in each of the sequences ([~124] and [~125]) can be syntactically coreferential. As in ellipsis, the complement recovered for the first verb is then copied to the second. If, for example, the pragmatically recovered object of '(not) forget' is 'atrocities', then this may be copied as the object of 'forgive' (that is, metonymically, not forgive the perpetrators of the atrocities). Here, though, the prevailing reading assigns two distinct complements, one to each verb. The vow splits in two: (1) a commitment by the survivors and the public, directed at the victims and at the perpetrators alike, that the victims and their sufferings will be remembered (not forgotten); and (2) a commitment by the survivors and the public directed at the victims and at the perpetrators that the atrocities executed by those assailants will not be forgiven. [~127] voices an additional commitment directed at the victims, perpetrators and the world in general: that the survivors and the public will never allow such atrocities to recur. The complements of 'forgive' and 'not forget' differ not only in denotation but also in disposition:

one is compassionate, attached to pain and grief, and the is other ferocious (in times also revengeful):

[~124^S] We will not forget S_1 and not forgive S_2

We now broader our discussion of sequential complement vs. The verb 'forgive' includes an element of letting go. Like the illocution 'apologise', the successfulness of 'forgive' does not depend on its acceptance by the beneficiary; 'forgive' is a mental process. Rubinstein (1980: 9) outlines the LF of the verb 'forgive' as:

x forgave y == BECOME (NOT (y's deed CAUSE [BECOME (x FEEL anger)])).

A detailed rewrite of [~124^S] yields:

[~124'] ((NOT (BECOME (NOT [we KNOW y=S_1]))) and (NOT (BECOME (NOT (y's deed=S_2 CAUSE [BECOME (we FEEL anger)]))))).

As explained, the fear that ordinary words may distort or belittle the gravity of both the oppressors' deeds and the painful feelings of the victims and survivors may lead to the conclusion that leaving the complements uninstantiated is the only way to give voice to the exceptional severity involved (see §4.6.4). However, leaving such complements uninstantiated has an additional affect here. Setting such two complements, which are incompatible from any rational and emotional perspective, in a syntactic equivalence (parallel conjunction) dramatically emphasises the differences.

Proof of the presence of clear specific content in [~124] and [~125], conveyed through vs and signalled by the failure to copy what appears as a trace antecedent of the second verb's complement in that sequence, comes from the emotional response to an advert published in Israel (in Hebrew). The advert, promoting the use of shortened phone numbers, was split so that the upper 80 per cent of the page replicated [~124] appended with an asterisk. The lower 20 per cent is much smaller, with fainter typefaces and split horizontally. Two-thirds of the space declared: 'Associate your business with an asterisk and short number. / Your customers won't forget, your competitors won't forgive you'. The remaining third read: 'Asterisk. Memorising-Remembering [gerunds]. Calling. *2552. The national Asterisks' Centre'. Had the uninstantiated complements been void of meaning, waiting to be filled unreservedly, the disgusted claims that the advert scorns and disrespects the memory of the Holocaust's victims could not have been raised.[79] This demonstrates the crucial difference between vs and ellipsis. While the contents of other omissions could be filled or replaced freely, the content expressed here using vs is

---

[79] www.the7eye.org.il/36530 (in Hebrew, accessed 2 January 2018).

3.2.4 Syntactic Verbal Silence

not a void to be eliminated or replaced. It is a presence conveyed through the absence of instantiation combined with its forerunners.

This uniqueness of vs as presence makes sequential complement vs, in which the trace attempt collapses, an important eye-opener to linguistic theory and to the syntactic study of ellipsis in particular. This failure points to vs, offering a challenge for the conventional ellipsis recovery models. Tolerating syntactic absences made present forces us to reconsider ellipsis: allowing vss contributes, as here, a means for testing the structure of what seems to be two identical surface vps. It reveals and acknowledges the difference between cases which originate from multiple vps governed by one and the same s node (in which case the former is the trace antecedent of the latter) and others which originate from two separate-independent sentences, where the technical trace fails to point to deliberate vs.

3.2.4.5 Leaving Syntactic Function Words – Prepositions and Connectives – Uninstantiated

Function words signal relations between parts of clauses and sentences and so tie them together, thereby directing syntactic parsing and contributing to textual coherence (§3.2.3 and §3.2.4.4). In order for these little words to determine phrase structure, they must be singled out by the syntactic parser as belonging to the (synchronically) closed class of function words.

We examined vs involving determiners under morphosyntactic vs rather than syntactic vs (see §3.2.3.1). The justification for this division of function words is crucial for vs in general, and for the role played by function words as forerunners pointing to vs in particular. While determiners only affect the noun or adjective which they modify, syntactic function words such as prepositions and connectives signal relations between syntactic constituents and so dominate entire clauses and sentences. While prepositions are inherently asymmetric, connectives divide into connectives which establish symmetry and connectives (like prepositions) which constitute asymmetry. Sketching prepositions as semantically non-lexical and syntactically case assigners (see §3.2.4.4) makes their typical role functional: to determine the syntactic-semantic relations between the nominal constituent which they govern and other constituents. Chomsky (1981: 48–50) confined his analysis to substantives and predicates, and did not include connectives in the above system. If included, they too may be sketched as $[-N, -V]$. Unlike prepositions, however, they are not case assigners but logical operators; their scope is not restricted to nominal constituents and they can also dominate vps and ss. This fundamental difference between prepositions as case assigners and connectives as logical operators is examined in detail when we also show their role, alongside (pragmatic) discourse markers but not prepositions, in forming and guaranteeing the coherence of the text.

164   Verbal Silence: Forms

Since the syntactic raison d'être of both prepositions and connectives is to signal relations between syntactic constituents, a full syntactic instantiation of such relations consists of the relation and its two (dyadic) or more (triadic) syntactic constituents. Leaving out such a particle, or leaving out a constituent instantiating that relation, if intended and not a technically recoverable ellipsis, constitutes a case of conjunction syntactic vs.

Deliberately refraining from instantiating the NP (or s̄) complementing the PREP of a PP was discussed together with other cases of complement vs (see §3.2.4.4.2). Here we focus on deliberately unarticulated prepositions and unarticulated connectives silencing the syntactic form – the relations between the elements. In §3.2.4.6 we focus on syntactic vs uninstantiating elements of conjuncts (dyadic and other).

Unlike the PREP complementation dealt with in §3.2.4.4.2, we are concerned here with function words syntactic vss (hereinafter – 'function words vs') signalled not by the uninstantiation of a particle required by syntactic rewrite rules, such as a verb, VP, PP (or s̄) but rather by those function words which formally dictate the choice of rewrite rules. This should become clear if we compare [~128] with [~128'] to [~128''']:

[~128]   Speech is silver silence is gold;

[~128']   Speech is silver [and] silence is gold;

[~128'']   Speech is silver [but] silence is gold;

[~128''']   [If] speech is silver [then] silence is gold;

The absence of function words in [~128] leaves the syntactic structure, and thus the syntactic relations, undetermined. On the basis solely of what is articulated, [~128] can be parsed and interpreted as two syntactically independent sentences:

[~128'''']   Speech is silver[.] Silence is gold.

For [~128] to be parsed as a single sentence, function words connecting the elements must be introduced either phonetically or by way of vs (as in [~128'] through [~128''']). But while the quote, as an English or multicultural expression,[80] does not instantiate any of the potential functions words, the semantic-lexical parallelism suggests some sort of cohesion, which in turn

---

[80] Its origin dates back to a first-century AC equivalent to [~128]:

[~128$^{\text{Hebrew-T}}$] 'A word is [worth] a sela [coin] silence two' (*Megilla* 18a).

3.2.4 Syntactic Verbal Silence

encourages the rejection of [~128″″]. This observation points to deliberately leaving out the function words as an instance of vs:

[~128ˢ] {𝑆₁}Speech is silver 𝑆₂ silence is gold (see note 74).

The essential question in this section is: what do function words vss express and add to their fully instantiated counterpart? One interesting observation concerning cohesion is that while function words physically interrupt the dyad, this is bypassed using vs. Seeing cohesion from the iconic perspective, we would expect function words' vs to take over prepositions and connectives expressing conjunction and unification (such as 'with' and 'and') but not disjoining ones (such as 'without' and 'but'), for which this effect seems counter-iconic (see [~132″^{Hebrew}]).

Leaving out function words as part of a pathological symptom is attested in psychotic speech. Such unorganised, incoherent speech both results from and depicts the speaker's inner psychic state: an 'attack of linking'[81] experienced as blurring boundaries and as incoherence. Amir (2014: 31–47) describes this dual function of the psychotic syntax as 'the split between voice and meaning'. Nevertheless, because this phenomenon is symptomatic of a mental state and not the product of a deliberate expressive choice made by the speaker, it is not a case of function words vs (see §2.2.1).

However, the experience of blurring language separation (such as punctuating discrete constituents) can also emerge from non-pathological states, such as swiftness and haste. For these to be cases of vs, they must be expressed intentionally (mimicking an uncontrolled symptom). The first example comes from Latin:

[~129^{Latin}] Veni vidi vici

This dictum is attributed to Julius Caesar following his swift victory in the Zela battle (47 BC). [~129^{Latin}] is comprised solely of three successive inflected verbs:

[~129$^{\text{𝑆-Latin}}$] Veni 𝑆₁ vidi 𝑆₂ vici

---

[81] Bion (1959: 314) concludes his psychoanalytically oriented paper by remarking that:

> The main conclusions of this paper relate to that state of mind in which the patient's psyche contains an internal object which is opposed to, and destructive of, all links whatsoever from the most primitive (which I have suggested is a normal degree of projective identification) to the most sophisticated forms of verbal communication and the arts.

It is worth mentioning here that empirical studies on the language of psychotic patients show a significant correlation between successful treatment (medication) and the elimination of language impairments (such as cohesion and organisation, compared with non-psychotic speech). This must be controlled for experiments involving the verbal behaviour of psychotic persons who did not receive any treatment or whose treatment did not include medication.

The analytic English adoption retains the iconic sense of swiftness conveyed by leaving out connectives and loosens the tightness of the synthetic Latin morphology, in which no temporal or other space interrupts the successive actions. The swiftness conveyed using function words vs ($Ş_1$ and $Ş_2$) is strengthened by leaving the required VP complements of each of the verbs uninstantiated ($Ş_3$, $Ş_4$ and $Ş_5$):

[~129$^{ŞŞ\text{-Latin}}$] Veni $Ş_3$ {$Ş_1$}vidi $Ş_4$ $Ş_2$ vici $Ş_5$

This complement vs (see §3.2.4.4) contributes to the elimination of the distance between the articulated verb forms to further convey swiftness: the actions were so swift as not to allow space for their objects (see Johansen 1996: 46–49).

In subsequent years, [~129^{Latin}] inspired many advert and campaign slogans (on intertextuality see §3.2.5.2), all using the punctuated rhythm emphasising function words vs to iconically convey swiftness and determination. Two examples will suffice here (see also §4.6.2.2). The first is the Olympic motto

[~130] Faster, higher, stronger

which, like [~129^{Latin}], originated in Latin:

[~130^{Latin}] Citius, Altius, Fortius

Like [~129^{Latin}], this combines function words vs with complement vs, leaving the comparative 'than NP' uninstantiated:

[~130^{Ş}] Faster $Ş_3$ {$Ş_1$} higher $Ş_4$ $Ş_2$ stronger $Ş_5$

$Ş_3$, $Ş_4$ and $Ş_5$ stand for 'than NP$_3$', 'than NP$_4$' and 'than NP$_5$' accordingly. In addition, NP$_3$, NP$_4$ and NP$_5$ may corefer or not. These properties gained using vs depict the spirit of the Olympic games – the contestants and the human body stretching and pushing beyond their limits.

The second example is the modern

[~131] Signed, Sealed, Delivered,

a name given to a North American television series (2014, produced by Martha Williamson) featuring four postal employees determined to track undelivered mail. The themes of punctuality, swiftness and determination, again transmitted by means of function words vs, acquire an ironic twist in the context of the failure of the post to do its job (successfully deliver the mail to its recipients) and the mission assumed by the four (determined) postal workers. The uninstantiated VP complements (see §3.2.4.4) depict the postal authorities' failure to complete the task but may also be attributed to the syntax of headings (see [~45$^{a\text{-}Ş}$] §3.2.2.2.2).

3.2.4 Syntactic Verbal Silence

The biblical commentator Rashi notices the deliberate leaving out of connectives in Psalm 8:3–5:

[~132$^{\text{Hebrew-T}}$] When I consider thy heavens, the work of thy fingers, the moon and the stars, which thou hast ordained; What is man, that thou art mindful of him? and the son of man, that thou visitest him? For thou hast made him a little lower than the angels, and hast crowned him with glory and honour.

Rashi is exceptionally sensitive to the use of vs as a biblical means of expression (see [~115$^{\text{s-Hebrew-T}}$]). He explains the vs of connectives and connection (cohesion) in [~132$^{\text{Hebrew-T}}$] as a means to convey spontaneity and the modesty of the human being facing the divine. Rashi supplies a fabricated rationalised paraphrase filling in the pragmatic context (and connective 'and'):

[~132'$^{\text{Hebrew-T}}$] [...] [And when I look at your heaven etc. I wonder in my heart] What is man, that thou art mindful of him? [...]

This paraphrase makes salient the iconic role of the function words vs, confining the left-out connective and speaking subject to the conjunction between the first clause denoting the divine and its subsequent clause denoting the nothingness of mankind. This depicts the dual iconic phase of connectives mentioned earlier in this section: leaving out the connective, that is, eliminating space and distance between the words uttered, merges their denotation, expressing swiftness and authenticity. But this spontaneity in [~132$^{\text{Hebrew-T}}$] comes at the expense of the iconic quality of disjoining connectives (such as 'but') to create distance between the divine and the human. Accordingly, an alternative rephrasing would yield:

[~132''$^{\text{Hebrew-T}}$] [...] [But when I look at your heaven etc. I wonder in my heart] What is man, that thou art mindful of him? [...]

The third advantage gained using connective vs in [~132$^{\text{Hebrew-T}}$] is that of syntactic indeterminacy. As a form of non-articulation, vs tolerates, and so leaves open, otherwise conflicting connectives (and relations).

Interestingly, the same three traits of connectives vs function in other genres. For example,

[~133^{a}] No, it is not 'mask-like', my face, her face

comes from Doris Lessing's short story 'An Unposted Love Letter'.[82] The broader context is:

[~133] We were sitting in her dressing-room and I was looking at her face as she wiped the make-up off. We are about the same age, and we have both been

---

[82] See lexical vs [~174] 'unposated' (§3.2.5.1.4).

acting since the year – – I recognized her face as mine, we have the same face, and I understood that it is the face of every real actress. No, it is not 'mask-like', my face, her face. Rather, it is that our basic face is so worn down to its essentials because of its permanent readiness to take other guises, become other people, it is almost like something hung up on the wall of a dressing-room ready to take down and use. Our face is – it has a scrubbed, honest, bare look, like a deal table, or a wooden floor. It has modesty, a humility, our face, as time wears on, wearing out of her, out of me, our 'personality', our 'individuality' (p. 32).

Deliberately leaving out the conjuncture 'and',

[~133$^{a-\delta}$] No, it is not 'mask-like', my face $\mathcal{S}$ [= and] her face

iconically depicts the story's narrative (see [~133]). The two actresses, similar in gender, age, prestige and even appearance, share yet another trait: their faces, their primary acting medium, are denuded of their singularity, so that even their ownership of these organs is denied – 'it is almost like something hung up on the wall of a dressing-room ready to take down and use'.

The comma standing for the missing connective expresses the unification of the distinct faces once they become a tool. This connective vs is supported by the grammatical mismatch between singular and plural: 'Rather, it is that our basic face is so worn down'. The two distinct (singular) faces merge completely (lack of connective, plural) once they become public (performance: 'readiness to take other guises, become other people'). As in [~132$^{Hebrew-T}$], leaving out the conjunction eliminates distance and differentiation, but this absence in turn enables the retaining of the conjunctive as well as the disjunctive reading (this may explain the comma in [~133^a]).

As a purely impressionist aside, it seems to me that, as iconicity predicts, function words vs – and prepositions in particular – occurs significantly more often with close relations than with more distant ones. The latter occur mostly when the addresser wishes to leave the nature of relations (additive or disjunctive) undetermined. Such selective instantiation or uninstantiation of prepositions seems to support Radden and Matthis's (2002: 234) observation that some languages favour zero marking (or no spatial marking) for closeness, while this is not attested regarding distance.

The opening verse of Robert Creeley's poem 'Later' is a neat case of iconic function words vs depicting the notion of merger, not by way of similarity and closeness, which entail a relation between distinct entities, but, as the poem states, through 'muddle':

[~134]   It feels things
         are muddled again
         when I wanted
         my head straight – (p. 90)

3.2.4 Syntactic Verbal Silence

The uninstantiated comparison (similarity) preposition ṣ̌ ='like',

[~134ᵃ⁻ṣ̌] It feels ṣ̌ things

not only minimises the (verbal) distance between feelings and things but more so, the sense of muddle eliminating separateness and obliterating relations. This theme is expressed here lexically as well as formally through vs.

As we show ([~285^Japanese] in §4.5.2), the absence of function words is one of the salient properties of the Haiku. The entire poem consists syntactically of the nominal construct 'Matsushima' and exclamations. But what seems striking is that due to the sensitivity of vs to the entirety in which it functions (context and form, as well as the repetitive meditative invariance), unlike the swiftness and determination communicated in [~129], [~130], [~131] and [~132], function words vs (eliminating relations: prepositions and connectives) depicts there a unique experience of unification (see also [~90] §3.2.4.3.1).

The last case to be examined in this section points to the use of function words vs to tuning and so attributing logic affirmations. It involves the difference between 'all' as a syntactic predeterminer and a logically (generic) universal quantifier, on the one hand, and 'all of' as a PRO (see, for example, Quirk et al. 1985: 257–259).

[~135ᵃ]   I Wrote All The Words!

comes from a blog[83] in which Lola Davina, who worked for over fifteen years in the sex industry, enthusiastically announces the completion of her book, *Thriving in Sex Work: Heartfelt Advice for Staying Sane in the Sex Industry*. The syntactic and thematic context of [~135ᵃ] is the blog's heading:

[~135]   'Thriving in Sex Work' Progress Report: I Wrote All The Words!

Syntactically, [~135ᵃ] seems to be a fully non-elliptic sentence, instantiating the subject (S/NP: 'I'); the predicate's main verb (VP verb: 'wrote'); and finally that predicate's verb assigned object (VP/NP: 'all the words'). Syntactically, 'all' appears to be a determiner, and examined from its LF perspective it seems to function as a universal quantifier.

The question to be answered with vs in mind concerns the scope of 'all' in this specific sentence and context. Is it totally universal – that is, does it carry a generic reading, true in all possible worlds? Or is its scope limited to a specific universe, in which case it is a PRO to be followed by the PREP 'of' and a complementiser, here left out – an omission which, if intentional, constitutes a case both of function words vs and of complement vs.

---

[83] www.loladavina.com/blog/2017/4/11/thriving-in-sex-work-progress-report-i-wrote-all-the-words (accessed 16 July 2019).

170   Verbal Silence: Forms

The saying in [~135ᵃ] is exclaimed and positioned not as a restrictive clause, such as in:

[~135ᵃ'] Progress Report: I Wrote All of 'Thriving in Sex Work' Words {!}
(VP/NP/PP: of 'Thriving in Sex Work').

Comparing [~135] and [~135ᵃ'] (compare also genres such as Jeremiah 36:9–18) with [~135ᵃ] points to the deliberate absence of the PP: preposition 'of' and the NP complementing and so restricting the scope of VP/NP:

[~135ᵃ⁻ˢ] I wrote all S_1 the words

S_1 stands here for constituents (PP), which while not traditionally or formally obligatory in all syntactic constructions are required in this specific utterance and context. The absence of this restricting PREP and its complementiser, using VS, communicates totality and universality ('all') rather than idiosyncratic ('all of'). Detailing the progress leading to the final stage prior to the book's publication, Lola Davina says, 'I have no idea how anyone else will receive it, but reading it over (and over and over again), at least to my eye, it flows. I cover a ton of territory, but the book still holds together'.

Our final class of function words VS concerns a major phenomenon: the use of conditionals stated by means of function word VS as affirmations. [~128'''] compared with [~128] and [~18ˢˢ] (§3.2.4.4.3 see note 74) were examples of this.

As illustrated, the difference between [~128] and [~128'''] lies in the nature of the logic and pragmatic relations between its two parts. While [~128'''] instantiating the conditional operators (if P then Q) communicates material uncertainty [~128], not instantiating the conditional functions words 'if . . . {then}' appears a declarative in which the two assertions are affirmed (not conditioned).

When the addresser's motive for presenting that which s/he knows is conditional as unconditioned is to conceal, though deliberate, this is not a case of VS. But this logical double-fold message is frequently initiated as a rhetorical strategy, not in order to conceal or deceive but rather to create a reality in which the cause–effect relations are not questionable, they are guaranteed.

Such cases are encountered daily in commercial language, such as [~118] and [~119] (§3.2.4.4.5), in which the condition

[~120]   [if] buy 1 [then] get 1 free

is presented not as a condition but a statement. This communicates the impression of a *fait accompli*, which encourages taking the steps to make the protasis true. [~119], unlike [~120], discourages the (potential) customer from seeking alternative ways to obtain the desired result (getting one free).

A trickier case is the last example for this section:

[~136]   Good, a woman who can fart is not dead.

3.2.4 Syntactic Verbal Silence

This citation, attributed to Comtesse De Verscellis, comes from a small ontology of *Famous Last Words* (Robinson 2003: 82). Robinson contextualises this citation saying that, 'In 1728, after breaking wind, the aristocratic comtesse uttered these words to an embarrassed visitor. Moments later she was dead – though not from flatulence'.

The countess had implied the conditional:

[~136']   Good, [if] a woman$_1$ can fart [then {ϵ woman$_1$}] is not dead$_1$.

Overlooking the embarrassing, yet comical, reference, the function words vs in [~136] portrays the idea that no matter what a person says or does, the very fact that she speaks asserts – both in logical calculus terms and in plain reality – her aliveness. The biographic fact that minutes after so doing and so saying the countess passed away adds an additional inverted layer, so that [~136] is transformed into a conditional in which the premises are false. However, not only are this claim and fact beyond the countess's control, as she is now dead, but more so they point to the difference between material implicature as a calculus and natural language in which the resultant (apodosis: 'is not dead') may be true even if she cannot fart.

3.2.4.6 Leaving a Conjunct of a Coordinating or a Subordination Construction Uninstantiated

In §3.2.4.5 we looked at vs leaving function words uninstantiated as a means of expression. We now focus on the other side of function words, when a conjunctive function word is instantiated while one of its conjuncts is left uninstantiated.

By their nature, conjunctors are functional particles. Examined as structural (logico-linguistic) operators, they signal the relations between syntactic entities, such as addition, contrast, causation and time. Examined from a textual perspective, they may function as cohesion markers relating to the text – that is, function words which specify 'the way in which what is to follow is systematically connected to what has gone before' (Halliday and Hasan 1976: 227). As Halliday and Hasan (1976: 226–273) appropriately demonstrate, while the two classes do not exclude each other, each has its typical formal and other features.

Functional-structural conjunctors divide into ones signalling coordination and others signalling subordination. Those can be identified using the following operative definitions:

If all of the constituents are of the same syntactic category and this is also the category of the whole construction, then this is a coordination construction.[84]

---

[84] These are operative rewrites of Haspelmath's (2004: 33) syntactic definitions. See also Haspelmath (2004: 34) for an alternative definition less useful for our syntactic focus here.

By contrast,

If the category of the whole construction is determined only by its head constituent, while the other constituents (the dependents) play no role in this respect, then this is a dependent (subordination) construction.

The two modes of linking, parataxis and hypotaxis, are not included in the operative definition because while all coordinations are paratactically linked and all subordinations are hypotactical, there are other (non-coordinative) paratactic constructions and other (non-subordinative) hypotactic constructions.

Coordinative constructions are symmetric while subordinate constructions are asymmetric. Unlike cohesion markers, conjunctors are signalled formally. These formally detected syntactic-logic function words and structures raise expectations of a semantic parallelism between form and meaning.

§3.2.4.6.1 is devoted to syntactic vs in complementary-paratactic symmetric coordinations and §3.2.4.6.2 to syntactic vs in subordinative-hypotactic asymmetric constructions.

3.2.4.6.1 Leaving a Coordinand of a Coordinating Symmetry Uninstantiated

Two key structural features of syntactic coordinates are that they function more or less anywhere in the structure of a language, and that their pair coordinands (or sets of multiple coordinands) constitute a single whole. Quirk et al. (1985: 46–47) define 'coordination' as a syntactic construction in which 'two or more units of the same status on the grammatical hierarchy may constitute a single unit of the same kind'.

Haiman (1985: 73–74) provides the following formulation for 'conceptual symmetry':

Two elements A and B are symmetrical with respect to a relation 'r' whenever

(1)   a. A r B and B r A are both true,
       or
    b. A r C and B r C are both true.

For example, there is conceptual symmetry in both sentences.

(2)   a. Max and Harry hit each other
    b. Max and Harry left at the same time.

Symmetry, as a reciprocal relation, necessitates (at least) two (distinct) coordinands. Emerging in varied forms (visual and acoustic, and for people intersubjective), symmetry bears, among other traits, economical value. Symmetry, constituting a well-defined (formally, sensually and aesthetically) whole, makes even the slightest deviation stand out (see, e.g. Koffka 1935: 177–210).

3.2.4 Syntactic Verbal Silence

Despite the regular occurrences of a hollow dyad, this phenomenon has not received linguistic attention beyond the context of technical ellipsis. Rare mentions include, for example, Bolden's (2010) description of 'and' appearing in an initial position to name that which has not been said but might or should have been said. Another is Ross's formulation of what he terms 'the coordinate structure constraint': 'In a coordinate structure, no conjunct may be moved, nor may any element contained in a conjunct be moved out of that conjunct' (1967: 89, quote from Haspelmath 2004: 28). This constraint explains why displacement, such as raising, results in ungrammaticality but overlooks cases in which movement results in no trace or there is no conjoin to begin with.

Following the syntactically based definition above, coordination is symmetrical in terms of its structural-syntactic relations. A symmetrical coordinator serves as a vs forerunner when it points to an uninstantiated coordinand. Because coordinate function words establish – and so require – symmetry, the uninstantiated coordinand is most salient, and so, when checked for symmetry, its absence becomes presence.

The function word 'and' serves different roles, chiefly as the basic coordinator of a symmetric dyad: '$C_1 {\wedge} C_2$'. The absence of a coordinand (C_1, or C_2 or more), signalled using the coordinator 'and' in its basic role, points to vs.

Illustrating vs leaving the initial coordinand (C_1) of the coordinate dyad (C_1 and C_2) uninstantiated as a means of expression can be seen in the opening lines of Ezra Pound's Cantos:

[~137]   And then went down to the ship,
Set keel to breakers, forth on the godly sea, and
We set up mast and sail on that swart ship,
Bore sheep aboard her, and our bodies also
Heavy with weeping, and winds from sternward
Bore us out onward with bellying canvas,
Circe's this craft, the trim-coifed goddess [...] (Pound, *Cantos*, I, p. 3)[85]

---

[85] Lines 1–3 of Homer's Greek source read

[~137^{Greek}] αὐτὰρ ἐπεί ῥ' ἐπὶ νῆα κατήλθομεν ἠδὲ θάλασσαν, / νῆα μὲν ἄρ πάμπρωτον ἐρύσσαμεν εἰς ἄλα δῖαν, / ἐν δ' ἱστὸν τιθέμεσθα καὶ ἱστία νηὶ μελαίνῃ [...]

Lines 1–3 of Andread Divus's Latin translation – which is saliently present in Pound's English translation (also mentioned in the Canto, see [~138]) – read:

[~137^{Latin}] *At postquam ad navem descendimus, et mare, / Nauem quidem primum deduximus in mare diuum. / Et malum posuimus et vela in navi nigra [...].*

174   Verbal Silence: Forms

Pound's translation of 'The *Nekuia*' – Odysseus' journey to Hedas, the underworld of the dead – to find out his future, as told by Homer in the Odyssey, takes up the first sixty-eight lines of Canto 1 (on quotation as vs, see §3.2.5.2.1). Pound prefaces his translation of this long fragment from the *Nekuia* with one single word – the function word 'and'. The entire Canto (1), and so the entire poem (consisting of 116 Cantos), thus begin with the symmetric coordinator.

Before examining this coordinator ('and') as a vs forerunner, it is important to point out that Homer tells the story of the *Nekuia* (book xi of the Odyssey) not chronologically, from beginning to end, but from its middle point, when its protagonist (Odysseus and his crew, but see later in this section) reach the ship. The Greek equivalent of the English coordinator 'and' is 'καί' (see line 3 in [~137]). 'αὐτάρ' in Homer's Greek, and its Latin equivalent '*at*', are conjunctors indicating contrast or transition (such as 'but' and 'however', and temporal 'as soon as').

The 'And' placed by Pound at the beginning of an entire poem is clearly a case in which its first coordinand is left uninstantiated and in which interpreting that 'and' token as denoting narration sequence (such as Greek 'αὐτάρ' and Latin '*at*') may compound – but not oust – its primary role as a coordinator.

Some scholars have noted that Pound's supplementing 'and' is not reflected in Homer's Old Greek source, nor in Divus's Latin translation (on the latter's influence on Pound's translation and poem, see note 85). In addition, they have also noticed the grammatical diversity resulting from the author's choice to supplement the coordinator but not to instantiate its expected symmetrical coordinand. The quote (Kenner 1971: 349) which follows proceeds in what seems to be Kenner's handwritten replica of the Canto's opening line:

And then went down to the ship

What comes before 'And'? In mankind's past, before even Homer, a foretime; a foretime even before the dark rite of confronting shades which Pound thought *older* than the rest of the *Odyssey*, reclaimed by Homer as he reclaims Homer now. In the *Odyssey*, the ten books that precede. In Ezra Pound's life, the time at Wyncote and Pennsylvania and Hamilton and Wabash, before he took ship for what was not meant as exile. And in the history of the poem, much precedent groping and brooding, out of which mostly unspecifiable darkness the poem as we know it emerges. In that darkness, aided by clues, we can locate a few of the standpoints Pound once occupied, as he pondered a chord that should comprise four of history's beginnings: the earliest English ('Seafarer' rhythms and diction), the earliest Greek (the *Nekuia*), the beginnings of the 20th-century Vortex, and the origins of the Vortex we call the Renaissance, when once before it had seemed pertinent to reaffirm Homer's perpetual freshness.

In this quote, Kenner seems to verbalise the content of the C_1 coordinand which Pound left uninstantiated. In so doing, he captures and justifies Pound's choice to express that content using vs. In particular, the long and detailed

3.2.4 Syntactic Verbal Silence

chronicles alluded to intertextually (see §3.2.5.2) could not have been smoothly integrated as part of the poem. This, in turn, points to two benefits gained through the use of vs. The first is that by expressing content without introducing phonetic material (signifiers), vs can overcome linearity (see §4.6.3.3.3). The second gain is aesthetic: by detailing content without interrupting the poetic sequence, vs can retain, and sometimes even emphasise, the poetic sequence, thereby projecting the principle of equivalence from the axis of selection into the axis of combination (see §4.5).

To take Kenner's explanation one step forward, we return to the theme of Canto 1, which essentially presents the theme of the entire poem. Pound is preoccupied in the Cantos with the authenticity of chronicles. While the speaking self in Homer's *Nekuia* is Odysseus and his crew, the protagonist of Pound's (Canto 1) *Nekuia* is Pound himself and mankind, in their journey through history, culture and personas. Playing around with these topics, Pound incorporates in the Cantos old and modern languages (with their vocabulary, grammar and even script); domestic and foreign; standard and exotic. He skips from one period, persona or style to another, sometimes without any formal or other indication. To serve and enact these themes, the initial coordinand (C_1) of 'and' does not confine itself to the list delineated by Kenner. In fact, Pound's ostensible starting point is the Hellenic Odyssey. All that preceded is alluded to by the uninstantiated C_1 coordinand, iconically depicting the cultures and personas preceding Odysseus (his *Nekuia*) as well as Pound's. This vs adds to Kenner's ordered, definite topics, Pound's *Nekuia*: calling his dead spirits to reveal the future.

This is supported by the concluding words of Canto 1:

[~138] Lie quiet Divus. I mean, that is Andreas Divus,
In officina Wecheli, 1538, out of Homer.
And he sailed, by Sirens and thence outward and away
And unto Circe.
Venerandam,
In the Cretan's phrase, with the golden crown, Aphrodite,
Cypri munimenta sortita est, mirthful, orichalchi, with golden
Girdles and breast bands, thou with dark eyelids
Bearing the golden bough of Argicida. So that: (p. 5)

'So that' is a subordinator function phrase marking adverbial clauses expressing result (or purpose, see, e.g., Quirk et al. 1985: 920; 1108–1109). While, as discussed, the 'and' beginning Canto 1 ([~137]) leaves the initial (past) coordinand uninstantiated, the Canto ends ([~138]) leaving out the apodosis constituent of the cause–result dyad, that is, the future.

These two conjunctive vss further depict the work's theme of the past (uninstantiated 'and' initial coordinand); present (the grammatical, narrative and even lexical) gaps within and among the Cantos; and future – the uninstantiated 'so that' – an answer which motivates Odysseus and Pound (and their companions and contemporaries) to set off, each to his *Nekuia*.

As mentioned, Haiman (1985) incorporates relation as an integral player in the determination and definition of symmetry. As a central coordinator expressing contrast, 'but' yields symmetrical syntactic linking. As an adversative coordinator, however, the logical relations between its coordinands (C_1 but C_2) are not symmetrical (C_2 but C_1 is not necessarily true). Quirk et al. (1985: 920–928, 935) rephrase 'contrastiveness' as 'the unexpectedness of what is said in the second conjoin in view of the content of the first conjoin [... or] a repudiation on positive terms of what has been said or implied by negation in the first conjoin'. Likewise, Schiffrin (1987: 152–177) stresses the discursive function of 'but' to contrast an upcoming unit with a prior one. Among these, Schiffrin mentions the role of 'but' to mark a return to a previously raised issue. These descriptions of the contrastive contexts of 'but' acknowledge that for 'but' to function as a coordinator (linking and contrasting) it must instantiate both of its coordinands (in fact, Schiffrin never refers to 'but' initialising a discourse). The addresser's choice to use 'but' as a function word yet leave one of its coordinands uninstantiated is a case of vs.

Our first example, one of the most memorable opening lines of English prose, is frequently the object of literary trivia quizzes:

[~139ª]   But, you may say, we asked you to speak about women and fiction – what, has that got to do with a room of one's own?

This is the opening line of Virginia Woolf's monograph *A Room of One's Own*. As recalled (see [~102] §3.2.4.4.1), the monograph is based on a series of lectures Woolf delivered in October 1928 at two women's colleges (see also [~122] §3.2.4.4.5 and §3.2.5.5.2).

Following Quirk et al.'s description (1985: 935), opening the book or the lecture with the coordinator 'but' signals the contrasting of the first coordinand, which Woolf deliberately leaves uninstantiated. Immediately after the 'but', Woolf verbalises the unexpectedness (mentioned by Quirk et al.): what has 'A Room of One's Own' to do with women and fiction? Had this been the only coordinand of the 'but' in [~139'], there would be no vs involved. But reading the entire paragraph, the possible uninstantiated coordinands, expressed using vs, pile up, leading to Woolf's conclusion that 'the great problem of the true nature of woman and the true nature of fiction [is left] unsolved':

[~139]   But, you may say, we asked you to speak about women and fiction – what, has that got to do with a room of one's own? I will try to explain. When you asked me to speak about women and fiction I sat down on the banks of a river and began to wonder what the words meant. They might mean simply a few remarks about Fanny Burney; a few more about Jane Austen; [...] But at

3.2.4 Syntactic Verbal Silence

second sight the words seemed not so simple. The title women and fiction might mean, and you may have meant it to mean, women and what they are like, or it might mean women and the fiction that they write; [...] But when I began to consider the subject in this last way, which seemed the most interesting, I soon saw that it had one fatal drawback. I should never be able to come to a conclusion. [...] All I could do was to offer you an opinion upon one minor point – a woman must have money and a room of her own if she is to write fiction; and that, as you will see, leaves the great problem of the true nature of woman and the true nature of fiction unsolved. (pp. 5–6)

We now move to Robert Frost, who in [~140] leaves the initial coordinand of the 'but' coordination uninstantiated as an iconic and poetic means of expression:

[~140]   But outer Space,
         At least this far,
         For all the fuss
         Of the popul*ace*
         Stays more popul*ar*
         Than popul*ous*. (p. 469)

Frost's poem could not have begun with any other word other than 'but', which serves, here, as the forerunner of vs, followed by the text from 'but' onwards, creating a universe. It is this specific 'but' which marks the semantic and thematic contrast between inner space and outer space; between the close and the distant; the reached (by populous) and the not-reached; the preserved and the lost. In addition, 'S but' could indeed signal that the poem is an answer to a question asked using vs either by the addresser of the poem (in which case it constitutes self-reply) or by a separate – here missing – interlocutor (see §4.3.3.2.2).

The two next cases briefly illustrate widespread coordinative vss involving more marginal coordinators. We start with 'also' and conclude with 'me too'.

'Also' is an adverb which, when indicating identity or similarity, may either combine with 'and' ('and also') or stand by itself functioning syntactically as a coordinator. Suffice to look at Tata Steel's neat jingles:

[~141]   Tata Steel – we also make steel

[~142]   Tata Steel – we also make tomorrow.

Fernando (2006: 71) takes the story of Tata Steel – a successful international company based in India – as his case study for investigating the theory and practice of corporate governance. He cites at length the personal account of the company's first jingle ([~141]) offered by the company's vice president, Muthuraman:

To me the statement represents everything Tata Steel does. It is pregnant with so much meaning and conveys a lot of things that making steel is not our only business, but a whole lot of other things define our business like corporate social responsibility, being ethical, spending effort and money on sports, having a green town caring for society ....

Detailing here the syntactic symmetry (signalled in the jingle by the use of 'also') and the vs it expresses, seems superfluous in light of Muthuraman's elaborated verbalisation of this vs.

Tata Steel's vision statement declares its intention 'to seize the opportunities of tomorrow and create a future that will make us a EVA positive company. To continue to improve the quality of life of our employees and the communities we serve' (Fernando 2006: 71–72). This statement seems to unfold the vs, expressed in [~142], similarly signalled using 'also'.

We turn now to our last case, that of:

[~143]   Me too

'Me too' is a recently formed worldwide movement and viral hashtag fighting sexual harassment and sexual assault (particularly in the workplace), and encouraging victims to speak out. It thereby seeks to associate strength and courage with the victims and cowardliness with the assaulters.

As should be clear by now, an expression such as 'me too' encompasses successive vss. This enacts the silence bridging intimate and public dominance, victimisation, gender and sexual harassment in particular. Focusing here on what is articulated, signalling the varied and meaningful vss, we notice the first-person pronoun 'me', as well as 'too', which like 'also' is an adverb functioning syntactically as a (symmetric) coordinator. This seems to say it all: it fixes the 'me' as a speaking subject in a symmetry. This also suggests why the chosen pronoun is 'me' (the speaking subject contextualised as object) and not 'I'. Being the first-person pronoun of the speaking subject, the pragmatic instantiation of its particular referent – the addresser who speaks and stands out – alternates from one speaker-subject to another. Using symmetric function word vs, such which necessitates a coordinand, makes absence presence. The instantiation of the second coordinand using vs appears open and unlimited. Each such speaking subject is no longer alone, hidden and detached; s/he are not only part of the symmetry ('me', not an isolated 'I') but a significant contributor to the whole.

With this we conclude the presentation of the forms of syntactic vss involving coordination and proceed to syntactic vss involving subordinative asymmetric constructions.

3.2.4.6.2   Leaving a Conjunct of a Subordinative-Hypotactic Asymmetric Construction Uninstantiated

Unlike symmetric coordinations, the conjuncts of asymmetric syntactic constructions differ in their syntactic positioning and roles: the conjunct sharing its

3.2.4 Syntactic Verbal Silence

syntactic category with the dominating construction is the superordinate constituent, while the non-sharing conjunct is its subordinate.

We concentrate here on conjunct vs signalled by the expected 'if P (s_1) then Q (s_2)' syntactic form. Although we have not yet used the term 'conditional', it will probably be clear that this vs revolves around real and hypothetical conditionals.[86] These conditionals raise and face interesting syntactic (and semantic-pragmatic) challenges, which have direct consequences regarding vs (and vice versa).

The first issue to note is the nature of the relations between the two constituents. Following the operative definition of asymmetry (introduced earlier in this section), the syntactic role is determined by its apodosis ('then' or syndetic adverbial) superordinate clause, while its protasis – 'if' clause – is a subordinate and hypotactic-dependent constituent.

While the (deliberate non-technical) absence of a coordinand is a trivial indication of vs involving coordinands (see §3.2.4.6.1), there is no formal symmetry to count on when examining 'if P (s_1) then Q (s_2)' vss. In turn, relying on the logic-syntactic and linguistic-pragmatic dependency between its two parts constituting the conditional, the absence of one conjunct likewise points to what we term here for short 'conditional vs'.

Elder and Savva (2018) examine 'incomplete conditionals' and explain that conditionals adhere to the

criterion that *p* provides a restriction on *q*. [...] in the case of incomplete conditionals, the two-part conditional thought is only partially expressed: while the linguistic input of the 'if *p*' form signals what the structure of the complete thought will look like, it is necessary to fill in the consequent to obtain a full conditional proposition. (2018: 48)

Interestingly, both a protasis and an apodosis could be expressed using vs. Moreover, and as demonstrated earlier (see note 74), conditional function words could also be left uninstantiated. We shall detail the restrictions enabling the involvement of such vss. This necessitates that at least one conjunct will be instantiated, and that the 'if' function word will be retained (followed or not by its syntactic complementation, and followed or not by the 'then' clause). This is reflected in Evans's (2007: 367) term 'insubordination' to denote 'the conventionalized main clause use of what, on prima facie grounds, appear to be formally subordinate clauses'.

To focus on conditional vss, we must first weed out syntactic structures which begin with the conjunctor 'if' but are not conditionals (A). We then organise the presentation moving gradually from closed groups in which conditional vss is the unmarked option (B1) to open cases of free conditional vss (B2).

---

[86] For vs involving other subordinate complementations, see §3.2.4.4.

A   Forms which begin with 'if' but not being conditionals an apodosis is not expected

Examples [~144] and [~145] consist of what, at least formally, appears as a fragmented conditional conjunct:

[~144]   If push comes to shove.
[~145]   If pigs have wings.

[~144] and [~145] are idioms because their meanings are not equivalent to the sum of their lexical components, their non-literal meanings (see §3.2.5.2.2). [~144] means 'to take steps at this cardinal state' while [~145] means 'if the unreal circumstances become true'.

While in both examples substituting the concrete image implied by the lexical content words results in the emergence of an alternative – generalised – situation, the examples differ in regard to the 'if' function word. While it retains its function in the paraphrase of [~145], in [~144] this function dissolves along with the lexical content words, yielding a non-conditional meaning.

Examined literally, [~145] appears as a conditional in which the articulated protasis points to a neutral-real possibility; this is sufficient for its idiomatic meaning as an indirect (conative) illocutionary act (see §4.3) urging the addressee to act (see later in this section). Idioms, such as [~144], not being a conditional, an apodosis is not to be expected and so it is not left out.

The next group to weed out of our discussion consists of formulaic expressions (see §3.2.5.2.2), which unlike idioms such as [~144] their meaning being, essentially, the sum of the meanings of the lexemes composing the utterance, they too are non-conditionals. They are face-saving expressions beginning with 'if'. Formulaic parentheses share, in part, the metalinguistic features of discourse markers (see §4.3.1.1). Examples are numerous. Three such parentheses are:

[~146]   If I'm not mistaken.
[~147]   If you see what I mean.
[~148]   If life depends on this.

The three differ regarding their syntactic subject: the subject of [~146] is the first-person who coincides with the speaking self; the subject of [~147] is the second-person (refers to the addressee); and the subject of [~148] is the third-person. They also differ in reference: [~146] is cataphoric, [~147] is anaphoric, while [~148] could be either. Logically, each of the protases is contingent (true or false) but set in the face-saving context (see §4.7), and not that of prepositional calculus, for this speech-act to be successful a sincere production of the formulaic expression is sufficient. The convention of face-saving strategy,

3.2.4 Syntactic Verbal Silence

according to which the addresser does not wait for hes interlocutor's approval (confirming the truth value of what seems its protases), is a direct outcome of the fact that these formulaic expressions are non-conditionals. This plainly explains the absences of conditional apodoses. Note, however, that if the same words serve in a genuine conditional (the protasis is not a formulaic expressions and not parenthetic), then the subordinate conjunct syntactically and logically necessitates (expects) an apodosis (subordinator).

B1 Closed groups in which conditional vss is the unmarked option
Touching on face-saving or avoiding face-threatening (see §4.7) strategies advances our discussion to conditional 'if' forms in which not instantiating the apodosis is the default option.

Unlike formulaic expressions, polite directives, as for example

[~149] If we may proceed

are not lexicalised: they are generated and phrased by the addresser. Comparing [~149] with its interrogative paraphrases

[~149^a] May we proceed?

reveals its pragmatic role as indirect speech-acts, for which, as Elder and Savva (2018: 45) contend, 'p functions not as a condition for the truth of q, but as a condition for the felicity of q as performing a successful speech act'. Further examining polite directives (such as [~149] and its interrogative counterpart [~149^a]) shows that viewed syntactically as a structure involving a dyad exposes the absence of the expected apodosis of the seeming conditional (or the expected answer to what is phrased as a 'yes/no' question). But viewed in their role as indirect speech-acts, their expected matching conjunct is not a syntactic constituent but rather a deed (such as moving forward spatially or in discourse). This is not vs, primarily since no speech is expected (see §4.3).

In addition, such a combination of indirectness and the conditional or interrogative phrasing serves both parties. Phrased as a conditional, it saves the addresser's face when the indirect speech-act does not obtain the outcome s/he desired. From the addressee's perspective, its indirect phrasing as a conditional vs rather than a direct imperative leaves hem a non-threatening way out.

This brings us closer to another unmarked conditional vs. As much as the conditional and interrogative phrasing of polite directives downplays their direct role as commands, they still constitute demands imposed by the addresser on hes addressee. The true apodosis of the 'if' in the protasis is the addresser's feeling of gratitude and its expression (an additional speech-act):

[~149'] If we may proceed [I'll be most grateful]

In fact, taking this apodosis as shared by all polite directives suggests that although all indirect interrogatives should be included in this conditional scheme, it is left unarticulated as part of the face-saving strategy serving the addresser, toning down hes need (and possibly dependency) in the event that hes request is declined.

This takes us a step forward to a special set of illocutionary acts, that of promises and threats, which are likewise phrased conditionally and involve default conditional vs in a unique way.

[~150]   Class cancelled

uttered by a teacher could be interpreted referentially as a statement (which can turn out to be true or false, see §4.1). But it can equally be a commitment interpreted as a promise or a threat. In the event that despite stating [~150] class is resumed, one student may respond claiming 'but you promised' while another might exclaim 'hurray'.

Castelfranchi and Guerini (2007) examine the conditional phrasing shared by promises and threats. They point to a crucial asymmetry regarding the addresser's perception of the addressee's desired outcomes. The addresser articulates hes commitment to the fulfilment of the promise's apodosis perceiving that its outcome is in the interest of hes addressee while downplaying the counterposed threat. In a statement intended to intimidate, it is the commitment of the promise which will be toned down. In the context of our [~150] example,

[~150']   If you pass the exam {then} class will be cancelled [but if you don't {pass the exam}{then} class won't be cancelled]

[~150"]   If you fail {then} class will be cancelled [but if you don't {fail}{then} class won't be cancelled]

that is, the counter-option – a threat when uttering a promise ([~150']) or a promise when making a threat ([~150"]).

Promises and threats are motivated – and so differentiated – by the addresser's needs and the desires s/he attributes to the addressee. Because threats, unlike promises, lack the commitment to execute what is perceived not to be desired by the addressee, stating this non-committed apodosis may weaken the threat. There are motives for phrasing threats using conditional vs exclaiming only the protasis (without articulating its apodosis):

[~150^S]   If you fail S

[~151^S]   If you (dare) touch my car S. (Evans 2007: 393)

Expressing this through vs not only tones down the absence of commitment but also communicates determinism through brevity, focusing on the protasis and iconically enacting a conspiracy of silence.

3.2.4 Syntactic Verbal Silence

The last group of default conditional vs are irrealis wishes. Returning now to [~145] we see that it points to a hypothetic – rhetorical – apodosis. Being an idiom, the verbal absence of its (syntactically expected) apodosis is not here the choice of the addresser, and so [~145] does not adhere to our definition of vs (see §3.2). In this respect the conditional and the syntactic forms are complete.[87] But such wishes, expressed non-idiomatically, are indeed cases of default conditional vs.

The protasis of hypothetical (irrealis) wishes, and hypothetical conditionals in general, not only restrict the situations under which the apodosis obtains but also communicate

> the speaker's belief that the condition will not be fulfilled (for future conditions), is not fulfilled (for present conditions), or was not fulfilled (for past conditions), and hence the probable or certain falsity of the proposition expressed by the matrix clause. (Quirk et al. 1985: 1091)

As Quirk et al. stress, the phrasing of the hypothetical conditionals is sensitive to, and so depends on, sensitivity to the time of reference.

Here, as Quirk et al. outline, the grammatical distinction between real-factual wishes and hypothetical wishes comes into play. The tendency not to articulate the false apodosis of hypothetical wishes and conditionals may not come as a surprise. Like [~145], the absence of the otherwise syntactically expected apodosis is a default means to signal the absence of factual support. [~152] seems to be the textbook example of a hypothetical wish:

[~152]   If I were God ø S_1.

The zero stands here for the irrealis apodosis (on the crucial difference between zero and vs see §3.2.2.2). Recalling the claim made earlier in this section that a wish in itself communicates that its outcome is favoured and so desired by the addresser, it seems that in addition zero marking the irrealis counterfactual apodosis, the addresser producing a hypothetical wish uses conditional vs to communicate hes giving up the hope for fulfilment which goes with a wish (S_1, this is unique to hypothetical wishes).

The next example of a hypothetical wish comes from Virginia Woolf's novel *The Waves*. Says Neville, one of *The Waves*' protagonists:

[~153]   It seems as if the whole world were flowing and curving – on the earth the trees, in the sky the clouds. I look up, through the trees, into the sky. The match seems to be played up there. Faintly among the soft white clouds I hear the cry 'Run', I hear the cry 'How's that?' The clouds lose tufts of whiteness

---

[87] This follows the natural language intuition whereby 'if' conditional equals 'if and only if' (iff) in the logic prepositional calculus and not its material conditional (in which the entire argument is true if its apodosis is true, irrespective of the truth value of its protasis).

184   Verbal Silence: Forms

> as the breeze dishevels them. If that blue could stay for ever; if that hole could remain for ever; if this moment could stay for ever – (p. 22)

The story interweaves nature (the movement from dawn to sunset and the sea's surf) with the matching and contrasting unfolding of the biographies of the novel's six living and one dead (Percival) protagonists. Like the changing cosmic and aquatic states, every protagonist represents, within each state, hes distinct selfhood. Woolf allots Neville [~153] a clearly hypothetical set of wishes concerning stability and temporality. Neville – an intellectual – epitomises the huge gap between the limits of reality and the unlimited ability of speech and storytelling to conceive and express unrealistic events. This is also matched by his concern with the ongoing play between variability (fluidity) and invariability (solidity).

We now examine [~154ª], which Jespersen quotes as an example of protasis 'without any continuation [...] taken at more than its face value and becomes, to the speaker and to the hearer alike, a complete expression of wish':

[~154ª]   If she could only get a hearing!

His example comes from Sir Caine Hall's novel *The Christian*. Told by an extradiegetic narrator, the indirect wish should be phrased as:

[~154ª']   If I could only get a hearing!

Following is the entire passage:

[~154]   There was a scene in the performance in which the three girls sang together, and Glory crept out to the head of the stairs to listen. When she returned to the dressing-room her heart was bounding, and her eyes, as she saw them in the glass, seemed to be leaping out of her head. It was ridiculous! To think of all that fame, all that fuss about voices like those, about singing like that, while she – if she could only get a hearing!
>   But the cloud had chased the sunshine from her face in a moment, and she was murmuring again, 'O God, do not punish a vain, presumptuous creature!' (p. 183)

Unlike [~152] and [~153], in which the wishes were objectively unrealistic, in the context of [~154], the wish of a theatre worker preparing the costumes to realise her artistic talent on stage is only subjectively unrealistic. In the story it turns out to be factually possible, and is indeed attained. Here the zero sign and conditional vs combine to serve as a significant literary strategy leading us to believe, as Glory does, that this wish is hypothetical and she will never realise the apodosis. The vp (see §3.2.4.2):

[~154$^{b\text{-}\delta}$]   To think of all that fame, all that fuss about voices like those, about singing like that, while she ̶S̶

3.2.4 Syntactic Verbal Silence

likewise depicts her disbelieve that the option that she, like others, will perform on stage, is possible.

B2 This, finally, brings us to unmarked conditional vss: neutral factual conditionals generated by an addresser who chooses to express one of the conditional syntactic constituents, the subordinate protasis or the superordinate apodosis, using vs

Jespersen, describing aposiopesis in which the sentence is abbreviated (Jespersen's terminology) and its end left out, explains that:

> After saying 'if only something would happen' the speaker stops without making clear to himself how he would go on – whether 'I should be happy,' or 'it would be better,' or 'things would be tolerable,' or what ever he might think of. But even without any continuation the *if*-clause is taken at more than its face value and becomes, to the speaker and to the hearer alike, a complete expression of wish [...] (1949: vii, 118)

Jespersen himself seems to offer an alternative explanation to the 'speaker stops without making clear to himself how he would go on', namely that this is a complete expression of wish. In

[~155]   If only something would happen

the addresser fully expresses hes desire that the protasis come true. This is true of all genuine wishes concerning realistic future events in which the addresser focuses on the wish's protasis to communicate hes certainty that the truth of the protasis is sufficient for the fulfilment of any welcomed outcome. This is not a matter of vs but of relevance.

A common example of conditional vs expressing the protasis (its apodosis is stated as a syntactic wh-proform),

[~156]   But what if –

comes from the novel *Between the Lines*, authored jointly by Jodi Picoult and her teenage daughter Samantha van Leer. The daughter is cited, on the book cover, recalling the birth of the novel:

> I was daydreaming in French class (I know, I should have been focusing ...) when I started to wonder what happens when a book is closed. What's it like for the characters? Can they see us? What does it feel like for them, when we read? Through the rest of that period, I tossed around the idea of what would become our book.[88]

Read in this context, the conditional vs is the novel's anchor, depicting together with the novel's title its theme: the protagonists' and the book's silence, as a written-static text and particularly, as Samantha van Leer says, a

---

[88] www.jodipicoult.com/between-the-lines.html#more (accessed 21 October 2019). See also the 'about the book' rubric.

finite corpus that ends once the book is closed. To see that, here is the broader textual context:

[~156ᵃ] 'I could close the book and you could be gone, forever'.
Oliver takes a step forward. 'Try it.'
'Try what?'
'Closing the book.'
'But what if – ' I realize that I don't want him to disappear. I may not fully believe he's real; I may not understand why I can hear him speaking to me – but I sort of like it. (p. 61)

Unlike the zero marking the apodosis of hypothetical wishes, the theme of Between the Lines – truth and imagination as they emerge facing authentic and mediated speech and silence – reverses the vs. Here it is the protasis that is expressed using conditional vs:[89]

[~156ᵃ⁻ˢ] But what if $

As Delilah verbalises immediately following the vs of the protasis, her fear that what she experienced as reality will turn out to be unreal emerges in her reluctance to allow conditioning and to confront the protasis as a contingent statement that may also turn out to be false.

Our final three examples illustrate non-default conditional vs standing for the superordinate apodosis.

The first example is:

[~157]   Westron wynde when wyll thow blow
the smalle rayne downe can Rayne
Cryst yf my love were in my Armys
And I yn my bed Agayne.

The identity of the author of this touching poem is unknown, as is the date of its composition (estimates range from 1300 to 1600). As if this were not enough, there is much controversy among scholars regarding the genuine version of the poem (for an overview see Frey 1976, which will also inform our discussion here).

A crucial point concerning the interpretation of the poem (and the choices of versions and punctuations) is the relationship between the wind and the rain as they are experienced or foreseen by the speaker. Is the rain undesirable, in which case the lover wishes for the wind to draw the rain away? Or is it desired, in which case the wind is to induce the rainfall? As seen in the following quote, silence's centrality both in the poem's theme and as verbal

---

[89] As becomes apparent reading [~156ᵃ], 'but' continues here the previous sentence and so is not a case of coordinative vs (see §3.2.4.6.1).

3.2.4 Syntactic Verbal Silence

means of expression underlie, albeit implicitly, Frey's analysis of the poem. He says:

> The overall tone of the song, however, is hardly buoyant. Its music suits a serious, if not sad, theme, and the nostalgic ending presents an almost-despairing emphasis upon gaps between past comfort and present pain. [...] To contemplate the coming of the rain is to admit its unwanted absence; to imagine its surcease is to admit its unwanted presence. In all cases the rain is present in mind. The rain forever comes or goes, and, whichever state we seek, impermanence is the one constant. (1976: 262–263)

Referring specifically to the conditional, Frey contends that 'Taken as a whole, the song stirs both memory and desire, an awareness of love gained and gone. We cannot say that the speaker only hopes or only despairs. The poem's "yf" is both promising and forlorn, just as "Cryst" connotes both death and life' (1976: 263).

This in itself justifies expressing the apodosis using conditional vs. Love and yearning are both thematically and verbally absent and present in this love song: we cannot long for someone (or something) we have never experienced (see 'agayne' as the poem's closure). But analogical in a way to the stand towards the winds and the rain, the uninstantiated apodosis iconically voices reservations: is there a partner? Or is the strive for partnership experienced as one that cannot be attained (hypothetical)?

In light of the key role played by the conditional, the nature of the protasis must be examined. This, I hope, is the contribution our focus on vs can make to the understanding and enjoyment of this poem. The poem's closing line is phrased elliptically: 'and' as a symmetric coordinator (see §3.2.4.6.1) joins two protases (see [~157^a]). Syntax also points to the left-out verb in the final protasis. This can be technically resolved adding an AUX (see elliptic recovery, §3.2.4), which yields:

[~157$^{a'}$]   Cryst yf my love were in my Armys
                And [Є yf] I [Є were] yn my bed Agayne.

However, this seems too easy a way out, and moreover it is antithetical to the poem, overlooking its play between presence and absence. For intimacy to attain, the two must share bodily or spiritual proximity. That is, they must unite, yielding a 'we' (see Frey 1976: 268): 'yn my armys' and 'yn my bed' must be coreferential. This condition is expressed once we replace the elliptic solution with a non-technical conditional vs interpretation:

[~157$^{a''}$]   Cryst yf my love were in my Armys
                 And $\mathcal{S}$ [[yf my love] [and] I [were] yn my bed Agayne.

The uninstantiated apodosis is absence made present, positioning predicament, the cause for the lover's torment, as the poem's theme. What the conditional vs captures and expresses by its silence is the indeterminacy of past and future:

hope and remembrance; life (promise) and death (threat, see earlier in this section); hope and despair. It enables and depicts an indeterminacy that is both climatic and anti-climactic.

The second example comes from Elder and Savva's (2018: 49):

[~158] (Casual conversation about operations)
A: But a friend of mine pulled some cartilage in her leg when she was playing squash, and she had that done under local. And it was awful because they had to give her uh uh uh injection in her back. It was apparently really dangerous because *if they get the wrong point there* ...

Elder and Savva suggest that 'in the absence of complete syntactic structures, rather than applying these truth conditions to conditional sentences, we apply them at the level of thought' (2018: 48). They therefore replace the formal test with what they term a 'level of thought', an intuitive truth condition meaning. Applying this to [~158] (which they discuss at length), after ruling out the possibility of syntactic ellipsis, they first turn to pragmatic inferencing based on context and world knowledge. This, they claim, retrieves a consequent along the lines of 'there could be negative effects'. They then, successfully, determine the left-out apodosis (2018: 56, 'she could be left paralysed').

Despite turning to 'the level of thought', however, they do not consider why the addresser chose the 'incomplete' strategy to communicate a fully fledged conditional thought. This does not replace a syntactic (formal) solution, a pragmatic one or a graded continuum, all of which are needed and employed as forerunners. But once these absences are spotted and complied with by the addresser and addressee, an inspection of what is added by leaving out the apodosis ('target of the condition') must follow. Elder and Savva (2018) do not allow for this seeming 'incompleteness' to be a means of expression in itself (our conditional vs). Moreover, they are mistaken to claim concerning [~158] that 'recoverable consequent does not correspond to a unique syntactic structure [... and that] such examples would be excluded from syntactically oriented accounts' (2018: 56). The main reason for this is that the syntactic subordinate and superordinate structure is that which raises expectations, and so enables us to talk of incompleteness (see §3.2.4.6). At the level of thought, treating such apparent syntactic incompleteness as a vs forerunner likewise necessitates a syntactic account.

Elder and Savva (2018: 57) rightly show that the context in which [~158] is uttered rules out any proposition that is incompatible with the new information offered by the incomplete conditional itself, such as the proposition that the risk of the operation is low, or that 'it leaves open a relatively constrained set of consequents that communicate the message that negative effects could be caused if the surgery does not go well, e.g. that the speaker's friend could be left paralysed, or that some other serious harm could be caused'. However,

3.2.4 Syntactic Verbal Silence

from a vs perspective we must question their conclusion that 'because the contextual contribution in these cases is greater, the contribution of linguistic information can be kept minimal'. Note that [~158] and Elder and Savva's (2018) contribution are discussed here regarding conditional (syntactic) vs. Having spotted this forerunner, the questioning of the motivation for its use, that is, the meaning expressed through vs, brings us to vs functions (see §4.6.1.4). From this angle, examining [~158] in light of taboo, as a metalinguistic motivated vs, we show that

[~158$^{a\text{-}\delta}$]   [...] if they get the wrong point there *s̶*

like all taboo signifiers, is not a case demoting the referent – here the agent – but a metalinguistic forerunner announcing the silence of taboo signifier: 'she could die' (see §3.2.5.3).

The last illustration of apodosis vs seems now an irresistible, real-life example:

[~159]   If Brexit means Brexit

This originates and intertextually (see §3.2.5.2) corresponds to Theresa May's declaration that

[~159^a]   Brexit means Brexit.

May, a 'remain' supporter, decided to stand for office, hoping to make the most of the dramatic new state of affairs engendered in the United Kingdom by the referendum vote for Brexit. During her campaign in July 2016 to head the Conservative Party, throughout the subsequent election and in her speech after emerging as prime minister, May pronounced [~159^a], the words that have since become identified as her slogan:

[~159^b]   Brexit means Brexit and we are going to make a success of it.

As became increasingly apparent after the remarks were made, what seems a clear-cut tautology proved to be highly equivocal. This encouraged countless memes based on [~159] that offered ever more creative instantiations interpreting the vs in May's apodosis.

Employing conditional vs [~159] states that because the protasis 'if Brexit means Brexit' is undetermined (or even worse, a meaningless premises), then not only can the entire condition not be determined but also any instantiation of the vs apodosis will be contaminated by the indeterminacy of the protasis. This is illustrated when we examine such possible instantiations as:

[~159^c]   If 'Brexit means Brexit', what does Brexit mean?[90]

---

[90] *Readyforbrexit*, 4 April 2018, https://readyforbrexit.co.uk/if-brexit-means-brexit-what-does-brexit-mean/ (accessed 19 October 2019).

[~159ᵈ] If Brexit means Brexit, what does Ireland mean?[91]

These instantiations, particularly in the context of the debates regarding Brexit, highlight the power of vs to encompass uncertainty, on the one hand, but also to offer openings blocked once words take over.

These examples bring us to the end of our presentation of the various forms of syntactic vs.

3.2.5 Lexical Verbal Silence

Bloomfield (1933: 178) defines words as 'minimal free forms', adding that 'for the purpose of ordinary life, the word is the smallest unit of speech'. Referring to the lexicon and to words, he adds:

> [A] complete description of a language will list every form whose function is not determined either by structure or by marker; it will include, accordingly, a *lexicon*, or list of morphemes, which indicates the form-class of each morpheme, as well as lists of all complex forms whose function is in any way irregular. (1933: 269)

Chomsky (1972: 39) describes the lexicon of a language as an inventory of the lexical entries specifying for each item 'just those properties that are idiosyncratic, that are not determined by linguistic rules'.

Lexical vs forerunners are lexical entries – mostly words – pointing to vs. Silence as a means of expression never occurs in isolation – it is always surrounded by the speech which grounds it. This feature, which distinguishes vs from stillness (see §2.1), uses that speech as its forerunner. Having discussed formal-grammatical forerunners, we now focus on lexical forerunners.

Unlike the forms described in §3.2.1 through §3.2.4, words in general, and words as vs forerunners in particular, are not determined by grammar and grammatical rules. For this reason they are learned and used idiosyncratically. The matter of lexical vs becomes even more tricky when they themselves denote silence. Lexical vs is confined to cases in which lexical items, mostly words belonging to the semantic fields of speech and silence, point not to themselves but to what the addresser chooses to leave out as a means of expression and to hes signalling this choice.

A key means of distinguishing between the use of lexemes to denote silence and their use to signal lexical vs is, of course, context.

---

[91] *Ireland Times*, 26 May 2018. www.irishtimes.com/opinion/if-brexit-means-brexit-what-does-ireland-mean-1.3508275?mode=sample&auth-failed=1&pw-origin=https%3A%2F%2Fwww.irishtimes.com%2Fopinion%2Fif-brexit-means-brexit-what-does-ireland-mean-1.3508275 (accessed 19 October 2019).

3.2.5 Lexical Verbal Silence

Rimmon-Kenan (2002: 88) contends that there is always a teller in a tale. She defines the narrator as the 'agent which at the very least narrates or engages in some activity serving the needs of narration'. Accordingly, she refines the classification of voices: instead of the traditional dichotomies between a present and an absent narrator, and between a narrator who is also a character in the story (a homodiegetic narrator) and one who is not (a heterodiegetic narrator), she proposes to distinguish forms and degrees concerning the perceptibility of the narrator in the text. She stresses that such criteria may result in non-exclusive categories and so allow for a mixture of the different types (2002: 94–96).

A narrator who is, as it were, superior to the story s/he narrates is an 'extradiegetic' narrator. A narrator may be a diegetic character in the first narrative told by the extradiegetic narrator, in which case s/he is a second degree, or 'intradiegetic' narrator, and so forth. Both narrators can be either heterodiegetic or homodiegetic characters. But the most important eminence Rimmon-Kenan attributes (after Ewen 1974: 144–146) to the extradiegetic-heterodiegetic narrators is their

> familiarity, in principle, with the characters' innermost thoughts and feelings; knowledge of past, present and future; presence in locations where characters are supposed to be unaccompanied (e.g. on a lonely stroll or during a love-scene in a locked room); and knowledge of what happens in several places at the same time. (Rimmon-Kenan 2002: 95)

These are materials which the author puts, so to speak, in the narrator's mouth, and which, as Rimmon-Kenan rightly contends, make the covert narrator part of the story. Such a narrator contributes hes insights regarding the entire story and its details, and this role belongs at the thematic level.

Our study of vs lexical forerunners highlights the need to separate the actions which Rimmon-Kenan attributes to such extradiegetic-heterodiegetic narrators into two distinct categories. The first includes the narrator's role in presenting and describing the characters, their histories and whereabouts, as well as expressing the narrator's attitude towards the characters and the story (such as opinions and judgements). The second category consists of the narrator's role in voicing the characters' innermost thoughts and feelings – often ones of which even the character hemself is unaware. While in the first category the extradiegetic-heterodiegetic narrator plays an active role, contributing hes perspective to the story, the second category typifies the extradiegetic-heterodiegetic narrator as a textual tool, in which s/he functions as a neutral mediator who conveys things that the characters do not voice. These may be phrased as the character's direct or indirect speech, or as thoughts and feeling which the character did not allow hemself to express or even experience, or which the character felt but refrained from sharing. These do not belong to the narrator but instead they are part of the characters' vss. As such, they originate in the characters' verbal choices and the textual sequences they produce. It is hardly surprising that, more often than not, it is the extradiegetic-heterodiegetic narrator's duty to indicate the coming of such lexical vss. This function may also be played by a homodiegetic narrator (such as first-person 'I' or 'said to him/herself', or in a play Hamlet's 'the rest is silence', [~163]).

The first group to discuss consists of speech and silence lexical entries pointing to an impending vs (§3.2.5.1). Next come lexical vss involving intertextuality (§3.2.5.2). From there we proceed to taboo words (§3.2.5.3); personal names involving lexical vs (§3.2.5.4); and, lastly, part–whole vss (§3.2.5.5).

3.2.5.1 Speech and Silence Lexical Entries Signalling Verbal Silences
Naturally, not every token of nominal, verb or adjectival lexemes belonging in the semantic fields of speech and silence is a vs forerunner. Such lexical entries signal vs only when the setting is that of a specific verbal interaction in which speech is expected, and the speech and silence semantic field articulated lexeme does not point to itself but rather to the expected speech which the addresser left out as a deliberate means of expression.

The passage from Huxley's *Eyeless in Gaza* (Table 3.5) describes the walk and interaction between Brian (who has a stammer) with Joan. Brian loves Joan, but seeking proof of her love to him stifles his desire to kiss her. Matching intersubjective silences (including vss) against the stillness and silences of nature, Huxley highlights here their rich modes and their external and internal power. [~160] serves, then, to intuitively embody the above provisions (emphases added here to signal silence-words but not necessarily vs). Lexical forerunners dealt with in the specific sections are indicated here by bracketed numbers.

3.2.5.1.1 Words of Silence
The first group of lexical vs forerunners consists of lexical items denoting silence, confined here to the absence of expected speech. [~160^e] is the extradiegetic-heterodiegetic narrator's verbalisation of the contents of 'secret silence of their unexpressed emotions' ([~160^d]): Joan's unexpressed complaints at being denied a hug and body contact with Brian, an emotion which her sense of loyalty made her leave out; and Brian's unexpressed sense of pity, aroused in the absence of Joan's complaint, as well as his unexpressed regret due to desires he did not wish to feel (see end of §3.2.5.1.4).

3.2.5 Lexical Verbal Silence

Table 3.5. Silences from Huxley's *Eyeless in Gaza* (pp. 176–177)

[~160]	*Eyeless in Gaza* – text	Silences
[~160ª]	The sky was still overcast, and beneath the low ceiling of grey cloud the air was soft and as though limp with fatigue, as though weary with the burden of too much summer. In the woods, into which they turned from the high-road, the *stillness* was oppressive,	*Stillness* of nature (see §2.1): while external to interaction, here it coalesces with the experiencer's mood.
[~160ᵇ]	like the intentional *silence* of sentient beings, pregnant with *unavowed* thoughts and hidden feelings.	See §3.2.5.1.4 Negating *verba dicendi*
[~160ᶜ]	An invisible tree-creeper started to sing; but it was as if the clear bright sound were coming from some other time and place.	Even when there is sound, it is distanced and eradicated as such.
[~160ᵈ]	They walked on hand in hand; and between them was the *silence* of the wood and at the same time the deeper, denser, more secret *silence* of their own *unexpressed* emotions.	Stillness (§2.1) See below and see §3.2.5.1.4 Negating *verba dicendi*
[~160ᵉ]	The *silence* of the complaints she was *too loyal to utter* and the pity that, unless she complained, it would, he felt, be insulting for him to *put into words*; her longing for the comfort of his arms and those desires he did not wish to feel.	See below and see §3.2.5.1.4 Negating *verba dicendi*
[~160ᶠ]	Their path led them between great coverts of rhododendrons, and suddenly they were in a narrow cleft, hemmed in by high walls of the impenetrable, black-green foliage. It was a *solitude within a solitude*, the image of their own *private silence* visibly hollowed out of the greater *stillness* of the wood.	Solitude *Private silence* (see phatic §4.4) Stillness (§2.1)
[~160ᵍ]	'Almost f-frightening,' he *whispered*, as they stood there listening – listening (for there was *nothing else for them to hear*) to	Whisper (§3.2.5.1.3 paralanguage) Nothing else to hear
[~160ʰ]	their own heart-beats and each other's breathing and all the *words that hung unspoken* between them.	Words hung unspoken §3.2.5.1.4.

Table 3.5. *(cont.)*

[~160^i]	All at once, she could bear it no longer, 'When I think of what it'll be like at home...' The complaint had *uttered itself*, against her will. 'Oh, I wish you weren't going, Brian!'	The complaint *uttered itself*, against her will (see end of §3.2.5.1.5).
[~160^j]	Brian looked at her and, at the sight of those trembling lips, those eyes bright with tears, he felt himself as it were disintegrated by tenderness and pity. *Stammering* her name, he put his arm about her.	Stammering (symptom §2.2.1)
[~160^k]	Joan stood for a little while quite still, her head bent, her forehead resting on his shoulder. The touch of her hair was electric against his lips, he breathed its perfume. All at once, as though waking from sleep, she stirred into motion and, drawing a little away from him, looked up into his face. Her regard had a desperate, almost inhuman fixity.	Still (§2.1)
[~160^l]	'Darling,' he *whispered*.	*whisper* (§3.2.5.1.3 paralanguage)
[~160^m]	Joan's *only answer* was to shake her head.	Only answer (§3.2.5.1.7) and nonverbal (§2.2.2) and (silence as answer §4.3.3.2.1)
[~160^n]	But why? What was she denying, what implication of his endearment was she saying no to? 'But J-joan ...?' There was a note of anxiety in his voice.	
[~160°]	Still she *did not answer*; only looked at him and once more slowly shook her head.	*did not answer*, nonverbal (§2.2.2) (see note 94)
[~160^p]	How many negations were *expressed in that single movement*!	Nonverbal (§2.2.2), see note 94, its contents is detailed in [~160^q]
[~160^q]	The *refusal to complain*; the denial for herself of the possibility of happiness; the sad insistence that all her love and all his availed nothing against the pain of absence; the resolution not to exploit his pity, not to elicit, however much she longed for it, another, a more passionate avowal	Refusal to complain, see [~160^e] Denial, avowal, see [~160^b]

3.2.5 Lexical Verbal Silence

The next example comes from the patient's remark in a psychotherapeutic session:

[~161]   It is as if I come here and talk about my leg cramps but keep silent about a surgical glove sewn in my stomach.

The therapist explains that the patient's words 'keep silent' helped him 'speak of her fear that there was something very disturbing inside her which she felt should not be there and might require rather careful surgery. In the meantime, she would prefer to talk about something else' (Budden and Horne 2017: 443). The psychotherapist manifests here his use of 'keep silent' as a forerunner pointing to the content which the patient expressed using vs and which he verbalised as a narrator-psychotherapist.

A passage from 'The Death of Stalin' by Leonardo Sciascia (p. 57) will serve to illustrate vs communicated ironically. The English translation preserves the lexical forerunner 'keep quiet' (*'tacere'*) in the original:

[~162[Italian-T]]   A friend let him have Dimitrov's speech, the one which said that the USSR would hold back and observe the two Imperialist blocks; which speech Calogero held to be true up to a certain point. According to him, what Dimitrov was keeping quiet about, and could not do anything but keep quiet about, was the fact that Russia was waiting for the moment when the German forces, even if victorious, were at their most exhausted, and then she would attack. He used to imagine the secret preparations [...]

The narrator begins by replicating the wording of Dimitrov's speech, but he voices, using Calegro as an intradiegetic-homodiegetic narrator the content about which Dimitrov remained silent. While in the unsaid (§2.2.3.1) the content not articulated by the speaker is left out, in the above cases such content is voiced using the narrator's lexical vs.

We close the presentation of this category with dying Hamlet's last words:

[~163]   HAMLET Oh, I die, Horatio –
  The potent poison quite o'ercrows my spirit.
  I cannot live to hear the news from England,
  But I do prophesy th'election lights
  On Fortinbras – he has my dying voice.
  So tell him, with th'occurrents more and less
  Which have solicited – the rest is silence.
  [He dies.]
HORATIO Now cracks a noble heart. Good night, sweet prince,
  And flights of angels sing thee to thy rest.
  [Drums sound within.]
  Why does the drum come hither? (Shakespeare, *Hamlet*, Q2 V.
ii.330–338, *Norton³*, p. 1282)

We here follow the Q2 version. Q2's phrasing and staging of the dying Hamlet's dictum '[. . .] The rest is silence' includes two silences, not one: the lexical vs forerunner ('silence') denoting the object silence, but not in itself silence, heralds the coming silence: silence as a sound-vehicle signifier: 'the rest is silence:"   "'. Focusing now on that silence as a sound-vehicle (and not on the word 'silence'), its semiotic status depends on the identification of its object and its interpretation in that specific discursive context. As the immediate narrow context reveals, and as supported and elaborated by its internal co-text (as well as external sources and theories), the narrow – immediate – object denoted here by silence is the silence of the dead. Silence as a signifier denotes here the absolute absence of sounds. The living human object changes on hes death into a still inanimate object (see §2.1). The dead person loses the capacity to speak. One of the distinctive characteristics of humankind is demolished upon death. This then is the first, straightforward, interpretation of the dying Hamlet's last words. Being a sound-vehicle directly imitating the stillness and muteness of the dead, this silence is a vs onomatopoeic image of the dead (see §3.2.1). The play's versions, such as the Folio version phrase this verse: 'The rest is silence. *Oh, oh, oh, oh'*. *Norton* comments that 'These exclamations, which appear in F but not in Q2, might be suggestive stage directions for death throes, rather than descriptive cries' (see *Norton³*, p. 1282 note 3). This is most enlightening, compared with versions such as Q2 – as it leads prima facie to the following readings – all involving silence as onomatopoeia:

[~163ª] The rest is silence Oh, oh, oh, oh. (i.e. The rest is silence: 'Oh, oh, oh, oh,' dying throe);

[~163ᵇ] The rest is silence Oh, oh, oh, oh,   . (i.e. The rest is silence: 'Oh, oh, oh, oh,' death throe – followed by onomatopoeic silence);

[~163ᶜ] The rest is silence   ., (i.e. The rest is silence: onomatopoeic silence).

The figure of Hamlet, as well as Hamlet's last words, have drawn many interpretations, some confined to the immediate text and play and some exceeding it. The best known is the significant tie-in between Oedipus Rex and Hamlet by Freud and thereafter (e.g. Oremland 1983). Referring to Hamlet, Freud (1900: 265) says: 'I have here translated into conscious terms what was bound to remain unconscious in Hamlet's mind'. Under this paradigm, Shakespeare's ingenious talent and understanding of the human mind makes onomatopoeic silence a vs residue expressing the inevitable struggle between unconscious, conscience and morals (the super-ego). On his impending death, Hamlet faces not merely (conscious) guilt about his stabbing Claudius with the poisoned sword in order to avenge Claudius's becoming King of Denmark through the sins of murder (his brother, Prince Hamlet's father) and incest (taking Prince Hamlet's mother as a wife), but more significantly the unconscious and universal guilt complex of a son who wishes to commit exactly the same two deeds, and against the same individuals: his parents. This further promotes many possible interpretations of the coming silence, but these come second and third adding to the first silence, that is, the onomatopoeic image of the dead.[92]

3.2.5.1.2 Concealing Words

One of the prominent roles attributed to silence in olden times as the negation of speech (and interaction) is its function as a fence to wisdom. The thesis underlying this role is outlined in Proverbs (17:28):

[~164] Even a fool, when he holdeth his peace, is counted wise: and he that shutteth his lips is esteemed a man of understanding.

In *The Merchant of Venice* (I.i.95–99, *Norton³*, p. 283), Shakespeare allots the announcement of this truism to Graziano, Antonio's loquacious friend:

[~165] GRAZIANO O my Antonio, I do know of these
That therefore only are reputed wise
For saying nothing, when I am very sure
If they should speak would almost damn those ears
Which, hearing them, would call their brothers fools.

This is not silence as a means of expression but rather silence masking means of expression – silence concealing information, and particularly concealing the truth.

In our context of lexical forerunners pointing to vs, concealing words function (like words of silence in §3.2.5.1.1) as metatextual means used by the addresser to inform on what is considered a secret. This must not be mistaken with divulging the secret by sharing it. The speaker or narrator using vs does not reveal the secret; it remains a secret.

A most impressive example comes from Viktor Frankl's constitutive monograph *Man's Search for Meaning*, in which he interweaves his Holocaust diary with his professional observations:

---

[92] We cannot extend our discussion here to the many interpretations of that silence. Suffice it to point out one line of interpretations that bears on Freud's view of healthy mourning-work as opposed to melancholia (1917). Talking of the elegy, Ogden (2001: 152) says that it 'must capture in itself not the voice that has been lost, but the voice brought to life in the experiencing of that loss – a voice enlivened by the experience of mourning. The new voice cannot replace the old ones and does not attempt to do so; no voice, no person, no aspect of one's life can replace another' (see also Amir 2008). This interpretation is supported by Horatio's immediate text [~163] ensuring continuation, thus enabling Hamlet's eternal rest, as he goes silent and Fortinbras assumes the voice of the dying Hamlet (see also Oremland 1983: 508, and see §3.2.5.4.1 Amir (2008) on the actual and possible dimensions).

[~166^(German-T)] That brought thoughts of my own wife to mind. And as we stumbled on for miles, slipping on icy spots, supporting each other time and again, dragging one another up and onward, nothing was said, but we both knew: each of us was thinking of his wife [...]
Then I grasped the meaning of the greatest secret that human poetry and human thought and belief have to impart: the salvation of man is through love and in love. (pp. 56–57)

As is apparent from Frankl's words, he did not divulge the secret. What he communicates is the secret's significance: that which may be revealed once the secret is disclosed. What makes this, in this context, a case of vs is that by narrating this stream of thoughts, Frankl verbalises the secret's contents (for additional lexical forerunners entailing concealment, such as 'don't tell your friends about', see [~176] §3.2.5.1.4).

3.2.5.1.3 Words Designating Paralanguage as Vs Forerunners

Paralinguistic signals in general, and pauses in particular (see Figure 2.1), are not means of expression and so are to be distinguished from vss. But when words pointing to paralanguage, both literally and figuratively, are followed by content (such as content informed by a narrator), this may constitute a lexical forerunner pointing to vs. We shall offer some examples here, beginning with physical vocal barriers repressing speech and then presenting some vocal qualifiers lessening speech.

Excerpt [~167] comes from a conversation between Francis (the father of Brit), and his son-in-law (Brit's husband Turk; emphases in the original):

[~167] [...] Francis replies, and then he looks at me shrewdly. 'Everything all right?' he asks, and by *everything* he means *Brit*. When I shrug, he purses his lips. 'You know, when Brit's mama left, I didn't understand why I was still here. Thought about checking out, if you know what I mean. I was taking care of my six-month-old, and I still couldn't find the will to stick around. And then one day, I just *got* it; the reason we lose people we care about is so we're more grateful for the ones we still have [...]. (Picoult, *Small*, p. 261)

Schefer and Karlins (2015: 134) explain the connections between physiological gestures and the speakers' struggle to verbalise their message:

Lip purse display is a slight, almost imperceptible, puckering or rounding of the lips. This gesture signals dissension or disagreement. The more pronounced the lip purse, the more intense is the dissension or disagreement. Pursed lips mean the person has formed a thought in their mind that is in opposition to what is being said or done.

At first sight, since Francis did share his thoughts with Turk, this does not seem to be a case of vs. But the author plays on Turk's double role as the homodiegetic narrator (reporting also metonymically on Francis pursing his

3.2.5 Lexical Verbal Silence

lips) and as Francis's interlocutor, and Francis's thoughts in pursed lips is enclosed to signal their status as the contents of vs.

'Purse lips', like 'bit my tongue', may be used literally, denoting a paralinguistic obstacle preventing the production of speech; for example:

[~168] Nay, hear me speak, Mosbie, a word or two; I'll bite my tongue if it speak bitterly. (*Arden of Faversham*, see MacDonald 2014: 31)

But when the physical description moves away from its literal physical denotation and is used metonymically to denote the particular mental state with which it is associated, it constitutes an idiom; and when this idiom points to contents not articulated, it is a vs forerunner (see 'But more than he her poor tongue could not speak' [~225] in §3.2.5.4.2). This is particularly salient concerning paralinguistic forerunners involving physical vocal barriers repressing speech.

To show this we synoptically report Davis's (1991) and Lacan's (as cited by Davis) contributions to Freud's self-analysis of his 'Irma' dream. [~169] replicates Freud's report of the initial part of his dream:

[~169] A large hall – numerous guests, whom we were receiving. – Among them was Irma. I at once took her on one side, as though to answer her letter and to reproach her for not having accepted my 'solution' yet. I said to her: 'If you still get pains, it's really only your fault.' She replied: 'If you only knew what pains I've got now in my throat and stomach and abdomen – it's choking me' – I was alarmed and looked at her. She looked pale and puffy. I thought to myself that after all I must be missing some organic trouble. (Davis 1991: 26)

Davis comments on Freud's auto-interpretation, saying:

In Freud's reading of his own dream, for example, there is an interpretive misrecognition and blindness, like something stuck in the throat, important for understanding the function of interpretive schemes – namely, Freud's repression of the body and of the material ('bodily') nature of the text. (1991: 30)

As for Lacan, Davis explains that:

In Lacan's version the voice of Irma's throat says to Freud, [...] 'You must find your own place in language amid all that is foreign and "other" to you.' [...] In this way, Lacan reads Freud's dream as a theatricalization of psychoanalysis's encounter with language and its suppression of the body – as both an acknowledgment and an evasion of limits. (1991: 29)

Focusing here on idioms as paralinguistic vs forerunners (and not on Davis's critique of the notion of subjectivity, particularly in the cultural context), we notice the shift of 'lump in one's throat' from a literal description of a bodily condition (in which a throat could be replaced with any other body organ) to an idiomatic sense describing, and at times pointing to, an extreme emotional state, resulting in the suppression of speech (as if stuck in the throat while waiting to be articulated). Davis's phrasing, 'like something stuck in the throat', serves as a forerunner, pointing to the vs contents: the body and the material ('bodily') nature of the text.

We now proceed to forerunners involving vocal qualifiers lessening speech. The examples quoted in [~170] also come from *Small Great Things* (pp. 375–376). The setting is the cross-examination of Ruth's supervisor (Marie), who on Turk's demand orders Ruth, an African-American nurse in the delivery ward, not to attend to his son. This takes place in the court hearing of Turk suing Ruth for being responsible for the death of his infant son:

[~170] [...] What if,' Kennedy says, [...] and the only nurse remaining on the floor was in fact African American?'
Marie's mouth opens and closes, but no sound emerges.
'I'm sorry, Ms Malone – I didn't quite get that.'
'David Bauer was not left unsupervised at any point,' she insists. 'Ruth was there,'
[...]
'Did you advise Ruth that in certain circumstances her Nightingale pledge as a nurse should supersede what you'd ordered?'
'No.' Marie murmurs.

Two lexical forerunners involving paralanguage serve here to point to lexical vs: 'mouth opens and closes, but no sound emerges' and 'murmurs'. While in [~167] the vs forerunner bears on the image of the vocal track's blockage, [~170] seems half way between [~167] and murmuring, in which the vs is pointed to using a speech-accompanying feature: not full speech but a murmur.

The two forerunners differ, however. While the latter is primarily a paralinguistic description of a speaking subject who is not wholehearted about her own words, and only secondarily a narrative strategy, an additional trait appears in the former: that of the defendant (Kennedy) forcing the supervisor to testify.

Picoult reiterates for her readers the vs forerunners and the contents of these silences, now from Ruth's perspective, playing the double narrative role: the homodiegetic narrator reporting the cross-examination of her supervisor.

It is important to note that it is by no means the case that whenever the narrator mentions a paralinguistic quality involving the speaker, this constitutes a lexical vs forerunner. As seen, whispered speech can involuntarily communicate emotions (such as fear [~160^g]) or serve as an intentional devise (such as with endearment, soothing and expressing tenderness, [~160^l]). Only when such qualities are used to point to what is not said, or not fully shared, is a vs flag raised.

3.2.5.1.4 Negating *Verba Dicendi* and Preterition

A message can inform on the production or completion of an action or, using negation, it can inform on the failure to perform an otherwise expected action. This is true regarding any action. The twofold peculiarity of speech – being both a verbal action and metalinguistically (see §4.6) serving as the contents of that action – may result in a tricky outcome of the negation of *verba dicendi*. When an addresser seeks to inform hes addressee that a verbal action was not taken, this is not a case pointing to vs (see, e.g., 'unavowed thoughts and hidden feelings' [~160^b]; 'words that hung unspoken' [~160^h]; and [~160^q] 'refusal to complain'). But when, despite the negation, the addresser phrases the contents, the negation of the *verba dicendi* is a lexical forerunner pointing to vs.

The first example, which dates back to the sixteenth century (William Creitchton's letter to Sir Francis Walsingham, 20 February 1585, see Holinshed et al. 1808: 572), illustrates a straightforward lexical vs forerunner: 'I dare not say' pointing indeed to its contents:

[~171]   RIGHT honorable sir, when your honor demanded me if maister Parrie did aske me, if it were leason to kill the queene; indeed and varitie, then I had no remembrance at all thereof. But since, thinking on the matter, I haue called to mind the whole fashion of his dealing with me, and some of his arguments: for he dealt verie craftilie with me, I dare not say maliciouslie.

Examples [~172] and [~173] illustrate the role of the extradiegetic-heterodiegetic narrator in voicing the characters' innermost feelings – often ones that the character hemself does not openly admit. The author of Lou Andreas-Salomé's biography, describes Salomé's mother reluctance at having a baby girl and not a sixth son, he depicts the stance of Salomé's father ('the general'):

[~172]   The General, on the other hand, had wanted a daughter for a long time, but being a discreet and polite man, he had never voiced such hopes openly, and perhaps by now he had given them up. (Peters 1962: 26)

Another illustration comes from Susan Lewis's novel *Never Say Goodbye* (pp. 222–223). In the following exchange, Nick, Bel's brother-in-law and the husband of her late sister Talia, informs Bel that he and Kristina (his new wife) plan to leave for Sidney:

[~173]   [...] we have to give Kristina a chance,' he'd cut in raggedly, 'because she is their mother now, Bel.'
Not you. He hadn't said those words, he'd never have been so cruel, but they'd been there anyway, stark and uncompromising in their truth.
'Let's not discuss it any more tonight,' he'd said. 'I can see you're upset, and I think it would be good for you to have some time to think it over before we speak again.'

Nick is close to Bel and appreciates her support and love for his children. Cutting off the children, who were comforted by their aunt (Bel) while they were undergoing the loss of their mother, is an extremely difficult step for Nick to take. The narrator not only points to the vs through the painful words 'not you' (note that these words are not reported speech) but also verbalises the difficulty speaking them out.

Because communication may be transmitted in writing, that is, not orally (or manually), negated *verba dicendi* in their role as lexical vs forerunners may also denote writing. Such is, for example, Doris Lessing's

[~174]   An Unposted Love Letter

While this description appears only as the short story's title, it is a vs forerunner pointing to the contents of that letter, which once replicated carries and so constructs the story's narrative. As shown for the extradiegetic-heterodiegetic narrator, here it is the love letter not being posted which allows the vs expression and thereby the articulation of what the homodiegetic speaker would have not otherwise shared with her former lover. 'No use telling you' is an additional lexical vs forerunner, the contents of which follow within this unposted letter:

[~175]   After we had all separated, and I had watched you drive off with your wife, I came home and ... no, it would be no use telling you, after all. (Or anyone, except, perhaps, my colleague and rival Irma Painter!) But what if I said to you – but no, there are certain disciplines which no one can understand but those who use them. [...] So I will translate into your language, [...] and I'll tell you how when I came home after meeting you my whole body was wrenched with anguish, [...] for, meeting you, it was being reminded again what it would be like to be with a man [...]. (p. 39)

We now return to [~160^e], discussed in §3.2.5.1.1. Although 'too loyal to utter' and 'insulting for him to put into words' lack a formal negation, their positive phrasing expresses the negation of a speech action. The signalling of this negation constitutes a lexical vs forerunners.

A special case negating *verba dicendi* is preterition: a rhetorical 'figure in which attention is drawn to something by professing to omit it' (OED: Preterition, N). Such was Jerome K. Jerome's

[~55^s]   Three Men in a Boat (S_1 To Say Nothing of S_2 the Dog).

'S_1 to say nothing of' can refer forward, stating that no further information will be provided. But when interpreted backwards, it is a means of vs, metalinguistically highlighting the mention of the dog: by this very phrasing something has been said of the dog (see §3.2.3.1.1).

This seems the most regular lexical vs strategy used by narrators, copywriters and speakers verbalising the contents of their own vs.

3.2.5 Lexical Verbal Silence

A common example is a commercial, such as:

[~176]   Don't tell your friends about our half-price special offer.

Literally, the advertiser urges the addressee to keep a secret. In the context of a commercial (see §4.4.3.3.1), however, the addresser not only points to the contents of the secret and verbalises its contents but connotatively encourages the addressee to spread the message.

This vs strategy is also frequently used as a diplomatic conduct, here with a humorous wink:

[~177]   Boris Yeltsin: '*Let's not talk about* communism. Communism was just an idea, just pie in the sky.'[93]

And see in detail (Peraldo 2016) on Daniel Defoe's significant use of the preterition, as a rhetorical and poetic strategy. Such is

[~178]   I shall not concern the Union in this discourse

which Defoe prefaced to Caledonia. Caledonia is not only a poem he wrote to advocate the union treaty between England and Scotland (1706), but more so, Defoe wrote it under his cover as a poet concealing his non-poetic position as Harley's (England's secretary of state) spy, a service he assumed in return to being released from prison (see also [~184] §3.2.5.1.7).

3.2.5.1.5 Lexical Entries Indicating the Relinquishing of the Intention to Communicate Contents

The text may inform on the addresser relinquishing hes intention to communicate specific contents. But when the focus is not the relinquishing as such, but the contents s/he initially wishes to be shared, this is a lexical forerunner pointing to vs. The most common forerunner is some variation of negated 'meant to say'.

Unlike §3.2.5.1.4, here it is not only the negation of *verba dicendi* that indicates vs but also the withdrawal from performing such a verbal action. This is illustrated in [~179], taken from Edith Wharton's novel *The Age of Innocence*:

[~179]   She paused for a long interval; so long that, not wishing to keep his eyes on her shaded face, he had time to imprint on his mind the exact shape of her other hand, the one on her knee, and every detail of the three rings on her fourth and fifth fingers; among which, he noticed, a wedding ring did not appear.

---

[93] On a visit to the USA (13 September 1989). *The Guardian, News>Europe>Russia*. www.theguardian.com/world/2007/apr/23/russia2 (accessed 12 November 2019).

'What harm could such accusations, even if he made them publicly, do me here?'

It was on his lips to exclaim: 'My poor child – far more harm than anywhere else!' Instead, he answered, in a voice that sounded in his ears like Mr. Letterblair's: 'New York society is a very small world compared with the one you've lived in. And it's ruled, in spite of appearances, by a few people with – well, rather old-fashioned ideas' (p. 78).

Taking on the role of the extradiegetic narrator, the difference between the intended but withdrawn message and the one communicated is signalled by prefacing the forerunner 'was on his lips to exclaim' to the content expressed using vs.

Before concluding this category, a comment must be made regarding 'the complaint had uttered itself, against her will' (see [~160^i]). Because vs comes into play only once the addresser chooses to express content by not verbalising it, this, as the text states, is not the case in [~160^i]. But shifting our perspective to that of Huxley, the author's literary choice, as it were, to spare the diegetic speaker (Joan) the complaint but instead to point to this message's silent mode of articulation and to name its contents (a complaint) in itself constitutes a case of vs, particularly since it is followed by the vs verbalisation in [~160^e].

3.2.5.1.6 General Words

The range of correspondence between the world and the signifiers offered in the lexicon is huge. The choice of a lexeme depends on many parameters, such as the speaker's active lexicon, hes neurological condition (chronic and sporadic) and linguistic circumstances. Clearly, a speaker may refer to corn using 'food' when the focus of utterance is food (such as having eaten) rather than its specifics (see §3.2.4.4.4). Moreover, as language philosophers contend and lay speakers experience daily, any lexeme is doomed to generalise. But, when within the communicative interaction, the expected lexeme is a specific rather than general one, yet the addresser chooses a more general lexeme, this constitutes a forerunner pointing to lexical vs.

The most general mode of reference is the hypernym 'thing', which covers all concrete, abstract, real and imaginative substantives (see §3.2.4.4.2 [+N]). The phrasing chosen ([~180]) by the father of a newborn suffering a fatal facial deformity (Picoult, *Small*, p. 12, see [~170]) illustrates such vs:

[~180] I turned to the father. 'Would you like to hold your son?'
He looked like he was about to be sick. 'I can't,' he muttered and bolted from the room.
[...]
I cornered the father in the parents' lounge. 'your wife and your son need you.'
'That's not my son,' he said. 'That ... thing ... '

3.2.5 Lexical Verbal Silence   205

The father's deliberate and painful choice to refer to his newly born son as 'that ... thing ... ', leaving out the expected wording, depicts the absence of the envisioned human features, those which every new parent searches for in order to confirm the baby's well-being as well as to search eagerly for family similarities, such as seeing hes own eyes or mouth in the newborn. This is here iconically expressed using lexical vs signalled by the use of the most general and generic word: 'thing'.

The next example comes from Shakespeare's *Hamlet* (I.ii.64–65, *Norton³*, p. 1200):

[~181]   KING   But now, my cousin Hamlet, and my son –
         HAMLET A little more than kin and less than kind.

Shakespeare offers one of his renowned puns here, playing on King Claudius's kinship with Hamlet. Scholars have noticed the sarcastic linking of the adjectives 'kin' and 'kind'. Adding to, and by no means replacing, these associations, the perspective of vs pointed here choosing 'kind' as a general-generic term, such as Shakespeare's 'a kind of nothing', has a contrasting effect of distancing: not kin-intimacy but kind-categorical.

3.2.5.1.7 Modifiers Qualifying Speech or Silence

Saville-Troike (1985: 10) quotes Abrahams' statement that 'the greater the level of sound or noise, the more profound will the silence be interpreted *to be, to mean* ... silence is employed as one of the most important devises in the vocabulary of intensification'. Abrahams refers to the silence itself as an intensifier. We shall here examine the role of lexical modifiers as vs forerunners.

When ADJs and ADVs are not in head position, they modify their syntactic head. As modifiers their effect on their heads can be primarily attributive (emphasisers) or it can rank the head (intensifiers). Amplifiers have a heightening affect usually scaling upwards from an assumed norm, while downtoners have a lowering affect usually scaling downwards (see, e.g., Quirk et al. 1985: 428–474 and especially 583–604). Others restrict the reference of their head (usually nouns). For such modifiers to serve as lexical vs forerunners, the heads they modify must belong in the semantic field of speech and silence and the content of the *verba dicendi* must follow. This resembles the negation of *verba dicendi* (see §3.2.5.1.4), but here the issue is modification rather than negation.

Their affect as lexical vs forerunners depends on their kind, which is in turn determined by the nature of the head. If the head (*verba dicendi* or its nominal form) concerns speech as a verbal expression then its vs forerunner will typically be a downtoner (see [~182] and [~183]). If, on the other hand, the head denotes silence then its forerunner can be any modifier heightening that silence ([~184]).

The first example is a common device whereby a writer says 'I nearly wrote x'. Unlike speech, a writer using artificial devices has the privilege to overwrite what s/he has written, leaving no trace of the former. The writer signals the erased content when s/he wishes to move that event to the fore. The connection to vs in such cases is that while focusing on replacement of one content, the writer communicates the ostensibly 'erased' content in a telling and by no means accidental manner. The examples are numerous. One such illustration, using the archetypical downtoner approximator 'nearly' as a lexical forerunner, comes from William Vollmann's 'Widow's Weeds' (p. 518):

[~182] Just as in Paris they open the long green coffins bolted to the wall of the quai, and the books and prints within get resurrected, so my capacity for affection – I nearly wrote infection – got once more disinterred within my breastbone by Mrs. Wenuke Lei McLeod. I almost believed she has no heart to hurt me.

'Only answer' in [~160^m] is a downtoner diminisher. But as becomes apparent reading [~160^n] and [~160°], because 'only answer' does not here point to content, it is not here a vs forerunner.[94]

A downtoner vs forerunner is illustrated in Doris Lessing's *Children of Violence: Martha Quest*, whose eponymous heroine constantly seeks to lead her own life and free herself from her mother's dominance. The passage is an excerpt of Martha's words while driving her mother:

[~183] 'I'm not taking you to tea with Mrs. Anderson, what do you want to see her for – ' She stopped, on the verge of saying, 'behind my back.' As usual she was feeling the impotent resentment that as soon as she made a friend, created anything of her own, her mother followed her, assuming first place. (p. 132)

The idiomatic collocation 'on the verge of' serves here as a downtoner approximator, denying the truth of the performance of the speaking action. It is here Martha the homodiegetic narrator who signals the vs and who shares with her readers its contents behind her mother's back.

A hopefully straightforward example illustrating a head denoting silence, and a maximising intensifier forerunner heightening that silence to the upper extreme of its scale, comes from Melvin M. Johnson Jr, who is best known as an American firearms designer. In an epilogue to his unpublished manuscript (*Unpardonable Guns*), Johnson notes his concern at the use of his weapons by the 'bad guys':

---

[94] It is worth noting that while [~160°]: 'still she did not answer; only looked' immediately follows a question, this is not the case with [~160^m]: 'only answer' (see in detail §4.3.3.2). The context of [~160°] and [~160^n] also exposes the limited extent of such nonverbal responses to fulfil what seems the expectancy for a verbal answer (but see the intensity of 'movement' in [~160^p] as nonverbal means of expressing all that is detailed in [~160^q]).

3.2.5 Lexical Verbal Silence   207

[~184]   [...] recently pictures of Cuban Castro's Revolutionists showed Johnson Emmas and Betsy rifles; even some very complementary comments were made about their superiority. Though I am utterly silent about the Cuban situation I finally established that Castro got their guns from the Dutch West Indies and several other second to fourth-hand sources. (Canfield 2002: 219)

Moderating the totality of maximisers such as 'utterly' and 'absolutely' through the use of approximators such as 'almost' is not the case in [~184]. The non-restrictive 'utterly silent' uttered using the first-person present and immediately followed by the contents included in the maximiser (that which Johnson said he is utterly silent about, see on preterition §3.2.5.1.4), is a clear case of a forerunner pointing to lexical vs.

3.2.5.2 Intertextuality as Verbal Silence

Julia Kristeva (1966: 36) defines intertextuality as the 'permutation of texts, an intertextuality: in the space of the text, many utterances taken from other texts intersect with one another and neutralize each other'. Kristeva's broad definition led scholars to narrow the scope of the term 'intertextuality' in various ways; some even wind up contradicting it.

Given the central role Kristeva attributes to spaces as the locus of intertextuality and the fragmentation involved, the connection between intertextuality and vs seems to be apparent. We may illustrate this with the opening verse of Hejinian's poem 'Writing Is an Aid to Memory':

[~185–1^S] S_1 apple is shot S_2 nod

Nowhere are the signifiers 'Wilhelm' and 'Tell' articulated. The tale of Wilhelm Tell slips into the space [~185–1^S] created by Hejinian's positioning of 'apple' and 'shot' (and 'nod', and see Hejinian 2007: 60). Wilhelm Tell is introduced as the agent performing the shooting act (by S_2) via intertextuality as a means of vs. This is the commonest and broad form of intertextuality, according to which any text is partial encompassing spaces. But for intertextuality to be a vs means of expression, the spaces must be deliberately initiated by the addresser (not overlooking the addressee's role in noticing these spaces and the external segments intersecting them). Hejinian's use of intertextuality interweaving vs in the poem's opening verse (also regarding the apple of Eden as knowledge) enacts the poem's theme: writing is an aid to memory.

Kristeva's notion of intertextuality is strongly dependent on writing as the bearer of literate individual and collective heritage and memory.

Emily Dickinson's verse 'Himself – abide with Thee – ' (see [~83^d]) also exemplifies intertextuality. As detailed there (§3.4.2.2), 'abide with thee' creates echoes for Christian readers, like Dickinson herself, of its occurrences in the Scriptures, which not only resonates these pre-texts involving faith and free will but also evokes the role of the sinner. Having interpreted this poem in light of vs, we now focus on the intertextuality it exemplifies. Unlike Hejinian [~185–1^s], who generated 'apple is shot nod' anew, Dickinson ([~83^d]) signals intertextuality by reciting 'abide with thee', which as described is recognised as an external textual quote, one she had not generated.

As will be apparent, Kristeva does not limit intertextuality to cases of explicit quotation such as [~83^d]. Her notion of intertextuality is determined not by the nature of the segments (such as being quotes, or their magnitude) but by the semiotic relations they produce and resonate.

Lexemes are stored in the lexicon and incorporated in syntactic and discourse units by the activation of grammar rules and pragmatics. This is the basic difference between lexicon and grammar. For intertextuality, including ready-made formulaic expressions, to serve as a vs forerunner, the addresser is not expected to know the exact identity of that corpora or its author. Moreover, unlike cases in which the addresser deliberately improvises an external segment, when the addresser innocently misquotes, this too may constitute a case of intertextuality. The addresser must know that the segment comes from an external source (which may also be a pre-text of hes own, see for example [~190] and note 98).

One can envisage Kristeva's definition of intertextuality as ranging over a scale with explicit full quotations at one end (§3.2.5.2.1) and implicit thematic allusions, such as Hejinian's [~185–1^s], at the opposite pole. In between we find formulaic expressions and idioms (see §3.2.5.2.2). Following Kristeva's definition, all intertextual stumps along that spectrum (including partial quotations, see [~188^a] and [~189] §3.2.5.2.2), which originate from the addresser's choice, involve vs.

Ziva Ben-Porat (1976: 107) defines 'literary allusion' as 'a device for the simultaneous activation of two texts' and divides the movement from the recognition of the marker through the intertextual patterning into four mandatory and successive stages: the spotting of the allusion markers; identification of the evoked text which ties the marker with intertextuality; the modification of the initial local interpretation of the signal; and finally, the activation of the evoked text as a whole (Ben-Porat 1976: 111). While the initial stage not only draws attention to the marker but also entails a recollection of the original form of the marker, the final stage leads to maximal deconstruction of the intertextual pattern.

It is not coincidental that these steps coincide with those that lead from the identification of vs forerunners to deciphering and integrating vs in the local and macro context. Vs forerunners are stumps pointing to all forms of meaningful uninstantiated signifiers (see §3.2), including intertextuality in one of its forms:

Intertextual vs is confined to cases in which the addresser fragments hes authentic text alluding to another which being external introduces spaces as means of expression.

3.2.5 Lexical Verbal Silence

An important issue related to intertextual vs is linearity. Vs, and intertextuality included, transmitted within the verbal channel are linear, but as a device for simultaneous activation (Ben-Porat, above), by creating spaces activating intersection and neutralisation (see Kristeva 1966), and particularly by expressing content through its very non-articulation (vs), they overcome linearity. [~185–1^s] is just one example with its vs intertextual spaces which reconstructs a narrative bringing together Hejinian's twenty-first-century messages and experience with fourteenth-centaury Wilhelm Tell and biblical Adam and Eve's Garden of Eden. We further discuss overcoming linearity in §3.2.5.2.1.

3.2.5.2.1 Quotation

When, in addition to the insertion of pre-text segments in hes authentic speech (or text), the addresser also signals to hes addressee that that segment is not authentic – and frequently, in doing so, also indicates what Plett (1991: 12) terms 'the seams between quotation and context' (the location where hes authentic text is fragmented, and the resumption of hes text), s/he thereby adds an additional layer of vs. In so doing that addresser metalinguistically (§4.6) communicates using vs hes reliance on the external source (text and speaker) as authoritative,[95] common heritage or alternatively indicating hem relinquishing hes own voice.

Quotation as a lexical vs forerunner adds to (and does not replace) intertextuality as vs.

Plett's (1991: 9) definition – 'a quotation repeats a segment derived from a pre-text within a subsequent text, where it replaces a *proprie*-segment' – diverges from Kristeva's notion of 'intertextuality' and Ben-Porat's notion of 'literary allusion'. Though Kristeva emphasises the blurring of texts (they 'neutralise each other') and Ben-Porat talks of 'simultaneous activation', they seem to describe a syntagmatic relation, while Plett claims that the repeated segment replaces a *proprie*-segment, suggesting a paradigmatic relationship. We shall return to this point, including the matter of linearity mentioned in section §3.2.5.2, after examining Plett's notion of seams. Seams are not part of his definition because, as far as he is concerned, not all quotations include seams.

Plett (1991: 11–12) spells out a system of diacritic markers required by what he terms 'the grammar of quotation', distinguishing between explicit signals (such as 'I quote'; 'quote – unquote') and implicit signals (such as a phonological pause or graphemic indications, including spaces). But as Plett,

---

[95] Using quotes to point to lexical vs must be set apart from cases in which social practices such as legal or scientific writing compel the use of quotes (see Plett 1991: 13–15).

Ben-Porat and others contend, all markers must be examined in light of the specific context in which they appear.

We may illustrate this by enumerating the markers indicating seams in Wyatt's 'Who So List to Hunt'. We do so from Gregerson's (2013) point of view. Focusing on what she terms 'open voicing', that is, supple movement into and out of an implied character, Gregerson (2013: 151) presents and interprets 'Who So List to Hunt', Wyatt's adaptation of Petrarch's 190 *'Rime Sparse'*. The following is Durling's prose translation of Petrarch's poem, fully quoted by Gregerson:

[~186[Italian-T]] A white doe on the green grass appeared to me, with two golden horns, between two rivers, in the shade of a laurel, when the sun was rising in the unripe season. Her look was so sweet and proud that to follow her I left every task, like the miser who as he seeks treasure sweetens his trouble with delight. 'let no one touch me,' she bore written with diamonds and topazes around her lovely neck. 'it has pleased my Caesar to make me free.' And the sun had already turned at midday; my eyes were tired by looking but not sated, when I fell into the water, and she disappeared.

Gregerson points out that in 'Who So List to Hunt' Wyatt turns the structure of Petrarch's sestet on its head. Wyatt's final octave, as quoted by Gregerson (2013: 153),[96] reads:

[~186[a]] And graven with diamonds in letters plain
There is written her fair neck round about:
'Noli me tangere for Caesar's I am,
And wild for to hold though I seem tame.'

Explicit quotation markers signalling the seams between authentic speech and the external segments are essential in legal and official documents, scientific writing and other fields. They are least expected in poetry, which in the name of poetic licence and aesthetic gratification (see §4.5) is encouraged to defy even rigid grammar rules, let alone notational conventions.

Examining here quotation vs signalling movement into and out of an implied character, a distinction must be made between Wyatt's forerunners and punctuation marks introduced by his editors (see note 96). In the final octave ([~186[a]]) Wyatt provides over two intertextual seams: the first – 'there is written' – is an explicit verbalisation, equal to 'I quote' (see Plett, earlier in this section). An additional diacritic marker is the varying of the typeface, here through italicising the font, to signal the micro seam: a quotation within a

---

[96] Gregerson (2013: note 2) relies on R. A. Redholz's (1978) edition of Wyatt's poems. Redholz (1978) explains that wishing to make the poems intelligible he introduced, among other additions, quotation marks for dialogue and soliloquy (compare, for example, Foxwell 1913: 327). Despite her focus on movement into and out of implied characters, Gregerson seems to overlook this most important and relevant matter of fact.

3.2.5 Lexical Verbal Silence 211

quotation. This also marks code switching (from English to Latin, see later in this section). Identifying the formal seam's forerunners provided in the text is merely the first technical step in the search for vs and its meaning (Ben-Porat's initial stage). Referring to the final couplet, Gregerson (2013: 195) says that

> The couplet is both disclaimer (It is not I who speak; it is 'they.') and coup, designed to expose both lady and lady's lord. It is also a highly impacted instance of multi-vocality. Caesar speaks his power through the lady; the lady speaks resistance through her 'wildness'. Caesar's vanity speaks the words of Christ. The players speak their privilege in diamonds. The system speaks its ultimate triumph, and the ultimate entrapment of everyone else, in a collar. The poet speaks his mastery, and also his collusion, in an inherited piece of fourteen-line machinery.

Each case involving the identification of the speaking voice and the message s/he communicates is, in fact, a case of intertextual vs. Gregerson successfully illustrates here the movement into and out of the implied character (Ben-Porat's initial two stages) and the local and macro deconstructed meanings this communicates (Ben-Porat's final two stages). Focusing here on the forms of quotes as intertextual vs forerunners, we may see what Gregerson has to contribute to the unfinished dispute between Plett's notion of replacement suggesting paradigmatic (substitution) relations between the *proprie*-segment and the external segments, on the one hand, and on the other hand Kristeva's notion of neutralisation and Ben-Porat's notion of simultaneity suggesting syntagmatic relations between the texts. The question is, what is the authentic segment that is replaced by the external (quoted) segment? Taking Gregerson's disclaimer as an example, is 'it is not I who speak; it is "they"' the authentic segment? For the answer to be yes, we must acknowledge that unarticulated content, that is vs, fills the intertextual space. This is not mere substitution, and not solely neutralisation, but precisely the intertextual thirdness (in fact, all vss' thirdness) obtained not by selection or combination, nor by replacement or neutralisation, but instead by reconstruction: simultaneous selection and combination (see also §4.6.2.2 and §4.6.3.3.3). Ben-Porat (1976: 109) explains that the 'substitution of one signifiant for another – the most crucial element in the actualization of allusion in general – can never take place in the actualization of a literary allusion'. As described, the italicised *'Noli me tangere'* marks both code switching and a change of speaker-voice. Gregerson (2013: 154) points to the fact that while Wyatt's code switching goes from English to Latin, that Latin translation stands for Petrarch's Italian code. Gregerson associates this with the role played by quotation and intertextuality (though she does not use these terms) in indicating the change of voices ('Caesar's vanity speaks the words of Christ'), explaining that it is rather the Latin (Vulgate) phrasing which replicated the words of the risen Jesus (John 20:17). Replicating here the first words the risen Christ uttered facing Mary Magdalene next to his own tomb clearly does not constitute the substituted authentic segment. It is a segment which, like Dickinson's 'abide with thee' ([~83^d]), intersects with the various texts to form, using quotation intertextual vs, a reconstructed third narrative resulting from the integration of some of the textual segments and the neuturalisation of others. Looking here at quotation intertextual forerunners, it must be pointed out that in light of Waytt's forerunners, the two quotation diacritics, which aren't Wyatt's (see note 96), are entirely superfluous for both the poem and its analysis.

Having looked at the intertextual vs forerunner involving quotations, we now focus on the message communicated using vs informed by such markers (forerunners). 'It is not I who speak; it is "they"' seems to capture the archetypal meaning, not limited to disclaimers. By providing hes addressee with suitable markers, the addresser either shares the credit for the message with others (tradition, sages, culture, professional or other authorities, such as 'the doctor ordered'; or renounces authenticity such as Wyatt's above disclaimer, [~186^a]).

Quotations relegating the speaking agent's authentic voice, that is, depicting the experience of the annihilated speaker, form the theme of Joshua Sobol's novel *Silence*, told as the autobiography of its eighty-year-old protagonist. The novel opens (p. 7, translated from Hebrew) with the following passage:

[~187$^{Hebrew-T}$] From the day I knew how to read and write I have not written a word of my own. I've only copied what others wrote. When I was a small boy I copied passages out of books. Later I begun to copy the manuscripts of the writer who lived in our village, so that he could send them for publication. I remember the day when the writer invited me over to his house to copy his manuscript. I was ten or eleven, I can't remember exactly. But I remember the day and the hour. This is how the writer described them in a passage I found in his novel 'The Forbidden Village' when copying it:
'It was a hot summer day [...]'

The speaker – the homodiegetic narrator – says in his own authentic words what he soon depicts through citation: that until the age of eighty he did not write a single word of his own. This protagonist explicitly marks the quotation seams, providing vs forerunners – 'this is how the author described them' – detailing the exact reference (the novel *The Forbidden Village*), adding the diacritic colon and inserting a quote (the length of a passage) within quotation marks. The local meaning depicted within these intertextual spaces is that even what the homodiegetic protagonist experienced first hand, and describes as highly significant for him, is not reported through his own voice but delegated to an external voice. The conflict the protagonist experiences between holding on to elective silence (mutism) or daring to regain his own voice (giving up the not-I voices) forms the macro theme of Sobol's novel, reconstructed here through the use of quotation intertextuality as a vs forerunner.

3.2.5 Lexical Verbal Silence 213

While Kristeva argues that intertextuality runs in all texts, Plett (1991: 5, like Ben-Porat) narrows its scope, saying that:

A text may be regarded as an autonomous sign structure, delimited and coherent. Its boundaries are delimited by its beginning, middle and end, its coherence by the deliberately interrelated conjunction of its constituents. An intertext, on the other hand, is characterized by attributes that exceed it. It is not delimited, but de-limited, for its constituents refer to constituents of one or several other texts.

The text in [~187$^{\text{Hebrew-T}}$] loses its independence (chiefly defined by boundaries), and consequently it, and more so its authentic speaker, disappear as a distinctive and unique self.[97] From the perspective of the novel as a text, 'it was a hot summer day [...] ' is a chain consisting of a quote within quote, illustrating the position expounded by Kristeva (following Lacan) that language is a sequence of signifiers pointing to the absence of the signified (*das Dind*). This is surely the most iconic representation of the pact that forms the essence of our study between vs as means of expression and absence (see also §4.5.1).

3.2.5.2.2 Formulaic Expressions

Formulaic expressions share with quotes, as with all instances of intertextuality, the trait of a non-linear text: that is, a current-authentic text fragmented by external stumps of pre-texts, with the textual and semiotic consequences this entails. In addition, formulaic expressions share with quotations their use as vs forerunners communicating the authentic addresser's wish, not only to evoke and integrate pre-texts but also to make this an issue in its own right.

Fischer and Yoshida (1968: 35) define a formulaic saying as 'any sort of stereotyped saying, usually but not necessarily of anonymous traditional origin, which can be quoted to provide a forceful statement of some point with a sort of backing of public opinion'. This useful definition explains their peculiarity as efficient sociolect-dependent stumps pointing to intertextual vs. Unlike non-formulaic quotations, quoting such idioms and clichés in full (or even partial stumps thereof) relieves the addresser of the need to inform addressees sharing hes sociolect that that segment was not hes own authentic production, and provides them with markers (see Plett in §3.2.5.2.1 and Ben-Porat in §3.2.5.2) indicating its source and boundaries.

It must be emphasised here that if the intersection of a formulaic expression is mandatory (in that sociolect), its use is not the addresser's choice and hence is not an instance of intertextual vs (though such compliance may indeed belong to the given-off information, see Goffman 1959: 2).

---

[97] See also Vince Vawter, *Copyboy*, 2018, pp. 2–3.

However, if the addresser electively intersects hes own authentic speech with a formulaic expression, this is a case of intertextual vs. This also explains why it makes no semiotic difference, within the sociolect, whether the addresser replicates that expression in full or quotes only part of it: the message communicated using this as a means of vs is one and the same. Compare

[~188ᵃ]   If the mountain will not come to Mohammed

with

[~188]   If the mountain will not come to Mohammed then Mohammed will come to the mountain.

In English sociolects, this expression is detached from its Muslim source (see also [~189ᵇ] and [~144] and [~145] § 3.2.4.6.2).

[~189]   Better late than never

seems a good illustration of a formulaic expression as an intertextual vs forerunner. A dictionary search (for example OED: Late, Adj.p3) shows that [~189] originates in Greek and Latin (for example, documented in Livy and Dionysius). The earliest documentation of its use in English dates to the late thirteenth century. However, most speakers are unaware of its source and use the expression not because of its attribution to Livy, Dionysius or Chaucer but because of its social strength and backing.

Example [~189ᵃ] comes from Picoult and van Leer's novel *Between the Lines* (see [~156] §3.2.4.6.2). The context is a short incident in a biology class doing a lab dissection on a frog:

[~189ᵃ]   The door opens, and in walks Allie McAndrews, with two black eyes. She looks like a raccoon, and has a criss-crossed strip of tape over the bridge of her nose too. She hands Mrs. Brown a hall pass. 'Sorry I'm late,' she says.
         'Better late than never,' the teacher says. 'Allie, why don't you pair up with Delilah?' (p. 150)

It comes as no surprise that teachers are inclined to use formulaic expressions. This releases the specific teacher from taking full responsibility for the implied criticism, had she been the authentic producer of the text:

[~189ᵇ]   Better late than never but better never late.

This usage also places her as part of a longstanding heritage. This is achieved by the space of intertextual vs.

Harvey Sacks' (1992: 104–110) findings concerning truth value in the case of proverbs would seem to be applicable to all formulaic expressions. He argues that in addition to stability, they offer 'something independent from any occasion of use', unlike other statements, because their truth value is taken

3.2.5 Lexical Verbal Silence

for granted: only their application, and not their truth, may be questioned. This is valid irrespective of the understanding that while formulaic expressions are 'correct about something', they are unlikely to constitute 'the whole truth'. This is taken to an extreme in the context of [~190^e].

The second formulaic expression we examine in light of intertextuality as vs is

[~190] Like lambs to the slaughter.

This image communicates the cruelty and asymmetry inherent in the mass killing of helpless and innocent people. It is widely used as a formulaic expression, as for example here:

[~190^a] The rank-and-file membership of the union are meekly following their so-called leaders like lambs to the slaughter. (*Daily Telegraph*, 10 February 1982, 16/5; quoted from OED: Slaughter, N.4)

The use of the formulaic expression vs here conveys a twofold message. The first, concerning authority and continuity, implies that this description is not merely the judgement of the individual reporter but is backed by society's perception of other such incidents. The second message carries a softening affect, directing the blame not at the innocent union members but at 'so-called' leaders who dominate and manipulate the workers. [~190^b], which at first seems to replicate [~190^a], further illustrates vs at work:

[~190^b] People continue to flock to the psychoanalytic couch as lambs to the slaughter, many of them ignorant of what lies in store for them. (Bobgan and Bobgan 1979: 75)

The authoritative impact conveyed by the use of formulaic expression vs, irrespective of its contents, is probably even stronger here than in [~190^a]. However, this instance is taken from a book written by two well-known Christian advocates, addressing Christian worshippers and urging them to seek redemption through Christian spirituality, and not to be tempted by Freud's psychoanalytic counselling. In this context, [~190] evokes the following intertextual sources:

[~190^c] He was oppressed, and he was afflicted, yet he opened not his mouth: he is brought as a lamb to the slaughter, and as a sheep before her shearers is dumb, so he openeth not his mouth (Isaiah 53:7);
[~190^d] The next day John seeth Jesus coming unto him, and saith, Behold the Lamb of God, which taketh away the sin of the world (John 1:29).

The text of [~190^b] seems trapped in the radical transformation which 'like lambs to the slaughter' underwent on its way to become a formulaic expression. The intertextual spaces filled in by vs [~190^b] encompass contradicting messages from the Jewish ([~190^c]) and Christian ([~190^d]) Scriptures, respectively. The spaces are also filled by traditions eulogising the martyrdom narrative (on silencing, see §2.2.4.1), whereby the analysands are compared to Jesus. Simultaneously, the disapproving message of the modern formulaic expression portrays the analysands on the couch as passive and seduced victims.[98] It seems most unlikely that Bobgan and Bobgan ([~190ᵇ]) overlooked this duality. Had these messages been articulated, the full utterance would have appeared incompatible, but this linearity and dichotomy is easily obscured using intertextual vs.

As a formulaic expression vs communicating and enacting the speaker's annihilation, [~190] is further illustrated in light of the excerpt Amir (2016) analyses to illustrate a psychotic mode of testimony, termed 'empty grammar', in which an attempted reconstruction of an event results in its erasure. As Amir notes, this in itself constitutes evidence of a traumatic lacuna. [~190ᵉ] quotes the testimony (quoted in Amir 2016: 628) of Lea, a Holocaust survivor born in 1934:

[~190ᵉ] I was living with my sister, brother, and mother in Rafalovka, when the murderers, the Germans, took over our city, and when I saw them I said to my mother: 'I cannot [bear to] look in their direction. I want to live, I am young, I cannot look on as the German murderers torture us, I must get through this and take revenge on these criminals.' A whole year went by, full of troubles, hunger, contempt . . . . Then suddenly, one lovely summer's day, SS people arrived and sealed the city and everybody got ready to die. I was 12 years old. I go to my mother and I say: 'Mummy, let's go, let's escape, let's not go like lambs to the slaughter.' I kiss my mother: 'I want to live, come on let's escape, let's escape!'

Amir states, following the editor's note to [~190ᵉ], that

[. . .] The witness is unlikely to have been familiar with the expression *like lambs to the slaughter* at the time of these events, and probably inserted it in her previously cited words after she came across it following liberation. [. . .] The expression *like lambs to the slaughter* does not represent rich metaphoric usage, in that sense, but rather pours the personal experience into a given format while blocking any authentic link with it.

Amir's explanation clarifies that in the excessive-psychotic mode of testimony, a rhetorical splint, such as a formulaic expression ([~190]), does not serve communication or aesthetics but rather depicts the psychic lacuna of the black hole, attacking the prospect of linkage and transformation. These expressions saturate texts, factual and narrative linearity and perspective. This process forms the basis for many uses of formulaic expression vs obliterating the self, but the case of [~190ᵉ] seems particularly salient in this context. First, an

---

[98] On the history of this expression and its turning point, see https://en.wikipedia.org/wiki/Like_sheep_to_the_slaughter (accessed 7 January 2020).

3.2.5 Lexical Verbal Silence

exceptional correspondence emerges between the psychotic rhetoric preserving 'the traumatic object in a saturated condition which blocks any possible movement either towards it or away from it' (2016: 630) and formulaic expressions as external stumps fragmenting authentic voice (in the excessive-psychotic context, Kristeva's (1966) notion of neutralisation serves as obliteration).

'Like lambs to the slaughter' is not only not authentic, but, as Amir notes, it is a prochronism, which Lea employs in her report on a conversation with her mother that took place decades before [~190] had become a formulaic expression in Israeli and other sociolects (see note 98). This prochronism further saturates the narrative linearity and truthfulness, and serves Lea as she condenses two rivalling narratives. The first of these is the authentic narrative of twelve-year-old Lea, who fearing her coming death as the German SS seals her city begs her mother to resist and not to become a victim:

[~190^{c-a}] I want to live, come on let's escape, let's escape!

This is fragmented by the stereotyped reproachful post-war Israeli and Western narrative (which was later renounced) adopted using the prochronistic formulaic expression ([~190]).

In so doing, Lea distances her report from the status of an authentic personal story by a Holocaust survivor who underwent the war as a child, told in the setting of a one-to-one intimate interview and offering an opportunity to bear witness and allow transformation, and moves towards the register of official legal proceedings. This shift is not articulated but is expressed by Lea through her use of the prochronism embodying responsibility, blame and innocence (see discussion of [~190^a] to [~190^d]). Formulaic expressions are not only instances of excessive-psychotic rhetoric but also constitute the prototype of non-personal, high-language, truth-preserving verbal forms. Their truth value is taken for granted (Sacks 1992: 100). [~190] – the prototypical sociolect representation of the Holocaust atrocities signals Lea's experience of the testimony as one that belongs not to the arena of personal witness (Amir 2016) but to the arena of a testimony of a defendant, under oath in a public court, who seemingly does not even attempt to fight for her innocence.

An additional correspondence between formulaic expressions as vs forerunners and the excessive-psychotic mode of testimony concerns the openness of silence as a means of expression, compared with the rigidity of articulation, for better and for worse. The addresser can use formulaic expressions to encourage a plurality of relations, narratives, voices, cultures and eras that shelter in the spaces offered by intertextuality. But formulaic expressions can also be used to deceive by fragmenting the authentic and preserving stagnation.

3.2.5.3 Verbal Silence Pointing to Taboo

Unlike usual content words, denoting is not the primary function of taboo signifiers; their primary function is to activate the performative force. Because this performative force is indissoluble from the taboo signifier, forms pointing to the tabooed signifier, not by articulating it but instead by using a vs forerunner, offer a way of avoiding its mana force and the associated ambivalence

Freud (1913) observed that the use of taboo language, among members of primitive societies, neurotic patients and normal speakers alike is an indication of emotional ambivalence. Two aspects crucial to our study are the ambivalence inherent in the notion of 'taboo' condensing two diverging meanings, that of the sacred and that of the uncanny (as it emerges in 'holy dread', 'owe'), and the magic power of the taboo.

Freud details lexical taboo as a derivative of the physical taboos surrounding contact and usage. Based on the animistic omnipotence of thought, whereby neurotic patients, like 'savages' and children, treat words as objects, and on contiguity, the uttering of a taboo word is equivalent to performing or activating the taboo itself. That is, whereas the lexical function of content words is to denote the reference they signify, taboo words do not denote but act: producing results in reality. Due to their magic (mana) power, they do not signify the prohibited object but are part of that object and of the associated prohibitions, with all their consequences. This is the foundation for the grounds for the Hebrew Talmudic (*Brachot* 19a) warning 'never open your mouth to the Satan', whose original literal meaning was that speech can tempt faith, and which only later evolved into its idiomatic meaning, 'speak of the devil and he doth appear'.

The relevance of taboo words to our study of vs centres on the fact that the prohibition on the use of taboo words denudes those words of their primary lexical-denotational function. This leaves the addresser with three lexical metalinguistic options:

1. To comply completely with the prohibition, refraining from any reference to the taboo (including the word).
2. To comply with the prohibition and bypass the taboo word through the use of alternative strategies.
3. To break the taboo, that is, ignore the prohibition using the taboo word as any denotative-content word.

Interestingly, none of these three options leads to the annulment of the taboo word. The first two options eliminate the production of the taboo word and ostensibly exclude it from the lexicon, but it persists as a lexical absence made present. Benveniste (1974: 255) defines 'linguistic taboo' as 'un certain mot ou

3.2.5 Lexical Verbal Silence

nom ne doit pas passer par la bouche' – 'words which must not leave the mouth'.

The first option is that of silencing (see §2.2.4.1). An addresser may break the taboo (third option), implying that s/he refuses to fall into the mystic threat (see e.g. Jaworski 1997: 392–394; this may indeed belong in given-off information, see Goffman 1959: 2). Alternatively an addresser may metalinguistically enclose the taboo word in quotation markers (see §3.2.5.2.1, and see Casas Gómez 2018: 23, also §4.6.1.4). But unlike the second option, the distancing of oneself from the authentic production of the taboo word does not deprive the taboo of its performative force.

Vs as a means of expression emerges in the context of the second option, aimed at bypassing the performative form and force. Benveniste (1974: 257) claims that while euphemism does not prevent blasphemy, it does dismantle the taboo's performative force. It is precisely at this point that bypassing assumes its role as a metalinguistic taboo forerunner.

The best example comes from the third commandment:

[~191]   Thou shalt not take the name of the LORD thy God in vain (Exodus 20:7).

There is one single name which is the tetragrammaton, yhwh (see [~211]). This is the ineffable and explicit name of God, the name of all names. Not taking this name in vain confines its use only to specific holy persons (such as the high priest on the Day of Atonement) as part of the worship. Magicians using the name in vain as part of their witchcraft to trigger its magical performative force (the third option) were said to have been automatically punished by the deity.

Many names are attested for the deity in the Scriptures of the three monotheistic faiths. These are not substitutes for the tetragrammaton ineffable but rather taboo vs forerunners pointing to the explicit taboo name. Benveniste (1974: 255) says 'tout ce qu'on possède de Dieu est son *nom*'.

Unlike usual content words, denoting is not the primary function of taboo signifiers; their primary function is to activate the performative force. Because this performative force is indissoluble from the taboo signifier, forms pointing to the tabooed signifier not by articulating it but instead, by using a vs forerunner, offer a way of avoiding its mana force and the associated ambivalence (the second option).

Here lies the crucial difference between taboo and most cases of euphemism, which have nothing to do with taboo.[99] Most euphemisms, such as euphemisms for derogatory words, serve on the one hand semiotics (denoting

---

[99] Many modern scholars did not observe this essential distinction. Because groups of words considered socially inappropriate are large and open ended, while the set of taboo words is limited and static, empirical experiments on euphemism either merged the two or confined their

the particular reference) and on the other hand social propriety, face-saving, political correctness and so forth (see Orwell 1946: 77–92). Zerubavel (2006: 28) labels euphemism 'the deodorant of language', since it covers rather than removes the underlying 'smell'. While euphemisms, as content words, point to the denoted object, this is not the case with taboo words, which metalinguistically (see §4.6.1.4) serve to create the taboo lexical vs.

We now concentrate on taboo and taboo vs. Due to the ambivalence inherent in taboo words, dissecting them into separate semantic fields such as death, bodily organs and deity, which at first seems a satisfactory classification, proves artificial and misleading. As Freud (1913) argues, taboo does not consist of five, four or even two distinct domains but rather embodies ambivalent feelings regarding the emotional relations of the savage, the neurotic and the modern person. He further explains (Freud 1915: 295) that 'what came into existence beside the dead body of the loved one was not only the doctrine of the soul, the belief in immortality and a powerful source of man's sense of guilt, but also the earliest ethical commandments'. Freud crystallised this ambivalence in 'Beyond the pleasure principle' (1920), which he devotes to the interplay between the drives eros and thanatos and the pleasure principle and reality principle, elevating the latter.

Looking at the attempted classifications (see, for example, Allan and Burridge 2006: 1; Napoli and Hoeksema 2009: 615) it becomes apparent that they do not constitute distinct taboos but rather each represents an instance of animism. Taboo enters where boundaries are crossed, such as between the mortal and eternal; human and occult; purity and impurity (sinful); attributing power and will to inanimate objects (including names, that is symbols); blurring the distinction between the psychical (internal) reality and material (external) reality; and merging mortality, illnesses and religious faith as indispensable. In his seminal paper 'On obscene words: Contribution to the psychology of the latent period', Ferenczi offers an interesting explanation for this merge: 'words that once denoted the most highly treasured objects of the infantile pleasure recur in the form of oaths and curses, and, characteristically, associated very often with the idea of the parents or the sacred beings and gods that correspond to them (blasphemies)' (1911: 128, see also Freud 1919a, 1919b).

---

cases to social-derogatory euphemisms. Overlooking this distinction, their conclusions erroneously include also taboo words.

Casas Gómez (2018) contributes important observations on the matter. To mention just two, he maintains a distinction between what he terms 'word/lexical/taboo' and 'conceptual interdiction', and he focuses on the linguistic process of breaking the association with the forbidden reality, rather than on its outcome (substitution).

3.2.5 Lexical Verbal Silence

We may add briefly that this crossing of boundaries blurs the separation between a divine (totemistic) father and the real (human) father (see Mettinger 1988: 50–73). Lacan's notion of 'The name of the father' (1963) elaborates Freud's concept of totemism and usefully combines attention to the aspects of reproduction (the realm of the real, such as drives), morals (as the internalisation of Freud's super-ego and Lacan's explanation of the parental role in initiating the child into the social order) and signification (language – the symbolic, see also [~203^{French}]).

Freud (1913: 21) explains that these prohibitions 'are necessary because certain persons and things are charged with dangerous power, which can be transferred through contact with them, almost like an infection'. Ferenczi (1911: 114) suggests that hearing such words agitates in the adult hearer '"a new edition" of the impressions made by overhearing in infancy actual sexual performances'.

It then follows that due to the indispensable merge between the taboo signifier and its contagious performative forces, they cannot be broken but only bypassed. We now examine taboo vs metalinguistic forerunners, that is, the lexical strategies that serve the second option: bypassing the taboo spell while pointing to that word which must not leave the mouth. As the reader may notice, unlike the former mode of presentation, here the vs forerunners are not confined to one single form (such as phonetic or syntactic vs) but employ various forms. These are detailed here under lexical vs because they constitute the main strategies serving and pointing to lexical taboo vs (see §4.6.1.4, and see also Ferenczi 1911: 114; Benveniste 1974: 257; Casas Gómez 2018: 19):

3.2.5.3.1 Generalisation-Metonymy

The vs forerunner is the hypernym of the taboo word (one of its hyponyms, see §3.2.4.4.4). Such is, for example, the common noun

[~192]   God

for the particular taboo proper name *yhwh*; or the hypernym of hypernyms, that is the Hebrew (definite noun)

[~193^{Hebrew}]   הַשֵּׁם (*hašem*=the name).

A fictitious and witty bypassing of the taboo spell can be found in J. K. Rowling's series, *Harry Potter* concerning Voldemort's name:

[~194]   He Who Must Not Be Named.

Other examples of generalisation as a taboo vs forerunner are

[~195^{French}] la maladie (=the illness)

[~196]   Long battle against illness

and other such hypernyms avoiding uttering the hyponym: 'cancer'. These exemplify Freud's (1913: 21) idea of the contagious power of taboo: the fear that uttering this word will bring about the illness in reality. In each age these hypernyms point to the name of the deadly illness of the day (recently it is Covid-19). The contagious quality also explains the numerous metonymic forms that circumvent the taboo lexeme 'to die', for example:

[~197]   Passed away

[~198]   Gone to a better world. (see e.g., Joyce, *Dubliners*: 'The Sisters', p. 14)

Accordingly, this emerges relating to cemeteries:

[~199]   Resting place.

Menstruation touches on the central themes of primeval ambivalence: sexual desire, illness, gendered blood and religion (see Leviticus 15:19–25). Freud (1913: 120) remarks, regarding totemism: 'The totem is of the same blood as the man and consequently the ban upon shedding blood (in connection with defloration and menstruation) prohibits him from sexual relations with a woman belonging to his totem' (see also Allan and Burridge 2006: 162–172; Freitas 2018: 169–197).

[~200]   period

being a hypernym of the lunar cycle, is another example of metonymy (and see [~205], [~213]). A different example is the general hypernym

[~201]   facilities (for 'toilet').

We may close this section by mentioning the use of the inanimate pronoun 'it' to refer to sexual intercourse (see also [~92] (§3.2.6.2):

[~202]   (to) do it /doing it.

3.2.5.3.2   An Unrelated Innocent Term
The forerunner is a signifier which is unrelated to the taboo word. Benveniste (1974: 257) gives the example

[~203[French]]   nom d'une pipe

pointing to the taboo name of god (but this also involves mutilation (see §3.2.5.3.4).

A common practice is the use of proper names not for names (as in [~191]) but for taboo notions, such as 'john' (not capitalised) for penis:

3.2.5 Lexical Verbal Silence

[~204]   O daughter dear daughter I think you are a fool to run against a man with a john like a mule (from T. S. Eliot, as cited in OED: John, II.6).[100]

Examples for menstruation are:

[~205]   I've got Fred/George/Jack; little Willie/Aunt Susie is here (Allan and Burridge 2006: 167)

[~205] could also be interpreted as a far-fetched, and so innocent but unrelated, metaphoric forerunner, comparing menstruation to a visitor. Due to the contagious taboos encompassed in menstruation (see [~200]), menstrual bleeding is, more often than not, left out of adverts promoting sanitary protection products and the packaging of these products (see Freitas 2018: 169–195; see also [~218^s]).

3.2.5.3.3 Foreign Language

The use of a foreign language as a mode of distancing is a most common individual and collective forerunner pointing to taboo VS. It is widely used in socially motivated obscene euphemisms (see, for example, in psychoanalysis, Ferenczi 1911: 114). Examples are the use of technical or scientific nomenclature, such as the prototypical, both from Greek,

[~206^{Greek}] Tetragrammaton (see by [~191])

[~207^{Greek}] Phallus

The use of finger spelling in British Sign Language (BSL) as a VS taboo forerunner (and euphemisms) is just as much an instance of the use of foreign words: firstly because BSL uses finger spelling for foreign words, while here the spelling refers to BSL; and more importantly because finger spelling – unlike the taboo lexemes – are void of the iconic features so prominent in many BSL taboo words (see Sutton-Spence and Woll 1999: 243–251, see also [~217^{bsl}] in §3.2.5.3.5).

3.2.5.3.4 Mutilation

Mutilation is a clear case of phonetic VS (see §3.2.1) in which the stump points to the unarticulated taboo signifier. A common practice is letter stumps, such as

[~208]   I never think myself impowered to excommunicate thereupon either the postchaise, or its driver – nor do I take it into my head to swear by the living G – (Sterne, *Tristram Shandy*, Vol. VII, Ch. 8, p. 432)

[~209]   big C ('cancer')

[~210]   F-word ('fuck')

---

[100] Nänny's (1999: 192) explanation of 'O' in [~216] might shed new light on Eliot's 'O daughter' particularly when adjacent to 'john'.

Leaving out the word's vowels in writing mutilates the phonetic ability to pronounce them as words. This is the case with the tetragrammaton

[~211^{Hebrew}] יהוה (*yhwh*, see [~191])

[~36]   G-d (see §3.2.1)

and

[~212]   h-ll

In some cases this is signalled introducing non-pronounceable symbols:

[~213]   f**k

(see also [~216]). Another common practice involving phonetic mutilation takes the stump as a lexical base and creates a non-existent hybrid form. Benveniste's (1974: 257) example, concerning the name of god is

[~214^{French}] pardi! ('par Dieu!')

or what he terms 'nonsensical form'. A known example for 'hell' is

[~215]   heck

The contagious pact of taboo and taboo words is so strong that it extends even to words which merely resemble a taboo word. As Allan and Burridge (2006: 44, 243) and others point out, this may even result in the dropping of innocent words from the lexicon, such as 'fuk' (a sail).

An extreme form of literary mutilation pointing to taboo comes from none other than Shakespeare (*Romeo and Juliet* III.iii.85–91, *Norton*[3], p. 1087):

[~216]   NURSE Oh, he is even in my mistress' case,
          Just in her case. Oh, woeful simpathy,
          Piteous predicament! Even so lies she,
          Blubb'ring and weeping, weeping and blubb'ring.
          – Stand up, stand up! Stand an[d] you be a man!
          For Juliet's sake, for her sake, rise and stand.
          Why should you fall into so deep an O?

Nänny (1999: 192) points out that:

[T]he nurse's four lamenting 'O's acquire their sexually iconic force due to the bawdy punning context and their vicinity to, or juxtaposition with, the quibble on 'case' for pudendum [...] seen in the context of such quibbling words as 'stand', 'rise' and 'fall' the letter 'O' is [...] an icon for the vagina.

This example is interesting since, from a visual perspective, the 'O' is much more blunt than the word. However, veiled as a word, or a mutilated word, it functions here as a taboo vs forerunner (see note 100, see also on BSL [~217^{bsl}]

in §3.2.5.3.5). As Nänny points out, scholars who interpreted that 'O' as a groan failed to recognise the taboo aspect.

3.2.5.3.5 Uninstantiated Morphemes or Syntactic Constituents Pointing to Taboo Words

These morphological and syntactic VSS (see §3.2.3 and §3.2.4) are motivated by taboo VS: leaving a constituent to be instantiated with a taboo word uninstantiated.

An example of morphologic VS comes from BSL. In BSL a prominent taboo VS forerunner (alongside finger spelling, see §3.2.5.3.3) is the changing of the location of the taboo word. This morphological change detaches the taboo signifier from its expected, and frequently iconic, special location. The example described by Sutton-Spence and Woll (1999: 243–251) is:

[~217^{BSL}] TESTICLES.

The two-hand-shape balls moved to sign in an upper location: in front of the signer. This VS forerunner comes under morphology since location is a morphemic component of the signed entry (alongside hand shape, movement, orientation and non-manual components). Such morphological change moving the entry away from its conventional location results in mutilation distancing the signifier from its taboo role, destroying its visually motivated iconic transparency.

One example of an uninstantiated syntactic constituents (see §3.2.4.2) due to taboo is [~218^{S}], which plays on [~205]:

[~218^{S}] I've got S [= period).

Another example of syntactic VS can be found in Joyce's 'The Sisters'. When in the evening the narrator and his aunt visited the sisters of the late Reverend's James Flynn at the house of mourning, the aunt asks:

[~219] 'Did he ... peacefully?'
'O, quite peacefully, ma'am. You couldn't tell when the breath went out of him. He had a beautiful death, God be praised.'
'And everything ... ?' (*Dubliners*: 'The Sisters', p. 14)

The narrator's aunt leaves the VERB 'die', and all that is associated with it, 'and everything NP' uninstantiated. Eliza, the late Flynn's sister, replies in accordance with the syntax of answers (see §3.2.4) by repeating the ADV 'peacefully'; she goes on to instantiate 'death' but camouflages it with the ADJ 'beautiful'.

3.2.5.3.6 The Absence of a Forerunner as a Forerunner

The last group is unique in the absence of a forerunner, which retroactively stands out as the VS forerunner pointing to the taboo. Turning again to the taboo of menstruation, our example comes from the wording on standard packages of 'Always' sanitary towels:

[~220]   Up to 100% dryness & comfort always clean and dry

Not only is menstruation not mentioned in any way, but each word is in fact an antiphrasis of the taboo. As pointed by Freitas (2018: 174–195), such packaging and adverts replace the warm red universally associated with danger (blood) and passion (again the ambivalent uncanniness concerning taboo) with prototypically cold colours. These colours semiotically designate the negation of red, in the same manner as in traffic lights and sign posts, where red serves for alerting and blue and green for permitting and informing.

3.2.5.4 Proper Names and Verbal Silence

Proper names – people's given names included – differ from other linguistic categories such as common nouns in that they point to individuals rather than classes. John Stuart Mill (1843: 27) asserted that:

> All names are names of something, real or imaginary; but all things have not names appropriated to them individually. For some individual objects we require, and consequently have, separate distinguishing names; there is a name for every person, and for every remarkable place.

Given that proper names do not link signifier and signified (denotation, class description), they are not part of the lexicon. Proper names have extension but lack intension. For this reason, two individuals, two mountains, two journals, two buildings, two diseases, two feasts or two dogs may share the same proper name yet share nothing in terms of class. Mill (1843) illustrates this by noting that while many people are named 'John', a proposition concerning John does not claim to apply to all persons called 'John'. This difference is manifested linguistically in that syntax allows the conjoining of proper names but not common nouns: 'John and John graduated yesterday' (but not 'the student and the student graduated yesterday'). Some languages have a specific case marking for proper names and some designate proper names graphically by means of an initial capital letter.

Looking specifically at people's given names as a unique class with regard to onomastics in general, and anthroponomy in particular, we soon find that they have unique supplementary qualities. In most societies given names are officially registered. Although they lack semantic features, personal names, and given names in particular, reflect and create personal and social identities. The subcategory of personal names consists of a person's official name (given name, family name and, if relevant, middle name) as well as unofficial names, such as nicknames, epithets and pen names (see, e.g. Morgan et al. 1979; Holland 1990).

3.2.5 Lexical Verbal Silence

Given that the role of personal names is to impart singularity to the individual, the best sign might seem to be a phonetic sequence generated from scratch, lacking any relationship with the language lexemes and hence having no meaning. Nevertheless, even in societies where parents are free to invent a name, most parents make use of existing names. Others borrow lexemes from the common lexicon of words either as they are or as the basis for deriving a new form. Still, women called 'Pearl' have nothing to do with pearls.[101]

The legal status of personal names and their protection differ from culture to culture and are reflected accordingly in various legal systems. Many such systems share two characteristics: the responsibility and obligation for any person to bear a registered name, and the steps taken within those legal systems to protect the individual's rights to hes name (see UNICEF's Children's Rights document states, Articles 7–8).[102] This formal and mandatory state of affairs results in a fundamental difference between common nouns and personal names. Whereas lexicography is quite familiar with the notion of a 'lexical void', this option is legally ruled out for the personal official names.

In literary works the author has the freedom to decide whether or not to name fictitious protagonists and which names to choose for those who are named. As literary analysis and criticism have established, in many cases names chosen or left out further the poetic function of the language by adding meaning and emphasis and reflecting a point of view (see Uspensky 1970: 17–32). Names such as Verne's 'Nemo', Odysseus's 'Noman' and 'Mr. Zero' of the 'Adding Machine', as well as Emily Dickinson's 'Nobody' and 'Somebody' and E. E. Cummings' 'Anyone' are all literary given names for unique individuals. The author's decision to name or not to name a protagonist can also be a vs forerunner.

Individuals identify themselves with and by their name and are identified by others with and by that name: 'I have a name, therefore I am (an individual, a person, a subject)'. The explicit mention of a person's name is anticipated either in isolation or along with the explicit mention of the names of other persons. It is also expected when one addresses that person (vocative role), when one alludes to the name bearer or in unique settings and rites involving the granting or pronouncing of a (new) name (appellative role). Clearly, the mention of a person's name is not anticipated when the name is unknown to the addressers, or when they do not wish or are not free to disclose that person's name. However, this anticipation in itself serves as a vs forerunner signifying to the addressee that the specific name has been left out.

---

[101] In special cases, due to metonymy, a proper name may enter the lexicon as a common noun or adjective.
[102] www.unicef.org/rightsite/files/rights_leaflet.pdf (accessed 28 January 2014).

An addresser may leave out a given name as a deliberate means of expression. S/he may use proper name vs to reflect a state of commonness and a lack of uniqueness and singularity, to express the construction or obliteration of identity or to bypass taboos involving proper names.

We now detail the main forerunners pointing to given name vs. As seen for taboo (§3.2.5.3), here too the various forerunners do not fall into one homogeneous form. Because their role is to mark the coming vs they do not substitute the anticipated name and therefore do not eliminate its absence.

In light of the above distinction between common nouns and proper names, an addressee will assume (in the absence of clues to the contrary) that when an addresser chooses to use a descriptive expression s/he wishes to emphasise not the individual as such but a member of a group, and so a proper name is not expected. A key clue signalling that such forms are proper name vs forerunners is contrast, for example when the addresser refers to all other individuals by their name. Depriving a character of a name can express the character's lack of importance or deny hes existence as a person or subject. It may also be a verbal means signifying potentiality.

The various proper name vs forerunners are detailed here under six groups (see also Ephratt 2015a).

3.2.5.4.1 Generalisation

Leaving out an individual's given name and referring to hem using a common noun is a proper name vs forerunner since it places that individual as part of a class, without the expected unique-distinguishing form.

Examples [~192] and [~193^{Hebrew}] (§3.2.5.3.1) were such generalisations devised to bypass the taboo of the deity's proper name.

Another example pointing to generalisation as a proper name vs forerunner is Edgar Allen Poe's short story

[~221]   'The Man in the Crowd'.

The story is told by a first-person narrator who is peering into the street from his seat near a large bow window in London's D Coffee House. At first he observes the masses; he then focuses on details and seeks to differentiate individuals: 'With my brow to the glass, I was thus occupied in scrutinizing the mob, when suddenly there came into view a countenance (that of a decrepit old man, [...]) which at once arrested and absorbed my whole attention' (p. 243). The narrator hurriedly makes his way into the street, and for the next twenty-four hours follows the man as he roams through the streets of London, until he gives up. He realises that this mysterious old man in the crowd will remain 'a secret not permitting itself to be read'.

Commentators have interpreted this short story in many ways. Reading the story in light of proper name vs, we notice the unique texture interweaving the

3.2.5 Lexical Verbal Silence

dominance of the crowd on the one hand and the details of 'many individuals' (p. 241) on the other. Although the narrator never learns the old man's name, he observes him cheerfully and in great detail. After describing the man's general appearance, he goes on to notice details such as a dagger hidden in his roquelaure. Had he wanted to, the author could have easily embroidered a name on that fringe or sleeve. The story is set in urban London and tells the story of the crowd and the individuals making up this crowd. The narrator and the old man go round and round in endless loops, eliminating the differences between them. Who is chasing/leading whom? Is 'the man in the crowd' the old man, the narrator or every man, which is best reflected in them being nameless. The main point to notice is that Poe does not overlook individuality. On the contrary, it is predominantly by observing, chasing and studying the individuals that the 'singular being' (a phrase used here by Poe, p. 245) fades away.

An example of opposition comes from De Amicis' notorious *Heart* Stories, in which unlike northern Italian children such as Enrico and Marco, Coraci – a southern child – is not referred to by name but instead stereotyped as:

[~222]   The Calabrian boy.

Maria Truglio (2018: 39–40) comments:

[T]his pupil joins Enrico's Turinese class where he is met with exuberant warmth from the paternal teacher, Signor Perboni. In perhaps the best-known passage from the novel, Perboni uses the arrival of the Calabrian boy as an opportunity to remind the class (and the readers) that this very event – this union of south and north – exemplifies the marvellous fruit of the hard-fought unification movement: [. . .] 'Remember well what I am telling you. In order for this event to take place, for a Calabrian boy to feel at home in Turin, and for a boy from Turin to feel as if in his own home in Reggio Calabria, for this our country fought for fifty years and thirty thousand Italians died'. While Pebroni's stirring words imagine a kind of balance and reciprocity, the text itself dramatizes only the first scenario – that of the southern boy coming north.

The next illustration of opposition comes from B. S. Johnson *House Mother Normal* (see [~31] §3.2.1). The eight residents are introduced and referred to among themselves by their names, whereas the house-mother is introduced and referred throughout (including the book's title) by her role:

[~223]   House Mother

This creates a proper name vs forerunner. The meaning communicated using this vs seems to lie in the two dimensions Amir (2008) describes for the experience of loss: the actual dimension, which being according to Amir, inherent in the absence of the lost object from the objective world, is responsible for shaping reality and the possible dimension which is responsible for the subjective process internalising the aspects in the lost object which, despite its actual absence, may not have been annihilated. The house-mother's clarification, 'You should understand the simple fact that they are all approaching death very quickly ... ' (198), depicts the residents' actual position. From this perspective, the house-mother, as the only person who can experience mourning, is set in both dimensions. The naming contrast illustrated here depicts the name as fixed, final and actual.

The last example of a common noun

[~224]   The old lady

as a proper name vs forerunner when contrasted with designating other individuals by their names is cited here from two different sources. The first is traditional Chinese culture. Asking whether Chinese men and woman convert from anybody to somebody in the same way, Watson opens her paper (1986: 619) saying that:

In Chinese society names classify and individuate, they have transformative powers, and they are an important form of self expression. [...] Many people have a confusing array of names while others are nameless. [...] For the male villagers of rural Hong Kong, naming marks important social transitions: the more names a man has the more 'socialised' and also, in a sense, the more 'individuated' he becomes. [...] By the time a male reaches middle age, he may be known by four or five names. Village women, by contrast, are essentially nameless. Like boys, infant girls are named when they are one month old, but unlike boys they lose this name when they marry. Adult women are known (in reference and address) by kinship terms, teknonyms, or category terms such as 'old woman.'

Watson explains that the namelessness of adult women and their inability to participate in the naming of others highlights in a dramatic way the vast gender distinctions that characterise traditional Chinese culture.

The second illustration for [~224] comes from the children's story *Babar*. Each of the elephant characters in the series have a name, while the old lady who Babar met on his journey, and whom Babar adores, is not named. This contrast in naming depicts her status; while Babar is sad to leave her on his return to the forest (de Brunhoff, *Babar*, pp. 32–33) she is not one of them; she is the Other. Being ethnocentric, each species is differentiated between its members and others. In Chinese rural male culture men have names while women, being members of the other group, are not expected to be individuated. The same holds within Babar's elephant kingdom: they are the individuals, and we – as the old lady – are the others perceived not as individuals but as members of a group.

3.2.5.4.2 Pronouns

When a given name or family name is expected, and the addresser knowing that name, not wishing to conceal it and not motivated by stylistic preferences (see ellipsis, §3.2.4) chooses to use a pronoun, this pronoun constitutes a proper name vs forerunner (see [~225] and [~227], and see [~287[French]] in

3.2.5 Lexical Verbal Silence

§4.5.3). This is even more significant when the absence of an expected proper name is indicated by an impersonal pronoun such as 'it' ([~228]).

In 'The Argument' section of Shakespeare's 'The Rape of Lucrece', each of the men who participate in the after-dinner chats in the tent of Sextus Tarquin (King Lucius Tarquinius's son) extols the virtues of his own wife. After Collatine praises the incomparable chastity of his wife Lucrece, Sextus Tarquin becomes inflamed with her reported beauty, departs from the rest and heads to Collatine's estate. He sneaks into Lucrece's chamber and at first asks for her consent, before going on to threaten her reputation and suggest that he will murder a slave and place her dead body in the arms of that dead slave's body. After she persists in her refusal, he violently rapes her, and then leaves swiftly the next morning. Lucrece sent messengers for her father and for Collatine, who arrive with Junius Brutus and Publius Valerius. After Lucrece demands revenge, she names her rapist 'He, he,' before stabbing herself (see [~225]). All of Tarquin's family is then exiled, and the state government changes from kings to consuls. Through 'The Argument' section and in his poem, Shakespeare communicates a parallelism between the private and the political. In addition, unlike the Ovidian narrative source, Shakespeare introduces an active heterodiegetic narrator who quotes the protagonists and speaks on their behalf.

We examine the pronoun 'he' in [~225] as a proper name vs forerunner:

[~225] Here with a sigh as if her heart would break
She throws forth Tarquin's name.
'He, he,' she says –
But more than he her poor tongue could not speak,
Till after many accents and delays,
Untimely breathings, sick and short essays,
She utters this: 'He, he, fair lords, 'tis he
That guides this hand to give this wound to me' (lines 1716–1722, *Norton*[1], p. 679).

Shakespeare's heterodiegetic narrator describes the drama at length. The vs forerunner emerges in:

[~225[a]] She throws forth Tarquin's name;
'He, he,' she says.

Lucrece repeats the pronoun 'he' when Tarquin's name as a singularity identifier is the object of her utterance, and so expected. Yet, the narrator (like Shakespeare in 'The Argument') contends that she 'revealed the actor, and whole manner of his dealing'. Scholars recognised this discrepancy as a constitutive means of expression signalling the climax of the poem (see Fineman 1991: 207–208) and offered answers in line with their contextualisation of the story (personal or political, a feminist analysis of a woman gaining her voice, or alternatively a woman serving male dominance) as they sought to interpret the meaning of this proper name vs. Lucrece's proper name vs both communicates and enacts the matters of speech versus reticence, power versus submissiveness and inner intimacy (chastity) versus external remoteness (pride), the poem's theme:

[~226] Haply that name of chaste unhapp'ly set (line 8, *Norton[1]*, p. 642).

In this context, a man's honour demands that his wife's virtues be made public as part of his assets. Collatine's compliance with this requirement aroused Tarquin's passion and motivated his actions. The (masculine) rationale that whatever is left unnamed does not exist is here matched by Lucrece's repetitive pronoun 'he' as a proper name vs forerunner. The suicide which immediately follows highlights the message of [~225] in the context of control, and the repeated pronoun is seen as an intentional refrain depriving Tarquin and his brutal violation of Lucrece of the status of a subject and so making Lucrece the subject. Not cancelling out matters of subjectivisation, Lucrece's leaving the naming to Collatine is a reparation for his initial responsibility for making her chastity public [~226]. In the context of submissiveness, this silence is perceived as a symptomatic inability to name (see for example Fineman 1991: 172–173; 207–208; Belsey 2001: 325–327, and see [~238] §3.2.5.5.1).

The next example coming from Doris Lessing's short story 'He' (*Works*, pp. 94–99) is set in Annie Blake's kitchen. Its first part is told via a conversation between Annie and her friend Mary Brook who dropped by. The conversation soon turns to the misery Annie experienced while her husband was living at home (before her husband left her for a young woman), as does Annie's obsessive struggle for perfectness, which surfaces in her cleaning compulsion and her preoccupation with doing the right thing.

The story's title

[~227] 'He'

indicates Rob Blake's central role in the story. Throughout the story Annie and Mary designate him using the personal pronoun ('he', 'him'). This deliberate avoidance of his name is highlighted by Annie's references to each of the couple's three sons by their name. Most of the story is carried by the character's direct speech. The readers are informed of Rob Blake's name by the heterodiegetic narrator, who tells us that after Mary left, Annie returned to her domestic chores, and

[~227[a]] Not a moment too soon. The door opened, and Rob Blake stood there.

This is the only time the narrator calls Rob by his name (the narrator too uses the pronoun). Rob and Annie converse, and in his repetitive warm appeal to Annie, Rob calls her by her name. The contrast between this use of the name and the ongoing avoidance by Annie, Mary and the narrator of referring to Rob

3.2.5 Lexical Verbal Silence

by name serves as a vs forerunner. In addition, Rob's young lover is heard, first calling

[~227^b] 'Rob! Rob' [...]
'Rob! You there, Rob?' it was a loud, confident, female voice

and then knocking on Annie's door. The story goes on to describe how Rob turned the woman away:

[~227^c] [...] said in a low, furious voice: 'Don't you do that, now. Do you hear me!' He shut the door, leaned against it, facing Annie. 'Annie,' he said again, in an awkward appeal. 'Annie ... '.

The naming asymmetry, as well as Annie's obsession with never doing anything one should not do, is embodied in Rob's words before he leaves Annie's home and in the renewed conversation between Annie and Mary, who returns after Rob leaves. The story ends with Annie's ambivalent feelings: her tender longing for Rob to return home and her sturdy justification for letting what she perceives as justice and rightness rule (or ruin) her life.

'He' as a proper name vs forerunner seems to bear the weight of the entire narrative, including the story's turning point. At first, the avoidance of mentioning Rob's name communicates castigating him as an immoral husband, father and person. This not only reflects what appears to be Annie's feelings but also encourages the readers to take her side. Annie's repeated complaints about her hard life extrapolate the story from a personal case to a general 'he' (Annie concludes one of her complaints by commenting: 'Bone lazy. Men are all the same').

What at first seemed to be a contrast between the proper name as intimacy and the pronoun as distancing is challenged in light of proper name vs. Awareness of the function of contrasts as vs forerunners enables us to identify the moment when the woman shouts out Rob's name as a narrative turning point. While the actions of the young woman in chasing Rob and shouting his name conveys unquestioned possession, 'he' as the proper name vs forerunner offers an opening – a chance to move the ambivalent relations between Rob and Annie from the actual to what is possible (see my discussion of Amir 2008). The same is communicated alluding to the collective experience (gender dominance or being versus doing): one may take the collective past ('men are all the same') as aphorisms blocking the personal present in the actual (thus having no future); or alternatively, this 'he' can be seen as signalling a possibility in which each person can manage hes choices and formulate hes unique meanings (proper name) for hes personal and collective subjective and intersubjective past, present and future.

The use of the impersonal pronoun 'it' when given names are expected illustrates an entirely different case of proper name vs. One such example comes from Joyce's 'The Sisters'. The mode of reference to Reverend James

Flynn, in the context of the improper nature of his relationships with the young homodiegetic narrator, moves from proper name basis to the impersonal pronoun:

[~228] 'The youngster and he were great friends. The old chap taught him a great deal, mind you; and they say he had a great wish for him.'
'God have mercy on his soul,' said my aunt piously.
Old Cotter looked at me for a while. [...] He returned to his pipe and finally spat rudely into the grate. 'I wouldn't like children of mine,' he said, 'to have too much to say to a man like that.'
'How do you mean, Mr. Cotter?' asked my aunt.
'What I mean is,' said old Cotter, 'it's bad for children. [...] '
'It's bad for children,' said old Cotter, 'because their minds are so impressionable. When children see things like that, you know, it has an effect ... '
(Joyce, *Dubliners*: 'The Sisters', p. 8)

Vanderbeke et al. (2017) explain the 'gaps and holes and silence' in 'The Sisters', commenting regarding the move in [~228]:

However, there is also a shift from 'he' to 'it': not 'he is bad for boys', but 'it is bad for boys'. The priest now becomes part of something larger, a more abstract situation, which does not only affect the narrator of the story, but also other children in similar circumstances. The relationship between the boy and Father Flynn, which seemed to be in some way exceptional, thus becomes less unique and more typical of a specific Irish environment in which the priest plays a contributing role.

These observations support the treatment of this usage as a vs forerunner, which seems to imply that Joyce introduced these gaps primarily as a means of expression and only secondarily as a stylistic strategy depicting authentic Irish speech (see also [~78] §3.2.4.1).

3.2.5.4.3 A Given Name Other than the Person's *Proprie* Name

Various (ethnic, professional, cultural) societies encourage, force or allow individuals to add additional names to the name they officially carry since birth. Some such names are pet names (which may function as the default name within a reference group), aliases, pen names and so forth (see for example §3.2.5.4.1 on rural Chinese men). Cases such as pseudonyms or the generic use in the legal contexts to secure anonymity go even further to constitute a means masking one's true identity.

While these can indicate status, or lever expectations as given-off information (see Goffman 1959: 2), these are not cases of vs. Our discussion is confined to the use of a *non-proprie* given name to point to the missing *proprie* name as a deliberate means of expression.

The conferring of a name on a new pope is a unique phenomenon concerning the creation of a new identity, in which a man now becomes the vicar of God on earth (Wood 1989: 1). This is a case of leaving out the *proprie* name as the designator of one's uniqueness as a human being. It is therefore not coincidental that only when the pope dies does he finally do so with the sounds of his mother tongue and his given name, like any other mortal.

The next example comes from André Aciman's novel *Call Me by Your Name*. The story concerns the developing relationship between Oliver and Elio. Oliver arrives to spend a summer in Italy as a visiting student with Elio's father, who is a professor of archaeology. Elio resents Oliver's arrival, as he does each of the annual graduate student visitors. However, his resentment gradually wanes, and the teenager Elio and Oliver (ten years his elder) discover their mutual passion for each other. The novel explores the different feelings this arouses: love, fears, confusion, their relationships with others (such as Elio's parents and girlfriend) and their parting when Oliver's stay comes to its end. The novel takes its name from Oliver's request after he and Elio had become intimate:

[~229]   Call me by your name and I'll call you by mine.

This at first sight seems an expression of love. But from the perspective of proper name vs, such a request is interpreted not as one motivated by mature love between two distinct individuals but as a quest for complete merger, as if swallowing the other; not merely bridging but completely obliterating their separateness.

3.2.5.4.4   A Single Letter

Like pronouns and names other than the person's *proprie* name, a single letter is often used to refer to a person without disclosing hes true identity. Inspired by the role of 'x' as an algebraic variable holder, 'x' is frequently used as a generic name initial.

The most notorious example of a letter pointing not to concealment but to proper name vs would seem to be Franz Kafka's 'κ.'.

The following are the opening line of *The Trial*'s first chapter ('The Arrest'):

[~230$^{\text{German-T}}$]   Someone must have been telling lies about Joseph K., for without having done anything wrong he was arrested one fine morning. (p. 7)

and the opening paragraph ('Arrival') of *The Castle*:

[~231$^{\text{German-T}}$]   It was late evening when K. arrived. The village lay deep in snow. The Castle hill was hidden, veiled in mist and darkness, nor was there even a glimmer of light to show that a castle was there. On the wooden bridge leading from the main road to the village K. stood for a long time gazing into the illusionary emptiness above him. (p. 9)

Many commentators have pondered on Kafka's 'κ.': Joseph κ. in *The Trial* and κ. the land surveyor of *The Castle*. Levi (1966) claims that 'from his earliest works to his last, Franz Kafka's central character was Franz Kafka'. Detailing the various names (not only к. but also Franz, Samsa and Gracchus), she concludes that '[T]ogether with the many who have no name, all these characters echo the crucial question asked by the land-surveyor's old assistant, "Then, who am I?"'

Doležel (1983: 519 note 19) quotes Jaffe (1967: 13) who argues that 'the question of whether or not the "K" stands for "Kafka" is less important than the fact that the protagonist has been deliberately deprived of a surname'. This important insight underscores that what matters is not the specific name but the significance derived from that name or the absence of a name when contrasted with other names.

To demonstrate what he terms the 'intentional function of naming', that is, the author's choice to name hes characters using rigid proper names or definite descriptions, Doležel (1983: 519–522) breaks up the names in *The Trial* into five groups: (1) the protagonist forms a one-member subset, singled out by his exclusive proper name, abbreviation; (2) other individuals are designated by standard surnames; (3) others are assigned only first names; (4) agents are named using an unstable, changing definite descriptions; or alternatively (5) a set of individuals are assigned a fixed definite descriptions. Referring to *The Trial*'s protagonist's name in the context of the latter four groups, Doležel (1983: 522) contends that '[t]he intension of exceptionality, uniqueness, which is given by this singling out of the protagonist within the system of fictional characters, outweighs by far the intension of anonymous commonness which this mode of naming evokes in isolation'. Further applying the notion of possible worlds to *The Trial*'s domain of social institutions, Doležel (1983: 524) shows how attention to such oppositions exposes the intentional macrostructure of the novel and so constructs the novel. He then shows how what at first seemed a disjoint set formed by the one-member protagonist proves, when accounting for oppositions, to be the intersection of all three main sets of fictional agents of *The Trial*: the 'private group', the bank and the court. Doležel does not stop here: in light of the above naming groups, he finally attends to the absence of the expected mode of naming Joseph к'.s killers, interpreting this not as an exception or error but as a proper name means of expression. Tying this proper name vs with fictional worlds, Doležel (1983: 524–525) suggests a twist in the line of the story: it is not by the order of the court that Joseph к. is executed: 'there exists a mysterious domain of an absolute, unattached, noninstitutionalized randomness, hiding behind the institutionalized randomness of the Court'.

From the start (see [~230$^{German-T}$] and [~231$^{German-T}$]), the proper name vs forerunners ('Joseph к.' and 'к.') are placed in the context of estrangement. Each of these novels deals in its unique way with the protagonist's identity in the face of the alienation and arbitrariness of bureaucracy. Despite apparent similarities between the themes of the two novels, they are by no means the same. While *The Trial* is rooted in the institution perspective, in which the individual is not only lost and trapped (arrested) but eventually executed, *The Castle* is grounded in the individual perspective, in which the individual surveyor, after getting caught in the alienation and arbitrariness of bureaucracy, becomes active and refuses, resisting borders, attempting to exceed the limits and fighting the option to surrender.

The difference between Joseph к. and к. seems to be communicated also by the proper name vs. The decrementing shaping of the names is its forerunners. To see that we now tie Doležel's (1983) distinction between the notion of a single (fictional) world and that of possible worlds with Amir's distinction (2008) between the actual and possible dimensions. The use only of the first letter of the protagonist's family ('Josef к'.), who would eventually be executed, suggests that the protagonist of *The Trial* is rooted in the actual dimension. *The Castle*'s evolving protagonist, designated solely by the letter 'к.' (which presented in isolation is not necessarily a family name) is less specific and points to an ability to move beyond the actual towards the possible. It is worth noting that Kafka does not offer a happy ending in either novel or for either of these protagonists. This is not only due to Kafka's well-known practice of leaving his novels unfinished. Kafka does not render an optimistic resolution since for all the crucial differences between the two novels, neither of his protagonists wins his freedom. This is portrayed looking at the other side of the proper name vs. which involving non-articulation can tolerate equivocal or even contrasting messages. Not articulating the name also enacts here the dialectical tragedy of the ongoing quest for a reply to (Levi's) universal question 'Then, who am I?'

Kafka's novels, and particularly the name 'к.', have inspired many subsequent works (such as Orson Welles's 1941 *Citizen Kane*). Being intertextually (see §3.2.5.3) inspired, each era, medium, production, location and artist used the notion of 'к.' for hes unique needs, but they all sprout from the quest for a personal and collective answer to 'Then, who am I?' in light of the actual and possible dimensions set within institutional Others.

3.2.5.4.5 Numerals

Referring to individuals by a number when the use of personal names would be expected is the cruellest onomastic practice obliterating one's identity as a unique person. It is important to distinguish between the use of identity numbers alongside names and their use in place of names. The transition from purely bureaucratic identity numbers to the non-innocent use of numbers is clearly indicated by the outcome of such practices.

The Nazis' elimination of the names of the inmates at Auschwitz, leaving them nameless by the categorical use of the tattooed serial number, was not only a means of dehumanisation and annihilation of identity; it was unique in its brutality as part of the Nazi extermination machine. Such was, for example, Primo Levi's

[~232]   A-174517.

Levi (1958: 28–29) recalls his first days in the camp: 'For many days, while the habits of freedom still led me to look for the time on my wristwatch, my new name ironically appeared instead, a number tattooed in bluish characters under the skin'. Primo Levi's description of the 'Null Achtzehn' (1958: 42) is testimony to this practice:

He is Null Achtzehn. He is not called anything except that, Zero Eighteen, the last three figures of his entry number; as if everyone was aware that only a man is worthy of a name, and that Null Achtzehn is no longer a man. I think that even he has forgotten his name, certainly he acts as if this was so. When he speaks, when he looks around, he gives the impression of being empty inside, nothing more than an involucre [...].

As Neumann (2010: 236–238) correctly argues, the foundation of the Nazis' atrocities was the transformation of the victim from a person into an entity whose existence was evident only as a number. The Nazis, of course, committed countless acts of brutality and murder, yet as Primo Levi suggests (1958: 27–28), the tattooing of the identity number, though barely painful and not life-threatening in itself, formed the basis for all that was to come.

3.2.5.4.6   The Absence of a Forerunner as a Forerunner
The absence of a forerunner retroactively stands out as a forerunner pointing to the proper name vs.

We begin with an example from a study conducted by von Hippel and colleagues (1997) who looked at the outcome of programmes concerning the management of temporary employees. To illustrate the negative attitude of the permanent employees towards the temporary employees (prior to the programme), the researchers noted that the former would not bother to learn the names of the temporary workers. '[F]urthermore, temporary workers were issued jumpsuits without their names on the pockets' (1997: 98). Intentionally leaving out the names of the temporary employees expressed the negative attitude of the organisation and the permanent workers to them. By refusing to refer to them by name, they denied their existence, making them inconsequential and lacking individuality. Such actions highlight the status of the name as an indication of identity, both in the eyes of the organisations and their employees (permanent and temporary) and from the researchers' perspective.

The next example comes from a vow made by New Zealand's Prime Minister Jacinda Ardern following a terror attack in Christchurch that killed

3.2.5 Lexical Verbal Silence

fifty people and injured dozens. During a special session of parliament, she said:[103]

[~233]   I implore you, speak the names of those who were lost rather than the name of the man who took them. He is a terrorist. He is a criminal. He is an extremist. But he will, when I speak, be nameless.

Justifying her call, the prime minister verbalises not only the message she communicates using this proper name vs but also the use of such vs alongside the contrastive explicit mention of the victims.

The next example comes from Judi Picoult's novel *My Sister's Keeper* (pp. 99–100). Anna, the younger sister of the Fitzgerald family, was conceived in order to provide a bone marrow match for Kate, her leukaemia-stricken sister (see §3.2.4.4.3 [~114]). Sara Fitzgerald, seated between two other pregnant women under the dryers at the hairdresser's, discusses the names they picked for their coming newborn:

[~234]   The woman on my left grins at me. 'Is this your first?'
[...]
'I have a boy and a girl,' I tell her. 'Five and three.'
'Do you know what you're having this time?'
I know everything about this baby, from her sex to the very placement of her chromosomes, including the ones that make her a perfect match for Kate. I know exactly what I am having: a miracle, 'It's a girl,' I answer.
[...]
'You have any names picked?'
It strikes me that I don't. Although I am nine months pregnant, although I have had plenty of time to dream, I have not really considered the specifics of this child. I have thought of this daughter only in terms of what she will be able to do for the daughter I already have.
[...]
I plan for her to save her sister's life.

The missing name for the baby who Sara Fitzgerald carries depicts that baby's sad status: not a person, daughter or sister in her own right but, as her mother admits and as the unfolding story shows; merely a means to save her sister's life.

The last example of the absence of a name as a proper name vs forerunner is unique in that the addresser of the proper name vs is the name bearer himself. Tabachnick and Klugman (1965) noticed a series of anonymous suicidal telephone calls made to an emergency suicide prevention clinic. Anonymous callers were defined as those who refused to give their name during their first call. The textual analysis of the calls showed that the no-namers made the calls

---

[103] www.bbc.com/news/world-asia-47620630 (accessed 19 March 2019).

to the centre with the unconscious intention but ultimate result of manipulating others, provoking hostility as a way of enacting their experiences of life. They used the no-name to put others through what had been done to them (a conative function, §4.3). Those who did give their names, on the other hand, actually sought help.

3.2.5.5 Part–Whole Relations and Verbal Silence

Not all part–whole incidents involve silence in general or vs in particular. Such are common cases in which the part – rather than the whole – is the focus of the message. We focus here on the forms of part–whole when the addresser uses these lexical containment relations as a vs forerunner: while the message centres on the whole – not as an example but as the subject matter – the addresser articulates (as a vs forerunner) only a part of that whole.

The forerunners of part–whole vs fall into two categories: 'part of a binary contrast' (§3.2.5.5.1) and 'the missing link in a series' (§3.2.5.5.2). For our purposes, suffice it to note that a 'SET X' is equivalent to all members which share the property x. There are non-finite sets and finite ones, there are series and unordered sets.

3.2.5.5.1 Part of a Binary Contrast

A binary set is a finite set consisting of two members excluding and complementing each other. In such sets, the mention of one member is justified when that member is the focus of the message. But when the entire set is expressed only by articulating one member of that contrast this is a binary part–whole vs forerunner.

This is illustrated here with the opening line of Grimm's fairy tale 'The Twelve Brothers':

[~235$^{German-T}$]   Once upon a time a king and a queen lived together peacefully and had twelve children, all boys.

Discussing the silences in this tale (see §2.2.4.1), Raufman and Ben-Cnaan (2011: 147) note:

Thus, from the very beginning, the story expresses a sense of absence; the lack itself is described by this absence. By mentioning the number of sons, we understand that the king and queen have no daughters. The heroine is expressed by her absence, both on the plot level (she does not exist, and this absence is expressed in the opening sentence), and also through the expression that describes an absence by focusing on the existence solely of sons. This represents a textual silence, which expresses the lack of a daughter. On a meta-linguistic level, we see here a foreshadowing of the preference for silence over speech, and a declaration that there is something lacking in this situation, something that is necessary in order to achieve completion.

3.2.5 Lexical Verbal Silence

Another binary vs forerunner involves incidence of incest in sixteenth-century Venice (Ferraro 2008: 45–64). For over six years Sebastian Stanghelin forced sexual relations on his daughter Mattia, as a result of which she gave birth to several babies. Sebastian was jailed. The incident is documented in the testimonies of members of the Stanghelin family. Orsola, Mattia's sister, tells how she decisively rejected their father the first time he approached her, after which he never dared to repeat his attempt. Mattia's brother, Francesco, opens his testimony saying

[~236]   I have three good sisters, and another from my stepmother. My father is a widower. Sir, I'll tell you the truth. My father does some things he should not do [...] Many times I heard my father get up from our bed and go over to Mattia [...]

The father's status as a widower is an objective fact. But coming from that father's son, in the context of his sister's abuse, it serves as a vs forerunner pointing to the subjective context of their mother's death; the fact that he, and more significantly his sisters, grew up without their mother; and their subsequent life with a stepmother, after whose death their father was left a widower for the second time.

Throughout his account of the Stanghelin case, Ferarro expresses uncertainty about Mattia. Her subsequent fate after she was detained, says Ferarro, is unknown. However, Ferraro does ponder on Mattia's choices. For example, he suggests 'that Sebastian eventually succeeded in seducing his daughter. She tacitly assumed a wifely role for him, suggesting that Sebastian's attitude was of critical importance to her own development'.

This paraphrases Francesco's vs:

[~236ᵃ']   *S* [=My mother died] My father is a widower.

This vs depicts the missing (dead) family's maternal figure as the source of affection and protection for her daughters and son, and as an intimate partner to her husband.

The next example is taken from one of the daily reports provided by Dr Shlomo Mor-Josef (Head of Hadassah Medical Centre) on the condition of Israel's Prime Minister Ariel Sharon, who was hospitalised in critical condition following a massive intracerebral haemorrhage in January 2006. In one particular report to journalists and the public, Mor-Josef said that

[~237^(Hebrew-T)]   The left side is preserved.[104]

---

[104] [~237^(Hebrew)] *Ha-cadd ha-jmali šamur* (Hebrew source).

Referring to the left hemisphere is a binary vs forerunner setting the conditions of the two hemispheres apart, and so expressing serious reservations concerning the right hemisphere:

[~237$^{\textit{Ş}\text{-Hebrew-T}}$] The left side is preserved Ş [=while the right side is damaged].

This is not only a matter of two halves constituting a whole but of two complementary halves whose condition dictates the patient's prospect of personal recovery, and more so his ability to resume his role as prime minister (see for example Fisher et al. 2014: 95).

For a literary use of opposition as binary vs, both thematically and linguistically, we return to Shakespeare's 'The Rape of Lucrece' (see [~225] §3.2.5.4.2). As recalled, Shakespeare's heterodiegetic narrator role voicing the protagonists, quoting their speech and speaking on their behalf (see §3.2.5.2.1) is particularly constructive concerning Lucrece, who speaks of being voiceless: 'so much grief and not a tongue' (1462).

In the following lines (659–665, *Norton^1*, p. 656) the narrator quotes Lucrece as appealing to Tarquin's senses and urging him to release her:

[~238] 'So shall these slaves be king, and thou their slave;
Thou nobly base, they basely dignified;
Thou their fair life, and they thy fouler grave;
Thou loathèd in their shame, they in thy pride.
The lesser thing should not the greater hide.
The cedar stoops not to the base shrub's foot,
But low shrubs wither at the cedar's root.

All the scholars who have examined this poem have noted the prominent use of synoecioses to form oxymoronic or paradoxical truths (see for example Belsey 2001: 319). The contrast between superior and inferior (royals and slaves; material and moral; possessing and objectified; voice and voiceless) runs through the poem and is particularly prominent in this stanza. Line 662 is particularly fascinating:

[~238^a] Thou loathèd in their shame, they in thy pride.

The pronouns 'thou'/'they' and 'their'/'thy', while not logically binary, are binary in this context (and in many others). The nominal of opposition of 'shame'/'pride' is indeed binary. While 'shame' is the object of the verb 'loath' the verb of object 'pride' is left uninstantiated:

[~238$^{a\text{-}\textit{Ş}}$] Thou loathèd in their shame, they Ş in thy pride.

In light of this stanza's rigid structure and parallelism, [~238$^{a\text{-}\textit{Ş}}$] appears as a binary vs forerunner. The question is what verb is to be instantiated here, and why it was expressed using part–whole vs. Quoting Lucrece's plea, 'thou' and

3.2.5 Lexical Verbal Silence   243

'thy' refer to Tarquin as a private person and as a representative of a class (royal, aristocrat, male, possessor). Accordingly, 'they' and 'their' refer to antithetical opposites:

[~238^b] So shall these slaves be king, and thou their slave

In [~238^b] Lucrece communicates these opposites to Tarquin both literally, with personal and collective force, and figuratively, as morals: mastering impulses as contrasted to being slaves to them while renouncing one's values. The uninstantiated verb may be that of [~238^b] yielding an elliptic trace of the couple's initial verb:

[~238$^{a'}$] Thou loathèd in their shame, they [Є loathèd] in thy pride

that is, you will be shameful and despised for not succeeding in controlling your own impulses, and these deeds will not render you satisfaction, but instead your pride and your lack of fear and morals will ruin you (here both personally and politically).

However, in light of the central role played by the matter of pride in the poem (see [~225] and [~226] §3.2.5.4.2) and in sustaining the poem's synoeciosis, an alternative to elliptical reduplication seems more plausible. An antonym of 'loathe' is particularly salient in the poem's context of pride inaugurating the rape of Lucrece:

[~238$^{a\text{-}\mathcal{S}'}$] Thou loathèd in their shame, they $\mathcal{S}$ [= praise/glory/lever] in thy pride.

This vs expresses the drastic personal and political turn by which Tarquin, who is unable to control his own impulses, will lose his pride (be shameful and despised), while the objects of his weakness and violence will gain pride.

Lucrece leaves the verb 'praise' of the [~238$^{a\text{-}\mathcal{S}'}$] synoeciosis uninstantiated as a binary vs forerunner in order to express her chastity in thematic and metalinguistic terms (see §4.6). She follows moral standards but does not name her pride; this is the essence of the true modesty she has maintained all her life, that for which her husband extolled her and which triggered her rape (see [~225] §3.2.5.4.2).

Our last examples of binary vs are unique in that they come from animal communication. In his monograph *The Social Contract* (1970: 75), Ardrey explains that '[A]n undisturbed elephant party in a Uganda woodland makes a communal purr which they can hear and we cannot. With any disturbance the purr stops. The elephant's alarm call is silence'.

Sherlock Holmes elucidates the clue that led him to decipher the theft of Silver Blaze from its stable in the King's Pyland estate:

[~239] Before deciding that question I had grasped the significance of the silence of the dog, for one true inference invariably suggests others. The Simpson incident had shown me that a dog was kept in the stables, and yet, though someone had been in and had fetched out a horse, he had not barked enough to arouse the two lads in the loft. Obviously the midnight visitor was someone whom the dog knew well. (Conan Doyle, 'Silver Blaze', p. 331)

The question to be asked here is how, in the context of the Ugandan woodland elephant, vs conveys an alert, while for the domestic dog it is a sign of familiarity. The answer demonstrates how vs, like speech, is context dependent: elephants being the largest mammals on earth care for themselves, and so while vibration can be tracked its absence is not only a means of communal interaction but is also, regarding others, a practical act of camouflage. Dogs, on the other hand, are not only considerably smaller in size but being domesticated depend on their human keepers. They use their bark to communicate impending danger to humans (see also §4.7).

Before moving on to the next group of part–whole vs forerunners, the following comment seems appropriate. The leaving out of formally expected morphological forms (see §3.2.2) or syntactic constituents required by grammar rules (such as a coordinand in a dyadic symmetry, see §3.2.4.6.1, or what seems a probable antecedent for the expected missing VP or verb, see §3.2.4.3.4) as a deliberate means of expression is rightly described as a case involving part–whole vs. Like the part–whole discussed here, there too the notion of the whole precedes its members; for example, the set characterised as a dyadic symmetry precedes this or that coordinant. These morphological and syntactic vss are discussed in §3.2.2, §3.2.3 and §3.2.4 and not here (but see [~238]) because their forerunners are formal, while the lexical vs forerunners discussed here are lexical.

3.2.5.5.2 The Missing Link in a Series

The second part–whole forerunner is confined to series. For a set to be fully ordered, the relations between its members must be transitive and asymmetrical. Ordered sets may be designated as having a lower or upper bound.

The archetypal example of such a set are the ordinal numbers. Its subsets have 'zeroth' or 'first' as their lower bound; some have an upper limit and others do not. As noted, any addresser producing a speech event is doomed to leave things out (see quote from Rescher (1998: 93) in §2.2.3.1). If the focus of the addresser is on the Third Reich, not alluding to the First and Second Reich is probably insignificant. But if the focus of the addresser is on the entire set, leaving out a member of that set when enumerating the set is a serial part–whole vs forerunner.

The best example is depicted in what has been lexicalised as the idiom

[~240]   On second thought.

The second member of an ordered series is always preceded by its first member. The idiom captures the human tendency firstly to react emotionally

3.2.5 Lexical Verbal Silence 245

and only then to consider matters in a rational manner. Virginia Woolf illustrates and explains this in the opening of *A Room of One's Own*. As seen in [~139] (§3.2.4.6.1), Woolf details the two sequential modes of thought: the first conceived while sitting by the river and wondering, and the second reached by consideration. Detailing the two no silence is involved. But when, as in [~19^s] (§3.1) and [~240], the missing link (here – the first thought) is left out, this is a serial part–whole vs forerunner. Such is

[~240^a] On second thought Digital.

Digital Equipment Corporation was known for its PDP and VAX minicomputers. The advert communicates using serial vs:

[~240$^{a\text{-}s}$] $\mathcal{S}$ [= on first thought IBM, but] on second thought Digital.

That is, the consumer's instinct may favour IBM, which was the dominant company through the 1970s and beyond. But considered professionally (the second thought), the consumer will take a different decision and opt for Digital's products.

The next example comes from Kazuo Ishiguro's novel *The Remains of the Day*. The butler Stevens, the first-person homodiegetic narrator of the novel, keeps a diary of his first motoring holiday. The diary tells of his deeds, as well as the autobiographical memories that revive during his six-day trip. Stevens makes regular entries each day, sometimes even several times a day, with one exception: Day Five. The chapter 'Day Four – Afternoon' is followed by 'Day Six'. Says Wolf (2003: 125):

Stevens, in his discourse, establishes a pattern of signifiers [...] from which he deviates by almost an imperceptible omission. Curiously, Stevens does not explain this omission, [...] this missing explanation is a further deviation from the established pattern, this time from a pattern of signifie*ds*, and together with the missing diary entry forms a classic *Leerstelle sensu* Iser.

On 'Day Six', Stevens recounts that on the fifth day he met up with a former friend who disclosed to him that she was unhappy in her married life and actually dreamt of a better life – as his wife. In that 'Day Six' entry, Stevens also mentions that 'her eyes had filled with tears', to which he responded with a smile. Wolf concludes:

The fact that Stevens refrains from explaining why, or even mentioning that, he has not made a diary entry on that important day takes on an iconic value: it corresponds to the absence, or rather suppression, of emotional reactions, of feelings or regrets that would have required an immediate outlet. The *Leerstelle* of the unexplained missing of 'day five' thus mimes a negative content: the sadly missing feelings in Stevens.

As Wolf points out, this iconic semantic gap is brought to the fore by skipping a member of the finite ordered set. Within the structure of the diary, we thus have:

246   Verbal Silence: Forms

[~241']   'Day Four – Afternoon' (ending on page 228)
          ⸱S [= Day five]
          'Day Six – Evening' (starting on page 229)

This serial vs serves an emotive function (see §4.2), as it iconically exhibits aloofness, illustrating Stevens's emotional blindness (in particular when his emotions conflict with his official stance, see §4.7).

Other hierarchical sets may also lend themselves to serial part–whole vs. We now illustrate two cases in which not a single name (see §3.2.5.4) but rather a finite set of titles attached to names create ordered sets involving serial vs.

The first illustration comes from the Talmud maxim:

[~242$^{Hebrew-T}$]   Greater than *Rav* – *Rabbi*;
                     greater than *Rabbi* – *Raban*;
                     greater than *Raban* – his name. (free translation, emphasis added, *Tosefta* 'Testimonies' Ch. 3:4)

The Talmud lays out a hierarchy expressing superiority, this finite series consists of four distinct grades. To distinguish superiority and express respect, the appropriate title is attached to the name, as in:

[~242$^{a-Hebrew-T}$]   Rav Huna;
                       Rabbi Akiva;
                       Raban Gamliel
                       ⸱S Hillel

The most honoured, that is, the fourth degree, is designated using serial vs: the name-person in hes own right is the most honourable.

A similar mannerism is known in Modern English regarding honorific titles for respected surgeons in Britain and the Commonwealth. A journal item published in 1844 in *The Lancet*[105] ends with a list of 'eminent professional gentleman [that] have borne testimony to the valuable properties of the Patent Unfermented Bread &c.' The list is arranged in the alphabetical order of the surname. We reproduce here a small chunk from the list:

[~243]   Dr. J. Blundell
         T. W. Brande, Esq., F. R. S., Professor of Chemistry in the Royal Institute of Great Britain
         Dr. J. Bright
         Sir B. Brodie, Bart. F. R. S., Sergeant Surgeon to the Queen, Surgeon to H. R. H. Prince Albert
         B. Brookes, Esq., Surgeon
         H. Brown, Esq., Surgeon to the Queen

---

[105] *The Lancet*, No. 18, Vol. I, Saturday, 20 July 1844, p. 516 (James G. Wakley Sergeon, ed.), advert following p. 516. https://books.google.com (accessed 28 August 2015).

3.2.5 Lexical Verbal Silence

The serial part–whole vss in [~242$^{\text{Hebrew-T}}$] and [~243] communicate that those who have not reached the highest distinction depend on a title to exhibit their distinction. Those who have earned the highest distinction are honoured and valued on their own merits.

We conclude our presentation of serial vs, as well as the entire chapter on lexical vs, with what has been interpreted as a humorous case entailing not the leaving out a member of a series but rather the jumbling of the order governing that series. The ordered set in question consists of Zelophehad's daughters. The Bible details this set twice:

[~244^a] [. . .] and these are the names of his daughters; Mahlah, Noah, and Hoglah, and Milcah, and Tirzah (Numbers 27:1).

[~244^b] [. . .] For Mahlah, Tirzah, and Hoglah, and Milcah, and Noah, the daughters of Zelophehad, were married unto their fathers brothers' sons (Numbers 36:11).

Puzzled by the different ordering of this set, Radday (1990: 37) adopts an interpretation first proposed by Jellinek (a nineteenth-century Viennese preacher), who explained that 'it is well known and evident to Him, who created the world by His decree, that ladies hate to have their age divulged, for which reason He left the sequence of the births of the five girls undetermined in his Torah by jumbling their names'. To this Radday remarks humorously, 'thus, it would seem that the Jewish God enjoys a good joke'. As Freud and others have argued, in every joke there is some truth as well as humour. This brings us back to serial vs: the truth does not lie only in the claim regarding women and their age complex but also regarding the addressees' grasp that the inconsistency between the ordering of what in reality is one and the same set is significant. Silencing the order is here serial vs – an intentional means of expression.

We here conclude Chapter 3 of our study. As the reader has no doubt noticed, illustrating the different vs forerunners in Chapter 3, we have not confined ourselves to the form of the example. To identify, illustrate and interpret vs we, as the addressees, must consider the meaning of the specific vs in that specific context, referring occasionally to its broader function. In Chapter 4 we focus on the communicative-pragmatic functions played by vs.

4   Verbal Silence
Functions

Vs is defined here as a means of expression: '*unarticulated verbal signifiers chosen by the addresser, that is the speaker (holding the floor) as a verbal means of expression (in place of particular articulated speech) signifying meaningful content*' (see §3.2). Vs shares this arche-function with most instances of speech (but see §2.2.3.2), while it likewise sets vs apart from other silences (see Chapter 2). As a means of expression (like speech), vs is an arche-function covering diverse and distinct functions.

The examination of the functions fulfilled or not by a particular means can take various forms. The functions involving vs can be examined inductively, in a bottom-up order: first detecting vs forerunners and then itemising each of the functions performed in such transactions using vs. Alternatively, one can proceed top down, examining the functions fulfilled or not using vs in light of an existing function theory or model. This could be a general model such as Maslow's (1954: 35–58) motivational and personality-based hierarchy of needs. It could also be a more specific model relating to language and communication.

The perception of vs and speech as mutually complementary means of expression encourages the adoption as our starting point of the model Jakobson (1960) considered the definitive model of the communicative functions of language.

Jakobson developed the model proposed by Bühler (1937; see also Lyons 1977: 51–52). Bühler claimed that three factors participate in every verbal communicative event: the addresser, hence the first-person ('I'); the addressee (the second-person, 'you'); and the world (the referent in the outside world, the third-person, 'it', 's/he', 'they'). To these, Jakobson added three more factors: the channel of communication (belonging both to the outside world and to language); and two factors from the realm of language – the organisation of the message and the code as the object of communication. His model does not end with the identification of these six factors, however. Jakobson's significant contribution was his observation that each of these six factors participates in the communicative event, yet in each such communicative transaction one of the six factors is the most salient. This predominance determines the communicative function of that event.

When the context-world is the centre of the communicative event, the referential function prevails; when the addresser is at the fore, the event serves the emotive

4.1 The Referential Function

function. When the addressee is the focus of the addresser's utterance, the conative function takes over. When the aesthetic traits of the message are at the fore, this establishes the poetic function, while when the focus of the communicative event is the code itself – that is, language as an object – the metalinguistic function prevails. Finally, when the contact – that is, the channel of communication – moves to the fore, the phatic function is at work. While for each communicative transaction the one factor which is salient in that transaction determines that message's function, it is hardly the case that a message serves only a single function.

Each of Jakobson's six functions is considered here in terms of the manner in which it is served by vs in general, and particularly by iconic depictions of absences and presences (§§4.1–4.6). It is our hope that in addition to illuminating the functions served by vs, this examination will throw new light on the communicative functions of speech (see §4.7).

4.1   The Referential Function

A major part of mass and intersubjective communication is directed towards one objective: the transfer of information – making statements regarding the world as the third-person (external in reference to the addresser and to hes addressee). Declarative utterances are the unmarked means of this function.

Examining vs in the context of the referential function requires confirming the ability to use vs to express propositions. As part of his examination of what he terms 'communicative silence' and markedness theory, Sobkowiak (1997) divides the latter into four criteria: content, form, distribution and function. He begins his discussion of the functional criteria by stating that 'speech is capable of fulfilling all six of the Jakobsonian "functions of verbal communication"'. Relating to the referential function, Sobkowiak (1997: 46) asserts that:

Silence, however, is functionally deficient. It is by now commonplace in pragmatic literature that the referential or locutionary force of cs [communicative silence] is nil. While cs is of course not devoid of meaning or contextual sense, it remains referentially void [...]. On the other hand, it does retain the illocutionary force of speech (an aggregate of emotive and conative functions in Jakobson's terms, I presume) in that it is fully capable of actualizing the common speech acts of apologizing, refusing, complaining, questioning, etc.

As discussed (§3.2.2.2), we may compare the different truth values attributed to the propositions here due to the opposition between the zero sign and the non-zero sign signalling different referents:

[~245^a]   Zeiss manufactures glassES (True);

[~245^b]   Zeiss manufactures glassø (False).

However, being lexically or grammatically prescribed sets the zero sign apart from vs. For example [~43^g],

[~43^S̶] Two boyS̶ but one bodyø

(see §3.2.2.2.2) illustrates the addresser's deliberate use of VS serving the referential function, postulating that while the two brothers share one body and their physical unity is indivisible (boyS̶), they are two distinct individuals. Other examples of the use of VS to make assertions were the part–whole lexical forerunners (§3.2.5.5) such as [~235^German-T].

We now add new examples of the use of VS to make assertions, that is, to fulfil the referential function. Examples [~246] and [~247] highlight the default practice in everyday contexts.

The first is the Christian marriage ceremony:

[~246] The minister turns to the participants inviting: 'If anyone here can show just cause why this man and woman should not be joined together in matrimony let him speak now or forever hold your peace'.
Participants: S̶.

This individual and collective VS is the unmarked verbal mode referentially expressing a negative answer:

[~246^S̶] S̶ [= No, I have no just cause to claim].

This is not limited to Hollywood films or to real-life marriage ceremonies; the same usage can be heard daily at the dining table when the family is asked whether they fancy a second helping; in meetings in response to the chairperson's questions, etc. The silence of each individual is an efficient way of indicating the unmarked answer (see also consent, §4.3.3.2.1).

The next example is taken from the UK's visa application form for 'visit and short term stay' (Figure 4.1):

[~247]

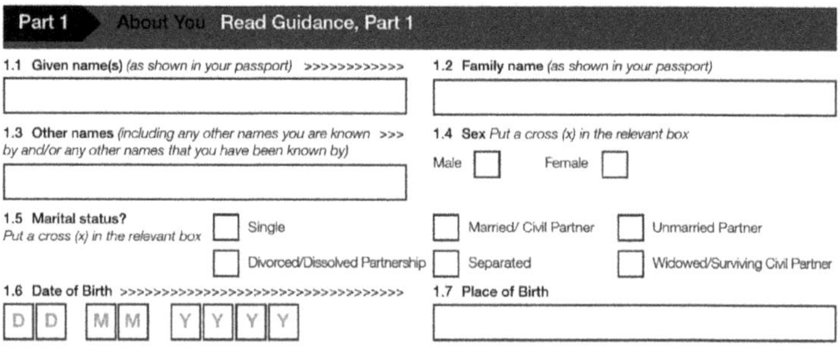

Part 1 About You Read Guidance, Part 1

1.1 **Given name(s)** *(as shown in your passport)* >>>>>>>>>>>>
1.2 **Family name** *(as shown in your passport)*

1.3 **Other names** *(including any other names you are known by and/or any other names that you have been known by)* >>>
1.4 **Sex** *Put a cross (x) in the relevant box*
Male ☐ Female ☐

1.5 **Marital status?**
Put a cross (x) in the relevant box
☐ Single ☐ Married/ Civil Partner ☐ Unmarried Partner
☐ Divorced/Dissolved Partnership ☐ Separated ☐ Widowed/Surviving Civil Partner

1.6 **Date of Birth** >>>>>>>>>>>>>>>>>>>>>>>>>>>>>>>>>>
D D M M Y Y Y Y
1.7 **Place of Birth**

Figure 4.1 UK visa application form for 'visit and short term stay'. Contains public sector information licensed under the Open Government Licence v3.0.[1]

[1] https://assets.publishing.service.gov.uk/government/uploads/system/uploads/attachment_data/file/752360/vaf1a-visitandshorttermstay-11-18.pdf (accessed 9 March 2020).

4.1 The Referential Function

Typically, all forms are issued to draw information, that is, to serve the referential function. Leaving a section blank may be the outcome of carelessness or it may reflect a conscious desire not to provide the requested information (see §2.2.4.1). Alternatively, the person or organisation filling this form may leave a section blank indicating that they lack the needed information; or they may do so indicating that this detail is not applicable in hes specific case. The latter will not be permissible when a legally competent person fills in sections such as hes given name or place of birth. But this is indeed the default way of indicating the unmarked situation in which the person has no names other than a given name and a family name (1.3 of [~247]), and see §3.2.5.4). The justification for this use of vs to fulfil the referential function is not only its iconic trait (being transparent: void for void) but more so the unequivocal nature of its practical efficiency. Once a sign – any sign – is entered it may be unclear whether it should be interpreted as content or as a meta-sign. This also holds for multiple possibilities (such as 1.4 and 1.5 of [~247]), in which one is expected to mark one of the possibilities and leave the others blank, indicating that they are irrelevant.

The truth or falsehood of a proposition expressed using vs is applicable only when one assumes that silence carries content. Tiersma (1995: 44–45) focuses on the legal-referential status of silence, noting that in the courtroom context the distinction between communication and inference is crucial. As he explains, 'it does not suffice, for a perjury conviction, that someone might draw a false inference from the silence of someone under oath. Instead the silence must communicate a message, for only then can the witness willfully make a false statement'. He illustrates this with various cases brought to court. One such case involves a taxpayer who completed an Internal Revenue form which included questions about several specific sources of income. The taxpayer had an additional source of income that was not explicitly included in the requests for information. In response to a catch-all question asking the taxpayer to list all income of any type not reported on the form, the taxpayer placed nothing on that blank. He then signed a declaration under penalty of perjury that the information on the form was accurate. Tiersma (1995: 45) summarises this case quoting a court observation that 'failure to [fill in the blank] was equivalent to an answer, and a false one at that'.

The next example we consider here presenting vs serving the referential function is:

[~248]   If u c rd th msg
         u c bkm a sec
         & gt a gd jb
         learn shorthand
         in as little as 6 weeks.

This is a case of iconic phonetic vs (see §3.2.1) in which, as appears from the text's verbalisation, the vs provides objective information concerning the world and thus serves the referential function. This example is also interesting in that it demonstrates Jakobson's claim that:

> The verbal structure of a message depends primarily on the predominant function. But even though a set (*Einstellung*) toward the referent, an orientation toward the CONTEXT – briefly the so called REFERENTIAL, 'denotative,' 'cognitive' function – is the leading task of numerous messages, the accessory participation of the other functions in such messages must be taken into account by the observer. (1960: 353)

Dressler (1987: 117), our source for this example, reveals that he saw it in a New York subway station. [~248] is, of course, an advert, and as such it seeks to activate the addressees (to enrol in the shorthand course) and belongs in the conative function (see §4.3.3.1). Employing the code – that is, the message's form – both to draw the attention of the potential addressees and to iconically convey the message is an instance of the metalinguistic function (§4.6). In this case, both the referential and the metalinguistic function support the predominant conative function of the text.

Our last example of vs serving the referential function comes from Grice (1989: 33):

[~249]   Dear Sir, Mr. X's command of English is excellent, and his attendance at tutorials has been regular. Yours, etc.

The basic assumptions underlying Grice's (1989: 28) model is that the purpose of conversation is a maximally effective exchange of information. Furthermore, Grice contends that talking is a form of rational behaviour. His major contribution is the integration of these expectations into a theoretical inferential phase that takes place between formal language (logic) and natural language. This is the phase which Grice (1989: 26) defines as the cooperative principle: 'Make your conversational contribution such as is required, at the stage at which it occurs, by the accepted purpose or direction of the talk exchange in which you are engaged'. Grice breaks down the cooperative principle into four maxims: quantity, quality, relation and manner. He quotes example [~249] to illustrate the flouting of the maxim of quantity by what is said. The maxim is particularly challenging in the context of vs in general and its fulfilment of the referential function in particular.

Grice provides the following context for [~249]: 'A is writing a testimonial about a pupil who is a candidate for a philosophy job'. Examining [~249] in that context, he contends that the letter observes his cooperative principle (and even the maxim of quantity) by what is implicated, he glosses:

> A cannot be opting out, since if he wished to be uncooperative, why write at all? He cannot be unable, through ignorance, to say more, since the man is his pupil; moreover,

4.1 The Referential Function

he knows that more information than this is wanted. He must therefore, be wishing to impart information that he is reluctant to write down. This supposition is tenable only if he thinks Mr. X is no good at philosophy. This then is what he is implicating. (1989: 33)

Referencing this very sample, Kasher (1976: 211) suggests that at first glance such a case may involve deviation from the principle of relation ('be relevant') and possibly also flouts the principle of quantity. However, he goes on to say that at second glance, the picture changes. Grice's description of the situation (as cited above) makes it clear that the addresser is, in fact, cooperative. S/he is writing the letter; s/he does not opt out; s/he cannot say more.

We use Grice's example ([~249]) to consider whether vs always flouts Grice's cooperative principle or its maxims, or whether, as a deliberate means of expression, it may sometimes (like speech) comply with the cooperative principle and so serve communication, here the referential function.

Maintaining the same circumstances, and assuming (as do Grice 1989 and Kasher 1976, at least for this case; and see also Kasher 1976: note 15) that the addresser is cooperative, s/he had two options: vs or speech. Had s/he chosen the latter, s/he might have phrased hes statements in this form:

[~249'] Dear Sir, Mr. X's command of English is excellent, and his attendance at tutorials has been regular. In connection with X's candidacy for the said academic post, my opinion is negative. Yours, etc.

[~249"] Dear Sir, My opinion in connection with Mr. X's candidacy for the said academic post is negative. Yours, etc.

Clearly, the three texts ([~249], [~249'] and [~249"]) all boil down to one and the same message: the addresser's negative evaluation of the candidate. As a letter of recommendation initiated not by the candidate or hes teacher but by the hiring party, its goal is to help its recipients arrive at the best decision about the most suitable applicant. As such, it has its own very specific rules (which we might collectively call the 'cooperative principle' of recommendation letters).

For example, the list of tips on 'what helps' and 'what hurts', gathered by a survey at Yale,[2] reveals that there is an expected checklist of what should appear there, such as an indication of distinctions and outstanding achievements, especially relative to the candidate's peers. Among these tips we also find a clause encouraging the letter writer to give examples to support any claims made. Their list of grounds for opting out makes clear that the letter writer in our example was not in a position to get away with saying 'no'. Had

---

[2] Responses to an informal survey of Truman Scholarship selection panel members asking: 'What do you like to see in a letter of recommendation, and what leaves you cold?' www.yale.edu/yalecollege/academics/fellowships/application/writing.html (accessed 19 June 2011).

s/he wanted to write the letter in spite of hes negative stance, s/he could have written [~249"]; had s/he been eager to express hes negative opinion, s/he could have gone through the checklist in detail.

The Yale survey respondent's saying, '[W]e have also found that, unless a student is first in a class, it is often not helpful to give a class ranking', reflects this point. This same point produced Grice's original example [~249].

In the wording of example [~249], the writer mentions two qualities of Mr X, even though s/he knows that these are not the qualifications needed. S/he does so not with the intention of flouting the maxim of quantity and the maxim of relevance ('be relevant'). On the contrary, [~249] illustrates a situation in which the norm-expectancy makes the use of vs the only permissible way to provide the required relevant information and so fulfil the referential function. Returning to Grice's use of [~249] in the above description, example [~249] shows that vs may be the optimal way to comply with the quantity maxim, enabling the contribution to be just as informative as required and not more so.

It is important to note that unlike the implicatures, such as those drawn by the addressee as to A's cooperation (see Grice above), A's assessment that X is not qualified for the job is provided explicitly using vs.

In summary, not only have we seen many daily communicative events in which, contrary to Sobkowiak's (1997) argument, verbal referential or locutionary force is by no means nil – we have also seen that cases in which meaningful vs and not speech is the expected answer are by no means rare. This realisation might seem to challenge our condition limiting vs to communicative events in which speech is expected (see §4.0, the introduction to this chapter). However, this challenge is easily resolved by noting that in examples [~246], [~247] and [~249], as well as in the case cited from Tiersma (1995: 44–45), the answer or statement provided using vs is not the only possible one. Vs is informative because these are not rhetorical questions (see §4.3.3.2.1). A person may have additional names (1.3 of [~247]); a participant may speak out against a marriage ([~246]); the teacher writing a recommendation letter may make positive statements describing a qualified candidate. In each such case, vs is merely the expected unmarked default practice.

We conclude our presentation of the vs serving the referential function by quoting two sayings: 'silence speaks louder than words' (see Jensen 1973: 252–254 on the 'revelational function') and 'if you do not understand my silence, you will not understand my words' (see Tannen 1985: 95).

4.2   The Emotive Function

At the centre of the emotive function stands the addresser as the speaking 'I'. Within the emotive function, this self is not stated as a referent in the world but

4.2 The Emotive Function

instead 'aims a direct expression of the speaker's attitude toward what he is speaking about. It tends to produce an impression of a certain emotion whether true or feigned' (Jakobson 1960: 354). While any use of a pronoun other than the first-person singular can be ambiguous, 'I' ('me') always refers to the person speaking and is unequivocal, although of course its referent changes as the speaker changes ('I' can only be ambiguous in fictive speech, such as quoting in general and the speech of actors in particular; see §3.2.5.2 and [~143] in §3.2.4.6.1). The expression of emotion as the shortest disposition (distinct from feelings, mood or temper) can only refer to the self 'I': 'I now feel' (see also Weisman 1955: 242). And so 'you feel happy' and 'I felt sad yesterday' are not emotive expressions but rather assertions belonging to the referential function (and hence true or false).[3] Since the speaking self is pragmatically determined, the explicit mention of the pronoun is often superfluous.

Jakobson (1960: 354) contends that 'the purely emotive stratum in language is presented by the interjections' (see also Volek 1987: 12). To properly present the close iconic trait between vs and emotions in general, and the emotive function in particular, we may take a quick look at interjections. Peirce (1965: V, 180–183, §§299–300) clarifies that while the image is not monadic (as a pure icon) it is the closest a genuine icon can get. '[T]he lowest form of language is the exclamation, by which an entire idea is vaguely conveyed through a single sound' (OED: Exclamation, N4.b Grammar=interjection, after Henry Spencer (1862: ii, 162)). Pure interjections are symptoms. Peirce (1965: III, 211, §362) defines a symptom as a sign which 'signifies its object solely by virtue of being really connected with it'. Onomatopoeias are the imitation of natural noises by speech sounds (see §3.2.1). Interjections, unlike animal calls or the sounds of water dripping or the wind whistling, are produced by the same agents and vocal organs as speech. They therefore partake in simple qualities of their object and so constitute the prototypical verbal image. A common example will suffice:

[~250]   a(h) (or 'ouch').

These sounds are produced not as signs – communicating to and sharing with others – but as physiological outlets. The 'a(h)' or 'ouch' are the sounds of air exiting when exhaling. It is important to point out that the above applies only

---

[3] This is why the singular 'I' and the plural 'we' (exclusive) are not symmetrical. 'We are proud', involving emotions of others than the addresser himself, is referential.

to such simple interjections and not to lexemes used interjectionally. This limits 'symptomatic expressions' to 'a sign that is a sign through the fact of its production' (Volek 1987: 5–6, after Morris 1946; see also Volek 1987: 28–29; and see §2.2.1).

To that we add the explanation that these are 'so called because, when so used, it is interjected between sentences, clauses, or words, mostly without grammatical connection' (OED: Interjection, N2.a. Grammar) and because they differ from means of referential language both by their atypical sound patterns and by their syntactic role (being equivalent not to sentences' constituents but to entire sentences, see Jakobson 1960: 354). Interestingly, the OED remarks that '[M]iddle English $\bar{a}$ in this interjection ['ah'] did not generally undergo the Great Vowel Shift, apparently owing to its connection with the natural utterance which it ultimately represents' (OED: Ah, Int. and N).

Examining VS as a verbal signifier reveals that in the context of absence VS is an onomatopoeic image (see the earlier quotes from Peirce 1965 and Spencer 1862). Onomatopoeic silence as a verbal signifier emerges as one of the most intuitive and iconic modes of representation (see §3.2.1). Indeed, it is unique in the sense that, when examined on the basis of the notion of silence as void, its transition from its source occurrence to the verbal-linguistic system (VS) does not involve translation or modification. This encompasses psychosomatic symptoms emerging in silence as well as silence as enactment.

Because the onomatopoeic VS signifier, that is, null articulation, appears identical to other silences (see Chapter 2), not only is it a universal signifier but together with the image interjection 'ah' these are the only universal verbal signifiers. While its use varies among cultures and eras, it is shared one way or another by all humans. Tied with Jakobson's insight that 'the purely emotive stratum in language is presented by the interjections' and the indispensable association between those and psychosomatic symptoms and acting out, VS seems to reign over the emotive function. In fact, all scholars who investigate silence as a means of expression seem to agree on the emotive force of silence. The addresser may use VSs to express and share hes inner world: that which is the focus of the emotive function.

While silence in general and VS in particular are made apparent by the absence of expected sounds, silence is strongly associated with intense emotion, which, in turn, is associated with reduced control and consciousness. This may seem to counter the deliberate choice of VS as a means of expression. For silence to belong in the emotive function that silence must be a mode of expression such that is focused on the addresser's inner world (Figure 4.2).

4.2 The Emotive Function

We each carry in our heart, yearning or with dread, that silence:

[~251]

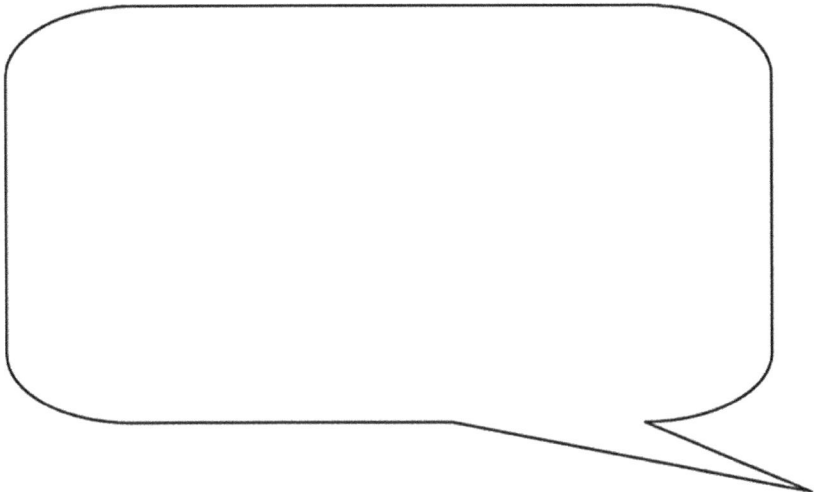

Figure 4.2 That silence which I carry.

Each of us is invited to mint here the impression of an emotive silence s/he carries: an equivocal or unequivocal silence; one which was comforting or not; sharp or tender, happy or sad; connecting or distancing.

Starting here in the context of the emotive function with the personal and unique emotive silence each reader has just contributed is appropriate given the focus of the emotive function on the experiencing addresser. This process also evinces that emotive vss, like other functions of vss, are not a theoretical matter confined to literary works and copywriters but occur in daily interpersonal interactions.

Bruneau (1973: 33–34) states that:

Deep emotion need not be expressed by outburst. Often, deep emotional states are expressed in silence. Intense grief, sorrow, and great disappointment are quiet states – words are difficult to find.[4] [...] The deepest fears and the most intense joys are wordless – or undifferentiated, repetitive sounds. In short: Silence is the language of all strong passions: love, anger, surprise, fear.

This statement must be taken with a grain of salt, as Bruneau fails to distinguish between emotion as the content of expression, such as in the emotional function, and emotion as blocking expression. This reservation applies

---

[4] See also §4.6.4.

likewise to Heinrich Heine's statement that silence is a precondition for happiness, and to the question posed by Marcel Marceau – the world's greatest mime: 'Do not the most moving moments of our lives find us all without words?' Shakespeare's 'Silence is the perfectest herald of joy' (*Much Ado About Nothing*, II.i.270, *Norton*[3], p. 363), on the other hand, is silence as a forerunner (herald) and unequivocally represents vs as a means of expression.

To the many examples detailed throughout our study illustrating emotive vs associated with intensive emotive experiences, we discuss here new examples. The first example dates back to Lincoln's Gettysburg Address (19 November 1863). Olinick (1982: 463) reminds us that at the closure of this famous address the audience responded with silence and refrained from clapping, as a manifestation of the intensive emotions experienced by the individuals comprising that crowd. The sound of applause is a nonverbal means by which an audience express appreciation, and its absence when expected is usually taken to express the lack of appreciation. It may also indicate symptomatic behaviour resulting from exceptional intensive emotional states blocking expression. But as people present in the audience (over 15,000 participants) reflected, the Gettysburg event was an example of a unique moment when the sound of clapping was sensed as superfluous: interrupting (see also two-minute silence as a linking mode, §4.4). Silence was thus chosen by most of the individuals present as a deliberate action, expressing a deep emotional experience.

The next example is quite recent and was covered extensively by the world media as well as in scholarly publications. These are the emotive vss so strongly associated with the tragic death of Diana Princess of Wales. Naturally, the huge number of people who left messages on the ground by the railings of Buckingham Palace and at other sites around the UK, and those who wrote tributes in condolences books, all chose words over vs. However, the following are two of many reports on emotive silence as a prominent device among the mourners:

[~252]   I live in central London. On the morning of the funeral I began to watch television as the cortege began its journey through Hyde Park, and then through familiar streets. Most striking perhaps was not the expected silent crowds nor the crunching hooves and feet, but the rhythmic tolling of the Westminster Abbey bell, once every minute [...] Some time around 10.15, as the procession neared Whitehall, my wife and I decided to walk to the Abbey [...] to take in the atmosphere, the silence, the emptiness of the city, the strangeness of it all (Silverstone 1998: 81–82).

[~253]   We must also beware of being misled by the media that September 1997 revealed a peculiarly emotional populace. Those actually present spoke not of hysterical, Mediterranean crowd of keeners, but of a haunting silence, punctuated by sobs. The weeping was noticeable only because it stood out

4.2 The Emotive Function

from the silence [...] It was, therefore, a remarkable achievement that the television coverage of the funeral itself managed to convey an awesome silence, itself a liminal contrast to the images of weeping and speaking that had dominated the screens for the previous six days. (Walter 1999: 25)

In 'Mourning and Melancholia' (1917), Freud ponders in depth on the fact that in mourning 'it is the world which has become poor and empty'. This explains why vs is an iconic means for the mourner (see [~284] in §4.5.1). Mourning is not confined to feelings towards the deceased but also triggers emotions centred in the mourner. In this context, silence – and not speech – offers a suitable framework for varied emotions, freeing the mourner from the obligation to choose fixed and objective terminology. These two elements are particularly relevant when looking at cases, such as Princess Diana's death, in which the personal emotions were experienced by a vast number of individuals who had never met or had any personal contact with the Princess.

For an example of emotive vs as the burst of a personal-private intensive emotion, we point to Bashō's Haiku [~285^{Japanese}] Matsushima. The parsimonious wording, comprising a single noun ('Matsushima'), an interjection, a cutting silence word and syntactic vs, onomatopoeically expresses what Yasuda (1957: 34–40) terms 'ah-ness': the state of mind in which the beholder can only give one breath-long exclamation of delight: 'Ah' (see §4.5.2).

The emotive first-person present 'I' is absent both from the collective Gettysburg non-applause and from the most personal [~285^{Japanese}] Matsushima astonishment. Nevertheless, the first-person and hes inner self are present, as the experiencing speaker, by hes eloquent use of vs to serve the emotive function.

The emotive vs in the next two cases is not triggered by intensive 'ah-ness' but by a tender and personal emotion of loss and longing, echoing, as it were, the proverb 'still waters run deep'. Despite the unequivocal preference of psychoanalysis ('talking cure') for verbalisation as the optimum means of expression, Arlow (1961: 48) delineates here emotional states in which speech, that is, words as the unmarked means of expression, seems to be unable to serve the emotive function. He says that: 'In the course of regression, derivatives of preverbal experiences may appear or highly complex emotional states or physical sensations may be experienced; situations which are not only confusing, but for which a ready reserve of verbal images is hardly available' .

A most impressive example is reported by Serani (2000). Serani experiences Sara as a textbook 'good patient': 'very likable person, and both she and I found ourselves very drawn into the work that we were doing. Over the next year a silence fell within each session' (2000: 508). In her case report, Serani describes this repetitive, prolonged silence; she reflects that while Sara's prolonged unexplained silences were distressful and annoying for her, Sara appeared calm and content. She also describes this silence as undemanding – an 'unusual silence'. She then reveals the external circumstances which shifted the metalinguistic focus (see §4.6.4) to these silences. Sara's therapist knew that Sara's mother had died when Sara was a year old. Sara now disclosed to her therapist that her mother had been deaf and dumb (and had been unable to speak or sign). It thus appeared that Sara's silence in the therapeutic sessions re-enacted her interactions with her mother. Using the same code she had practised as an infant with her mother, Sara's metalinguistic vs expressed an emotional silence. Says Serani: '[T]he next several weeks were spent just having the silence. Remaining in the quietness was now not a curious or frustrating exchange, but one of a union of sorts' (2000: 517). This working through gave voice to Sara's memories of compassion and holding she experienced in silence with her late mother and to her longing for such a calm and bonding relationship (see also Weisman 1955: 252).

The next example comes from Elisabeth Kübler-Ross's (1998) report on the tremendous discord between the needs of the dying person (here a sixteen year old) and those of the surrounding family and medical staff:

[~254] [...] I introduced the girl and explained that she had generously volunteered to answer their questions on what it is like to be terminally ill. [...] Obviously the students were uncomfortable. When I asked for volunteers, nobody raised a hand. Finally I selected a handful of students, called then onto the stage and instructed them to ask questions. All they could muster were questions about blood count, the size of her liver [...]

When it was clear they weren't going to ask anything about her personal feelings, I decided to steer the interview in the direction I envisioned. But I didn't have to. In a passionate fit of anger, Linda herself lost patience with her interrogators. Fixing her unimpressed brown eyes on them, she posed and answered the questions she had always wanted her physician and team of specialist to ask her. What was it like to be sixteen and given only a few weeks to live? What was it like not to be able to dream about the high school prom? [...]

After nearly half an hour, Linda tired and returned to her bed, leaving the students in a stunned, emotional, almost reverential silence. Quite a change had overtaken them. Although the lecture time was over, no one got up to leave. They wanted to talk but didn't know what to say until I started the discussion. Most admitted that Linda had moved them to tears. [...] They couldn't help but think about what it would be like if they were in Linda's place.

'Now you are reacting like human beings instead of scientists,' I offered. Silence.

'Maybe now you'll not only know how a dying patient feels, but you'll also be able to treat them with compassion the same compassion that you'd want for yourself'. (1998: 132–133)

This report illustrates the roles played by the varied silences: from silencing death and the emotions it raises by asking other questions (see §2.2.3.1 on 'the

4.2 The Emotive Function

unsaid'); to emotive vs as a means of expression: the 'almost reverential silence' (see also phatic silence on identification §4.4); and the peak with the entire turn consisting of the individual silence in response to Kübler-Ross's suggestion, or rather rebuke. Each of the students may have experienced and so expressed a different emotion using this silence: blame, regret or shame; pity and sorrow; or insight prompting courage and determination.

Emotive vs is strongly associated both in phenomenological and ontological terms with the expression of intensive and deeply personal emotions (see also [~103] §3.2.4.4.1). But emotive vs is likewise extensively used to express aloofness or self-detachment. To the examples of aloofness discussed when looking at form (see for example [~10] in the introduction to Chapter 2 and [~241'] §3.2.5.5.2) we add T. S. Eliot's 'The Waste Land': II 'A Game of Chess'. The poem involves different speakers and voices discussing marital relations. Unlike the mono-dialogue (see §4.5.3), here both voices are exposed. To differentiate the utterances, Eliot inserts that of the desperate wife in quotation marks, while those of her husband are indicated using indentation:

[~255]   'My nerves are bad to-night. Yes, bad. Stay with me.
         Speak to me. Why do you never speak? Speak.
             What are you thinking of? What thinking? What?
         I never know what you are thinking. Think.'

         I think we are in rats' alley
         Where the dead men lost their bones.

         'What is that noise?'
                 The wind under the door.
         'What is that noise now? What is the wind doing?'
                 Nothing again nothing. (p. 67)

As part of his exploration of ellipsis and recoverability (see §3.2.4), Wilson (2000: 51–54) analyses short extracts from 'A Game of Chess' to find that recoverability fails. Wilson interprets Eliot's distinctive use of the quotation mark and indentation notations as a poetic means enforcing the reinterpretation of the entire part. Those are not to be overlooked as external arbitrary notations but instead as the location of silence (indicated by Wilson using square brackets):

[~255ª]   ... 'What shall we do tomorrow?
         What shall we ever do?'
         * [tomorrow we shall do] The hot water at ten.
         * And if it rains, [we shall do] a closed car at four.

But this is not a matter of syntax and form here, as Wilson (2000: 54) explains:

> This is Eliot's way of representing an anxious and fretful woman talking aloud to an indifferent husband who maintains his silence, but answers in his head. The husband's final unvoiced enumeration of routine events underlies

the atmosphere of mental unease. Here we have a failing relationship in 'The Game of Chess', Eliot's suggestive metaphor for the marital relationship he depicts.

Intensive emotions, deep tender emotions and indifference are each associated with silence and constitute iconic instances of vs. The distinction between paralinguistic symptomatic silences and vs as means of expression may blur when such symptoms are the topic of verbalisation, such as in literary works or naïve daily reports. Examples of this include the symptomatic silences we discussed when looking at vs forerunners, some of which resulted from intensive positive emotions, which when not overwhelming are most welcome, such as astonishment and surprise in S_1 of [~7^S] (§2.0), while others resulted from negative emotions, such as for example fear in [~292] (§4.6.3.3.2), or turmoil in S_1 of [~8^S] (§2.0): the urge to speak out and the fear to speak out (and so be resented or be misunderstood), [~82] (§3.2.4.2) or the experience of an alienated false self, such as, for example, in [~103] (§3.2.4.4.1), [~190^e] (§3.2.5.2.2) and [~241'] (§3.2.5.5.2).

4.2.1   The Diminutive

Before concluding the presentation of vs serving the emotive function, we must consider the diminutive. As explained in §3.2.1, the diminutive was first studied as a linguistic grammatical category from the perspective of its form, that is, phonetic and morphologically derivatives, denoting small size. Only later did the semantic and pragmatic (contextual) qualitative interest in diminutives arise. Barbara Strang (1962: 121–122) comments on what she terms 'mature diminutive':

Diminutives are usually forms that have begun by meaning 'a small one of its kind' but have undergone a development whereby they come to express not merely an assessment of size, but also, or even exclusively, the speaker's response to small things, a response ranging from affection through condescension to contempt; we might say that a diminutive is mature when it carries only this 'response'-meaning.

Examples are

[~256]   Aggressive → aggro (milder aggression, troublemaking);

[~257]   Mistress → Miss (suggesting, as Sundén, 1904: 67 points out, a tone of sneer and disregard).

Forms such as [~256] and [~257], derived using truncation, indeed have a distinct meaning to their full form, and this additional meaning may indeed be emotive. However, they are lexicalised, and as such are not the product of the addresser's choice of vs as a means of expression. Moreover, their emotive force often fades, as is the case with [~256] and [~257]. Volek (1987: 38) adds

4.2 The Emotive Function

to Strang's above observation a semantic differentiation between notational-evaluative diminutives and emotive diminutives: the latter may not be associated with any positive or negative attitude towards the stimulus, and they contain an *Excitizer*, that is, 'an emotive component of meaning present in a sign in an expressive way (i.e. relating directly or through an associative component to its object-emotion)'.

Examining here the diminutive phenomenon as an instance of emotive vs, three questions arise: where does vs emerge, what does it communicate and why is that so?

Clearly, not all diminutive forms involve vs. Affixation is a common morphological device across languages and language families (see [~262]). Derivation can either add the emotive component (to the base) or modify a base incorporating an emotive component. Bare truncation, such as

[~258]   Mother → Maś

that is, the reduction of the base not followed by suffixation or duplication, is the vs forerunner of the diminutive serving the emotive function. Thus the truncation of the form functions as a forerunner to the vs emotive-diminutive meaning.

Yet, irrespective of the languages examined, most studies completely ignore the formation of diminutive by truncation (Volek 1987 is such an example). This is surprising, since regardless of language this non-prototypical formation not only prevails in infants' pre and protomorphology but is also believed to be the first derivational morphology rule they acquire (for discussion, see Dressler and Karpf 1994; Schneider 2003: 9–11, 233–234).

As Volek and others show, the association between the quantity sememe and the *Excitizer* is by no means accidental. It evolved both phylogenetically (concerning languages) and ontogenetically (concerning speakers) from the objective quantity physical sememe: reduced size (compared to a norm) through metonymic and metaphoric semantic shifts to its subjective and contextual *Excitizer* emotive components. In the anthropocentric setting of languages and their speakers, young animate offspring, and children in particular, are both the prototypical objects denoted by the [– quantity] sememe and the triggering users and consumers of diminutives.

This contiguity between content (smallness) and form (diminutives) triggers the qualitative metonymy introducing and so attaching the emotive components to diminutives. These include familiarity, affection and endearment, as well as negative emotions such as hatred (see also Volek 1987: 241). The OED quotes Edmund Burke (1757), who contends that '[i]n most languages, the objects of love are spoken of under diminutive epithets' (OED: Diminutive, Adj and N A.1 Grammar).

In addition to the overall association between smallness, children, familiarity and emotions, the bare truncation diminutive is iconic in respect to smallness: the reduction of form communicates the emotive and physical qualities associating with smallness.

A chief category iconically expressing affection using vs as an emotive forerunner is spontaneous hypocoristics. Hypocoristics are shortened or abbreviated forms of people's given names (or in specific social groups surnames):

[~259]   Elizabeth → ⌽Beth; Elizabeth → Liz⌽

[~260]   Lady Diana → Lady Di⌽ (see §4.2).

Spontaneous hypocoristics are either private hypocoristics or known and even lexicalised truncated forms deliberately chosen by the addresser to express emotion when the full form is expected (see §3.2.1). While the addressee-referent of 'Ma' and the like emotive flavour is the maternal kin, this is not the case with

[~261]   Brother → Bro⌽

which when not directed at one's brother is an affectionate hypocoristic by its lexeme (brotherhood) and its emotive-diminutive vs.

Due to the association between diminution and affection, conventional diminutive suffixes (such as 'i', 'ie' and 'y') also likewise serve as affection morphemes forming 'pet names' and more appellation forms. In fact, many affectionate names are formed by combining subtraction (phonetic vs) with addition:

[~262]   Robert → Rob⌽ → Robby.

4.3   The Conative Function

Despite the fact that all functions are initiated by the verbal behaviour of the addresser, the conative function centres on the second person, that is the Other ('Thou').

Jakobson explains that 'orientation toward the ADDRESSEE, the CONATIVE function, finds its purest grammatical expression in the vocative and imperative, which syntactically, morphologically, and often even phonemically deviate from other nominal and verbal categories' (1960: 355). He confines the conative function to a grammatically explicit instructing form. This is not surprising bearing in mind that this function was proposed by Bühler in the 1930s and adopted by Jakobson, two scholars preceding the pragmatic turn. Before discussing pragmatic conative vs, including other addressee oriented utterances, a note must be made regarding Jakobson's observation that imperatives and vocatives deviate from other categories. The most apparent morphosyntactic characteristic of the imperative, but not of the vocative, is that its subjectless structure leaves out the second-person nominal PRO, thus (Jakobson's 1960: 355 example):

[~263]   Drink!

Leaving out the second-person, that is, the focus of the communicative event, may seem odd at first glance. However, for an imperative to serve its function, the addresser must produce it in the presence of hes addressee, and accordingly it is the mention of the addressee which either becomes odd or presents the utterance as a vocative rather than an imperative. Leaving out the redundant subject PRO, being a means dictated by grammar, is a case of the zero sign and not one involving vs (see §3.2.2.2).

But the conative function focusing on the addressee exceeds the signifier–signified verbal relation. As a communicative event initiated by the addresser to activate hes addressee, it resides in the use of language, that is, pragmatics, and particularly speech-act theory. This is not to say that all speech-acts belong in the conative function.

Pragmatics is a relative newcomer to the field of linguistics that highlights the call for a distinction between using language to say (constative utterances) and using language to do (performatives). But as Austin discovers half way through his book *How to Do Things with Words* (1962: 109), utterances are not exclusively constative or performative; they may in fact serve three non-exclusive verbal acts or modes: locutionary acts, illocutionary acts and perlocutionary acts.

This distinction is at the basis of speech-act theory. While the locutionary act is associated with the referential function (§4.1), the last two modes are strongly associated with the conative function. To show this we chose a 1930s Marmite advert:

[~264]   MARMITE Definitely Does You Good
         and you'll enjoy it too[5]

In terms of verification, [~264] is stated as a constative utterance performing a locutionary act. This utterance, in turn, is composed of two concatenated assertions, which while making claims regarding the second-person, that addressee is here the referent of a claim concerning facts in the world (the referential function). Examined in its pragmatic context as an advert, [~264] indicates that the motivation triggering the addresser's utterance is not referential, and so the second-person is not just any referent. The addresser here

---

[5] From Tom Smith's write-up 'marmite-v-vegemite-whats-the-difference', *The Culture Trip*, 7 November 2017, https://theculturetrip.com/pacific/australia/articles/marmite-v-vegemite-whats-the-difference/ (accessed 30 July 2019).

does not wish to make a statement; s/he initiates [~264] as an illocutionary act performed to influence the addressee, indirectly encouraging hem to purchase the product. This, in turn, raises various likely and less likely affects, which are accounted for as the perlocutionary component of the conative function.

Compared to [~263], [~264] is not structured and not performed to instruct. Wilson (2000: 178–179) adds to Jakobson's instructive phase Leech's notion of 'influencing the addressee in some way' and Kinneavy's notion of the 'persuasive'. These, supported also by the Latin etymology of 'conative', lead Wilson to extend the function centred on the addressee to any rhetoric initiated by the addresser to get others to do things. Illocutionary and other acts within the conative function are evaluated according to their capacity to accomplish their aim (what Austin terms 'happiness' or 'felicity') – that is, to communicate to the addressee the addresser's expectation that s/he do something. In line with Kinneavy and Leech's expansions, this is by no means limited to material actions; it includes, for example, undergoing a change of opinion, will, preferences, etc.

We now examine how the addresser uses vs to get others to do things. The pragmatic phenomenon of speech-acts performed using words is in itself intriguing, and speech-acts performed using vs are even more so. Austin (1962: 119) discusses the conventional phase of illocutionary acts and argues that '[s]trictly speaking, there cannot be an illocutionary act unless the means employed are conventional, and so the means for achieving it non-verbally must be conventional. But it is difficult to say where conventions begin and end'. Referring, among other phenomena, to silence, Austin (1962: 120) says that:

Similar difficulties arise over giving tacit consent to some arrangement, or promising tacitly, or voting by a show of hands. But the fact remains that many illocutionary acts cannot be performed except by saying something. This is true of stating, informing (as distinct from showing), arguing, giving estimates, reckoning, and finding (in the legal sense); it is true of the great majority of verdictives and expositives as opposed to many exercitives and commissives.[6]

We look here at the conative roles in which vss are the conventional means (§4.3.1) and those in which speech is the convention (§4.3.3), some of which are quoted by Austin as illocutionary acts performed only by saying something. While our study presents vs as a verbal means (alongside speech) to say something, the above quote shows that this is not the case regarding Austin. We undertake this challenge, showing that among these are familiar (illocutionary) acts performed using vs. It seems worth remembering that in the context of the conative function, too, it is the addresser's vs and not the addressee's silence which serves the conative function.

---

[6] On vs serving locutionary acts, such as stating and informing see §4.1.

4.3 The Conative Function   267

Bearing in mind that self-esteem facilitates people's compliance to perform deeds which they perceive as stirred by their own free will, the addresser who seeks to generate deeds will tend to conceal the conative function using indirect speech-acts, that is, utterances toning down or silencing hes endeavour or presenting the utterance as serving another function. This explains the two forms verbally activating the other: direct or indirect speech-acts (compare [~264] and [~111] with [~112] and [~113] §3.2.4.4.3).

An interesting feature that underlies and hence connects vs and the illocutionary force triggering the conative function is a physical and psychological *horror vacui* which demands the filling in of the void, triggering movement and action. Indeed, this dimension renders the conative function a secondary one when the addresser uses vs in non-conative utterances to stimulate the addressee to fill in a signifier. An apparent exception (see §4.4) is the 'being rather than doing' phase of the vs in the phatic function.

4.3.1   Conative Roles Served by Verbal Silence as the Unmarked Means

For some conative roles vs is not only the unmarked means – that is, the means preferred to speech – but also the conventional default means for performing the specific illocution. We also ask why in such cases the illocutionary act – that is, the utterance itself and not external elements such as preparatory and sincerity conditions – is performed using vs.

4.3.1.1   Turn-Switching: A Verbal Silence Discourse Marker

The vs at the centre of example [~14^S] had no bibliographic reference, as it – or variants thereof – participates as the default unmarked turn-switching means in every verbal exchange (see also S_3 of [~7^S] (§3.1) and [~8^S]).

Holding the floor of a communication event constitutes a social resource. Managing turns is economically motivated to make the most of this resource. When, as in most settings, transitions of turns occur which are not fixed for length, an efficient distribution of the turn resource will seek a smooth flow of turns free of gaps or overlaps. This is true concerning all turns as social resources, be these the turns of a card game, couples dancing, vehicular and pedestrian traffic lights or discourse (see Sacks et al. 1974: 699 note 8).

Models describing the mechanism underlying turn-transitions in conversation detail the sociopragmatic conditions and rules governing this behaviour. Sacks et al. (1974) seem to offer the most influential contribution on this topic. In their paper, Sacks and his colleagues outline what they describe as 'a simplest systematics for the organization of turn-taking for conversation'. In §4.6.2.1 we examine this conative vs convention as a metalinguistic discourse marker. Examined here from an addressee-centred perspective, this deliberate vs is a direct speech-act performed by the addresser holding the floor in order to signal metalinguistically the termination of hes turn and so activate hes addressees (either the one s/he had selected as next addresser-speaker or a self-selected speaker) to take over. For this to take place, the interlocutors, and particularly the next addresser, must embrace this metalinguistic and conative indexical role of the turn-switching vs.

As a matter of fact, the use of a vs discourse marker to switch turns is so conventionalised that any attempt to find an example for daily informal phrasing of this illocution using words, that is, Austin's 'saying something' and not the vs discourse marker, sounds positively artificial. Even forms such as 'Roger' in military discourse for 'received', or Latin '*dixi*' for 'I have spoken', do not replace the vs marker. This is particularly significant in light of Austin's categorical argument.

4.3.1.2 The Silent Treatment

Williams et al. (1998: 117) define the silent treatment as 'primarily punitive and social (carried out in the presence of the target), and [...] composed mostly of avoidance of eye contact and absence of verbal communication'. This description captures the illocutionary characteristics of the conative vs at the heart of the silent treatment.[7] This is a punitive act, carried out by the addresser's silence in the presence of hes addressee with the intention not only of informing that addressee that s/he caused the addresser dissatisfaction, unhappiness or pain (a locutionary act) but more importantly of performing a punitive speech-act punishing and correcting hes behaviour. This illocutionary force surfaces using 'treatment' as well as collocations such as 'to give/get the silent treatment'. The perlocutionary outcome of the addresser's punitive act ranges from affects wished by the addresser to affects s/he may not desire.

The addresser may verbally announce the coming speech-act, that is, say 'I refuse to talk with you'. Such speech when perceived as a vs forerunner announcing the coming silence is indeed agreeable, while for the speech-act to be successful, such an utterance must be followed by the conventional conative vs. For the silent treatment is performed using silence; otherwise not only does a referential clash takes place, but we are now faced with an instance of illocutionary infelicity.

Examining the silent treatment as conative vs, we show that it is performed using silence due to its *horror vacui* suction quality. The silent treatment as an illocutionary act creates, or threatens to create, a void. Clearly the perlocutionary outcomes of the act are varied, partly directly prescribed by the act and partly depending on personality variables and social-circumstantial

---

[7] The illocutionary elements just mentioned regarding the silent treatment as a punitive act highlight the fact that, contrary to arguments made in the social sciences, ostracism is not the same as the silent treatment, primarily because the former is not an illocutionary act.

parameters, such as the extent and nature of the objective and subjective relationships between the addressee receiving the treatment and the addresser giving it. This no doubt determines the threat of loss. Williams et al. (1998) found that while all four fundamental needs (belonging, self-esteem, meaningful existence and control) were lost when receiving the 'treatment', the effects on the addresser were different. While performing the act fortified the addresser's control, it threatened – as for the addressee – the need for belonging. This seems to support the paradigm of a *horror vacui* suction propelling to fill in the void. Their studies ignored personal variables, which had they been accounted for would no doubt have shown a significant link between the extent of an initial – that is, personal or circumstantial – sense of void and threat and the perlocutionary effects of the silent treatment. This applies to both addresser and addressee, indeed determining whether the addresser will choose to perform this act, regarding it, for example, as a last resort, or the extent to which these relations are important to hem. The magnitude of the threatening void, that is, its suction capacity, surfaces, for example, in the observation that an addressee seeking belonging may experience the addresser's act as indicating hes (the addressee's) importance (which in turn also explains the addresser's threat of belonging). Last but not least, the advantage of vs over speech, in the case of the silent treatment, stands out. Perceived as what Williams et al. (1998: 135) term 'nonbehaviour', this practice relieves the addresser not only of the need to admit using it but also of the need to accept responsibility, for example by apologising for the deed or its consequences.

4.3.1.3 *Silence as Consent*

A special case of conative silence is '*qui tacet consentire videtur*' – he who keeps silent is assumed to consent. It is a convention which uses conative vs to perform a social act of consent as an answer to questions or allegations (see §4.3.3.2.1).

The OED defines consent as 'voluntary agreement to or acquiescence in what another proposes or desires; compliance, concurrence, permission' (OED: Consent, N1.a). As this definition implies, consent constitutes a social pact between the addresser and hes addressee. 'Silence as consent' belongs in the conative function because vs serves to perform consent; that is, it serves the pact. Through the admission of consent, the speaker permits the addressee to do things or refrain from doing things.

As a speech-act of exposition (Austin 1962: 85–86), its verbal code consists of three parts: the illocution's declarative first-person present phrase (here, 'I admit') and its complement, structured as a locution, that is, a proposition P:

[~265] 'I didn't know what to say to you on the stand,' I admit. (Picoult, *Sister's*, p. 353)

A third part is social perlocution of the admission, that is, the social permission transferred to the other. Exceptions, which raise doubt about whether the act is performed, are culturally prescribed silences in which the subordinate is even deprived of the social option of actively participating in the act. Examples of this can be found in the status of women in a traditional Japanese marriage proposal [~21$^{Japanese-T}$] (see §3.1, and see Loewenstein 1957 on passivity disclaiming agency, in §3.2.3.2.2 by [~66]).

For 'silence as consent' to serve the conative function, vs must occupy at least the expositive's second part, that is, the referential (see §4.1) locutionary part, syntactically imbedded as the subordinate clause.[8]

This conative consent convention, seen from a cost-effective perspective, turns out to be an extremely efficient cooperative strategy. As an anaphoric PRO ranging over the entire (two-part) act, this conative vs covers all that was claimed referentially and paradigmatically, be its range a proposition, charge sheet or discourse. This reduces significantly the need for conversation analysis and interpretation, such as comparing the wording of the admission with the wording of the previous statements, testimonies or investigations. Moreover, the recoverable feature inherent in anaphoric PRO carried over to this vs obviates the need to inquire and verify the locutionary part, that is, to examine information that would have been brought up had the admission been performed using words.[9]

And what about the third part, the conative phase, motivating the entire act? Set in a specific social pragmatic context, in performing the expositive act the addresser-speaker disclaims control and transfers power. In most cases, particularly in official or semi-official settings such as work or a judicial proceeding, circumstances (see §4.7) make vs the only appropriate means expressing that illocutionary component. The same may not be the case in more equal or close relationships such as an intimate couple.[10]

In addition to 'silence as admission (of guilt)', vs also serves as a judicial convention in 'the right to silence'. On the face of it these two practices seem to conflict: in the former the addresser chooses silence to admit guilt and so acquiesce to prosecution and penalty, while in the latter s/he keeps silent as a safeguard against self-incrimination. But the perspective of vs neatly resolves

---

[8] Compare, for example, the negation test: (1) 'I admit P (and P)'; (2) 'I admit P (and ~P)'; as opposed to (3) 'I do not admit P (and P)' or (4) 'I do not admit P (and ~P)'.

[9] On language as a human system governed by the principle of least effort, see Zipf (1949: 55) and Martinet (1949).

[10] While Wyatt's sonnet 'Hate whom ye list' (see [~103] §3.2.4.4.1) and its vss are clearly set in the poetic function, it does have the flavour of a conative consent, explicitly (see particularly [~103^e]) and repeatedly ordering his addressee on her deeds.

4.3 The Conative Function

the apparent contradiction, showing that each of the two legal practices focuses on a different component of the interaction and so serves a different function. While 'silence as consent' is a conative vs activating the addressee, 'the right to silence' is code oriented and so serves the metalinguistic function (see §4.6.5).

4.3.2 When Speech and Verbal Silence Jointly Complement to Produce an Illocution

Before we move on to cases in which conative vs may be used but is not the unmarked case, a note should be made concerning illocutionary acts in which speech – that is, articulation – and vs equally serve the conative function. In such cases neither is the marked option. In addition, these typically employ both, so that not the entire illocutionary component is performed using vs.

To see that we return to our discussion of threats and the difference between promises and threats (§3.2.4.6.2). Examining their syntactic vs leaving a conjunct of a subordinative-hypotactic asymmetric construction uninstantiated, we explained the different roles played by silence as concealment (see [~150'], [~150"]) and vs as a conative means of expression. The addresser assumes that hes addressee desires the outcome of the promise, that is, its perlocutionary act, and so in performing the promise the addresser commits hemself to that outcome. Threats are illocutionary acts in which the reverse takes place. To paraphrase [~151^S]:

[~151']   If you (dare) touch my car I'll kill you

Here the addresser initiates the threat, assuming that hes addressee does not want the outcome. In addition, because the intimidation is performed as a conative means to get the addressee to do something desired by the addresser, even if the condition persists (the addressee goes on approaching the addresser's car), the latter is not committed to the apodosis (killing hes addressee). Accordingly,

[~151^S]   If you (dare) touch my car $\mathcal{S}$ (Evans 2007: 393),

not articulating the threat itself, that is the apodosis ($\mathcal{S}$), strengthens the threat, not only because it leaves out the non-commitment, but because it communicates determinacy in terms of the illocutionary act. Alluding here also to the judicial perspective, a distinction must be made between a threat as a didactic means and a threat as a legal offence. Regarding the latter, performing the offence using vs ($\mathcal{S}$) rather than articulated-explicit speech formally prevents any attempt to file a lawsuit on the grounds of a threat to cause the perlocutionary illegal or even criminal outcome (killing). All these explain the use of conative conditional vs as a common means for forming threats.

4.3.3 Conative Roles Served by Verbal Silence while Speech Is the Unmarked Means

Describing the metalinguistic use of vs to focus on the code, and particularly to communicate the shortage of words, we turn to Pope John Paul II's address commemorating the Holocaust and its victims (see [~293] in §4.6.4). The Pope referred to

[~293[a]] Silence because there are no words strong enough to deplore the terrible tragedy of the Shoah.[11]

This is an example of a forerunner indicating the coming metalinguistic vs, since in this particular context the code is not fit to perform the illocution of deploring. One cannot deplore by executing a deed, such as physically stoning an opponent or blocking hes bank account. In an exceptional context in which words – the unmarked means – are found inadequate, vs as the marked option may take over.

Deploring illustrates the many situations in which vs serves as the marked conative option to perform conative roles conventionally performed using speech (see [~293[a]]). Because the examples and situations are many – in fact endless – we focus here on two fundamental phenomena: propadverts – persuasive campaigning (§4.3.3.1) – and the question–answer adjacency pair (§4.3.3.2).

4.3.3.1 Propadverts: Propaganda + Adverts

Besides instructive utterances, such as Jakobson's imperatives and Wilson's (2000: 180–183) example of the genre of recipes, the conative function includes other events that seek not to order the addressee but to persuade and influence hem. While in the former the addresser directs the addressee on hes actions, in the latter the addresser directs the addressee's attention to get hem to act in a desired manner. Clearly any communicative event can result (in terms of perlocution) in a change in the addressee's behaviour. Confining ourselves within the conative function to illocutions performed to direct the addressee's attention, we look at advertising and propaganda; unfortunately, English lacks a general term covering both directive illocutions. The two differ only in the object of the conative illocutionary attention: while adverts promote goods or services, propaganda advances ideas, attitudes, causes and so forth. For simplicity, we coin the neologism 'propadvert' to cover 'condensed media artefacts composed to direct the addressee's attention to consume goods or services or to propagate ideas, attitudes or causes'. Such are, for example, [~264], [~17], [~18] (§3.1); [~96] (§3.2.4.3.4) and [~159[a]] (§3.2.4.6.2).

---

[11] From Yad Vashem, www.yadvashem.org/il (accessed 16 August 2013).

4.3 The Conative Function

The addresser performing the propadvert's illocution is the person, company or organisation wishing to direct the addressee's attention and so persuade hem and influence hes actions.

As Grice (1989) elucidated, for verbal interaction to be successful, the interlocutors must cooperate with each other. This holds true for all the communicative functions, but the conative function is tricky in this respect. As a function initiated by the addresser to activate hes addressee, such interaction may easily split apart when interests clash. This explains why, of all the functions, the conative risks being the least cooperative. Despite – or perhaps due to – the fact that ever since infancy people are accustomed to being instructed, people resent being controlled and particularly manipulated. On the one hand, propadverts are not instructive and do not threaten the addressee's sense of control; on the other hand, they are still conative means for activating hem. To overcome likely resistance, a skilful propadvert's campaigner will tone down its illocutionary intent. This is accomplished, firstly, by directing attention to the desired object rather than imposing directives. Additional softening is attained by wrapping the conative intention in other functions, such as sharing emotions (§4.2), providing information (§4.1) or being a piece of art (§4.5).[12] We have here not silence as means of expression but silence as a manipulative means. This explains why, unlike [~110], [~112], [~267] and [~268] (see below), most propadverts are not phrased in the second-person.

We should now examine what it is about vs that makes it an attractive means of expression in text-based propadverts.[13]

Factors such as the size of the propadvert, its duration and the platform on which it is broadcasted or published all determine its price. The cost gap encourages the maximum exploitation of these factors. Two key benefits offered by vs stand out in this conative context:

1. From the addresser's-campaigner perspective, vs, unlike wording, does not consume space and time.
2. From the addressee's perspective, it does demand an additional processing effort, yet this advances its purpose: the conative feature of vs triggered by the suction quality of the void activates the addressee to fill in that void. This makes that addressee the creator, and hence owner, of the message.

---

[12] See Jakobson (1960: 357):

[~266]   I like Ike

On the reverse, a literary work presented as an advert, see [~19⁶] §3.2.3.2.3.

[13] Graphic silence predominates visually based propadverts; see, for example, Wilson (2000: 187–189). Interestingly, these allow much space and blanks, not in the expense of size, to communicate space, wealth, freedom, ubiquity and such.

Instead of being directed and manipulated, the addressee becomes, in fact, the (current) addresser who again regains hes sense of control, which in turn makes hem committed to that message. While, as seen throughout our study, this dynamic operates and surfaces for vss in all functions, it is particularly significant in the conative function (focusing on the addressee).

We illustrate these by returning to

[~113$^\delta$] [Schweppes] Drink different ₷

In §3.2.4.4.3 we proposed a vs reading of [~113] as a comparative vs forerunner: 'different than ₷', adding that this does not alternate with the absolute interpretation, such as 'think big'. 'Different' unlike 'big' inherently denoted comparison, which is further induced in contexts such as 'drink' (distinct from 'think different' in [~112]). To see how this syntactic vs serves the two key conative benefits in [~113], we first compare [~113] with Jakobson's example of the imperative [~263]. Examined grammatically the two employ the same token: the imperative form 'drink'. But while [~263] is placed in a manding context, this is not the case with [~113] in general, and particularly its televised version. In addition, the complement 'different' not only breaks the laconic instructive form and tone of the imperative, but by integrating vs, that is, a void, it captures the addressee. The syntactic void attracts the addressee's attention, activating hem to fill in the uninstantiated syntactic constituent. Moreover, the allusion to pragmatic and emotional needs (void) motivates the addressee to invest in hes own desires. By its essence 'different' tolerates any realistic and imaginary complementation. This vs transforms what is the addresser's (here Schweppes's) direct conative illocution into the addressee's most personal self.

[~267] For once,
Don't Do It.[14]

The opening screen in Nike's video response to the killing of George Floyd in Minnesota (May 2020) intertextually (see §3.2.5.2) corresponds with Nike's slogan-advert

[~268] Just do it.

Both [~267] and [~268] are phrased as Jakobson's clear-cut determinant instructives. Yet [~268] is an advert promoting the firm's commodities, while [~267] falls towards the propaganda end of the conative illocution spectrum. In responding to current events, Nike contributing its share performs the conative

---

[14] White letters on a black background. See, for example, www.independent.co.uk/life-style/nike-ad-george-floyd-racism-dont-do-it-a9540956.html (accessed 5 August 2020).

4.3 The Conative Function

act of drawing the attention of its customers to racism and personal and institutional violence, recruiting them to join in combating such ideologies and imperfections.

The two above-listed key profits are supported by additional benefits:

3. In addition to the conative transformation, making the message one of the addressee – discussed in (2) – the additional processing consumed of that addressee also has immediate cognitive impact, imprinting the message, which is now that of the addressee (as current speaker), in hes declarative memory and thereby fruitfully completing the conative function.
4. By wrapping, as explained, the conative illocution in other functions, vss serving those functions are integrated into those propadverts, and used to draw the attention of the potential addressee (see, for example, [~111] poetic rhyming (§3.2.4.4.3), [~86^s] §3.2.4.3.1 referential wrapping or even logic [~159^a] (§3.2.4.6.2) and [~248] (§4.1) metalinguistic challenging).
5. This is particularly affective (in perlocutionary terms) when the use of vs, that is, the integration of uninstantiated signifiers, induces creativity, humour and surprise.
6. Vs experienced as saying without saying (see §4.3.1.3) serves to express ideas, denote competitors or promote political organisations without having to name them. This is a very useful practice that enables the circumvention of social taboo ([~92] §3.2.4.3.2) and legal ([~124] §3.2.4.4.5 by note 79), commercial ([~18] §3.1; [~240] §3.2.5.5.2) or other restrictions.

4.3.3.2 Question–Answer Adjacency Pair

The question–answer dyad is a fundamental occurrence in the conative function, as in real life. Questioning is a basic illocutionary act which invites the addressee to supply verbally information that the addresser lacks and needs, and which s/he knows or assumes hes addressee possesses. The addresser may perform this conventionally using direct or indirect questions.

The illocutionary status of the interrogative sentence depends on its 'integrative distribution', that is, its being the first conative constituent of the question–answer adjacency pair. This presents the asymmetry between the two: while the question is formally marked, the answer has no peculiarities. Its identification as the answer – that is, the second constituent of the dyad – is its content filling in the requested information posed in the question.

While statements, as utterances serving the referential function, allow any form of responses (statements, direct and indirect illocutionary acts, or even nonverbal responses), the adjacency pair quality of the interrogative conventionally predicates an answer as the only behaviour following a question. Acceptable, but exceeding the dyad, are illocutionary acts such as refusal, turning the question back to its initiator, etc. Looking into the nature of this adjacent pair, it is worth bearing in mind that while the answer is expected to immediately follow the question, different cultures allow, expect or prescribe a varied length of time in between the two. Goffman (1981: 25–26) gives as an example five to ten minutes passing – in silence or discussing matters other than the matters questioned – before a Warm Springs Reservation Native American person would offer hes answer.

As we all know and experience as speakers of the language, the use of words for asking and answering a question is predominantly the unmarked option. Vs is also an option: usually a marked one, but in specific illocutionary situations even the unmarked option.

4.3.3.2.1   Questions Signalling a Verbal Silence Answer

The adjacency pair question–answer is a canonical minimal dialogic unit. As illocutions performed to activate the addressee to provide an answer, questions impose 'conditional relevance' upon whatever occurs in the slot that follows. This faculty signals the coming answer, mostly using words but also by vs.

The absence of an answer to a true question creates or risks the breakdown of the dialogue. A distinction must be made between the absence of a (required) answer and an answer performed using vs. Says Goffman (1981: 6): 'whatever comes to be said there will be inspected to see how it might serve as an answer, and if nothing is said, then the resulting silence will be taken as notable – a rejoinder in its own right, a silence to be heard'.

In line with the firm understanding underlying our study that vs is a unique form alongside non-communicative silences (see Figure 2.1), Goffman's point must verify for each dialogic unit the nature of the silence heard. That silence may be found to be a symptom ('I can't speak'), the result of silencing (that is, not the addressee's free choice) or the product of resistance (see, for example, Kurzon 1998: 48). But it may also be an adequate cooperative reply to the addresser's question, and in this instance, like any adequate cooperative reply using words, it will constitute a complete utterance.

To examine answers (adequately) supplied using vs, one must note different sorts of (sincere) questions. These we classify here according to the canonical forms of their (expected) answers. Questions requiring affirmation or negation as the missing information (answer) are yes/no nexus/polar questions and tag questions. WH- questions are open and anticipate new information as their answers. Pragmatically speaking, even the addresser presenting a yes/no question also usually expects additional information alongside the affirmation or denial. The form and content of the admissible answers to a question are determined by the canonical type of that question. This aspect is discussed by Hiz (1962: 255), who describes 'explicit questions as similar in some way to generalizations [...] you obtain a sentential function: an expression that is not a sentence but a sentence with one phrase replaced by a variable' (see also

4.3 The Conative Function

Lyons 1977: 757). Accordingly, the answer is obtained by dropping the question prefix and replacing the free variable of the sentential function with a phrase of the proper syntactical category.

This, particularly when vs is involved, determines the nature of the answer – in Goffman's wording, the nature and contents of the rejoinder silence to be heard.

If one asked people whether silence can be an answer to a question, many would immediately mention rhetorical questions as the epitome. Wikipedia embraces this lay assumption, saying that '[a] *rhetorical question* is one for which the questioner does not expect a direct answer'.[15] Sobkowiak (1997: 51) elaborates: 'in the unmarked context of a rhetorical question no speech-coded answer is expected'. Examining these two representative descriptions of rhetorical questions in light of the above definition of a question as an adjacency pair illocution seeking information to be provided by the addressee's answer, it becomes clear that rhetorical questions are not in fact questions. They are referential statements phrased indirectly as questions. As a statement, they may stand on their own or elicit responses from the interlocutor, but they do not elicit answers, which are reserved for the second part of the question–answer adjacency pair. Says Schmidt-Radefeldt (1977: 377):

> Rhetorical questions do not have an answer (because they are not questions), and on the other hand, questions (wh-questions) always have more than one possible direct answer. [...] questions are to be considered as requests for information, whereas rhetorical questions are intended to provide information.

Another category of indirect speech-acts performed as questions are phatic greetings, such as:

[~269]   How are you doing?

[~270]   What's up?

These are true questions when, for example, performed by a physician during a medical check-up but not when initiated by the addresser as greetings, showing hes addressee that s/he is noticed. This has nothing to do with the conative function (activating the addressee); it belongs to the phatic means maintaining the channel (§4.4).

The last category to note is one described by Hiz (1962: 261):

> Silence is the best possible answer to a nonsense question. Instead of answering such pseudoquestions one rejects them.

A pathologist of questions must therefore distinguish among those questions to which only a negative answer is true, those questions to which all answers including

---

[15] https://en.wikipedia.org/wiki/Rhetorical_question (accessed 3 August 2020).

the negative answer are false, and those questions to which there is no grammatical answer.

Hiz refers here to 'pseudoquestions', such as

[~271]   What kind of ink was used by Homer to write the Odyssey?

for which the appropriate response is no answer because the question's constative (see §4.3) that Homer wrote the Odyssey is, according to Hiz, undetermined. Silence then is not an answer (conative VS) but a symptom of the collapse of felicity and dialogue.

Having ruled out rhetorical questions, greetings and pseudoquestions as not actually questions, and so not representing the question–answer adjacency pair, we now focus on VSs as accepted cooperative fulfilment of the question–answer adjacency pair.

Two cases in which VS is the conventional unmarked answer were discussed earlier. The first is the individual and collective VS in reply to the minister's true question in the marriage ceremony ([~246]). As discussed in §4.1, the answer using VS is an informative answer to a yes/no question. Moreover, it is not limited to such a ceremony but instead is an efficient way of indicating the unmarked answer, in daily encounters, as noted there. The second case is silence as consent (see §4.3.1.3).

Comparing [~246$] and silence as consent with rhetorical questions or greetings (see [~269]) illuminates the difference between questions and non-questions, and between conative VS as verbal informative and cooperative answers to true questions. To these conventional conative VS answers we add an example of a non-conventional, and hence marked, VS answer. This comes from Beckett's play *Waiting for Godot* (1962: 91), known for its explicit and implicit iconic use of silence:

[~272] VLADIMIR: What does he do, Mr. Godot? *(silence)* Do you hear me?
BOY: Yes, Sir.
VLADIMIR: Well?
BOY: He does nothing, Sir.

Should the discourse proceed as presented in the raw text ([~272]), the silence indicated as stage directions[16] and the three subsequent lines do not seem to add any information. Their only justification may be in their iconically enhancing tiresome boredom to convey the play's theme: arbitrariness, the eradication of causality and freedom of choice (see Kane 1984: 115). Such a justification is *ipso facto* contrary to relevance, such as Grice's (1989) relevance maxim which is an efficiency measure. However, combining here

---

[16] On silence in stage directions, see, for example, Jaworski (1993: 94); Wilson (2000: 163–175).

4.3 The Conative Function

Beckett's intensive use of silence and the interpretation of the interaction as cooperative, this fragment of the very same discourse can be rearranged ([~272']), introducing conative vs as the boy's informative answer to Vladimir's question:

[~272']   VLADIMIR: What does he do, Mr. Godot?
          BOY: ∫
          VLADIMIR: Do you hear me?
          BOY: Yes, Sir.
          VLADIMIR: Well?
          BOY: He does nothing, Sir.

To Vladimir's question about Godot's occupation the boy answers using conative vs: nothing for nothing ('he does nothing'). Vladimir's next question indicates that he does not recognise this silence as an answer and hence suspects that the boy has not heard his question. From the boy's perspective, as an obedient cooperative speaker, his silence is a sincere direct answer to Vladimir's request for information. This is why, having answered the initial question, the boy interprets Vladimir's second question as a fresh one rather than an indirect illocution invoking an answer to the first, and so the boy answers it accordingly ('Yes, Sir'). Vladimir's 'Well?' expresses his renewed attempt to get the boy's answer to his initial question. Thus, 'He does nothing, Sir' is the boy's verbalised paraphrase of his first informative answer expressed using vs (see end of note 28 in §4.6.3.3.3).

4.3.3.2.2 Questions Posed Using Verbal Silence

Sobkowiak (1997: 47) argues that 'communicative silence' is unheard of in the first part of a conversational adjacency pair (see also §4.1). Yet vs may indeed constitute the first constituent of a dyad (see §3.2.5.5 and §3.2.4.6; see also Jaworski's comment in Sobkowiak 1997: 57 note 2).

Drawing on Aristotle, Hiz contends that 'knowledge can be classified according to what questions it answers' (1962: 253). If the answer is the filling in of the information missing in its question, then by substituting the answer with the variable the question's sentential function will be recovered. This seems most fruitful when considered from a question–answer logic framework. But when vs constitutes the answer, the open nature of silence makes this trace insufficiently boundless. This is why, both intuitively and practically, while vs is attested as the unmarked answering option in particular conversations and specific conventions, a question posed using vs is definitively a marked option.

Describing a question as one that was not asked may refer to either lexical vss indicating the relinquishing of the intention to communicate (see §3.2.5.1.5) in which case no illocution is performed or to the question's illocution performed using conative vs. We focus here on the latter. As the marked option, an expectancy signalling the uninstantiated question frequently emerges from specific settings or contexts.

The first example of expectancy illustrating a question performed using conative vs concerns institutional interrogation, such as police questioning. Example [~273] comes from the novel *The First Directive*, written by Joseph McNamara, a former police officer (pp. 71–72). The text, describing the detective's investigation of a murder of a young female, seems self-explanatory, illustrating expectancy:

[~273] We went into the hall. Neither wanted to say anything. The Block avoided my eyes. English stared into them as if seeking some deep truth.
Finally, I demanded of English, "Well?"
He said, 'Lisa,' and stopped.
[...]
'Cause of death?' I questioned mechanically, shocked despite myself.
'Not sure.' Paul was uneasy, aversive.
'Come on, Paul, neither one of us is a cherry. Spit it all out'.
'The body had been dismembered,' he answered, as I started. 'They still don't have it all. Remember, I haven't been there. This is what I got on the phone.'
'Dismembered,' I repeat stupidly. Ugly pictures of other such cases floated unbidden into my mind. I hoped that she had died quickly.
'When?' I asked.
'The old man found her this morning.'
He looked away from my glare. He had answered a question not asked and he knew it.

The rationale behind the forensic notion of 'concealed information', and more so its implementation in interrogation, involves the idea that such information provided by a suspect is an answer, that is, the filling in of the variable of an unasked question.

The second setting of questions performed using vs motivated by expectancy is psychotherapeutic practice. A question mark hovers at the opening of each and every therapeutic session for which the patient's words are attempted answers. In his chapter on the 'initial analytic meeting', Thomas Ogden (1989: 169–194) recommends that when the therapist and the new patient walk together from the waiting room to the counselling room, the therapist should refrain from small talk. Ogden contends that such talk, though intended to ease tension, is unkind, belittling the patient (as if s/he were an infant) or communicating the therapist's responsibility towards the patient. Ogden explains:

Furthermore, this sort of comment is an act of theft: it robs the patient of the opportunity to introduce himself to the analyst in the way that he consciously and unconsciously chooses. [...] One must not deprive him of his opportunity to write the opening lines of his own analytic drama by burdening him with the analyst's own unconscious contents before he even sets foot in the counselling room.

4.3 The Conative Function

Here, Ogden's emphasis is on the analyst's fundamental commitment to accept the patient in each session 'without memory, desire or understanding' (Wilfred Bion). The therapist must allow hemself to be surprised anew, to be caught unprepared, to discover things over and over again as if for the first time. This indeed underlies Freud's notion of the analyst's 'hovering attention'. This leads further to the matter of questions. Ogden notes:

> The patient brings to the first interview many questions and worries (usually unspoken) about what it means to be an analysand. The analyst's attempts at answering these questions in the form of explanations [...] are not only futile but invariably highly limiting of the patient's opportunity to present himself to the analyst in his own terms. (1989: 175–177)

But the matter of answers to questions not asked is, in the psychoanalytic paradigm, not only a formal exterior matter (as may be the case in interviews). Local, general and ongoing questions asked using conative vs play a significant role in psychotherapeutic discourse in general, and in the psychoanalytic encounter in particular. The utterance or theme with which the patient opens the therapeutic session, or hes entire treatment, constitute an answer to the question of hes life. Returning to Aristotle's equation of knowledge with the questions it answers, it is the questions posed by both the therapist and the patient using conative vs, and not the answers, which are to be worked through and discovered/recovered in therapy. Lacan (1988: 242), who, as explained, places speech at the forefront of psychoanalysis (see end §3.2.5.3), claims that speech in general, and particularly speech in therapeutic transference discourse, comprises a chain of signifiers in search for the missing object: the primary desire. The unique, intensive experience of answers to most significant personal-intimate questions (including 'The Question') performed using conative vs, also iconically and emotionally depicts the constitutive experience of absence (the absent question) as a motivator (see §4.3 and §4.3.1.2 on *horror vacui* and suction).

Although questions performed using conative vs are the marked case, they are not restricted to settings raising expectancy, such as interrogation and psychoanalysis. They may also appear in contexts that do not raise expectancy.

A moving example was cited in our presentation of emotive vs ([~254] §4.2). Linda, a youngster dying of leukaemia, appeared before a class of medical students:

[~254ª] [S]he posed and answered the questions she had always wanted her physician and team of specialists to ask her. What was it like to be sixteen and given only a few weeks to live? What was it like not to be able to dream about the high school prom? [...]. (Kübler-Ross 1998: 132)

Example [~274] illustrating a casual intersubjective encounter comes from Goffman (1981: 48):

[~274] A: [Enters wearing new hat]
        B: 'No, I don't like it.'
        A: 'Now I know it's right.'

Goffman introduces this example by suggesting that the interactional unit, and not the conversational one, underlies natural talk. The crucial difference, he asserts, is that while artificial texts such as literary works confine systematic transformation to words, this is not the case with real-life interactions. In place of the adjacency pair, Goffman suggests a three-part unit, the first part of which is likely not to involve speech at all. He cites [~274] to illustrate what he considers to be a question asked using nonverbal clues (such as body language, see §2.2.2).

Goffman's argument concerning literary works being confined to words is peculiar, particularly since he himself mentions plays, that is, works that go beyond the written medium. The many examples throughout our study of surfacing vss may be offered in humble support for the contrary view (see also [~275]).

[~274] may indeed not involve nonverbal clues but rather constitute a question performed exclusively using conative vs. The third part of the interaction, that is, A's verbal response, is a clear confirmation that B's utterance was an answer filling in information asked by A's question asked using vs.

To conclude, we cite an example drawn from a literary work par excellence – the opening verse of Emily Dickinson's poem 510:

[~275] It was not Death, for I stood up,
        And all the Dead, lie down –
        It was not Night, for all the Bells
        Put on their Tongues, for Noon. (Dickinson, *Complete*, pp. 248–249)

Like several of Dickinson's poems, [~275] is phrased as an answer to an unarticulated question. The deliberation, manifested in negation and reason from the outset, signals syntactically and pragmatically an answer to a question performed using conative vs. This is here a poetic-rhetoric means but one which not only poetically portrays real-life experience but is also frequently attested in daily interaction.

In addition, [~275] serves here to touch on the matter of self-reply, that is, the adjacency question–answer pair performed and successfully concluded by one and the same speaker. This might seem to contradict the notion of a conative illocution activating the addressee. But, as Lyons (1977: 756) explains, distinguishing between posing a question and putting a question, this is not the case:

[O]ne can ask questions of oneself, in soliloquy and discursive reasoning; just as one can make statements or issue mands to oneself; and to ask a question of oneself is to perform a mental or illocutionary act which is governed by the same felicity-conditions as those which govern information-seeking questions addressed to others (see also Goffman 1981: 45).

This happens either when that addresser-speaker has recalled what s/he had forgotten or by hem reaching such information. This holds true for both questions asked using words, or, as here, questions asked using conative vs. Because the question is asked using vs, it is difficult to determine whether the case is self-reply or involves two separate interlocutors. Real-life examples provide the necessary context to distinguish between the two, but this is not the case with written texts, literary or other (see discussion of Goffman earlier in this section). Dickinson's [~275], like Frost's [~140] (§3.2.4.6.1), poetically maintains ambiguity in this respect.

4.4 The Phatic Function

To the three functions postulated by Bühler (1937), Jakobson (1960) added three more communicative functions, the first of which is the phatic function, centred on the channel by which the communicative act is carried and maintained. Says Jakobson (1960: 355): 'There are messages serving primarily to establish, to prolong, or to discontinue communication, to check whether the channel works ("Hello, do you hear me?")'. Jakobson further explains that '[t]he phatic function, may be displayed by a profuse exchange of ritualized formulas, by entire dialogues with the mere purport of prolonging communication' (1960: 355). He adds that the 'phatic function of language is the only one [birds, animals] share with human beings. It is also the first verbal function acquired by infants' (see Olinick 1982; Winnicott 1958 later in this section regarding silence).

Being the residue between the world and language, that is, the carrier of the language in the world, utterances serving the phatic function are such that the content (addresser, addressee or outside world) and the form (language) are secondary or latent and by no means primary. The prototypical example is checking the channel to make sure it is open and can convey the utterance to the addressee. Because the content and form are irrelevant, customarily calling out numbers or uttering 'hello' can serve this function, but reading out classics, singing a tune or expressing a political statement may equally serve this function. Indeed, any sound (voices or other, such as tapping) can do the job. Institutions, companies and so forth utilise this unique facet of the phatic function to supplement its primal purpose to inform and ensure the customers who initiated the phonecall that the phone – the channel – is working, while also securing a secondary – conative – purpose, such as promoting their goods and services (see §4.3.3.1). This explains why in place of the regular, insignificant sounds we encounter long, detailed commercials.

Žegarac (1998) devotes his paper to the question 'What is phatic communication?' Among the answers he provides we find 'minimum of information vs. [versus] maximum of supportive chat' (1998: 328). The most apparent example is 'small talk' among strangers, such as passengers sharing a train cabin, or Olinick's description of the chatting of barbers (1982: 463). Serving the phatic function, 'small talk' such as chatting about the weather or superficial non-personal, uninformative matters operates within a situational limited shared channel without penetrating the interlocutors private space. While it is most typical of chance encounters between strangers, it also emerges in public channels in which speech is expected no matter whether or not there is content (referential, emotional, etc.) to be conveyed.

Such an example comes from a paper by Jaworski et al. (2005) entitled 'Busy saying nothing new: Live silence in TV reporting of 9/11'. Analysing the BBC coverage on 9 September 2001, from the start of the attack, the authors point to a shift in live broadcast news from serving the referential function (reporting) to serving a phatic function of 'keeping in touch with the audience'. The authors show that this latter function was fulfilled on 9/11, as in other 'disaster marathons', not by reporting fresh updates but instead by repetitive verbosity.[17] In addition, they touch on the distinction between 'small talk' and 'empty speech' (see §2.2.3.2), showing that while the former does not substitute or displace anything, 'empty speech' is introduced only to distract the interlocutors' attention from a known and so more anticipated theme.

Returning now to the prototypical articulated signifier with no content quality serving the phatic function, three challenges seem to arise: (1) examining the relations between the phatic function and vs; (2) determining whether vs can serve this function; and (3) discriminating between utterances serving the phatic function and those performing empty speech.

Vs seems to be the mirror image of the utterance in the phatic function: while vs constitutes content conveyed choosing an unarticulated signifier, at the centre of the phatic function stands an articulated signifier with no content. This supports the impression that the phatic function can be served only using sounds, including articulated speech, but ruling out vs. Interestingly, while linguists follow this approach, others such as psychotherapists conceive vs as a vital natural trait serving the phatic function.

The linguists' stance confining the phatic function to speech – ruling out vs – is most apparent in Leech's (1983: 142) phatic maxim phrased once positively, 'go on talking', and once negatively, 'avoid silence'.

---

[17] Compare with [~253] (§4.2) regarding the coverage of Princess Diana's funeral.

4.4 The Phatic Function

Opposing views challenge the fitness of silence in general and in serving the phatic function in particular. Jensen (1973) mentions the maintenance of contact (a phatic role) as the prime role he attributes to silence (followed by roles such as expression of sympathy and revelation):

> Not only does silence link us with those near us but also with those removed in distance, time, or point of view. In silence we think of and feel linked with an absent sweetheart, friend, parent, child or spouse. In moments of silence we sense a bond with generations gone before us. (1973: 250)

Psychologists in general, and followers of the various psychoanalytic schools in particular, seem most interested in theorising on and examining the practice of phatic silence in intersubjective conducts, including psychotherapy.

Sidney J. Baker (1955) introduces an interpersonal theory on silences, which he builds on the role of psychic tension. Baker arrives at the theory that:

> The underlying (unconscious and unpremeditated) aim of speech is not a continued flow of speech, but *silence*, for the state of complete equilibrium, marked by elimination of interpersonal psychic tension, is possible only when the position S+ in the speech field has been reached. (1955: 161)

Baker observes that 'there are two basic forms of interpersonal silence, when speech breaks down or words become irrelevant'. The former (s−, in Figure 4.3) is typical of situations in which no reciprocal identification holds between subjects: social encounters between strangers. The latter (s+) occurs in situations of complete reciprocal identification.

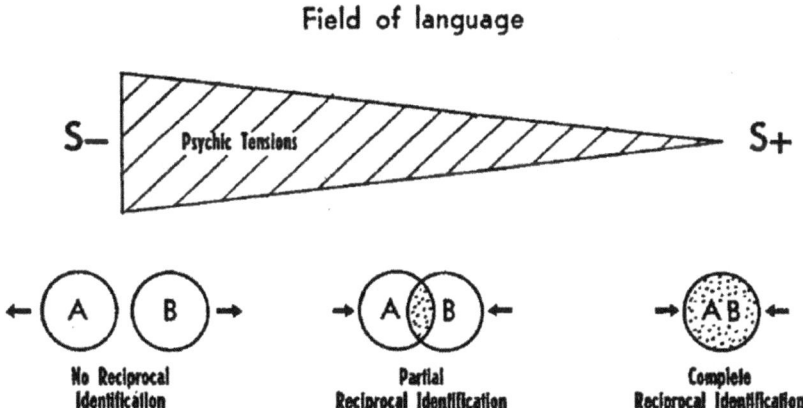

Figure 4.3 Baker's (1955: 159, figure 6) model of the silences in the field of language.
Reprinted by permission of Taylor & Francis.

Baker places speech in the locus of the partial reciprocal identification, that is, between what he terms s− (= negative silence / stimulus): absolute lack of reciprocal identification (blocked type, see also Basso 1972: 71) and s+ (= positive silence / stimulus): not disturbed − complete reciprocal identification. That is, speech takes place in the common situations of partial reciprocal identification, between the experiences of alienation (at one extreme) and intimacy (at the other).

The next two examples move us closer to the phatic silence, that is, Baker's positive silence. Both of the following poets, by informing on the distractive outcome of empty speech, endorse the internal quality of phatic silence resulting from tranquillity as well as facilitating it.

The first comes from the opening line of Gibran Khalil Gibran's poem 'On Talking' (*The Prophet*, p. 59):

[~276] You talk when you cease to be at peace with your thoughts:
And when you can no longer dwell in the solitude of your heart you live in your lips, and sound is a diversion and a pastime.
And in much of your talking, thinking is half murdered.

Henry Wadsworth Longfellow expresses an identical stance in the closing lines of 'Three Silences of Molinos', addressed to his friend Whittier:

[~277] Hermit of Amesbury! thou too hast heard
Voices and melodies from beyond the gates,
And speakest only when thy soul is stirred! (Vol. IV, p. 336, see [~117] in §3.2.4.4.4)

Gibran ([~276]) and Longfellow ([~277]) illustrate the fact that while Baker's model is limited to a channel connecting two individuals (intersubjective intimacy relationships), the phatic function, and silence serving this function, also include the intrasubjective psychic channel: connecting a person to hemself.

Focusing now on intersubjective communication and its channel, we note that the chief innovation offered by Baker is that within this field of language, constituting negative silence (s−), speech and positive silence (s+), the aim of speech is to arrive at complete reciprocal identification; hence the aim of speech is to lead to positive, intimate silence.

In her paper on 'Emily Dickinson and the discourse of intimacy', Margaret Freeman (1996) discusses formal (syntactic and morphological) and particularly cognitive semantic recoverability not as a linguistic grammatical strategy but as an indication of intimacy. Freeman contends that 'Dickinson is remarkable precisely because she is able through silence to capture the essence of true intimacy that gives her poetry its power'. As she notes, this is a boomerang, as '[t]he cognitive principles of conversational discourse which iconically reflect the closeness of its participants turn out to be the very elements that make a

4.4 The Phatic Function

Figure 4.4 The less semantic content the more intimate knowledge sets. Reproduced with kind permission of the author (Freeman 1996: 199).

Dickinson poem "difficult" for its readers'. At first glance, Freeman appears to be talking about intimacy as addresser centred, that is, within the emotive function (see §4.2). But a closer reading suggests that the issue at stake is shared knowledge as a cognitive actuality: the open or blocked channel connecting the speaker-addresser (Dickinson) and her readers. Figure 4.4 replicates the diagram which Freeman lays out surfacing Helen Hunt Jackson's (HHJ) response 'I wish I knew just what "dooms" you meant, though!' a response to the poem her friend and co-poetess Emily Dickinson (ED) had sent her as a wedding congratulation:

Mapping Baker's triangle onto Freeman's diagram and circle constellation reveals a complete overlap: Baker and Freeman agree entirely on the intersubjective states and on the resulting relations between silence and speech. This is straightforward regarding the two left-most states, but the correspondence between Freeman's right square and Baker's positive silence requires consideration. Freeman (not mentioning Baker) phrases Baker's positive-phatic silence using clear linguistic terminology: 'the less morphophonological forms are used in the discourse, the closer the hearer/reader falls to the speaker/writer' (1996: 192). To this she appends the requirement that the cognitive domain must also be shared. Yet an examination of the specific example she discusses for the right square suggests that had Jackson (HHJ) and Dickinson (ED) been in a state of complete reciprocal identification, there would have been no need for Jackson to ask for clarification regarding 'what "dooms" you meant, though!'. The conative request (see §4.3) indicates that the two circles (representing the participant's knowledge or the nature of the channel) are not overlapping; the residue of the demand is left unfulfilled.

An example Freeman brings to illustrate Dickinson's discourse of intimacy, which is a case of intimacy focusing on the channel, that is, silence serving the phatic function, is manifested graphically. In addition to her analysis of Dickinson's text and its linguistic characteristics in light of cognitive principles, Freeman also examines Dickinson's use of the channel: the layout of the poem on the page. Pointing to the important difference between the original facsimiles of Dickinson's poems and their printed versions, Freeman (1996: 207) argues that 'the actual spaces that occur in the original manuscript, [...] make[s] one physically feel a sense of absence or silence'. These, she explains, serve to slow down the reading, to imprint the poem physically in the mind.

But returning in conclusion to Dickinson's texts and the phatic channel, I wish to cite poem 1681:

[~278]   Speech is one symptom of Affection
         And silence one –
         The perfectest communication
         Is heard of none –
         Exists and its indorsement
         Is had within –
         Behold, said the Apostle,
         Yet has not seen! (*Complete*, p. 686)

The poem's first stanza is open to varied interpretations, based partly on the differentiations perused in our study between speech and silence as symptom (see §2.2.1), and within the communicative framework, between speech and vs serving the emotive function (§4.2) or focused on the channel. Examined from this perspective, and after eliminating symptomatic speech and silence, the poem states that 'the perfectest communication / is heard of none'. This seems to shed new light on the role of silence within the phatic function, suggesting that what maintains the channel is not silence per se but rather silence as the outcome of discharging, so making room for the endorsement of being and togetherness as such.

This also explains the human personal and intersubjective striving for phatic silence, bringing together Baker's innovative observation that the aim of speech is to arrive at positive silence and the observation by paediatrician and psychoanalyst Donald Winnicott that:

[I]n the development of the individual infant living arises and establishes itself out of not-living, and being becomes a fact that replaces not-being, as communication arises out of silence [...] I have tried to state the need that we have to recognize this aspect of health: the non-communicating central self, for ever immune from the reality principle, and for ever silent.

Here communication is not non-verbal; it is, like the music of the spheres, absolutely personal. It belongs to being alive. And in health, it is out of this that communication naturally arises. (1963: 191, 192)

Dickinson's 'the perfectest communication / is heard of none' [~278] seems to poetically reverberate Winnicott's notion of the 'ability to be alone'. Pointing

4.4 The Phatic Function

out that while the psychoanalytic literature was occupied with the fear and wish to be alone, it overlooked the ability to be alone, Winnicott (1958: 32–33) devoted what is now considered a formative paper to the understanding of the maturation of the capacity to be alone. He argues that the adult capacity to be alone evolves from

> Being alone in the presence of someone can take place at a very early stage, when the *ego immaturity is naturally balanced by ego-support* from the mother. In the course of time the individual introjects the ego-supportive mother.
> [...]
> 'I am alone' is a development from 'I am', dependent on the infant's awareness of the continued existence of a reliable mother whose reliability makes it possible for the infant to be alone and to enjoy being alone, for a limited period.

Winnicott connects the capacity for emotional maturity with the ability to be alone in the presence of someone. In his paper on 'Communicating and not communicating' (1963: 189, see quote above), Winnicott further explains that this capacity of being alone in the presence of someone first appears as a natural event in a good-enough childhood, and is only later a matter of acquisition. Accordingly, exemplifying such adult phatic silence, Winnicott (1958: 31) introduces the silence of partners after satisfactory intercourse. This, Winnicott contends, is the exemplary case of the capacity to be alone, that is, the ability of the adults involved 'to wait for the natural return of id-tension, and to enjoy sharing solitude, that is to say, solitude that is relatively free from the property that we call "withdrawal"'.

Olinick (1982: 461) opens his paper 'Meanings beyond words' by remarking that '[i]t is hardly a novelty for the psychoanalyst to reflect on silence, whether his own or his patients'. Nor is it a revelation to hear that there are many varieties of silence'. Olinick emphasises that phatic silence is not confined to the clinic. Like Winnicott and others, Olinick sees the silence of intimates as the prime classic case of phatic silence (1982: 469; see also Reik 1927). Phatic silence, that is, keeping the channel of communication open via silence, is thus the locus of intimacy and individuation (reciprocal identification between two separate individuals, as opposed to merge resulting in being swallowed up, annihilated, see [~229] in §3.2.5.4.4). Winnicott (1958, 1963) links these with object-relating communication, suggesting that 'there is room for the idea that significant relating and communicating is silent' (1963: 184).

This portrayal of intimate relations is not limited to the psychoanalytic paradigm. Martin Buber (1932: 189–205) explains 'silence which is communication' by referring to that which is attained and conducted by the very discharge of the expression of gesture or of physical attitude of the one to the other. In so doing, he introduces the notion of 'the sphere in between' (*Weltanschauung*):

Just as most eager speaking at one another does not make a conversation [...] so no sound is necessary for a conversation, not even a gesture. Speech can renounce all the medium of sense, and it is still speech [...].

Unreservedly, communication streams from him, and the silence bears it to his neighbour [...] For where unreserve has ruled, even wordlessly, between men, the word of dialogue has happened sacramentally. (1932: 189–190)

Buber (1932: 196) stresses that this silence is not metaphorical but real. In fact, he recognises such phatic communication as the genuine dialogue, 'no matter whether spoken or silent – where each of the participants really has in mind the other or others in their present and particular being and turns to them with the intention of establishing a living mutual relation between himself and them' (unlike technical dialogues and monologues disguised as dialogues).

We began our exploration of the phatic function puzzled as to how vs can serve a function which centres on the channel: how can vs serve the same function as small talk, whose very raison d'être is to maintain the communication channel by avoiding silence? The straightforward answer lies in the distinction between different silences. This is in line with the thesis perused in our study and in the writings of the scholars just cited and discussed. While empty speech and silences of alienation jeopardise contact, phatic silence fulfils the phatic function by keeping the channel of communication alive and open. This occurs in cases of closeness and intimacy, when silence iconically depicts the content (such as intimacy or when confronting loss and absence) or when silence in the form of empty speech is threatening to take over. While in the first two cases vs avoids the silencing of the authentic connecting silence, in the last it avoids fake silence.

We now examine excerpts illustrating vs serving to maintain the communicative channel. The first case comes from the above-mentioned paper by Jaworski et al. (2005: 129) analysing the BBC coverage on 9 September 2001. Despite focusing on speech shifting in the 'disaster marathon' from serving the referential function (reporting) to serving a phatic function, extract [~279] seems most interesting examined here from the perspective of the phatic function served by both verbalisation, that is, small talk, and vs:

[~279]   JH [JANE HILL – ANCHOR]: and uh let's get a quick update now (.) from Washington D.C. itself *live* to our correspondent Rob Watson. (to RW) Rob just give a feeling a sensation of the of the mood of what people are saying the atmosphere where you are. (1.0).
    RW [ROB WATSON – CORRESPONDENT]:   one word. Numb.

4.4 The Phatic Function

As Jaworski et al. (2005: 130) explain, the anchor's phrasing 'as elaborate a fashion as possible' laced with emotional references does not request an update but instead is framed to fill in airtime and so keep the communication channel going despite the absence of (expected) referential information. The correspondent's part cited in [~279] is, as the authors indicate, the beginning of Rob Watson's answer (after which he reports on the emotion on the scene, rather than offering any new facts or news), while his opening, which the authors cite but do not recount, is a case of the phatic function fulfilled by vs:

[~279^a]   one word: numb.

What follows (and is not transcribed) is, like the anchor's verbalisation, the conventional media means serving the phatic function: confirming the channel (the centre of this function) open.

[~279] illustrates two apparent ways of serving the phatic – connective – function: small talk and vs. 'Apparent' because both means may serve this function but also because, for some people, some cultures and in specific situations, small talk will do the job, while in others vs would seem fit. Sociologists distinguish between restrained societies and cultures and bursting (noisy) ones. Naveh (1993: 101–104) points to a correlation between these tendencies and the response to death in general, and mourning expressions and rites in particular. Examining here the phatic function and [~279] in particular, small talk prevails as a phatic means in bursting societies, while vs is associated with restricted societies. For the latter, particularly in this unique 'disaster marathon' setting, endless verbosity – a must dedicated by the rolling broadcast format – clashes with the silence of bewilderment, shock, death and fear. Instead of getting people together by their silence – such as with the ceremonial minute of silence – talk is experienced not as small talk but as empty and distracting speech. As Bilmes (1994: 82) observes, 'some silences are obscured by words'. To support this, he cites a Chinese saying that 'one should speak only if the quality of what one has to say is greater that the quality of the silence that one interrupts' (1994: 74).

Fascinatingly, Baker's two poles of silence (s– and s+) are illustrated in the narrator's description of Lou Salomé's reunion with her husband Andreas after she was hospitalised following a serious operation:

[~280]   After living together and yet separate – for almost half a century they suddenly confronted each other in a hospital room. Andreas, now in his mid-eighties, [...] Lou herself nearing seventy was not old either; [...] At first they did not know what to say to each other. They felt like two people who had met again, unexpectedly, after a long time and difficult journey. But there was not much need for talking. Had they not both reached, following their separate paths, the most difficult gaol that life has to offer: maturity without disenchantment? Quietly they looked at each other, barely able to suppress a subtle smile as they remembered the obstacles they had had overcome before reaching the high plateau of peace and serenity. (Peters 1962: 289)

While the first silence is that of the emotional distance coming in between them after years of living separate lives (Baker's s−, see Figure 4.3), the second tender silence, coming as if after the first sudden shock, is an example of phatic intimate silence, that which makes talking superfluous (Baker's s+ in Figure 4.3).

The next illustration of phatic vs comes from Zane Grey's novel *The Rainbow Trail*. Shefford is a newcomer to the West in search of a woman he once loved (though they never met). The following is an interchange between him and Nas Ta Bega, the Indian who offers to help Shefford find his way around.

[~281]   'Nas Ta Bega will show you the trails and water-holes and how to hide from Shadd.'
    'For money – for silver you will do this?' inquired Shefford.
    Shefford felt that the Indian's silence was a rebuke. He remembered Wither's singular praise of this red man. He realized he must change his idea of Indians.
    'Nas Ta Bega, I know nothing. I feel like a child in the wilderness. When I speak it is out of the mouths of those who have taught me. I must find a new voice and a new life... You heard my story to Withers. I am an outcast from my own people. If you will be my friend – be so.'
    The Indian clasped Shefford's hand and held it in a response that was more beautiful for its silence. So they stood for a moment in the starlight (p. 61).

While the first silence is, as the heterodiegetic narrator verbalises, the Navaho mode for expressing rebuke (see the conative function, §4.3), the second silence is phatic. This (beautiful) sustained silence, alongside the gesture, depicts and indeed enacts the constitution of the bond – a channel of friendship, trust and need – between Shefford and Nas Ta Bega (see also §4.6.3.3.1).

We conclude our presentation of phatic vs by considering one of its most impressive manifestations: the 'two-minute silence'. The iconic affinity between death as eternal absence (and stillness) and vs as a means of enacting death and communication with the dead is the foundation on which restrained societies use silence as a space for communion. This is overtly apparent in [~253] (§4.2) Walter (1999: 25) made a comparison between what he termed a 'hysterical, Mediterranean crowd of keeners' and the British mourning Princess Diana in 'haunting silence'. The two-minute silence was introduced in the UK on November 1919 to mark the anniversary of the armistice ending of the Great War (Armistice Day, see Gregory 1994). This tradition then spread to other nations and occasions, such as v-Day (8 May) and International Holocaust Remembrance Day (27 January). In Japan, it is signalled by the sounding of gongs to commemorate the victims of the Hiroshima bombing (6 August) and the earthquake in Kanto (1 September). A special version of the two-minute silence is practised on 9 September at the Ground Zero service commemorating the dead of the Twin Towers in New York. The names of the 2,749 victims are read aloud accompanied by background music. However, the reading stops four times (for a minute), signalling the exact time each plane hit its target. Spontaneous minutes of silence are also observed (see, for example [~253] §4.2).

The two-minute silence ritual is not only observed in silence, but unlike other rituals in which participants are silent while texts, addresses or parades supply contents, this ritual centres on and is occupied with the silence of the channel. Gregory (1994: 13), describing press reports on the public's impression on its first observance (11 November 1919), quotes the *Daily Express* saying that 'nobody can imagine what a silent London – still for two minutes – is like', adding that 'it was urban Britain which felt the sensation of silence, most powerfully'. Revisiting Dickinson's verse 'the perfectest communication / heard of none' [~278] in the context of the two-minute silence, such phatic silence constitutes the maximal communion between the living and the dead. Interrupting and halting the routine at once, enforced by the iconicity of that silence replicating both the silence of the guns the moment they ceased fire and the silence of the commemorated dead, draws the living as close as possible to the deceased (see Ephratt 2015b).

Turning to the literary realm, the pause Mark Antony announces in the closing lines of his famous oration for Caesar, responding to Brutus, is a minute of silence that signifies or enacts Mark Antony's phatic merge with the dead Caesar lying in front of him:

[~282] – Beare with me;
My heart is in the Coffin there with Caesar,
And I must pause till it come back to me. (*Julius Caesar*, III.ii.103–105, *Norton*^{3}, p. 1157)

Moreover, 'beare with me' may indeed be a conative turning to the audience urging them to actively participate in this phatic pause.

Before closure, one clarification is called for. Phatic vs, like the phatic function in general, is odd in that it focuses on the channel which habitually is the most latent component of the communicative event. This explains why, as seen regarding the still city of London, this silence is most impressive and compelling but equally why the silence cannot last long. Its gripping and its maximal reciprocal identification in the intersubjective realm either fade (inviting speech) or nurture emotions and thoughts.

4.5 The Poetic Function

The functions which Jakobson added to Bühler's model included two centred on language – the signifier axis. Because of this similarity, Jakobson (1960: 358) stresses, '[p]oetry and metalanguage, however, are in diametrical opposition to each other: in metalanguage the sequence is used to build an equation, whereas in poetry the equation is used to build a sequence'.

The poetic function is not defined by the genre – poem, prose, play, diary and so forth – but by the factor placed at its centre. Jakobson (1960: 356) elucidates: 'Any attempt to reduce the sphere of the poetic function to poetry or to confine poetry to the poetic function would be a delusive oversimplification. [...] when dealing with the poetic function, linguistics cannot limit itself to the field of poetry' (see for example [~26] §3.2 or [~111] §3.2.4.1.4). At the centre of the poetic function is the autotelic quality of the message. Once the unique arrangement of the signifiers creates an aesthetic sequence, its effect is pleasure. This explains the poetic function's responsibility for the aesthetic experience triggered by language, and in particular, for our purposes, it explains the use of vs, ambiguity and indefiniteness, as if flouting Grice's (1989) maxims, to enrich the poetic challenge and its aesthetic reward (pleasure).

Many literary works of all genres use words to speak of silence: to describe it, praise it, despise it, etc. Dealing here with vs serving the poetic function, discussion of silence as one of the themes of a particular literary work may play a merely secondary role (such as when searching for iconicity). In light of Jakobson's (1960: 358) definition '[t]he poetic function projects the principle of equivalence from the axis of selection into the axis of combination', we set out to examine the primary issue, namely the author's choice to incorporate the complementary correspondence between vs and articulation into the poetic sequence.

As explained in §4.4, because vs is defined by its lack of phonetic realisation, its role serving the phatic function seems at first counterintuitive; however, the opposite seems to pertain regarding the poetic function. The unique trait of vs as a signifier not phonetically realised offers unique possibilities of poetic projection and sequencing.

As detailed in Chapter 3, vs forerunners range from single phones to entire discourse chunks. Some trivial examples of vs forerunners as part of the formation of the poetic sequence are the zero sign, prosodic and other caesuras, ellipses and blank lines.

Cy Coben and Charles Grean's 'Sweet Violets'[18] illustrates rhythm and rhyming as ultimate sequences (wholes) based on equations:

[~283] There once was a farmer who took a young miss
        In back of the barn where he gave her a ...
        Lecture on horses and chickens and eggs
        And told her that she had such beautiful ...
        Manners that suited a girl

---

[18] https://wikivisually.com/wiki/Sweet_Violets
https://en.wikipedia.org/wiki/Sweet_Violets (accessed 5 March 2018).

It is only by the equation that anticipates the final syllable rhyming that the silenced words 'kiss' and 'legs' emerge in the sequence.[19]

This seems a plain example of the principle of equation, that is, the paradigmatic axis of selection (the final stressed syllable of the line) projected onto the axis of combination. Introducing this rhyme by a terminal caesura (rather than instantiated phonetic and prosodic material rhyme) suspends any possible substitution, and alongside poetic licence this exceeds the possibilities found in existing lexicons. Making use of the non-linear quality of vs (see §4.6.3.3.3), 'miss', the vs and 'kiss' combine rather than compete. This equality shapes both the poetic sequence and its effect: phonetic aesthetics and pleasure. The vs here carries the poetic projection, simultaneously concatenating 'miss', the vs and 'kiss'; this is not only surprising and hence amusing, but it also communicates the semantic and pragmatic equivalence between 'Miss' (noun or ADJ), 'miss' (verb denoting absence), 'kiss' (as a noun or a verb) and vs.

Vs signalled not by phonetic uninstantiation but by the uninstantiated syntactic complements required for 'not' in Wyatt's 'Hate Whom Ye List' was examined in [~103] (§3.2.4.4.1) in the context of projection iconically enacting a two or threefold monotonous effect.

To explain and illustrate poetic vs we focus on three genres in which vs actively partakes in poetic projection, each highlighting a different mode and mood of vs: the ballad (§4.5.1), Haiku (§4.5.2) and the mono-dialogue (§4.5.3).

4.5.1 Poe's 'The Raven': Verbal Silence Projected to Build the Ballad's Poetic Sequence

Edgar Allan Poe's legendary ballad 'The Raven' (Poe, 'The Raven', *Works*, pp. 707–710) interweaves syntactic and lexical vss together with phonetic and prosodic vss, creating an iconic poetic effect which by projection renders absence – as form and theme – present.

The ballad first appeared in print in 1845. Our analysis draws on the essay 'The philosophy of composition', published by Poe a year later (1846), in which he traces (faithfully or not) the steps that guided him in crafting 'The Raven'. We also refer to external sources to illuminate the momentous role poetic vss play in the formation of the ballad and the portrayal of its narrative.

---

[19] In this case the forerunner is phonetic (rhyming) but the vs is lexical.

296 Verbal Silence: Functions

Table 4.1. *Poe, 'The Raven': prosodic patterning illustrated with the opening stanza*

[~284]		Syllables and rhythmic patterning	Rhyming
	Once upon a midnight dreary,	16: / ˇ / ˇ / ˇ / ˇ	– eary (a)
	while I pondered, weak and weary,	/ ˇ / ˇ / ˇ / ˇ	– eary (A)
	Over many a quaint and curious	15: / ˇ / ˇ / ˇ / ˇ	
	volume of forgotten lore,	/ ˇ / ˇ / ˇ /	– or (B)
	While I nodded, nearly napping,	16: / ˇ / ˇ / ˇ / ˇ	– apping (c)
	suddenly there came a tapping,	/ ˇ / ˇ / ˇ / ˇ	– apping (C)
	As of some one gently rapping,	15: / ˇ / ˇ / ˇ / ˇ	– apping (c)
	rapping at my chamber door.	/ ˇ / ˇ / ˇ /	– or (B)
	"*Tis* some visitor,' I muttered,	15: / ˇ / ˇ / ˇ / ˇ	
	'tapping at my chamber door –	/ ˇ / ˇ / ˇ /	– or (B)
	Only this, and nothing more.'	7: / ˇ / ˇ / ˇ /	– or (B)

The poem comprises 108 lines, arranged in eighteen six-line stanzas. We present in Table 4.1 the poem's opening stanza. The metric and rhyming (left columns), discussed afterwards, remain constant throughout the entire poem.[20]

Over a century prior to Jakobson's (1960) portrayal of the poetic function, Poe identifies beauty as the province of poetry: 'Beauty is the sole legitimate province of the poem'. To this he adds that 'a poem is such only inasmuch as it intensely excites, by elevating the soul; and all intense excitements are, through a psychal necessity, brief'. Since, according to Poe, the poetic function – that is, beauty – is responsible for the elevation of a pure effect, these must also render the work universally appreciable. Bringing together form (aesthetics) and content (theme), Poe concludes that melancholy is the highest manifestation of all the poetical tones. He then proceeds to implement these ties as he creates his poem.

The rationale Poe outlines for his choice of the refrain as the poem's pivot again pre-empts Jakobson's portrayal of the poetic function as the projection of the principle of equivalence onto the axis of combination:

The pleasure is deduced solely from the sense of identity – of repetition. I resolved to diversify, and so heighten the effect, by adhering, in general, to the monotone of sound,

---

[20] Notations: italicised syllables in the poem are stressed; in the second column: '/'=stressed syllable; 'ˇ'=unstressed syllable; bracketed upper-case letter=external rhyming; bracketed small case letter=internal rhyming.

4.5 The Poetic Function

while I continually varied that of thought: that is to say, I determined to produce continuously novel effects, by the variation of the application of the refrain – the refrain itself remaining, for the most part, unvaried.

To achieve this effect, Poe adopted a strict trochaic meter (/ˇ) and a sonorous word that closes each stanza. Poe chose the word 'nevermore' since it permits the poetic projection of selective variations onto a repetitive and melancholic monotony in order to produce beauty. The same consideration, he reports, led him to choose the raven – a non-reasoning creature capable of speech – as the addresser of this monotony. This, he continues, dictated the poem's theme and its unfolding narrative: 'the death, then, of a beautiful woman is, unquestionably, the most poetical topic in the world – and equally is it beyond doubt that the lips best suited for such topic are those of a bereaved lover'. Poe proceeds to describe the evolvement of the narrative and its turning towards the final stanza from the real to the transcendental, and concludes by asserting that '[t]he reader begins now to regard the Raven as emblematical – but it is not until the very last line of the very last stanza that the intention of making him emblematical of Mournful and never-ending Remembrance is permitted distinctly to be seen'.

Paraphrasing Poe's above justification of his choices, we here replace 'nevermore' with 'poetic vs':

The sound of the refrain being thus determined, it became necessary to select a word embodying this sound, and at the same time in the fullest possible keeping with that melancholy which I had pre-determined as the tone of the poem. In such a search it would have been absolutely impossible to overlook (poetic) vs.

As Poe (1846) himself testifies, the word 'nevermore' depicts phonetically, that is as an ideophone, the denotation of ongoing absence. This is further highlighted by the ballad's unique prosodic setting. As illustrated, the external rhyming pattern in the opening stanza, as in all the stanzas, is A B C B B B. The poem also follows systematic internal rhyming and the figure of alliterations (see Table 4.1). The rhythm alternates, in accordance with the rhyming, between full octameter in the A and C lines and a final incomplete foot, leaving out the second unstressed syllable in the B lines. The closing line of each stanza – also a B line – is confined to half a trochaic heptameter: three and a half syllables.[21] Interestingly, some editions, such as (Poe, 'The Raven', *Works*, pp. 707–710), graphically indent this final tetrameter catalectic line, as if leaving an empty space for its vs (initial) half.

The meter decrementing in each stanza is in itself an expression of absence through poetic vs. But further examination of this pattern shows that the

---

[21] Twice, in succession, Poe (1846) outlines the poem's versification. Poe was right in his verbal description of the meter but erred in the preceding description, where he described lines two, four and five as heptameter catalectic.

catalectic lines, that is, the metrically incomplete lines, are all the B lines and only these lines: all those ending with a stressed ' – or', including the final 'Nevermore' (and its variants 'nothing more' and 'evermore'). This layout emphasising the ' – or' as the line's final syllable is a deliberate use of poetic vs. The repetitive missing syllable serves not only to express void but to make the presence of this void the semiotic and poetic theme, depicting and enacting melancholy.

To see this delicate construction of the melancholic we may connect the decrementing versification with what Kristeva describes as poetic projection of non-idempotence. Idempotent signifiers are signifiers that retain the same meaning, irrespective of their iteration. Idempotence is the basis for logical relations such as tautology. Kristeva (1968: 50, adopting the term from mathematics) contends that 'la multiple répétition du vocable jamais identique (comme sens) à lui-même, joue sur la non-idempotence du langue poétique' (the multiple repetition of a term, never being identical (as meaning) to itself, plays on the non-idempotence of poetic language). According to Kristeva, compared, for example, with codes such as logic, mathematics and what she terms 'everyday language', poetic language not only uniquely negates idempotence, but more so its non-idempotent quality is a key element in the projection of selection to the axis of composition, or that which Poe named variation within repetition. Not surprisingly, Kristeva (1968: 50) designates Poe's repetition of 'nevermore' in 'The Raven' as the first exemplar in modernity of a poem founded on the negation of the idempotence.

To say that the poetic repetition negates idempotence is to admit the idemponent quality of repetition. To portray repetitions in the poetic setting in general, and in 'The Raven' in particular, contrary to Kristeva, not as dichotomous (idempotence versus non-idempotence) but instead as a twofold phenomenon, will not only be more faithful to the poetic setting as such but will also elucidate the uncanny flavour of the ballad and its portrayal of the melancholic. The idempotent quality of the repetitions, unchanging and untouchable, captures as a symptom the melancholic experience. Conversely, the non-idempotent quality of the poetic repetitions, as emphasised by Kristeva, projected from the selection axis to the combination axis (such as meter, rhyming, wording, questions and other means such as decrementing signifiers) depicts – for the reader – movement and transformation (mirroring that processed by the mourner). In addition, the non-idempotent quality (novelty) not excluding the idempotent (familiarity) depicts the uncanny (see §3.2.5.3): familiar and estranged, calmly embracing repetition and mysteries veiling presence and absence, speech-language and vs.

Drawing together Poe's designation of melancholy as the tone of 'The Raven', Kristeva's (1968) view of the founding of the ballad on the negation of the idempotence and Kelly's (2016) contribution, 'Staging nothing: The

4.5 The Poetic Function

figure of das Ding in Poe's "The Raven"', positions poetic vss as the carriers expressing and enacting the object of melancholia.

While mourning – painful and intense as it may be – is invested in the acceptance of the loss of the actual object, and so, despite resistance, works through to withdraw all libido from its attachment to that object (Freud 1917: 244), melancholia clings to the lost object. This not only mitigates against mourning as a healing process but blocks the self from hes grief and from hemself. Kelly (2016) examines how the void is staged through aesthetic means in 'The Raven' and 'filled' by the enigmatic raven, which takes on the function of a sublime object in the speaker's fantasy. She says:

> [M]uch of the imagery and rhetoric of 'The Raven' serves to dramatize not the metaphorical coherence of language but, on the contrary, the fundamental incapacity of language to achieve its aim, the tendency of signification to generate excesses of (non) meaning in symptomatic expression of its constitutive lack. For Poe, this lack accounts for the material opacity of language, which, like a veil, induces the specter of some palpable – be it ideal or terrible – 'beyond.' It is ultimately the speaker's traumatic repeated confrontation with this lack in the uncanny figure of *das Ding*, in the image of the mysterious tapping, the fantasy of his angelic beloved, and his encounter with the enigmatic raven itself, that mirrors his own lack and provokes his melancholic despair into madness. (2016: 123–124)

Amir (2008), differentiating between actual and potential dimensions underlying the experience of loss, identifies two ways in which the melancholic subject resists the actual loss: s/he either clings to the actual non-existent object, putting himself to death together with it, or, when the potential dimension predominates, clings to the psychotic illusion that the lost object still exists (see [~223] §3.2.5.4.1). If we consider these two modes of melancholic resistance with Kelly's (2016: 117) above-cited description of *das Dind* and the inanimate quality of language as oral substances, it appears that words and ideophones as inanimate ideation portray the first melancholic mode of resistance, while the extensive use of form, that is repetitions, enact psychotic madness.

Accordingly, the melancholic effect is not confined in 'The Raven' to the tone, that is, the idempotent quality of the ongoing metric monotonous repetition. It is also complemented by lexical vss, such as in Table 4.2.

The lexical vss in Table 4.2, addressing the theme of silence, stillness and darkness versus speech, movement and light, transmitted in the fixed repetitive rhyming and meter, poetically delineate an uncanny and melancholic fixation to the void while at the same time rendering present the signifiers pointing to the missing object. The shortage of language to express the void makes vs the preferred means of expression for this purpose (see §4.6.4). While vss are non-articulated signifiers as deliberate means of expression – that is, they carry

Table 4.2. *Poe, 'The Raven': lexical verbal silences*

Lexical vs	Citation	Section
Words of silence And Negating speech words	But the silence was unbroken, And the stillness gave no token (V)	§3.2.5.1.1 §3.2.5.1.4
Downtoner speech-diminishing modifier Negating speech words	But the Raven, sitting lonely on the placid bust, spoke only That one word, as if his soul in that one word he did outpour. Nothing farther then he uttered	§3.2.5.1.7 §3.2.5.1.4
Relinquishing the intention to communicate contents	This I sat engaged in guessing, but no syllable expressing (XII)	§3.2.5.1.5
Words pointing to paralanguage	And the only word there spoken was the whispered word, 'Lenore?' (V) This I whispered, and an echo murmured back the word, 'Lenore!' –	§3.2.5.1.3
Quotation as vs General words	Quoth the Raven 'Nevermore.'	§3.2.5.2.1[22] §3.2.5.1.6
No name as vs	For the rare and radiant maiden whom the angels name Lenore – Nameless *here* for evermore (II)	§3.2.5.4

meanings – empty speech covers the excessive articulation of signifiers deliberately detached from meaning. As Kelly mentioned with regards to *das Ding*, by its very definition, language makes present the absence of the object (see end of §3.2.5.2.1, and see also in §4.6.4 Amir (2014: 1) on psychic language being first and foremost a depressive achievement). Moreover, as the sounds, the wording and the protagonist of 'The Raven' all convey, words as oral substances and semantic content generalisations are ideations and idealisations (see Kelly 2016: 117; and see §3.2.5.1.6) which, like wholeness and perfection, present and serve as a defence against the void of death. In fact, it is only due to this ideation that one can use words, that is, language, to deceive: 'Leave no black plume as a token of that lie thy soul hath spoken!' (XVII).

In concluding our discussion of the differentiation around speech and silence, presence and absence and absence made present serving the poetic function in 'The Raven', a word is called for regarding Poe as the poet and as the author of the essay. Whether or not Poe's (1846) essay faithfully describes

---

[22] And see there Plett's (1991: 9) definition tying quotation with repetition.

4.5 The Poetic Function 301

the stages leading to the composition of this extraordinary ballad, his preoccupation with form in general and repetition in particular, so that the content or narrative comes last, itself mimics the melancholic empty signification. This seems particularly significant in the context of the poetic function, since the stages Poe outlines proceeding from beauty and tone (the melancholic tone) through to the selection of signifiers – that is, the message – all accord with Jakobson's (1960) portrayal of the poetic function: the message – the aesthetic organisation of the code – dominates the content. But this may conversely play into the hands of the melancholic empty signifiers. As 'The Raven' demonstrates, the successful aesthetic investment in the message that forges poetic language in no sense constitutes empty speech. The use of poetic vss (including forms of repetition) as it were projects the melancholic investment in the empty signifier onto the axis of combination, that is, the figure–ground relations of speech as forerunners and vs as meaning.

4.5.2   Haiku

We now focus on Haiku, a genre strongly associated with silence. In many ways Haiku seems to be the mirror image of 'The Raven', yet their common poetic motivation (see Poe's description of his poem which 'intensely excites, by elevating the soul; and all intense excitements are, through a psychal necessity, brief') illuminates the important role played by poetic vs, not least in poetic projection and the quality of idempotence.

Though Haiku is now the best-known Japanese poetic genre, its original motivation was not to serve the poetic function but rather to constitute one of the many meditative practices of Zen Buddhism (alongside yoga and the mandala, for example), and to be used by Shinto practitioners (together with such Japanese arts as the tea ceremony and calligraphy). Each particular piece of artwork takes one of the four Zen moods – *Sabi*, *Wabi*, *Aware* and *Yugen* – as its dominating mood (for an overview, see Raz 2010). We shall return to these moods as we consider silence.

In addition to its beginning as a spiritual practice rather than poetry per se, Haiku did not begin as an autonomous text. In the eighth century, it formed the opening verse of the *Tanka*, a traditional Japanese genre constructed of five 'on' morae (that is, vowel nucleus sound units) grouped in two: the upper verse (consisting of 5/7/5) and the lower verse (7/7). Around the twelfth century the *Renga* took over as a collaborative poetic genre, in which the *Tanka*'s upper verse, that is, the 5/7/5 opening verse (Haiku 俳句), was written by one poet, the 7/7 lower verse by another, and so forth. This became a social creative event that sometimes yielded hundreds of verses. The opening verse, the Haiku, set the *Renga*'s theme and atmosphere. Due to its special status, the composition of that opening verse was allotted to the most skilled poet, or alternatively to the guest of the house. From the seventeenth century on, these unique properties gave the Haiku a life of its own as an independent poetic creation. This was far beyond a technical matter. The detachment of the Haiku from the *Renga*'s chain and from the *Tanka*'s two-verse composition further distilled its Zen poetic qualities, particularly the essence of being rather than doing. The Haiku, then, is not an aim (such as doing poetry) but a state of being – a mood. The contemporary Haiku scholar Kenneth Yasuda (1995: 146) termed this 'a haiku moment': an 'aesthetic moment – a moment in which the words which created the experience and the experience itself can become one'. An obvious question is why an aesthetic genre purifying an ephemeral instant is subject to so many formal and thematic restrictions. The answer is that what makes the Haiku moment is the unique selection within the rigid formal and thematic constraints set by immanent qualities (such as mood, season or scene) projected onto a composition that is again constrained by regulations. Both the rules and the selections and compositions are not rhetorical devices artificially imposed on the genre but rather qualities making words and experience become indivisible. This is in itself an aesthetic oneness experience. All these involve silence as essence and as means: by its presence and by its absence.

To illustrate this, we turn here to the master Matsuo Bashō's Haiku as an extraordinary exemplar of the poetic vss crafting Haiku as a poetic genre:

[~285[Japanese]] Japanese source: 松島や　　/ あ あ 松 島 や　/ 松 島 や
　　　　　　　　Transcription:　　matsu shima ya / a a matsu shima ya / matsu shima ya
　　　　　　　　Morae count:　　　 1　2　3 4 5/ 1 2　3　4 5 6 7/ 1　2　3 4 5
　　　　　　　　Translation 1 nouns: pine　isle ʂ / ah ah pine　isle ʂ / pine　isle ʂ
　　　　　　　　Translation 2 toponym: Matsushima ʂ / ah ah Matsushima ʂ / Matsushima ʂ

As illustrated in [~285[Japanese]], Haiku is expressed in a seventeen *ons*-morae, that is, phonetic vowel nucleus characters (to be differentiated from syllables which instead of being one unit are a concatenation of consonants and vowels). The number seventeen, being equivalent to the average optimal breath length, is in no way arbitrary. These cluster in Haiku in a rhythm of 5/7/5 stressed *ons* (see morae count, above). Yasuda (1957: 34–40) coins the term 'ah-ness' to describe a state of mind in which the beholder can only give one breath-long exclamation of delight: 'Ah'. Thus the length of the Haiku, Yasuda asserts, is dictated by physical necessity. This neatly demonstrates the delicate build-up of the poetic prosodic sequence by that which is (the ah-ness rhythm) and that which isn't (rhyming, experiencing as noise veiling the naturalness of the 'a').

In lexical terms, [~285[Japanese]] repeatedly combines three words: *Matsushima* – a content word that is a compound constructed of two Japanese nouns but also serves as a toponym; *Ah* – a universal exclamation;

4.5 The Poetic Function

and the *kireji* cutting word *ya* (designated above by our vs signifier ꙅ). The last two constituents participating in the selection axis occupying (5/7/5) morae are thus neither content nor function words; they are natural sounds (see §2.2.2 and §4.2) – one of breathing and the other of pausing. Set in the poetic-centred function, they project to the combination axis, like all selection constituents. But these two expressions also by no coincidence happen to be the two constitutive parts (not discrete constituents) of experience: the *Yugen* ah-ness and the *Wabi* poverty-emptiness. The ah-ness, as we saw, is, as it were, a state of fullness: full seventeen *ons* of the breath – a whole Haiku moment, but the breath cycle goes from fullness to emptiness (pause). Breath and ah-ness being an ephemeron (*Aware* impermanence) make present *Sabi* (loneliness). As seen, the experience of silence-void is present in all four moods. The *Sabi* mood deserves special attention in this respect, as it indicates not isolation and loneliness as a rigid external experience but rather a tender and quiet experience of aloneness reminiscent of Winnicott's (1958) 'capacity to be alone' (see §4.4).

The expression of the Haiku moment with its moods is not confined to a single vs means, such as the 5/7/5 non-rhyming prosody. The essence of Haiku nature is enhanced through other vss.

Sam Hamill, the English translator of *Narrow Road to the Interior*, Bashō's diary of his travels in northern Japan, suggests that:

The theory of co-dependent origination infuses seer and seen, making them not two things, but one. Seeing the more than two hundred beautiful pine-covered islands off the coast of Matsushima, he wrote:

> *Matsushima ya*
> *ah Matsushima ya*
> *Matsushima ya*

This is the sort of poem that can be done once, and once only. But it is quintessentially Bashō, both playful and inspired, yet with a hint of *mono-no-aware*, a trace of the pathos of beautiful mortality. A literal translation: 'Pine Islands, ah, / Oh, Pine Islands, ah! / Pine Islands, ah!'

Simple as it is, the poem implies co-dependent origination, physical landscape, and a breathless – almost speechless – reverence. [...] [for Bashō] Each moment is the only moment in which one can be fully aware. Standing on the shore, he saw hundreds of tiny islands carved by tides, wind-twisted pines rising at sharp angles. *Matsu* means pine; *shima* is island. *Ya* indicates subject, but also works simultaneously as an exclamation. It functions as a kireji or 'cutting word'. The township on the mainland is itself called Matsushima. (Hamill 1999: xviii–xix)

Phrasing Hamill's observation in terms of vs seems to be a matter of no more than surfacing.

Morphological vss confining to aktionsart and gerund (see [~90]) in §3.2.4.3.1) and lexical vs in the form of a simple everyday lexicon communicate here tenderness and reverence. The clearly intentional lack of functional words such as syntactic connective or prepositions (see §3.2.4.5) relaxing causality and logic depicts a unique (cosmic) experience of unification: the observer and the observed nature are one. These selections projected onto the Haiku sequence result in a condensed, non-linear, rationale-free expression of the Haiku moment.

The essence of a here-and-now experience is also captured by the double function of *ya* as an exclamation and the Japanese 'cutting word' (termed *Kire-ji* or *ma*). This is another form of vs that seems to the non-Japanese reader to be a special feature of the Haiku, though it is actually an integral part of Japanese culture and language. As Shirane (1998: 101–104) explains, cutting words fragment and pause but also link and emphasise (see also Takeda 2013).

As neatly demonstrated in [~285^{Japanese}], the 'ya' (and see also 'ya' and 'no' in [~286^{Japanese}]) cutting words are not silence but instantiated signifiers that simultaneously may even have denotative meanings alongside their function as lexical vs forerunners (see §3.2.5). The latter, as seen, introduces silence into the selection axis.

This brings us to examine the repetitions in [~285^{Japanese}] in light of Kristeva's (1968) claim concerning poetic non-idempotence.[23] As suggested, from an entirely different perspective regarding 'The Raven', to say that the poetic repetition negates idempotence is to admit the idempotent quality of repetition. In [~285^{Japanese}], and generally in Haiku as a genre and an experience, this captures the banal and humble mood of experience: as much as it is an 'ah' (*Yugen*), it is also a 'ya' (*Wabi*) nothing. Coexisting with the idempotent quality is the non-idempotent quality of the poetic repetitions, emphasised by Kristeva, which enacts dualism. The repeated forms projected from the selection to the combination axis in Haiku not only depict the cyclic experience of movement and transformation from fullness to emptiness but iconically mimic the experience of *Aware*: there is no true repetition, for each instance is not a token of a type but the type itself. This exceptional idempotent and non-idempotent poetic effect of the repetition is again enhanced by other vss. Had, for example, connectives and prepositions (causality and time) intersected [~285^{Japanese}], the exceptional repetition would have been ruined (see the above quote from Hamill (1999: xix).

Haiku depicting the *Sabi* transient momentary experience does not emerge only by vss in the form of the absence of function words, contextual morphemes and articles but also lexically through the absence of rhetorical ornamentation (such as rhyming, uncommon vocabulary and figures of speech).

---

[23] It is interesting to note the similarities and differences between the stances of Yasuda (1995: 132) and Kristeva (1968) regarding the difference between the scientist or logician and the Haiku poet.

4.5 The Poetic Function

The unique combination of repeating three words in [~285^{Japanese}] – *Matsushima*, a content word constructed of two Japanese nouns but also a toponym, 'A' a universal exclamation and a cutting word *ya* – easily lends [~285^{Japanese}] to translation. But this is the exception.

Due to the significant phonological, syntactic and morphological differences between Japanese and other languages, the breath element so immanent to the Haiku poetic affect, as well as function words vss, are scarcely retained in translations of the genre.

One of the many English translations of another of Bashō's Haikus will illustrate this point:

[~286^{Japanese}] 古池や蛙飛ンだる水の音
                Japanese source: 古 池 や   / 蛙飛び込む   / 水 の 音
                Transcription: Furuike ya / kawazu tobikomu / mizu no oto
                Morae count: 1 23 4   5 / 1 2 3 4 5 6 7 / 1 2   3 4 5
                Translation: old pond *s* / frog jump-in   / water *s* sound

The rhythm of *on* is not retained in translation, and moreover English 'additions' such as articles and tense, not to mention poetic words and metaphors, introduce foreign noise, purging the Haiku moment from that text. Blyth's translation in [~286^{Japanese-T}] is just one such example (cited by Takeda 2013: 37, see references there).

[~286^{Japanese-T}]   The old pond;
                         A frog jumps in –
                         The sound of the water.

Before making two remarks on Pound, Dickinson vss and Haiku, and before moving on to the final illustration of vs within the poetic function, we return to Haiku as an opening verse. Although, as explained, Haiku became an independent genre, a claim is made that Haiku is to be regarded as an opening verse followed by an unrealised and, as it were, lower verse to be initiated by the reader. This could be true of any text (see §4.3.3.2; and see also §3.2.5.2 on Kristeva's notion of intertextuality), but seen from the Haiku moment, the moods and poetic vss, this does not seem to be the case here. The reader, no doubt, has hes own singular ah-ness on reading a Haiku, and a Haiku moment is experienced anew with each such encounter. But this is not part of the Haiku. Claiming otherwise seems to negate the silences and voids being part of the oneness. As discussed regarding the inseparable oneness of the *Yugen* and the *Wabi*, a saturated Haiku is not a Haiku moment.

This leads us to two remarks. The first concerns Ezra Pound's poem 'In a Station of the Metro' ([~90]), which we discussed at length (§3.2.4.3.1) illustrating syntactic vs signalled by a verbless form vp (v)s, for which there are no antecedents to be instantiated. We cited there Pound's (1914: 205) reference to *Hokku* (Haiku) as his direct model for [~90]: 'I make the following *hokku*-like sentence', as well as his poetic-artistic conceptualisation of 'imagism' and 'vortex'. Examined here from the perspective of poetic vs, in which, as seen for Haiku, the essence is not only what there is but equally what there isn't, [~90] shares with Haiku syntactic vss, that is, the more extrovert formal means, but differs dramatically in terms of the tender inner means and moods.

The next remark refers to claims of similarities between Dickinson's poetry and Haiku. Confining ourselves again to aspects involving poetic vs, I agree with Takeda (2013) regarding the centrality of the residual in both Dickinson's poetry and Haiku, which surfaces in both cases with the unique use of the notion of cutting (Takeda refers to this by the Japanese '*ma*') so prominent in Dickinson's extensive use of dashes (see [~83] §3.2.4.2). But here, too, the similarity ends. A crucial difference between the two lies in the starting point: while Dickinson's starting point is fragmentation (such as I–not-I; life–death; reality–fiction; sacred–profane; past–present–future), the Haiku, as just discussed, begins from an experience of wholeness–oneness, albeit one that is ephemeral and empty (empty wholeness, indeed).

In conclusion, a comparison between the discussion here of Poe's ballad 'The Raven' and the exploration of the nature and role of poetic vss typifying Haiku in general, as illustrated here with Bashō's two Haikus, demonstrates the central role played by vs in the projection within the poetic function, as well as the open-ended variations of poetic vss. This comparison also emphasises the fact that the particular nature and role of vs in general, and within the poetic function in particular, is the outcome of the unique setting (selection and projection) in which it partakes.

4.5.3 The Mono-Dialogue

To illustrate the significance of the setting (selection and projection) of poetic vs we touch on an additional unique poetic means based on vs – the mono-dialogue. A mono-dialogue differs from a monologue or soliloquy. While the latter consists of a single addresser-speaker, a mono-dialogue is a conversation in which two addressers participate by taking turns (on turns, see §4.3.1.1). In this respect it is a dialogue. But its poetic-rhetoric defining feature is that only the turns of one of the two interlocutors are reported, while those of the other addresser are left out, leaving in the exposed addresser rejoinders which serve as vs forerunners of the hidden addresser's turns. Bakhtin (1984: 197) describes this as a 'hidden dialogue':

Imagine a dialogue of two persons in which the statements of the second speaker are omitted, but in such a way that the general sense is not at all violated. The second speaker is present invisibly, his words are not there, but deep traces left by these words have a determining influence on all the present and visible words of the first speaker. We sense that this is a conversation, although only one person is speaking, and it is a

4.5 The Poetic Function

conversation of the most intense kind, for each present, uttered word responds and reacts with its every fiber to the invisible speaker, points to something outside itself, beyond its own limits, to the unspoken words of another person.

Mono-dialogue, as a deliberate poetic technique, projects a gap from the selection axis (alternating addressers) to the combination axis, that of local and macro-overall meaning and significance. This projection accentuates the gap, making the hidden exchange present and attuning the reader to its poetic role. Unlike the protagonists of the mono-dialogue, the reader is exposed to only one of the two voices, and so this poetic vs conatively activates hem to fill in the hidden turns (see §4.3) to align with the protagonists. This poetic vs is signalled by formal (lexical, pragmatic and discursive) clues planted in the speech of the reported addresser as vs forerunners, thus clarifying its quality as a mono-dialogue. On the one hand this format silences one addresser-speaker's words and world; on the other hand, and unlike monologues, poetic vs renders hes voice and world present. In fact, the poetic vss convey two silences: the silence of the genre and silence of the hidden speaker. Unsurprisingly, more often than not the two go hand in hand; that is, the poet chooses this poetic vs to iconically depict alienation, miscommunication and passivity.

To see this unique poetic vs we look at this genre's epitome: *La voix humaine*, a single-act play written in 1927 by Jean Cocteau. The play features the last telephone conversation between 'Elle' (a proper name but also the French third-person feminine PRO, see §3.2.5.4.2) and her lover who left her for another woman. The audience is verbally exposed only to the turns of Elle, a suicidal woman. In the décor, and throughout the text (in italics), Cocteau provides detailed instructions as to staging and acting. [~287^{French}] is a short extract (pp. 66–67), Elle answering the telephone call:

[~287^{French}] : *Elle raccroche et se trouve presque mal. On sonne.*
Alló! Ah! Chéri! C'est toi? .... On avait coupé .... Non, non. J'attendais. On sonnait, Je décrochais et il n'y avait personne............ Sans doute .... Bien sûr .... Tu as sommeil .... Tu es bon d'avoir téléphoné .... très bon. *(Elle pleure.)* .... *(Silence.)* .... Non, je suis là .... Quoi? .... Pardonne ..... C'est absurde .... Rien, rien .... Je n'ai rein .... je te jure que je n'ai rein .... C'est pareil .... Rien du tout. Tu te trompes .... Le même que tout à l'heure .... Seulement, tu comprends, on parle, on parle, on ne pense pas qu'il faudra se taire, raccrocher, retomber dans le vide, dans le noir .... alors .... *(Elle pleure.)* .... Ecoute, mon amour. Je ne t'ai jamais menti .... Oui, je sais, je sais, je te crois, j'en suis convaincue .... non, ce n'est pas ça .... C'est parce que je viens de mentir .... Tout de suite .... là .... au téléphone, depuis un quart d'heure, je mens. Je sais bien que je n'ai plus aucune chance [...]

The telephone is a modern mechanical device, a channel for linking and hence admitting separation yet overcoming physical distance. At the same time it also depicts that very distance and, among intimates, the absence of intimate bodily interaction. In *La voix humaine*, the telephone together with the mono-dialogue which it so naturally brings about play an active role in the unfolding of the plot, enacting estrangement and the breakdown of communication. As a material object in its own right, the telephone adjoins its own technical interruptions of the channel (see §4.4). More so, the *horror vacui* absence of physical contact allows the telephone to take over, further exposing that absence. Elle informs her interlocutor that the telephone cord is wrapped around her neck, enacting both an erotic phallic scene and an image of the potentiality of a thanatos suicidal act with which the play ends.

Poe's 'The Raven', Haiku and the mono-dialogue illustrate here three poetic genres in which vs actively partakes in poetic projection, each highlighting a different mode and mood of vs. While these epitomise poetic vs, as seen throughout our study, varied modes of poetic vs take part, to a greater and lesser extent, in all poetic genres, as well as in communicative events not focused on the message and its aesthetics.

4.6 The Metalinguistic Function

Jakobson (1960) contends that the code takes part in every communicative event, and accordingly he therefore devotes the sixth function to the metalinguistic factor. Many communicative events are such that the code remains in the background, while other factors conveyed using that code, such as the content, occupy the figure. But when language is pursued not as a means but as the object of study, the event revolves around the metalinguistic function, and so the code is at the centre of the event. Jakobson stresses that while the metalinguistic function is strongly associated with linguistic discourse, it is not confined to linguistics; rather, it surfaces in non-professional contexts such as common discourse. His example is Molière's Jourdain, who used prose without knowing it: 'Par ma foi, il y a plus de quarante ans que je dis de la prose, sans que j'en susse rien', on which Jakobson comments that we practice metalanguage without realising the metalingual character of our operations.

Like any book on language and linguistics, this present study employs language to talk about language. Such is, for example, our definition of vs as '*unarticulated verbal signifiers* chosen by the *addresser, that is, the speaker* (holding the *floor*) as a *verbal* means of *expression* (in place of particular *articulated speech*) *signifying meaningful content*', in which thirteen of the seventeen content words refer to the code. We illustrate speech serving the metalinguistic function with [~288] and [~163°]. If we ask, for example,

[~288] What is longer, an ox or a caterpillar?

4.6 The Metalinguistic Function

we get two different answers depending on whether we are referring to the objects denoted or we are referring to English code.

To clarify the distinction between speech as the means serving the metalinguistic function and silence as its object and silence serving as code, that is, as the means of the metalinguistic function, we return here to dying Hamlet's notorious last words:

[~163ᶜ]   The rest is silence

Silence appears in [~163ᶜ] on both sides of the equation: 'in metalanguage the sequence is used to build an equation' (Jakobson 1960: 358). First, as the lexical metalinguistic forerunner, and second, as the object of the metalinguistic claim, onomatopoeic referential vs denoted by the code and announced by its forerunner (for elaboration, see §3.2.5.1.1).

For silence to serve the metalinguistic function, this silence must be or belong in the code.

As seen in §4.1, Sobkowiak (1997) is certain that silence is inferior to speech, since it does not function referentially and metalinguistically. He argues that silence 'cannot be used to comment on, or express a query about the structure of language itself' (1997: 46). Yet below we present and discuss five major classes in which silence serves the metalinguistic function. The examples presented not only counter Sobkowiak's claim but also show cases in which vs is the default unmarked code serving the metalinguistic function.

4.6.1   Pointing to a Mismatch between Code and Meaning

The first group we consider comprises cases in which vs is at the centre of the communicative event, pointing to a mismatch between the utterance's form, that is, what is instantiated, and its contents.

4.6.1.1   The Passive Pointing to a Mismatch between Subjecthood and Agenthood

Examined here from the metalinguistic perspective, the addresser's choice not to instantiate the agent as the expected subject s(NP) constituent (as classified and illustrated in §3.2.3.2) is a case of metalinguistic vs communicating here the discord between what surfaces as code: the morphosyntactic structure of the sentence and the meaning of the utterance.

Of the many examples given, we repeat here

[~73]   For sale: baby shoes, never worn

to show that Hemingway could have phrased this in the active voice placing the baby in its syntactic role as agent. But instead he chooses the middle voice (§3.2.3.2.3), that is, metalinguistic vs enacting and so pointing to the mismatch between the code (phrased as facts of a commercial: 'shoes' are the subject and 'baby' its modifier) and the heartrending reality of the untimely loss of the baby.

4.6.1.2 Uninstantiated Syntactic Function Words Pointing to the Structure of the Code

The raison d'être of function words in general, and prepositions and connectives in particular, is to signal relations between syntactic constituents. This involves the code. As discussed in §3.2.4.5, when considered metalinguistically as uninterrupted code, vs connectives communicate cohesion, such as merger (see [~134]), unification (see [~285^{Japanese}]) or swiftness and determination (see [~129^{Latin}]).

Alternatively, focusing attention on the incoherent code, vs leaving out function words may communicate detachment and a lack of (expected) connections. This is symptomatically attested in psychotic speech (see Amir 2014: 31–47) but also appears as a deliberate vs in literary works enacting this psychic or momentary experience, conveying a harsh sense of emotional, and even physical, detachment and disorientation.

Another major group involving metalinguistic function words vs is leaving an expected 'if' conjunctor uninstantiated as a rhetorical strategy to create an illusion that the cause–effect relations are not questionable but guaranteed (see, for example, [~118'] §3.2.4.4.5 and [~159^a] §3.2.4.6.2).

4.6.1.3 Partial Binary Code Accenting Its Counterpart

As explained in §3.2.5.5.1, the choice of an addresser who when wishing to refer to an entire set of a binary contrast articulates only one member of that contrast is a binary part–whole vs forerunner. But, when as in

[~235$^{a\text{-German-T}}$] [...] had twelve children, all boys

(illustrated from Grimm), this vs refers not only to the missing object (here girls, see §3.2.5.5.1) but primarily serves to focus on the code as theme, this is a case of vs serving the metalinguistic function. Raufman and Ben-Cnaan's (2011: 147) argument referring to Grimm's [~235$^{German-T}$] that 'On a metalinguistic level, we see here a foreshadowing of the preference for silence over speech' emerges as a frequent metalinguistic practice. Vs serves as code pointing to silence as code (see, for example, [~238^a] §3.2.5.5.1). This complements examples such as [~163^c] (see §4.6) in which silence as a lexical metalinguistic vs forerunner is articulated (the word 'silence' pointing to the onomatopoeic referential vs).

4.6.1.4 Taboo: The Words Pointing to the Prohibited Code

To dismantle the taboo magic performative force the use of taboo words is prohibited. The taboo vs forerunner does not replace the unarticulated taboo

4.6 The Metalinguistic Function   311

word in its referential role but instead brings the code to the fore: as if saying, 'I point to the denotative – expected but uninstantiated – signifier which must not be used: not leave the mouth' (see the examples in §3.2.5.3).

4.6.1.5 Distorted Code as Metalinguistic Verbal Silence

While groups §4.6.1.1. through §4.6.1.3 overlap with specific formal linguistic properties discussed and illustrated in Chapter 3, the current group involves many forms of vs serving to focus on the discord between code and meaning. It constitutes a group on its own because it is not the particular linguistic form of vs which carries the metalinguistic function; rather, the experience of distortion and the hampered code point to the discord between code and meaning.

An example is Wyatt's

[~25]   My word nor I shall not be variable
        But always one, your own both firm and stable (Wyatt, 'Of change in minde')

As an art poetic poem, it is set within the metalinguistic function (hence serving the poetic function). As explained (§3.2.1), the rhyming of 'variable' with 'stable' introduces juncture silence [ˈvə-ri##ˈable] and so draws attention to the code play. As Gregerson (2013: 157) contends, while the text speaks of stability (of code and of object) this fracture of the code 'enacts in miniature the selfsame instability that is the subject, and the larger method, of this poem [...] the speaker's firm and stable is anything but'.

Distortion attained by introducing vs to serve the metalinguistic function, that is, to focus on the fractured code, is also illustrated in [~37] Hejinian's 'Writing Is an Aid to Memory'. The many morphological vss serve to highlight the fiction of representation in the context of memory and parallax (see §3.2.2).

Likewise, vs carries the metalinguistic function in Ernst Jandl's consonantal lipogram poem 'schtzngrmm' [~33^{German}]. As discussed in §3.2.1, Jandl chooses not to instantiate any vowel, that is, to leave out the phonetic particles that imbue the code (speech) with its sonority and syllabic flow (life), in order to portray war as destruction.[24]

4.6.2   Activating the Addressee as an Encoder

As detailed in §4.3, when the addressee occupies the focus of the communicative event, the primary function of that event is the conative function. Thus,

---

[24] From a metalinguistic perspective, [~33^{German}] involves binary contrast (consonants vs. vowels) and hence also belongs in §4.6.1.3.

the cases involving metalinguistic vs activating the addressee, outlined here, belong in the conative function. They are considered here because the focus of these events is both on the addressee and on the code: the addresser uses metalinguistic vs to signal to hes addressee that it is that addressee's job as the encoder rather than decoder to handle that code (see §4.1 by [~248] the quote from Jakobson 1960: 533 allowing for the possibility of multiple functions).

4.6.2.1 The Unmarked Turn-Switching Discourse Marker

We now return to turn-switching, examined in §4.3.1.1 from the perspective of a speech-act performed using vs to activate the addressee, explaining why this conative vs indicating turn-switching in conversation is a discourse marker.

Managing turns as a social resource is economically motivated (see §4.3.1, and see Sacks et al. 1974: 699 note 8). Sacks and his colleagues formed a model (1974) based on fourteen premises, of which the most relevant to our discussion of metalinguistic vs as a turn-switching discourse marker are that turn-switching occurs (1), and that the order and length of turns as well as turn-switching are not fixed (5, 6). Also, overwhelmingly, one party talks at a time (2, 3) and transitions (from one turn to the next) with no gap and no overlap are common (4); talk can be continuous or discontinuous (11); and finally, the turn may be allocated by either the current addresser who selects a next addressee, or parties self-select and start to talk (12).

Based on their fourteen premises, Sacks et al. formulated a set of ordered turn-constructing rules to be activated on every transition-relevance place.

Interestingly, they admit using 'transition-relevance place' as a way of avoiding

choosing, with a term, between alternative and possibly compatible features of transition coördination which we are currently investigating. There are aspects of transition coördination which seem to require the notion of a 'space' for transitions, e.g. inter-turn silences which are not treated by participants as gaps or pauses. And there are aspects of transitions for which the notion of a transition 'point' seems correct; e.g., the end of a question which selects a next speaker seems often to constitute transition point – a new turn starts there whether or not talk by another is immediately begun. 'Space' and 'point' need not be mutually incompatible, as later discussion will indicate. The concerns of this paper seem to us not to turn on this order of detail, and we avoid prejudicing the issue by the use of 'place', of which both 'space' and 'point' are possible specifications. (1974: 705–706 note 15)

This, finally, brings us to metalinguistic vs. As indicated in the above quote, and as discussed in Chapter 2, there are different sorts of silences. Deliberate silence in our context signals and so metalinguistically constructs a transition-relevance place. It is therefore a conative vs direct illocutionary act performed by the addresser holding the floor in order to metalinguistically signal the termination of hes turn, and in so doing activate hes interlocutors (either the

4.6 The Metalinguistic Function

one s/he had selected as next addresser, or a self-selected one) to take over. Most significant is Sacks et al.'s mention of the difference between these and 'inter-turn silences'. The addresser may pause within hes turn (see premise 11 above). Under normal discursive conditions, participants are inclined to treat this as part of the addresser's turn. Not treating it as a gap, they will not usually interrupt hes speech. There is a fundamental pragmatic-discursive difference between inter-turn silence and the metalinguistic vs turn-switching discourse marker. The latter is the unmarked form structuring and constructing the conversation and conatively activating the addressee.

After a chronological overview of the concept of discourse markers, Maschler and Schiffrin (2015) examine apparent pairs from English and Hebrew. Their detailed study reaches the conclusion that it is impossible to offer a single definition encompassing all the broad roles, and even more the multiple functions of all markers and the different aspects of their meanings and uses. Referring to her initial study on discourse markers, Schiffrin (1987; Maschler and Schiffrin 2015: 191–192) characterises discourse markers as non-obligatory, sequentially dependent utterance-initial items, which function in relation to ongoing talk and text to bracket it into units of talk. She further specifies their characteristics, such as being 'syntactically detachable, initial position, range of prosodic contours, operating at both local and global levels operate on different planes of discourse'. To break the barrier between markers displaying meaning and particles creating meaning, Schiffrin suggests treating discourse markers as multifunctional indexicals.

Maschler contributes an operational definition of a prototypical discourse marker as an utterance fulfilling a semantic requirement, such that it must have a metalingual interpretation in the context in which it occurs and a structural one: 'the utterance must occur at intonation-unit, initial position, either at a point of speaker change, or, in same-speaker talk, immediately following any intonation contour *other than continuing intonation* [unless it follows another marker in a cluster]' (Maschler and Schiffrin 2015: 197).

The scholars do not consider silence indicating turn-switching to constitute a discourse marker, whether explicitly or implicitly. But examined here from our perspective, vs turn-switching appears to share most of the characteristics enumerated for discourse markers (regarding the exception, see below). Since, as explained, such vss are motivated by interaction bracketing, they are focused on the code and so serve the metalinguistic function. Signalling and so constructing turn transition, they meet Schiffrin's justification for treating discourse markers as multifunctional indexicals. In addition, they accord with prosodic features concerning intonation contours interacting with discourse segments distributed in transitional boundaries. Nevertheless, vs turn-switching seems to challenge two important features defining discourse markers.

The first is the requirement that discourse markers must be lexical expressions. Although conventional linguistics – pragmatics included – overlook the differences between the various silences and so also ignore silence as a verbal means of expression (vs), this is not our position. Our study provides theoretical arguments as well as practical illustrations demonstrating that vss are verbal expressions. A trickier point is the second requirement restricting discourse markers to the initial position. Maschler and Schiffrin's (2015: 193) contention that Fraser focuses on how discourse markers 'signal a relation between the discourse segment which hosts them and the prior discourse segment' highlights the question: which discourse segment hosts vss turn-switching? Customarily discourse transcriptions mark overlap but do not mark turn-switching.[25] This notational absence seems indicative of overlooking its role as a sign, let alone a discourse marker.

As formulated by Sacks et al. (1974), vs turn-switching is initiated by the addresser relinquishing hes turn. S/he may do so using a delicate composition of that vs marker, discourse segments and final (dropping) intonation contour, as well as nonverbal clues such as head positioning and gaze (and their signed languages counterparts).

All silences within interaction, vss included, are interpreted retroactively (see Figure 2.1). For vss to be metalinguistically interpreted as a turn-switching marker, the interlocutors, and particularly the next addresser, must, so to speak, embrace this silence, making it an intermediately positioned vs marker. As Sacks et al. (1974: 715) explain: 'In selecting a next speaker to follow its possible completion, no lapse can properly occur; i.e., a silence after a turn in which a next has been selected will be heard not as a lapse's possible beginning, nor as a gap, but as a pause before the selected next speaker's turn-beginning'. This accords and so supports attributing a multifunctional (metalinguistic and conative) indexical role to vs turn-switching. Various moves can follow vs turn-switching (see §4.3.1.1). These include, for example, a next addresser's turn: an answer to a question, a response to a statement, the opening of a new topic, an action (such as mands, advises and other illocutions) or the conclusion of the interchange, that is, retroactively elevating the vs turn-switching to a final closing marker (see [~14^{s}] §3.1).

4.6.2.2 Intertextual Stumps Metalinguistically Activating the Addressee as an Encoder

In light of §3.2.5.2, intertextuality pointing to the non-authentic text fragmenting and so introducing spaces within the authentic text is a lexical metalinguistic vs forerunner. When in addition the partial quote of the formulaic

---

[25] By convention, turn-switching is implied typographically by allocating a new line; and in texts such as plays, discourse transcriptions and such like, it is usually indicated by preceding the text of that new line with a name or label introducing the speaker (see, for example, [~62] in §3.2.3.2.1 and [~272] in §4.3.3.2.1).

4.6 The Metalinguistic Function

expression or of an original (though external) text points to unarticulated code, thus activating the current addressee to join the current addresser in becoming an addresser filling in the code, this is another prototypical case encompassing the multifunctional (metalinguistic and conative) indexical role of vs. To the many illustrations discussed in §3.2.5.2.1 and §3.2.5.2.2 we add here one more example:

[~289^{Latin}]   Veni Vidi Futui

This is the title of Stafford's (2007) book on 'sexual imagery and social class in Roman art'. This is, of course, a metalinguistic vs forerunner pointing to the dictum attributed to Julius Caesar following his swift victory in the Zela battle,

[~129^{Latin}]   Veni vidi vici

which as explained in §3.2.4.5 iconically communicates the sense of swiftness and determination.

Intertextuality is not a case of substitution, nor solely of neutralisation (see §3.2.4.5 and §3.2.5.2.1). Rather, it is precisely the intertextual thirdness:

[~289$^{S\text{-}Latin}$]   Veni Vidi Futui S [= *Caesar: Veni vidi vici*]

Such thirdness is not obtained by selection or combination, nor by replacement or neutralisation, but instead by reconstruction: simultaneous selection and combination (see also on linearity §4.6.3.3.3). [~289^{Latin}] does not substitute '*vici*' ('win') with '*futui*' ('to have intercourse with'). Metalinguistically pointing to intertextuality, it activates the addressee to join the addresser, to create the intertextual thirdness, whereby a new message is (jointly) created and communicated intersecting speakers, spaces, codes, eras, heroes and authenticities: Caesar's triumphs and sexual conquests.

4.6.2.3 Formal Stumps Activating the Addressee as an Encoder
While intertextuality is content driven, there are also metalinguistic vss signalled by grammar. An addressee faced with a stump of a left-out grammatical expected constituent, prior to attempting to decode and interpret that text, must first move to the addresser's position sharing the encoding with the authentic addresser. By way of illustration, we return to:

[~92']   Does she S_1 or doesn't she S_2? Only her hairdresser knows [$S_{1=}S_2$ / ∈ PRO] for sure.

As discussed in §3.2.4.3.2, the metalinguistic unease evoked by vs (leaving out the expected verb heads) causes cognitive and emotional tension that can be discharged only once that addressee steps in as an encoder, reconstructing the message to resolve the riddle. In the rhetoric of persuasion, such as in adverts and propaganda, the immense benefit of such metalinguistic vs is that by conatively (see §4.3.1.1) moving the potential customer to the encoder's position, the text becomes hes own, and so s/he do not experience himself as submitting to an externally imposed message or instruction.

4.6.3 The Metalinguistic Verbal Silence: Dot Dot Dot

Punctuation signs are metalinguistic graphic marks fragmenting the written text into linear or hierarchal clusters, such as syntactic constituents and structures, prosodic patterning, thematic frames, intertextual spaces or script representations of floor and turn organisations.

The three-dot punctuation mark shares with all other marks this metalinguistic role: focusing on the code and its segmentation. However, this mark is unique in its role pointing to metalinguistic vs.

The three-dot mark merits its own section here because, in addition to its metalinguistic function supporting, for example, lexical vs ([~175] §3.2.5.1.4) or syntactic vs (see [~92] §3.2.4.3.2), it also serves to point to a mismatch between code and meaning (see §4.6.1), to activate the addressee as an encoder (see §4.6.2) – at times even filling these tasks simultaneously – and last but not least, to draw attention to and focus on authentic void as metalinguistic essence (rather than its being marginalised, ignored or even eliminated).

We cluster here those metalinguistic roles of vs dot dot dot in three groups. The groups and their subsections are not necessarily exclusive. They are presented separately to emphasise a unique role or feature of the three-dot metalinguistic vs.

4.6.3.1 The Paradigmatic Role of the Three-Dot Mark

The three-dot mark fulfils the metalinguistic paradigmatic role pointing to a left-out code, such as a phone, word, clause or discourse turn. An example of this was seen in illustration [~283] from 'Sweet Violets', in which 'a … ' in line 2 points to the left-out form rhyming with 'miss' of line 1. This, as explained (§4.5), was a case of phonetic vs serving the poetic function as well as wittily bypassing the ban on disrespectful language (see §4.7). A similar illustration is 'he … peacefully' of [~219] (see §3.2.5.3.5) from Joyce's 'The Sisters'.

But vs in general and the three-dot mark in particular are seldom confined to substitution, that is, to the paradigmatic role; even in their paradigmatic settings (such as [~283], [~287^{French}] and [~219]) they do not confine to substitution: the meaning of the silence is carried over.

4.6.3.2 The Syntagmatic Role of the Three-Dot Mark

Here the three-dot mark is a metalinguistic vs forerunner not by local replacement but by metalinguistic addition which extends beyond the textual segment,

4.6 The Metalinguistic Function

such as adding interpretation, evaluation, reflections or back setting atmosphere. These, too, are not articulated but instead expressed using vs. This is attained not by words but by the three-dot mark metalinguistically pointing to the entire message, as if notifying the reader of the mismatch (see §4.6.1) between the literal meanings of the message and its ironic meaning, the addresser's doubts, etc. (see, for example, [~62] in §3.2.3.2.1), and so activating that reader (§4.6.2) to encode – that is, to introduce the additional layer(s).

The first example comes from an imaginative text by Donald Winnicott describing the end of his life, in fact, his death in retrospect (beginning stating: 'I died'):

[~290]   [...] When the time came I knew all about the lung heavy with water that the heart could not negotiate, so that not enough blood circulated in the alveoli, and there was oxygen starvation as well as drowning. But fair enough, I had had a good innings: mustn't grumble as our old gardener used to say....
(Winnicott 1989: 4)

This three-dot metalinguistic mark calls for reflection, noticing the mismatch between the literal words just stated ('mustn't grumble') and the grumble performed in this very passage (and possibly also grumbling about the gardener, who likewise rebuked grumbling while grumbling).[26] This seems a softened mode of sarcasm.

As illustrated in [~291], verbalisation explaining the metalinguistic meaning of the three-dot mark often follows. As Toner (2015: 164) details, this is a common practice in Virginia Woolf's writing, for example:

[~291]   One went to the counter; one took a slip of paper; one opened a volume of the catalogue, and ... the five dots here indicate five separate minutes of stupefaction, wonder and bewilderment. Have you any notion how many books are written about women in the course of one year? (Woolf, *Room* p. 40)[27]

Despite what seems here a paradigmatic role, in fact, destroying the mark as a mark so that each dot stands for a distinct object, these dots here metalinguistically add an extra layer to the code conveying an atmosphere of stupefaction.

Having stipulated the syntagmatic metalinguistic role played by the three-dot mark, it must be pointed out that, ranging on the entire code: utterance or conversational floor, this role can be fulfilled not by a local single three-dot mark but instead by combining many such marks (Toner 2015: 153 counts

---

[26] This is proceeded (and so inserted) by intertextual vs, that of a quote, see §3.2.5.2.1.
[27] See [~139] (§3.2.4.6.1). On the significance of the three dots as a conventionalised mark, in place of the varying number of dots, see Toner (2015: 151–153). For a historical overview of the evolvement of the three-dot mark replacing the dash, see Eeckhout (1996) and Toner (2015: 151–170).

over 400 occurrences in Ford and Conrad's *The Inheritors*, see also [~287^{French}] in §4.5.3). One should, therefore, be very careful when attempting to analyse each mark locally.

4.6.3.3 The Three-Dot Mark Signifying Authentic Metalinguistic Void

While the paradigmatic and syntagmatic metalinguistic roles played by the three-dot mark focused solely on the code as means, the current section looks at authentic absence. As outlined in §§4.1–4.5, authentic absence appears as a typical issue in functions other than the metalinguistic function. We look here at authentic absence – that is, absence in the real world made present and figured in the code, using the three-dot mark. Unlike the paradigmatic and syntagmatic roles just outlined, when the three-dot mark metalinguistically points to authentic absence, the mark in the code is not to be substituted (§4.6.1) nor the code complemented (§4.6.2); instead, the absence left as-is is metalinguistically moved to the fore.

4.6.3.3.1 Retaining the Absence to Move It to the Fore

Paralinguistic fragmentation such as stammering and pauses (see §2.2.2) necessarily involve speech, that is, here vocalisation. On the other hand, the metalinguistic role of the three-dot mark signifying authentic metalinguistic void, examined here, introduces the coded script, thus writing as intervention. While authentic speech (that is, such that is not otherwise transcribed) materialises in time, and so lapses once it is articulated, script materialising in space behaves differently. It remains after it has been inscribed, and so the writer – or any other person having access to this text – can erase parts of it. The readers see and so notice the text as it is finally submitted or presented (the writer may also leave a part but strike it through as a sign of erasure).

The writer transcribing or reporting speech may deliberately choose not to utilise the benefit of script enabling the complete elimination of speech lapses but instead to retain them using the three-dot mark. By so doing the writer indicates hes choice to move this absence to the focus of attention.

This is particularly commonplace in cases involving symptomatic speech lapses, such as stammering, hesitation or confusion, as well as cases entailing the birth of a thought (for such erasure retained and pointed using lexical vs see [~182] in §3.2.5.1.7). Toner (2015: 156–157) presents the birth of a thought as one of the chief roles played by the three-dot marks in literature. She ties this in with the stream of thought, providing examples from James Joyce, Laurence Sterne (*The Life and Opinions of Tristram Shandy*) and Virginia Woolf (see also note 29). Berg (1987: 43–47) examines the differences concerning the stream of thought between its English exponents, such as Sterne, and the French, such as Diderot's rationale doctrine.

4.6 The Metalinguistic Function   319

Stammering, a physiological or psychosomatic symptom (see §2.2.1) experienced by 1 per cent of the population, features in many youth and adult novels as a literary-rhetorical plot carrier. These local or reoccurring blockages in the articulation flow are iconically (and graphically) signalled using the three-dot mark. Examples include the protagonist of Vince Vawter's novels *Paperboy* and *Copyboy*, and Felix Grandet's somewhat aberrant speech impairment, as Balsac portrays in *Eugénie Grandet*.

For an iconic illustration of a birth of a thought signalled by the three-dot mark and verbalised by the homodiegetic narrator, we return to [~281] (§4.4), Zane Grey's novel *Rainbow Trail*:

[~281^a] [...] He [Shefford] realized he must change his idea of Indians.
         Nas Ta Bega, I know nothing. I feel like a child in the wilderness. When I speak it is out of the mouths of those who have taught me. I must find a new voice and a new life ... You heard my story to Withers. I am an outcast from my own people. If you will be my friend – be so. (p. 61)

This verbalisation of the three-dot vs mark adds an extra metalinguistic layer, that of a thought about emergence: the birth of a new life and with it the (again metalinguistic) emergence of a new voice.

4.6.3.3.2 Our Blind-Spot as Authentic Absence

Another authentic absence, metalinguistically signalled by the three-dot vs mark and so moved to the fore, is the blind-spot, narrated by the addresser or otherwise. To illustrate this we return to [~3] which served in §2.1 to illustrate the first-hand experience of the stillness of nature following the 2015 earthquake in the Himalayas. Photographer Roberto Schmidt begins his written report thus:

[~3^a]   We heard this most horrifying sound, it was like a train but came from so deep ... and then finally there was this stillness, this complete stillness [...]

The three-dot vs mark may communicate here a specific emotion (such as fear, see §4.2). Alternatively or additionally, it may contribute a non-local but atmospheric sense of collapse and fragmentation. But attaching the metalinguistic three-dot vs mark to the NP constituent 'came from so deep' seems to bring to the fore the experience of the blind-spot: that which is there but beyond the reach of the preceptor.

We may speculate that had punctuation marks in general, and the three-dot mark in particular, existed at the time when the Bible was standardised, Isaac's question to his father, when led to the altar,

[~292]   Behold the fire and wood: but where is the lamb for a burnt offering? (Genesis 22: 7)

would have used the metalinguistic vs three-dot mark[28] to signal Isaac's moving experience involving a blind-spot:

[~292']   but where is the lamb for a burnt offering? ...

Toner (2015) talks of obscurity. She illustrates this analysing the three-dot punctuation in Ford and Conrad's novel *The Inheritors*. The science fiction plot set in London is told by Etchingham Granger, the novel's homodiegetic narrator who falls in love with a girl from the 'Fourth Dimensionists', a group which infiltrated London's society to inherit the earth. Says Toner (2015: 155):

> On Granger's first meeting with the Dimensionist girl, his vision of the landscape he looks over is obscured and yet he has a vague sense of being able to see 'something beyond' (p. 8). Ellipsis points are like this 'gate-gap' into 'another world; to another order of things'. (p. 20)

But applying the distinction between ellipsis and vs (see §3.2.4), it is ellipsis as a mark ('ellipsis mark') as a metalinguistic vs forerunner and not ellipsis which depicts the unrealised dimensions (the blind-spot of authentic absence).

4.6.3.3.3   The Brake of Linearity as Authentic Absence

While non-vss fragmenting speech, such as pauses, cannot co-occur with speech and so must be aligned sequentially with speech, thus confirming linearity, the study of vs as a verbal signifier challenges the axiom on the linearity of the linguistic code.

According to de Saussure (1913: 69–70), 'the linguistic signal, being auditory in nature, has a temporal aspect, and hence certain temporal characteristics: (a) *it occupies a certain temporal space*, and (b) *this space is measured in just one dimension*: it is a line'. De Saussure considers the principle of linearity as one of the two fundamental linguistic principles (alongside the principle of the arbitrariness of the linguistic sign).

The unsaid in no way takes up any time, while what could be chronometrically measured concerning empty speech is the concurrence of the empty-false speech with the not verbalised signifier of the true speech (see §2.2.3).

As a signifier in its own right, and a figure grounded by speech as forerunners, vs has its own structure and conduct. Vss are not isomorphic with the expected verbalised signifier(s) as being means of expression they add more content. Communicating the specific content does not substitute that silence – that is, it does not eliminate it. While many critics have pointed out that de

---

[28] The fact that, although some modern translations of the Bible into English have introduced punctuation such as the colon, none of them has used the three-dot mark here (as suggested in [~292']) is easily explained by its absence from biblical translations, presumably because it is regarded as anachronistic. Isaac's ostensible double question is a case of turn-switching in which his first question is answered using vs (see §4.3.3.2.1).

4.6 The Metalinguistic Function

Saussure arrived at and so restricted the principle of linearity to the vocal channel, vs being primarily a case of concurrent vocal signifiers, overcoming the linearity of the auditory verbal sign. While, as any of the examples of vs in our study demonstrate, this holds regarding all forms and functions of vs (see also Ephratt 2016: 60–65), it is no coincidence that linearity is introduced in the context of the three-dot mark as metalinguistic vs (see also §3.2.5.2 on intertextual vs).

From its outset, the three-dot punctuation mark is to the full stop as silence is to speech. The full stop (also in the metonymic semantic shift it underwent) signals and denotes determinacy, completion and closure of both meaning (message) and form (such as code and grammar). And so, in this respect, it is correlated with linearity. The three-dot ('ellipsis' or 'suspension') punctuation mark, on the other hand, metalinguistically makes absence present, signalling and denoting the opposite, that is – indeterminacy, incompletion and openness of both meaning and form. Associating final silence with death, Eeckhout concludes his paper (1996: 269) by saying that 'maybe this is the primary function of suspension points, then: to illustrate the permeability of our written sentences, to signal how, once in a while, desire springs all bounds ... '.[29]

The three-dot mark's graphic appearance (unlike the non-appearance of most vs forms), which is retained in writing and physically presented with its role pointing to a mismatch between code and meaning, thereby activating the reader, both realises and signifies metalinguistic condensation and displacement. Not only do codes (the existing code and the absent one), addressers (the original speaker, the reader taking on the role of the addresser) and at times additional speakers, such as the intertextual speaker (see §3.2.5.2) surface concurrently using the three-dot metalinguistic mark, but the mark may displace time, exceeding chronometric boundaries, such as cultural-historic eras introduced intertextually, or quotes (including self-citations) merging past and present. All these displacements, retained in the text by the writer, serve hem as metalinguistic vs means focusing on the code's authentic silence: that which is beyond linearity. As seen from the above quote, Eeckhout regards this as the primary role of the mark (but see note 29).

4.6.4 The Shortage of Words

Codes, words included, are primarily means for connection and expression. Means are evaluated in light of their suitability to the task at hand. Any

---

[29] While Eeckhout rightly emphasises the indeterminacy of the three-dot mark, he also tones down the categorical difference between the three-dot mark and the full stop, saying that 'A "full stop" in actual fact, is never truly such, but only a makeshift stop-log in the stream of consciousness' (1996: 269). And see, accordingly, the absence of an expected full stop mark as a (graphic) vs forerunner in [~72] (§3.2.3.2.3).

instrument is sized measuring cost and effect; the parameters involved include efficiency, availability, prerequisites such as experience and temporal and spatial requirements. For words to constitute a successful code, they must not only be accurate and fit (for example, by belonging to the expected register) but they must also be handy, that is, shared by both addresser and addressees: the two parties must be familiar with the word and agree on its meaning.

While iconic vs is motivated by content, that is, by the object or experience in the real world, silence in face of language's insufficiency originates in the failure of words – as code – to fulfil their semiotic and metalinguistic task of signification. But more often than not, the shortage of words – manifested in lack of words – goes hand in hand with iconic vs. On reflection, this makes sense: form and substance match – rather than mismatch – when void is represented by void.

To grasp metalinguistic vs iconically pointing to the shortage of the code facing void, we first look at example [~293] (see §4.3.3 note 11). In March 2003, Pope John Paul II opened his speech in the Hall of Remembrance at *Yad Vashem* (Israel's official memorial site for the victims of the Holocaust), saying:

[~293]   In this place of memories, the mind and heart and soul feel an extreme need for silence. Silence in which to remember. Silence in which to try to make some sense of memories which come flooding back. Silence because there are no words strong enough to deplore the terrible tragedy of the Shoah.

In this moving address, the Pope lists the roles of silence as an emotional need, a means for recollection and a slow time for processing memories and experiences. The last role he mentions is silence performing an illocutionary act of condemnation. The Pope felt obliged to deplore. Deploring is a speech-act (see §4.3.3) conventionally performed using words. The topic of [~293] is not the Holocaust but rather the failure of the code (words) to do their job, to carry out an illocutionary act: that of deploring. Does the Pope deplore here? He deplores by using vs. 'There are no words (strong enough)' is a metalinguistic forerunner commenting on the code (counter to Sobkowiak's 1997: 46 argument) indicating: now comes vs as a means of expression – not because I have nothing to say (paralinguistic pause) but because in this particular context the code – the unmarked conventional means – fails to perform the act. The idiomatic characteristics of 'there are no words' is also an indication of its role as a marker (see Maschler and Schiffrin 2015: 191).

Not surprisingly, metalinguistic vs pointing to language's insufficiency appears frequently in the writings of poets, authors of other literary genres and philosophers of language. As explained in §4.1 (by example [~249]), Grice (1989) breaks down his cooperative principle into four maxims:

4.6 The Metalinguistic Function

quantity, quality, relation and manner. The maxim of manner focuses on metalanguage: the utterance's form. Grice expects a cooperative response to avoid obscurity of expression, avoid ambiguity, be brief and orderly, etc. (1989: 27). But what happens in face of language's insufficiency? An example Grice provides to illustrate the flouting of the manner maxims (not mentioning silence as a cooperative means of expression) is Blake's lines:

[~294]   Never seek to tell thy love, Love that never told can be.

To avoid the complications introduced by the presence of the imperative mood, Grice (1989: 35) paraphrases:

[~294']   I sought to tell my love, love that never told can be.

The focus of Blake's verse is language deficiency. As Grice contends, flouting here the maxim of manner, such as not naming each reading ('my love': a state of emotion or an object of emotion; 'never told can be': cannot be told, or if told cannot continue to exist, 1989: 35), and so maintaining rather than eliminating the ambiguity, serves as a cooperative means of expression.

Metalinguistic vs merging the shortage of words and iconic void combines with yet another factor, which is truth: the correspondence between the code (what is stated) and the real world. This is accounted for in Grice's (1989) quality maxim. When failing to provide information which not only involves void but such that is beyond words, the maxims 'make your contribution one that is true' and 'don't say what you lack adequate evidence for' reinforce silence as both cooperative and iconic. This, as discussed at length in Ephratt (2012), constitutes communicative events in which vs fulfils Grice's cooperative principle while speech (such as false or empty speech) flouts it (and see on Kierkegaard and Wittgenstein later in this section).

Gerzi (2007: 144, 148) describes silence in general, and in the psychoanalytic context in particular, as both the lack of registration and the registration of absence. Interestingly, the most typical phenomenon in which vs points to language's insufficiency (such as the shortage of words or the addresser's inability to guarantee the truth of the statement) concerns cases in which it represents, and so informs on, the lack of registration. Prototypical phenomena are preverbal experiences and experiences involving trauma.

Babies experience events, and these may even be imprinted in their procedural emotional memories. But because such events were experienced prior to the maturation of the infant's conceptualisation and verbalisation capacities (that is, code skills), they defy registration as distinct components, and so are not integrated as parts of the self that the individual can identify, access and share (see, for example, Bion 1970: 10–13). To illustrate this we refer back to the case reported in detail by Serani (2000) and discussed here under the emotive function (§4.2). Winnicott (1958, 1963) and many others emphasise the intrasubjective and intersubjective sequences in adulthood of the initial interaction between newborn and mother being in silence (see, for example, Amir 2014). The unique circumstances of Sara's early upbringing by her mother, who not only died when Sara was a year old but was also deaf and mute, explain Sara's repetitive, prolonged, yet comfortable silences in the therapeutic sessions: metalinguistic vss re-enacting the code she had experienced as an infant with her mother. Sara uses this metalinguistic vs to reconstruct in the transference of the therapeutic setting her longing for the comfort preverbal space-contact (see §4.4) she had with her late mother and to inform her therapist of the past and present emotions involved (see §4.2).

It is no accident that the example we chose for metalinguistic vs enacting preverbal code involves compassion and longing. Many examples of negative events experienced in the preverbal stage expressed in adulthood using metalinguistic vs also involve trauma. Trauma, as will be recalled, was the second prototypical case of metalinguistic vs involving the shortage of code, the lack of registration, that is, no testimony, which results in the indeterminacy of truth.

The many incidents of post-traumatic stress disorder surfacing among war veterans (see, for example, Freud 1920), focused attention on the enigmatic nature of trauma. This unveiled the widespread presence of such trauma, not only among soldiers but also victims of mass atrocities (such as concentration camps) and rape, as well as more latent daily offensives such as abuse within the family. Trauma figures as a central theme in the theoretical as well as practical dealings of clinicians and scholars within psychoanalysis and other therapeutic paradigms, neuropsychiatry and many other disciplines.

The key features encompassing trauma are the psychic black hole absorbing the substance including the subject (self) in response to an intolerable intrusion severely rupturing the protective shield. One is annihilated from hes own inaccessible experience and hence trapped in repeated symptoms. The traumatic experience is always met only retroactively. Past and present, self as experiencer and as non-experiencer, truth and fiction are experienced not as complementing an integrated whole but instead as both undifferentiated and detached (see, for example, Caruth 2001; Amir 2016).

The association which many scholars make between silence, formally or thematically ruptured, partial and incoherent language and trauma emerges as a vital link. Language is both a means and an authentication of symbolisation. Naming necessitates the distinction between concepts, communication sprouts from separateness (I–not-I). However, the traumatised subject excluded as the owner of hes own narrative cannot tell hes story, and moreover the enigmatic nature of trauma makes the distinct, communicable and linear code (see §4.6.3.3.3.3) metalinguistically unfit. Amir (2014: 1) marks psychic language as 'first and foremost a depressive achievement, involving both the concession

4.6 The Metalinguistic Function

of what cannot be articulated – and the giving up of the symbiosis with the other by acknowledging him or her as a distinct subject'. Amir shows that for the newborn to attain this achievement, the mother must play an active supportive role. Traumatising this twofold position may lead to what Amir describes as two modes negating language materialising as concrete language and as pseudo-language – in fact, two modes of empty speech. But bearing the traits of language and those of trauma, it appears that an adult, even one who was fortunate as a baby to have supportive caregivers and to attain language, when facing trauma as an adult is in no position to maintain this achievement. Metalinguistic vs, then, is not only the inevitable result of the black hole but also the messenger of this shortcoming.

Individual and collective atrocities, such as systematic extermination in concentration camps or rape, appear frequently as archetypal cases of trauma: the experience–non-experience of the black hole and detachment from one's own self. The case of the Holocaust adds two additional metalinguistic phases, associating trauma and code, and so making vs its voice. For the victims born in the regions occupied by the Nazi regime, the local languages were their mother tongue. But due to the sudden rupture of familiar routines, the native language associated with family, a protective and happy childhood and normality, now came to be identified with the oppressors. This imbued the use of this language with a traumatic and unbearable flavour. The dissonance may have been particularly great in the case of German-speaking victims during World War II, for whom the German language was not only a mother tongue but also the language of culture and humanity.

This ambivalent approach to language in the wake of trauma appears in the works of Holocaust survivors both as themes and as form. This is here voiced clearly in Aharon Appelfeld's confession in his autobiography, *The Story of a Life*: 'I've carried with me my mistrust of words from those years. A fluent stream of words awakens suspicion with me. I prefer the stuttering, for in stuttering I hear the friction and the disquiet' (p. 103; see also pp. 105–109). These gaps, the deliberately fragmented and broken language, serve Celan, Appelfeld, Wiesel and others as metalinguistic vs depicting the code as part of the trauma (see [~33^{German}] in §3.2.1; and see, for example, Yra van Dijk 2011).

In addition, Appelfeld and other writers and survivors who following their liberation from the camps have emigrated to other countries and cultures also express their metalinguistic fear that words serving for mundane matters are worn out. These words cannot serve to express the unique trauma and horrors they experienced, and indeed the very use of such common words belittles the atrocities, equating them with normal life.

This brings us to the last phenomenon: the shortage of language being a means of abstraction and generalisation (see also §3.2.5.1.6). While the inherent faculty of words linking signified and signifier is to denote, and so to convey meaning from addresser to addressee, this quality achieved by the generic trait of words proves to be a severe weakness when it comes to singularity. This was the case when Pope John Paul called for metalinguistic vs in light of the unique tragedy of the Holocaust (see [~293]).

Discussing Kierkegaard's stance on language and silence, Kenaan (2001: 256) explores Kierkegaard's understanding of the place of language in philosophy in light of the biblical story of Abraham. Kierkegaard contends that Abraham made a deliberate decision to betray and murder his beloved son. However, when examined in a manner which transcends language, Abraham's action is not meaningless, as Kenaan explains (2001: 256):

Nothing makes Abraham different from a murderer. But we may also say, that what makes Abraham different from a murderer is *nothing*, and that this nothing is precisely where we should look for individual existence. This is, existence is found in the lacuna which, in the space of language, appears in the form of a nothing. Here however, we are lead back to the question of silence.

Silence here serves as a metalinguistic means not only for transcending language which obscures existence but more so for bringing the lacuna to the fore, and so allowing existence, that is, singularity, to exist. Kenaan says that 'for Kierkegaard, Abraham's silence is a manifestation of an authentic disposition towards his exile from the sphere of the intelligible'.

I conclude this presentation of metalinguistic vs facing language's deficiency by noting that Kierkegaard's stance on the matter, as outlined by Kenaan, appears to match Wittgenstein's perfectly:

'7.0 What we cannot speak about we must pass over in silence' (1922: 151).

That is, that, Wittgenstein too contends that the only correct method of philosophy is to say nothing except what can be said, namely propositions concerning natural science and not mysticism (see also the immediately preceding propositions, 6.522 through 6.53 in the *Tractatus*).

This, I must admit, raises severe concern as to the suitability, as in our study, of discussing the language of silence in general, particularly insofar as we exceed the factual realm of science. The reader shall judge.

4.6.5 The Right to Silence

While 'silence as consent' belongs in the conative function (see §4.3.1.3), 'the right to silence' belongs primarily in the metalinguistic function. In fact, understanding that each of the two legal practices focuses on a different component of the interaction, and so serves a different function, resolves what at first glance seem to be contradicting practices.

The right to silence is not administrated uniformly in all juristic systems. The systems vary not only in acknowledging the privilege but also in

4.6 The Metalinguistic Function

determining who is granted this right, its juristic implications and the modes of its administration.

In the USA, the right to silence is based on the Fifth Amendment: 'No person shall be held to answer for a capital, or otherwise infamous crime, unless on a presentment or indictment of a Grand Jury, [...] nor shall be compelled in any criminal case to be a witness against himself'. Following *Miranda* v. *Arizona*, this privilege must not only exist but must be stated explicitly. The statements read out to suspects, witnesses and so forth employ words to perform an illocutionary act of warning (see Constable 2006: 156; and see note 30). While the *Miranda* (US) wording announces the right to (remain) silent, the British warning (1994 Criminal Justice and Public Order Act) states that one does not have to say anything unless s/he wishes to do so. In addition, unlike the US warning, the British warning stresses that the police, court or jury may draw inferences from that silence.

These warnings inform the suspect, accused or witness on the stand of the following metalinguistic threats: first, that speech in interrogation and court works differently than in other (everyday) exchanges and registers and thus might have different consequences (see Constable 2006: 150); and second, that silence in interrogation and court may be interpreted in different ways.

Only two matters surface when the silence (granted by the right to silence) is seen as code denoting content: the interpretation of silence in interrogation and court as indicating guilt (particularly where the burden of proof rests on the accused) and its interpretation as the appropriate response (see Kurzon 1998: 55; Constable 2006: 151). All other matters revolve around form. Despite the fact that in those cases silence is not a means of expression but rather a fence to wisdom (see §3.2.5.1.2 [~164] and [~165]), the right to silence as a special phenomenon focusing on code (form) and involving functional silence justifies its inclusion in our examination of vs serving the metalinguistic function. As Mirfield (1997: 61) explains: 'Just as conduct may sometimes be equivalent to words, so may words be equivalent to conduct. In some cases the substantive content of speech or text may not matter, but rather the manner in which it is spoken, written or expressed'.

Metalinguistically, the silence granted in the right to silence serves as a safeguard against the legal consequences of the use of code (that is here speech – not silence). We mention here three such issues.

The first is a practical matter involving incriminating identification. Identifying suspects usually relies on fingerprints or identity parades. But when no fingerprints are found, or when the suspect was heard but not seen, evidence relying on the idiosyncratic voice-print may be applied in a voice parade. In such cases the right to silence is a metalinguistic right to refrain from producing code (sounds) as a practical code safeguard.

The last two issues highlight the aim of the right of silence to protect the uneducated and inarticulate. Because investigators, jurors and even professional judges cannot be immune from subjective impression, the linguistic conduct of the defendant may influence or even determine the verdict. Both issues concern the pragmatic observation that speech works differently in interrogation and court proceedings than in everyday registers. The first of these metalinguistic issues protected by the right to silence is poor vocabulary, stammering language, difficulties in verbal expression and lack of experience in speaking in public (in general and in such official settings in particular). The second is the protection of the innocent person who, being ignorant of the unique legal register, may not only fail to convince or inform the tribunal but may actually be convicted due to the use of code unfit for the court register. In fact, being accused of misleading the court may result both from a failure to understand a question due to poor vocabulary as well as from ignorance of the court register.[30]

Legislation and rulings excluding the presentation of documents in court and excluding public representatives from the protections granted by the right to silence are based on the above metalinguistic considerations.

With this we conclude the presentation of the metalinguistic function played by vs.

4.7   The Circumstantial Function

We devoted §§4.1–4.6 to the examination and illustration of vs fulfilment of the six functions of language included and presented in Jakobson's (1960) model. We now look at vs fulfilment of the circumstantial function, a function that was overlooked in Jakobson's model.

In addition to its benefit in completing a comprehensive study of the functions of language, this aspect seems to offer a constitutive illustration of the theoretical contribution made by the linguistic study of vs. Circumstantial vs stands out as a central phenomenon concerning silence. Together with other silences, it touches on cultural silences, such as silence in distinct places, ritual silences and silence as a means for saving face. As indicated when looking at silencing (§2.2.4.1), much scholarly effort is devoted to such silences.

This examination of Jakobson's model of the functions of language makes this absence very apparent. For each communicative event, the context, addresser, addressee, channel, message and code must be set within a

---

[30] It must be pointed out that since the warning (Miranda or its equivalents) is itself communicated verbally, it is subject to the same shortcomings. Legislators dispute the consequences and interpretation of silence; what, then, is the uneducated and inarticulate person on the stand or in interrogation expected to make of the warning?

4.7 The Circumstantial Function

particular environment. This may be a particular physical surrounding or an intersubjective setting or ambiance. Using Goffman's (1981: 128) notion of 'footing' (see also Jaworski 1998: 142), we argue that *when the interaction aligns with a circumstantial factor, that event is set in the 'circumstantial function'. And when vs serves to fulfil this function, that silence is circumstantial vs.*

As seen concerning each of Jakobson's six functions, for vs to serve the specific function it must be chosen and performed by the addresser as a means of expression. This is particularly important to note concerning the circumstantial function.

To examine this additional function, we begin by providing, as Jakobson (1960) did, an example relating to a case in which speech serves the function discussed. The example comes from the court setting in which the participants honorifically address the judge on the bench using 'your honor' (but see later in this section on the use of the third-person). From this illustration of speech we turn to vs.

The court is a location and an institution that structures a cultural reality. This structuring also covers the speech and turns during the proceedings: allocating turns and determining what may be said in such a turn by the particular participant in terms of style and content (see §4.6.5). The defendant, or any other participant in the court proceedings, may only talk in hes particular slot. This is not silencing or vs. But in a legal system which denies a defendant hes slot on the basis of hes formal or informal social affiliation, this is silencing. When the defendant is allowed and expected to talk in hes slot and yet chooses silence – not as a means serving the metalinguistic function (see 'the right to silence' §4.6.5) or any of Jakobson's other functions but instead as a means to express hes rejection of the court's very legitimacy, this constitutes circumstantial vs. The following is one example of this:

[~295]   Man charged with attempted murder of PSNI officer in Co Derry
A man has appeared at Derry Magistrate's Court charged with attempting to murder a police officer.
A device was found under a car in Glenrandel in Eglinton, Co Derry last June in what police described as a 'clear attempt' to kill officers.
Sean McVeigh (35), of Victoria Street in Lurgan, is accused of attempted murder and possessing Semtex with intent to endanger life on June 18 last year.
He did not acknowledge the court and refused to stand during his appearance on Monday.
When asked if he understand the charges he sat in silence.[31]

---

[31] *The Irish New*, Staff Reporter, 9 May 2016, www.irishnews.com/news/northernirelandnews/2016/05/10/news/man-charged-with-attempted-murder-of-police-officer-in-co-derry-515010/ (accessed June 2020).

330   Verbal Silence: Functions

Another recurrent and typical form of circumstantial vs involves the expression of respect. In this sphere, we first look at silence saving face. Many sociological, anthropological, ethnographic and other cultural studies focus on silence as saving face (see, for example, Basso 1972; Bruneau 1973: 36–41; Tannen 1985; Blum-Kulka 1987; Jaworski 1993; Kurzon 1998: 26–28).

Brown and Levinson (1987) designate silence as the super-strategy for saving face. This, they claim, reflects not only silence's softening effect in tense situations but also the direct consequences of refraining from speech, which in itself saves face and masks diversities. This strategy is strongly endorsed in the Scriptures, for example 'Keep thy tongue from evil, and thy lips from speaking guile' (Psalms 34:13) and the apostle's adage 'Whoever would love life and see good days must keep their tongue from evil and their lips from deceitful speech' (1 Peter 3:10). Commenting on such truisms, Jensen (1973) cautions that the 'linking function' (see §4.4) in general, silence included, can 'bind together people or it can sever relationships'. Face-saving silences essentially embodying the lack of pervasive speech are not a case of silence as a means of expression but rather of silence as a cover-up.

Yet when silence is performed not to hide but to embrace personal, political or other diversities, that is, to convey the message that despite their diversity, the opponents respect the particular, location or situation and so restrain their diversity, this is circumstantial vs. While such cases involving world leaders and political rivals are well known, we illustrate this type of such circumstantial vs with an example from Edward Thomas' play *Fallen Sons* (discussed by Jaworski 1998: 145), in which the twins' mother says:

[~296]   No arguing on your birthday.

Examining the silences between the twins in terms of bonding and separation (see Baker's 1955 model in §4.4), Jaworski cites the mother's urge at the closure of '[t]he only longer piece of dialogue which they engage in is an argument at breakfast over whether Iorry knows how to skin rabbits, which the boys' father has brought home this morning for dinner on their birthday. The argument comes suddenly to an end when their mother declares "No arguing on your birthday"'. Jaworski explains that 'the ease with which the boys come in and out of the argument and slip back into silence without any mitigating talk emphasizes their closeness'. This is generally acceptable, and more so, as Jaworski shows, in the particular narrative of this play. But the significance of the birthday within the play makes the event – the birthday – the circumstantial focus of vs as respect. This in turn explains why no mitigation (another silence) was needed to easily slip the boys away from the argument into their bonding silence. The play shifts across three of the twins' birthdays: their twelfth birthday, when soon after the above scene Iorry erroneously and fatally shoots his father, a constitutive event that switches silence from bonding to

4.7 The Circumstantial Function

alienation; their estranged fortieth birthday; and their reconciliation on their seventieth birthday.

Silence is a prominent means for expressing respect. This no doubt originates in both speech and silence as social resources (see §4.3.1.1) as well as in emotive silence in light of the extraordinary, such as the deity (Psalms 65:2). Cultural circumstantial silence is manifested in registers pertaining to verbal interaction between superiors and inferiors (such as rulers and their subjects, employers and employees, and majority and minority groups). But while these silences are cultural structures, and as such imposed, vs is a chosen means of expression for showing respect. Specific locations and situations prescribe silence. In such cases, breaking that expected silence, rather than maintaining it, is a means of expression. But when an individual or a group chooses to observe silence to show respect, not because it is officially or culturally prescribed, this silence is a circumstantial means for expressing respect. As illustrated in [~296], this may take the form of total silence, but it can also assume linguistic forms. A prominent example concerns modes of address. Three modes of address are relevant here: titles and epithets (mostly adjectival), onomastic proper names and pronouns. The circumstantial function is most salient in the choice of the mode of address in light of social status and the linguistic register. The use of the third-person rather than second-person in addressing the judge is circumstantially dictated conventionally and so not the product of circumstantial vs choice.

Circumstantial vs is illustrated looking at non-reciprocal addressing convention known as 'first-name basis'. The convention, as Jaworski (1998: 141) points out (after Brown and Ford 1961) is that 'the superior can address the inferior with his/her first name but is addressed in return with title and last name' (see also §3.2.5.4 and [~242$^{\text{a-Hebrew-T}}$] and [~243] in §3.2.5.5.2). Circumstantial vs of a first name as a manifestation of respect is encountered, for example, in official or professional events, when close relatives silence their private intimate mode of addressing to express respect for the event. This can be seen, for example, when at official events Prince Charles, the heir to the British throne, invites his mother to speak or announces her presence while referring to her as

[~297] Her Majesty the Queen $\mathcal{S}$

and not Mummy. Being emotively rather than officially motivated,

[~297^{a}] Your Majesty, Mummy[32]

is the exception that proves the rule.

---

[32] www.youtube.com/watch?v=mGDujdUQNVg, 2:20 (accessed 17 July 2018).

The following example relates to the world of professional societies and their conventions. Again, the examples are many, and in a sense trivial. [~298] is indicative of the circumstantial function, as it is taken from the opening words of Anna Freud's official clinical case presentation delivered at the Vienna Psychoanalytic Society as a final requirement to become a member of that institute:

[~298] In his paper 'A Child Is Being Beaten' Freud (1919) deals with a fantasy which, according to him, is met with in a surprising number of persons who seek analytic treatment on account of a hysteria or an obsessional neurosis. [...] I shall take for granted that you are familiar with the content of Freud's paper. (Freud 1923)

Onomastic vs is only one manifestation of the circumstantial setting: to be approved as a psychoanalyst by her father's society – not to mention his entire movement – Anna Freud, as she states in the opening, chooses to clutch on to her father's recent paper (see [~66] §3.2.3.4.2).

Having looked here at respect, we now turn to its mirror image as embodied in the use of vs involving pronominalisation. In [~29^{French}] (§3.2), we considered Adler's (2007) example of vs in French signalled by the deletion of the animate pronoun '*sur lui*' to express the protagonist's treatment of the criminal as inanimate, excluding him from the class of humans (animate, rational). This was set in the conative function (§4.3) negatively activating the addressee. Example [~299], on other hand, relies on the circumstantial force and basis of honorific pronouns and here illustrates circumstantial vs. In many languages the use of a distinct second-person pronoun is dictated socially according to register, formality and status. Such an honorific distinction emerges in what Brown and Gilman (1960) tag v versus T (English 'thou'/'you'), exemplified in French '*vous*' and '*tu*'. Traditionally this circumstantial power distinction expresses non-reciprocal relations in which inferiors addressed their superiors using v and were addressed using T. In symmetric equality a reciprocal pronoun prevails, that is, a pronoun that is neutral regarding superiority. As the authors show, in modern times English has moved to a reciprocal designation in which the pronoun 'you' has assumed the neutral mutual designation. To illustrate the French move in a similar direction, Brown and Gilman (1960: 261) provide the following example:

[~299] We have a favorite example of this new trend given us independently by several French informants. It seems that mountaineers above a certain critical altitude shift to the mutual T. We like to think that this is the point where their lives hang by a single thread.

Both this example and Brown and Gilman's comments highlight the circumstances (altitude) dictating not only language but more so the use of circumstantial vs: leaving out the honorific convention so deeply embedded in French

4.7 The Circumstantial Function

grammar. This vs seems particularly interesting: while circumstantial vs involving proper names and titles served to express respect ([~297] and [~298]), here the addressers (the mountaineers) deliberately wish to leave out formal respect in unique circumstances which motivate their choice of this particular vs.

The proximity between silence conventionally enforced in particular locations, situations (such as ceremonies and rituals) and positions (embodying superiority versus inferiority) and circumstantial vss is so close that when examined behaviourally the two seem to overlap. The distinction becomes apparent only when they are examined from the perspective of the intention and choice in the given circumstances (see [~299]). This seems to explain why while silences other than vss dominate non-circumstantial functions, circumstantial vs is the exception. But interestingly, while this is true regarding people, circumstantial vs is widespread in the animal kingdom. We alluded to two such examples looking at 'part of a binary contrast' (§3.2.5.5.1). The first vs, the purr stop of the Uganda woodland's elephants as their alarm call (Ardrey 1970: 75), is both conative (§4.3) and circumstantial. The second was Sherlock Holmes's account of the dog not barking [~239], which Holmes interpreted as circumstantial vs leading him to decipher the theft of Silver Blaze. As discussed above, it is the focus on the circumstantial function which brings to light this difference between the use of speech and silence, in the animal kingdom as with humans. As the largest mammals on earth, elephants care for themselves, and so while vibration can be tracked, its absence may be a means of communal interaction, but in other instances it constitutes a practical act of camouflage. Dogs, on the other hand, are not only considerably smaller in size but as domesticated animals they depend on their human keepers. They use their bark to communicate to those humans impending danger.

With this we conclude the examination of vs serving the circumstantial function, as well as our dealing with the functions of vs (Chapter 4) and its forms (Chapter 3).

5 S S S

My words now come to closure in the hope that they triggered the reader's inquisitiveness about silence as a verbal means of expression, and that they pave the way for deepening an intriguing and lively scholarly and personal dialogue with silence S S S

References

Abd-Alkareem Massalha, 2005, *The Agentive Passive Construction in English and Its Translation into Arabic*, MA thesis, Haifa: University of Haifa.

Adell Jordi, Bonafonte Antonio, and Escudero David, 2007, 'Filled pauses in speech synthesis: Towards conversational speech', in *Proceedings of 10th International Conference on Text, Speech and Dialogue*, LNCS 4629, Plzen: Springer, pp. 358–365.

Adler Silvia, 2007, 'Silence and the French connection', in Ephratt Michal (ed.), *Silences: Silence in Culture and in Interpersonal Relations*, Tel-Aviv: Resling Publishing, pp. 177–191 (in Hebrew).

— 2015, 'Liaisons "non marquées" de prédications dans l'accroche publicitaire', *Langages*, 200: 121–136.

Al-George Sergiu, 1967, 'The semiosis of zero according to Panini', *East and West*, 17 (102): 115–124.

Allan Keith and Burridge Kate, 2006, *Forbidden Words: Taboo and the Censoring of Language*, Cambridge and New York: Cambridge University Press.

Alter Robert, 1981, *The Art of Biblical Narrative*, New York: Basic Books.

Amir Dana 2008, 'Naming the nonexistent: Melancholia as mourning over a possible object', *Psychoanalytic Review*, 95(1): 1–15.

— 2014, *Cleft Tongue: The Language of Psychic Structure* (translation: Mirjam Hadar), London: Karnac.

— 2016, 'When language meets traumatic lacuna: The metaphoric, the metonymic, and the psychotic modes of testimony', *Psychoanalytic Inquiry*, 36(8): 620–632.

Ardrey Robert, 1970, *The Social Contract*, London: Collins.

Arlow Jacob A., 1961, 'Silence and the theory of technique', *Journal of the American Psychoanalytic Association*, 9: 44–55.

Aronoff Mark, Meir Irit, Padden Carol and Sandler Wendy, 2004, 'Morphological universals and the sign language type', in Booij Geert and van Marle Jaap (eds.), *Yearbook of Morphology*, Dordrecht: Kluwer Academic Press, pp. 19–39, https://doi.org/10.1007/1-4020-2900-2904_2.

Austin John L., 1962, *How to Do Things with Words*, Sbisà Marina and Urmson J. O. (eds.) (2nd edition), [1975], Oxford: Clarendon Press.

Baker Sidney J., 1955, 'The theory of silences', *The Journal of General Psychology*, 53: 145–167, https://doi.org/10.1080/00221309.1955.9710142.

Bakhtin Mikhail M., 1984, *Problems of Dostoevsky's Poetics* (translation: Caryl Emerson), Minneapolis: University of Minnesota Press.

Bar-On Dan, 1995, *Fear and Hope: Three Generations of the Holocaust*, Cambridge, MA: Harvard University Press.
Basso Keith H., 1972, '"To give up on words": Silence in Western Apache culture', in Giglioli Pier P. (ed.), *Language and Social Context*, London: Penguin Books, pp. 67–86.
Belsey Catherine, 2001, 'Tarquin dispossessed: Expropriation and consent in the Rape of Lucrece', *Shakespeare Quarterly*, 52(3): 315–335.
Ben-Porat Ziva, 1976, 'The poetics of literary allusion', *PTL: Journal for Descriptive Poetics and Theory of Literature*, 1: 105–128.
Ben-Ze'ev Efrat, Ginio Ruth and Winter Jay (eds.), 2010, *Shadows of War: A Social History of Silence in the Twentieth Century*, Cambridge: Cambridge University Press.
Benveniste Émile, 1974, 'La blasphémie et l'euphémie', in Émile Benveniste, *Problèmes de linguistic général*, Paris: Gaillimard, II, pp. 254–257.
Berezowski Leszek, 2009, *The Myth of the Zero Article*, London and New York: Continuum, http://ezproxy.haifa.ac.il/login?url=https://search.ebscohost.com/login.aspx?direct=true&db=e000xww&AN=283768&site=ehost-live&scope (online resource, accessed 10 November 2018).
Berg Michael Vande, 1987, '"Pictures of pronunciation": Typographical travels through Tristram Shandy and Jacques le Fataliste', *Eighteenth-Century Studies*, 21(1): 21–47.
Bilmes Jack, 1994, 'Constituting silence: Life in the world of total meaning', *Semiotica*, 98(1/2): 73–88.
Bion Wilfred R., 1959, 'Attacks on linking', *International Journal of Psycho-Analysis*, 40: 308–315.
  1970, *Attention and Interpretation: A Scientific Approach to Insight in Psychoanalysis and Groups*, London: Tavistock.
Blackmur Robert P., 1957, 'The language of silence', in Ansher Ruth N. (ed.), *Language: An Inquiry into Its Meaning and Function*, Vol. VIII, New York: Harper and Row, pp. 134–152.
Bloomfield Leonard, 1933, *Language*, [1954] New York: Henry Holt.
Blum-Kulka Shoshana, 1987, 'Indirectness and politeness in requests: Same or different?', *Journal of Pragmatics*, 11: 131–146.
Bobgan Martin and Bobgan Deidre, 1979, *The Psychological Way*, Minneapolis: Bethany Fellowship.
Bolden Galina, 2010, '"Articulating the unsaid" via and-prefaced formulations of other's talk', *Discourse Studies*, 12(1): 5–32.
Bréal Michel and Jules Alfred, 1877, *Mélanges de mythologie et de linguistique*, Paris: Librairie Hachette, Cambridge University Press (online publication date: October 2014), https://doi-org.ezproxy.haifa.ac.il/10.1017/CBO9781139839181.
Brown Penelope and Levinson Stephen, 1987, *Politeness: Some Universals in Language Usage*, Cambridge: Cambridge University Press.
Brown Rogers and Gilman Albert, 1960, 'The pronouns of power and solidarity', in Sebeok Thomas A. (ed.), *Style in Language*, New York: Wiley, pp. 253–277.
Bruneau Thomas J., 1973, 'Communicative silences: Forms and functions', *The Journal of Communication*, 23: 17–46.
Buber Martin, 1932, 'Dialogue', in Biemann Asher D. (ed.), 2002, *The Martin Buber Reader: Essential Writing*, New York: Palgrave, pp. 189–205.

Budden Mark and Horne Ann (eds.), 2017, 'Clinical commentary', *British Journal of Psychotherapy*, 33(4): 442–455.
Bühler Karl, 1937, *Sprachtheorie: die Darstellungsfunktion der Sprach*, Jena: Gustav Fischer Verlag.
Cage John, 1961, *Silence: Lectures and Writings*, Middletown, CT: Wesleyan University Press.
Canfield Bruce, 2002, *Johnson Rifles and Machine Guns: The Story of Melvin Maynard Johnson*, Woonsocket, RI : Andrew Mowbray Pub.
Caruth Cathy, 2001, 'Parting words: Trauma, silence and survival', *Journal for Cultural Research*, 5(1): 7–26.
Casas Gómez Miguel, 2018, 'Lexicon, discourse and cognition: Terminological delimitations in the conceptualizations of linguistic taboo', in Pizarro Pedraza Andrea (ed.), *Linguistic Taboo Revisited: Novel Insights from Cognitive Perspectives*, Berlin, Boston: De Gruyter Mouton, pp. 13–31.
Castelfranchi Cristiano and Guerini Marco, 2007, 'Is it a promise or a threat?', *Pragmatics & Cognition*, 15(2): 277–311.
Ceramella Nick, 2014, '"Silence Symphony" conducted by Pinter and Eduardo, two world theatre maestri', in Onic Tomaž (ed.), *Harold Pinter on International Stages, Frankfurt am Main*, Berlin, Bern, Bruxelles, New York, Oxford and Vienna: Peter Lang, pp. 31–51.
Cherry Shai, 2007, *Torah through Time: Understanding Bible Commentary from the Rabbinic Period to Modern Times*, Philadelphia: Jewish Publication Society.
Chilton Randolph and Gilbertson Carol, 1990, 'Pound's "'Metro' Hokku": The evolution of an image', *Twentieth Century Literature*, 36(2): 225–236.
Chomsky Noam, 1965, *Aspects of the Theory of Syntax*, Cambridge, MA: MIT Press.
1972, *Language and Mind* (2nd edition), New York: Harcourt Brace Jovanovitch.
1981, *Lectures on Government and Binding: The Pisa Lectures* (3rd revised edition), [1984], Dordrecht and Cinnaminson: Foris Publications.
Chovanec Jan, 2003, 'The uses of the present tense in headlines', in Chovanec Jan (ed.), *Theory and Practice in English Studies*, Brno: Czech Republic Masaryk University, I, pp. 83–92.
Clark David R., 1977, 'After "silence", the "supreme theme": Eight lines of Yeats', in Ronsley Joseph (ed.), *Myth and Reality in Irish Literature*, Waterloo, Canada: Wilfrid Laurier University Press, pp. 149–174.
Constable Marianne, 2006, *Just Silence: The Limits and Possibilities of Modern Law*, Princeton and Oxford: Princeton University Press.
Cornelis Louise H., 1997, *Passive and Perspective*, Amsterdam and Atlanta, GA: Rodopi.
Corver Norbert and Riemsdijk van Henk, 2001, 'Semi-lexical Categories', in Corver Norbert and Riemsdijk van Henk (eds.), *Semi-lexical Categories: The Function of Content Words and the Content of Function Words*, Berlin and New York: Mouton de Gruyter, pp. 1–22.
Courtenay Charles, 1916. *The Empire of Silence*, New York: Sturgis and Walton.
Crumbley Paul, 1992, 'Dickinson's Dashes and the Limits of Discourse', *The Emily Dickinson Journal*, 1(2): 8–29.
Crystal David and Quirk Randolph, 1964, *Systems of Prosodic and Paralinguistic Features in English*, The Hague: Mouton.

Dauenhauer Bernard P., 1980, *Silence: The Phenomenon and Its Ontological Significance*, Bloomington: Indiana University Press.
Davis Robert Con., 1991, 'Freud, Lacan, and the subject of cultural studies', *College Literature*, 18(2): 22–37.
De Saussure Ferdinand, 1913, *Course in General Linguistics* (translated and annotated: Harris Roy), [1983/1993], London: Duckworth.
  2006, *Writing in General Linguistics*, Bouquet, Simon, Engler, Rudolf, Sanders, Carol and Matthew, Pires, Oxford and New York: Oxford University Press.
De Zutter Hank, 1993, *Who Says a Dog Goes Bow-wow?*, New York: Doubleday.
Didier Franck, 2012, *Nietzsche and the Shadow of God* (translation: Philippe Farah), Evanston, Illinois: Northwestern University Press.
Doležel Lubomir, 1983, 'Proper names, definite descriptions and the intensional structure of Kafka's "The Trial"', *Poetics*, 12: 511–526.
Dressen Dacia F., 2002, 'Identifying textual silence in scientific research articles: Recontextualizations of the field account in geology', *Hermes*, 28: 81–107.
Dressler Wolfgang U., 1987, 'Word formation as part of natural morphology', in Dressler Wolfgang U., Mayerthaler Willi, Pangal Oswald and Wurzel Wolfgang U. (eds.), *Leitmotifs in Natural Morphology*, Amsterdam and Philadelphia: John Benjamins, pp. 99–126.
Dressler Wolfgang U. and Karpf Annemarie, 1994, 'The theoretical relevance of pre- and protomorphology in language acquisition', in Booij Geert and VanMarle Jaap (eds.), *Yearbook of Morphology*, Dordrecht: Kluwer Academic Press, pp. 99–122.
Druckman Daniel, Rozelle Richard M. and Baxter James C., 1982, *Nonverbal Communication: Survey, Theory and Research*, Beverly Hills: Sage Library.
Eeckhout Bart, 1996, 'When language stops ... Suspension points in the poetry of Hart Crane and Wallace Stevens', in Grabher Gudrun M. and Ulrike Jeßner (eds.), *Semantics of Silence in Linguistics and Literature*, Heidelberg: Universitätsverlag C. Winter, pp. 257–270.
Elder Chi-Hé and Savva Eleni, 2018, 'Incomplete conditionals and the syntax–pragmatics interface', *Journal of Pragmatics*, 138: 45–59.
Ephratt Michal, 2012, '"We try harder": Silence and Grice's cooperative principle, maxims and implicatures', *Language and Communication*, 32: 62–79.
  2014a, 'Grice's cooperative principle in the psychoanalytic setting', *The Psychoanalytic Review*, 101(6): 815–845.
  2014b, 'A model is born – Presenting the derivation in Modern Hebrew', *Hebrew Studies*, 55: 129–170.
  2015a, 'What's in no-name?', *Onomstica Canadiana*, 94(1): 1–34.
  2015b, 'The minute of silence as solidarity and individuation: A conceptual model of an Israeli ritual', *Journal of Ritual Studies*, 29(1): 1–20.
  2016, 'Verbal silence as figure: Its contribution to linguistic theory', *Poznan Studies in Contemporary Linguistics*, 52(1): 511–549.
  2017, 'Wondering about silence: Considerations from over fifty translations of Goethe's "Wandrers Nachtlied II" into Hebrew', *Hebrew Studies*, 58: 201–242.
Evans Nicholas, 2007, 'Insubordination and its uses', in Nikolaeva Irina (ed.), *Finiteness: Theoretical and Empirical Foundations*, Oxford: Oxford University Press, pp. 366–431.

Fanshel David and Moss Freda, 1971, *Playback: A Marriage in Jeopardy Examined*, New York and London: Columbia University Press.

Ferenczi Sandor, 1911, 'On obscene words: Contribution to the psychology of the latent period', in *Sex in Psychoanalysis* (translation: Ernest Jones), [1965], New York: Dover Publications, pp. 112–130.

Fernando A. C., 2006, 'A case study – Tata Steel: A company that also makes steel', in *Corporate Governance: Principles, Policies and Practices*, New Delhi, India: Pearson Education, pp. 69–74.

Ferraro Joanne M., 2008, *Nefarious Crimes, Contested Justice: Illicit Sex and Infanticide in the Republic of Venice, 1557–1789*, Baltimore: Johns Hopkins University Press.

Fillmore Charles, 1968, 'The case for case', in Bach Emmon and Harms R. (eds.), *Universals in Linguistic Theory*, New York: Holt, Rinehart and Winston, pp. 1–88.

Fineman Joel, 1991, 'Shakespeare's will: The temporality of rape', in *The Subjectivity Effect in Western Literary Tradition: Essays toward the Release of Shakespeare's Will*, Cambridge, MA: MIT Press, pp. 165–221.

Fischer John L. and Yoshida Teigo, 1968, 'The nature of speech according to Japanese proverbs', *Journal of American Folklore*, 81: 34–43.

Fisher Mark, Franklin David L. and Post Jerrold M., 2014, 'Executive dysfunction, brain aging, and political leadership', *Politics Life Science*, 33(2): 93–102.

Foxwell A. K. (ed.), 1913, *The poems of Sir Thomas Wiat: Edited from the Mss. and Early Editions*, London: University of London Press.

Freedman Morris, 1958, 'The seven sins of technical writing', *College Composition and Communication*, 9(1): 10–16.

Freeman Margaret H., 1996, 'Emily Dickinson and the discourse of intimacy', in Gudrun M. Grabher and Ulrike Jeßner (eds.), *Semantics of Silences in Linguistics and Literature*, Heidelberg: Universitätsverlag C. Winter, pp. 191–210.

  1997, 'Grounded spaces: Deictic-self anaphors in the poetry of Emily Dickinson', *Language and Literature*, 6(1): 7–28.

Freitas Elsa Simões Lucas, 2018, *Taboo and Advertising*, Amsterdam and Philadelphia: John Benjamins.

Freud Anna, 1923, 'The relation of beating-phantasies to a day-dream', *International Journal of Psychoanalysis*, 4: 89–102.

Freud Sigmund, 1900, 'The interpretation of dreams', *SE* 4/5: 1–630.

  1913, 'Totem and taboo', *SE* 13: 1–162.

  1915, 'Thoughts for the times on war and death', *SE* 14: 273–300.

  1917, 'Mourning and melancholia', *SE* 14: 237–58.

  1919a, 'A child is being beaten', *SE* 17: 175–204.

  1919b, 'Ein kind wird geschlagen', *Gesammelte Werke* 7: 197–226.

  1920, 'Beyond the pleasure principle', *SE* 18: 1–64.

Frey Charles, 1976, 'Interpreting "Western Wind"', *ELH: English Literature History*, 43(3): 259–278.

Gerzi Shmuel, 2007, 'What do silences express in the psychoanalytic process?', in Ephratt Michal (ed.), *Silences: Silence in Culture and in Interpersonal Relations*, Tel-Aviv: Resling, pp. 137–160 (in Hebrew).

Gifford Don, 1982, *Joyce Annotated: Notes for Dubliners and a Portrait of the Artist as a Young Man*, Berkeley: University of California Press.

Gilead Amihud, 2008, 'How few words can the shortest story have?', *Philosophy and Literature*, 32: 119–129.
Givón Talmy, 1993, *English Grammar: A Functional Based Introduction*, Amsterdam and Philadelphia: John Benjamins.
Goffman Erving, 1959, *The Presentation of Self in Everyday Life*, Garden City, NY: Doubleday.
  1981, *Forms of Talk*, Philadelphia: University of Pennsylvania Press.
Greenberg Jay, 2005, 'Conflict in the middle voice', *Psychoanalytic Quarterly*, 74(1): 105–120.
Greenberg Joseph H., 1963, 'Some universals of grammar with particular reference to the order of meaningful elements', in Greenberg J. H. (ed.), *Universals of Language*, Cambridge, MA and London: MIT Press, pp. 73–113.
Greenblatt Stephen, 2016, 'Introduction to Hamlet', in Greenblatt Stephen, Cohen Walter, Gosset Suzanne, Howard Jean E., Maus Katharine Eisaman and McMullan Gordon (eds.), *The Norton Shakespeare* (3rd edition), New York: W. W. Norton, pp. 1181–1188.
Gregerson Linda, 2013, 'Open voicing: Wyatt and Shakespeare', in Post Jonathan (ed.), *The Oxford Handbook of Shakespeare's Poetry*, Oxford: Oxford University Press, pp. 151–67.
Gregory Adrian, 1994, *The Silence of Memory Armistice Day 1919–1946*, Oxford: Berg.
Grice Paul H., 1989, *Studies in the Ways of Words*, Cambridge, MA and London: Harvard University Press.
Haiman John, 1983, 'Iconic and economic motivation', *Language*, 59(4): 781–819.
  1985, 'Symmetry', in Haiman John (ed.), *Iconicity in Syntax*, Amsterdam and Philadelphia: John Benjamins, pp. 73–95.
Hall Donald, 1957, *Writing Well*, Boston: Little, Brown and Company.
Halliday Michael A. K., 1985, *Introduction to Functional Grammar* (2nd edition), London and New York: Arnold.
Halliday Michael A. K. and Hasan Ruqaiya, 1976, *Cohesion in English*, London: Longman.
Hamill Sam, 1999, 'Translator's introduction', in Bashō Matsuo and Hamill Sam, *The Essential Bashō*, Boston and London: Shambhala, pp. ix–xxxi.
Harris Zellig S., 1951, *Methods in Structural Linguistics*, Chicago: University of Chicago Press.
Harrison Matthew, 1856, *Rise, Progress, and Present Structure of the English Language*, Philadelphia: E. C. and J. Biddle.
Haspelmath Martin, 2004, 'Coordinating constructions: An overview', in Haspelmath Martin (ed.), *Coordinating Constructions*, Amsterdam and Philadelphia: John Benjamins, pp. 3–40.
Hassan Ihab, 1967, *The Literature of Silence: Henry Miller and Samuel Beckett*, New York: Alfred A. Knopf.
Hawkins John A., 1978, *Definiteness and Indefiniteness*, London: Croom Helm and Atlantic Highlands, New Jersey: Humanities Press.
  1991, 'On (in)definite articles: Implicatures and (un)grammaticality prediction', *Journal of Linguistics*, 27(2): 405–442.
Hejinian Lyn, 2000, *The Language of Inquiry*, Berkeley: University of California Press, http://ezproxy.haifa.ac.il/login?url=https://search.ebscohost.com/login.aspx?

direct=true&db=e000xww&AN=66018&site=ehost-live&scope=site (accessed 27 March 2018).

2005, 'I am suddenly aware that phrases happen', Lyn Hejinian at Kelly Writers House, 22 February 2005, https://jacket2.org/interviews/i-am-suddenly-aware-phrases-happen (accessed 25 March 2018).

2007, 'LH', in *The Grand Piano: An Experiment in Collective Autobiography*, San Francisco 1975–1980, Detroit, Part 3, pp. 55–67.

Hempel Carl G., 1966, *Philosophy of Natural Science*, Englewood Cliffs, NJ: Prentice-Hall.

Hewson John, 1972, *Article and Noun in English*, The Hague: Mouton.

1997, *Tense and Aspect in Indo-European Languages: Theory, Typology, Diachrony*, Amsterdam and Philadelphia: John Benjamins.

Hiz Henry, 1962, 'Questions and answers', *Journal of Philosophy*, 59(10): 253–265.

Holinshed Raphael, Hooker John, Thynne Francis, Fleming Abraham, Stow John and Ellis Sir Henry (eds.), 1808, *Holinshed's Chronicles of England, Scotland, and Ireland*, London: J. Johnson et al., Vol. IV *HeinOnline*, https://heinonline-org.ezproxy.haifa.ac.il/HOL/P?h=hein.cow/holceni0004&i=572 (accessed 20 November 2019).

Holland Theodore J. Jr., 1990, 'The many faces of nicknames', *Names*, 38(4): 255–272.

Horobin Simon, 2012, 'The language of Chaucer', in Bergs Alexander and Brinton Laurel J. (eds.), *English Historical Linguistics: An International Handbook*, Berlin and Boston: Walter de Gruyter, pp. 567–588.

Hundt Marianne, 2007, *English Mediopassive Constructions: A Cognitive, Corpus-based Study of Their Origin, Spread, and Current Status*, Amsterdam and New York: Rodopi.

Hurford James R., 2014, *Origins of Language: A Slim Guide*, Oxford: Oxford.

Hydén Margareta, 2005, '"I must have been an idiot to let it go on": Agency and positioning in battered women's narratives of leaving', *Feminism and Psychology*, 15(2): 169–188.

Jakobson Roman, 1937, 'Zero sign', in Waugh Linda R. and Morris Halle (eds.), 1984, *Russian and Slavic Grammar: Studies 1931–1981*, Berlin, New York and Amsterdam: Mouton de Gruyter, pp. 151–160.

1960, 'Concluding statement: Linguistics and poetics', in Sebeok Thomas A. (ed.), *Style in Language*, New York: Wiley, pp. 350–377.

Jaworski Adam, 1993, *The Power of Silence: Social and Pragmatic Perspectives*, Newbury Park, CA: Sage.

1997, '"White and white" metacommunicative and metaphorical silences', in Jaworski Adam (ed.), *Silence Interdisciplinary Perspectives*, Berlin and New York: Mouton de Gruyter, pp. 381–401.

1998, 'The silence of power and solidarity in *Fallen Sons*', *Studia Anglica Posnaniensia*, 33: 141–152.

2006, 'Silence', in Brown Keith (ed.), *Encyclopedia of Language and Linguistics*, Amsterdam: Elsevier, pp. 377–379.

Jaworski Adam, Fitzgerald Richard and Constantinou Odysseas, 2005, 'Busy saying nothing new: Live silence in TV reporting of 9/11', *Multilingua*, 24: 121–144.

Jensen Vernon J., 1973, 'Communicative functions of silence', *ETCA Review of General Semantics*, 30: 249–257.

Jespersen Otto, 1922, *Language: Its Nature, Development and Origin*, [1949], New York: Macmillan.
  1924, *The Philosophy of Grammar*, [1935], London: George Allen & Unwin.
  1949, *A Modern English Grammar*, [1961], London: George Allen & Unwin and Copenhagen: Munksgaard, Part 7: Syntax.
Johansen J. D., 1996, 'Iconicity in literature', *Semiotica*, 110: 37–55.
Kane Lesley, 1984, *The Language of Silence: On the Unspoken and Unspeakable in Modern Drama*, Rutherford: Fairleigh Dickinson University Press.
Kasher Asa, 1976, 'Conversational maxims and rationality', in Kasher Asa (ed.), *Language in Focus: Foundations, Methods and Systems*, Dordrecht and Boston: D. Reidel, pp. 197–216.
Keenan Edward L. and Comrie Bernard, 1977, 'Noun phrase accessibility and universal grammar', *Linguistic Inquiry*, 8(1): 63–99.
Keenan Edward L. and Dryer Matthew S., 2007, 'Passive in the world's languages', in Shopen Timothy (ed.), *Language Typology and Syntactic Description* (2nd edition), Cambridge: Cambridge University Press, pp. 325–361.
Kelly Seam James, 2016, 'Staging nothing: The figure of Das Ding in Poe's "The Raven"', *The Edgar Allan Poe Review*, 17(2): 116–141.
Kemmer Suzanne, 1993, *The Middle Voice*, Amsterdam and Philadelphia: John Benjamins.
Kenaan Hagi, 2001, 'Kierkegaard and the language of silence', in Jäkel Siegfried and Timonen Asko (eds.), *The Language of Silence*, Turku: Turun Yliopisto, pp. 249–258.
Kenner Hugh, 1971, *The Pound Era*, London: Faber and Faber.
Kjellmer *Göran*, 2002, 'Must down: On non-occurring verbs of motion in modern English', *Nordic Journal of English Studies*, 1(2): 339–353.
Klima Edward S. and Bellugi Ursula, 1976, 'Poetry and song in a language without sound', *Cognition*, 4: 45–97.
Koffka Kurt, 1935, *Principles of Gestalt Psychology*, [1963], New York: Harcourt, Brace & World.
Koulidobrova Elena, 2017, 'Elide me bare: Null arguments in ASL', *Natural Language and Linguistic Theory*, 35(2): 397–446.
Kristeva Julia, 1966 'The bounded text', in Roudiez Leon S. (ed.), *Desire in Language* (translation: Th. Gora A. Jardine and L. S. Roudiez), [1980], New York: Columbia University Press, pp. 36–63.
  1968, 'Poésie et négativité', *L'Homme*, 8(2): 36–63.
Kübler-Ross Elisabeth, 1998, *The Wheel of Life: A Memoir of Living and Dying*, New York: Simon & Schuster.
Kurzon Dennis, 1998, *Discourse of Silence*, Amsterdam and Philadelphia: John Benjamins. https://benjamins.com/catalog/pbns.49.
  2007, 'Towards a typology of silence', *Journal of Pragmatics*, 39: 1673–1688.
Lacan Jacques, 1956, 'The function and field of speech and language in psychoanalysis', in Lacan Jacques, [1966], *Écrits* (translation: Alan Sheridan), London and New York: Routledge and Kegan Paul, pp. 33–125.
  1963, 'Introduction to the names-of-the-father', in Lacan Jacques, [2013], *On the Names-of-the-Father* (translation: Bruce Fink), Cambridge: Polity, pp. 51–91.
  1988, *The Seminar of Jacques Lacan: Book I. Freud's Papers on Technique 1953–1954* (translation: John Forrester), Cambridge: Cambridge University Press.

Leathers Dale G., 1997, *Successful Nonverbal Communication* (3rd edition), Boston and London: Allyn and Bacon.
Leech Geoffrey N., 1983, *Principles of Pragmatics*, London: Longman.
Lees Robert B., 1963, *The Grammar of English Nominalizations*, [1966], The Hague: Mouton.
Levi Margot P., 1966, 'K., an exploration of the names of Kafka's central characters', *Names*, 14: 1–10.
Levi Primo, 1958, *Survival in Auschwitz: The Nazi Assault on Humanity* (translation: Stuart Woolf), [1986], New York: Touchstone Simon & Schuster.
Löbner Sebastian, 1985, 'Definites', *Journal of Semantics*, 4: 279–326.
Loewenstein Rudolph, 1957, 'Contribution to the psychoanalytic theory of masochism', *Journal of the American Psycho-analytic Association*, 5(2): 197–234.
Lyons John, 1977, *Semantics*, Cambridge: Cambridge University Press.
MacDonald P. Jackson, 2014, *Determining the Shakespeare Canon: Arden of Faversham and a Lover's Complaint*, Oxford: Oxford University Press.
Magill Frank N., 2015, *Cyclopedia of Literary Characters* (revised 4th edition, original editions edited by Frank N. Magill). Ipswich, MA: Salem Press.
Mahoney Martha R., 1991, 'Legal images of battered women: Redefining the issue of separation', *Michigan Law Review*, 90(1): 20–94.
Malandro Loretta A., Barker Larry L. and Barker Deborah A., 1989, *Nonverbal Communication* (2nd edition), Reading, MA: Addison-Wesley.
Martinet André, 1949, 'George Kingsley Zipf, human behavior and the principle of least effort', *Word*, 5: 280–282.
Maschler Yael and Schiffrin Deborah, 2015, 'Discourse markers: Language, meaning, and context', in Tannen Deborah, Hamilton Heidi E. and Schiffrin Deborah (eds.), *The Handbook of Discourse Analysis* (2nd edition), Chichester: John Wiley & Sons, pp. 189–221.
Maslow Abraham H., 1954, Motivation and personality (2nd edition), [1970], New York and London: Harper and Row.
Mayerthaler Willi, 1987, 'System independent morphological naturalness', in Mayerthaler Willi, Pangal Oswald and Wurzel Wolfgang U. (eds.), *Leitmotifs in Natural Morphology*, Amsterdam and Philadelphia: John Benjamins, pp. 25–58.
McGregor Rafe, 2015, 'Literary thickness', *British Journal of Aesthetics*, 55(3): 343–360.
McGrew Timothy, 2011, 'Evidence', in Bernecker Sven and Pritchard Duncan (eds.), *The Routledge Companion to Epistemology*, New York: Routledge, pp. 58–67.
Mehrabian Albert, 1972, *Nonverbal Communication*, Piscataway and Chicago: Aldine.
Melčuk Igor A., 1976, 'On suppletion', *Linguistics*, 170: 45–90.
  1979, 'Syntactic, or lexical, zero in natural language', *Proceedings of the Fifth Annual Meeting of the Berkeley Linguistics Society*, Berkeley Linguistics Society, pp. 224–260. http://dx.doi.org/10.3765/bls (accessed 19 August 2018).
Merchant Jason, 2001, *The Syntax of Silence: Sluicing, Islands, and the Theory of Ellipsis*, Oxford: Oxford University Press.
Mettinger Tryggve N. D., 1988, *In Search of God: The Meaning and Message of the Everlasting Names* (translation: Frederick H. Cryer), Philadelphia: Fortress Press.
Mill John Stuart, 1843, *A System of Logic: Ratiocinative and Inductive*, [1973], Toronto: University of Toronto Press, Routledge and Kegan Paul, Vol. VII, Book 1.

Miller Cristanne, 1987, *Emily Dickinson: A Poet's Grammar*, Cambridge, MA: Harvard University Press.

Mirfield Peter, 1997, *Silence, Confession and Improperly Obtained Evidence*, Oxford: Clarendon Press.

Mirus Gene, Fisher Jami and Napoli Donna Jo, 2012, 'Taboo expressions in American sign language', *Lingua*, 122(9): 1004–1020.

Montefiore Simon Sebag, 2007, *Speeches that Changed the World*, London: Quercus.

Morgan Jane, O'Neill Christopher and Harré Rom, 1979, *Nicknames*, London: Routledge.

Nänny Max, 1999, 'Alphabetic letters as icons in literary texts', in Nänny Max and Fischer Olga (eds.), *Form Miming Meaning: Iconicity in Language and Literature*, Amsterdam and Philadelphia: John Benjamins, pp. 73–198.

Napoli Donna Jo and Hoeksema Jack, 2009, 'The grammatical versatility of taboo terms', *Studies in Language*, 33(3): 612–643.

Naveh Hanna, 1993, *Captives of Mourning*, Tel-Aviv: Hakibbutz-Hemeuchad (in Hebrew).

Nespor Marina and Sandler Wendy, 1999, 'Prosody in Israeli sign language', *Language & Speech*, 42(2–3): 143–176.

Neumann Boaz, 2010, *Die Weltanschauung des Nazismus–Raum, Körper, Sprache*, Göttingen: Wallstein Verlag.

Noelle-Neumann Elizabeth, 1974, 'The spiral of silence: A theory of public opinion', *Journal of Communication*, 24: 43–51.

Nofal Khalil Hassan, 2011, 'Passive voice as an inimitable linguistic phenomenon in the Holy Qur'an', *International Journal of Business and Social Science*, 2(18): 148–168.

O'Connell Daniel C. and Kowal Sabine, 2004, 'The history of research on the filled pause as evidence of the written language bias in linguistics', *Journal of Psycholinguistic Research*, 33(6): 459–474.

OED online, *The Oxford English Dictionary* (2nd edition), http://dictionary.oed.com Entries are indicated by 'OED' followed by the OED's lexical entry, its category, and the meaning's number and letter (the entries were accessed between December 2010 and June 2020).

Ogden Thomas H., 1989, *The Primitive Edge of Experience*, Northvale, NJ: Jason Aronson.

2001, *Conversations at the Frontier of Dreaming*, Northvale, NJ: Jason Aronson.

Olinick Stanley L., 1982. 'Meanings beyond words: Psychoanalytic perception of silence and communication, happiness, sexual love and death', *International Review Psycho-Analysis*, 9: 461–472.

Oremland Jerome D., 1983, 'Death and transformation in Hamlet', *Psychoanalytic Inquiry*, 3: 485–512.

Orwell George, 1946, 'Politics and the English language', in Orwell George, [1950], *Shooting an Elephant*, New York: Harcourt Brace, pp. 77–92.

Pane Greta L., 2017, 'The unreal path to a real place: Six strategies of representation in the novels of Thomas Hardy', *Style*, 51(1): 52–75.

Pavel Khoroshikh, 2014, 'Fonetic symbolism in the E. Jandl's work "schtzngrmm"', *Евразийский Союз Ученых* (ЕСУ), 4: 46–47, https://istina.msu.ru/media/publications/article/fc3/641/7028116/2014-2007-25_Strelets_I.E._

Sovremennyie_kontseptsii..._Evrazijskij_Soyuz_Uchenyih_Chast_11_4–2014_S
._158–162.pdf (accessed 6 February 2018).

Peirce Charles Sanders, 1965. *Collected Papers of Charles Sanders Peirce*, Hartshorne Charles and Weiss Paul (eds.), Cambridge, MA: Harvard University Press.

Peraldo Emmanuelle, 2016, '"I shall not concern the union in this discourse": Preterition and engagement in pro-unionist writing by Daniel Defoe, traveler to Scotland', *E-rea*, 14(1), https://doi.org/10.4000/erea.5582 (accessed 19 August 2020).

Peters Heinz F., 1962, *My Sister, My Spouse: Lou Andreas-Salomé's Biography*, New York: Norton.

Pfau Ronald and Quer Joseph, 2010, 'Nonmanuals: Their grammatical and prosodic roles', in Brentari Diane (ed.), *Sign Languages*, Cambridge: Cambridge University Press, pp. 381–402.

Plett Heinrich F., 1991, 'Intertextualities', in Plett Heinrich F. (ed.), *Intertextuality*, Berlin and New York: Walter de Gruyter, pp. 3–29.

Poe Edgar Allen, 1846, 'The philosophy of composition', www.gutenberg.org/5/5/7/4/55749/ (accessed 3 July 2020).

Polykoff Shirley, 2016, 'Does she . . . or doesn't she? The making of Miss Clairol hair coloring', *Advertising & Society Review*, 16(4), https://doi.org/10.1353/asr.2016.0001 (accessed 19 June 2019).

Pound Ezra, 1914, 'Vorticism', in Zinnes Harriet (ed.), [1980], *Ezra Pound and the Visual Arts*, New York: New Directions, pp. 199–209.

Poyatos Fernando, 2002. *Nonverbal Communication across Disciplines*, Amsterdam and Philadelphia: John Benjamins.

  2017, *Literary Thesaurus of Nonverbal Communication: A Tool for Interdisciplinary Research*, editorial académica Española.

Prasad Joshi P., 2009, *Vedic Aorist and Panini*, Delhi: Eastern Book Linkers.

Pribram Karl H., 1971, *Languages of the Brain: Experimental Paradoxes and Principles in Neuropsychology*, Englewood Cliffs, NJ: Prentice-Hall.

Quirk Randolph, Greenbaum Sidney, Leech Geoffrey and Svartvik Jan, 1985, *A Comprehensive Grammar of the English Language*, London: Longman.

Radday Yehuda Thomas, 1990, 'On missing the humour in the Bible', in Radday Yehuda T. and Brenner Athalya (eds.), *On Humour and the Comic in the Hebrew Bible*, Sheffield: Almond Press, pp. 21–38.

Radden Günter and Matthis Elizabeth, 2002, 'Why similar to, but different from?', in Cuychens Hubert and Raddan Günter (eds.), *Perspectives on Prepositions*, Tübingen: Max Niemeyer Verlag, pp. 231–257.

Radford Andrew, 1988, *Transformational Grammar: A First Course*, Cambridge: Cambridge University Press.

Raufman Ravit and Ben-Cnaan Rachel, 2011, 'Cursed by magic spell, cured by silence: A discussion on the functions of speech and silence in the Sephardic version "The Sister Who Turned Her Brothers into Goats" and its Grimm parallel "The Twelve Brothers"', *El-Prezente – Study in Sephardic Culture*, 5: 139–157.

Raz Jacob, 2010, 'Kill the Buddha: Quietism in action and quietism as action in Zen Buddhism thought and practice', *Common Knowledge*, 16(3): 439–456.

Redholz R. A. (ed.), 1978, *Sir Thomas Wyatt: The Complete Poems*, New Haven, CT: Yale University Press.

Reik Theodor, 1927, 'The psychological meaning of silence', *Psychoanalytic Review*, [1968], 55: 172–186.
Rescher Nicholas, 1998, 'The significance of silence', *European Review*, 6(1): 91–95.
Richardson Laurel, 1993, 'Poetics, dramatics, and transgressive validity: The case of the skipped line', *The Sociological Quarterly*, 34(4): 695–710.
Richter David, 1985, 'Two studies in iconic syntax: Tennyson's "Tears, Idle Tears", and Williams's "The Dance"', *Language and Style*, 18: 136–151.
Rimmon-Kenan Shulamit, 2002, *Narrative Fiction* (2nd edition), [1983], London and New York: Routledge.
Robinson Ray (ed.), 2003, *Famous Last Words*, New York: Workman.
Rodman Lilita, 1981, 'The passive in technical and scientific writing', *Journal of Advanced Composition*, 2(1–2): 165–172.
Römkens Renée, 2000, 'Ambiguous responsibilities: Law and conflicting expert testimony on the abused woman who shot her sleeping husband', *Law & Social Inquiry*, 25: 355–391.
Rubinstein Eliezer, 1980, 'A semiotico-syntactic study of verbs expressing an emotional state', *Lěšonénu*, 65(1): 5–16 (in Hebrew).
Ruipérez Martín S., 1953, 'The neutralization of morphological oppositions as illustrated by the neutral aspect of the present indicative in Classical Greek', *Word*, 9(3): 241–252.
Russell Bertrand, 1905, 'On denoting', *Mind*, 14(56): 479–493.
Sacks Harvey, 1992, *Lectures on Conversation*, in Jefferson Gail (ed.), Oxford and Cambridge, MA: Blackwell.
Sacks Harvey, Schegloff Emanuel A. and Jefferson Gail, 1974. 'A simplest systematics for the organization of turn-taking for conversation', *Language*, 50: 696–735.
Sandler Wendy, 2010, 'The uniformity and diversity of language: Evidence from sign language', *Lingua*, 120(12): 2727 – 2732.
Saville-Troike Muriel, 1982, *The Ethnography of Communication: An Introduction*, Cambridge, MA: Basil Blackwell.
  1985, 'The place of silence in an integrated theory of communication', in Tannen Deborah and Saville-Troike Muriel (eds.), *Perspectives on Silence*, Northwood, NJ: Ablex, pp. 3–18.
  1989, *The Ethnography of Communication: An Introduction* (2nd edition), Cambridge, MA: Basil Blackwell.
  1994, 'Silence', in Asher Ron E. and Simpson J. M. Y. (eds.), *The Encyclopedia of Language and Linguistics*, Oxford: Pergamon Press, 7: 3945–3947.
  2003, *The Ethnography of Communication: An Introduction* (3rd edition), Cambridge, MA: Basil Blackwell.
  2006, 'Silence: Cultural aspects', in Brown Keith (ed.), *Encyclopedia of Language and Linguistics*, Amsterdam: Elsevier, pp. 379–381.
Schachter Paul, 1977, 'Does she or doesn't she?', *Linguistic Inquiry*, 8(4): 763–767.
Scharf Peter M., 1996, *The Denotation of Generic Terms in Ancient Indian Philosophy: Grammar, Nyāya and Mīmāsā*, Philadelphia: American Philosophical Society.
Schefer Jack and Karlins Marvin, 2015, *The Like Switch: An Ex-FBI Agent's Guide to Influencing, Attracting, and Winning People Over*, New York: Simon & Schuster.
Schiffrin Deborah, 1987, *Discourse Markers*, Cambridge: Cambridge University Press.
Schmidt-Radefeldt Jürgen, 1977, 'On so-called "rhetorical" questions', *Journal of Pragmatics*, 1: 375–392.

Schmit John, 1993, '"I only said – the syntax – ": Elision, recoverability, and insertion in Emily Dickinson's Poetry', *Style*, 27(1): 106–124.
Schneider Klaus P., 2003, *Diminutives in English*, Tübingen: Max Niemeyer.
Scott Clifford W. M., 1958, 'Noise, speech and technique', *International Journal of Psych-analysis*, 39(2–4): 108–111.
Scott Robert and Wilson E., 2014, *The Voyage of the Discovery* (Cambridge Library Collection – Polar Exploration), Cambridge: Cambridge University Press.
Sebeok Thomas A., 1994, *An Introduction to Semiotics*, London: Pinter.
Serani Deborah, 2000, 'Silence in the analytic space, resistance or reverie?', *Contemporary Psychoanalysis*, 36: 505–519.
Sherwood Katherine and Dungan Elizabeth, 2005, 'Art Expedition Blind at Museum: Theresa Hak Kyung Cha', University of California, Berkeley Art Museum and Pacific Film Archive, http://archive.bampfa.berkeley.edu/art/AN0230 (accessed 14 July 2019).
Shibatani Masayoshi, 1985, 'Passives and *related* constructions: A prototype analysis', *Language*, 61(4), 821–848.
  1988, 'Introduction', in Shibatani Masayoshi (ed.), *Passive and Voice*, Amsterdam and Philadelphia: John Benjamins, pp. 1–8.
Shirane Haruo, 1998, *Traces of Dreams: Landscape, Cultural Memory, and the Poetry of Bash*, Stanford, CA: Stanford University Press.
Silverstone Roger, 1998, 'Space', *Screen*, 39(1): 81–84.
Silz Walter, 1956, 'Longfellow's translation of Goethe's "Ueber allen Gipfeln . . . "', *Modern Language Notes*, 71(5): 344–345.
Skinner Daniel and Pludwin Steven, 2013, 'Unsought responsibility: The U.S. supreme court and the politics of passive writing', *Polity*, 45(4): 499–524.
Smith Paige H., Tessaro Irene and Earp Jo Anne, 1995, 'Women's experience with battering: A conceptualization from qualitative research', *Women's Health Issues*, 5: 197–182.
Sobkowiak Włodzimierz, 1997. 'Silence and markedness theory', in Jaworski Adam (ed.), *Silence Interdisciplinary Perspectives*, Berlin and New York: Mouton de Gruyter, pp. 39–61.
Sontag Susan, 1969, *Styles of Radical Will*, London: Secker & Warburg.
Sperber Dan and Wilson Deirdre, 1986, *Relevance: Communication and Cognition*, Oxford: Basil Blackwell.
Stafford Laura E., 2007, *Veni, Vidi, Futui: Sexual Imagery and Social Class in Roman Art*, Cambridge, MA: Harvard University Press.
Strang Barbara M. H., 1962, *Modern English Structure*, London: E. Arnold.
Sumner Ives, 1957, 'Defining parts of speech in English', *College English*, 18(7): 341–348.
Sundén Karl, 1904, *Contribution to the Study of Elliptical Words in Modern English*, Upsala: Almqvist & Wiksells Boktryckeri.
Sutton-Spence Rachel, 2005, *Analysing Sign Language Poetry*, New York: Palgrave Macmillan.
Sutton-Spence Rachel and Woll Bencie, 1999, *The Linguistics of British Sign Language: An Introduction*, Cambridge: Cambridge University Press.
Tabachnick Norman and Klugman David J., 1965, 'No name: A study of anonymous suicidal telephone calls', *Psychiatry,* 28(1): 79–87.

Takeda Masako, 2013, 'Emily Dickinson and Japanese Aesthetics', *The Emily Dickinson Journal*, 22(2): 26–45.
Tannen Deborah, 1985, 'Silence: Anything but', in Tannen Deborah and Saville-Troike Muriel (eds.), *Perspectives on Silence*, Northwood, NJ: Ablex, pp. 93–111.
Thomas Andrew L., 1979, 'Ellipsis: The interplay of sentence structure and context', *Lingua*, 47: 43–68.
Thurber Barton, 1984, 'Speaking the unspeakable: Conrad and the sublime', *Conradiana*, 16(1): 41–54.
Tiersma Peter, 1995, 'The language of silence', *Rutgers Law Review*, 48(1): 1–100.
Toner Anne, 2015, *Ellipsis in English Literature: Signs of Omission*, Cambridge: Cambridge University Press.
Trudgill Peter, 1974, *The Social Differentiation of English in Norwich*, Cambridge: Cambridge University Press.
Truglio Maria, 2018, *Italian Children's Literature and National Identity*, New York: Routledge.
Tsur Reuven, 2001, 'Onomatopoeia: Cuckoo-Language and Tick-Tocking – The constraints of semiotic systems', www.tau.ac.il/~tsurxx/Cuckoo_onomatopoeia.html).
   2006, 'Size-sound symbolism revisited', *Journal of Pragmatics*, 38: 905–924.
Tyler Stephen A., 1978, *The Said and the Unsaid: Mind, Meaning, and Culture*, New York: Academic Press.
Uspensky Boris, 1970, *A Poetics of Composition* (translation: Valentina Zavarin and Susan Witting), [1973], Berkeley, Los Angeles and London: University of California Press.
Van Dijk Yra, 2011, 'Reading the form: The function of typographic blanks in modern poetry', *Word & Image: A Journal of Verbal/Visual Enquiry*, 27(4): 407–415.
Van Oosten Jeanne, 1986, *The Nature of Subjects, Topics and Agents: A Cognitive Explanation*, Bloomington: Indiana University Linguistics Club.
Vanderbeke Dirk, Gast Volker and Wehmeier Christian, 2017, 'Of gaps and holes and silence: Some remarks on elliptic speech and pseudo-orality in James Joyce's short story "The Sisters"', *Literary Linguistics*, 6(1), https://doi.org/10.15462/ijll.v6i1 (accessed 27 February 2020).
Vargas Marjorie F., 1986, *Louder than Words: Introduction to Nonverbal Communication*, Ames: Iowa State University Press.
Vendler Helen, 2007, *Our Secret Discipline: Yeats and Lyric Form*, Cambridge, MA: Harvard University Press.
Verschueren Jef, 1985, *What People Say They Do with Words*, Northwood, NJ: Ablex.
Volek Bronislava, 1987, *Emotive Signs in Language and Semantic Functioning of Derived Nouns in Russian*, Amsterdam and Philadelphia: John Benjamins.
Von Hippel Courtney, Mangum Stephen L., Greenberger David B., Heneman Robert L. and Skoglind Jeffrey D., 1997, 'Temporary employment: Can organizations and employees both win?', *The Academy of Management Executive*, 11(1): 93–104.
Wajnryb Ruth, 2001, *The Silence: How Tragedy Shapes Talk*, Crows Nest, NSW: Allen & Unwin.
Walter Tony, 1999, 'The questions people asked', in Walter Tony (ed.), *The Mourning for Diana*, New York: Berg, pp. 19–47.

Watson Rubie S., 1986, 'The named and the nameless: Gender and person in Chinese society', *American Ethnologist*, 13(4): 619–631.
Waugh Linda R. and Newfield Madeleine, 1995, 'Iconicity in the lexicon and its relevance for a theory of morphology', in Lansberg Marge E. (ed.), *Syntactic Iconicity and Linguistic-Freezes*, Berlin and New York: The Human Dimension, pp. 189–221.
Websdale Neil, 1998, *Rural Women Battering and the Justice System: An Ethnography*, London and New Delhi: Sage.
Webster Michael, 1999, 'Singling is silence', in Max Nänny and Olga Fischer (eds.), *Form Miming Meaning*, Amsterdam and Philadelphia: John Benjamins, pp. 199–214.
Weisman Avery D., 1955, 'Silence and psychotherapy', *Psychiatry Journal for the Study of Interpersonal Processes*, 18: 241–260.
Wilkinson Elizabeth M., 1949, 'VIII. Goethe's Poetry', *German Life and Letters*, 2(4): 316–329.
Williams Kupling D., Wendelyn Shore J. and Grahe Jon E., 1998, 'The silent treatment: Perceptions of its behaviors and associated feelings', *Group Processes & Intergroup Relations*, 1(2): 117–141.
Wilson Peter, 2000, *Mind the Gap: Ellipsis and Stylistic Variation in Spoken and Written English*, Harlow: Longmman.
Winkelmann Carol Lea, 2004, *The Language of Battered Women: A Rhetorical Analysis of Personal Theologies*, Albany: The State University of New York Press.
Winnicott Clare, 1989, 'D.W.W.: A reflection', in Winnicott Clare, Shepherd Ray and Davis Madeleine (eds.), *Psycho-analytic Explorations*, London: Karnac, pp. 1–18.
Winnicott Donald W., 1958, 'The capacity to be alone', in Winnicott Donald W., [1990], *The Maturational Process and the Facilitating Environment*, London: Karnac Books, pp. 29–36.
  1963, 'Communicating and not communicating', in Winnicott Donald W., [1990], *The Maturational Process and the Facilitating Environment*, London: Karnac Books, pp. 179–192.
Winston Betsy, 2000, 'It just doesn't look like ASL! Defining, recognizing and teaching prosody in ASL', in Swabey Laurie (ed.), *Celebrating Excellence, Celebrating Partnership, Proceedings of the 13th National Convention, Conference of Interpreter Trainers Portland*. Silver Spring, MD: Rid Publications, pp. 103–117, www.cit-asl.org/new/2000-cit-conference-proceedings-download-pdf/ (accessed 30 May 2018).
Wiseman Hadas and Barber Jacques P., 2008, *Echoes of Trauma*, Cambridge: Cambridge University Press.
Wittgenstein Ludwig, 1922, *Tractatus Logico-Philosophicus* (translation: David F. Pears and Brian F.McGuinness), [1961], London: Routledge & Kegan Paul.
Wolf Werner, 2003, 'Non-supplemented blanks', in Meader Costantino and Fischer Olga (eds.), *Outside-in – in-side-out*, Amsterdam and Philadelphia: John Benjamins, pp. 113–132.
Wolfson Nessa, 1989, 'The conversational historical present', *Linx*, 20: 135–151.
Wood Diana, 1989, *Clement VI: The Pontificate and Ideas of an Avignon Pope*, Cambridge: Cambridge University Press.

Yasuda Kenneth, 1957, *The Japanese Haiku: Its Essential Nature, History, and Possibilities in English, with Selected Examples*, Rutland, VT: Tuttle.
— 1995, '"Approach to Haiku" and "Basic principles"', in Hume Nancy G. (ed.), *Japanese Aesthetics and Culture*, Albany: State University of New York Press, pp. 125–150.
Young Philip, 1966, *Earnest Hemingway: A Reconsideration*, University Park and London: Pennsylvania State University Press.
Yule George, 1998, *Explaining English Grammar*, Oxford: Oxford University Press.
Zapedowska Magdalena, 2006, 'A lesson in grammar: Dickinson's "Grasped by God" and "Drowning is not so pitiful"', *The Emily Dickinson Journal*, 15(1): 16–34.
Žegarac Vladimir, 1998, 'What is phatic communication?', in Rouchota Villy and Jucker Andreas H. (eds.), *Current Issues in Relevance Theory*, Amsterdam and Philadelphia: John Benjamins, pp. 327–361.
Zeligs Meyer A., 1961, 'The psychology of silence', *Journal of the American Psychoanalytic Association*, 9: 7–43.
Zerubavel Evyatar, 2006, *The Elephant in the Room: Silence and Denial in Everyday Life*, Oxford: Oxford University Press.
Zipf George K., 1949, *Human Behavior and the Principle of Least Effort: An Introduction to Human Ecology*, Cambridge: Addison-Wesley Press.

Literary Works

Aciman André, *Call Me by Your Name*, New York: Farrar, Straus and Giroux, 2007.
Appelfeld Aharon, *The Story of a Life* (translation: Halter Aloma), New York: Schocken Books, 2004.
Beckett Samuel, *Waiting for Godot*, London: Faber, 1962.
Blake William, 'Love's Secret', in Quiller-Couch Sir Arthur (ed.), *The Oxford Book of English Verse 1250–1918*, Oxford: Clarendon, 1939, pp. 580–581.
Byron George Gordon (Lord), 'The Destruction of Sennacherib', in Ashton L. Thomas (ed.), *Hebrew Melodies*, London: Routledge & Kegan Paul, 1972, pp. 180–182.
Caine Hall Thomas Henry, *The Christian*, New York: D. Appleton, 1897
Cocteau Jean, *La voix humaine*, in *Œuvres Complètes de Jean Cocteau*, Genève: Marguerat, 1946.
Coe Jonathan, *The House of Sleep*, London: Penguin, 1997.
Conrad Joseph, *Lord Jim*, London: Penguin, 1994.
   Nostromo, Harmondsworth: Penguin, 1904 [1963].
Creeley Robert, 'Later', in *The Collected Poems of Robert Creeley, 1975–2005*, Berkeley: University of California Press, 1982, Vol. II: p. 90.
De Brunhoff Jean, *The Story of Babar the Little Elephant*, London: Methuen.
Dickinson Emily, *The Complete Poems of Emily Dickinson*, Johnson Thomas H. (ed.), New York, Boston and London: Back Bay Books, 1960.
Doyle Arthur Conan, 'The Adventures of Silver Blaze', in *Sherlock Holmes. His Adventures. Memoirs. Return. His Last Bow and The Case-book. The Complete Short Stories*, London: John Murray, 1949, pp. 305–333.
Eliot T. S., 'The Waste Land': II 'A Game of Chess', in *Collected Poems (1909–1962)*, London and Boston: Faber and Faber, 1963, pp. 66–69.
   'Burnt Norton', V, 'Four Quartets', in *Collected Poems (1909–1962)*, London and Boston: Faber and Faber, 1963, pp. 189–195.
Epstein Helen, *Where She Came from: A Daughter's Search for Her Mother's History*, Boston : Little, Brown, 1997.
Frankl Viktor, *Man's Search for Meaning* (translation: Ilse Lasch), New York: Simon and Schuster, 1946 [1962].
Frost Robert, '[But outer Space . . .]', in Lathem E. C. (ed.), *The Poetry of Robert Frost*, Barre, MA: Imprint Society, 1971, p. 469.
Gibran Khalil Gibran, 'On talking', *The Prophet*, Tel-Aviv: Tammuz, 1923 [1980], p. 56.
Goethe Johann, *Goethe Werke*, Trunz Erich (ed.), Hamburg: C. Wegner, 1948.
Grey Zane, *The Rainbow Trail*, London and New York: T. Nelson and Sons, 1939.

Hejinian Lyn, 'Writing Is an Aid to Memory', 1996, http://eclipsearchive.org/projects/ WRITING/Writing.pdf (accessed 20 March 2018).
Hugo Victor, *The Hunchback of Notre-Dame* (translation: Catherin Liu), New York: Random House, 2002.
Huxley Aldous, *Eyeless in Gaza*, New York: Harper & Row, 1936 [1974].
Ishiguro Kazuo, *The Remains of the Day*, New York: Alfred A. Knopf, 1989.
Jandl Ernst, *Laut und Luise*, Olten und Freiburg im Breisgau: Walter-Verlag, 1966.
Jerome Jerome K., *Three Men in a Boat (to Say Nothing of the Dog)*, Bristol and London: Arrowsmith, 1924.
Johnson B. S., *House Mother Normal: A Geriatric Comedy*, New York: Directions Books, 1971.
Joyce James, 'An Encounter', in Joyce James, *Dubliners*, London: Penguin, 1914 [1996], pp. 18–28.
'The Sisters', in Joyce James, *Dubliners*, Great Britain: Penguin, 1914 [1996], pp. 7–17.
Kafka Franz, *The Castle* (translation: Muir Edwin and Muir Willa), Harmondsworth: Penguin Books, 1930 [1970].
The Trial (translation: Edwin Muir and Willa Muir), Harmondsworth: Penguin, Books 1953.
Lamb Charles, 'A Quakers' Meeting', *The Essays of Elia and Eliana*, London: Bell & Daldy 1868, pp. 58–63.
Lessing Doris, 'An Unposted Love Letter', in *The Story of a Non-Marrying Man and Other Stories*, London: Jonathan Cape 1963 [1972], pp. 31–42.
Children of Violence: Martha Quest, New York: Simon and Shuster, 1964.
'He', in Lessing Doris, *Stories*, New York: Alfred A. Knopf, 1978, pp. 93–99.
'Wine', in Lessing Doris, *Stories*, New York: Alfred A. Knopf, 1978, pp. 87–92.
Lewis Susan, *Never Say Goodbye*, New York: Ballentine, 2014.
Longfellow Henry Wadsworth, in Scudder H. E. (ed.), *The Complete Poetical Works of H.W. Longfellow*, Boston and New York: Houghton, Mifflin, 1894.
McNamara Joseph, *The First Directive*, New York: Crown Publishers, 1984.
Pennac Daniel, *The Fairy Gunmother* (translation: Ian Monk), London: Harvill Press, 1987, pp. 75–76.
Picoult Jodi, *A Spark of Light*, New York: Ballantine Books, 2018.
My Sister's Keeper, New York: Washington Square Press, 2004.
Small Great Things, London: Hodder & Stoughton, 2016.
Picoult Jodi and van Leer Samantha, *Between the Lines*, New York: Simon and Shuster, 2012.
Pizarnik Alejandra, 'Silence', in *Alejandra Pizarnik: Selected Poems* (translation: Cecilia Rossi), Hove: Waterloo Press, 2010.
Poe Edgar Allan, 'The Man in the Crowd', in *Works of Edgar Allan Poe*, New York: Gramercy Books Random House, 1985, pp. 240–245.
'The Raven', in *Works of Edgar Allan Poe*, New York: Gramercy Books Random House, 1985, pp. 707–710.
Pound Ezra, *The Cantos of Ezra Pound*, New York: New Directions, 1970.
Quindlen Anna, *Black and Blue*, London: Arrow, 1998.
Rebelle Alexander, *Light of the Waxing Crescent: The Sweet Dream*, Bloomington: Authorhouse, 2013.

Sciascia Leonardo, 'The Death of Stalin', in *Sicilian Uncles* (translation: N.S. Thompson), Manchester and New York: Carcanet, 1986, pp. 55–83.

Shakespeare William, *Norton¹: The Norton Shakespeare*, Greenblatt Stephen, Cohen Walter, Maus Eisaman Katharine, Howard Jean E., Gossett Suzanne, and McMullan Gordon (eds), (1st edition), New York: Norton, 1997.

Norton³: The Norton Shakespeare, Greenblatt Stephen, Cohen Walter, Maus Eisaman Katharine, Howard Jean E., Gossett Suzanne, and McMullan Gordon (eds) (3rd edition), New York: Norton, 2016.

Sobol Joshua, *Silence [Shtika]*, Tel-Aviv: Hakibbutz-Hemeuchad (in Hebrew).

Sterne Laurence, *The Life and Opinions of Tristram Shandy, Gentleman*, Holt Monk Samuel (ed.), London and Chicago: Holt, Rinehart and Winston, 1950 [1967].

Stevelork Yana, *Not Giving up on Forever*, www.wattpad.com/723534547-not-giving-up-on-forever-chapter-5 (accessed 15 September 2019).

Twain Mark, *Adventures of Huckleberry Finn*, Boston: Mifflin, 1958.

Vollmann William, 'Widow's Weeds', in *Vollmann William, Last Stories and Other Stories*, New York: Penguin, 2014, pp. 511–524.

Wharton Edith, *The Age of Innocence*, Orgel Stephen (ed.), Oxford, New York: Oxford University Press, 2006.

Woolf Virginia, *A Room of One's Own*, London: Hogarth Press, 1929 [1967].

The Waves, London: Vintage, 1931 [2004].

Yeats William Butler, 'After Long Silence', in Clark David R. (ed.), *Words for Music Perhaps and Other Poems*, Dublin: The Cuala Press, 1932, p. 36.

Index

actual and the potential, 119, 233, 237, *see also* world (the real __), *see also* factuality:fictitious:possible worlds
    mourning the lost object (*Amir*), 229–230, 299
    Pāṇini's zero, 62–63, 72
    Vortex (*Pound*), 121, 174
advertising, 3, 76, 95, 157–158, 170, 202–203, 251–252, 272–275, 283–284, 315–316
    adverts, 162–163
        Apple, 151
        Avis, 33, 48, 149–150
        Bounty, 150–151
        children who go missing (ACPO campaign), 50–51
        Clairol, 121–124
        Coca Cola, 34
        diet programs, 112, 148–149
        Digital, 245
        Hertz, 33, 48, 149–150
        If Brexit means Brexit, 189–190
        Marmite, 32–33, 38, 265–266
        Nike – George Floyd, 274–275
        Pepsi, 33
        sanitary products, 223, 225–226
        Schweppes, 151, 274
        Tata Steel, 177–178
        Walmart, 150
        World-Cup (2018) – domestic violence, 126–128
    taboo and __, 123–124
aesthetics. *see* poetic function (the)
age and stages (human), 32
    childhood
        psychosexual stages, 88–91
    infancy, 204–205, 220–221, 239, 288
        premature death, 95
        preverbal, 3, 259–260, 323–324
    old age, 9, 52–53
    premature death, 43, 200
    youth and old age, 112–116
aloneness, 15, 110, *see also* intersubjective loneliness, 13–14, 25, 146, 178, 202, 268–269
    abandonment, 140
    solitude, 21, 193
    The capacity to be alone (Winnicott), 288–289, 303
ambiguity, 22, 71, 74, 77, 87, 106–110, 116, 131, 255, 283, 294, 322–323
    semantic __. *see* semantics:ambiguity
Amicis de
    Heart Stories, 229
Amir Dana, 20, 165, 216–217, 229–230, 233, 237, 299–300, 310, 324, *see also* actual and the potential
animals' silence, 53, 76, 243–244, 283, 333
Ardern Jacinda (PM, New Zealand), 238–239
Aristotle, 44, 279, 281
authenticity, 62, 82, 101, 123, 140, 167, 175, 234, 290, 295, 300, 315, 318–321, *see also* corpus
    first-hand experience, 212–213, 216–217, 257, 259, 319, 324
    intertextual segments, 209–214, 314–315
    <>non-authentic, 219
    literature, 52, 87, 186, 282
    writing, 58, 318
axes. *see* paradigmatic and syntagmatic axes (the)

Bashō Matsuo
    Matsushima, 169, 259, 302–305
    Old pond, 305
Beckett Samuel
    Waiting for Godot, 20, 278–279
biographies, 3, 19, 94–95, 171, 184, 201, 291–292
    autobiographies, 19, 26, 113, 116, 123, 185, 212–213, 245–246, 257, 280–281, 325, *see also* first hand experience

Index

Bion Wilfred, 37, 165:fn 81, 281, 323
Blake William, 323
Bruneau Thomas J., 8, 11, 13, 24, 36, 257, 330
Buber Martin, 289–290
Byron George Gordon (Lord)
   The destruction of Sennacherib, 67–68

Cage John, 5–6
   4'33, 6
Cha Theresa Hak Kyung
   Aveugle Voix, 142–144
channels, 39–40, 42, 44, 209
   media, 25, 258–259, 273
      press (the), 68–69, 81–82, 215, 293
      publications, 23
      television, 20, 147, 166, 274, 284, 290–291
      video, 64, 274–275
      phatic function (the). *see* phatic function (the)
   telephone, 238–240, 283–284, 306–308
   vocal/nonvocal, 4, 39–46, 198–200, 320–321
      nonvocal, 10–11
choice of code, 5, 8, 13, 16, 18, 20, 32, 79, 112, 236, 253, 258, 280, 294
   vs, 1–2, 23, 30, 37–38, 46, 48–169, 185, 190, 205, 230, 256, 307, 309, 333
   vs versus grammar rules, 61–62, 65, 69, 73, 85, 154, 169, 176
   vs versus silencing, 24–25, 81, 331, *see also* silencing
Chomsky Noam, 88:fn 44, 144, 163, 190
   Lecture on Government and Binding, 97–98, 111–112
chronemics, 29, 44, *see also* linearity: chronemics
   breath, 302–305
   duration, 14–15, 18, 20–21, 23, 48, 273, 318
   time sequence, 68–69, 94, 114–116, 154, 173–176, 183, 187, 233, 312, 321, 324, 330–331
   atemporal, 69, 305
Cicero, 23
circumstantial function (the), 2, 74, 270, 328–333
   circumstantial vs (definition), 329
   court (judicial), 327–329, 331
   diversity, 330–331
   face saving, 180–182, 220, 330
   locations, 6, 15:fn 12, 329, 332–333
   official positions, 246, 331–332
   recommendation letters, 252–254
   respect, 331–332
      honorific vs, 246–247, 331–332

<>disapproval, 329
Cocteau Jean
   La voix humaine, 307–308
code non-realisation, 1, 8, 12, 21, 33–34, 44, 97:fn 50, 120, 209, 237, 275, 294, 299, 311, 315, 317, *see also* expected code
Coe Jonathan
   The House of Sleep, 154–156
cohesion, 33–34, 99, 163–165, 171, 310, 324–325, *see also* fraction: mutilation
   intertextuality and __, 207–217
collocations. *see* idioms and collocations
competence. *see* metalinguistic competence
conative function (the), 2–3, 38:fn 11, 264–283, 333
   activating the addressee, 33, 51, 112, 180, 251–252, 264–283, 293, 307–308, 311–316, 332
   horror vacui effect (the), 267–269, 273–274, 281, 307–308
   masked by other functions, 267, 273, 275
   propadverts – adverts and propaganda, 272–275
   questioning, 275–283
   silence as consent, 35, 269–271, 278
      right to silence (the) and __ (differences), 270–271, 326
   silent treatment (the), 268–269
   turn-switching. *see* turn switching
concealment, 10, 20–21, 47, 81, 197–198, 234–235, 244, 267, 291–330, 333
   blind spot (the), 319–320
   concealed information, 280
   secrets, 192, 197–198, 202–203, 228
conditionals, 126, 135, 184–185, *see also* syntax:subordination: conditionals
   guaranteed __, 150:fn 74, 170–171
   irrealis __, 182–185
Conrad Joseph
   Lord Jim, 128–132
   Nostromo, 129
content and form, 13, 16, 37, 47–48, 68, 79, 117, 174–175, 204, 296, 327, *see also* unsaid (the); *see also* empty speech
   discrepancy, 22, 56, 143–144, 309–311
   iconicity. *see* iconicity
   no content, 283–284, 291, *see also* phatic function (the)
   signifiers pointing to absence, 21, 213, 281, 299, 301
   wordness (rupturing __). *see* fraction: mutilation

Index

content words and function words, 70–71, 123, 302–303, *see also* function words
contribution to linguistics made by the study of vs, 1, 3–4, 38–39, 47–48, 64–67, 110, 163, 173, 266, 313–314, 328–329
cooperative principle (the), 3, 33, 47, 252–254, 273, 276, 278–279, 294
  implicatures, 21, 48
  vs and __ (differences), 251, 254
  maxims
    manner, 322–323
    quality, 323
    quantity, 252–254
    relevance, 19, 21, 37, 84–85, 253–254, 278
coordinatives, 103, 137, 171–178
  asymmetrical __
    but, 176–177, 186
  symmetrical __
    also, 177–178
    and, 173–176, 187
    too (#me too), 178
corpuses, 3, 49–50, 208, 297
  authenticity of __, 14, 210:fn 96, 288, *see also* intertextuality
  drafts, 113, 118–120, 124, 137–139
  manuscripts, 186
  manuscripts, 196, 206, 212
culture, 25, 42, 212, 315, 325
  heritage, 209, 212, 214, 229
  restrained versus bursting __ (*Naveh*), 291–292
cultures, 143, 164, 175, 256, 321
  African-American, 26
  Bukidons (southern Philippines), 42–43
  Chinese (rural Hong Kong), 230
  Christian, 108, 207, 215–216, 250, 278
  Irish (Dublin), 100–101, 234
  Japanese, 35, 40–41, 43, 270, 301
  Native American, 275–276, 292, 318–319
  New York, 204
  Nigeria (Igbo), 43–44
  savages, 218, 220
  Western, 217
  white (Caucasian), 132
Cummings E. E.
  Birds, 53

death, 2, 8, 80, 116–118, 145:fn 69, 170–171, 230, 282–283, 306, 317, *see also* mourning
  danger of __, 151–152, 189, 217, 237–238, 260–261
  eros and thanatos, 105–107, 112–116, 186–188, 220–221, 308

murder. *see* victimhood:murder
premature __, 95, 200, 309–310
rituals, 234–235, 258–259, 293
  condolence, 43–44, 225
  two minute silence (the), 258–259, 291–293
silence of the dead (the), 54–55, 94, 115–116, 195–197, 288, 293, 321
suicide, 13–14, 95, 107, 232, 238–240, 307–308
taboo and __, 220–222, 225
war, 54–55, *see also* Holocaust (the)
widowhood, 32, 241
definite and indefinite articles (the), 70–78, 163, 221, 236
  expected articulation of __, 76–77
  exposition (the), 74–76
desire, 146–147, 182–183, 186–188, 192, 233, 271, 274, 281, 321, *see also* psychoanalysis:*das Ding*
diagrammaticality, 31–32, 55, *see also* iconicity
Diana Princess of Wales, 258–259, 264, 292
Dickinson Emily, 227, 286–288
  Haiku and __, 306
  It was not Death, 282–283
  No prisoner be, 107–110, 207–208, 212
  Speech is one symptom, 288, 293
diminutive (the), 56–57, 129, 262–264
  lexicalisation of __, 56, 262
disappearance, 50–51, 68, 92–93, 161, 186, 210, 213
  faiding, 52–53, 129–132, 180
discourse, 3, 17, 38, 48, 208, 289–290
  dialogues, 16
    mono-dialogue (the), 306–308
  discourse markers, 163, 180, 312–314, 322, *see also* turn-switching
  sign languages, 41
  interviews, 260–261
  monologues
    soliloquy, 82–84, 105–107, 306
  multi-vocality, 211, 261–262
  public __. *see* public addresses
  questions-answers, 275–283
  registers. *see* pragmatics:registers
distribution, 14, 249, 267, 313
  integrative __. *see also* speech and silence
    comparatives (__ of), 33, 48, 149–152, 274
    coordinatives. *see* coordinatives
    questions-answers (__ of), 275–283
    series (__ of), 34, 244–245

Eliot T. S., 223
  Four Quartets, 36
  The Waste Land, 261–262

Index

ellipsis, 97–190, 294, *see also* syntax
  binding, 97–98, 108–109, *see also* Chomsky, Noam
  grammar rules violation. *see* grammar: grammar rules
  hollow dyad as vs forerunner, 164, 173–175, 244
  PRO-DROP, 101–107
    as a vs forerunner, 106–107
  propredicates, 121–123
  recoverability, 97–101, 107–111, 188
    collaps as a vs forerunner, 116–118, 128–130, 135, 261–262
    pragmatic __, 103, 112, 121–123, 126
  redundancy, 33, 97–101, 107, 264–265
  vs and __, 136–141, 161–163, 187, 243, 295
    differences, 33, 48, 98–99, 103, 107–111, 121, 125, 320
emotive function (the), 2, 15, 19, 41, 120, 254–264, 288, 322, *see also* mourning, *see also* intersubjective; *see also* self
diminutive (the), 57, 262–264
dispositions, 8
  emotive blindness, 245–246
  empathy, 43, 109, 146, 161, 259–260
  turmoil, 15, 105–107, 262
  Zen moods, 301–304
emotions
  anger, 162, 257, 260
  anxiety, 116, 194, 281
  compassion, 324, *see also* emotive function (the):dispositions: empathy
  disappointment, 146–147, 257
  fear, 18, 115, 146, 162, 192–193, 257, 262, 319
    of isolation, 25, 268–269
    revealing emotions, 14, 192, 262
  frustration, 117, 131, 140
  guilt, 89–91, 117, 196–197, 261
  hatered, 89, 140, 238–240, 263
  hope, 18, 201
    <>despair, 183, 186–187, 299
  longing, 113–114, 186–188, 193, 233, 259–260, 323–324
  loss, 95, 259–261, 290, 292–293, 297–299, 309–310
  love, 89, 140, 186–188, 194, 263, 323
  pain and sorrow, 19, 105–107, 128, 140, 146, 161, 202, 224, 257, 299
  passion, 136–141, 235, 257
  pleasure, 89, 91, 220, 257–259, *see* poetic function (the):aesthetics
  pride, 242–243

357

  regret, 117, 192, 245–246, 261
  shame, 14, 242–243, 261
  surprise, 12, 23, 26, 257, 259, 262, 281, 317
feelings, 26
  admiration, 261, 303
  alienation, 21, 80, 235–237, 308, 331
  aloofness, 136–141, 261–262
  ambivalence, 14, 147–148, 218–220, 233, 325
  emptiness, 20, 140–158, 278, 303
  forgiveness, 160–163
  rivalry, 89, 202
first person I. *see* self:first person I
interjections. *see* interjections
empty speech, 2, 9, 16, 19–23, 284–286, 290, 299–301, 320, 323, 325
  enactment, 9, 114, 121, 125, 131, 139, 141, 148, 175, 182, 207, 217, 232, 278, 292–293, 295, 297–299, 308–309, *see also* iconicity
  acting out, 23, 238–240, 256, 259–260
Ephratt Michal, 16, 18, 33, 47–48, 51, 95, 105, 228, 293, 321, 323
eros and thanatos, 105–107, 112–116, 186–188, 220–221, 308
etymology, 55, 71, 97, 256, 266
expected code, 16, 48, 188, 258, 271, 277, 283–284, *see also* speech and silence, *see also* markedness
  articulation as __, 8, 15–16, 27, 47, 68, 74, 76–77, 92–93, 112, 114–115, 117, 128–129, 132, 148, 192, 259
  articulation or vs as __, 1, 3, 23, 39, 43–46, 70, 253–254
  discrepancy, 20, 36, 76, 168, 172, 231, 245
  hypernym for its hyponym as __, 204–205
  proper-names as __, 227, 233, 237
  speech-acts' __, 268–269, 272, 322
  vs as __, 20–21, 35, 38, 40–41, 268–269

factuality, 77–78, 82, 180, 214–215, 274, 297, 306, 323–324
  denial, 91, 140, 194, 206, 276
  fictitious, 76, 88–91, 221, 255, 299, 317, 332
    possible worlds, 169, 177, 236
  irrealis, 183–185
  realia. *see* world (the real __)
  words deceive, 143–144, 299–300, 325
figurative language, 108, 135, 243, 262, *see also* semantics shifts, *see also* rhetorics
figure–ground, 33, 38, 85, 132, 308
  attention, 36, 123, 315–316
  vs as figure, 1, 4, 36, 39, 47–48, 57, 76, 79, 117, 147, 190, 286, 318–321

Fillmore Charles, 133, 149
fraction, 11, 32, 47–48, 84, 306
   intertextual segmentation, 207–214
   Kireji-cutting word, 120, 259, 302–306
   mutilation, 33, 50–60, 223–225
   partial, 33, 49, 60, 77–78, 113, 152, 179, 207–208, 213, 240, 244–246, 278–283, 306–308, 310, 318
   segmentation, 36–38, 96, 316
Freud Sigmund, 8:fn 5, 148, 199–200, 215, 247, 281, 299, 324
   A child is being beaten, 88–91, 332
   Freudian slips, 206
   Mourning and Melancholia, 197:fn 92, 259
   Oedipus (complex), 88–91, 196–197
   taboo, 96, 220–222
Frost Robert
   But outer space, 177
function words, 70, 140, 171–172, 306
   connectives, 34, 118, 141
   coordinatives. *see*:coordinatives
   left out as vs forerunners, 163–171, 303–304, 310
   prepositions, 119–120, 144–149
   subordination. *see* syntax:subordination

Gandhi Mahatma, 124–125
gender, 1:fn 2, 31–32, 88–91, 201, 240, *see also* victimhood
   female, 159–160, 176–177, 247, 317
   feminism, 26, 133–136, 233
   male, 43–44
      dominance, 27, 35, 133–136, 231–232, 242–243, 270
   naming traditions, 230
   neutralisation of __ marking, 65
generalisation, 204–205, 221–222, 233, 276, 300, 325–326
   proper-names and __, 228–230
Gibran Khalil Gibran
   The Prophet, 21
given and given-off information, 9, 15, 18, 39, 48
   given information, 17, 23, 33, 36, 38, 49, 99
   given-off information, 213, 219, 234, 327
Goethe Johann Wolfgang von
   Wandrers Nachtlied II, 5, 103–105
Goffman Erving, 9, 16, 276–277, 282, *see also* given and given-off information
government (syntactic). *see* syntax:thematic roles
grammar
   headlines and titles __ of, 68–69, 113–114, 166
   prescriptive __, 67–68, 79–80, 84–85

quotations (the __ of) (Plett), 209–212
rules, 23, 32, 61, 208
   violation of __ as a vs forerunner, 38, 41–42, 49, 67–69, 76–78, 122–123, 146, 154, 168, 315–316, 332
Grice Paul H., 16, 33, 47, 95, 252–254, *see also* cooperative principle (the)
Grimm brothers (the)
   The Twelve Brothers, 26, 240, 310

headlines and titles, 75–78, 102, 120, 123, 138, 143, 177, 185, 202, 232
   grammar of __, 68–69, 113–114, 166
Heidegger Martin, 73
Heine Heinrich, 258
Hejinian Lyn
   intertextuality and __, 207–209
   Writing Is an Aid to Memory, 58–60, 207, 311
Hemingway Ernest, 95, 309–310
Holocaust (the), 18–19, 93–94, 162–163, 197–198, 216–217, 237–238, 272, 292, 322, 325
Homer, 278
   Odyssey – The *Nekuia*, 173–176
Hugo Victor
   The Hunchback, 142
humour, 37, 76, 171, 203, 224, 247, 275, 295
Huxley Aldous
   Eyeless in Gaza, 74, 192–195, 204

iconicity, 2–3, 33, 79, 105, 320
   indexicality, 13–14
   naming and not-naming and __, 161
   onomatopoeic vs, 54–56, 196–197, 255–256, 259, 309
   symptoms in literature, 8, 52–53, 141, 145, 310, 319
   unsaid (the) and __, 17
   visual __, 41–42, 224–225, *see also* sign languages, *see also* written texts:orthographic
   <>counter-iconic, 22, 55, 167, 225–226
   vs iconicly depicting
      absence, 61, 100, 205, 250–251, 253–299, 318–323, 326
      abyss, 94–95
      black hole (the), 18, 324–325
      boundaries (blurring), 82, 212–213, 298
      of desire, 21, 154–156
      for __, 21, 41, 213, 256, 280–281
      loss, 95, 146–147, 293, 297–298, 309–310
      weight __, 112, 148–149

Index   359

iconicity (cont.)
  nullification, 33–34, 48, 67–68, 149–150
  as presence, 163, 178, 187, 232, 240, 253–299, 307, 321
  of a responsible agent, 84–92
completion, 117–118
  determination, 165–166, 271
    <>inditermancy, 187–190, 310, 321
    <>failure, 166, 307, 319
    <>unattainable, 58–60, 142–144, 159–160, 176–177
  deception, 157–158
emotions and feelings
  aloofness, 136–141, 245–246, 278, 295
  turmoil, 105–107
equivalence
  synchronisation, 69
  unification, 53, 169, 304
  unique versus common, 159, 228–229
    individuation, 64–65, 133, 249–250
    <>contrast, 177
exclusion, 128, 142–144, 332
  alienation, 41–42, 94–95, 216–217, 235–237, 307
  dehumanisation, 49, 237–238
  distancing, 124–125, 167, 205
  isolation, 145–146
  suspension, 151–152
movement, 165–167, 210–211, 298, 304–305
  spontaneity, 167
  variation, 34–35, 37, 161, 177–178, 189–190, 259
    restoration, 51, 55
    <>stagnation, 26, 54–55, 216–217, 299
obscurity, 117–118, 319–320
  ambivalence, 14, 90, 99–167
  enigma, 130–132, 299
  unknown (the), 175–176
opening, 134–136, 151, 233, 273, 281, 321
  emergence, 318–319
  <>closure, 53
  determinism, 80, 182
plain form (the), 123
  generic __, 118–121
totality, 169–170
  merge, 167–169, 235
  <>partiality, 77
traits
  modesty, 242–243
  salience, 76
  tenderness, 215, 330
  tininess, 263–264

idioms and collocations, 93, 150, 198–200, 268
  breaking of __, 150–151
  formulaic expressions, 180–181, 213–217, 283
  greeting, 30, 277
  Like lambs to the slauter, 215–217
  formulaic silence, 39
idioms
  Abide with thee, 109
  Easy come easy go, 34–35
  If pigs have wings, 180, 182–183
  If push comes to shove, 180
  No more, 117
  On second thought, 33, 244–245
  On the verge of, 206
  Speak of the devil and he doth appear, 218
  Speech is silver silence is gold, 164–215
  Still waters run deep, 259
  There are no words, 322
inanimate (the), 6, 148, 220, 299
  versus animate, 49, 91, 103–105, 196, 332
intention, 9–10, 44, 121, 238, 268, 297, 304, *see also* choice of code
  deliberate, 17, 22, 33–36, 124, 207
  withdrawal (from sharing content), 203–204, 300
interjections, 10, 37, 103
  vs and __, 255–256, 259, 302–303
intersubjective, 2, 14, 17, 154, 257, *see also* aloneness
  I and not-I (the Other), 84, 230, 242–243, 306
  nothingness, 20, 237–238
  oneness, 115, 239, 245–246, 261–262
  twoness, 41, 168, 284–286, 288–289, 324
    activating the addressee, 264–283
    belonging, 268–269
      separation and __, 25, 83–84, 133, 187, 202, 291–292, 324–325
      <>alienation, 41–42, 306–308
    bonding, 259–260, 292, 318–319, 323–324
    individuation, 318–319
    or merge, 64–65, 167–168, 206, 235, 249–250
  intimacy, 263, 285–290
    romantic __, 41–42, 186–188, 192, 202, 235, 270, 291–292, 307–308
    failure, 232–233, 261–262
  silent treatment (the), 268–269
kinship, 201–202, 205–206, 264
  parenthood, 331–332

intersubjective (cont.)
    mother–child, 259–260, 323–325
    siblings, 151–154, 239
    twins, 330–331
        siamese, 64–65, 249–250
intertextuality, 77, 108–110, 143–144, 165–166, 189–190, 207–217, 237, 274–275, 305, 315–316, 321, 332
    cohesion and __, 207–217
    formulaic expressions, 213–217, *see* idioms and collocations:formulaic expressions
    intertextuality vs (definition), 208
    intimacy and __, 286–287
    linearity, __ and vs, 208–209, 211–212, 216–217
    literary allusion *(Ben-Porat)*, 208–213
    neutralisation, 207–217
    proprie and external segments, 209–214
    quotations, 175, 209–214
        grammar of __ (the) *(Plett)*, 209–212
        as vs, 208–214, 255, 300
intuition, 22, 30–36, 54, 128, 151, 244–245, 256, 279, 294, *see also* spontaneity
    birth of thought (the), 188, 318–319

Jakobson Roman
    functions, 54, 138, 155, 248–249, 252, 254–256, 264–266, 272–274, 283, 293–294, 296, 301, 308–309, 312, 328–329
    zero sign (the), 31, 61
Jaworski Adam, 5, 15, 17, 20, 26, 35, 39, 46, 278–279, 284, 291, 329–331
Jerome K. Jerome
    Three Men in a Boat, 75–76, 202
Jespersen Otto, 54, 56
    conditionals, 184–185
    definite article (the), 71–72, 75
    ellipsis, 98
    passive voice (the), 84
John Paul II (Pope), 272, 322, 326
Johnson B. S.
    House Mother Normal, 52–53, 229–230
Joyce James, 318
    The Dubliners, 100–101, 225, 233–234, 316
Julius Caesar, 211, *see also* Shakespeare: Julius Caesar
    Veni vidi vici, 165–166, 315
Jundl Ernst
    schtzngrmm, 54–55

Kafka Franz
    The Castle, 73, 235–237
    The Trial, 235–237
Kierkegaard Søren Aabye, 323, 326
Kristeva Julia
    idempotence, 298–299, 304–305
    intertextuality, 207–209, 213, 305
    neutralisation, 207, 209, 217
Kurzon Dennis, 5–6, 15, 18, 22, 38:fn 10, 44–47, 63:fn 25, 276, 327, 330

Lacan Jacques, 199–200, 213
    Name of the Father, 221
    parole vide, 21
    signifiers pointing to absence, 281
language. *see also* metalinguistic
    acquisition, 323
    mother tongue __, 234–235, 325
    silence __, 263, 283
    foreign __, 124–125, 175, 223
    interference, 125
    national identity and __, 124–125
    preverbal, 3, 259–260, 323–324
    shortage of words (the). *see* shortage of words (the)
    sociolects, 213–214, 217, *see also* cultures
languages (oral), 3, 31, 39–46, 175
    specific. *see also* translations
    Arabic (classical), 81
    Chinese, 291
    English, 2, 5, 11, 23–24, 31–32, 38, 56, 58, 61–62, 65–67, 70–75, 92–93, 101, 103–105, 112, 120, 124–125, 137, 144, 152–154, 164, 166, 195, 211, 214, 246–247, 256, 272, 302–305, 313, 318, 332
    French, 48–49, 58, 66, 142–144, 148–149, 221, 224, 307–308, 318, 332–333
    German, 54, 56, 58, 66, 88–90, 103–105, 240
    Greek, 92, 97, 173–176, 214, 223
    Hebrew, 57, 152–154, 162, 164:fn 80, 166–167, 212–213, 218, 221, 224, 241–242, 246, 313
    Hindi, 124–125
    Igbo (Nigeria), 43–44
    Irish (Dublin), 101
    Italian, 211
    Japanese, 40–41, 120, 301–306
    Latin, 17, 31, 55, 165–166, 173–176, 211, 214, 266, 268
    Sanskrit, 62
    Spanish, 94
    Turkish, 66
    Yiddish, 123

Index 361

languages sign. *see* sign languages
legal, 154, 158, 210, 227, 251, 266
   concealed information, 280
   court hearings, 86, 145–146
   in literature, 26, 200, 235–237, 269, 280
   testimony, 200, 217, 241, 270
   imprisonment, 107–110, 203, 241
   responsibility eradicating, 271, 275
   right to silence (the), 270–271, 326–329
   silence as an informative answer, 251
   silence as consent, 35, 269–271, 278
Lessing Doris
   Children of Violence, 206
   He, 232–233
   An unposted love letter, 167–168, 202
   Wine, 74–75, 146–147
lexicon, 149, 208, 303
   idioms and collocations. *see* idioms and collocations
   lexical vs, 33, 38–39, 57, 190–247, 279, 313–314
      generalisation, 9, 204–205, 221–222, 300
      lexical vs forerunners (definition), 190
      lexicalisation and __, 56, 134, 156–159, 181, 244, 262, 264
      modifiers, 205–207, 300
      paralinguistic allusions, 198–200, 300
      part–whole, 240–247
      proper-names and __, 226–240, 300
      taboo words, 218–226
      verba dicendi, 205, 300
         negating, 192, 201–203, 330–331
      withdrawal (from sharing content). *see* intention:withdrawal (from sharing content)
Lincoln Abraham
   The Gettysburg Address, 258
linearity, 324
   chronemics and __, 18, 22, 44, 318, 321
   condensation and displacement, 321
   intertextuality, __ and vs, 208–209, 211–213, 216–217, 315
   vs overcoming __, 174–175, 273, 295, 304, 320–321
linguistic schools, 284
   Jakobson's communicative model, 248–249, 328–329
   structuralism, 61–62, 320–321
   transformational grammar, 88:fn 44, *see also* Chomsky Noam
logic, 62, 105–106, 298, 304
   calculus, 34, 249, 275
      natural languages and __, 73, 163, 180, 183:fn 87, 188, 242, 252–254, 279

      tautology, 189, 298
      truth value, 169–171, 176, 217, 249–254, *see also* factuality
   idempotence, 298–299, 304–305
   singularity, 71, 74–76, 226–227
Longfellow Henry Wadsworth
   O'er all the hilltops, 5, 103–105
   Three silences of Molinos, 156, 286

Marceau Marcel, 258
markedness, 12, 249–251, 255, *see also* speech and silence
   default, 15, 44, 181–185, 250–251, 263, 267–271
   marked (the), 31–32, 66–67, 272–283, 322
   typical and atypical, 15–16, 18–23, 27, 39, 85, 271, 276, *see also* expected code
   unmarked (the), 30–31, 80–81, 185–190, 244, 259, 278, 312–314
   zero sign (the) and the __, 61–67
May Theresa (PM, UK), 189–190
memory, 162, 275, 281
   commemoration, 18, 258, 272, 285, 292–293, 297, 322
   demetia, 52–53
   recollection, 2, 18–19, 112–116, 187–188, 260, *see also* biographies
   Writing Is an Aid to Memory (*Hejinian*), 58–60, 207, 311
   <>forgetfulness, 18, 140–141, 160–163
metalinguistic competence, 1, 3, 30, 36, 47, 70, 85, 204
metalinguistic function (the), 1–2, 121–123, 148–150, 201–202, 240, 243, 259–260, 293–294, 308–328
   code, 15, 39–40, 272, *see also* choice of code
      switching __, 211
   pointing to a code-content mismatch, 309–311, 321
   binary part for the set, 310
   distortion, 50–57, 311
   function words left out, 163–171, 310
   passive voice (the), 309–310, *see also* passive voice (the)
   taboo, 218–219, 221–226, 310–311, *see also* taboo
   punctuation marks. *see* punctuation marks
   dot dot dot, 316–321
   blind spot (the), 319–320
   overcoming linearity, 320–321
   retaining symptomatic silences, 318–319
   right to silence (the), 326–329

metalinguistic function (the) (cont.)
  silence as consent and __ (differences), 270–271, 326
  serving the conative function, 251–252
    activating the addressee as encoder, 311–316
      intertextual segments, 209, 315, see also intertextuality
      turn-switching, 314, see also turn-switching
  serving the poetic function, 311
  shortage of words (the), 321–326, see also shortage of words (the)
metalinguistic processing, 11, 34, 36, 49, 151, 273–274, 288
Miles Dorothy
  Total communication, 41–42
Modi Narebdra (PM, India), 161
moral, 178, 220–221
  responsibility, 76, 107–110
  eradicating __, 43–44, 84–92, 214, 269, 280
  standards, 107, 124, 131–132, 196–197, 221, 242–243
  <>immoral, 49, 108–110, 234, see also victimhood
morphology, 1, 22, 57–69, 97, 103, 108, 166, see also morphosyntax
  diminutive (the), 56–57, 262–264
  gender. see gender
  inflection, 31, 66–67, 149
  morphemes, 38, 51, 58, 63, 190, 305
    bound __, 58–70, 80, 149–196
    zero (the). see zero (the)
  morphological vs (definition), 58
  taboo and __, 225
  tenses, 65–69, 94, 114–116, 124, 303
  verbs (finite __), 102–104, 121–124
morphosyntax, 69–96, 303–304, see also syntax
  auxiliaries, 104, 108, 120–125, 187
    as tense markers, 67, 124
  definite and indefinite articles (the), 70–78, 163, 221, 236
  imperatives, 264–265, 274, 323
  impersonal form (the), 34, 48–49, 80, 93, 103, 222, 233–234
  middle voice (the), 92–95, see also passive voice (the)
  passive voice (the), 78–96, 309–310, see also passive voice (the)
  pronouns, 34, 48–49, 51, 65–66, 230–234, 242–243, 332–333, see also self:first person I, see also reference:referents
  propredicates, 121–123
mourning, 230, 259, 291, see also emotive function (the):pain and sorrow, see also death
  melancholy, 155, 296–301
  Mourning and Melancholia (Freud), 259
muteness, 46, 141, see also symptoms:mental __:mutism

neutralisation, 24
  intertextuality __, 207–217
  of oppositions, 60, 65
  taboo and __, 218–219, 310–311
Nietzsche Friedrich W., 73
Noelle-Neumann Elisabeth
  spiral of silence (the), 25
noise, 5, 7, 20–21, 44, 205, 255, 302
nonverbal, 10–11, 15, 29, 39–40, 42–45, 101–102, 142–143, 194, 206:fn 94, 266, 275, 282
  artifactics, 24
  chronemics. see chronemics
  kinesics, 6, 12, 22, 40, 45–46, 122, 192, 216, 282, 295, 314
  oculesics-gaze, 22, 24, 26, 40, 81, 130, 132, 268, 314, 320, see also written texts:orthographic
    blind (the), 142–144
  paralinguistics. see paralinguistics
  proxemics, 40–44, 308
  silence and __, 39, 44, 102
  tacesics, 40, 192, 258
  vocal/non-vocal. see channels:vocal/non-vocal
norms, 17, 25, 39, 263, 312, see also circumstantial function (the)
  appropriateness, 42, 123
  conventions, 16, 21, 42, 75, 180, 258, 266–268, 278, 283–284, 291, 317:fn 27, 319, 331–332
  routine, 36, 94–95, 151, 206, 217, 293, 325
  stereotypes, 27, 86, 213, 217, 229, 318–319
  stigmas, 146

objectivity and subjectivity, 9, 34, 82, 105–107, 131, 184–185, 241, 244–245, 263, 268–269, see also factuality
  imagism, 121
  science versus
    arts, 298–299, 326
    human, 82–84, 326–328
occultness, 220, 297, 301, 304, 326, see also religion
  miracles, 142–144, 239

Index 363

occultness (cont.)
  taboo. *see* taboo
uncanny (the), 218, 226, 253–299
onomatopoeia, 48, 259, 303, 310
  vs as __, 54–56, 196–197, 255–256, 309–310
opposites, 205, 207, 215, 270–271, 286, 326
  diametrical __, 143–144, 293–294
  dichotomies, 16, 46, 92, 191, 216, 240–244, 298, 310, 333
  oxymorons, 13–14, 78, 109, 242
  part–whole, 54, 240–247, 310
  silence and speech as __, 20, 39, 43–44, 46, 197, 327–328
    something versus nothing, 61, 302, 326, *see also* zero (the)
  vs accomodating opposites, 53, 99–167, 215–216, 232, 237
order, 323, *see also* linearity
  chronology, 173–176
    backwards, 158, 202
    prochronism, 217
    retroactive, 12, 49, 60, 238, 314, 324
  rules, 62, 312
  series, 244–245
  sequences, 34
Orwell George, 79, 84, 220

Pāṇini, 46, 62–67, 72, 133
paradigmatic and syntagmatic axes (the), 46, 209, 211–212, 293–294
  paradigmatic axis (the), 61, 316
    substitution, 45, 67, 73, 211–212, 219, 228, 279, 320–321
  parallelism, 34, 52, 108, 115, 158, 162, 242
  projection, 138–139, 175, 294–298, 307, *see also* poetic function (the): projection
  syntagmatic axis (the), 316–318
paralinguistics, 6, 9–16, 26, 40, 44–45
  non-vocal. *see* channels:vocal/non-vocal
  pauses, 2, 9–15, 19, 23–24, 27, 33–34, 96–97, 148, 198, 203, 302–303, 312–314, 318–320, 322, *see also* phonology and phonetics:segmentation, *see also* turn-switching
    filled and unfilled __, 13–15
  prosody. *see* prosody
  vocal organs, 26, 198–200, 231, 242, 330
  vs and __, 15, 198–200
part–whole
  binary set (the), 240–244, 332–333
  missing link (the), 244–247
passive voice (the), 70, 78–96, 307, see also self:subjecthood

active and __, 27, 309
agency and responsibility, 84–92
agentless, 34–35, 68, 80, 85
epistemic ignorance, 80–84
middle voice (the), 92–95, 309–310
passivity, 26, 86–87, 91–93, 216, 270
taboo and __, 96
pauses. *see* paralinguistics:pauses; *see* turn-switching
phatic function (the), 148, 193, 259–260, 283–294, 308, 323–324, 330
  being (opposed to doing), 267, 285–290, 302–305, 326
  The capacity to be alone (Winnicott), 288–289, 303
  two minute silence (the). *see* rituals:death __:two minute silence (the)
  greeting, 277
  small talk, 20, 280, 284, 290–291
phonology and phonetics, 1, 22, 46, 48, 50–57, 251–252, *see also* transcriptions
  homophones, 142–143, 224, 295
  hypocoristics, 264
  letters (single __), 235–237
  lipograms, 32–33, 51, 54–55, 311
  onomatopoeia, 54–56, 196–197, 255–256
  phonemes and phones, 11, 33, 38, 45–46, 48–57, 60, 63, 294
  phonetic vs (definition), 50
  prosody. *see* prosody, *see also* poetic function (the):prosody
  segmentation __, 36–38, 96, 209
  sound symbolism, 55–57
    ideophones, 297, 299
  syllables, 51, 54, 59, 256, 297–298, 311
  taboo and __, 57
Picoult Jodi
  My Sister's Keeper, 151–152, 239, 269
  Small Great Things, 151–152, 198–200, 204–205
  Spark of Light, 158–159
Picoult Jodi and *Leer* van *Samantha*
  Between the Lines, 185–186, 214
Pinter Herold, 21
Pius XII (Pope), 19
Poe Edgar Allen
  The Man in the Crowd, 228–229
  The Raven, 295–301
poetic function (the), 2, 52, 94–95, 103–105, 121, 282–283, 293–308
  aesthetics, 95, 294, 296–297, 299–302, 308
  genres, 3, 294
    ballad (the), 295–301
    Haiku, 118–121, 169, 259, 301–306
      Haiku moment (the), 121, 302–305

poetic function (the) (cont.)
    mono-dialogue (the), 306–308
    sonnet (the), 136–141
poetic license, 41, 58–59, 67, 82, 150, 210, 295
projection, 36–37, 54, 107–110, 136–137, 155–156, 175, 294–308
prosody
    alliterations, 297
    rhyming, 37, 104:fn 54, 136–137, 143, 295–296, 311, 316
    rhythm (meter), 174, 295–296, 301–302, 305
    repetitions, 60, 117, 136–137, 150–151, 295–301
    idempotence, 298–299, 304–305
    serving other functions, 143, 203
    adverts, 150–151, 273
sign languages __, 41–42
Polo Marco, 17
Pound Ezra
    Cantos, 173–176
    In a Station of the Metro, 118–121, 305–306
    Laudantes Decem Pulchritudinis, 119
Poyatos Fernando, 6, 36:fn 7, 38:fn 10, 63:fn 25
pragmatics, 1, 61, 122, 133, 178, 208, 255, 313
    context, 2, 17–18, 25, 33, 43, 48–49, 58, 62, 70–75, 82, 88, 97–100, 107, 122–123, 126, 131, 134–144, 147–148, 166–171, 180, 184–186, 188–190, 196, 210, 241, 243–244, 252–253, 262, 270, 333
    cooperative principle (the). *see* cooperative principle (the)
    discourse. *see* discourse
    Jakobson's communicative model, 248–249
    pragmatic recoverability. *see* ellipsis: pragmatic recoverability
    reference. *see* reference
    registers, 35, 159, 231, 283, 308, 322, 328, *see also* written texts:genre, *see also* legal
        non-personal discourse, 217
        ordinary discourse, 30, 160, 298, 325
    speech-acts' theory, 264–266, *see also* speech-acts
    turn-switching. *see* turn-switching
processing. *see* metalinguistic processing
propaganda. *see* advertising
proper-names, 72–73, 221, 226–240, 300
    affection and __, 57, 233, 235, 264
    anonymity, 228–230, 235–238
    common nouns and __, 227
    contrast pointing to vs, 228–230, 232–233, 238–240

generalisation and __, 228–230
given-names, 307
    first-name basis, 331
    legal status of __, 227, 251
    non-proprie __, 234–235
    honorific vs, 246–247, 331–333
    hypocoristics, 264, *see also* diminutive (the)
    letters (single __), 235–237
    linguistic peculiarities of __, 226–227
    literary __, 227–230, 232–233, 235–237
    naming norms, 226–227, 230, 234
    numerals and __, 237–238
    ordered series (of __), 246–247
    pronouns and __
        distancing, 233, 307
        he, 231–233
    taboo and __, 57, 222–223
    toponyms, 302
prosody, 11, 14, 44, 96, 114, 166, 316, *see also* poetic function (the):prosody
    intonation, 23, 30–31, 38, 313
    vocal qualifiers, 10, 26, 37, 94, 193–194, 200, 233, 300
psychoanalysis, 199–200, 220–221, 259–260, 288–289, 323–325, 332
    Das Ding, 21, 213, 281, 298–300
    Freud Sigmund. *see* Freud, Sigmund
    Lacan Jacques. *see* Lacan, Jacques
    therapy, 22, 37, 93:fn 45, 215–216, 280–281
    transference, 88–91, 259–260, 281, 323–324
    Winnicott, Donald W. *see* Winnicott, Donald W.
psychotherapy, 13–14, 22, 31, 147–148, 195, 238–240, 324
public addresses, 2, 16, 20, 124–125, 134, 189–190, 195, 258, 272, 293, 322, 328, 331
    diplomatic discourse, 203, 330
punctuation marks, 95
    brackets, 75–76, 153
    capital letters, 95, 97, 155, 226
    colons and semicolons, 116, 118–121, 212, 320:fn 28
    commas, 168
    dashes and hyphens, 107, 110, 130, 306
    dot dot dot (ellipsis mark (the)), 316–321
    final punctuation, 155
    full stop (the), 95, 97, 321:fn 29
    quotation marks, 210:fn 96, 212, 219, 261

questions–answers, 15, 38, 275–283
    conative function (the), 275–283
    questions as indirect speech-acts, 277
    rhetorical questions, 35, 254

questions–answers (cont.)
   specific acts
      greet (phatic), 277
      rhetorical questions, 277
   questions asked using vs, 177, 260,
         279–283, 320:fn 28
      concealed information, 280
      self reply, 177, 282–283
      vs as an answer, 35, 40–41, 250, 278–279

racism, 26, 200, 274–275
Rashi (biblical commentator), 154, 167
reference. *see also* definite and the indefinite
            articles (the)
   familiarity, 71, 74–75, 263, 287
      <>anonymity, 213, 228–229, 234
      <>ignorance, 9, 80–84
   propredicates, 121–123
   referents, 108–110, 150, 180, 242–243
      coreferential, 155, 187–188
         <>not coreferential, 159–163
      reciprocal, 93, 152, 332–333
         <>non-reciprocal, 331–332
      reflexive, 93, 107–110, 135
   switch __, 126–128
   time of __, 183
referential function (the), 2, 15, 17, 149, 182,
         249–254, 265, 270, 277, 284,
         see also world (the real __)
Reik Theodor, 17, 22
relevance, 16–20, 185, 276, *see also*
            cooperative principle (the):
            maxims:relevance
   downplaying, 35, 85, 181–182, 267
   secondary, 75, 283–284, 294
   <>irrelevant, 17, 21, 35, 139, 142, 250–251
religion, 306, *see also* scriptures
   divine and the human being, 167, 221
   god, 88, 96, 103, 109–110, 167, 183,
         215–216, 219, 221–224, 331
   monotheism, 73, 219
   religions
      Christianity, 108–110, 143, 215–216
         Jesus Christ, 96, 109–110, 142,
            211–212, 215–216
         papacy, 234–235
      Hindu, 62, 143
      Judaism, 57, 73, 215, 219
      Muslim, 214
      Roman, 109
      Shinto, 301
      Zen Buddhism, 301
repetition, 11:fn 8, 160, 209, 232, 257, 259,
         284, 324, *see also* poetic
         function (the):repetitions
   avoidance of __, 98, 111–112

idempotence, 298–299, 304–305
monotony, 137–138, 295–297, 299
routine events, 69, 86, 159–160, 261–262,
         267–268
rhetorical questions, 35, 254, 277
rhetorics, 23, 266, 306
   irony, 117, 195
   sarcasm, 139–140, 205, 317
   rhetoric devices
      conditionals as __, 150:fn 74, 170–171
      lipograms, 33, 51, 54–55, 311
      personation (sign languages), 41–42
      preterition, 202–203
      puns, 205, 224
      synoeciosis, 242–243
rituals
   birthday celebration, 330–331
   death __, 234–235
      condolence, 43–44
      two minute silence (the), 258–259,
            291–293
   ethnic __, 42–43
   marriage __, 35, 40–41, 43, 250, 270, 278
Royal family (the), 331
   Diana Princess of Wales, 258–259, 264,
         292
Russell Bertrand, 71
Saussure Ferdinand de, 42, 61, 97
   linearity, 320–321
   zero sign (the), 46

Saville-Troike Muriel, 15, 18:fn 14, 20, 22, 26,
         35, 38–44, 46–140, 205
scriptures (the), 3, 143, 207, 218
   The New Testament
      John, 142, 211, 215–216
      Luke, 108–110, 142
      Matthew, 96
      Peter, 330
   The Old Testament, 73, 108–110, *see also*
            translations:commentators and
            translations of the bible
      Exodus, 219
      Genesis, 152–154, 319, 326
      Isaiah, 215–216
      Jeremiah, 170
      Leviticus, 222
      Numbers, 247
      Proverbs, 197
      Psalms, 166–167, 330–331
      Sirach, 108–110
self, 83–84, 267, *see also* intersubjective
   contemplation, 105–107, 112–116, 132, 187,
         191–192, 237, 282–283, 286
   detachment, 21, 93–95, 216–217
   from __, 53, 261, 299, 310, 324–325

self (cont.)
  first person I, 51, 178, 254–255, 259, see also emotive function (the)
  individuation, 51, 184, 226
  obliteration, 21, 228–229, 234–235, 238–240
  obliteration of __, 105–107, 138–139, 209, 212–213
  subjecthood, 107, 121, 171, 230, 232
  trauma. see trauma
semantics, 1, 11, 23, 27, 33, 97, 112, 122, 133, 135, 144
  ambiguity, 58–60, 103–104, 224, 322–323
  antonyms, 22, 243
  denotation, 51, 156, 167, 263
    taboo words' __, 218
  hypernyms, 138, 152–156, 204–205
    taboo words and __, 221–222
  lexicon. see lexicon
  semantic fields
    speech and silence, 190–198, 205–207, 294, 300
    taboo and __, 220–221
  shifts, 263, see also figurative language
  metaphors, 18, 120, 154, 223
    <>non-metaphorical, 18, 216, 290
  metonymies, 95, 158, 161, 199, 221–222, 227:fn 101
  synonyms, 156–158
semiotics, 10, 22, 42, 196, 208, 324
  iconicity. see iconicity
  imagism, 121
  indexicality, 8, 13, 268, 313–315, see also symptoms
  Peirce Charles, 8, 255–256
  semtiotic square (the) (*Aristotle*), 44
  symbolic (the), 54, 220–221, 297
sexuality, 56, 73, 122, 169–170, 224–225, 294, 315, see also gender
  eros and thanatos, 105–107, 112–116, 186–188, 220–221, 308
  incest, 88–91, 196–197, 240–241
  psychosexual stages, 88–91, 220–221
  reproduction, 221, 241
    menstruation, 222–223, 225–226
  sexual abuse, 24, 86–88, 145–146, 178, 231–232, 234, 242–243
  taboo and __, 220–223, 225–226
Shakespeare William
  Hamlet, 105–107, 195–197, 205, 309
  Julius Caesar, 117, 293
  King Lear, 9, 145:fn 69
  Much Ado About Nothing, 258–316
  Richard Duke of York, 112
  Romeo and Juliet, 224–225

The Merchant of Venice, 197
The Rape of Lucrece, 231–232, 242–243
Sharon Arik (PM, Israel), 241–242
shortage of words (the), 3, 18, 21, 23, 47, 118, 161, 199, 257–316, 321–326
  generalisation and __, 325–326
  trauma and __, 324–325, see also symptoms
sign languages, 3, 14, 40–42, 45–46, 259–260, 323–324
  conative function (the), 41
  discourse markers, 41
  ellipsis, 41
  morphology, 225
  nonverbal, 41, 314
  oculesics-gaze, 31, 41, 314
  paralinguistics, 41
  poetic function (the), 41–42
    personation, 41–42
  prosody, 41
  taboo, 223, 225
  theme, 41
  turn-switching, 41
  specific languages
    ASL, 41, 64:fn 27
    BSL, 41–42, 223, 225
    ISL, 41, 64:fn 27
silencing, 2, 23–27, 133, 276, 290, 307, 329, see also social order
  boycott, 24, 268:fn 7
  breaking of the __, 24, 26, 331
  censorship, 24, 26
  collective __, 19, 25–26
  self __, 25–26, 260
  spiral of silence (the) (*Noelle-Neumann*), 25
silent treatment (the), 268–269
Skripal Sergie (the Novichok poisoning), 68–69
small talk, 20, 280, 284, 290–291
social order, 84, see also cultures, see also circumstantial function (the), see also silencing
  authority, 19, 24, 212, 215
  control, 24, 26, 230–232, 242–243
  gender and __. see gender
  institutions, 26, 234–238, 280, 332
  official, 250–254, 327–328
  private and collective, 178, 217, 228–229, 231–233, 235–237, 242–243, 258–259, 274, 331–332
  silent treatment (the), 268–269
  submissiveness, 215, 232, 248–332
socialisation, 24, 221, 230, 273
sound symbolism, 55–57
  ideophones, 297, 299

Index 367

space, 312–315, 326
  gaps, 166, 312–314
  intertextual gaps, 207–217
  intervals, 21
  location, 42, 46, 121, 273
  orthographic __, 97
  outerspace, 177, 320
  respite, 13, 17, 273, 284, 324
  suspension, 10, 42–43
speech and silence, 15–16, 23, 27, 38–47,
    164–215, 291–330, *see also*
    expected code, *see also*
    markedness
  alternate, 13, 21–22, 27, 44, 112–116, 240,
    243–244, 286, 293, 333
  coincide, 22, 44, 320–321
  complement, 2–4, 22–23, 27, 128, 217, 240,
    248, 286, 323
  exclude, 45–108
  resources, 1–4, 24, 27, 102, 240, 248, 267,
    331
    efficiency, 17, 35, 97–99, 124, 250–251,
      270, 312, 321–326
  words deceive, 22, 143–144, 291
speech-acts, 16, 264–266
  direct and indirect __, 35, 153
    indirect, 82–83, 180, 267
      polite directives, 181–182
      rhetorical questions, 35, 254
  felicity of __, 9, 266, 268, 277–278
  instructive versus persuasive __, 265–266
  specific acts
    accuse, 82–83, 145–146, 322
    apologise, 249
    complain, 204, 249
    confess, 123, 158–159, *see also* testimony
    consent, 35, 141, 250, 278
    deplore, 272, 322
    greet, 30, 277
    instruct, 264–265, 314
    invite, 293
    persuade, 314, *see also* advertising
    promise and threat, 182, 268–269, 271
      threat, 9
    promise, 159
    propose, 35
    punish, 268–269
    question, 249, 275–283
    rebuke, 292
    refuse, 249, 275
    turn-switching. *see* turn-switching
    vow, 25, 160–163
    warn, 145, 327
spontaneity, 2, 93, 167, 264, 293, *see also*
    intuition

Sterne Laurence
  Tristram Shandy, 223, 318
stillness, 2, 5–7, 13, 23–24, 27, 55, 95,
    103–105, 190, 192, 196, 292,
    299, 319
style, 3, 175, 230
  high language, 79, 115, 217
  registers. *see also* pragmatics:registers
suppletion, 47–48
symmetry, 172, 332–333, *see also*
    coordinatives
  <>asymmetry, 182, 233
symptoms, 2, 8–9, 11–12, 34, 39, 199, 232,
    258, 262, 276–278, 288, 298
  blindness, 142–144
  in literature, 8, 53, 141, 145, 310, 318–319
  interjections as __, 255–256
  language __
    aphasia, 52–53
    nominal realism (the), 218
    stammering, 8, 192, 318–319, 325
  mental __, 15, 325
    battered woman syndrome (BWS), 86
    mutism, 7–8, 23, 196, 212
    perplexity, 141
    Post-Traumatic Stress Disorder (PTSD),
      324
    psychotic mode (the), 165, 216–217, 299,
      310
    regression, 259
  neurological __, 8, 241–242
    demetia, 52–53
syntagmatic axis. *see* paradigmatic and
    syntagmatic axes (the)
syntax, 1, 11, 34, 57, 96–190, 256, 313, 316,
    see also morphosyntax
  complementary constituents left out,
    132–190, 274
  coordinatives. *see* coordinatives
  ellipsis. *see* ellipsis
  logical form (LF), 137, 140–141, 157,
    161–162, 169
  passive voice (the). *see* passive voice (the)
  structural constituents left out, 97–132
  subordination, 104, 137, 159, 171–172, 175,
    270
    conditionals, 150:fn 74, 178–190, *see also*
      conditionals
  syntactic vs (definition), 98
  taboo __ forerunners, 103, 123–124, 189,
    225
  thematic roles, 34, 65–150
    case marking, 103, 226
    distinctive __ left out, 152–156
    nonlexicalised __ left out, 156–159

taboo, 25, 57, 310–311
  breaking of the __, 219
  derogatory words and __, 25, 219
  euphemism and __, 101, 219–220
  forerunners
    foreign language as __, 223
    morphological vs as __, 225
    mutilation as __, 223–225
    passive voice (the) as __, 96
    proper-names as __, 222–223
    syntactic vs as __, 103, 123–124, 189, 225, 316
  semantic fields and __, 220–221
Tennyson Alfred (Lord)
  Tears, Idle Tears, 116–118
terror attacks
  9/11, 20, 161, 284, 290–293
  Christchurch (2019), 238–239
  Pulwama terror attack (India), 161
testimony, 158–159
  battered women, 86–87
  bear witness, 19, 217
  legal __, 200, 241, 270
  personal __, 324
    psychotic mode (the), 216–217
  personal versus legal __, 217
theme, 117, 150, 191, 278, 294–295, 316
  silence as __, 95, 114, 116–117, 186, 212, 302, 309, 324
  thematic roles. *see* syntax:thematic roles
thirdness, 4, 211–212, 289–290, 315
tranquility, 7, 103–104, 259–260, 291, 303, *see also* phatic function (the); *see also* stillness
transcriptions of silence, 31, 291, 314, 318–319
translation, 202
  silence, 54, 256
translations
  commentators and __ of the bible, 152–154, 320:fn 28
  German-English, 88–90, 103–105
  Greek-English, 173–176
  Greek-Latin, 173–176
  Hebrew-English, 57, 152–154, 320
  Italian-English, 195, 210
  Italian-Latin, 211
  Japanese-English, 120, 302–305
  Latin-English, 166
  Spanish-English, 94
trauma, 8, 14, 18–19, 105–107, 299, 324–325
  black hole (the), 18, 216–217, 324–325
turn-switching, 15, 23, 148, 267–268, 312–314, 316, 329
  transition point, 312–313
  vs a __ discourse marker, 12, 30–31, 35, 37, 267–268, 312–314

Twain Mark, 77
  Adventures of Huckleberry Finn, 76–77
  The Adventures of Tom Sawyer, 77
typology, 48–49, 57–58, 166, 263, 305
  agglutinative languages, 66
  analytic languages, 69–70
  synthetic languages, 31

universals, 57, 62, 116, 256, 296, 302–303
  universal versus particular, 56, 103–105, 169–170
unsaid (the), 2, 16–20, 22, 26, 39, 195, 260, 281, 320
  argument from silence (the), 17
  elephant in the room (the), 16–17, 19, 26

verbalisation, 132, 201–202, 252, 259, 288, 291, 318–319, 323
  intertextual seams and __, 210
  paraphrasing, 176, 178, 191–192, 279, 323
  one's own silence, 14, 186, 202–203, 207
  Other's silence (the), 26, 88–91, 148, 195–196, 198–200, 204, 206, 212, 231, 242, 292
  silence, 23, 167, 197–198, 268, 297, 317
  preterition, 202–203, 207
  versus the refrain from __, 154, 174–175, 193
victimhood, 24, 216, 237–238, 324
  battered women, 24, 86–88, 126–128
  A child is being beaten (Freud), 88–91
  genocide mass atrocities, 161–163, 215–217, *see also* Holocaust (the)
  George Floyd, 274–275
  incest, 88–91, 240–241
  murder, 152–154, 195–197, 293, 329–330
  rape, 145–146, 178, 231–232, 242–243
vs (definition), 37, 50, 58, 98, 190, 208, 248, 308, 329
vs and other silences, 5–29, 54–56, 276, 290, 312–314
vs forerunners (definition), 38, 47–48

Winnicott Donald W., 288–289, 317, 323
  The capacity to be alone, 288–289, 303
Wittgenstein Ludwig, 323, 326
Woolf Virginia, 318
  A Room of One's Own, 112, 134–136, 159–160, 176–177, 244–245, 317
  The Waves, 183–184
world (the real __), 13, 21, 23, 25–26, 32, 55, 61–62, 76, 91, 93–94, 121, 133, 139, 184, 218, 220, 222, 229, 247, 282–283, 307, 318–321
written texts, 2–3, 11, 42:fn 16, 47, 97, 130–131, 202, 283, 316

written texts (cont.)
  genres
    academic, 82, 210
    legal, 210
    official forms, 250–251
    professional, 87–88
    recommendation letters, 252–254
    reports, 319
  orthographic, 22:fn 16, 48, 225–226, 321
    blanks, 52, 250–251, 294
    erasure, 206
    graphemes, 70
    homographs, 117
    iconic letters, 224–225
    indentations, 261, 297
    italics, 210, 307
    layout, 95, 297–298
    spaces, 97, 209, 273:fn 13, 288, 297

    punctuation. *see* punctuation marks
Writing Is an Aid to Memory (Hejinian), 58–60, 207
Wyatt Thomas (Sir)
  Each man me telleth, 37
  Hate whom ye, 136–141, 295
  Of change in minde, 311
  Who so List to Hunt, 210–212

Yeats W. B.
  Speech after long silence, 112–116

zero (the), 46, 99:fn 52, 183, 186
  definite article (the) and __, 70–78
  Pāṇini's zero, 62–63
  vs and __ (differences), 61–67, 249–250
zero sign (the), 31–32, 264–265, 294